FIFTEENTH-CENTURY
CARTHUSIAN REFORM

STUDIES IN THE HISTORY
OF
CHRISTIAN THOUGHT

EDITED BY

HEIKO A. OBERMAN, Tucson, Arizona

IN COOPERATION WITH

HENRY CHADWICK, Cambridge

JAROSLAV PELIKAN, New Haven, Conn.

BRIAN TIERNEY, Ithaca, N.Y.

A.J. VANDERJAGT, Groningen

VOLUME XLIX

DENNIS D. MARTIN

FIFTEENTH-CENTURY
CARTHUSIAN REFORM

FIFTEENTH-CENTURY CARTHUSIAN REFORM

THE WORLD OF NICHOLAS KEMPF

BY

DENNIS D. MARTIN

E.J. BRILL

LEIDEN • NEW YORK • KÖLN

1992

The paper in this book meets the guidelines for permanence and durability of the Committee on Production Guidelines for Book Longevity of the Council on Library Resources.

Library of Congress Cataloging-in-Publication Data

Martin, Dennis D., 1952-
    Fifteenth century Carthusian reform: the world of Nicholas Kempf
/ by Dennis D. Martin.
      p.   cm.—(Studies in the history of Christian thought, ISSN
00818607; v. 49)
    Includes bibliographical references and index.
    ISBN 9004096361 (cloth)
    1. Kempf, Nicolas, 1397-1497. 2. Theology—Middle Ages,
600-1500. 3. Carthusians—Europe—History. I. Title. II. Series.
BX4705.K378M37   1992
271'.7102—dc20
[B]
                     92-20135
                         CIP

ISSN 0081-8607
ISBN 90 04 09636 1

CAROLAE, QUAE CEPIT CAPITQUE

TABLE OF CONTENTS

TABLE OF CONTENTS

ACKNOWLEDGEMENTS

This book was written with encouragement from my teachers and colleagues, especially Mark Burrows (Washington, D.C.), Robert Clouse (Terre Haute, Ind.), Peter Erb (Waterloo, Ont.), Berndt Hamm (Erlangen), James Hogg (Salzburg), Heiko Oberman (Tucson, Ariz.), Werner Packull (Waterloo), and Michael Shank (Madison, Wis.). Kenneth Davis (Langley, B.C.), Peter Erb, Kent Emery, Jr. (Notre Dame, Ind.), and Thomas Tentler (Ann Arbor, Mich.) planted the seeds for research that led from a thesis to a book. Berndt Hamm, William Courtenay (Madison), Michael Shank, and Mark Burrows read part or all of the manuscript, offering valuable suggestions for improving it. John Van Engen read an earlier version of chapter six. None of them are responsible for the book's failings. I am grateful to Heiko Oberman for including it in the series Studies in the History of Christian Thought and for thoughtful counsel regarding the title.

Hugh of Saint Victor insisted that poverty was essential for genuine learning. I might have had too much of a good thing were it not for the financial support of the Fulbright-Hays program, the Austrian Bundesministerium für Wissenschaft und Forschung, the Hill Monastic Manuscript Library research travel program, the National Endowment for the Humanities Summer Stipends Program, the American Academy of Religion Research Assistance Program, the Eli Lilly Foundation, Associated Mennonite Biblical Seminaries, the American Historical Association's Bernadotte E. Schmitt Research Grant Program, and the Institute for Research in the Humanities at the University of Wisconsin-Madison.

Hugh's insistence on the pedagogical profit accruing to a stranger in a foreign land came home to me at the universities of Marburg and Tübingen, where I encountered a degree of cultural disjunction that might minimally have met Hugh's standard, and during twenty years as an academic "sojourner in the promised land . . . dwelling in tents . . . looking forward to the city with foundations." John Van Engen and David Lindberg, together with their colleagues and staff members at the Medieval Institute of the University of Notre Dame and the University of Wisconsin's Institute for Research in the Humanities were gracious hosts during the two most recent years of my academic wanderings. St. John's Abbey and Julian Plante of the Hill Monastic Manuscript Library at Collegeville, Minn., James Hogg, and the Carthusians at Pleterje extended hospitality for shorter, nonetheless valuable, periods of time.

A number of manuscript libraries made their books and manuscripts available *in situ*, furnished microfilms, and permitted me to quote from or publish excerpts from their holdings. These include the Hill Monastic Manuscript Library, with its extensive collection of *incipit* indexes and finding aids; the Bayerische Staatsbibliothek in Munich; the Nationalbibliothek in Vienna; the Universitätsbibliothek in Graz; the Stiftsbibliothek at Melk; the Diözesansarchiv in St. Pölten; the Stiftsbibliothek at Rein; the Stiftsbibliothek at Admont; the Öffentliche Universitätsbibliothek at Basel; the Österreichisches Staatsarchiv (Haus-, Hof-, und Staatsarchiv) in Vienna; Egyetemi Könyvtár and Orszagos Széchényi Konyvtár (University Library and National Széchényi Library) in Budapest, the Bibliothèque Nationale in Paris, and the Burke Library at Union Theological Seminary, New York. Other libraries generously furnished photocopies or portions of films and replied to queries from a distance: the Biblioteka Jagiellonska in Cracow, the Württembergische Landesbibliothek in Stuttgart, the Badische Landesbibliothek in Karlsruhe, the Universitätsbibliothek in Leipzig, the Biblioteca Civica Gambalunga in Rimini and Dr. Donatella Frioli of the University of Padua, the Herzog-August Bibliothek in Wolfenbüttel, and the Staatsbibliothek in Berlin.

The real and imagined wonders of word processing and desktop publishing and the vicissitudes of academic life in the 1970s and 1980s have "encouraged" more and more scholars to assume an increasing share of the clerical work of publishing their research. Circumstance and choice have induced me to carry out personally each stage in the production of this book from the initial typing to coding for the typesetting so capably carried out by Anita Davis Lauterstein. At the end of that path it is a pleasure to acknowledge the assistance of Michael Plishka with proofreading and indexing and Brian Fitzpatrick and Wendy Chiaramonte of the Loyola University Center for Instructional Design in drawing the manuscript *stemma* found in appendix C.

Earlier versions of parts of chapters two, three, five, and appendix A were published in the *Journal of the History of Ideas* (1990); *Religious Education* (1990); *Kartäusermystik und -mystiker*, Analecta Cartusiana, 55.5 (1982); and *Die Kartäuser in Österreich*, Analecta Cartusiana, 83.1 (1980). I am grateful to the publishers and editors of each publication for granting permission to reuse these materials.

The dedication page speaks of the largest debt I owe in the writing of this book.

Chicago, Laetare Sunday, 1992 Dennis D. Martin

ABBREVIATIONS

Note: Scripture citations are given according to the Vulgate, with variants in brackets. Manuscripts are normally cited by folio, column (where applicable), and line numbers, e.g., VS1, folio 12v, column A, lines 13-16. Bibliographical citations in the footnotes have been shortened, even at first mention, primarily by eliminating information on monograph series, publishers, and place of publication; occasionally also by eliminating subtitles. Enough information has been given to permit the reader to gain a sense of the title and nature of the work cited. For full information the reader should consult the Bibliography. In the following list of abbreviations, abbreviations for monograph series are not italicized; abbreviated journal titles are italicized. The most recent place of publication is given for journals.

AC	Analecta Cartusiana. Salzburg: Institut für Englische Sprache und Literatur, or, Institut für Anglistik und Amerikanistik, 1970-.
AC	*Analecta Cartusiana*. Pont-Saint-Esprit, France, 1989-.
ADB	*Allgemeine deutsche Biographie*. Published by the Historische Kommission bei der bayerischen Akademie der Wissenschaften. Leipzig: Duncker und Humblot, 1875-1912; reprinted Berlin: Duncker und Humblot, 1967-71. Cf. *NDB*.
AEKG	*Archiv für elsässische Kirchengeschichte*. Rixheim. 1926-43. [Continued as *Archives de l'église d'Alsace*].
AHDL	*Archives d'histoire doctrinale et littéraire du moyen âge*. Paris. 1926/27-.
AHR	*American Historical Review*. Bloomington, Indiana. 1895-.
AÖG	*Archiv für Österreichische Geschichte*. Vienna. 1848-.
ARG	*Archiv für Reformationsgeschichte*. Gütersloh. 1903-.
BGAM	Beiträge zur Geschichte des alten Mönchtums und des Benediktinerordens. Münster i. W.: Aschendorff, 1912-.
BGPhMA	Beiträge zur Geschichte der Philosophie [und Theologie] des Mittelalters. Münster i. W.: Aschendorff, 1891-.
Bibl. ascetica	Bernhard Pez, ed., *Bibliotheca ascetica antiquo-nova*, 12 vols. Regensburg: Johann Conrad Peez, 1724-40; reprinted in 3 vols., Farnborough, Hampshire: Gregg Press, 1967.
Böhm	Böhm, Constantin Edlen von. *Die Handschriften des kaiserlichen Haus-, Hof-, und Staatsarchivs*. Vienna: Wilhelm Braumüller, 1873. Supplement, 1874.
Cartusiana	Albert Gruys, comp. *Cartusiana: Un instrument heuristique*. Vol. 1: *Bibliographie générale, auteurs cartusiens* (1976). Vol. 2: *Maisons* (1977). Vol. 3: *Supplement, addenda, et corrigenda* (1978).

	Institute de Recherches et d'histoire des Textes, Bibliographies, Colloques, Travaux prépara- toires. Paris: Editions du Centre National de la Recherche Scientifique de France, 1976-78.
CCCM	Corpus Christianorum, Continuatio Mediaevalis. Turnhout: Brepols, 1966-.
CCSL	Corpus Christianorum, Series Latina. Turnhout: Brepols, 1953-.
CF	Cistercian Fathers series. Shannon, Ireland; Washington, D.C., and Kalamazoo: Cistercian Publications, 1970-.
CH	*Church History.* Chicago. 1932-.
clm	Codex latinus monacensis. Munich, Bayerische Staatsbibliothek, Handschriftenabteilung.
CS	Cistercian Studies monograph series. Shannon, Ireland, Washington, D.C., and Kalamazoo: Cistercian Publications, 1969-.
CS	*Cistercian Studies.* Spencer, Mass. 1966-90. Cf. *CSQ*.
CSEL	Corpus scriptorum ecclesiasticorum latinorum. Vienna. 1866-.
CSQ	*Cistercian Studies Quarterly* (continues *Cistercian Studies*). Spencer, Mass. 1991-.
cvp	Codex Vindobonensis Palatinus. Vienna, Österreichische Nationalbibliothek.
CWS	Classics of Western Spirituality series. New York: Paulist Press, 1978-.
DHGE	*Dictionnaire d'histoire et de géographie ecclésiastiques.* 21 vols. to 1988. Originally edited by Alfred Bau- drillart, Albert Vogt, and Urbain Roziès; cur- rently edited by R. Aubert, J. P. Hendrickx, and J. P. Sossons. Paris: Letouzy et ané, 1912-.
diss.	dissertation.
DSAM	*Dictionnaire de spiritualité, ascetique et mystique.* 15 vols. to 1989. Edited by Marcel Viller and others. Paris: Beauchesne, 1932-.
DThC	*Dictionnaire de théologie catholique.* 15 vols. and 3 indices. Edited by A. Vacant, E. Mangenot, E. Amann. Paris: Letouzy et ané, 1903-50, 1951-72.
DVfLG	*Deutsche Vierteljahrsschrift für Literaturwissenschaft und Geistesgeschichte.* Stuttgart. 1923-.
ET	English translation.
FC	Fathers of the Church. Washington, D.C., 1947-.
Guigo I, *Consuet.*	Guigo I, *Coutumes de Chartreuse* [Consuetudines Cartusienses]. Edited and translated by a Carthu- sian. Sources Chrétiennes, 313. Paris: Editions du Cerf, 1984.
HJ	*Historisches Jahrbuch der Görresgesellschaft.* Munich. 1880-.
JEH	*Journal of Ecclesiastical History.* Cambridge. 1950.
JHI	*Journal of the History of Ideas.* New Brunswick, N.J. 1940-.
JLNö	*Jahrbuch [des Vereins] für Landeskunde von Niederösterreich.* Vienna. 1902-.
JMRS	*Journal of Medieval and Renaissance Studies.* Durham, N.C. 1971-.

JTS	*Journal of Theological Studies.* Oxford. 1899-1949. new series, 1950-.
JVGSW	*Jahrbuch des Vereins für Geschichte der Stadt Wien.* Vienna. 1939-.
LThK	*Lexikon für Theologie und Kirche.* Edited by Josef Höfer and Karl Rahner. 2nd edition. 11 vols. Freiburg i. Br.: Herder, 1957-65. 3 vols. supplement, 1966-68.
Matrikel	*Die Matrikel der Universität Wien.* Vol. 1: *1377-1450.* Compiled by Artur Goldmann, Herman Göhler, Kurt Soukup, and Franz Gall. Publikationen des Instituts für Österreichische Geschichtsforschung, Reihe 6: Quellen zur Geschichte der Universität Wien, 1. Abteilung. Vienna: Böhlau, 1956.
MIÖG	*Mitteilungen des Instituts für Österreichische Geschichtsforschung.* Vienna. 1948-.
MÖIG	*Mitteilungen des Österreichischen Instituts für Geschichtsforschung.* Vienna. 1880-1914.
MTU	Münchener Texte und Untersuchungen zur deutschen Literatur des Mittelalters. Munich: Beck, later Artemis, 1961-.
n.	footnote, endnote.
NDB	*Neue deutsche Biographie.* 15 vols. to 1987. Edited by the Historische Kommission bei der bayerischen Akademie der Wissenschaften. Berlin: Duncker und Humblot, 1953-.
n.F.	neue Folge.
NPNF, ser. 1	Nicene and Post-Nicene Fathers. First Series. New York, 1886-93. Reprinted Grand Rapids, 1952-.
NPNF, ser. 2	Nicene and Post-Nicene Fathers. Second Series. New York, 1890-99. Reprinted Grand Rapids, 1952-.
Oeuvres	Gerson, Jean. *Oeuvres Complètes.* 10 vols. in 11. Edited by Palémon Glorieux. Paris: Desclée, 1960-73.
ÖNB	Österreichische Nationalbibliothek, Vienna.
Pez and Hueber	Pez, Bernhard, and Hueber, Philibert, editors. *Codex diplomatico-historico-epistolaris* (= vol. 6 of *Thesaurus anecdotorum novissimus*). Augsburg, Graz: Philip, Johannes, Martin Veit, 1729.
"Peziana"	Melk, Stiftsarchiv, correspondence of Bernard Pez (see appendix A).
PG	Patrologiae cursus completus, series Graeca. 168 vols. Edited Jacques-Paul Migne and others. Paris: Migne, 1857-68. Reprinted Turnhout: Brepols.
PL	Patrologiae cursus completus, series Latina. 217 vols. Edited by Jacques-Paul Migne and others. Paris: Migne, 1844-64. Reprinted Tournhout: Brepols.
QFIAB	*Quellen und Forschungen aus italienischen Archiven und Bibliotheken.* Rome. 1898-.
R	List of writings of Nicholas Kempf by Heinrich Rüthing in *DSAM*, vol. 8, cols. 1699-1703.
RAM	*Revue d'ascetique et de mystique.* Toulouse. 1920-71. Continued by *RHSp.*

RHSp	*Revue d'histoire de la spiritualité.* Paris. 1972-.
RQ	*Römische Quartalschrift für christliche Altertumskunde und für Kirchengeschichte.* Rome. 1887-.
RTAM	*Recherches de théologie ancienne et médiévale.* Louvain. 1929-.
S. Bernardi Opera	*Sancti Bernardi Opera Omnia.* 8 vols. Edited by Jean Leclercq, H. M. Rochais, and C. H. Talbot. Rome: Editiones Cistercienses, 1957-77.
SB	Staatsbibliothek.
SC	Sources Chrétiennes. Paris: Editions du Cerf.
SGR	Studien zu den Grundlagen der Reformation. Edited by Rudolf Damerau. Gießen: the Author, 1964-.
SHCT	Studies in the History of Christian Thought. Leiden: Brill, 1966-.
SMBO	*Studien und Mitteilungen aus dem Benedictiner- und dem Cistercienser-Orden, mit besonderer Berücksichtigung der Ordensgeschichte und Statistik.* Munich. 1882-1910.
SMGB	*Studien und Mitteilungen zur Geschichte des Benediktinerordens* (title varies). Munich. 1911-.
SMRT	Studies in Medieval and Reformation Thought. Leiden: Brill, 1966-.
SR	*Studies in the Renaissance.* New York. 1954-1974. [Continued as *Renaissance Quarterly.* New York. 1975-.]
StdtB	Stadtbibliothek.
STh	Thomas Aquinas, *Summa Theologiae.*
TRE	*Theologische Realenzyklopädie.* Edited by Gerhard Müller et al. Berlin: de Gruyter, 1976.
UB	Universitätsbibliothek.
UL	University Library.
Verfasserlexikon	*Die deutsche Literatur des Mittelalters: Verfasserlexikon.* Edited by Wolfgang Stammler and Karl Langosch. Berlin: de Gruyter, 1936; revised edition edited by Kurt Ruh, Franz Josef Worstbrock and others. 7 vols. to 1989. Berlin: de Gruyter, 1978-.
Vie monastique	*Théologie de la vie monastique: Études sur la tradition patristique.* Études publiées sous la direction de la Faculté de Théologie S.J. de Lyon-Fourvière, 49. Paris: Aubier, 1961.
W	List of writings of Nicholas Kempf by Leopold Wydemann in Melk, Stiftsbibliothek, cod. 683 and *Bibl. ascetica*, vol. 4: Preface.
WA	*Luthers Werke: Kritische Gesamtausgabe.* Abteilung Schriften. Weimar, 1883ff. Reprinted Graz, 1964-.
ZAM	*Zeitschrift für Askese und Mystik.* Innsbruck. 1926-.
ZDA	*Zeitschrift für deutsches Altertum und deutsche Literatur.* Wiesbaden. 1841-.
ZDP	*Zeitschrift für deutsche Philologie.* Berlin. 1869-.
ZKTh	*Zeitschrift für katholische Theologie.* Innsbruck. 1876-.
ZKG	*Zeitschrift für Kirchengeschichte.* Tübingen. 1876-.

ZKG	*Zeitschrift für Kirchengeschichte.* Tübingen. 1876-.
ZThK	*Zeitschrift für Theologie und Kirche.* Tübingen. 1891-.

Works of Nicholas Kempf

Cantica	*Explanatio in Cantica Canticorum* (appendix A, no. 20).
Discr	*De discretione* (appendix A, no. 6).
MTh	*De mystica theologia* (appendix A, no. 19).
Ost	*De ostensione* (see appendix A, no. 18).
Prop	*De proponentibus* (appendix A, no. 5).
Rect	*De recto studiorum fine ac ordine* (appendix A, no. 4).
Serm. epist.	*Sermones super epistolas* [appendix A, no. 14a].
Serm. evang.	*Sermones super evangelia* [appendix A, no. 14b].

WHY NOT LET SLEEPING MONKS LIE?

Cartusia sanctos facit, sed non patefacit. "The Chartreuse makes saints but does not make them known."

The Carthusians have made no effort to extol the saints and spiritually mature men in their midst. Thus a certain prior of this order always taught that one should avoid all ostentation, citing the words of the prophet: "I keep things to myself." When he died, a grace of healing began to work many miracles, and this caused people to flock to that monastery, disrupting the accustomed repose of the brethren. Pondering the problem the new prior went to his predecessor's grave and commanded him by virtue of holy obedience to work no more miracles—because they were disturbing the brethren. He told the dead man that he ought to observe in death what he had always taught in life: "I keep things to myself." He worked no miracles at all after that, and thus the flood of people ebbed away. That this order has always remained in good monastic observance is due in no small part to its having fled the favors and praises of men that arise from sanctity's signs and miracles.

This common Carthusian anecdote was retold by Nicholas Kempf in his history and defense of the Carthusian order.[1] Modern readers might expect the prior to have cashed in on the crowds, to have marketed the miracles. Medieval readers expected much the same. Nicholas Kempf,

---

[1] *De confirmatione et regula approbata ordinis cartusiensis* [see appendix A, no. 15], ch. 9/8 (Vienna, ÖNB, cvp 13904, fol. 12r, 27 - 12v, 14): "Nunquam autem curaverunt cartusienses suos extollere si quos habuere sanctos et perfectos. Unde quidam prior ordinis istius ostentacionem semper vitare docens, allegans illud propheticum 'Secretum meum michi, secretum meum michi' [Is 24:16], cum mortuus esset et sanitatis gratia, quia miracula facere cepit, multi ad monasterium illud confluerent, de quo fratres in sue quietis consuetudine erant turbati et impediti. Quod successor eius considerans, ad locum sue sepulture transivit [transunt in V5, transivit in V1], prohybuit ipsum in virtute sanctae obediencie ne amplius miracula faceret—unde fratres inquietarentur—allegans sibi quod mortuus deberet servare quid dum viveret docuisset, scilicet, 'Secretum meum michi' etc. Qui postea nullum penitus miraculum fecit et ita concursus cessavit. Et quod ordo ille semper in bona mansit observancia, inter alias est eciam non minima causa illa abstractio et declinatio a favore hominum et laude per sanctitatis signa et miracula." The story appears in the chronicles of the order as edited by Charles Le Couteulx, *Annales ordinis cartusiensis*, 3 (1888), 129-31, although Kempf's version differs in some details. Similar stories are told about Bernard of Clairvaux and other monastic figures. For Bernard see *Exordium magnum cisterciense*, dist. 2, ch. 20, Griesser ed., pp. 116-18.

the subject of this book, tells the story precisely to challenge commonly held assumptions—to drive home the point that even a miraculous voice from the grave must be silenced for the sake of monastic contemplation. What makes monastic contemplation so important? Even in his own day Kempf's fellow Carthusians, awakening to the presence of a literate, urban public and aware of consumer demand for religious goods, were beginning to ask whether contemplative claustration was all that important, whether it could not be compromised for the sake of other good ends. Yet Kempf positioned himself on the traditional wing of a traditional order and opposed the trend toward active involvement. His response to the theological, religious, social, and economic changes of his day seems odd to the modern reader. In the face of what modern scholars have (mis?)identified as an urban communalization and domestication of the church, he put all his eggs in the basket of rural monastic communities. In the face of growing, even if ambiguous, concern about freedom and a new understanding of the self-authentication, he trumpeted obedience and role-playing.

In the twentieth century how are we to make sense of his traditionalism? We might begin by seeking, in the words of Hans Kellner, to "get the story crooked"[2] and by paying attention to a monastic *modus loquendi* described in chapter two. Precisely because Kempf and the Carthusians contradict modern assumptions we are brought up short and given an opportunity to refract medieval and early modern history in the hope of catching a glimpse of something we have previously overlooked.

That the Carthusians have been overlooked is a problem largely of their own making—a problem for us and a boon for them. Like the Old Order Amish in contemporary North America, Carthusians have shunned publicity, and, as Nicholas Kempf points out, at least part of the constant rigor of their monastic observance results from their strenuous efforts to avoid outside contacts—for example, by refusing to attach their names to their writings,[3] or, by departing from the Benedictine tradition of receiving lay guests.[4] In the nineteenth century, Romantic nostalgia for the "Middle Ages" and for the anachronistic strictness of Carthusian religi-

---

[2] *Language and Historical Representation: Getting the Story Crooked* (1989).

[3] Johannes Hagen of the Erfurt Charterhouse had to be ordered by his prior to put his name on his writings. See Dieter Mertens, "Kartäuser-Professoren," in *Die Kartäuser in Österreich*, vol. 3 (1981), 75-87, at 82, citing Joseph Klapper, *Der Erfurter Kartäuser Johannes Hagen* (1961), 2: 140, 145.

[4] Guigo I, *Consuet.*, ch. 10, 18, 19, 36, 79. The *Consuetudines* abound in strictures intended to ensure the isolation of the Grande Chartreuse, including the instruction that the lay brother in charge of the winter shepherding duties take a hired servant with him to run errands and buy provisions in villages. See ch. 50 and 76.

osity made the Grande Chartreuse into a tourist attraction in an increasingly secularized France, receiving the "honor" of a visit from Queen Victoria and becoming the subject of a poem by Matthew Arnold.[5] The difficulty of maintaining intact an ancient way of life under the impact of such notoriety, even though many would-be visitors were in their own romantic way kindly disposed toward the monks, compelled the order to shun all lay visitors since reoccupying the Grande Chartreuse during the Second World War. Late in the twentieth century, unlike their closest monastic cousins, the Trappists and Discalced Carmelites, Carthusians do not participate in publishing scholarly or devotional journals and have not embarked on an apostolate to teach meditation techniques to lay people.[6]

Why not let the Carthusians have their contemplative *quies*, their sabbath of anonymity? Like the Amish they are willing to live surrounded by a certain degree of misinformation—the inevitable result of their isolation. Already in the fifteenth century Nicholas Kempf and others set about refuting the worst misinformation, e.g., the claim that the Carthusian Order had never received papal approval, or that Carthusian strict abstinence ruined the monks' health.[7] Yet they remain a much misunderstood community. Accounts of Carthusians in textbooks[8] or world-

---

[5] James Hogg, *Dom Edmund Gurdon* (1988), 100-120. In the fifteenth century, indeed already in the twelfth century, Carthusian rigor and isolation fascinated outsiders. Peter the Venerable and Guibert of Nogent have left accounts from the twelfth century, although scholars debate whether Guibert actually visited the Grande Chartreuse personally. From the late fifteenth century comes a remarkable description by an Italian visitor (see chapter one, below).

[6] The parallels with the Old Order Amish are remarkable yet incomplete. They have found a *modus vivendi* with the tourist trade and have begun publishing journals that serve the practical needs of teachers in the private elementary schools they have established in response to rural school consolidations. See Donald B. Kraybill, *The Riddle of Amish Culture* (1989).

[7] This was the purpose of Kempf's *De confirmatione*. Similar tracts were written by Jacob de Paradiso, Heinrich Egher of Kalkar, and others. For the Carthusian diet see Guigo I, *Consuet.*, ch. 33, and James Hogg, "Everyday Life in the Charterhouse," in *Klösterliche Sachkultur* (1980), 133-35.

[8] In the course of a series of short summaries of the various religious orders, Steven Ozment's excellent textbook, *The Age of Reform, 1250-1550* (1980), 87, tells us that "the Carthusians attached special importance to silence, manual labor, and the strict suppression of sexual desire. They continued to practice self-flagellation after Pope Clement VI forbade flagellant processions in 1349. . . ." Of the four putative characteristics, only silence received special emphasis among Carthusians. Carthusian "distinctives" that might have been mentioned include their unique liturgy and chant, their semi-eremitical life in cottage-like "cells" with gardens and workrooms, the wearing of hair-shirts, the night-office, the order's centralized constitution and system of frequent and authoritative visitations, and the special interest Carthusians exhibited for the copying of books, including their own system of punctuation.

historical syntheses[9] often focus on minor details misleadingly reported. A recent survey of Christian spirituality devotes one paragraph to the Carthusians in the twelfth century[10] and completely ignores them in the fourteenth-sixteenth centuries—when they reached the height of their expansion and were one of the most significant spiritual forces in western Christendom.[11]

Precisely as the western church struggled with the transfer of the papacy to Avignon and papal schism, as Europe faced the Black Death, as the creation of new orders that had characterized the twelfth and thirteenth centuries ended, the Carthusian Order enjoyed its golden age. Fifty percent more charterhouses were founded in the fourteenth century (99) than during the two hundred years between 1084 and 1300 (62). Much of this growth took place in Germany, where the first monastery was established at Mainz in 1320. Fourteenth-century German charterhouses tended to be located near but not in major cities—Mainz, Cologne, Straßburg, Trier, Nürnberg—and were endowed by leading princes, burghers, and bishops, who viewed the Carthusians as "leaven" that would raise the spiritual level of the church in general.[12]

---

[9] E.g., Fernand Braudel mentions the Carthusians twice in *Civilization and Capitalism* (1981), 1: 331-32, 379. In discussing the coming and going of fashions in men's facial hair, he notes that "Louis XIV entirely abolished short beards. Only the Carthusian friars did not abandon them." Aside from the translator's misnomer in calling the Carthusians "friars", the image of the mysterious and bearded Carthusians employed here once more recalls popular images of the bearded and bowl-tonsured Amishmen. Braudel's second reference to the Carthusians has to do with the debate over their innovative practices in metallurgy. On this subject see Auguste Bouchayer, *Les chartreux: Maîtres de forges* (1927); Joelle Dupraz, "Bovinant, une mine de fer dans les limites du désert de la Grande Chartreuse (XIIème-XVIIIème siècles)," in *La naissance des Chartreuses*, ed. Bernard Bligny and Gerald Chaix (1986), 489-500, and Gerardo Posada, *Der Heilige Bruno* (1987), 127.

[10] Cheslyn Jones and others, eds., *The Study of Spirituality* (1986). The Carmelites and other mendicants receive nearly 30 pages, the Cistercians 3, and the Benedictines 13.

[11] In his discussion of various critiques of scholasticism in the late Middle Ages, Jean Leclercq says concisely, ". . . always in the background and sometimes to the fore is the Charterhouse." See "Monastic and Scholastic Theology, Fourteenth to Sixteenth Century," in *Cloister to Classroom* (1986), 184. For literature regarding the significance of the Carthusians in sixteenth-century Catholic reform see Gerald Chaix, *Réforme et Contre-Réforme Catholique*, 3 vols (1981); Joseph Greven, *Die kölner Kartause* (1935); Chaix, "Contributions cartusiennes" aux débuts de la réforme Catholique," *Revue d'histoire de l'Eglise de France*, 75 [= no. 194] (1989), 115-23.; T. H. Martín, "Los misticos alemanes en la España del XVI y XVII," *Revista de Espiritualidad*, 48 (1989), 111-28; Ildefonso M. Gómez, "Los Cartujos y los estudios," *Los monjes y los estudios* (1963), 163-207.

[12] See Heinrich Rüthing, "Zur Geschichte der Kartausen in der Ordensprovinz Alemannia inferior von 1320 bis 1400," in Zadnikar and Wienand, *Die Kartäuser*, 139-67. Rüthing gives the following list of Carthusian foundations: 1084-1200: 37; 1201-1250: 10; 1251-1300: 15; 1301-1350: 55; 1351-1400: 44; 1401-1450: 24; 1451-1500: 16.

Another major survey of Christian spirituality, which includes very welcome essays on the spirituality of late medieval scholasticism and renaissance humanism, begins its single-page discussion of the Carthusians in the late Middle Ages by admitting that "the true significance of the mediating role of the Carthusians in medieval spiritual life and in medieval spirituality has in no way been properly recognized." As have many other scholars, the author turns to the readily accessible writings of Denys of Rijkel (Denys the Carthusian) to represent the Carthusians in general.[13] Although there is no such thing as a "typical Carthusian" (the semi-eremitical Carthusian life permitted considerable latitude in spiritual development), the affective contemplative theology of Hugh of Balma, Guigo de Ponte, or Nicholas Kempf would all serve to illustrate Carthusian mystical theology better than Denys's Thomist and Albertist speculative inclinations.

Yet the order founded by Saint Bruno and his six companions is currently being discovered. Robin Bruce Lockhart has written a popular introduction to the Carthusians growing out of his own spiritual experience as a lay guest at St. Hugh's Charterhouse, Parkminster, England.[14] The heroic witness of the London Carthusians under Henry VIII has never been entirely forgotten. A lay publisher in Cologne, a center of the Carthusian publishing apostolate during the sixteenth-century Catholic Reformation, has issued two volumes intended to introduce to the Catholic reading public the order founded by a native son of the city.[15] Building on the work of the Benedictine André Wilmart earlier in this century

---

[13] Alois M. Haas, "Schools of Late Medieval Mysticism," in *Christian Spirituality: High Middle Ages and Reformation* (1987), 165. While Denys's writings are widely accessible, the late nineteenth-century edition of his *Opera* is little more than a reprint of the sixteenth-century Cologne collection, whereas critical editions of significant but lesser-known Carthusian writings have appeared in the series Sources Chrétiennes and Analecta Cartusiana. *Christian Spirituality: High Middle Ages and Reformation* contains essays by William J. Courtenay on late medieval scholasticism (109-20) and by William Bouwsma (236-51) and James D. Tracy (252-67) on renaissance humanism. Two of these three essays begin by admitting that readers may be surprised to find these essays included. Via Denys of Rijkel, the Carthusian Order briefly makes an entrance in the essay on scholasticism! The preceding volume in the same series, *Christian Spirituality: Origins to the Twelfth Century*, (1985), omitted any mention of the Carthusians in the twelfth century, while giving considerable attention to the Victorines and Cistercians.

[14] *Halfway to Heaven: The Hidden Life of the Sublime Carthusians* (1985). Although the Grande Chartreuse remains closed to nonreligious visitors, other charterhouses have on occasion received lay guests.

[15] Marijan Zadnikar and Adam Wienand, eds., *Die Kartäuser: Der Orden der schweigenden Mönche* (1983); Posada, *Der heilige Bruno*. The Posada volume was translated from Spanish into German by the librarian at the Charterhouse of Marienau, Humbertus Maria Blüm—this illustrates the ad hoc and carefully limited involvement of members of the order in this sort of publishing venture.

and that of the Grenoble professor Bernard Bligny and the Paris Benedictine scholar Jacques Dubois after World War II, a circle of lay and religious *Cartusiana* specialists emerged in the 1970s. James Hogg has
played a leading role in this development, both with the publication of
the monograph series Analecta Cartusiana and the organization of a series of international conferences.[16] Students of English literature in the
late Middle Ages are paying greater attention to the Carthusians.[17] The
Centre Européen de Recherches sur les Congrégations et Ordres Re-
ligieux has announced plans to inaugurate a series of historical atlases of
religious orders with a volume devoted to the Carthusians. Gordon Mursell has further developed the work of Gaston Hocquard and André Wilmart to demonstrate that a coherent theology lies embedded in the
eclectic borrowings of Carthusian spirituality.[18] The Carthusian Order itself has permitted some of the fruits of its members' textual and historical scholarship to be published in the series Sources Chrétiennes.[19]
Private owners and local historical societies at Molsheim in Alsace,
Aggsbach and Gaming in Austria, and Buxheim in southern Germany, to
name only a few examples, have restored or plan to restore the remnants
of charterhouses ravaged by the "enlightened" and revolutionary politics

---

[16] After two decades the Analecta Cartusiana series of books and articles published
by Professor Hogg in Salzburg has given way to a semiannual journal carrying the same
title and published at Pont-Saint-Esprit, France. See Hogg's review of studies through
the late 1960s in his 1970 Berlin dissertation, *Die ältesten consuetudines der Kartäuser*
(published Salzburg, 1973), 7-12.

[17] For samples see some of the articles in Michael G. Sargent, ed., *De Cella in Saeculum* (1989) and Rosemary Ann Lees, *The Negative Language of the Dionysian School of
Mystical Theology*, 2 vols. (1983), which, although focusing on Thomas Gallus to a large
degree, also deals with Hugh of Balma and Guigo de Ponte and cites much of the other
literature dealing with Carthusian influence on vernacular English devotional literature.

[18] Mursell, *The Theology of the Carthusian Life in the Writings of St. Bruno and
Guigo I*, AC 127 (1988); Gaston Hocquard, "Les idées maîtresses des *Meditations* du
Prieur Guiges Ier," in *Historia et Spiritualitas Cartusiensis* (1983), 247-56; André Wilmart, "Les écrits spirituelles des deux Guiges," *RAM*, 5 (1924), 59-79, 127-58, repr. in
Wilmart, *Auteurs spirituels et textes dévots du moyen âge latin* (1932), pp. 217-60. Additional references to Hocquard and Wilmart are found in Mursell. It may be only a slight
exaggeration to compare Wilmart's, Hocquard's, and Mursell's work with that of
Etienne Gilson in *The Mystical Theology of Saint Bernard* (1940), in which he demon-
strated that Bernard was a significant theologian and not merely a pious monk. One of
the aims of the present study is to remind us that monks traditionally have been central to
the theological task of the church in the West.

[19] Guiges I, *Coutumes de Chartreuse*, SC 313 (cited here as *Consuet.*); *Lettres des
premiers Chartreux*, 2 vols, SC 88, 274 (1962, 1980). Jacques Dubois, O.S.B., severely
criticized the first volume's scholarship in "Quelques problèmes de l'histoire de l'ordre
des Chartreux à propos de livres recents," *Revue d'histoire ecclésiastique*, 63 (1968), 27-
54. See James Hogg's defense of its Carthusian editor in "The Carthusians and the 'Rule
of St. Benedict'," in *Itinera Domini* (1988), 281-318.

of the late eighteenth and early nineteenth centuries. Former charter-houses across Europe house museums, including a Carthusian documentation center at Ittingen in Switzerland and a major exhibition in 1991 at Cologne, where the former charterhouse belongs to a Protestant parish.

The present study does not aim at awakening slumbering monastic history out of nostalgic antiquarian interest. Carthusian history is not alone in suffering neglect. In recent decades historians of ideas have rehabilitated the late medieval *via moderna* and have thoroughly revised the interpretation of humanism. Yet students of the late medieval church have concentrated on "high theology"—on the scholastic theology of the universities,[20] and the revisionist view of humanism, while emphasizing its Christian piety, has examined late medieval monasticism only superficially.[21]

Monastic history has received some attention in the context of "late medieval studies," which, ranging from popular religion to literature to social and economic history, have become a growth industry. Kaspar Elm has called for sustained attention to monastic history in the late Middle Ages and his students and colleagues have produced a number of excellent studies.[22] Jacques LeGoff and Jean-Claude Schmitt organized a remarkable study of the mendicant orders in urban France during the late Middle Ages.[23] Dieter Mertens, Klaus Schreiner, Heinrich Rüthing, Barbara Frank, Dieter Stievermann and others have studied Benedictines and Carthusians in Germany, pointing to the complex network of politi-

---

[20] One example may serve to illustrate this point. In a thorough and important study of the idea of repentance in Johann von Staupitz's sermons, Lothar Graf zu Dohna and Richard Wetzel conclude that Staupitz steered a course between the Scylla of attritionist laxness and the Charybdis of a contritionism based on human ability and merit-theology, offering a way out of the *cul-de-sac* of late medieval scholastic teaching on penitence. Kempf's theology of repentance (chapter four) anticipates Staupitz on almost every point. When compared to the scholastic tradition, Staupitz is strikingly refreshing. But the scholastic tradition need not be the sole point of comparison. See "Die Reue Christi," *SMGB*, 94 (1983), 457-82, at 481.

[21] E.g., Giles Constable, "Petrarch and Monasticism," in *Francesco Petrarca: Citizen of the World* (1980), 53-99 (reprinted 1988); Charles Trinkaus, "Humanist Treatises on the Status of the Religious," *SR*, 11 (1964), 7-45 (reprinted 1983); Paul Kristeller, "The Contribution of Religious Orders to Renaissance Thought and Learning, *American Benedictine Review*, 21 (1970), 1-54 (reprinted 1974).

[22] Published primarily in the joint series Berliner Historische Studien / Ordensstudien, sponsored by the Arbeitskreis für vergleichende Ordensforschung of the Friedrich-Meinecke-Institut der Freien Universität Berlin.

[23] See Jean-Claude Schmitt, "Où en est l'enquête 'Ordres mendiants et urbanisation dans la France médiévale?" in *Stellung und Wirksamkeit der Bettelorden in der städtischen Gesellschaft* (1981), 13-18, reporting on progress made by the research team investigating the theses articulated by LeGoff in his well-known article, "Apostolat mendiant et fait urbain dans la France médiévale," *Annales*, 23 (1968), 335-52.

cal, social, and economic forces at work: growing consolidation by territorial princes, monastic reform, growth of towns, founding of universities in Germany, and the "crisis" of the nobility.[24]

Yet in virtually all of these studies, the focus is on change. This has
meant that a "traditional" contemplative order[25] like the Carthusians is of
minimal interest because scholars conventionally assume that "traditional" means "static and unchanging." When scholars discover that even
the most traditional orders changed and developed, the party that favored
change receives most of the attention.[26] We find an example of this in
Klaus Schreiner's study of the Melk and Bursfeld Benedictine reforms.[27]
He argues that differences between the two are visible in greater "openness toward the world" at Melk, referring to more space for reading and
study in the daily *horarium* at Melk compared to the Bursfeld emphasis
on liturgy and manual labor. Schreiner leaves no doubt as to where his
sympathies on this point lie (with Melk). To the medieval mind, however, liturgical worship and manual labor might possibly have represented the greater openness and universality, since worship transcended
monastery walls and penetrated to the throne of God, and since manual
labor involved some degree of personal interaction, whereas the private
study and meditation favored by Melk may have seemed more idiosyn-
cratic and privatized. *Zeitanpassung*, adjusting to the present, is present
not only in the movements historians study, it is part and parcel of their
own interpretive reconstruction of history—the present study included.

Tradition itself is a genuine vehicle for change, a particular approach to change that sets a high priority on faithfulness to the past by
measuring innovations against the norm of what has been handed down
across time. Carthusians did change—a shift from contemplation to limited pastoral activity was underway in the late fifteenth century (see

---

[24] Works by these scholars are listed in the Bibliography. Perhaps the most significant volume is Kaspar Elm, ed., *Reformbemühungen und Observanzbestrebungen im
spätmittelalterlichen Ordenswesen* (1989).

[25] For a description of what I mean by the term "traditional contemplative monastic
order," see Leclercq, "Monastic and Scholastic Theology," 182-83. See also Mertens,
"Kartäuser-Professoren," 79, for evidence that the Carthusians viewed the Cistercians,
and Benedictines as their closest monastic cousins, since all three orders consisted of *viri
contemplativi*.

[26] Steven Rowan, "Chronicle as Cosmos: Hartmann Schedel's Nuremberg Chronicle,
1493," in *Literatur und Kosmos* (= *Daphnis*, 15, no. 2-3 [1986]), 127-59, offers Gregor
Reisch's remarkably secular activity: professor at Freiburg, author of a widely used "encyclopedia," consultant to Hartmann Schedel, confessor to Emperor Maximilian. Reisch
has often been claimed as an example of a Carthusian who remained a university professor after entering religion. Mertens refutes these claims in "Kartäuser-Professoren," 76.

[27] "Benediktinische Klosterreform als zeitgebundene Auslegung der Regel," *Blätter
für württembergische Kirchengeschichte*, 86 (1986), 107-95, at 134.

chapter six below), a shift so significant as to be compared to the Copernican revolution in astronomy by one scholar. From a "traditionalist"
standpoint,[28] however, the issue was whether the changes beginning in
the late fifteenth century were faithful to the Carthusian tradition or
whether they might destroy what had kept the Carthusians faithful—
were they treading close to the edge that had led to laxity in other orders?
A traditional order must constantly ask these questions if it is to remain
traditional. Nicholas Kempf asked these questions and answered them
very traditionally.

Why not let monks who allegedly were fast asleep in traditionalism
already in their own day continue to slumber through the late twentieth
century? Because attempting to view their era through their sleepy eyes
might possibly give us a new angle of vision, might refract our own view
and help us to "get the story crooked." Our effort at seeing things crookedly might begin by taking seriously the spiritual, psychological, and institutional context of monasticism. In doing so, we must be aware of a
dual temptation: *historians of ideas* are tempted to leap easily back and
forth over the monastery wall, mining monastic authors for their theology without asking about the context in which monks lived that theology. Whether lack of attention to context produces a intolerable level of
distortion when dealing with university theology is something I leave to

---

[28] Referring to Jerome Aliotti (1412-80), an Italian Benedictine reformer, Leclercq
comments, "In particular, he wanted to remedy the ignorance, the *indocta simplicitas*, of
monasticism. On the other hand, however, he does not want monks to fall into the 'sub-
tleties', the 'distinctions', the 'vain curiosity' which he combats in words very similar to
the terms used by Saint Bernard. . . . In short, he was an authentic representative of the
monastic tradition; but he belonged to his own century and no longer to the twelfth. The
fundamental convictions were the same, but an historical evolution had taken place, and
he noticed this, . . ." "Monastic and Scholastic Theology," 185-86. Coming from one of
the leading "filio-pietistic" writers on monastic culture, these words amply refute the
charges made by Schreiner and other secular historians that modern monastic scholars
create a static, idealized, unchanging portrait of monastic history. Schreiner yields to the
opposite temptation—rather than measure change against the putative "timelessly valid
norms" of the filio-pietists, he prefers simple relativism, insisting that the monks denounced by fifteenth-century reformers were often merely trying to convince their order
or community to take account of changing times. One might ask whether Schreiner has
not anachronistically employed modern assumptions that give the benefit of the doubt to
"changing times." Traditionalists, whether twentieth-century Amish or fifteenth-century
Benedictine reformers, are ready to accept change, but believe that *Zeitanpassung* can be
either good or bad depending on whether the times to which one is adjusting are good or
bad, hence the need to evaluate change within the context of tradition. Ironically, the
same charge of static idealism was directed by the Benedictine professor Jacques DuBois
against the anonymous Carthusian editor of the Sources Chrétiennes edition of the Carthusian *Consuetudines*. See Hogg's defense of the editor in "Carthusians and the 'Rule
of St. Benedict'" and Hogg's own account of change and development in the order in his
article, "Daily Life."

others to decide.[29] Ignoring the context is disastrous when the subject is monasticism, for monastic theology is simply monastic life: the *horarium*, role-formed identity, the patterns of liturgy and labor, the cycle of sounds and silences in a highly structured manner of living, indeed, a mannered way of life. Contemplative theology and mystical union take on different meanings when divorced from their original context in the monastic life, as was typical of some late medieval mendicant spiritual writers.[30] The difference was not lost on fathers of the Council of Trent.[31] Yet temptation shows a second face: *social historians* may too readily subordinate ideas to structures and contexts. In the present study we are concerned with contemplative monasticism's regulative, notional, psychological, and spiritual context as a tool, as a set of lenses, to help us understand the meaning of the monastic life, to help us glimpse the monastic *mentalité*. Thus the present study resembles conventional history of ideas. Before we can profitably address monasticism in the context of late medieval and Reformation politics, economics, and religion we must have a better understanding of monastic *mentalité per se*.

Lucien Febvre, one of the founders of the Annales School, wrote about the history of mentalities by giving exquisite attention to the structures of everyday life, yet also writing what can be called "a work of intellectual history." Unfortunately, "after Febvre, historians with an interest in *mentalité* have not done studies of great writers and thinkers," concentrating instead on the economic and social life of the common folk.[32] In a study of the symbolic world of the French nobility in the sixteenth century, Kristen Neuschel[33] reminds us that

> People in the sixteenth century were different from us, not simply because they had different ideas about certain things, but because they constructed their world in wholly different terms. *Notions* of theirs which look familiar to us are nevertheless not and cannot be the same notions we hold.

---

[29] Among recent efforts to take account of the institutional and spatial context while focusing on the history of ideas, one of the most successful is William J. Courtenay's, *Schools and Scholars in Fourteenth-Century England* (1987).

[30] See Thomas Renna, "Wyclif's Attacks on the Monks," in *From Ockham to Wyclif* (1987), 267-80, at 272.

[31] See Klaus Ganzer, "Monastische Reform und Bildung: Ein Traktat des Hieronymus Aliotti (1412-1480) über die Studien der Mönche," in *Reformatio Ecclesiae* [Iserloh Festschrift] (1980), 181-99, at 181, where the debate between the Benedictine abbot Isidor Chiari and the Dominican theologian, Domingo Soto, is summarized: contemplative monks meditate on scripture; mendicants teach it in the schools.

[32] The quotations are from Beatrice Gottlieb's translator's preface to Lucien Febvre, *The Problem of Unbelief in the Sixteenth Century* (1982), xxiii-xxiv.

[33] Kristen B. Neuschel, *Word of Honor* (1989), 19-20, emphasis added.

In his most famous example, Febvre argues that while the term 'atheism' existed then as now, it expressed a notion that was understood by means of a radically different symbolic and linguistic environment in the sixteenth century.

In Nicholas Kempf's symbolic world, what is absent may signify as loudly and vibrantly as what is present. Our crooked view and dissonant audition of his world must watch and listen for presences and absences, sounds and silences: The absence of an inner-directed sense of self and the presence of a Rule (chapter four); the absence of speaking[34] and the presence of a spiritual director's word (chapter four); the "easy way out " of spiritual *securitas* and *vacatio*[35] and the "womanish" avoidance of "virile" spiritual risk-taking (chapters three, six, and seven)—all of these shaped the world in which Nicholas Kempf lived his life. They frame his understanding of ecclesial and pastoral leadership (chapter six) as well as his view of mystical union (chapter five).

The desert monastic tradition with its slogan, "Abba give me a word," has echoed through the centuries, even when the word was an absurd one designed to test the radical commitment of the novice. The word, codified in the Rule but still requiring interpretion by the sages and seniors of the community, shaped monastic life in ways that were different from the world's commerce in words. At the conclusion of her thorough study of the way monasticism was embedded in the social and economic networks of twelfth-century Burgundy, Constance Bouchard[36] commented that

> The life of the reformed monastery appealed [to local nobles] exactly because it was so diametric to the normal noble life in the world. The donors were independent agents, wealthy, living a life in which family ties and the begetting of heirs were of major importance; and they rushed to

---

[34] Paul F. Gehl, "Mystical Language Models in Monastic Education Psychology," *JMRS*, 14 (1984), 219-43; idem, "Competens Silentium: Varieties of Monastic Silence in the Medieval West," *Viator*, 18 (1987), 125-60; Paul Saenger, "Books of Hours and Reading Habits," *Scrittura e civiltà*, 9 (1985), 239-69; idem, "Physiologie de la lecture et séparation des mots," *Annales*, 44 (1989), 939-52; idem, "Silent Reading," *Viator*, 13 (1982), 367-414.

[35] These terms translate literally as "freedom from cares" and "leisure" or "lack of busyness." However any translation of these terms into English involves words with pejorative connotations, even as the English cognates to the Latin originals ("security" and "vacation") run counter to the modern, activist work ethic. The purpose of chapters three, six, and seven of the present work is to explain more precisely what these terms meant for monks. At this point it should be sufficient to warn the reader that they do not mean what they seem to mean.

[36] Constance Brittain Bouchard, *Sword, Miter, and Cloister* (1987), 246.

make gifts to monasteries where the monks relinquished their self-will for humble obedience and forsook all personal possessions for an austere life in which the only 'family' that mattered was the brotherhood of the community. Because knights and nobles knew well that their lives were not the holy life Christ had recommended, the reformed monastic life that was opposed so thoroughly to their own seemed almost by definition a holy life, and the monks those men most likely to have the ear of God.

This sense of disjunction, of ana-chronism rather than *Zeitanpassung*, a disjunction that made monasticism perversely attractive, increased as the aristocratic-peasant culture of the high Middle Ages gave way to an urban-commercial-scholastic culture in the late Middle Ages. In Nicholas Kempf we find someone still speaking the silent language of the desert and the early medieval monastery. The very anachronism of the Old Order Carthusians on the eve of the word- and print-saturated age of Reformation casts a different light on the changes underway between the twelfth and the eighteenth centuries.

The present study pursues two interrelated objectives. On its most literal level, it recounts the life and letters of a fifteenth-century Vienna University master of arts and Carthusian prior (chapters one and two and appendix A) placed in the historical context of reform and renewal, Renaissance and Reformation (chapter seven and the Epilogue). On another level—what the monks might have called the "higher senses" of the text composed by Nicholas Kempf's life, writings, and context—it explores the significance and symbolism of that life and context (chapters three through six).

Chapters three through six return again and again to the theme of voluntary meekness and affectivity as "means" of hidden strength. Human incapacity as the result of sin and human receptiveness in the light of God's mercy dominate Kempf's monastic theology. His understanding of spiritual direction, repentance and salvation, pastoral leadership and ecclesial reform, withdrawal into contemplative repose (*otium*, *vacatio*), and mystical theology, are based on the assumption that initiative lies with the Creator God, with the Rule, with the spiritual director. The centrality of this affectivity was hammered home to me as I struggled to find a concise term that adequately translates the cluster of Latin terms derived from *ad-ficio* and *ad-facio*: to do something to someone, to exert an influence on someone, to be brought into such a state, to be affected. *Affectio* thus means "the relation to or disposition toward a thing produced in a person by some influence" (Lewis and Short, *A Latin Dictionary*). The only activity of the "affected" person is to be disposed toward someone by virtue of having been influenced by someone or something. The affective spirituality of the Carthusian mystics Hugh of

Balma, Guigo de Ponte, and Nicholas Kempf (chapter five) and the twelfth-century love-centered spirituality of Bruno and Guigo I[37] constitute a receptive theology, an impacted rather than impacting, a being-acted-upon-theology, a sagging-back-to-let-oneself-be-overwhelmed-by theology. At the heart of affective theology is the word *desiderium*—a yearning, loving longing for something indescribable and ungraspable yet unceasingly desirable.[38] Affective theology "knows" that the object of its yearning cannot be grasped, at least not in this life. Instead of grasping, instead of apprehending, it seeks and yearns. As Plato suggests in the *Symposium*, one cannot love what one has already grasped, one can only love what one still lacks. In the language of the affective mystics, even the "clinging" union with God is simply the outstretched yearning of an affected, acted-upon, spirit.

Affective theology's foil is the investigating, out-looking, linear, speculating, logocentric theology of the schools (and of modern science and technology). *Speculatio* connotes casting one's line of sight forward, reaching out to take hold of and perceive, grasping, comprehending, penetrating. In the words of Hans Kellner,[39]

> The problem . . . is how to speak within a discourse of reason and representation that has . . . generally repressed the possibility of speaking as a woman from our very imaginations. "Woman un-thinks the unifying, regulating history that homogenizes and channels forces, herding contradictions into a single battlefield" [Hélène Cixous]. Logocentrism, the term that denotes Derrida's concept of the word-centered, conceptual history of Western metaphysics, is equated [by Cixous] with phallocentrism, the need to claim authority by defining, clarifying, making sequential points, leading to conclusions.

Centuries ago contemplative monks linked and relativized the functional equivalents of "logocentrism" and "phallocentrism."[40] Yet, in an

---

[37] For the earlier Carthusian tradition, not discussed in detail in the present volume, see Gordon Mursell's fine book.

[38] One of the best studies of Bernard of Clairvaux's spirituality is constructed around this theme: Michael Casey, *Athirst for God: Spiritual Desire in Bernard of Clairvaux's Sermons on the Song of Songs* (1988).

[39] Kellner, *Language and Historical Representation*, 302-3, citing Cixous's linkage of Lacan and Derrida. Kellner notes that, for Lacan, "[The phallus] is not a human organ of any sort, but rather a reference to the ancient processions in which a veiled phallus was carried about. For Lacan, the phallus is a signifier that creates desire for the unveiling of a signified, of meaning and truth; . . ."

[40] Many Carthusians insisted that women had a special aptitude for non-scholastic (i.e., non-logocentric) contemplative theology. Jacob de Paradiso used the standard medieval reference works, among them, Vincent of Beauvais's *Speculum historiale*, to

age of thrusting, driving activism eager for "empowerment," advocates of modern causes are likely to read the silent and receptive[41] *sola gratia* religion of the blind, maimed, lame, and poor Carthusians as defeatist "self-victimization." It is not surprising that traditional contemplative theology was denounced as "womanish" and "cowardly" already in the fifteenth century (chapter six).

Thus the present study offers a "crooked" reading in place of modern and postmodern orthodoxies: the "womanish" contemplative men whose flight from leadership is studied in this book were truly farsighted leaders in their day, even though they looked backwards and moved more by touch than by sight, more by yearning than by accomplishment.[42] This "crooked" reading is not entirely my own invention: it is in fact an effort to take these contemplatives at their word, to read them in a straight, literal sense. Taking *them* literally and straight means that they will be "crooked" whether viewed through our modern, enlightened and postenlightened lenses or the "worldly" lenses of their own contemporaries. As a German drinking song reminds us, a drunken man is convinced that it is the lamp-posts that stagger and the streets that run crooked.[43] To the monks, mystical union was *sober* inebriation.[44]

The hermeneutic optics employed by monastic theology to make what seemed crooked to the world appear straight was *discretio* (chapter four). Instead of *critical* analysis (*discretio* and *critical* come from the

---

compile a list that included Marie d'Oignies (ca. 1177-1213), Hedwig of Silesia (ca. 1174-1243), Elisabeth of Thüringia (1207-31), Gertrude the Great (1256-1302), Birgitta of Sweden (ca. 1303-1344), Dorothea of Montau (1347-1394) and his favorite, Catherine of Siena (1347-80). See Dieter Mertens, "Jakob von Paradies über die mystische Theologie," in *Kartäusermystik und -mystiker*, vol. 5 (1982), 43. The same was true of Vincent of Aggsbach. See Johann Auer, "Die *Theologia mystica* des Kartäusers Jakob von Jüterbog (d. 1465)" in *Die Kartäuser in Österreich*, vol. 2 (1981), 42-45.

[41] That a feminine-receptive epistemology underlies Carthusian spirituality, which in turn draws on patristic sources, is evident in the quotations from Guigo de Ponte in chapter six, below and especially in Guigo I, *Meditation* 249 (SC 308: 182), which portrays outer forms as masculine and phallic, leaving an imprint in the human mind that has wrapped herself around them.

[42] Alison Weber's book, *Teresa of Avila and the Rhetoric of Femininity* (1990), would have benefited from familiarity with the affective, "womanish" monastic tradition. The "rhetorical strategy" by which Teresa purportedly subverts the misogyny of her age is in fact of one piece with the monastic spirituality in which Teresa was formed. Weber never mentions Teresa's monastic tradition.

[43] "Grad aus dem Wirtshaus, komm' ich jetzt heraus, / Straße, wie wunderlich siehst du mir aus! / Rechter Hand, linker Hand, beides vertauscht, / Straße ich merk' es wohl, du bist berauscht. . . . Und die Laterne erst, was muß ich sehen? / Die können alle nicht gerade mehr stehen! / Wackeln und fackeln die kreuz und die quer: / scheinen betrunken mir, allesamt schwer."

[44] See Kempf, *Cantica*, prologue, ch. 6 (G1, 136v, 35 - 137r, 11; Pez, *Bibliotheca Ascetica*, 11: 23-24), cited in ch. 2, n. 52, below.

same Greek root) that pushed forth to distinguish truth from falsehood and sought demonstrative knowledge in the sense of Aristotle's *Posterior Analytics*, the monks began by abandoning sexuality, family, words, possessions, cognitions, even their own (false) self-identity, in order to discover a deeper and more encompassing language and identity, which they expressed both in persuasive rhetorical "logic" (chapter two) and in silent contemplation. Monastic *discretio* cannot be pinned down to a particular set of concepts or fixed rules, yet it was firmly based on the vow of commitment to the monastic Rule. It was the kaleidoscopic result of years of experience of living within the Rule, the cumulative yet charismatic wisdom of the *seniores* (the Old Men of the desert) and the pastor-abbot-spiritual director. The Rule, which itself was a symbol of the Creator's provident, fore-seeing, directing reality, established a framework whose givenness permitted the monk to probe himself to the core, stripping away the falsities out of which he had constructed his selfhood: pride; his inability to manage his eating, sexuality, or acquisitiveness; his anger and envy; his listless lack of commitment. This process is *discretio*, discernment. From the simple and oft-repeated words and deeds of a highly patterned life of liturgy and labor emerged a language that permitted one to dis-cover, to un-cover, to "invent" (in the medieval sense) oneself by discerning, i.e. by separating out, the falsities of the jury-rigged ego constructed in the wake of the Fall. The Rule and its human interpreters remained but pale shadows of the provident Logos directing the universe, but they permitted one to draw closer to that provident Logos precisely because they codified a radical renunciation of so much that makes up the normal human commerce in words and deeds: pride, acquisitiveness, anger, comparisons with others' possessions and qualities, words, sex, food.

All too often scholars have described the religion of certain "affective" late medieval groups and theologians (e.g., the Devotio Moderna) as "interiorized" and obscurantist piety. Far from being merely a reaction to scholastic theology, this late medieval affective theology is a survival from an earlier age when all Christian theology sought to persuade, to move, to *affect* the hearts as well as the minds of believers.[45] In its very method the rhetorical and metaphorical theology of the Church Fathers (up to and including Bernard of Clairvaux) moved and shifted, discovering means of clarification ("arguments" in the Latin sense of the word), arranging them, couching them in suitable words, learning them well,

---

[45] On parallels and distinctions between humanist and monastic critique of scholasticism, discussed in greater detail in chapter two below, see Leclercq, "Monastic and Scholastic Theology," 184-85.

and forming voice and gesture to convey them optimally. The message could be, indeed had to be, massaged to fit the audience at hand, just as the spiritual director took a hard and fast Rule and, drawing on his wise experience, adapted it to each novice under his care, creating from the fixed grammar of the Rule a remarkably flexible pastoral language with which to mold and shape the young monk—a far cry from the cogent and demonstrative technical language of speculative knowledge.

Peter Brown[46] offers a perceptive description:

> There was always a moment, then, when the thoughts of the monk could be sensed as no longer belonging wholly to the human mind, but to the demons or to the angels whose subtle presences were registered in the unaccustomed force of the flow, through the heart, of powerful trains of thought—the *logismoi*. Hence the crucial importance of the gift of discernment, of *diakrisis*, among the Desert Fathers. This meant far more than self-knowledge and good sense, though it might, in fact, often include a large measure of both. It meant the rare spiritual gift of being able to see clearly what one could no longer call one's own in one's own stream of consciousness. It was the ability to heed a warning signal to depend on others.

Kempf lived in full continuity with this vision, thanks to the reverence for the Desert Fathers that pulsed more vibrantly through the Carthusian *eremus* than anywhere else in the late medieval Western monastic landscape. Here lies the heart of Kempf's hermeneutic—a person only really knows himself when he knows enough to depend on another, on someone outside himself. That insight is discretion, the text is the heart, and years of experience together with the illumination of the Spirit teach one how to exegete it. Genuine self-knowledge leads *beyond oneself*, ultimately to the image of God *in oneself*.

Against the background of a monastic culture which cultivated an extrinsic rather than intrinsic self, the present study seeks to make a contribution to our understanding of the Renaissance and Reformation. Burckhardt's "individualism" as the key to the Italian Renaissance is no longer in fashion, and Kristeller's insistence that those devoted to the *studia humanitatis* were part of the medieval rhetorical tradition has largely been accepted, while Giuseppe Toffanin's effort to demonstrate continuity with medieval scholasticism has not.[47] As chapters two, four, and seven suggest, medieval contemplative monasticism flourished in a prescholas-

---

[46] Peter R. L. Brown, *The Body and Society* (1988), 228-29.

[47] See Albert Rabil, Jr., in the preface to volume one of *Renaissance Humanism*, ed. Albert Rabil, Jr. (1988), xi-xii.

tic rhetorical culture that offers parallels to the first stirrings of human-ism in fifteenth-century Germany. Yet for all the affinities between monastics and humanists on both sides of the Alps, something of Burck-hardt's Renaissance individual is visible in Petrarch precisely when he is viewed *against* the Carthusian tradition his own brother espoused.

The same fundamental issues of extensive and intensive self-iden-tity in the Carthusian tradition can be applied to Martin Luther, who agreed that humility was nothing more than the humble recognition that human works are *stercora*, excrement. Yet Luther came to view the mo-nastic Rule, which Nicholas Kempf embraced gladly as an aid to his weakness, lameness, and complete inability to save himself, as nothing but an effort at self-salvation. This illustrates most effectively the shift-ing of the prism, a refocusing that made what Kempf saw "straight" seem "crooked" to Luther. In the wake of four hundred years of the mod-ern version of authentic self-identity this refocusing now mandates that we try to see things crookedly in order to understand what animated Kempf.

We should not be surprised that the Carthusians in the twelfth cen-tury, having chosen the rhetorical over the demonstrative, the affective over the speculative, the feminine-receptive over the masculine-phallic, meekness over power, "cowardly" *securitas* over courageous risk-taking, silence over words, and repose over action, silenced even a voice from the grave. Half a millennium later, one of their contributions to Reforma-tion Catholicism was a voice straight from hell as recast by a Jesuit play-wright.

The Carthusian life began after Bruno and his friends left the elev-enth-century schools for the Alpine wilderness just as proto-modern European scholarship, in the form of medieval scholasticism, was begin-ning to bud. With exquisite irony a seventeenth-century Jesuit school-master-playwright, Jacob Bidermann, employed the "Paris professor" of the Bruno-legend to turn the respected *Herr Professor* of his day into a "Dean of Liberal Arts in Hell."[48] In the intermission between these two acts of the medieval (Bruno) and early-modern (Bidermann) historical drama we find a fifteenth-century Carthusian pedagogue articulating the wisdom of the cloister. We need to listen carefully, for Carthusian articu-lation proceeds mostly by eloquent silence. This book utilizes words. It employs the imagery of vision (skewed, to be sure) to trace out a theol-ogy that gropes affectedly in yearning blindness. It necessarily proceeds

---

[48] See the Epilogue for details, including the 1991 musical theater revival of this play as part of the quincentenary celebration of the birth of Ignatius of Loyola.

in the sort of ordered arrangement required by a scholarly, indeed, a scholastic, community. It cannot be otherwise—how does one write wordlessly? The Carthusians will remain obscure and unnamed in their pursuit of the inexpressible, obscure Song of songs, for the words of this book aim to enlighten a different group of *viri obscuri*. The sleeping monks will continue to slumber.[49]

Trahere in affectum—affected and dimwitted groping rather than clever and grasping comprehension—was the key to Nicholas Kempf's approach to education, his method of enlightenment. *Qui potest capere, capiat* (Mt 19:12).

---

[49] Respect for the Carthusian tradition of anonymity has led me to cite anonymously those modern works of Carthusian scholarship that were published anonymously, even in those instances where "outside" scholars have revealed in secondary literature the name of the Carthusian scholar involved.

CHAPTER ONE

MONK

People who spend their time acquiring books without reading or understanding them injure themselves. For, if "to read without understanding is to be negligent" [prologue to *Disticha Catonis*], how much more careless it is to copy or collect books with great effort without ever reading them! For if, as often happens, the soul of a collector of many unread books is collected by death, who will then own his books? If you have few books and modest knowledge you are better able to give account for them. One ought above all to acquire virtues and good works, which cannot be misused. Seek first the kingdom of God through these virtues and everything else will be added—perhaps not as much as you inordinately desire but enough to suffice for your soul's salvation. [Kempf, *Rect.*, I.9.]

1. Novice

On September 6, 1440, at the charterhouse known as the Throne of Mary, located at Gaming in Lower Austria, a former regent master of arts from the university at Vienna, Nicholas Kempf, prostrated himself before God and the community and asked to be received for mercy's sake as a member of the community and servant of all.[1] He arose and, after hearing a description of the rigors of the Carthusian life, reaffirmed his desire to undertake it. Then he knelt and placed his clasped hands between those of the community's prior in order to be received as probationary member. He was reminded that, just as he would be free to leave before making his solemn profession about a year later, so too the community was free to reject him after a year's probation if, God forbid, he lacked a genuine monastic vocation. After exchanging the kiss of peace,

---

[1] The following reconstruction is based on the procedures for receiving novices and making profession outlined in the *Statuta antiqua* (1259, 1271), part II, ch. 23-24 (= AC 99.2, pp. 205-11), which fleshed out details left untreated in Guigo I's *Consuetudines*, ch. 22-25. For the thirteenth- and fourteenth-century legislation I have used the *Statuta ordinis cartusiensis* published by Amerbach in Basel in 1510. For convenience, I have added the page numbers from the AC 99 reprint edition, since the original edition lacked consecutive pagination. Kempf dealt with this subject in *Prop* [see appendix A, no. 5], I.30. Vienna ÖNB cvp 2731, 2r-11r, a codex written at Gaming during Kempf's tenure as prior, contains an *ordo* for clothing a novice, including musical notation for the psalmody and chant.

he exchanged his own clothes for a novice's habit. Then he was led to the church, where the monks chanted a "Veni Sancte Spiritus" in a penitential mode (minus the alleluia) and the prior prayed that God would "confirm what he has done in us."

The novice was then led in a procession, with the prior in front and the psalm-chanting community ranked by seniority following, to the door of his cell (which was actually a small two-story cottage). There the prior took him by the hand and led him into the cell, with much of the symbolism of a wedding ceremony. As the novice knelt at the oratory of his cell, the psalmody concluded with a "Kyrie Eleison," an "Our Father," and several prayers, including one addressed to "God who justifies the unrighteous."[2] This phrase did not simply wash over Nicholas Kempf's head. As we shall see in chapter four, it became a central part of his understanding of salvation by faith and by grace alone.

The ceremonies concluded with the prior exhorting the novice to keep the observances and exercises of the order for the remission of his sins, hearing his confession, and absolving him of vows made in the world,[3] if he should persevere in the order.

Approximately a year later Nicholas Kempf made his profession as a monk, his commitment to the Carthusian way of life. "Confiding more in the Lord's love and in the prayers of the community than in his own

---

[2] *Statuta antiqua*, part II, ch. 23 (AC 99, pp. 206-8): [par. 12] "Induitur igitur novitius et preparatus, ducitur ad ecclesiam et instruitur ut ad gradum altaris faciat orationem suam. Interim conventus cantat in ecclesia versum, "Veni Sancte Spiritus" sine alleluia. Quo finito, dicat prior, 'Confirma hoc deus,' et respondeatur a conventu, 'quod operatus es in nobis,'; 'Deus vobiscum,' 'Et cum spiritu tuo.' . . . Quo dicto, . . . eundo ad cellam precedit prior cum stola et aspersorio, sequitur novitius, deinde conventus, precedentibus antiquioribus. [par. 13] Veniens autem prior ad celle ostium, aspergit novitium et ipsam cellam, dicens 'Pax huic domui.' Tenens manum novitii, introducit eum et ducit ad oratorium. [par. 14] Finito vero psalmo sive psalmis cum gloria patri, sequitur 'kyrieleison, christeleison, kyrieleison'; 'pater noster,' 'et ne nos inducas,' 'salvum me fac, servum tuum,'. . . 'Deus qui iustificas impium,' et cetera. . . . . [par. 15] Dum ista dicuntur, est novitius flexis genibus in oratorio. Quibus completis, prior iniungit ei celle et aliorum que ad ordinem nostrum pertinent observantiam et exercitium, in remissione peccatorum, et, audita eius confessione, absolvit eum a votis factis in seculo, si perseveraverit in ordine." (emphasis added). The *Nova Statuta* (1368) made no changes in this procedure. In the Gaming *Ordo* the key phrase reads "qui vivificat impium." Cvp 2731, 2r, line 23.

[3] Kempf described the process later in the following manner: "Indutus et ante gradum altaris prostratus iacens humil{l}ime et omni devocione qua potest se Deo et Beate Marie Virgini committat et Spiritus Sancti graciam invocet, ut eum confirmet et usque ad professionem suum propositum deducat, dicendo, 'Confirma hoc Deus quod operatus es in me, quod incepi pro tuo honore et mea salute. Dirige gressus meos in semitis tuis, in quibus ambulare incepi, ut non moveatur vestigia mea declinando extra ea et revertendo ad viam pristinam secularem.' Postmodum vero cella sibi in remissionem peccatorum iniungitur, {et} unus sibi ex patribus assignatur, qui ipsum informet ut suum propositum salubriter exitu terminare valeat, scilicet solempnem professionem attingendo, . . ." *Prop*, I. 30 (VS1, 20v B, 33 - A, 10).

prayers," he would have taken off his clothes as a public witness to his readiness to put off the old man [Eph 4:22, 24][4] and put on the new man symbolized by the habit of a choir monk bearing the sign of the cross (the yoke of Christ) over which the following prayer had been offered:

> Lord Jesus Christ, who are the way without which no one can come to the Father, we beseech you in most gentle mercy to lead this your servant, who has turned away from fleshly yearnings, along the path of rule-bound observance. And because you have deigned to call sinners, saying 'Come to me, all you who are burdened, and I shall refresh you,' grant that this your voice of invitation might grow so strong in him that, setting aside the burdens of sins and tasting how sweet you are, he might deserve to be nourished by your own repast . . . [Guigo I, *Consuet.*, ch. 25.1; SC 313, p. 218.]

Then he would have been told: "From this moment onward, the day you were received by us, you must regard yourself as a stranger to everything in the world. Without permission from your superior, you will have control over nothing, not even your own will."[5] Once more, the phrase was not lost on Nicholas Kempf, for we shall encounter his incorporation of this principle into his work as a monastic pastor in chapter four. His commitment, made to God rather than men, was to be impressed on his memory like a seal on wax, a seal that God alone could remove. Thus, in the midst of each future action, it could serve as a reminder of the commitment he had made.[6]

In the early months of 1441,[7] on the other side of the Alps at the court of the king of Naples, Lorenzo Valla was writing a dialogue (*De professione religiosorum*) that wittily attacked precisely this type of sur-

---

[4]   *Prop*, II.23 (VS1, 34v A, 7-31): "Deinde humiliter et ex corde petit pro se orari, ut ipsis conjungatur per amoris osculum et vere, in Domino caritatis, plus confidens in eorum oracionibus quam proprijs, exuitur vestibus in publico, ut publice testetur se veterem hominem exuere et nigram suam conversacionem secularem, que undique eum circumdabat sicut cappa, penitus deponere. Induitur autem cruce veste que habet figuram crucis et crucifixi, ut cognoscat se amplius crucifixum mundo et crucem Domini portare et iugum Christi. Professionem eciam in cartula conscriptam propria manu signo crucis sigillat, ut se non hominibus, sed Deo et Christo crucifixo obligatum sciat, nec per hominem potest illud sigillum amoveri sed per solum Deum. Professionem memorie suam imprimat et in omnibus suis actibus recogitet, 'Tu promisisti Deo et sanctis eius conversionem morum tuorum et quid iam facis? Nunquam iterum post veteres declinas mores tuos consuetudines' etc. Amen."

[5]   Guigo I., *Consuet.*, 25.2.

[6]   See the passage from *Prop*, II.23, quoted in n. 4, above.

[7]   See the introduction to *Laurentii Valle De professione religiosorum*, ed. Mariarosa Cortesi (1986), xxxiii, where the editor concludes her argument for the early months of 1441 as the date of composition.

render of one's own will.We shall devote the rest of this book to an effort to understand Nicholas Kempf's motives and inspiration and their contexts. In an age of self-assertion, self-discovery, and "empowerment," Lorenzo Valla's arguments are likely to need much less interpretation.

Nicholas Kempf's story does not end with his solemn vows. From 1447 to 1451 he was prior of the second-oldest charterhouse in "German" lands, Geirach, in Slovenia. He then returned to Gaming as prior from 1451 to 1458. A number of masters of arts and other former university students followed Kempf to Gaming, which in turn supplied leaders for Carthusian monasteries in Austria, Moravia, Hungary, Slovenia, and Switzerland. By 1458 former Vienna academics made up more than half of the professed monks of the Gaming community (which included those living and giving leadership in other Carthusian monasteries).

2. Scholar

Who was this man? We know little about his life before 1440. All modern biographical sketches rest on data supplied in the eighteenth century by the Gaming librarian Leopold Wydemann to the Benedictine monk Bernard Pez at Melk and to the Jesuit Anton Steyerer at Vienna, pioneers in the modern writing of Austrian history.[8] Based on a set of verses entered in a Gaming manuscript that appears not to have survived, Wydemann believed Kempf had been born ca. 1397, since the verses, written by a contemporary of Kempf, refer to Kempf's death as a centenarian in 1497.[9] Were this to be taken literally, Kempf would have been

---

[8]   On Pez see appendix A. Pez published a biographical sketch in the preface to volume 4 of his *Bibliotheca ascetica antiquo-nova*. Wydemann's comments on the lives of various Gaming monks were interspersed in a copy he made for Steyerer of a list prepared by Wilhelm Hofer in 1458 for a visitation of the Gaming charterhouse. Hofer's original list is found in Vienna, ÖNB cvp 12811; Wydemann's copy is in Steyerer, "Collectanea historica Austriaca," part 6, Böhm 86/6, in the Österreichisches Haus-, Hof-, und Staatsarchiv, Vienna, 377r-379v (new foliation). Further biographical information on Kempf is found in Joseph Karl Newen von Newenstein, *Pandectae saeculares*, 56-57; *Topographie von Niederösterreich*, (1893), 3: 281; Nikolaus Paulus, "Der Kartäuser Nikolaus Kempf von Straßburg," *AEKG*, 3 (1928), 22-46; Engelbert Krebs, "Kempf, Nikolaus von," *Verfasserlexikon*, 2 (1936), 784-86, and, in greater detail in Alois Hörmer, "Der Kartäuser Nikolaus Kempf als Seelenführer" (1959).

[9]   Text in Pez, *Bibl. ascetica*, 4: b2-b3. Cf. Pez and Wydemann correspondence, "Peziana" collection, Melk, Stiftsarchiv (no shelf number), for Wydemann's letter of January 22, 1718, to Pez, in which he speculates that many of Kempf's works had been lost—because he died a centenarian and must have written other works before entering the charterhouse at the age of forty-three. This late fourteenth-century birthdate was as-

functioning as prior of the Charterhouse at Geirach at the age of ninety-three when he asked to be relieved of his duties in 1490.

Nor can a birthdate of 1397 be easily reconciled with what is known about Kempf's university studies. The entry, "Nicolaus Kempf de Argentina, pauper," appears in the Vienna matriculation register under the Rhenish nation for the spring term in 1433. The arts faculty *Acta* testify to a normal academic arts curriculum for Kempf: bachelor of arts in 1435, *magister artium actu regens* during the years 1437 and 1438.[10] If Kempf was born ca. 1497 he would have been thirty-six when he began his studies. Hörmer explained this unusual situation by pointing to an entry for a "Nicolaus de Argentina" in the matriculation register for 1416.[11] He reasoned that Kempf could have begun his arts studies at a somewhat more conventional age in 1416, with the entry for 1433 referring to the beginning of his theological studies—all in all, a rather unlikely explanation.[12] We conclude that Kempf began his university studies in 1433. If he began university at an age that was common in the early fifteenth century, he may have been born between 1412 and 1416. Since Vienna university regulations set the minimum age for the master of arts degree at twenty-one,[13] presumably Kempf was born not later than 1416.[14] More-

sumed by Nikolaus Paulus, Engelbert Krebs, Alois Hörmer, and initially, by Heinrich Rüthing in *Der Kartäuser Heinrich Egher von Kalkar, 1328-1408* (1967), 27, n. 31. Rüthing revised this assumption in *DSAM*, 8 (1974), 1699, and *NDB*, 11 (1974), 486. In what may be a typographical error, Bernard Baillie, who completed the edition of Kempf's commentary on the Song of Songs after Bernard Pez's death in 1735, placed Kempf's birth in 1393. *Bibl. ascetica*, 11: 4r.

[10] *Matrikel*, 1: 182. The arts faculty *Acta* after 1416 remain unpublished. Professor Paul Uiblein of the Institut für Österreichische Geschichtsforschung at the University of Vienna, who edited the *Acta* prior to 1416 for publication, was kind enough to verify the following citations from Hörmer: *Acta*, vol. 2, fol. 122: BA in 1435; vol. 2, fol. 125: licentiate in 1436; vol. 2, vol. 128v: Kempf is mentioned as a *magister regens artium* for the first time on May 3, 1437, having been granted the regency, or authority to lecture as a master; vol. 2, fol. 129: lectures on Alexander de Villa Dei's *Doctrinale* in 1437; vol. 2, fol. 132: lectures on the *Summa iovis* (*ars dictaminis*) in the summer semester, 1438.

[11] Hörmer, "Kempf," 12; *Matrikel*, 1: 111. A "Nicolaus sacrista de Ehenheim" (Oberehnheim, today's Obernai in the Alsace) in the matriculation register for the summer semester of 1434 was also known as "Nicolaus de Argentina." No "Nicolaus de Argentina" appears in the published arts faculty *Acta* (up to 1416).

[12] The *Matrikel* and the arts faculty records clearly place Kempf in that faculty, 1433-38; moreover, Kempf's name does not appear in the acts of the theological faculty at all. Paul Uiblein, ed., *Die Akten der Theologischen Fakultät der Universität Wien (1396-1508)*, 2 vols. (1978).

[13] Paul Uiblein, "Zur Lebensgeschichte einiger Wiener Theologen des Mittelalters," *MIÖG*, 74 (1966), 98.

[14] In the preface to vol. 4 of *Bibl. ascetica*, Pez and Wydemann described a manuscript presumably no longer extant, that contained a *Dialogus inter monachum et religionem de causis ruinae ordinum, religionis, et regularum*. Its style and contents

over, since Nicholas of Dinkelsbühl died in 1433, the year of Kempf's matriculation, Kempf could not have been a direct disciple of Nicholas of Dinkelsbühl, as many have asserted.[15]

In the eighteenth century, Joseph Karl Newen von Newenstein assumed that Kempf came from the patrician Kempf family of Straßburg. Paulus noted the existence of a cooper family by the same name,[16] and, with Hörmer, we can agree that Kempf's matriculation at Vienna as a *pauper* argues against patrician origins, although it does not mean his family was without means.[17] The *Chartae* of the Carthusian General Chapter mention an "Elisabeth Kempis de Argentina" (1461), an "Elisabeth Kempfin de Argentina" (1467), and a "Mathias Kempf, civis Argentinensis" (1474), among the deceased lay benefactors of the order. That these are Kempf's mother, sister, and brother, respectively, as Hör-

---

corresponded in Wydemann's view to that of Kempf's other writings. But, assuming the 1397 birthdate, they were puzzled that the author of this dialogue said he had entered the Carthusian order at the age of twenty-four. Assuming a 1412-16 birthdate would solve this puzzle.

[15] Although Kempf obviously knew Nicholas of Dinkelsbühl's writings, he seems to quote Heinrich of Langenstein and Jean Gerson more frequently, although any such assessment is impressionistic in the absence of critical editions of Kempf's works. Despite Rüthing's debunking in *DSAM* (1974), the image of Kempf as a student of Nicholas of Dinkelsbühl remains a commonplace in the secondary literature. See, e.g., Bernhard Schnell, *Thomas Peuntner, "Büchlein von der Liebhabung Gottes"*, MTU, 81 (1984), 48, who repeats Hermann Maschek, "Thomas Peuntner," in *Verfasserlexikon*, 3 (1943), 863-69, at 864-65, on this point. Pez and Wydemann thought that Kempf translated into German the *Our Father*, the *Decalogue*, and *Apostles' Creed* for Duchess Elisabeth of Austria and submitted them to Nicholas of Dinkelsbühl for approval. They were unable to locate copies of these translations, and it is unlikely Kempf was responsible for them.

[16] *Pandectae*, 56; Paulus, "Kempf" (1928), 25.

[17] To cite one of many examples, Gregor Heimburg enrolled as "pauper" at Vienna in 1413, although he was from a well-to-do burgher family in Schweinfurt, where his father seems to have been *Bürgermeister* repeatedly. See Peter Johanek in *Verfasserlexikon*, rev. ed., 3 (1981), 629-42, at 31. At Vienna monks and paupers were to pay nothing, commoners in the arts faculty paid four groschen, and commoners in the higher faculties paid eight groschen. However it was possible to evade payment in various ways. The matriculation registers not only record names of many people who were not really students, they also lack the names of many genuine students who failed to enroll. See James H. Overfield, Nobles and Paupers at German Universities to 1600," *Societas: A Review of Social History*, 7 (1974), 175-210, at 179-81; Rainer Christoph Schwinges, "Pauperes an deutschen Universitäten des 15. Jahrhunderts," *Zeitschrift für historische Forschung*, 8 (1981), 285-309, at 292-93, and idem, *Deutsche Universitätsbesucher im 14. und 15. Jahrhundert* (1986), 441-85; and Fletcher and Paquet as listed in the Bibliography. Vienna enrolled a higher number of poor students than other German universities. Between 1411 and 1435 the percentage of *pauperes* among students enrolled at Vienna grew from 27.3 to 40.8 (1421-25) and then fell back to 28.9. Already in 1381-85 *pauperes* made up 30 percent of the enrollment. This percentage continued to decline after 1435 (20 percent by 1450-55, 10 percent by 1465-70 and hovered between 2 and 10 percent during the sixteenth century.

mer assumed,[18] is suggested by data from the *Livre de bourgeoisie de la ville de Strasbourg*, which indicate that Matthias Kempf's daughter Barbara married Leinhart Krüg (from Eltmann in Franconia) and joined the grain merchants' guild in 1474, after Matthias's death. Matthias was a citizen of Straßburg—he may be the Mattheus Kempf of Geispoltzheim who bought his citizenship in 1455 and joined the *Gärtner* guild. A Paulus Kempf married the daughter of the late Peter Westerman in 1452 and also entered the gardeners' guild; an Arbogast Kempf from Geispoltzheim married Barbara, daughter of Hans Stouffer, in 1453 and likewise entered the gardeners' guild.[19] Thus Nicholas Kempf probably came from a Straßburg family that acquired citizenship rights by mid-century but still belonged to the lower echelons of the guild hierarchy. At Nicholas's birth early in the century, his family either had recently immigrated to the city or was still resident in Geispoltzheim, one of the villages in the immediate environs of the imperial city. Nicholas Kempf appears not to have been directly related to the prominent family that produced Elisabeth Kempf (1415-1485), prioress of the Dominican convent in Colmar ("Unterlinden").[20]

Kempf's brief regency in the arts faculty at Vienna could have been intended as a short prelude to theological studies and he may have actually begun the theological curriculum.[21] His writings clearly show his concern about the academic study of theology and a familiarity with the *Sentences* of Peter Lombard, the *Summa Theologiae* of Thomas Aquinas, and the pastoral-ethical writings of Robert Holcot (*Super sapientiam Salomonis* etc.) alongside the Vienna luminaries, Heinrich of Langenstein, and Nicholas of Dinkelsbühl.[22] Yet this familiarity with fundamental

---

[18] *Chartae . . . 1457-65* (1985), 106; ibid., *1466-74* (1985), 35, 214; Hörmer, "Kempf," 6. If the entries do refer to Nicholas Kempf's relatives, the dates of their deaths could have been either 1460 or 1461, 1466 or 1467, and 1473 or 1474, since the obituary lists for the preceding year were assembled from reports brought by priors of the various charterhouses to the Chapter General in May.

[19] Charles Wittmer and J. Charles Meyer, eds., *Le Livre de bourgeoisie de la ville de Strasbourg, 1440-1530*, 3 vols. (1948), nos. 1021, 1099, 1225, 2797.

[20] Karl-Ernst Geith, "Elisabeth Kempf (1415-1485)," *Annuaire de Colmar*, 29 (1980-81), 47-73. This is the judgment of Professor Geith, communicated in a letter of July 13, 1984, to the present writer. Diebolt Kempf, the grandfather of Elisabeth Kempf of Unterlinden, emigrated from Straßburg to Colmar in 1389; another Diebolt Kempf renounced his Straßburg citizenship in 1446. Wittmer-Meyer, no. 523.

[21] His brief time as a regent master may have been more the norm than the exception, although statistics for Vienna have not yet been carefully analyzed. See Courtenay, *Schools and Scholars*, 25-28, 118, 190; Gordon Leff, *Paris and Oxford Universities in the Thirteenth and Fourteenth Centuries* (1968), 7-8.

[22] Occasionally Kempf makes general references to the commentaries of various "doctors" on the *Sentences*—e.g., in *Ost* [see appendix A, no. 18], ch. 27 (G1, 18v, 22-

theological textbooks could also have been acquired after he became a monk. In any case, his later writings are critical of university theological education, not of the university in general or of the arts faculty. Indeed he said much that was positive about the liberal arts in their proper place, while warning against an inordinate love of studies.[23]

Kempf's name does not appear in the arts faculty *Acta* after the summer semester of 1438. He began his novitiate in September 1440. One surviving copy of his disputation on the *Posterior Analytics* was copied in 1439 in Vienna. It is clearly a student transcription which Wolfgang Kydrer carried with him in his later career as a schoolteacher and monk. This may imply that Kempf continued to teach in 1439.

One is tempted to seek an explanation for Kempf's decision to become a monk in the turbulent temporal and ecclesiastical politics of fifteenth-century south-central Europe. As far as civil politics were concerned, the 1430s were a relatively tranquil period for Lower Austria and Vienna—but only relatively so, when compared with the turmoil of the revolt by the "young patrician party" late in the fourteenth century, the execution of the upstart *Bürgermeister* Vorlauf in 1408,[24] and the ravages of the Hussite wars in the Lower Austrian countryside during the 1420s.[25] However, the sudden death of Albrecht V (emperor Albrecht II, 1437-39) in 1439 led to a struggle to dominate his posthumous heir, Ladislaus. This led to a particularly chaotic period in the 1450s and early

---

23) [cf. chapter three, p. 77, below), *Cantica* I.1, or *Discr*, ch. 4 (VS1, 38r B; Pez 9: 402).

[23] We catch glimpses of Kempf's application of standard assumptions of natural philosophy to theology in his comments on the illumination of the human mind in comparison to the illumination of rays of light (*Ost*, ch. 31 [G1, 23v, 31 to 24r, 1]); on the subtlety of the human soul compared to fire and air (ibid., ch. 32 (G1, 24v, 24 to 25r, 15); and on the influence of celestial bodies in relation to God's grace (ibid., ch. 38 (G1, 29r, 17-30), cf. ch. 46 (G1, 34v, 31-35) and ch. 44 (G1, 33r). In *Rect* [see appendix A, no. 4], III.12 (V1, 69va, 18-22; *Bibl. ascetica*, 4: 458), Kempf apologized because he could not discuss the matter at hand *assertive et scolastice* due to the brevity of the work he was writing. *Ost*, ch. 10 (G1, 7v, lines 10-32) is structured along the lines of and employs the terminology of a scholastic *quaestio*. Studies of Carthusian library catalogues confirm the importance given to the liberal arts. At Basel they formed a category second only to devotional literature. See Max Burckhardt, "Bibliotheksaufbau, Bücherbesitz, und Leserschaft im spätmittelalterlichen Basel," in *Studien zum städtischen Bildungswesen* (1983), 33-52, at 39. For Erfurt see Erich Kleineidam, "Die Spiritualität der Kartäuser im Spiegel der Erfurter Kartäuser-Bibliothek," in *Die Kartäuser*, ed. Zadnikar (1983), 185-202 (originally published in 1962). For Kempf's cautions about inordinate love of studies see *Prop*, I. 13/12 (VS1, 9r, B - 9v B).

[24] See Peter Csendes and Helmut Größing, "Schrifttum zur Geschichte Wiens (1954-1974)," *MIÖG*, 83 (1975), 415-72; Max Vancsa in *Geschichte der Stadt Wien*, vol. 2 (1904), 518-48.

[25] Ferdinand Stöller, "Österreich im Kriege gegen die Hussiten (1420-1436)," *JLNö*, 22 (1929), 1-87.

1460s,[26] especially when combined with the growing threat from the Ottoman empire to the south after the defeat of the crusaders at Varna in 1444 and John Hunyadi's failure at Kossovo in 1448.[27] In the city of Vienna, the story of Wolfgang Holzer's rise and fall reads like historical fiction: although he was born in humble circumstances, his own self-confidence, the political intrigues of the day, and the permeability of the Vienna patriciate permitted him to rise to wealth and a powerful political position, only to be executed for high treason by being drawn and quartered.[28]

Perhaps it was fortunate that political turmoil subsided briefly during Kempf's time at the university, for the 1430s were a turbulent period in the ecclesiastical politics of Western Christendom. Support for the councils of Constance and Basel was strong at Vienna, as it was in university circles generally across Europe.[29] In the Vienna of the 1430s, Benedictine reform circles supported the council of Basel, despite irritation over the council-ordered visitation of Austrian monasteries that interfered with existing monastic reform.[30] Carthusians, including Kempf, supported the council firmly, with the prior at Aggsbach, Vincent, becoming one of the most notable examples of diehard conciliarism.[31] Sup-

[26] Otto Brunner, "Beiträge zur Geschichte des Fehdewesens im spätmittelalterlichen Österreichs," *JLNö*, 22 (1929), 431-507; Peter Csendes, *Wien in den Fehden der Jahre 1461-63* (1974); Karl Schalk, *Aus der Zeit des Österreichischen Faustrechts, 1440-1463* (1919).

[27] John V. A. Fine, Jr., *The Late Medieval Balkans* (1987).

[28] Richard Perger, "Wolfgang Holzer: Aufstieg und Fall eines Wiener Politikers im 15. Jahrhundert," *JVGSW*, 41 (1985), 7-61. Perger comments that Holzer, who had once expressed doubt in the Christian faith and in life after death, was conscious enough during the execution, that he could call on the Virgin Mary.

[29] Johannes Helmrath, *Das Basler Konzil 1431-1449: Forschungsstand und Probleme* (1987), 132-57; Antony Black, "The University and the Council of Basle," *Annuarium Historiae Conciliorum*, 6 (1974), 341-51; and idem, "The Universities and the Council of Basle: Collegium and Concilium," in *The Universities in the Late Middle Ages* (1978), 511-23; Heiko A. Oberman, "University and Society on the Threshold of Modern Times: The German Connection," in *Rebirth, Reform, and Resiliance: Universities in Transition, 1300-1700* (1984), 19-41; Paul W. Knoll, "The University of Cracow in the Conciliar Movement," ibid., 190-212.

[30] Hartmann J. Zeibig, *Beiträge zur Geschichte der Wirkung des Basler Concils in Österreich* (1852), 515-618, at 515-16; Gerda Koller, *Princeps in Ecclesia: Untersuchungen zur Kirchenpolitik Herzog Albrechts V von Österreich* (1964), 107-11. See also the letters exchanged between Stephan of Spanberg, Johann Schlitpacher of Weilheim, and Vincent of Aggsbach in Pez and Hueber, *Cod. dipl.- hist.- epist.*, pt. III: 280-90, 327-82; Martin of Senging, "Tuitiones pro observantia regulae Sancti Patris Benedicti in concilio Basileensi," in *Bibl. ascetica*. 8: 504-50; and Franz Hubalek, "Aus dem Briefwechsel des Johannes Schlitpacher von Weilheim" (diss., 1963), 41-49.

[31] For Kempf's affirmation of a general council's supreme authority in the church see *Rect*, II.16 (59r B, 10-32; pp. 349-50): "Quippe cum nunquam priori tempore tantam le-

port from within the university was perhaps less unanimous than has been frequently asserted,[32] but it too lessened only under direct pressure from Friedrich III (1440-93) after the Vienna Concordat of 1447-48.[33] Throughout the 1430s, when Kempf was a student at Vienna, the university was firmly behind the council at Basel.

When Kempf left the arts faculty in 1439 the council's prospects were unclear, but certainly not propitious.[34] Although the imperial electors had shifted to a neutral position, the council still enjoyed support in the empire in March 1438. The Acceptation of Mainz (March 1439) might have given some hope that the council's reform decrees, now formally acknowledged by the imperial electors, other metropolitan bishops, and representatives of the German king, would be enforced by bishops throughout Germany.[35] Yet careful private diplomacy attracted increasing support for Eugenius IV among the German electors, 1440-41, laying the groundwork for the concordat. Although Johannes Nider left Basel in disgust and despair as early as 1437, convinced that a total reform of the church was impossible and turning his hopes for reform to the observant Dominican reform,[36] Jacob de Paradiso, a leading proponent of conciliarism from the University of Cracow, actively supported the council until 1441 and left the Cistercian Order to join the Carthusians at Erfurt.[37]

---

gitur fuisse contradictionem et iniquitatem in civitate ecclesie militantis, que iam raro diu stat sine scismate, et iam tali, de quo a seculo non est auditum, ita quod nec generalibus concilijs, a quo est tocius ecclesie auctoritas, obeditur." On Vincent see Joachim W. Stieber, *Pope Eugenius IV, the Council of Basel, and the Secular and Ecclesiastical Authorities in the Empire*, SHCT, 13 (1978), 84, 100-102, 338-40; Hubert Jedin, *Geschichte des Konzils von Trient*, vol. 1 (1949), trans. by Ernest Graf as *History of the Council of Trent*, vol. 1 (1957), 43-44; Helmrath, *Basler Konzil*, 127.

[32] A moderately revisionist view is found in Isnard W. Frank, *Der antikonziliaristische Dominikaner Leonhard Huntpichler* (1976); cf. Walter Jaroschka, "Thomas Ebendorfer als Theoretiker des Konziliarismus," *MIÖG*, 71 (1963), 87-98, and Virgil Redlich, *Tegernsee und die deutsche Geistesgeschichte* (1931, 1974), 195.

[33] John B. Toews, "Pope Eugenius IV and the Concordat of Vienna (1448)," *CH*, 34 (1965), 178-94. On the reluctance of Vienna academics to accept the change of position by Friedrich III during the years from 1446-48, see Stieber, *Eugenius IV*, 313, 336-38, and Lhotsky, *Ebendorfer*, 43-44. For a survey of interpretations of the concordat, see Helmrath, *Basler Konzil*, 314-22.

[34] Toews, "Concordat," 178-80.

[35] For a survey of various interpretations see Helmrath, *Basler Konzil*, 297-306.

[36] Koller, *Princeps*, 35.

[37] On Cracow, see Jerzy Kloczowski, "Le conciliarisme à l'université de Cracovie," in *The Church in a Changing Society* (1978), 223-26; and Knoll, "University of Cracow." On Jacob de Paradiso, see Jedin, *Council of Trent*, trans. Graf, vol. 1, p. 35; Dieter Mertens, *Iacobus Carthusiensis* (1976), 32-34, 223; and Stieber, *Eugenius IV*, 100-101. Disillusionment with the council was not his sole reason for becoming a Carthusian.

To what degree Kempf shared the growing pessimism is hard to determine. His *De recto fine* of 1447 expresses disappointment over the failure of both pope and council to bring about reform.[38] In *De discretione*, written before the schism ended in 1449, he castigated both the adherents of the papal council at Ferrara and the neutral party for their intransigence, asserting that the biggest hurdle to settling the controversy was selfishness and pride.[39]

The Council of Basel did send a commission to conduct a visitation of the university in 1436. It called upon the theological faculty to conduct its disputations "with peace, love, and with decency (*honestas*)." No one was to berate another, rather, all were to stay on the subject and avoid impertinent and sophistical arguments. Citing Augustine on the fundamental role of scripture and invoking the authority of Duke Albrecht, the commission called for two special lectures on scripture.[40] All these themes are echoed in Kempf's *De recto studiorum fine*.

Other passages in Kempf's writings shed more light on his decision. Given his choice of the austere Carthusian life, it is not farfetched to interpret his repeated warnings about the perils of academic pride as an expression of genuine fear for his salvation, rather than as mere cliches. Disappointed at the realities of life as a teacher and at student apathy, he warned his readers, among whom were university students and masters,[41] not to comfort themselves with the thought that their anxiety would cease after the baccalaureate, nor, having acquired it and finding themselves more anxious and burdened than before, to hope for relief by obtaining a master's degree. "[With its] acquisition, anxiety and wretchedness of heart only just begin, especially for those who must support themselves by their own labor." The new master of arts faces greater obligations than before, if he is to live in accordance with his new status. With the author of Ecclesiastes, Kempf insists that "he who increases knowledge increases toil [Eccl. 1:18]." The higher academic degrees bring the perpetual burden of a struggle against avarice and pride.[42]

---

[38] *Rect*, I.3 (V1, 41r-v; *Bibl. ascetica*, 4:266-70).

[39] *Discr*, ch. 3 (*Bibl. ascetica*, 3:393-94), quoted in chapter four, pp. 128-29.

[40] Text in Kink, *Universität Wien*, 2: 279-90.

[41] Pez cites the colophon to a copy of Kempf's *Memoriale primorum principiorum in scholis virtutum* (see appendix A, no. 13): "This little work was put together nearly fifty years ago by a famed master, whose fame, knowledge, and books . . . are praised and embraced by Vienna students in preference to many others." *Bibl. ascetica* 4: b-b2.

[42] *Prop*, I.9/10 (VS1, 8r B, 20-34): "Primo enim quanta sit anxietas quilibet studio adherens potest in se experiri. Quamdiu quippe scolaris est, putat solo baccalauratu adepto quietari aliquam; quo obtento, plus anxiatur. Item sperans se eciam magisterij dignitati liberari; qua acquisita, incipit primo recte cordis miseria et anxietas, ymmo duplatur, precipue eorum quos suo labore se oportet nutrire—plura enim sibi sunt necessaria

Kempf found teaching itself to be a constant temptation to pride. His
ideal for a teacher was one of teaching by humble example; inadequately
digested learning vitiated that ideal.[43]

Kempf's decision to enter religion was undoubtedly encouraged by
his realization that the "school of virtues" in the monastery had a place
for pedagogues. The need for wise, discretion-filled direction from a *magister*, a spiritual director, an architect of the religious life, is a theme
that recurs throughout his writings.[44] No monk is wise enough to educate
himself in the religious life. On rare occasions God even calls monks out
of their cloistered existence to reform other houses or entire territories,
turning simple monks, even Carthusians, into bishops.[45]

Among the "schools of virtues," the Carthusian order had a special
attraction for Kempf. He took seriously the apocryphal story of the "Professor of Paris" whose revelations from his funeral bier shocked St.
Bruno into the wilderness of the Grande Chartreuse (see the Epilogue).

---

pro sui status condicione quam prius. Et diversis se facultatibus adaptat, arcium
tamen sophismata et questiones predominantur. Quod bene considerans Salomon ecclesiastes primo dixit, 'Qui addit scienciam, addit et laborem, . . . " Likewise ibid., I.10/11
(8v A, 14-16): "Qui cum scienciarum altis gradibus superbie avaricieque perpetuo coni-
ugio copulatur, . . ."

[43] *Ost*, 51 (G1, 38v, 10-17): "Qui enim comedit nimium de melle non sibi prodest,
cum non digerit sed evomit, et sic vertitur sibi in amaritudinem evomendo. Sic qui
nimium comedit de sciencia intellectuali, eciam sacre scripture (que per mel designatur)
quando non digerit eam in affectum per amorem trahendo, tunc evomit per vanitatem
alios docendo et in se vacuus remanendo. Comedat ergo unusquisque de melle, id est
sciencia sacre scripture, quantum sibi sufficit pro amore Dei, ut in eo plus crescat quam
in sciencia, quia 'sciencia inflat, amor ad vitam eternam edificat et perducit' [1 Cor
8:1]." For the context see appendix B. A parallel passage is found in Kempf's *Rect*, II.8
(V1, 53r A, 23-36; Pez, *Bibl. Ascetica*, 4: 321) as cited in chapter three, p. 83, below.

[44] *Prop*, II.14 (VS1, 30r A, 32 - 30r B, 1): "Et quia ad huiusmodi edificium constru-
endum requiritur sciencia, experiencia, et discrecio, quas [MS *quos*?] homo inexpertus in
construendo et in huiusmodi indoctus, licet alias multa sciat, non habet. Ideo necessario
habebit architectorem seu magistrum expertum et discretum qui novit quo ordine sit in-
structura procedendum, et lapides virtutum pollire, et malos a bonis discernere." On the
monastery as *schola*, see Karl Suso Frank, "Vom Kloster als scola dominici servitii zum
Kloster ad servitium imperii," *SMGB*, 91 (1980), 80-97, at 81-86.

[45] *Prop*, I.17/16 (VS1, 12r B, 26 - 12v, A, 6): "Et satis mirabile est quot tales timent
quod Deus suos electos perire permittat, nisi ipsi propria voluntate et presumpcione in
seculo remanerent. Cum tamen ipse per prophetam promiserit se suum gregem in necces-
sitate per seipsum visitare et pascere. Nec considerant quod nullus est status religionis in
toto mundo a Deo contrarius profectui proximorum, quin si Deus vult ipsum preesse, et
si ipsum elegerit, eciam velit nolit ipsum alijs preficit. Numquid non invenit Gregorium,
Augustinum, Benedictum, et plures alios in monasterio reclusos aut in speluncis et tamen
in eternum exaltavit cornu ipsorum? Et adhuc hoc, quamvis rarius ex causa supra tacta,
per tales qui tamen indignos se ad huiusmodi reputant? Nec umquam aliquem profectum
alijs per ipsos fieri putant subito divino nutu trahuntur ut tota patria aut multa monasteria
per ipsos reformentur, ut tempore meo per simplices vidi fieri et quandoque ad episcopalis dignitatis curam quamvis inviti trahuntur, eciam ex ordine kartusiensium."

Kempf had no doubt that the Carthusian order had been miraculously instituted to save masters and students of the University of Paris from the
perils of pride in learning, academic degrees, and ecclesiastical offices
that threatened their eternal destiny. He had no sympathy for those who
entered the mendicant orders to gain an education and pursue a scholar's
career.[46]

3. Prior

The charterhouse Kempf joined, the *Thronus Sanctae Mariae* at
Gaming, was located in a narrow valley south of Scheibbs on the opposite side of the Ötscher Mountains from the pilgrimage center of Mari-
azell. It had been founded by Duke Albrecht II of Austria, who survived
an attempt on his life in 1330 and was moved thereby to fulfill a vow
made several years earlier. Accepted by the Carthusian order in 1337,
Gaming was initially populated by monks from Mauerbach (founded in
1314) near Vienna and maintained close legal and economic ties to Mauerbach and to the *Schottenstift* in Vienna.[47] Its endowment was generous
and centralized, so generous in fact that the monks told Duke Albrecht
"sufficit Domine" ("enough, enough")—out of fear that wealth would
undermine their rigorous asceticism. Albrecht's response evoked pro-
phetically the hard times that descended on Gaming in the late fifteenth
and early sixteenth centuries: "Take what is gladly given, for a time will
come when it will be far too little. Preserve and take care of what I am
giving you, my children."[48] The Benedictine abbey of Melk and the

---

[46] *Prop*, I.20/19 (VS1, 14r B, 7-13, 31-39): ". . . si ad ordines mendicancium proponit
quis ingredi, non ideo moveatur ut ibi possit studio vacare, et magnus in sciencijs fieri et
solempnis predicator, quia omnia ista posset consequi et non ad propriam salutem, sed
aliorum utilitatem et sui dampnacionem. . . . Non enim est finis principalis huius ordinis
[Cartusiensis] multum scire, sed multum amare, cantare, obedire, legere, et ea que ordo
instituit, quanto quis melius poterit expedire, ad que ut melius expediat; omnia alia debet
moderare et ordinare. Unde non mirum quod tales [who enter mendicant orders for purposes of scholarship] iuste Deo permittente sepe periclitantur se in corpore destruentes."

[47] On Gaming see James Hogg, "Gaming," *DHGE*, 19 (1981), 988-97, with exhaustive bibliographical citations, including the following listed in the Bibliography to the
present volume: Niederberger and Jelenik; Paulhart; George Grausam; Newenstein;
Zeißberg; Erdinger (largely dependent on Zeißberg); Alois Müller; Haselbach; *Topographie von Niederösterreich*, 3: 269-301; Spreitz; Frieß; Brunhilde Hoffmann; Winner,
Klosteraufhebungen, ch. 7. Some materials from Gaming's archives have survived and
are found in the Haus-, Hof-, und Staatsarchiv in Vienna. For the fifteenth century these
include Böhm, nos. 55, 56, and Böhm Supplement, 190, 229, 305, 339.

[48] Edmund Ferdinand Spreitz, "Zur ältesten Geschichte der Kartause Gaming" (diss.
1929), published as AC, 58.4 (1986), 45: "Nembt dieweil man euch gibt gern, es chumbt

charterhouse of Aggsbach were nearby. Together with Abbot Angelus of
the Cistercian Abbey of Rein near Graz, it was Prior Leonhard Paetraer
of Gaming (d. 1435), a personal acquaintance of Duke Albrecht V, who
conducted the visitation of Melk (1418) that inaugurated the Melk Benedictine reform.[49] Gaming had experienced a steady influx of postulants
during the 1430s, with a significant number coming from Vienna university circles. The community flourished at mid-century: in 1461 monks
professed at Gaming headed nine other charterhouses.[50] The monastery
was full to overflowing: out of humility Johannes of Eßlingen, who entered nine months after Kempf (June 9, 1441), lived for thirty years in
the monastic lockup (in carcere).[51] As civil strife grew and Hungarian
and Turkish invasions threatened during the last half of the century, the
Gaming priors were forced to retrench, struggling to maintain the community in the face of increased levies from the Lower Austrian Landtag
and reduced income because of the poverty of the monastery's dependent peasantry in the wake of invasions and floods.

Internally the convent was not entirely free of problems. In 1444 the
Carthusian General Chapter admonished the lay brothers in effect to
"shape up or be shipped out" to other houses in the order. The cryptic nature of the General Chapter's Ordinationes dealing with such matters
make it impossible to determine exactly what the problem was.[52] A series of admonitions between 1452 and 1463 sought to discipline quarrel-
some monks from Lövöld in Hungary temporarily residing (in part under

---

die zeit, das sein alles zuwenig wirdt werden. Meyne Chynder, waß ich euch werdt
geben, das huett und pfleget gar ebem." Böhm Supplement 305, the account book for the
year 1440 (containing accounts for 1439), gives an overview of Gaming possessions, income, and moneylending activity on the eve of Kempf's entry: note, e.g., the summary
of livestock found on Gaming's granges (fol. 21r): 17 horses, 13 oxen, 107 cows, 58
nonbreeding animals, 410 goats, 175 sheep, 36 pigs. Note also Bernard Bligny, "La
Grande Chartreuse et son ordre au temps du Grand Schisme et de la crise conciliaire
(1378-1449)," in Historia et spiritualitas Cartusiensis (1983), 35-57, at 35-37, where
Gaming is listed among the wealthiest third of the order's houses (most of which are
German, Italian, and Belgian urban foundations, with most of the French and German rural houses found among lower and middle two-thirds.)

[49] Ignaz Keiblinger, Geschichte des Benedictiner-Stiftes Melk, 2nd ed. (1867-68), 1:
486. For Prior Leonhard's active role in monastic reform, see H. Rüthing, "Die
Kartäuser und die spätmittelalterlichen Ordensreformen," in Reformbemühungen, ed.
Elm (1989), 35-58, at 50-52.

[50] Zeißberg, "Gaming," 566-67.

[51] Zeißberg, "Gaming," 586.

[52] 1444: "Conversi vero dicte domus Throni per Visitatores de quampluribus in ordi-
nationibus notati se studeant efficaciter emendare si sui dispersionem per domos Ordinis
sub gravibus disciplinis voluerint evitare. . . . Chartae . . . 1438-46, p. 152.

incarceration) at Gaming and also ordered the Hungarian charterhouse at Tarkan to repay money owed to Gaming.[53]

We know little about Kempf's first seven years as a Carthusian. One of his better known works, *De recto studiorum fine*, was written in 1447. It is possible that he also wrote the *Memoriale primorum principiorum in scolis virtutum, De proponentibus religionis ingressum, De confirmatione*, and part of *De discretione* (appendix A, no. 6), during this period of his life. But all these works, except *De recto fine*, more likely were written during Kempf's first priorate, at Geirach, 1447-51.

Geirach, the charterhouse *Vallis Sancti Mauritii* (today's Jurkloster, near Celje in Slovenia, followed its neighbor Seitz in the initial Carthusian expansion into the "German" Empire. Founded by Bishop Henry I of Gurk in 1170s with a meager endowment, it belonged briefly to but was not inhabited by, the Austin Canons of Gurk before being restored to the Carthusian Order between 1209 and 1212 under the sponsorship of Archduke Leopold VI of Austria and Styria.[54] A description of the neighboring charterhouse of Seitz recorded by an Italian visitor in 1487, offers a remarkable contemporary glimpse of Kempf's environment: Geirach may not be "surrounded by a garland of hills" like its neighbor, Seitz,[55] but it does lie in a narrow valley along a rushing stream. It too fell on hard times in the late fifteenth century, passing into Jesuit possession in the late sixteenth century. Its library was dispersed.

After Prior Christoph Hüpfl of Gaming died in January 1451,[56] Kempf was elected to succeed him as prior. The first documentary evidence of his return to Gaming is a letter to the abbot of the Benedictine house at Admont in May.[57] Wydemann tells us that Kempf constructed a cemetery chapel, three altars in the cloister and church, a new library, and completed the winter refectory.[58]

---

[53] *Chartae . . . 1447-1456*, pp. 65 [1449], 91 [1450], 139 [1452], 160 [1453], 183, 184 [1454]; *Chartae . . . 1457-65*, p. 165 [1463]; *Chartae . . . 1466-74*, p. 135.

[54] James Hogg, "Geirach," *DHGE*, 20: cols. 258-62, with an exhaustive listing of previous literature, including Reiner Puschnig, "Zur Geschichte des untersteirischen Klosters Geirach," *Zeitschrift des historischen Vereins für Steiermark*, 34 (1941), 13-32. See also Zadnikar and Wienand, *Die Kartäuser* (1983), 98-110 for information from Zadnikar's architectural studies of Slovenian charterhouses (Seiz, Geirach, Pleterje) previously available only in Slovenian.

[55] Rudolf Egger, *Die Reisetagebücher des Paolo Santonino, 1485-1487* (Klagenfurt, 1947) as excerpted and translated in Zadnikar and Wienand, *Die Kartäuser*, 96-97.

[56] *Chartae 1447-56*, 1451 (obituary section), p. 101.

[57] *Bibl. ascetica*, 11: 4v-5r; Hörmer, "Kempf," 20-22; Wydemann in Steyerer, "Collectanea," 377r. See appendix A, part 5c, below.

[58] *Bibl. ascetica*, 11: 5r-v; added by Wydemann to the Hofer list, Steyerer, "Collectanea," 377r. Acquisition of new land holdings during Kempf's priorate are referred to in

During his seven years as prior at Gaming, we have several hints of Kempf's activity as the prelate of one of the most prestigious monasteries in Austria. He obviously maintained contact with university circles, indeed, the favorite student of Georg Peuerbach, one of the university's first "humanist" professors, was Reimbert Mühlwanger, who, according to Karl Großmann and subsequent scholars was "a monk from Gaming." Mühlwanger died of the plague in 1453, soon after taking up a pastorate, probably in a parish incorporated into Melk's holdings. The pastoral activity is scarcely congruous with the Carthusian life, and Mühlwanger does not appear on any lists of Gaming monks, because he never professed. He apparently was clothed as a novice in 1451 but left sometime during his novitiate.[59] However the story does illustrate Kempf's ties to the university and early humanist circles: Peuerbach effusively expressed regret at not having become a novice with Mühlwanger and he learned of Mühlwanger's death after returning to Melk with Johann Schlitpacher from a visit to Gaming. Another member of the earliest Vienna humanist circle,[60] Paulus (Chrysogonus) Hebenkrieg, became a monk at Tegernsee in 1467 and transferred to Gaming in 1473, becoming prior at the charterhouse in Olomouc, 1490-92, and then at Gaming, 1502-10.

Kempf also had political responsibilities: a nineteenth-century summary of a letter to the abbot of Admont dated January 17, 1458, explains that Kempf would not be able to attend the coming *Beschautag* (visitation) at Admont because his presence was required at the *Landtag* ses-

---

the indexes to Gaming archival materials (some of which have not survived) found in Böhm 56, 39r, 43v, 45r-v, 47v, 50v, 64r-v, 93r-v; Böhm Supplement, 190, 50r.

[59] Karl Großmann, "Die Frühzeit des Humanismus in Wien," *JLNö*, 22 (1929), 150-325, at 238-39, 249, 251; repeated nearly verbatim in Großmann, "Begründung der modernen Himmelskunde durch die Wiener Mathematikerschule des 15. Jahrhunderts," *JVGSW*, 21/22 (1965/66), 209-10. The most detailed treatment of the extremely intimate relationship between Peuerbach and Mühlwanger is found in Helmuth Grössing, "*Astronomus poeta*: Georg von Peuerbach als Dichter," *JVGSW*, 34 (1978), 54-66, which includes extensive quotations from Peuerbach's poems celebrating his love for Mühlwanger. Grössing drew on the 1948 Vienna dissertation on Peuerbach by Hermann Wallner, "Georg von Peuerbach," which I have not seen. Mühlwanger matriculated at Vienna in the winter semester of 1447 but had not yet finished even a bachelor's degree by 1451. All of these scholars seem to have assumed that being invested as a novice simply meant becoming a monk; none entertained the possibility that he might not have stayed long at Gaming and none realized how much a parish pastorate was incongruous with Carthusian life. A Mühlwanger family from the local gentry was associated with Aggsbach in the late fifteenth and through the sixteenth century. See Heribert Roßmann, *Geschichte der Kartause Aggsbach* (1976), 75-76, 167, 171, 177.

[60] Großmann, "Frühzeit," 228-29. Jerome of Mondsee, who enthusiastically read Kempf's writings, also fits into this proto-humanist circle at Vienna in some respect. See chapter two, p. 68, for a discussion of Vienna, ÖNB cvp 3520, containing autograph copies of Peuerbach's poems collected by Jerome.

sion in Vienna.[61] This was during the struggle between Emperor Frie-drich III and his brother Albrecht VI of Austria for the inheritance of Al-brecht V. Indeed, in 1458 Friedrich managed to occupy the city of Vienna. Perhaps the burdens of the political responsibilities that came with the priorate of a monastery like Gaming, when combined with the internal problems reflected in the *Chartae* of the order as described above, moved Kempf to ask to be released from his office during a No-vember 1458 visitation. More probably, as in the examples of Gregory the Great and Augustine that he was fond of citing, he longed for con-templative solitude. In any case his request was granted.

Kempf must have spent some of the following four years at Gam-ing. A letter from Leonhard Huntpichler of the Dominican convent in Vienna, addressed to Kempf as a member and not as prior of the Gaming community, was probably written during this period. From one of Ulrich Gossembrot's correspondents (1462) we learn of Kempf's hospitality to-ward a group of students from Vienna who, late in 1461, sought refuge in Gaming from the plague.[62] Kempf sent his greetings via Ulrich to Ul-rich's father, Sigmund Gossembrot, the Augsburg patrician, whom he knew from their student days in Vienna.

Nikolaus Paulus also drew attention to Kempf's sojourn in Straßburg and an invitation to him to join the Carthusian community at Nürnberg (the latter being found in a codex containing Hartmann Sche-del's historical writings, clm 215).[63] The visit to Straßburg may have been related to Kempf's mother's death. Kempf undoubtedly spent much of the period 1458-62 at Gaming, and he may have composed there his *De mystica theologia*, portions of his *Expositiones in Cantica Canti-corum*, and his *De ostensione regni Dei* (appendix A, nos. 18-20).

In April 1462 Kempf became prior of the young foundation at Pletriach, or Pleterje in Slovenia. Founded by the counts of Celje (Cilli) in 1403-6, the Pleterje community's first members came from Gaming. It alone among the charterhouses of the old Austro-Hungarian empire houses a Carthusian community in the late twentieth century. Of the fif-teenth-century monastery, only the old church, constructed in 1420, still

---

[61] Jakob Wichner, *Geschichte des Benediktinerstiftes Admont* (1878), 3: 198-99. Wichner did not cite his source, which was undoubtedly from the Admont Stiftsarchiv. References to Kempf's correspondence with Admont are found under "Lade C" in the seventeenth-century index to Gaming's archives that is now preserved in Böhm Supple-ment, 313. Other letters, related mostly to affairs in villages or parishes owned by Gam-ing, were listed under Lade D, no. 46; E 26-27, F 97-102.

[62] Paulus, "Kempf," 27; "Erhard R[iderer?] to Ulrich Gossembrot" in *Hermann Sche-dels Briefwechsel, 1452-1478*, ed. Paul Joachimsohn (1893), 89.

[63] Quoted in Paulus, "Kempf," 27.

stands. During Kempf's priorate Pleterje found itself on the periphery of the Turkish advance and was attacked repeatedly, including considerable destruction just before Kempf became prior.[64] The three works on mystical spirituality mentioned above, if not written at Gaming between 1458 and 1461, were probably composed at Pleterje, since all three appear in a Graz (formerly Seitz) manuscript dated 1468.

In the fall of 1467 Kempf was named prior at Geirach for the second time. He spent twenty-three more years there, and, with Wydemann, we may assume that he wrote additional works that have been lost. Geirach documents establish his presence there as prior as late as 1479.[65] The *Chartae* of the order indicate that he had his share of internal problems.[66] In 1490 he asked to be relieved of office on account of his advanced age—if born in 1415 he would have been seventy-five. His request was granted by the General Chapter in May 1490. Both the records of the General Chapter and the poem in the Gaming manuscript cited by Wydemann[67] place his death on November 20, 1497 (Vigil of the Presentation of the Virgin Mary). A Budapest manuscript contains a note in an early sixteenth-century hand which gives the year as 1499[68]; it is probably the result of an error in copying.

Such are the meager data of the life of Nicholas Kempf of Straßburg. Diligent archival searching might add some details but the vicissitudes of central European geopolitics during and since the Second World War have further clouded the manuscript and archival records of the Slovenian charterhouses. A survey of the surviving copies of Kempf's writings and of data in fifteenth-century catalogues suggests that the extant writings probably all predate 1468; certainly all his major writings that have survived were composed before 1468.[69] Leopold Wy-

---

[64] Zadnikar and Wienand, *Die Kartäuser*, 321. The *Chartae* of the Chapter General for 1462 refer to the community's "loss and desolation." See *Chartae . . . 1457-65*, (1985), 141.

[65] Paulus, "Kempf," 28.

[66] [1468] "Priori domus Vallis Sancti Mauricii in Gyrio non fit misericordia. Et quantum ad eductionem illorum duorum incarceratorum super quibus petit provideri, committimus vices nostras Visitatoribus provincie." [1470] "Priori domus Vallis Sancti Mauricii in Girio non fit misericordia. Et de fratre Martino clerico reddito professo eiusdem domus declaramus quod obligatur ab observancias Ordinis ut monachi nisi per Priorem suum emittatur foris, vel occupetur in exterioribus. Et si obedire noluerit, serventur Statuta qua de inobedientibus faciunt mentionem. Et de hoc quod scribit dominus Philippus monachus eiusdem domus, committimus Visitatori principali." *Chartae . . . 1466-74*, 72, 124-25.

[67] *Bibl. ascetica*, 4:2v; cf. Steyerer, "Collectanea," 377r.

[68] Budapest, Egyetemi Könyvtár (University Library), cod. 77, fol. 157v.

[69] Only the *De tribus essentialibus* (no. 7), the sermons on the gospels and epistles (no. 14), and the missing liturgical writings, might possibly have been written after 1468.

demann was undoubtedly correct to speculate that much of Kempf's
written legacy has been lost.[70] Thus the last twenty-five years of
Kempf's life, his second period as prior at Geirach, are framed by question marks. Many, if not most, of the codices described by Wydemann
and Pez can be identified as extant in modern collections. The Gaming
manuscripts described by Wydemann, in most instances, were not
unique copies but were present at Seitz, Tegernsee, Melk, and Aggsbach,
and most of these have survived. Thus it was the destruction of the Pleterje and Geirach monasteries in the sixteenth century rather than the
Josephine dissolution in the eighteenth century (after Wydemann) that
has deprived us of the rest of Kempf's supposed legacy.

This is all the more tantalizing since one can discern a steady development in the subject matter of Kempf's writings up to 1468: if the
1440s and 1450s were characterized by works on the monastic life, the
later 1450s and 1460s appear to have been dominated by questions of
mystical theology, although one should not overlook the fact that one of
his earliest writings, *De recto studiorum fine*, sets forth his entire program: from schooling in virtues and carrying into one's behavior what
one reads, the true theologian moves to the *finis omnium scientiarum*,
mystical theology. We turn now to the context that produced that early
work.

---

[70] Wydemann to Pez, January 22, 1718, f. 3r.

CHAPTER TWO

MAGISTER

Does it seem that I pummel knowledge too hard, that I scold scholars and proscribe the study of letters? God forbid! I am not ignorant of how much the Church has profited and still profits from her scholars—both from their refutation of her opponents and their instruction of the simple. . . . I have read that the learned will shine as brightly as the vault of heaven, and those who have instructed many in virtue as bright as stars for all eternity. But I know I have read elsewhere that knowledge puffs up, and "Whoever stores up knowledge stores up sorrow." You see then how knowledge can be differentiated: as one kind of knowledge inflates, another makes one sad. I should very much like to know which of the two you think is more useful or necessary to salvation, the one that makes you swell with pride or the one that makes you weep. [Bernard of Clairvaux, *Sermones super Cantica canticorum*, 36.2.]

1. The Vienna University Milieu

Some understanding of the university setting that Nicholas Kempf knew as a student in Vienna is necessary for understanding chapter three's discussion of one of Kempf's best-known works (*De recto studiorum fine*) and its outline for the training of "true theologians." It is no accident of history that Nicholas Kempf developed his brief for a monastic-based affective theology at a university dominated by a conservative and pastoral theology, one that drew upon the living tradition of patristic-monastic rhetor-theologians, a tradition that could readily convert Cicero's model *orator* into a model theologian. This was a setting in which a professor of theology (Konrad Säldner) could declare Jerome, Augustine, Gerson, and Heinrich of Langenstein superior to the neo-classical poets of Italian humanism because the former skillfully employed language practically rather than artificially. The monastic culture to which much of the rest of this book is devoted became Kempf's home at least in part as an outgrowth of the unique set of intellectual and religious currents flowing through Vienna.

Michael Shank has sought to correlate intellectual currents at Vienna with sociopolitical developments there, suggesting tantalizing linkages between changes in theological apologetics and the violent fate of heretics and Jews in Austria during the first two decades of the fifteenth century. The present chapter presupposes Shank's work. The present work expands the late medieval intellectual context for Shank's study by looking at monastic and lay religiosity as it affected academic theology, language, and exegesis. It expands the chronological context by looking at the patristic and early medieval rhetorical background for Heinrich of Langenstein's challenge to heretics and Jews: "Unless you believe, you shall not understand."[1]

The history of the University of Vienna has been told only in part by the work of previous scholars, and the present study is not intended to fill the gaps so much as to suggest avenues for future research that are opened up by attention to Kempf and his fellow students of the 1430s. The basic outlines of an institutional history of the university are found in the studies by Kink, Aschbach, Wappeler, Sommerfeldt, Schrauf, Lhotsky, Uiblein, Gall, and Frank (see the Bibliography). The matriculation register, the fifteenth-century *Acta* of the theological faculty, and part of the *Acta* of the arts faculty (to 1416), together with an excellent monograph on the arts faculty's history, have been published (Lhotsky, Uiblein).

The history of ideas at the University of Vienna in its first century of existence has received less attention. We have monographs on several leading figures from the arts faculty and the theological faculty: Heinrich Heinbuche of Langenstein (d. 1397), Heinrich Totting of Oyta (ca. 1330-97), Franz of Retz, O.P. (ca. 1343-1427), Nicholas Prünzlein of Dinkels-bühl (ca. 1360-1433), Peter Zech of Pulkau (ca. 1370-1425),[2] Johannes Nider of Isny, O.P. (ca. 1380-1438),[3] Thomas Ebendorfer of Haselbach (1388-1464),[4] and Leonhard Huntpichler of Brixen, O.P. (ca. 1400-

---

[1] Michael H. Shank, *"Unless You Believe, You Shall Not Understand": Logic, University, and Society in Late Medieval Vienna* (1988), esp. 26-37. See also James Overfield, *Humanism and Scholasticism in Late Medieval Germany* (1984), 102-6; Lhotsky, *Umriß* (1964); Redlich, *Tegernsee*; Ludwig Glückert, "Hieronymus von Mondsee," *SMGB*, 48 [n.F. 17] (1930), 98-201; Anton Mayer, "Aus dem geistigen Leben Niederösterreichs im 15. Jahrhundert," in *Festgabe zum 100-jährigen Jubiläum des Schottengymnasiums* (1907), 187-201.

[2] On Langenstein see the works by Heilig, Kreuzer, and Shank; on Totting von Oyta see Albert Lang (1937); on Franz von Retz see Häfele; on Nicholas von Dinkelsbühl see Madre, Binder, Schäffauer, Justin Lang; on Peter Zech see Girgensohn.

[3] Schieler, Gieraths, Frank, *Hausstudium*. Nider studied at Vienna but spent a number of years at Dominican convents in Cologne and Basel. He taught theology at Vienna 1425-30, 1436-38. Of his writings, the most accessible is the *Formicarius* (reprinted, 1971). For the present study his most significant work is *De reformatione religiosorum* [or *Tractatus de reformatione status coenobitici*] (Paris, 1512; Antwerp, 1611). I have used the manuscript copy found in Salzburg, St. Peter, Stiftsbibliothek cod. b IX 7. Nider also translated and paraphrased into German John Cassian's writings.

[4] Lhotsky, 1957.

1478). The work of Johannes Geuß of Deining in the Oberpfalz (ca. 1398-1440), among the circle of influential university and court personages, remains sadly neglected.[5] Only a few of the writings of these personages have been published in modern editions (see the Bibliography). In the absence of useful editions of many of the works of Heinrich of Langenstein[6] and Nicholas of Dinkelsbühl,[7] our picture of the intellectual life of early fifteenth-century Vienna remains very incomplete, despite much progress in recent decades.

The university was reorganized, indeed, for all practical purposes, refounded, in 1384. It was patterned after Paris in many ways, although the influence of Prague is evident and three members of Vienna's first theological faculty (1384) were graduates of Bologna.[8] Vienna's university was the largest in German-speaking areas throughout most of the fifteenth century[9] and drew many of its students from the Danube regions in southern Germany, indeed, from as far west as Straßburg—until the founding of universities at Freiburg (1452), Basel (1460), Ingolstadt (1472), and Tübingen (1477). Beginning with the reorganization in 1384, when the university received papal permission to teach theology, theologians dominated the leadership of the university. By the late fourteenth century the prominent role of chairs in theology reserved for specific mendicant orders had declined even at Paris, and the absence of such Dominican, Franciscan, or Augustinian schools of thought at Vienna permitted such leading secular theologians as Heinrich of Langenstein, Thomas Ebendorfer, or Nicholas of Dinkelsbühl to play a large role in university affairs in general and to serve as diplomats and pastors for the

---

[5] On Huntpichler see Frank (1976). Geuß matriculated in 1412; taught as a master of arts 1416-33, then as a master of theology, 1434-40. He was confessor for Archduchess Elizabeth (after 1438, queen). See Franz Josef Worstbrock, "Geuß (Gaws, Gews, Geiz, Geyss), Johannes," in *Verfasserlexikon*, rev. ed., vol. 3, cols. 37-41, for a preliminary list of manuscripts. Cf. the article by A. Linsenmayer, "Johannes Geuß, ein Prediger des 15. Jahrhunderts," *Theologisch-praktische Monats-Schrift*, 3 (1893), 825-32.

[6] The best general overview is Kreuzer, *Heinrich von Langenstein* (1987). Cf. François Vandenbroucke in *DSAM*, 7 (1969), 215-19; Kreuzer in *TRE*, 15 (1986). Heinrich's *Sentences* commentary has been published by Rudolf Damerau (1979-80). Cf. Thomas Hohmann, "Initienregister der Werke Heinrichs von Langenstein," *Traditio*, 32 (1976), 399-426.

[7] In addition to Madre, *Nikolaus von Dinkelsbühl*, see Madre, ed., "Sermo magistri Nicolai ad clerum et ad religiosos De profectu et perfectione," in *Ecclesia militans* (1988), 1: 185-211.

[8] Uiblein, "Beziehungen," 177-79, 187-89; Hastings Rashdall, *Universities of Europe in the Middle Ages*, rev. ed. (1936), 2: 240-41.

[9] Schwinges, *DeutscheUniversitätsbesucher*, 61-73, esp. 63-64; Uiblein, "Quellenlage," 162; Gall, "Anfänge," 54; Conradin Bonorand, "Die Bedeutung der Universität Wien für Humanismus und Reformation, insbesondere in der Ostschweiz," *Zwingliana*, 12 (1965), 162-80, at 166.

Austrian court.[10] But regular clergy were not absent. Aschbach lists three Augustinian Eremites, three Carmelites, nine Dominicans, one Franciscan, and eleven Benedictines among the arts faculty masters for the period 1365-1465.[11] As we shall see, even the secular masters of theology took a strong interest in monastic reform alongside their active role in efforts to improve the education and zeal of parish clergy. In general, the University of Vienna had not advanced as far as French or English universities in the process of transformation from "independent centers of clerical culture to preparatory schools for future princely officials."[12]

2. Via Moderna and Apologetics at Vienna: Modes of Speaking

The labels "nominalism," "terminism," and *via moderna* have all been employed to describe the intellectual developments at Oxford and Paris in the fourteenth century. Despite the ongoing debates over the best label, many revisionist interpretations of the *via moderna* emphasize that its representatives explored the varied ways human language functions in relation to metaphysics, natural science, philosophy, and theology. The work of William J. Courtenay, Neal Gilbert, Zénon Kaluza, and others have contributed to this focus on rhetoric, language, and semantic logic—on methods and language rather than philosophic content.[13]

---

[10] There were institutes and *studia* of several mendicant orders at Vienna, e.g., the Dominican *Hausstudium* or the Carmelite or Augustinian convents' programs of studies. They did not, however, develop into schools of thought or theology. See Franz-Bernard Lickteig, "The German Carmelites at the Medieval Universities" (diss., 1977; published 1981), pp. 202-57 on Vienna; Friedrich Rennhofer, *Die Augustiner-Eremiten in Wien* (1956); Johannes Gavigan, "De doctoribus theologiae O.S.A. in universitate Vindobonensi," *Augustinianum*, 5 (1965), 271-364; Häfele, *Franz von Retz*, 126; Katherine Walsh, "The Observance . . . Augustinian Friars in the Fourteenth and Fifteenth Centuries," *Rivista di Storia della chiesa in Italia*, 31 (1977), 40-67. Frank, *Hausstudium*, 134-40, disputes Rennhofer's arguments for a nominalist "Augustinian school" at Vienna; cf. Lhotsky, *Artistenfakultät*, 31-32. The most recent summary is found in Shank, *Unless*, 17-18, 28-31.

[11] Aschbach, *Wiener Universität*, 1: 596-627.

[12] Jacques LeGoff, "How Did the Medieval University Conceive of Itself," and "The Universities and the Public Authorities in the Middle Ages and the Renaissance," in *Time, Work, and Culture in the Middle Ages* (1980), 122-34, 135-49, 318-24; cf. Stieber, *Eugenius IV*, 76.

[13] Neal W. Gilbert, "Ockham, Wyclif, and the 'Via Moderna'," in *Antiqui et Moderni* (1974), 85-125, and William J. Courtenay, Charles Trinkaus, Heiko Oberman, and Neal W. Gilbert in *JHI* 48 (1987), 3-50; William J. Courtenay, "The Reception of Ockham's Thought at the University of Paris," in *Preuve et raisons à l'université de Paris: Logique, ontologie et théologie au XIVe siècle* (1984), 43-64; idem, *Schools* (1987), esp. 219-40; Zénon Kaluza, *Les querelles doctrinales à Paris: Nominalistes et réalistes aux*

Shank has now applied recent interpretations of the *via moderna* to the
Vienna university. From his study it becomes clear that important ele-
ments of the Paris *via moderna* came with Heinrich of Langenstein and
Heinrich of Oyta and others to Vienna. Markowski's inventories of
manuscripts demonstrate at least a potential impact of the terminism of
Jean Buridan (d. ca. 1358) in the arts faculty at Vienna.[14]

Recent scholarship has also emphasized that Jean Gerson, whose
importance for Vienna theologians is undeniable, was educated within
the "school" of Jean Buridan at Paris in the late fourteenth century.[15] As
chancellor of the Cathedral of Notre Dame and the university (1395ff)
Gerson paid more attention to the theological faculty than the arts faculty, where the technical question of universal forms was debated early
in the fifteenth century. In the theological faculty, Gerson's concern was
the appropriate use of language and logic in theology, an application of
logic different from that required by the natural sciences and philosophical metaphysics. Gerson decried the effects on theology of the 'reified'
or metaphysical approach to language characteristic of the modist logic[16]
favored by Scotist theologians. Gerson's attitude is visible in his conviction that Jerome of Prague (d. 1416), John Hus (d. 1415) and John Wyclif (d. 1384) fell into error in part because they misunderstood the role
of metaphor in scripture, because they failed to realize that scripture has
its own semantic logic, its own *modus loquendi* (way of speaking).[17]
One might describe Gerson's efforts as a didactic, pious, "literary, perhaps aesthetic" application to theology of *via moderna* terminism, suitably modified from its role in the arts faculty's debates over universals.[18]

---

confins du XIVe et du XVe siècles (1988); Charles Trinkaus, *The Poet as Philosopher* (1979), 52-57, and idem, "Erasmus, Augustine, and the Nominalists."

[14] Mieczyslaw Markowski, "L'influence de Jean Buridan sur les universités d'Europe
Centrale," in *Preuve et raisons*, 149-63; idem, "Abhandlungen zur Logik an der Universität Wien in den Jahren 1365-1500," *StudiaMediewistyczne*, 22, no. 1 (1983), 53-77. As
Lhotsky, *Artistenfakultät*, 184ff., commented more than twenty years ago, until the unpublished commentaries and lectures on Aristotle and the arts curriculum are studied
much more thoroughly, we remain more in the dark about the nature of the arts faculty in
early fifteenth-century Vienna than about the theological faculty.

[15] Gilbert, "Ockham, Wyclif, and the 'Via Moderna'," 85-125, and Courtenay in *JHI*
48 (1987), 3-10.

[16] See Gilbert and Courtenay as cited in n. 12, above; see also Jan Pinborg, *Logik und
Semantik im Mittelalter* (1972), 77-126, but note Robert D. Anderson, "Medieval Speculative Grammar: A Study of the Modistae" (diss., 1989), and idem, "Laying Bare Speculative Grammar: Some Remarks," *New Scholasticism*, 61 (1987), 13-24.

[17] Kaluza, "Le Chancelier Gerson et Jérôme de Prague," *AHDL*, 59 (1984), 81-126,
esp. 108-115; cf. idem, *Querelles*; Shank, *Unless*, 176-85.

[18] Kaluza, *Querelles*, 122; "Chancelier Gerson," 110-12.

One of the outgrowths of *via moderna* terminism for theology was the way theologians began to draw limits around the use of logic in apologetic argumentation for belief in the Trinity.[19] This is especially true for Langenstein, for whom syllogistic logic had its role to play but not in the mysteries of theology, where one must believe in order to understand. In Shank's view this retrenchment of speculative courage converged with the general conservatism of the University of Vienna and, when combined with the anxieties of the Hussite wars, led to violence against heretics (notably Jerome of Prague) and a pogrom that obliterated the Vienna Jewish community.[20]

That the atmosphere in Vienna was conservative seems clear. Authorities moved quickly to stifle Hussite influence and, after the trial of Jerome of Prague, the movement had few adherents in the city.[21] In 1420 theologians from Vienna furnished learned opinions against the heresy of the "Twenty-Four Elders" that flourished in Judenburg (Styria), South Tyrol, Carinthia, and elsewhere.[22] Support for conciliarism at Vienna does not so much indicate openness to innovation as hope for church *re*form, hope for a *re*turn to the spiritual vigor of a previous age.

The Vienna theologians also seem to have been greatly concerned for the practical and affective. Indeed, the *via moderna* theologians' concerns about excessively speculative and reified logic and language correlate well with a general preference for the practical over the speculative, for rhetorical and affective effectiveness rather than abstract speculation.

---

[19] Courtenay, *Schools*, 276-82; Shank, *Unless*; Robert Holcot, *Exploring the Boundaries of Reason: Three Questions on the Nature of God by Robert Holcot, O.P.*, ed. Hester Gelber (1983), cf. Gelber, "Logic and the Trinity: A Clash of Values in Scholastic Thought, 1300-1335" (diss., 1974), 265-317. Alfonso Maierù, "Logic and Trinitarian Theology," in *Meaning and Inference in Medieval Philosophy* (1989), 247-95; idem, "Logique et théologie trinitaire dans le moyen-âge tardif," in *The Editing of Theological and Philosophical Texts from the Middle Ages* (1986), 185-212; idem, "Logique et théologie trinitaire: Pierre d'Ailly," in *Preuve et raisons* (1984), 253-68; Fritz Hoffmann, "Robert Holcot—Die Logik in der Theologie," in *Die Metaphysik im Mittelalter* (1963), 624-39; Johann Auer, "Die aristotelische Logik in der Trinitätslehre der Spätscholastik," in *Theologie in Geschichte und Gegenwart* [Schmaus Festschrift] (1957), 457-96 (including the text of a *quaestio* on the topic, but note the corrections by Shank, *Unless*, pp. 119-20).

[20] Shank, *Unless*, 87-200; Katherine Walsh, "Vom Wegestreit zur Haeresie: Zur Auseinandersetzung um die Lehre John Wyclifs in Wien und Prag an der Wende zum 15. Jahrhundert," *MIÖG*, 94 (1986), 25-48. On the general issues involved, see Guy Fitch Lytle, "Universities as Religious Authorities in the Later Middle Ages and Reformation," in *Reform and Authority in the Medieval and Reformation Church* (1981), 69-97, and William Courtenay's less eirenic assessment, "Inquiry and Inquisition: Academic Freedom in Medieval Universities," *CH*, 58 (1989), 168-81.

[21] Aschbach, *Wiener Universität*, 1: 255-65.

[22] Girgensohn, *Peter von Pulkau*, 42-45.

We shall look at two examples of the intersection of logic, affective-pragmatic theology, and proto-humanist pedagogical reform at Vienna. The first is Langenstein's sermon on St. Catherine, in which he set forth his vision for the university, a text that figures significantly in Shank's analysis. The second example is the "quarrel between the poets and theologians" of the 1450s, with possible roots in the student generation of the mid-1430s.

The principle expressed by Langenstein's phrase, "unless you believe you shall not understand," has a long history.[23] Although in the volatile political environment of Vienna studied by Shank it may have become a defiant challenge to "unbelieving" Jews and heretics, in its patristic and early medieval usage, from Augustine to Bonaventure, it was an expression of "pious ignorance," a confession: *credo ut intelligam.* Most recent studies of Heinrich of Langenstein have tended to deemphasize the importance of his Rhineland sojourn (late 1382 to 1384),[24] part of which was spent at the Cistercian monastery of Eberbach, most of which, however, was passed as a guest of Bishop Eckhard von Ders of Worms. Much of the case for Langenstein's "affective conversion" during his Eberbach sojourn once rested on the "Augustinian" overtones of a commentary on the *Sentences* in Munich clm 11591 that is now attributed to Langenstein's Eberbach host, a former professor at the Paris Cistercian house of studies, James of Eltville.[25] However, the reattribution of this one work does not rule out the impact of monastic piety and theology on Langenstein's subsequent career. The issue is larger than the question of Langenstein's turn toward academic or philosophical Augustinianism in the misattributed commentary. His widely disseminated devotional writings, both in Latin and German, require closer examination in this regard. One need not postulate a sharp "turning point" at Eberbach to recognize the presence of an affective, devotional piety in Langenstein's later writings.[26]

---

[23] E.g., Augustine, *Soliloquium*, I.12; II.9, II.19-34; *De utilitate credendi*, esp. 13.29 (CSEL 25: 36-37).

[24] For a summary see Kreuzer, *Langenstein*, 63-79.

[25] On James of Eltville, see Heinrich Denifle ed., *Chartularium Universitatis Parisiensis* (1891), 4: 412, doc. 1521, and Caesarius Bulaeus (Du Boulay), *Historia Universitatis Parisiensis* (1668; repr. 1966), 994. The challenge to Langenstein's authorship was first made by Damasus Trapp in a footnote in "Augustinian Theology of the Fourteenth Century: Notes on Editions, Marginalia, Opinions, and Book-lore," *Augustiniana*, 6 (1956), 146-274, at 252, n. 93.

[26] François Vandenbroucke in *DSAM*, vol. 7; Kreuzer, *Langenstein*, 63-78; F. Falk, "Der mittelrheinische Freundeskreis des Heinrichs von Langenstein," *HJ*, 15 (1894), 517-28; cf. Shank, *Unless*, 141-42.

Heinrich of Langenstein's St. Catherine's Day sermon[27] can be interpreted against the background of Augustinian affectivity as well as against the speculative theology studied by Shank.[28] In his *De contemptu mundi*, a "consolation treatise" written at Eberbach, Heinrich of Langenstein had portrayed the false world of "Egypt" and its vain pursuit of eloquence, the liberal arts, and that knowledge which puffs up, as a foolishness leading to perdition. Against this "Egypt" he offered "Jerusalem" with its humble wisdom and restrained tongue—its own way of speaking.[29] In his sermon for St. Catherine's Day, he offers St. Catherine as a model for members of the *universitas magistrorum et studentium* because her learning, or *disciplina*, fufills the threefold model for learning set forth by Robert Holcot (d. 1349): information, training in moral behavior, castigation of wrongdoing.[30] She had been trained in sciences and doctrine to the point that she could dispute with the emperor about the foolishness of idolatry. Admittedly, she had not gone to school to obtain this learning—it was a miraculous gift in her hour of need. This in itself indicates that *both* prayer and reasoning are useful in converting unbelievers. In fact, a holy life is a more effective champion of Christ than is brilliant scholarly accomplishment. Shank points out that Langenstein believed that the most "fundamental reasons for the failure of [Christian] apologetics" lay in the fact that

> We are deficient in holiness of life: our Church is in disarray and is in
> some sense answerable to no authority when we act against our law, since
> the infidels can argue from our perverse works that the things we preach to
> them are false and deceptive; nor do we believe the same articles with true
> and firm faith, since we constantly evince and carry out the opposite in
> deed.[31]

---

[27] Albert Lang, ed., "Die Katharinenpredigt Heinrichs von Langenstein," *Divus Thomas*, 26 (1948), 123-59, 233-50; cf. the discussion by Lang, "Die Universität als geistiger Organismus nach Heinrich von Langenstein," ibid., 27 (1949), 41-86.

[28] Shank, *Unless*, 158-69, 192-200.

[29] Gustav Sommerfeldt, ed., "Des Magisters Heinrich von Langenstein Traktate 'De contemptu mundi'," *ZKTh*, 29 (1905), 404-12. Something of the same "pious" and "Bernardine" development in Langenstein's theology is evident from Aquilin Emmen's examination of his Mariological views, "Heinrich von Langenstein und die Diskussion über die Empfängnis Mariens," in *Theologie in Geschichte und Gegenwart* [Schmaus Festschrift] (1957), 625-50.

[30] Holcot, *Super sapientiam Salomonis* (1494; repr. 1974), ch. 8, lect. 106 (not 107 as reported in Lang's edition of the St. Catherine's Day sermon).

[31] Translation by Shank, p. 167.

Not only Jews should believe if they wish to understand the mystery of the Trinity; Christians must believe in word and deed, must practice what they preach. Drawing on an entire tradition of pious ignorance, Langenstein affirms in this sermon a theme that reemerges as a fundament of Gerson's and Kempf's theology: the prayers of simple, unlettered lay people are more effective than the arguments of the learned.

Catherine had also been trained to be an example of virtuous, upright life and to struggle against vices, the second and third aspects of genuine *disciplina*. Here Langenstein is using the classic language of the monastic tradition, once dominant in the entire church: the monastery as a "school" of charity, the "active life" of combat against vices. We shall encounter all of these themes in Kempf, who repeatedly cites Heinrich of Langenstein alongside Gerson as the best of the "modern theologians."

Heinrich of Langenstein also uses the language of the nonmonastic schools: Catherine knew the "disciplines" of the university and *disputed* with masters in the various arts and sciences: law, medicine, theology, and all the liberal arts. He insists on the interdependence of the disciplines even while he leaves no doubt that theology belongs at the top of the pyramid. Each one has need of the other; none can do its task completely independently. In the background lurks the Pauline body metaphor (1 Cor 12), which assumes that the head is indeed superior to the rest of the body but also insists that the head cannot get along without the less showy members.

In his *quaestio* near the end of the sermon, Langenstein outlines the marks of a true and praiseworthy philosopher. These characteristics stress the practical over the speculative: to love wisdom and seek its true end with pure intention; to see to it that what one speculates about somehow contributes to the improvement of one's way of living; to live what one learns.[32]

Shank does not intend to exclude the "pious, Bernardine" element in Langenstein's development (p. 142); the present study certainly does not aim at excluding the apologetic debate with the Vienna Jewish community that Shank posits as a stimulus to developments in Langenstein's

---

[32] Albert Lang insisted that Heinrich of Langenstein typifies the "practical" concerns of the university's founders here. See "Universität," 83-85. Cf. Langenstein's *Genesis* commentary: "The earth is now full of the knowledge of the Lord [Is 11:9], as Isaiah says; the light of knowledge shines more clearly but the earth does not grow warmer, indeed, the love of many grows cold [Mt 24:12]. Where is he who burns with a profusion of knowledge and strives to live a holy life? It almost seems as if the words of Augustine are being fulfilled: 'The unlearned arise and reach for the heavens while we fall into hell with our knowledge.'" Quoted in Friedrich Wilhelm Oediger, *Über die Bildung der Geistlichen im späten Mittelalter* (1953), 13.

theology and that of his successors. It does, however, intend to place the
entire matter within the larger context of a rise and fall of confidence in
the logical demonstrability of the Christian faith—a rather modest rise
and fall that had long been bracketed by most theologians' awareness
that the mystery of the Trinity ultimately exceeded rational demonstration. Christian theology grounded on logic was itself a relatively recent
development, the product of the eleventh- and twelfth-century Christian
interaction with Jews, Muslims, and heretics.[33] Little more than a century after the rise of university theology at Paris, questions about the ap-
plicability of the Aristotelian logic to the mysteries of faith were
broached at Oxford early in the 1330s, where Robert Holcot's call for a
"new logic of faith"[34] built on elements already present in Ockham.[35]
Thus the reexamination of theological "science" began within scholastic
theology itself. Even as the new "English" logic and natural philosophy
were being exported to the continent, pastoral concerns became increasingly prominent in England.[36] The Vienna theology faculty's "practical"
and pastoral orientation in the early fifteenth century thus mirrors contemporary developments in Paris (Gerson, 1400ff.) and those of a generation earlier in England.

3. Vita Monastica: Monastic Rhetoric and Epistemology

The devotional, affective piety of the Vienna theologians also had
sources distinct from fourteenth-century scholastic revisionism. The re-
emergence of pastoral and practical priorities coincided not only with
growing interest in general (conciliar) church reform and a movement to
provide pastoral and devotional literature for the literate laity,[37] but also
with the growth of monastic reform north of the Alps. All of these movements brought northern theologians into contact with humanist stirrings

---

[33] See G. R. Evans, *Old Arts and New Theology: The Beginnings of Theology as an
Academic Discipline* (1980), 137-66; Joseph de Ghellinck, *Le mouvement théologique du
XIIe siècle*, 2nd ed. (1969), 225-26, 279-84, 289-93; Ludwig Hödl, "Die dialektische
Theologie des 12. Jahrhunderts," in *Arts libéraux et philosophie* (1969), pp. 137-47, at
141-43.

[34] Courtenay, *Schools*, 219-49, 276-78; Gelber, "Logic and the Trinity" (1974), 265-
317; Shank, *Unless*, 65-78.

[35] Courtenay, *Schools*, 205-8.

[36] Courtenay, *Schools*, 327-80; cf. 257.

[37] Courtenay identifies this as an important factor in the "pastoral" turn taken by English theologians of the last half of the thirteenth century. *Schools*, 373-80. See also the
discussion of Thomas Peuntner and other Vienna "translators," below.

in Italy. Yet, when viewed against the broad context of medieval theologizing, Langenstein seems to be returning to the prescholastic approach incorporated into the pronouncements on Trinitarian theology at the Fourth Lateran Council in 1215—as Shank points out, before Aristotelianism had made its full impact on theology.[38] Indeed, the movement to limit the scope of logic within theology eventually meant a larger role for imagination and metaphor in language about the mysteries of faith, the approach characteristic of the patristic and monastic world in which theologians were trained primarily as rhetoricians and secondarily as dialecticians.

Luke Anderson and others have shown that monastic writers in the twelfth-century, drawing on the patristic heritage, primarily employed a well-defined rhetorical logic rather than a strictly dialectical method to persuade and "subdue the will and move to action,"[39] leaning heavily on the incomplete syllogism, the enthymeme.[40] This monastic-patristic rhetorical and affective theology was no limp and mindless emotivism but a highly skilled method in which "a lively interplay between the abbot (orator) and his monks (audience), between the orator's eloquence and the audience's emotional and intellectual response" took place, combining "imaginative speech and creative listening" "to create a beauty of life altogether unique and especially claustral."[41]

The monastic teacher, the abbot, differed from the *magister*-educator. The latter's purpose was not primarily to move his hearers to action, thus intellectual acuteness, not personal moral virtue was essential to his task.[42] The monastic-patristic, rhetorical epistemology that resulted

> defines knowledge as *practical*, truth as *prudential*, and certitude as *probable*, but imperating. Bernard's perceptions, judgments, and argu-

---

[38] *Unless*, 121-24, 134-35.

[39] Luke Anderson, "Enthymeme and Dialectic: Cloister and Classroom," in *From Cloister to Classroom* (1986), 239-74, at 245. An unpublished paper by Anderson, delivered at the 1990 Bernard of Clairvaux nonacentenary proceedings at Kalamazoo and generously made available to me by its author, deals more specifically with Bernard, showing that he used a demanding and highly developed rhetorical methodology: "The Rhetorical Epistemology in Saint Bernard's Super Cantica" (forthcoming in *CSQ*). Note also Raymond D. DiLorenzo, "Rational Research in the Rhetoric of Augustine's *Confessio*, in *From Cloister to Classroom*, 1-26; and Ronald G. Witt, "Medieval Italian Culture and the Origins of Humanism as a Stylistic Ideal," in *Renaissance Humanism* (1988), 1: 29-70.

[40] Luke Anderson, "Enthymeme," 250, 258, citing Aristotle, *Prior Analytics*, Bk. 11, ch. 27, and John of Salisbury, *Metalogicon*, III.10.

[41] Luke Anderson, "Enthymeme," 253.

[42] Ibid.

ments are colored by his gift of *ingenium*. The linking of concepts and propositions is unfailingly contingent as Bernard addresses the mutable human situation. But the goal of his persuasion, by way of *logos*, *ethos*, and *pathos*, is never attained without the consent of his audience.[43]

The distinctions between monastic and scholastic theologies made by Jean Leclercq and M.-D. Chenu forty years ago have been challenged repeatedly. Brian Stock describes monastic communities as "textual communities," arguing that monastic allegory is predicated on first having isolated the literal text, placing monks closer to the emerging text-based world of the schools. In Stock's view, the distinctions drawn by Leclercq and others between monastic culture and scholastic culture must yield to a more complex set of intersections and interrelationships.[44]

Although it is possible to use "monastic" and "scholastic" reductively, as mere slogans, such misuse should not be permitted to obscure the contribution made by Oediger, Leclercq, Chenu, De Ghellinck, and others. The distinction between "monastic" and "scholastic" theology can and will remain an extremely useful interpretive tool.[45] And this dis-

---

[43] These sentences form the conclusion to Luke Anderson, "Rhetorical Epistemology."

[44] Brian Stock, *The Implications of Literacy* (1983). Cf. Stock, "Experience, Praxis, Work, and Planning in Bernard of Clairvaux," in *The Cultural Context of Medieval Learning* (1975), 219-62, discussion, 262-68, which, pursuing suggestions by Max Weber, attempts to draw connections between the monastic understanding of experience and the first faint stirrings of modern empiricism. This argument appears in a more subtle and revised form as pp. 410-54 of *Implications of Literacy*. Stock's cautions are helpful to some degree. Yet his summary argument in *Implications* (525-26, cf. 328-29, 405) is weak. He points out that Anselm, whom Grabmann called the "father of scholasticism," wrote primarily for monks, as if writing for monks itself meant that one wrote monastically rather than scholastically and as if Grabmann's label is beyond question. Stock also suggests that, although Bernard was a "charismatic" preacher, "textuality nonetheless played a major role in [the] production, audience relations, and transmission [of Bernard's sermons on the Song of Songs]. . . . His dicta became a set of quasi-sacramental bonds for the period's most exemplary textual community." (526). I am not convinced that the "textual community" label fits—as Brian McGuire's work on Cistercian story-telling after Bernard's era (in progress) suggests, Bernard's "text" was transmitted in an eminently monastic, imaginative, and pre-textual way. Like Stock, Ludwig Hödl also rejects the contrast between scholastic and monastic theology, considering Chenu's "symbolist theology" to be one subdivision of scholastic theology, alongside "dialectical theology." He rejects the term "monastic theology" entirely, arguing that the theology of monks in the twelfth century was scholastic theology. (Restricting his argument to the twelfth century sidesteps the main thrust of Leclercq's book and, to that degree, begs the question.) See Hödl, "Dialektische Theologie," esp. 137-38, 155-56.

[45] Slightly before Leclercq published his *Love of Learning*, Oediger had commented in *Bildung*, p. 13: "Es liegt an der einseitigen Richtung der bisherigen Forschung, dass wir zuerst an die Scholastik denken, wenn wir von der Theologie des späten Mittelalters

tinction is not simply the invention of modern scholars: already in the
fifteenth century Heinrich Arnoldi, the prior of the Basel charterhouse,
used precisely the terms *modus monasticus* and *modus scholasticus* to
define the method and purpose of his dialogue on the love of God and
neighbor.[46] Stock's profound and seminal book must be employed to
deepen, not to blur our understanding of the distinction they express.

The essentially rhetorical character of monastic-patristic hermeneutics can be observed in the commentaries of Bede. In the words of Lawrence T. Martin:

> Because of the linear, one-thing-at-a-time nature of discourse, a com-
> mentator generally is forced to discuss first the literal sense of a scriptural
> text, and then its spiritual significance, resulting in a kind of fragmentation
> of the scriptural message. Bede, however, breaks through this linear con-
> straint by his pattern of repetition of the same words, first with literal
> meaning, then with abstract, psychological meaning. In this way he can
> point to both levels of meaning, but at the same time remind his readers
> that both meanings are present in the scriptural text simultaneously and in-
> tegrally.[47]

Much the same simultaneity of multiple levels rather than linear, se-
quential progression can be seen in monastic writings on the ascent to
contemplative union.[48] Treatises on contemplation often seem repetitive
and convoluted to modern scholars, who routinely abridge and rearrange
them when translating for a popular audience, yet this repetition and in-
terlacing of various stages and substages is often essential to the author's

---

sprechen." In addition to Leclercq, *Love of Learning* (French, 1957; ET 1961); De
Ghellinck, *Mouvement théologique*; Marie-Dominique Chenu, *Nature, Man, and Society
in the Twelfth Century* (1968), see G. R. Evans, *Old Arts*; John W. Baldwin, *The Scholastic Culture of the Middle Ages, 1000-1300* (1971); idem, *Masters, Princes, and Merchants: The Social Views of Peter the Chanter and His Circle*, 2 vols. (1970); Lester K.
Little, *Religious Poverty and the Profit Economy in Twelfth-Century Europe* (1978).

[46] Pez, *Bibl. ascetica*, 6: 5. "Et quamvis materia haec originem ducat ex theologia
mystica, innitendo videlicet jam purgativae, jam illuminativae, et jam unitivae seu per-
fectivae viis; principalius tamen intendit viae unitivae, quae in dilectionis perfectione
consistit. Modus autem procedendi in subsequentibus non est directe scholasticus, sed
potius monasticus, qui decet religiosos, eo, quod hic agitur de his, quae magis et principalius ad devotionis affectum, quam ad inquisitionis intellectum pertinere videntur, prout
ea colligentis memoriae ex prius quandoque lectis occurrebant." Occasionally, however,
the scholastic will intrude, Arnoldi warns.

[47] Lawrence T. Martin, "Bede's Structural Use of Wordplay as a Way to Truth," in
From Cloister to Classroom (1986), 27-46, at 39.

[48] Karl F. Morrison illustrates the ambiguity found even in a work of political-pas-
toral counsel like Bernard of Clairvaux's *De consideratione*. See Morrison, "Hermeneutics and Enigma: Bernard of Clairvaux's De Consideratione," *Viator*, 19 (1988), 129-51.

method: it is a means to make clear to his reader that spiritual progress is not merely linear, that it defies abstract textual analysis in order to speak to the heart.[49] As Ann Astell argues, the "higher" allegorical senses of scripture fused with the literal/historical sense in the course of medieval contemplative exegesis, becoming a single rhetorical synthesis of meaning and effectively "reliteralizing" the allegorical levels. All the various levels of meaning together constitute the "factum," or historical meaning, and the gloss itself becomes an inseparable part of the text.[50]

Nicholas Kempf was well aware of the differences between scholastic and affective-contemplative monastic methodology. Having addressed a variety of hermeneutic issues in the prologue, he proceeds in the opening chapter of the first book of his commentary on the Canticle to address the "scholastic" question directly: the best sources for understanding this Song of Songs, this unique form of speech, include the Fathers (namely Gregory, Bernard, Anselm, Bede, and Origen), and Dionysius and his commentators (John Scotus Eriugena, Thomas Gallus, Robert Grosseteste,[51] and Hugh of Balma). He notes that *Sentences* commentaries on book 1, distinction 14 (the procession of the Holy Spirit) and elsewhere are also relevant, but insists that

> I have been helped by the writings of many devout people who write more out of their experience than out of naked knowledge, for they sing that Song with God their Beloved, not only from their mouths but in their hearts. . . . One should not be surprised that these writings endure much criticism, especially from those who are not moved by love. . . .

---

[49] A prime example is Guigo de Ponte, *De contemplatione*, ed. Philippe DuPont (1985), as discussed in chapter five, below. Hugh of Balma, *Viae Sion lugent* [also known as *De mystica theologia* and *De triplici via*] sets forth an analytical outline that makes use of scholastic terminology and concludes with a *quaestio*—but employs all of these to delimit sharply, though not exclude absolutely, the role of cognition in the affective ascent to God. He also insists that practice must precede theory and that outer moral practice leads to inner illumination. See Hugh of Balma, *Viae Sion lugent*, Prologue, ed. A. C. Peltier (1866), p. 3b (= par. 9 in the Sources Chrétiennes edition).

[50] Ann W. Astell, *The Song of Songs in the Middle Ages* (1990), 6, 17-18, 29, 55, 180, etc. Much the same point is made by E. Ann Matter, *The Voice of My Beloved: The Song of Songs in Western Medieval Christianity* (1990), e.g., pp. 4-8, 13-14; Beryl Smalley points out an instance in which Richard of St. Victor offered as the literal sense what Jerome explicitly called the spiritual sense of a passage from Ecclesiastes [see "Essay I" in *Medieval Exegesis of Wisdom Literature: Essays by Beryl Smalley*, ed. by Roland E. Murphy (1986), 3].

[51] Kempf mistakenly writes *Hugo linconiensis*, conflating Hugh of Lincoln, the Carthusian saint and bishop of Lincoln, with Grosseteste, who was also bishop of Lincoln. See G1, fol. 143v, line 9.

There is a place, he admits, for a "scholastic" approach full of citations of the various authorities, including scholastic theologians, and he has done that in his treatise *On the Revelation of the Kingdom* (= *De mystica theologia*, see appendix A, nos. 18-20). But in the present work, a commentary on a love song, he pursues knowledge by pursuing experience of God's love.[52]

In *De ostensione regni Dei* Nicholas Kempf weaves together a number of strands relevant to the present discussion. Under the chapter heading: "Through the anagogical sense the sweetness of honey is tasted, but through the other senses [of scripture] blossoms are gathered through the flow of divine grace from all of scripture and all symbols [*figurae*]" he comments

> The eye of the spirit [mens] is illuminated with light to understand the anagogical meaning in sacred scripture when the spirit [mens] herself reaches upward toward God through an affected, sighing, and longing love. This [anagogical] meaning lies hidden everywhere in the scriptures, and it cannot be effectively revealed except to a spirit [mens] that is cleansed and pure. This true anagogical meaning converts the gathered flowers into the sweetness of honey, just as the bees are accustomed to do. The blossoms of the scriptures are gathered by the other meanings of scripture, but it is through the anagogical meaning that the sweetness of honey is tasted through the affectedness of love. So too the bees gather flowers and from them are well able to draw out and concentrate nourishment. So too should all scripture be read in order that the honey of love might be gathered into the wax of Christ's divinity and humanity—but not only

---

[52] *Cantica*, I.1 (G1, 143v-144r; Pez 11: 52-53): "Adiutus eciam fui per multorum devotorum scripta magis ex experiencia quam ex nuda sciencia emanancia, qui illud canticum non solum in ore, sed in corde cum deo dilecto suo cantaverunt; . . . Nec mirum, si paciantur hec scripta contradictionem, precipue ab hijs qui non agitantur amore, . . ." Note also the use of *modus loquendi*, custom, and conventional words—even Peter did not *know* what he was saying after the Transfiguration—in *Cantica*, prologue, ch. 6 (G1, 136v, 35 - 137r, 11; Pez, *Bibliotheca Ascetica*, 11: 23-24): "Secunda causa huius [scilicet Cantici Canticorum] obscuritatis est ad designandum quod illa cantica, que cantantur inter Deum et animam, in sponsam electam et sibi unitam et copulatam in thalamo mentis, in ipsa imagine, sunt occultissima et omnino ineffabilia—ita quod nec ipsa anima que percipit exprimere valebit, uti patet ex verbis Beati Bernardi [*Sermones in Cantica*, Sermo 1.11] superius allegatis, quibus adjungit: 'Est quippe nupciale carmen, exprimens castos iucundosque complexus animorum, morum concordiam, affectuumque consentaneam ad alterutrum caritatem.' Huiusmodi autem affectus et iubilus, et ea quae sequuntur in mente non possunt exprimi verbis consuetis communiter. Quia, sicut ebrii a vino perdunt debitum et consuetum loquendi modum, ita et sponsa sic ebria sobria ebrietate non poterit loqui ut intelligatur ab omnibus, sed solum ab amantibus simili amore. Unde et Petrus nescivit quid diceret postquam gustaverit claritatis dulcedinem [Mt 16]." Though a commentary on the Song of Songs might seem to modern readers to be an unlikely context for this discussion of epistemology and hermeneutics, it was a most *logical* development for Kempf.

scripture, for indeed one should look at each creature in order to obtain not merely knowledge of God but also love of God. For every creature is like a picture or letter or trace that points to the Creator. Thus the apostle says "the invisible things of God are understood through the things that are made; his eternal power and divinity are seen clearly" (Rom 1:20).[53]

The above statement of Nicholas Kempf's hermeneutic assumptions is of one piece—down to the common prooftext from Romans that played such a central role in Augustine's conversion[54]—with Augustine's sacramental understanding of language.[55] The anagogical sense lurks everywhere in scripture and in the created universe. All signs interconnectedly manifest an uplifting mystery, and the manifestation is real yet the sign hides even as it discloses. Belief (affectedness, cleansing) is necessary to understanding. Far from isolating the literal text in order to practice allegory upon it, monastic hermeneutics wove historical and higher senses together into whole cloth.

The practical, rhetorical epistemology and logic and the circular, interlocking structures of exegesis characteristic of late antique and early medieval Christian writers fit the monastic context superbly: the fixed

---

[53] *Ost*, ch. 44 (G1, 32v, 24 - 33r, 6): *"Per sensum anagogicum gustatur dulcedo mellis, sed per alios sensus flores colliguntur ex omnibus scripturis et figuris per divine gracie influxionem.* Precipue illuminantur [MS: illuminatur] oculi mentis ad intelligendum sensum anagogicum in scripturis sacris quo ipsa mens conatur se extendere sursum in Deum per amoris affectum, suspiria, et desideria. Et ille sensus ubique latet in scripturis nec [MS hec] aperitur saltem effectualiter nisi mentibus purgatis et mundis. Ipse enim sensus anagogicus verus convertit flores collectos in mel dulcedinis sicut apes solent facere. Nam per alios scripture sensus colliguntur scripturarum flores, sed per anagogicum gustatur dulcedo mellis per amoris affectum. Nam ideo apes flores colligunt ut inde mel sugere et congregare valeant quo reficiantur. Ita et omnis scriptura [G1, 33r] est legenda ut mel amoris colligatur in cera divinitatis aut Christi humanitatis; et non solum scriptura, sed omnis creatura est inspicienda ut hauriatur non solum cognicio Dei sed eciam amor. Quia omnis creatura [corrected from "scriptura" in later hand] est quasi quedam pictura aut littera seu vestigium signans creatorem. Iuxta illud apostoli: 'Invisibilia Dei, per ea que facta sunt, intellecta, conspiciuntur, et sempiterna eius virtus et divinitas' [Rom 1:20]." The passage continues with a discussion of the special way in which human beings are signs of God. I have translated *mens* as "spirit" because the modern English word "mind" has taken on largely cognitive and rational connotations and would correspond more to the Latin *animus* than to either *mens* or *anima*. Medieval writers used *mens* to refer to the highest part of the human soul, which, in the tripartite psychology of many patristic and medieval spiritual writers, was the *spiritus*.

[54] See *Confessions*, VII.17-18, and John J. O'Meara, *The Young Augustine* (1965), 146-48.

[55] Robert J. O'Connell, *Art and the Christian Intelligence in St. Augustine* (1978), 164, reminds us that Augustine was deeply preoccupied with "showing us that the entire universe, open to the eyes of the believing—and understanding—Christian, is truly a sacramental universe: a forest of signs figuratively disclosing the creative and redemptive work of the Trinitarian Godhead," yet a sign that also veiled what it signified.

grammar of the rule was inseparable from the many interlocking layers of interpretation by spiritual directors who adapted it to individual monks. This monastic way of reading, teaching, and counseling will be encountered again and again through the course of this book. This is what is meant by "monastic *discretio*" in the present study, a term intended to denominate an encompassing epistemology, hermeneutic, pedagogical method, and way of spiritual life.[56] It is a full epistemological program but, precisely because it emphasizes the practical over the speculative[57] it is also a full-orbed way of life, a monastic culture rather than merely a monastic theology. Yet it is also a feature of the main prescholastic theological authorities, from Augustine to Peter Lombard, and as such it was accessible in the university even apart from the monastic context. These two sources—monastic and prescholastic patristic theology—both contributed to the academic world that Heinrich of Langenstein, Nicholas of Dinkelsbühl, Johannes Geuß, Franz von Retz, Johannes Nider, and others created at Vienna. Exactly how it did so is difficult to determine until more of the writings of these masters are available in scholarly editions.

At Paris a relationship between *via moderna* questioning of extreme confidence in logic *as applied to theology* and a concern for the metaphorical and rhetorical *modus loquendi* of scripture seems to parallel that at Vienna.[58] Paris debates on theology also led to violence—to the execution of Jan Hus at Constance, in part for his failure to understand the nature of metaphor in scripture. As at Vienna, the violence was partly the result of political fears. Yet we should not lose sight of the fact that the same terminist concern with *modus loquendi* also made it possible for someone like Gerson to be open toward the first stirrings of humanist, rhetorical renewal at Paris. Gerson, a "great reader of Horace," had friendships with leading early French humanists,[59] and German humanists valued his Latin poetry, his dialogue on the "consolation of theology," and his devotional and pastoral writings.[60] We turn now to a similar intersection of *via moderna*, monastic life, and pedagogical humanism at Vienna.

---

[56] I.e., what Anderson refers to as the gift of *ingenium* (see p. 49 above).

[57] Luke Anderson, "Epistemology" [unpublished].

[58] Courtenay in *Preuve et Raisons*, 48-50; Kaluza, *Querelles*; Shank, *Unless*, 181-82.

[59] Kaluza, *Querelles*, 42; Cesare Vasoli, "Les débuts de l'humanisme à l'université de Paris," in *Preuve et raisons*, 269-86.

[60] Paul Joachimsohn, "Aus der Bibliothek Sigismund Gossembrots. *Centralblatt für Bibliothekswesen*, 11 (1894), 249-68, 297-307; Herbert Kraume, *Die Gerson-Übersetzungen Geilers von Kaysersberg* (1980); E. Jane Dempsey Douglass, *Justification in Late Medieval Preaching* (1966; 1989).

4. Pedagogical Reform and Monastic Reform at Vienna

Tensions in the arts faculty at Vienna are evident during the turbulent decade of the 1420s. In 1422 Master Christian of Traunstein announced at a quodlibetal disputation that the arts faculty masters' disputations were a farce: anything, whether true or false, whether argued logically or illogically, was being defended in disputations from which students were learning nothing at all. He was disciplined by the faculty for his indiscretion and apologized without delay.[61] Christian of Traunstein was one of the "junior faculty" disgruntled because of restrictions on full participation by new masters in faculty decision-making and administrative structures. There may have been more involved than the normal tension between junior and senior faculty. Lhotsky speculates that many of the junior faculty were in close contact with an increasingly large number of students from south Germany, Bohemia, and Hungary, i.e., with foreigners. In a period of intense political upheaval in some of these areas, tension between native sons like Thomas Ebendorfer of Haselbach and "outsiders" would not be surprising.[62]

Yet a more likely explanation lies in the late medieval terminist critique of overly sophisticated logic.[63] In Vienna, six years after the Traunstein affair, an effort was made to reform one aspect of Latin grammar instruction in the arts faculty by deemphasizing precisely the metaphysical grammar that was under attack at Paris.[64] The arts faculty passed a statute regarding the review exercises (*resumptiones*) in grammar undertaken in preparation for the baccalaureate degree, asserting that those "reviewing in grammar ought to proceed grammatically [*grammaticaliter*] rather than metaphysically [*metaphysicaliter*] or logically [*logicaliter*], proceeding through cases, declensions, tenses, conjugations, comparatives, teaching them . . . not only how that which is thought might be suitably well expressed, but even how the declinable and indeclinable parts of speech might be aptly combined." Students should be given sentences in the vernacular and asked how they would

---

[61] Aschbach, *Wiener Universität*, 1: 345-46. The text of the faculty decision is published in Lhotsky, *Artistenfakultät*, 94-95.

[62] Lhotsky, *Artistenfacultät*, 95-97.

[63] Shank interprets the faculty's disciplining of Christian of Traunstein as another example of narrowing latitude for dissent in the Vienna of the 1420s, since Christian had attacked the role of logic even as understood by the terminist thinkers. *Unless*, 199.

[64] Kaluza, *Querelles*.

express similar sentences in Latin. They should be given definitions, rules, divisions, questions, sophisms, properties etc. and be asked whether such are well constructed. If they are, for the sake of a bit of practice, the students should retrace the argument step-by-step. If not well constructed, the students should be asked to explain why. "No one undertaking the review exercises should propose new *syncatagoremata* not commonly held by the ancients" and exercises "should not abandon common and well founded words of well-known authors."[65]

Lhotsky, Bauch, and others have concluded that the grammar reform of 1428 left no lasting mark.[66] Perhaps it did not; legislation reforming the *resumptiones* need not have had an impact on arts faculty masters' grammar lectures. We know far too little about the content of those lectures. Yet an impact of the 1428 regulation can perhaps be seen in the theology faculty and among arts faculty alumni of that era twenty-five years later. In the 1450s a "quarrel between the theologians and poets" took place when the Augsburg patrician, Sigmund Gossembrot (d. 1493), who had studied at the Vienna arts faculty (1433-36), defended the "poets"[67] against the criticisms of Conrad Säldner, a "scholastic" theologian at Vienna, who took his MA in 1437—within a year of Gossembrot and the same year as Kempf.

To understand what was happening in the Gossembrot-Säldner exchange much research is needed. Wattenbach published excerpts from the texts but his essentially Burckhardtian view of humanism was scarcely reconcilable with scholasticism.[68] Overfield was fully aware of Kristeller's revisionism but it lay beyond the scope of Overfield's study[69] to reexamine the manuscripts and incorporate revisionist interpretations.[70] This is an immense task that cannot be attempted here

---

[65] Text in Kink, *Geschichte*, 2: 274-75; improved text of the first part in Lhotsky, *Wiener Artistenfakultät*, 121-22. Cf. Großmann, "Frühzeit," 175-76.

[66] Lhotsky, *WienerArtistenfakulät*, 59, 121-26; Gustav Bauch, *Rezeption des Humanismus in Wien* (1903; repr. 1986), 9-10. Bauch calls it a victory of common sense yet a Pyrrhic victory that could not stem the tide of contemporary trends. Cf. Frank, *Hausstudium*, 140-44.

[67] For parallels see Joël Lefebvre, "Le poéte, la poésie, et la poétique," in *L'humanisme allemand (1480-1540)* (1979), 285-301; James V. Mehl, "Hermann von dem Busche's *Vallum humanitatis* (1518): A German Defense of the Renaissance *Studia Humanitatis*," *Renaissance Quarterly*, 42 (1989), 480-506; Concetta Carestia Greenfield, *Humanist and Scholastic Poetics, 1250-1500* (1981).

[68] W. Wattenbach, "Sigismund Gossembrot als Vorkämpfer der Humanisten und seine Gegner," *Zeitschrift für die Geschichte des Oberrheins*, 25 (1873), 36-69.

[69] James Overfield, *Humanism and Scholasticism*, 120-24.

[70] Charles Trinkaus, *In Our Image and Likeness*, 2 vols. (1970); Paul Oskar Kristeller, *Renaissance Thought and Its Sources* (1979); Albert Rabil, Jr. (ed.), *Renaissance Humanism*, 3 vols. (1988).

either. My reading of the published excerpts suggests that Säldner was rejecting an artificial, Ciceronian style that he considered to be as exaggerated, unreal, and unpractical as the speculative grammar the "terminists" had challenged at Paris and Vienna.[71] Gossembrot studied liberal arts alongside Säldner in the wake of the 1428 reform, and he admired the approach to teaching Latin represented by Guarino of Verona[72]—he sent his sons to study under Guarino's successors in Italy. Since Gossembrot himself could not write in the Ciceronian epistolary style he so admired, in a sense he only confirmed Säldner's point that the hard-won classical erudition of the "poets" threatened to make Latin into an impractical, elitist museum piece. Säldner was as much interested in rhetoric and in the *modus loquendi* of conventional theology as Gossembrot was fascinated by the new epistolography. But Säldner believed that "famous theologians"—Heinrich of Langenstein, Nicholas of Dinkelsbühl, Thomas Ebendorfer,[73] and Johannes Geuß—had already evolved an eminently practical rhetoric that kept Latin a useable, living language. He feared that this would be lost if theologians applied to Ciceronian style the energy needed to master it. The theologians that Säldner preferred were some of the same patristic, medieval, and contemporary masters of theological language whose writings were prominent in Gossembrot's own library: Jerome, Augustine, Bernard of Clairvaux, and the "moderns" Gerson, Langenstein, and Geuß.[74] Säldner's concerns

---

[71] Overfield, p. 121, insists that Säldner preferred precisely the modist grammarians. Although "ignorance of speculative grammar" is one of the charges Säldner directs against the "modern poets," he seems to equate "speculative grammar with Alexander's *Doctrinale*, and thus may have meant simply that they were ignorant of basic grammar. Moreover, the statement is part of an entire catalogue of the poets' "ignorance," including ignorance of all the liberal arts, traditional rhetoric, and logic: "Et quod plus est, non vidi audivive temporis modo nominatos poetas in septem liberalibus artibus perfecte fundatos, quin certe grammatice speculative seu doctrinalis ignaros, cum vere rethorice principiis modis et coloribus, prorsus quoque sine rationabilis scientie, scilicet logice, vero disputandi modo, sed alti spiritus tumore inflatos." (Wattenbach, 39).

[72] See Anthony Grafton and Lisa Jardine, *From Humanism to the Humanities* (1986), 1-28; W. K. Percival and Benjamin A. Kohl in *Renaissance Humanism*, ed. Rabil, 3: 5-22, 67-83.

[73] Lhotsky, *Wiener Artistenfakultät*, 123-25, disputes Säldner's claim regarding Ebendorfer's acquaintance with the classical poets on the basis of Lhotsky's analysis of Ebendorfer's sources carried out as part of his edition of Ebendorfer's *Chronica austriae*. Lhotsky showed that Ebendorfer depended on earlier chronicles and florilegia for his classical allusions. Yet Säldner must have had some basis for baldly asserting that Ebendorfer read the "poets." The fact that he used intermediary sources in assembling his chronicle does not necessarily give a complete picture of his reading. Ebendorfer wrote in other genres and a more thorough study of his use of classical sources would be helpful.

[74] Joachimsohn, "Aus der Bibliothek."

were not unfounded, for humanist insistence on neo-Ciceronian Latin
may indeed have helped turn a living European language into an antiquarian relic.[75]

That Gossembrot and Säldner admired many of the same theologians points to another side of Gossembrot. He was a deeply pious, contemplative man who ultimately gave up his civic roles as mayor of
Augsburg and his business activity to retire to monastic contemplation at
the Johanniter cloister in Straßburg. He valued Langenstein, Geuß, and
others for their piety but was also enthused about the Italian and classical
poets, especially the "epistolary style." In this he points forward to urban
south German humanism, for instance, to his Benedictine protégé, Sigmund Meisterlin,[76] who combined skill in epistolary style with an antiquarian interest in local history.

In short, the dispute between Gossembrot and Säldner, was something of a family spat, since both of them came out of the same combination of *via moderna* critique of improper use of *modus loquendi*,
affective piety, and the rhetorical tradition of patristic theology.[77] In
them we see how late medieval affective piety, so ubiquitous in the Devotio Moderna, in Gerson's reform efforts at Paris, in Langenstein's
"nisi credideritis," merged with humanist piety.[78] This happened not
only in the Augsburg humanist circle around Gossembrot and Bishop Peter von Schaumburg (d. 1469),[79] but also, e.g. in Petrarch (d. 1374), and
Gabriel Biel (d. 1495), in the grammar and pedagogical reforms of Alexander Hegius (d. 1498) and Johannes Synthen (d. ca. 1493) at Deventer,
and in humanist circles in mid-fifteenth-century and early sixteenth-century Nürnberg.[80]

---

[75] C. S. Lewis, *English Literature in the Sixteenth Century* (1954), 21.

[76] Paul Joachimson, *Die humanistische Geschichtsschreibung in Deutschland*, vol. 1:
Sigismund Meisterlin (1895).

[77] Some indication of what I have in mind under the rubric "rhetorical tradition of
patristic theology" may be seen in James L. Kinneavy, *Greek Rhetorical Origins of the
Christian Faith* (1987), and Frederik van der Meer, *Augustine the Bishop* (1961), part
III. Peter Erb first drew these works to my attention.

[78] See Lewis Spitz, *The Religious Renaissance of the German Humanists* (1963).

[79] Joachimsohn, "Aus der Bibliothek," esp. 297-307; Wattenbach, "Gossembrot";
Friedrich Zoepfl, "Der Humanismus am Hof der Fürstbischöfe von Augsburg," *HJ*, 62
(1949), 671-708, and Joachimsohn, *Humanistische Geschichtsschreibung*, vol. 1.

[80] Noel Brann in *Renaissance Humanism*, ed. Rabil, 2: 123-56, at 129-30, and Franz
Machilek, "Klosterhumanismus in Nürnberg um 1500," *Mitteilungen des Vereins für
Geschichte der Stadt Nürnberg*, 64 (1977), 10-45, at 15-16; Arnold Reimann, *Die
älteren Pirckheimer* (1944), 161-96; Peter Johanek, Heimburg, Gregor," in *Verfasserlexikon*, rev. ed., vol. 3 (1981), 629-42.

The combination of pragmatic concern for language and affective piety also produced vernacular spiritual literature in response to a growing literate readership among nobles and well-to-do burghers. With special encouragement from court circles, the devotional writings of Heinrich of Langenstein and Nicholas of Dinkelsbühl were transformed into German, along with catechetical materials, and other devotional and theological literature drawn from theologians ranging from Augustine to Aquinas.[81] The reworking of Nicholas of Dinkelsbühl's sermons on the love of God and neighbor by the Vienna court chaplain, Thomas Peuntner (d. 1439), became something of a late medieval bestseller.[82] Its dissemination in South Germany illustrates the linkages between university, parish, monastery, and *Ratsstube*: a pastor and canon at the Augsburg cathedral, Hans Wildsgefert (d. 1470); an anonymous Carthusian from Christgarten charterhouse near Nördlingen; the Carthusian's sister Christina in the Nürnberg Franciscan nunnery; a Salzburg goldsmith; and Augsburg's own mayor, Sigmund Gossembrot, among others, helped "market" this work.[83]

Although Nicholas Kempf cited Heinrich of Langenstein more frequently than Nicholas of Dinkelsbühl, the latter was the dominant figure in the recent past of the theological faculty. He shared with Heinrich of Langenstein a concern for the limits of logic in theological mysteries, citing Aristotle's *Posterior Analytics* regarding the nature of demonstrable knowledge and human inability to achieve demonstrable knowledge of

---

[81] Thomas Hohmann, "'Die recht gelerten maister': Bemerkungen zur Übersetzungsliteratur des Wiener Schule des Spätmittelalters," in *Die österreichische Literatur* (1986) 1: 349-65; Egino Weidenhiller, *Untersuchung zur deutschsprachigen katechetischen Literatur des späten Mittelalters* (1965); Thomas Hohmann, *Heinrichs von Langenstein "Untersuchung der Geister"* (1977), 257-76; Gabriele Baptist-Hlawatsch, *Das katechetische Werk Ulrichs von Pottenstein* (1980), esp. 69-72; Lhotsky, *Quellenkunde*, 312-13; Rupprich, *Wiener Schrifttum*, 154; Hohmann, "Deutsche Texte, 220-21; Lhotsky, *Wissenschaftspflege*, 61-65; idem, "Zur Frühgeschichte der Wiener Hofbibliothek," *MIÖG*, 59 (1951), 329-63 (repr. 1970); Peter Wiesinger, "Zur Autorschaft und Entstehung des Heinrich von Langenstein zugeschriebenen Traktats 'Erkanntnis der Sünde'," *ZDP*, 97 (1978), 42-60. Christoph Cormeau, "Wiens Universität und die deutschen Prosatexte im Umkreis Heinrichs von Langenstein," in *Milieux universitaires et mentalité urbaine au moyen âge* (1987), 35-45, at 39, persists in listing Kempf among the Vienna translators, even though no hard evidence of any translations by Kempf has been uncovered. Cormeau simply repeats Rupprich on this point.

[82] Schnell, *Thomas Peuntner*, esp. 1-2, 33.

[83] See Schnell's descriptions of the manuscripts (98-232), and his "sociological analysis" (238-59), which together show that it was popular among lay brethren (e.g., p. 113), pastors (e.g., p. 130), artisans (e.g., p. 122), patricians (e.g., p. 142), and noblemen (e.g., p. 119). Gossembrot had copies of both the long and the short version of this work as well as a copy of the German version of Langenstein's *Erkanntnis der Sund*. See Paul Joachimsohn, "Aus der Bibliothek," 249-68, 297-307, at 268. On Gossembrot see Schnell, 142-43, 164, 187, 242-43, 253-54, 268-71.

faith.[84] Shank believes that Nicholas of Dinkelsbühl was using Aristotle to buttress his own authoritarian epistemology, leading to the murder of the purportedly obstinate, unteachable, Jews. That Heinrich of Langenstein recognized more of a "spirit of reciprocity" in the disputation process than did Nicholas of Dinkelsbühl does not necessarily mean that Nicholas of Dinkelsbühl had moved beyond Heinrich of Langenstein into a narrow authoritarianism. Even within the disputation system there were clear distinctions between masters and disciples. And the classic Christian recognition that depths of the mystery of faith cannot be sounded by human reason alone had always given an important place to the authority of supernatural revelation and of the experienced master teaching neophytes. As we shall see in subsequent chapters, this principle is fundamental to the monastic, pre-scholastic context to which, I suggest, both Langenstein and Dinkelsbühl were returning. By itself, Dinkelsbühl's appeal to authority seems heavyhanded to modern minds. Yet in a patristic or early medieval theological context it was the norm, a norm interpreted through Augustine's hermeneutic principle of *caritas*.[85]

The context into which Dinkelsbühl spoke these words was, however, highly charged, and the breadth of *caritas* was overshadowed by the narrowness of *anxietas*. Nicholas of Dinkelsbühl had been heavily involved in political affairs, serving the Habsburg dukes at Constance. He thus played a leading role in the trial of Jerome of Prague.[86] And the Hussite threat to Lower Austria eventually became a devastating reality.[87] Modern minds tend to see heresy as harmless, and a truly sensitive historical perception must find a way to understand why heresy produced a "siege mentality"[88] in early fifteenth-century Vienna. This, too, is part of the social context of the University of Vienna against which its intellectual history must be read.

Nicholas of Dinkelsbühl concerned himself not only with Hussites and Jews. When he returned from Constance he became the leading theological proponent of the Melk Benedictine reform,[89] i.e., he became

---

[84] Shank, *Unless*, 117-27, 191-200.
[85] *De doctrina Christiana*, esp. Bk. I,ch. 35-38; Bk. II, ch. 10-15.
[86] In addition to Shank, *Unless*, 187-200, see Walsh, "Wegestreit."
[87] Stöller, "Hussiten."
[88] Shank, *Unless*, 187-88. See also Frantisek Smahel, "Krise und Revolution: Die Sozialfrage im vorhussitischen Böhmen," in *Europa 1400: Die Krise des Spätmittelalters* (1984), 65-81.
[89] Philibert Schmitz, *Geschichte des Benediktinerordens*, 3: 173-77; Joachim Angerer, ed., *Die Bräuche der Abtei Tegernsee unter Abt Kaspar Ayndorffer (1426-1461)*, SMGB, Ergänzungsband, 18 (1968); Anselm Schramb, *Chronicon Mellicense* (1702), 320-55, which include the *consuetudines* of Melk; Martin Kropff, *Bibliotheca Mellicensis*

intimately involved with the main reservoir of pre-scholastic, patristic theology—traditional contemplative monasticism. Yet monastic reform too was inseparable from the political questions of the day. The territorial princes had an interest in establishing a reformed monasticism that would be less closely tied to the aristocracy; in German-speaking areas monastic reform was thus often part of the emergent centralizing territorial state.[90] Andreas Plank, chancellor to Albrecht IV (1395-1404) and mentor to Albrecht V, had recommended that the duke reform existing monasteries rather than found new ones.[91]

On the other hand, monastic reform cannot simply be reduced to politics, and court theologians like Leopold Stainreuter, Heinrich of Langenstein, Thomas Peuntner, Johannes Geuß, and Nicholas of Dinkelsbühl were concerned about more than mere *Realpolitik*.[92] Its origins in Lower Austria are rooted in the university just after the death of Heinrich of Langenstein. In 1403, a former rector of the university, Nicholas Seyringer of Matzen, together with several masters of arts, left Vienna to enter the Benedictine observant house at Subiaco in Italy.[93] Recognition of the limits of rational theology that had begun with the *via moderna* and issued in Langenstein's "nisi credideritis" theme ran parallel to an actual return to the institution from which scholastic theology had sprouted. Our knowledge of the sources does not permit us to assert a causal connection between the two, although the circumstances surrounding Seyringer's departure deserve monographic study[94] to determine the degree

---

(1747), 302-55 (also containing the text of the *consuetudines*), Koller, *Princeps*, 78-111; and Redlich, *Tegernsee*.

[90] Dieter Stievermann, *Landesherrschaft und Klosterwesen im spätmittelalterlichen Württemberg* (1989); Dieter Mertens, "Riforma monastica e potere temporale nella Germania sud-occidentale prima della Riforma," in *Strutture ecclesiastiche in Italia e in Germania prima della Riforma* (1984), 171-205; Koller, *Princeps*. For examples of the very different, obstructionist, role played by territorial monarchs and Gallican bishops in France, see William J. Telesca, "The Cistercian Abbey in Fifteenth Century France: A Victim of Competing Jurisdictions of Sovereignty, Suzerainty, and Primacy," in *Cistercians in the Late Middle Ages* (1981), 38-58, and "The Cistercian Dilemma at the Close of the Middle Ages: Gallicanism or Rome" in *Studies in Medieval Cistercian History presented to Jeremiah F. O'Sullivan* (1971), 163-85.

[91] Koller, *Princeps*, 60-62, citing Schramb, *Chronicon Mellicense*, 308, and Kropff, *Bibliotheca Mellicensis*, 163.

[92] On monastic reform, see Kaspar Elm, "Reform- und Observanzbestrebungen im spätmittelalterlichen Ordenswesen," in *Reformbemühungen und Observanzbestrebungen*, ed. Elm (1989), 3-19; idem, "Verfall und Erneuerung des Ordenswesen im Spätmittelalter," in *Untersuchungen zu Kloster und Stift* (1980), 188-238.

[93] Barbara Frank, "Subiaco, ein Reformkonvent des späten Mittelalters," *QFIAB*, 52 (1972), 526-656.

[94] The writings of Petrus of Rosenheim, one of the Subiaco Austrian party, have been studied by Franz Xaver Thoma, "Petrus von Rosenheim, O.S.B.: Ein Beitrag zur Melker

of interdependence between the crisis of logic in matters of faith, the affective piety of the court theologians, the ecclesio-political crises of the Schism and Hussite troubles, and growing interest in revived monasticism is strong.

When Albrecht V asked Nicholas of Dinkelsbühl in 1415 to suggest the best procedure for reforming houses of Benedictines and Augustinian Canons in Austria, it was Dinkelsbühl who suggested calling the former Vienna academics back to their homeland from Italy.[95] He also proposed that the "Scottish" monastery in Vienna be opened up to Germans, leading eventually to the exile of the Irish Benedictines.[96] His address to a Carthusian chapter meeting, probably at Gaming or Mauerbach, illustrates his interest in and popularity among Lower Austrian Carthusians. It is probably not a mere coincidence that the prior of Gaming played a leading role in the visitations that launched the Melk reform.

Yet another interconnection between university and cloister resulted from the unsuccessful attempt by Albrecht V to gain Jean Gerson for his university—it meant that Gerson, whose writings were so influential for several generations of monastic and clerical reformers at Vienna, was present at Melk about the time the reform began. His *De consolatione theologiae*, written at Melk during his exile from France,[97] develops a theology based on "seeking," a theology of yearning for what one lacks, a theology of meekness very much like that of traditional, contemplative

Reformbewegung," *SMGB*, 45 (1927), 94-222, but primarily from the perspective of his important role in the extension of the reform to Tegernsee in Bavaria. See Thoma, "Die Briefe des Petrus von Rosenheim an Abt Kasper Ayndorffer von Tegernsee während der Klosterreform in Südbayern, 1426-1431," *Oberbayerisches Archiv für vaterländische Geschichte*, 67 (1930), 1-20. See also "Anonymi benedictini anno MCCC epistola de consuetudine et modo vivendi coenobitarum monasterii Sublacensis," in *Bibl. ascetica*, 8: 492-502 (cf. Melk, Stiftsbibliothek, cod. 979 [784], 1r-2v, written in 1400); Petrus of Rosenheim, "Sermo de statu vitae monasticae sui temporis," in *Bibl. ascetica*, 2:81-94, an attack on the "superbia praelatorum," on those who live carnally, on those who flatter and seek favors, and on those who are self-willed (the four beasts of Dan 7).

[95] The text is found in Schramb, *Chronicon Mellicense*, 308-12, and Kropff, *Bibliotheca Mellicensis*, 184-87. A brief analysis and summary is found in Madre, *Nikolaus von Dinkelsbühl*, 269-71. On Nicholas' activity as a monastic reformer see also Menhardt, "Deutsche Predigt," 21-24.

[96] Katherine Walsh, "From 'Victims' of the Melk Reform to Apostles of the Counter-Reformation: The Irish Regular Clergy in the Habsburg Dominions," in *The Churches, Ireland and the Irish* (1989), 69-88.

[97] Johann B. Schwab, *Johannes Gerson, Professor der Theologie und Kanzler der Universität Paris* (1858), 761ff; James L. Connolly, *John Gerson, Reformer and Mystic* (1928), 190; Lhotsky, *Wissenschaftspflege*, 85; E. Henry, "Gerson dans l'exil du 15. mai 1418 au 15. novembre 1419," *Travaux de l'academie impériale de Reims*, 25 (1857), 335-52; Koller, *Princeps*, 93-94; and Thoma, "Petrus von Rosenheim" (1927), 122; Keiblinger, *Melk*, 2: 1122.

monasticism[98] in the wake of Gerson's frustrated efforts to lead the university into a more pious path.

The reform began in 1418 at Melk. Nicholas of Dinkelsbühl watched over the growth of the observant movement and participated in many visitations, as did the duke's officials.[99] Later he further nurtured ties with the reform when he personally delivered lectures on the *Sentences* at Melk, significantly, on the fourth book, dealing with pastoral and devotional issues. In the view of the most thorough analyst of the political significance of the Melk reform,[100] with the involvement of the Subiaco monks, the reform shifted from mere ducal policy to a genuine monastic reform carried by monastics. As Albrecht V became enmeshed in the Passau and Freising bishops' disputes and the Hussite wars in the 1420s, the burden of the continuation of monastic reform fell upon the community at Melk. Nor were Benedictines and Austin Canons the only monastic reformers with connections to the Vienna university. Franz of Retz and Johannes Nider were heavily involved in the Dominican observant movement.

The monastic reform movement represents many interlocking sociopolitical and religious currents of the late Middle Ages.[101] Theologically it was characterized by the same patristic, affective, rhetorical, and contemplative orientation that dominated the church up to the twelfth century.[102] As renewed in the fourteenth and fifteenth centuries, traditional monasticism's critique of scholasticism[103] merged with the *via moderna*, the renewed interest in the *studia humanitatis*, and the affective piety described above, including the Devotio Moderna (which had a special relationship with the Carthusian order[104]). One can see this in personal

---

[98] See, e.g., Gerson, *De consolatione theologiae*, bk. I, prosa III (*Oeuvres*, IX, 193) on salvation for the deaf and lame, cf. Mark S. Burrows, *Jean Gerson and "De Consolatione theologiae"* (1991), 175-94.

[99] Pilgrim IV of Puchheim, who became *Landmarschall* in Austria in 1419, was sent by Albrecht V to accompany the visitors of monasteries in the reforms of 1418. Koller, *Princeps*, 67.

[100] Koller, *Princeps*, 88.

[101] In addition to the literature on monastic reform cited in nn. 90, 92, and 94, above, see Klaus Schreiner, "Benediktinische Klosterreform," and idem, "Mönchsein in der Adelsgesellschaft des hohen und späten Mittelalters," *Historische Zeitschrift*, 248 (1989), 557-621.

[102] Leclercq, *Love of Learning*; Chenu, *Nature, Man, Society*; De Ghellinck, *Mouvement théologique*; Anderson, "Enthymeme."

[103] Leclercq, "Monastic and Scholastic Theology."

[104] Otto Gründler, "*Devotio moderna atque antiqua:*" in *The Roots of the Modern Christian Tradition*, ed. E. Rozanne Elder (1984), pp. 27-45; Kaspar Elm, "Die Bruderschaft vom gemeinsamen Leben: Eine geistliche Lebensform zwischen Kloster und Welt, Mittelalter und Neuzeit," *Ons geestelijk Erf*, 59 (1985), 470-96; Willem Lour-

interconnections, e.g., in Jean Gerson, who maintained relationships with several religious orders, especially the Carthusians[105] and defended the Brothers and Sisters of the Common Life; in Heinrich of Langenstein's Rheinland sojourn; and in Nicholas of Dinkelsbühl's involvement in the Melk reform.

We also see interconnections when we realize that monks were just as concerned about the proper and improper use of language and logic as were humanists[106] and the terminist semantic theorists. Twelfth-century monastic humanism had combined the classical heritage with the legacy of such fourth-century rhetor-theologians as Ambrose, Chrysostom, Jerome, and Augustine, producing the consummate Latinity of a Bernard of Clairvaux.[107] A sizeable part of fifteenth-century monastic reform developed into monastic humanism.[108] Petrarch flirted with the monastic life in the 1340s and his writings inspired more of the same throughout the fifteenth century—although, as we shall see in a later chapter, a large gulf still separated him from the monastic life, and the resulting tension was the source of much of his "melancholy."

Before proceeding to Nicholas Kempf, a product of this matrix in the 1430s, let us look briefly at one more Vienna theologian, in this case

---

daux, "Kartuizers—Moderne Devoten: Een Probleem van Afhankelijkheid," *Ons geestelijk Erf*, 37 (1963), 402-18.

[105] Palémon Glorieux, "Gerson et les Chartreux," *RTAM*, 28 (1961), 115-53; Veronika Gerz-von Büren, *La Tradition de l'oeuvre de Jean Gerson chez les Chartreux: La Chartreuse de Bâle* (1973).

[106] For the intersection see especially Charles L. Stinger, "St. Bernard and Pope Eugenius IV (1431-1447)," in *Cistercian Ideals and Reality* (1978), 329-343, and idem, *Humanism and the Church Fathers: Ambrogio Traversari (1386-1439) and Christian Antiquity in the Italian Renaissance* (1977).

[107] Christine Mohrmann, "Observations sur la langue et le style de Saint Bernard," in *S. Bernardi Opera*, 2: IX-XXXIII, and "Le Style de Saint Bernard," in Mohrmann, *Etudes sur le latin des chrétiens* (1961), 2: 347-67, which originally appeared in *San Bernardo: Pubblicazione commemorativa nell'VIII centenario della sua morte* (1954), 166-184.

[108] Leclercq, "Monastic and Scholastic Theology"; Machilek, "Klosterhumanismus in Nürnberg"; Winfried Müller, "Die Anfänge der Humanismusrezeption in Kloster Tegernsee," *SMGB*, 92 (1981), 28-90; Joachimsohn, *HumanistischeGeschichtsschreibung*, vol. 1; A. Schröder, "Der Humanist Veit Bild, Mönch bei St. Ulrich," *Zeitschrift des historischen Vereins für Schwaben und Neuburg*, 20 (1893), 173-227; Newald, "Geschichte des Humanismus in Oberösterreich"; Klaus Ganzer, "Zur monastischen Theologie des Johannes Trithemius," *HJ*, 101 (1981), 384-21; idem, "Monastischer Reform und Bildung: Ein Traktat des Hieronymus Aliotti (1412-1480) über die Studien der Mönche," in *Reformatio Ecclesiae* [Festschrift Iserloh] (1980), 181-99; Noel Brann, *The Abbot Trithemius (1462-1516)* (1981). Paul O. Kristeller, "Contribution," includes the mendicants, unlike the other titles cited here. Cf. Kaspar Elm, "Mendikanten und Humanisten im Florenz des Tre- und Quattrocento," in *Die Humanisten in ihrer politischen und sozialen Umwelt* (1976), 51-85.

the product of the student generation just preceeding Kempf. Johannes Keck of Giengen in Swabia was *magister regens* in the arts faculty, 1426-29, and a *cursor biblicus* in the theology faculty, 1432-34. He spent most of the years between 1437 and 1441 as a priest in the diocese of Freising—as a beneficed priest in the Munich parish of St. Peter and as confessor for Bavarian Duke Albrecht III—before being sent to Basel for the council. While there he earned a doctoral degree in theology at the council's "university."

His inaugural lecture, ca. 1441-42, was titled "De laude scripturae."[109] According to Keck, the object of theology, the eternal word of God, eternal Wisdom, lends a certain grandeur to the subject itself. But theology is not merely an object of study—it is also a subject that affects its student, because the Word becomes flesh. Both in the historical incarnation and in a recurring spiritual incarnation, theology enters the life of the theologian. Therefore, theology is to be judged on the basis of a theologian's behavior: "By their fruits you shall know them [Mt 7:16, 20]." For "theology makes the theologian humble, heavenly, conscious of God's gracious deeds, worthy of royal majesty, a despiser of men of this world, rich in spiritual goods, powerful, cheerful, and safe from perdition in the end." Anyone who does not exhibit these characteristics is no theologian, but possesses only a hypocritical theological learning.[110] The prime purpose of theology for Keck is the searching of scriptures to find eternal life—the yearning, questing theology that lies at the heart of the "mystical theology" we shall encounter in later chapters. The slower, patient searchers often find what the sharper (*acutiores*) miss, because the slower searchers practice what they learn. Thus *simplices* can indeed be theologians.

The main elements of Langenstein's St. Catherine's Day sermon (the importance of a holy, virtuous life; the ability of *simplices* to be theologians; a seeking, yearning, loving attitude as the mark of a true philosopher) are repeated here, and they are the same themes that recur in Nicholas Kempf's writings, as well as in Gossembrot and others.[111]

---

[109] See Heinrich Karpp, "Ein Bibellob aus der Basler Konzilsuniversität," in *Studien zur Geschichte und Theologie der Reformation* [Bizer Festschrift] (1969), 79-96. For Keck's biography, see Virgil Redlich, "Eine Universität auf dem Konzil in Basel," *HJ*, 49 (1929), 42-101, and Heribert Roßmann, "Der Tegernseer Benediktiner Johannes Keck über die mystische Theologie," in *Das Menschenbild des Nikolaus von Kues und der christlichen Humanismus* [Haubst Festschrift] (1978), 330-52.

[110] For Keck's attack on scholastic theologians see Ganzer, "Monastische Theologie des Johannes Trithemius," 416-17, quoting from Keck's commentary on the Rule of St. Benedict in Munich, clm. 18150, fol. 151r.

[111] E.g., Johannes Nider's *Vier und zwanzig güldene Harpfen* (a paraphrase of John Cassian's *Institutes*). See also Gieraths, "Nider," 340.

This alone should suggest that affective, devotional, "credo ut intelligam" piety characterized the Vienna intellectual milieu in some significant way. Only when the writings of Geuß, Ebendorfer, and others are edited will we be able to ascertain how dominant it was and better evaluate the interrelationships between socio-political, economic, and religious elements in the violent upheavals of the 1420s-1440s in Vienna and Lower Austria.

The present study does not attempt a thorough analysis of the academic writings of Nicholas Kempf, for its concern rests primarily with his monastic writings. As we conclude this chapter on Kempf's Vienna, we can only look briefly at the academic works out of which Kempf's monastic career grew. To what degree this monastic outgrowth was by organic continuation, lateral branching, or dialectical antithesis to his academic years cannot be definitively determined, given the immense amount of manuscript research remaining to be done for all the leading university figures of the period. It is plausible that *via moderna* concerns about the limits of demonstration in theology (Kempf's disputation on Aristotle's *Posterior Analytics*) coupled with a pragmatic concern for simplifying the teaching of Latin grammar and training in the traditional rhetoric curriculum, combined to push him toward monastic culture.

5. Nicholas Kempf as Master of Arts

Kempf was presumably trained in the tradition of the Vienna *via moderna*. His disputation on Aristotle's *Posterior Analytics* follows precisely the list of questions dealt with by Albert of Saxony (d. 1390) in his commentary on the same work.[112] Further study is needed, however, to ascertain the precise degree to which Kempf's specific positions followed the terminism of Albert of Saxony and Jean Buridan that was popular at Vienna. His grammar lectures were copied twice at Vienna in 1442 and made their way to the libraries of Indersdorf and Mondsee.[113]

---

[112] On Kempf's *Disputata super libros posteriorum Aristotelis* (1439), see Mieczyslaw Markowski, "Abhandlungen zur Logik," and idem, "L'influence de Jean Buridan." In "Jean Buridan est-il l'auteur des questions sur les 'Seconds analytiques'?" *Mediaevalia philosophica polonorum*, 12 (1966), 16-30, Markowski pointed out that the manuscripts of Albert's commentary offer a text of the commentary on the first book of the *Posterior Analytics* that differs from the one published under Albert's name in Venice in 1497 and 1522 (reprinted Hildesheim, 1986).

[113] See appendix A for a discussion of the erroneous attribution of a number of sets of grammar rules to Kempf in G. L. Bursill-Hall's census of Latin grammatical manuscripts.

Alongside grammar, the branch of the liberal arts *trivium* most central to humanist concerns was rhetoric. One of two lecture series known to have been undertaken by Kempf in his arts faculty career covered the "Summa iovis," a thirteenth-century metrical *ars dictandi* that was popular in southern Germany and Austria.[114] At the end of the century Conrad Celtis insisted that it be replaced by a more up-to-date, i.e., neo-Ciceronian, textbook on epistolary style. It is unlikely that Kempf was familiar with the new style, but Georg Peuerbach, the leading "early humanist" at Vienna, was well acquainted with Kempf. It is tempting to attribute Peuerbach's inclination toward monasticism, 1451-53, as well as that of his intimate friend, Reimbert Mühlwanger, who briefly entered the novitiate at Gaming during Kempf's priorate, to Kempf's *De recto fine* dialogue, but there is no real evidence to confirm such speculation.

The impact of Kempf's *De recto fine* is clearer in the case of Johannes of Donauwörth (d. 1475). He studied at Vienna, 1439-45, and taught as a regent master in the Vienna arts faculty until 1451, when he entered the Benedictine monastery of Mondsee in Upper Austria, taking the name "Jerome." Among his readings as a novice were Nicholas Kempf's book on the monastic vocation and novitiate and Kempf's *De recto fine studiorum*. He probably also read Kempf's *De discretione*.[115] A copy of Kempf's grammar commentary, probably Jerome's personal copy brought from Vienna, is found today bound next to part of Jerome's own commentary on Alexander de Villa Dei's grammar textbook.[116] Jerome's reading notebooks from his university days and his monastic years reveal a wide-ranging interest in classical literature, history, and poetry, but also in mystical theology, monastic spirituality, and the Melk Benedictine reform. He was a prolific writer of Latin verse and letters, composed melodies for his hymns, studied astronomy, and seems to have

---

[114] According to arts faculty minutes Kempf lectured on the *Summa iovis* in the summer semester, 1438. Surviving manuscripts of the *Summa iovis* are listed by Franz Josef Worstbrock in *Verfasserlexikon*, rev. ed., vol. 4, cols. 429-30. Melk, Tegernsee, and Mondsee copies of commentaries on the text are known. It cannot be ruled out that one of these might be Kempf's, but without some hint of the approach taken in his lectures, it would be difficult to identify it. One candidate would be the copy of the *Summa iovis* in Munich clm 19697, 235r-255r. This codex is a collection of letters from monastic sources, including the correspondence related to the Tegernsee mystics controversy, that in part may have served as a model for teaching the *ars dictandi*. It includes a letter from Sigismund Phantzagel (Kempf's successor at Gaming) to Bernard of Waging (fol. 112r), and the collection begins with a letter from Wilhelm, the prior of Gaming, announcing the death of his predecessor, Frederick in 1432.

[115] Jerome may also have been responsible for the extended excerpts from Kempf's *De discretione* found in Vienna, ÖNB, cvp 4789.

[116] See Vienna, ÖNB, cvp 4966. The Kempf text is dated 1442. The codex also contains two treatises on *ars dictaminis*.

enjoyed a reputation as an accomplished and pragmatic teacher of grammar.[117] His training in the Vienna *via moderna* is apparent, yet a Mondsee codex[118] containing Jerome's collection of sample letters, poetry,
and history—including items by Guarino of Verona (d. 1460), Poggio
Bracciolini, and Georg Peuerbach alongside those by Prudentius, Bernard of Clairvaux, and contemporary Benedictine monastic reformers[119]—illustrates how he integrated patristic, monastic, and humanist
literary interests.

Thus, although scholars have conventionally placed the arrival of
humanism at Vienna in the 1450s, with intermittent periods of flourishing until it became established in the 1490s,[120] the *via moderna* and affective, pietistic, and patristic traditions transmitted by Langenstein and
Gerson may have permitted university theology and monastic renewal at
Vienna in the late fourteenth and early fifteenth century to establish important precedents for humanism at Vienna. It is in this context that
Kempf studied and taught.

Kempf understood his calling as that of a pedagogue. The treatise
on school administration, *De sollicitudine*, probably though not certainly
written by him, deals with the moral and religious training of school children, an important component of the pedagogical reforms underway in
the new schools of Vittorino da Feltre and Guarino of Verona, the
schools to which Kempf's fellow student, Sigmund Gossembrot, sent his
own son. Astrik Gabriel has pointed out the degree to which universities
undertook the grammar school education of young children.[121] Kempf
may have had oversight of such grammar school pupils. In entering the
monastery he very clearly found a new avenue for the same pedagogical
skills and concerns, sharing with Langenstein, Gerson, Dinkelsbühl, and

---

[117] Ludwig Glückert, "Hieronymus von Mondsee."

[118] Vienna, ÖNB, cvp 3520. Glückert, 113, accepts this codex as one of Jerome's
compilations. The Peuerbach letters and poetry have to do with his grief over the death
of Rembert Mühlwanger, whose connections with Gaming have been discussed in chapter one. This codex contains Peuerbach's autograph of these materials, illustrating his
continued contact with the university and its "proto-humanist" circles. The manuscript
also includes one poem by Jerome himself (115r), plus a variety of historical documents,
especially those relating to the history of Benedictine monasteries at Tegernsee,
Dietramszell, Beuron, Ettal, Steingaden, etc. (151r-209r, 216r-219v). More ominously, it
includes a report to Vienna authorities regarding an alleged sacrilege committed in 1453
by Jews in Breslau against a eucharistic host (232r-34r).

[119] E.g., fol. 151r contains a sample letter exhorting to perseverance in the monastic
life, written by professed monks of Melk.

[120] Summarized in Overfield, *Humanism and Scholasticism*, 68-70, 102-106, 120-42,
cf. Karl Großmann, "Frühzeit des Humanismus."

[121] Astrik L. Gabriel, "Preparatory Teaching in the Parisian Colleges during the Fourteenth Century," *Revue de l'Université de Ottawa*, 21 (1951), 449-83, repr. 1969.

others, a quest for an effective and affective way to seek the Wisdom that is theology.

The affective piety we have been observing throughout the Vienna university milieu runs throughout Kempf's corpus of writings. In the chapters that follow we shall encounter again and again both his insistence that a simple pious lay person is often more devout than a learned doctor and his affective method for appropriating cognitive learning. Although eighteenth-century scholars asserted that he translated catechetical materials into German, no clear evidence of such vernacular writings has turned up. Still, as prior, he preached in German to the lay brethren of his monastery, and this activity lies behind one of his three works on mystical theology.

With much of the humanist tradition Kempf shared both the desire for contemplative repose (*otium*) drawn in large part from Augustine[122] and a patristic view of the theologian as orator (in Kempf's case, an orator who declaims silently, in spiritual writing).[123] Whether Kempf read Petrarch's Latin "monastic" writings (*De otio religioso* and *De vita solitaria*) is unclear but they were popular in Carthusian circles, and Heinrich of Langenstein knew at least *De vita solitaria*.[124] As Kempf's acquaintance from student days at Vienna, Sigmund Gossembrot, who also knew Petrarch's writings, prepared to leave the cares of public service for humanist-monastic retirement in Straßburg, Kempf sent greetings to him through a friend of Sigmund's son.[125]

Yet as the remainder of this book will illustrate, Kempf ultimately identified more with prescholastic, affective monastic theology than with humanism or the *via moderna*. The Carthusian order's founder, St. Bruno, had abandoned his role as chancellor of the cathedral school at Reims ca. 1083. Kempf made this story, in a version conflated with a later legend of an exodus of academics from the university at Paris, central to his interpretation of the Carthusian order's mission, namely, to rescue scholars from peril.[126] (Ironically, Bruno may well have contrib-

---

[122] Jean Leclercq, *Otia monastica: Etudes sur le vocabulaire de la contemplation au moyen âge* (1963), esp. 23-26, 37-40,45-46, 54-56.

[123] See chapter three, p. 83, below, for a more detailed discussion of this theme, which Kempf took from Gerson's *De consolatione theologiae*.

[124] In his conciliarist *Epistola exhortatoria* he quotes from book 2, taking from Petrarch the complaints by an anonymous Italian who believes the emperor's title is in bad hands among the Germans. See Kreuzer, *Heinrich von Langenstein*, 58.

[125] Paul Joachimsohn, *Hermann Schedels Briefwechsel*, 89.

[126] Cf. Heinrich Egher van Kalkar's history of the Carthusian order as edited by Hendrina B. C. W. Vermeer, *Het Tractaat 'Ortus et decursus ordinis cartusiensis van Hendrik Egher van Kalkar* (published diss., 1929), esp. pp. 88-94, in which the "exodus from the university" theme plays a less significant role. See Louis J. Lekai, *The Cistercians*

uted to early scholastic theology and Guigo I employed textual criticism
on the letters of Jerome and other patristic writers.[127]) Gerson, Heinrich
of Langenstein, and others had begun to question the role of logic in matters of faith. Kempf took this to its logical conclusion and searched for a
better place to do theology and for a proper *modus theologizandi*. His
conclusions, set forth in his manual for monastic theological method, are
the subject of the next chapter.

(1977), 46-47, for similar stories about the effect of Bernard of Clairvaux on the
schools of his day.

[127] See Jean Châtillon, "La Bible dans les écoles du XIIe siècle," in *Le Moyen Age et
la Bible* (1984), 163-97, reprinted 1985); Gordon Mursell, *Theology*, 21-32. At issue is
Bruno's authorship of commentaries on the Psalms and Pauline writings. Anselme Stoelen, "Les commentaires scripturaires attribués à Bruno le Chartreux," *RTAM*, 25 (1955),
177-247, refers to Artur Landgraf's earlier work. See also Damian van den Eynde, "Literary Note on the Earliest Scholastic Commentarii in Psalmos," *Franciscan Studies*, 14
(1954), 121-54, and his supplementary article, ibid., vol. 17 (1957), 149-72. On Guigo
see Mursell, *Theology*, 75-80, 172-74.

CHAPTER THREE

THEOLOGUS

Two brothers went to see an old holy hermit at Scetis. One of them said to him, "Abba, I have memorized all of the Old and New Testaments." The old man said to him, "You have filled the air with words." The other said, "I have copied out the Old and New Testaments and have them with me in my cell." To this one he replied, "You have papered your windows. Do you not know who said, 'The kingdom of God is not words but power'? And again, 'For it is not the hearer of the law who is righteous before God, but the doer of the law who will be justified'." They therefore asked him for a way of salvation. He said to them, "'The fear of the Lord is the beginning of wisdom', and humility with patience." [*Verba Seniorum*, VII (Paschasius; PL 73: 1056D)]

1. Trahere in Affectum

Toward the end of his first period at Gaming (1447), Kempf wrote his *Dialogus de recto studiorum fine ac ordine et fugiendis vite saecularis vanitatibus*. *De recto fine* contains in programmatic fashion most of the elements in Kempf's theological and religious program. Thus it offers a convenient point of departure for the second objective announced in the introduction to this book, namely, a study of the contents of Kempf's writings as they indicate the meaning of monastic culture. At first glance, much in *De recto fine* seems to have been borrowed from Jean Gerson's efforts to reform the teaching and study of theology at Paris. Yet when Kempf's dialogue is compared with Gerson's pre-Constance writings, the outlines of a distinctively monastic theology emerge, a theology grounded in *otium*, in contemplative renunciation that means meekness and "uselessness"[1] to the world but brings freedom from anxiety (*securitas*) to its adherents. The monastic life is not superior to life in the world, so much as, by God's grace, it is more secure, because it provides an external crutch in the form of the Rule and spiritual direction. Monks are not stronger than lay people, rather, their strength consists in

---

[1] The role played by *utilitas*, in the sense of fruitfulness, within the framework of Carthusian renunciation is developed in Mursell, *Theology of the Carthusian Life* and in the notes to the Sources Chrétiennes edition of Guigo I, *Meditationes*.

their recognition of weakness and their grateful willingness to lean on
the Rule. That Kempf's message—both his warnings against the perils of
proud trust in one's own academic or ecclesiastical achievements and his
call to the care-less life of monastic "leisure"—did not fall on deaf ears
is evident from a sizeable list of Vienna academics who became monks
at Gaming. Many of these later took up positions of leadership in various
charterhouses, disseminating Kempf's writings as they went. The present
chapter takes up the contents of Kempf's call and the response given to
it.[2]

   De recto fine was written, ostensibly, for a student of theology who
had made clear his intention to enter religion in order to reach a harbor
safe from the tempestuous seas of life in the world.[3] Kempf puts his advice in the form of a dialogue between the student (Discipulus) and
teacher (Magistra—Mistress Sacred Theology). Kempf does not encourage the student to abandon studies immediately, but at the same time, he
leaves no doubt that the most secure and temptation-free pursuit of sacred theology is to be found in the cloistered religious life, especially in
the semi-eremitical Carthusian life. Thus, when Kempf counsels in part I
to continue studying theology, sets forth in part II the best manner of
study, and points out in part III which vices to avoid when studying, he
is also urging his readers to enter religion, to study in the *schola monastica*. After seven years as a Carthusian, if not before, monasticism and
theology are inseparable for Kempf.[4]

   Yet he does not ignore the university setting. He leaves no doubt
about the superiority of theology over all other disciplines taught at the
university. Indeed, the dialogue opens with the problem posed by the
various academic disciplines' competition for Discipulus's allegiance.

   Commenting on her pupil's habit of skipping lectures and his lack
of enthusiasm for studies, Magistra Theologia warns Discipulus about

---

   [2] Manuscripts are listed in appendix A. Citations will be made to part and chapter
numbers with folia and column numbers from Vienna cvp 4259 (= V1) and page numbers from the *Bibl. ascetica* edition in parentheses. To avoid overloading the footnotes, a
number of passages from this treatise are not cited from the manuscripts. Pez's edition is
generally faithful to the manuscripts (apart from his habit of changing future or present
indicative to subjunctive). The reader can thus refer to the printed Pez edition with rea-
sonable confidence. The date of the dialogue can be calculated from a reference (II.21 [p.
370]) to the founding of the Carthusian order in 1084, 363 years before the point of
Kempf's writing. The treatise may have been composed around Pentecost 1447, as indicated by II.31 and III.1.

   [3] *Rect*, preface (40r A; pp. 260-61), cf. I.9 (p. 285).

   [4] I find it difficult to agree with Mertens's assessment, "Kartäuserprofessoren," 83,
of the dialogue as a "wissenschaftstheoretische und wissenschaftspädagogische" work—
unless both terms are qualified by the adjective "monastic."

the danger of floating on one wave of enthusiasm after another, resolving first to enter religion, then to study theology, and soon thereafter setting his sights on law or medicine, or, then again, deciding he really wants to be a schoolteacher.[5] Even if the student manages to escape damnation, such inconstancy might well lead to his running aground in the mud of apathy. The study of canon law is clearly the most seductive temptation, since the path to the theological doctorate involves long years of study and, compared to the potential for advancement in ecclesiastical office offered by a degree in canon law, promises little in the way of material or social reward. Discipulus's presumption in desiring rapid academic prestige, a desire frustrated by his slow progress in theological studies[6] and his refusal to be satisfied in pursuing the theologian's proper goal—knowledge leading to love and praise of God—finds ample reproach from Theologia. Like so many in the church, Discipulus is seeking mere degrees and titles.

Larger ecclesiological issues are at stake in the competition between canon law and theology. Although canon law, in contending against secular forces for the rights and privileges of the church, appears superior to theology, Magistra Theologia reminds her pupil that the ultimate source and foundation of all laws and canons is divine law, the domain of sacred theology.[7] It is the duty of the theologian who is well grounded in the writings of the doctors of the faith to test the principles of existing ecclesiastical law against divine law and right reason, leaving only the minor details to the experts in canon law. Indeed, what appears right and just in the *forum ecclesiae*, where canon law dominates, is often illicit and unjust in the *forum conscientiosum*. Even though such ecclesiastical legislation was issued primarily to resolve problems of the soul in relation to God (over which the church had jurisdiction through the penitential system), much legislation has been twisted to apply mainly to litigation in the church. Despite the claims of canon lawyers that their discipline is more important because it applies to both letter and spirit, Kempf asserts that law belongs primarily to the exterior *forum contentiosum* or *forum ecclesiae*, not to the interior *forum conscientiosum*.

---

[5] *Rect*, I. 1 (40v A; p. 264).

[6] *Rect*, I. 2 (40v A - 41r A; pp. 265-66). Cf. *Prop*, I. 9/10 (VS1, 8r B.20-34).

[7] On Gerson's view of canon law and lawyers, see Christoph Burger, *Aedificatio, Fructus, Utilitas: Johannes Gerson als Professor der Theologie und Kanzler der Universität Paris* (1986), 85-97, with summaries of three sermons ("Conversi estis nunc ad pastorem" [1406], "Pax vobis" [1408], and "Dominus his opus habet" [1410]; *Oeuvres*, vol. 5: *L'oeuvre oratoire*, 168-79, 435-47, 218-29). Cf. Leclercq, "Monastic and Scholastic Theology," 180. Kempf acknowledges his use of Gerson on this subject in *Rect*, I.4 (V1, fol. 41v B, 46 - 42r A, 16), but this portion was omitted in the Pez edition.

Using figures drawn from Genesis 16:5-6 and Galatians 4:21-31, Kempf's Theologia complains bitterly that, ever since the Council of Constance, Mistress Theology (Sarah) has remonstrated to the Pope (Abraham) about the disrespect shown her by Maidservant Canon Law (Hagar). Yet the pope, unlike Abraham, chooses not to grant Theology authority over her maid, Canon Law. Indeed, the head of Christendom has defended the maidservant and suppressed Mistress Theology. Out of this situation, with the offspring of the maid, Canon Law, playing with the sons of the mistress, Theology, tempting them to evil and deriding them, arise the schisms and corruptions that plague the church. For neither pope nor prelates nor princes have had the courage to banish the maidservant and her children to the wilderness.[8] Kempf's Magistra Theologia continues with a warning that, more than any other discipline, the study of canon law sharpens one's appetite for things of the world (I.6).

In other words, canon law and lawyers have become the scapegoat for Kempf. With origins that run parallel to those of academic theology, the role of canon law had expanded with the fourteenth-century papal bureaucracy. Writing in the shadow of the final collapse of the Basel Council, Kempf, as had Gerson before him, bitterly laid the blame for the malaise of the church, especially in the conciliar epoch since Constance, at the feet of lawyers and ecclesiastical bureaucrats. Clearly more was involved here than the traditional proscription of canon law and civil law studies for monks (Second Lateran Council, 1139). Such antipathy, even animosity, toward lawyers was common in the later Middle Ages, finding expression in Gerson, Dante, Ulrich von Hutten, and popular poetry, to cite only a few examples.[9] Statistics for Oxford indicate that law was indeed expanding its turf within the university at the expense of theology in the early fifteenth century.[10] Kempf was reciting what became

---

[8]   *Rect*, I.3 (41r-v; pp. 269-70). The allegorical use of the Abraham, Sarah, Hagar story constitutes a long tradition, primarily as an illustration of the dangers of literal interpretation, which, in this case would seem to give approval to bigamy. Kempf's source for the application to the relationship between canon law and theology was undoubtedly Robert Holcot (d. 1349) in the prologue to *Super sapientiam Salomonis*, where both Esther with her two maids and the Sarah-Hagar story are applied to canon law and theology, without, however, the ecclesiological fulminations of the Kempf passage. See the discussion in Oediger, *Bildung*, 43-45. In Gerson's sermon to canon law graduates ("Conversi estis" in *Oeuvres*, 5:173-74), Hagar symbolizes canon law and Sarah symbolizes theology, but without the further allegorical development given here by Kempf.

[9]   See Charles H. Haskins, *The Renaissance of the Twelfth Century* (1927), 216; Gerald Strauss, *Manifestations of Discontent in Germany on the Eve of the Reformation* (1971), 198-207; and Oberman, *Werden und Wertung*, 143-60.

[10]   Courtenay, *Schools*, 365-66, summarizes the statistical analysis of Oxford biographical registers.

an old refrain: in the seventeenth century we find William Perkins preaching sermons designed to woo the most promising Cambridge students away from law studies toward theology.[11]

Theologia counsels patience with the apparent barrenness of theology, for, although Sarah endured derision for years, in her old age she became the mother of a much greater family than that of her handmaid. Above all, the goal of theology "is God, that he be known and loved. And what could be better than to know and love God?"[12] The student of theology must be ready to bear abuse, for "theologians are despised and derided as hypocrites and fools, thus seeming to be of no benefit to themselves or to others, in contrast to jurists."[13] From Kempf's Magistra Theologia and the words of Scripture, Discipulus learns that it is no shame to be considered a fool according to the wisdom of the world (1 Cor 1:26-29, Mt 11:25, and Lk 10:21). Besides, Theologia continues, claiming to quote a popular proverb, there are those who say that just as all theologians are hypocrites, so all jurists are simoniacs, all physicians are murderers, and all students of the arts are dreamers (I.7).

So much for the perils of the university. Even in the cloister the pursuit of theology is subject to dangers and temptations. Kempf's purpose in writing is to warn of those dangers and to outline a path avoiding such pitfalls. He devoted the second of the three parts of the *Dialogus* to that end.

The very desire to know, abused as an inordinate and insatiable curiosity to know good and evil, was the cause of Adam's sin. Thus the student of theology must take care to restrain with the tether of right reason his natural appetite for knowledge.[14] His intentions must be pure.

---

[11] Perkins, *On the Calling of the Ministrie* (1605); see Ian Breward, ed., *The Works of William Perkins* (1970), 41. Cf. William J. Bouwsma, "Lawyers and Early Modern Culture," *AHR*, 78 (1973), 303-27, at 318, citing the commonplace from the late Middle Ages: "A good lawyer makes a bad Christian." See also Oediger, *Bildung*, 43-45, for further examples from the thirteenth century onward.

[12] *Rect*, I.4 (42r B - 42v A; p. 273).

[13] *Rect*, I.7 (43v B - 44r A; pp. 279-81). In the memorandum acompanying his letter of April 1, 1400, to Pierre d'Ailly, Jean Gerson also complained about the abuse heaped upon theologians. See *Oeuvres*, 2: 26.

[14] *Rect*, II.1 (46r B; p. 291). Cf. *De confirmatione*, 3 (V5, 5r, 20-30), on the connection between desire for riches of knowledge and mankind's fall into sin: "Cupiditas equidem illarum diviciarum intellectualium, id est scienciarum, tam angelice quam humane nature lapsus causa fuit. Angeli siquidem propter scienciam ceciderunt, et similiter Adam cupiens scire bonitatem et malum. Et cum utraque natura, videlicet angelica et humana, concupivit esse dives in sciencia, facta est misera. Contra quas divicias principaliter Christus predicat cum dicit, 'Beati pauperes spiritu quoniam ipsorum est regnum celorum,' a quo angelica natura et humana ceciderunt, quia divites in spiritu esse voluerunt."

The vain desire for learning in order to gain riches or honors can only darken the eye of the soul. The theologian must continuously rectify his intention by directing his studies toward God. Above all, he must never pursue that which is useless at the expense of the necessary, that which is merely curious at the expense of the fruitful, that which is subtle to the neglect of that which is devout, or that which is verbose instead of what edifies (II.2). The language is reminiscent of Gerson's campaign "contra curiositatem studentium,"[15] although Gerson is probably not exclusively the source for Kempf's admonition, since the criticism of the vice of "vain curiosity" has a long history.[16] And the student must not be disappointed at missing opportunities to acquire benefices and temporal power because of his long years of theological study. Kempf insists that it is difficult both for those rich in temporal goods and those rich in accumulated knowledge and its attendant presumptuousness to enter the kingdom of heaven. A pedagogue at heart, he makes his point by extending the wordplay found at the beginning of the most elementary grammar text, the *Disticha Catonis*: "Legere et non intelligere est negligere"—if to read without understanding is not to read and to be careless [*negligere*], then to collect a large library by purchase or copying without reading is equally negligent.[17] The statement could be given an ironic

---

[15] See *Oeuvres*, 2: 26-27; 3: 230-31, 238-39, 247. Cf. Bernard of Clairvaux, *Sermones in Cantica Canticorum*, 8.6 (*S. Bernardi Opera*, 1: 39-40); Aelred of Rievaulx, *Speculum caritatis*, II.24, CCCM, 1: 99-101. From the Cistercian perspective, see Louis J. Lekai, *Cistercians*, 88, for comments on the problems of Cistercian students faced with the temptations and distractions of university life at Paris in the mid-fifteenth century. Cf. Thomas Aquinas, *STh* IIa.IIae, qu. 167, art. 1.

[16] Jean Leclercq, "*Curiositas* and the Return to God in St. Bernard of Clairvaux," *CS*, 25 (1990), 92-100 (published in French, 1983); Hans Blumenberg, "*Curiositas* und *veritas*: Zur Ideengeschichte von Augustin, *Confessiones* X,35," *Studia patristica*, vol. 6, pt. 4 (1962), 294-302, and *The Legitimacy of the Modern Age* (1983), esp. part III, pp. 229-435. Note Heiko Oberman's critique of Blumenberg in Oberman, "Reformation and Revolution: Copernicus' Discovery in an Era of Change," in *The Cultural Context of Medieval Learning* (1975), 397-429, and especially the discussion of Oberman's critique by symposium participants on pp. 429-35. See also Oberman, *Contra vanam curiositatem* (1973). Cf. E. P. Meijering, *Calvin wider die Neugierde: Ein Beitrag zum Vergleich zwischen reformatorischem und patristischem Denken*, Bibliotheca Humanistica und Reformatorica, 29 (1980).

[17] *Rect*, I.9 (46r A 20-39; pp. 289-90): "Nocent etiam sibi, qui tempus consumunt pro libris acquirendis et se negligunt ipsos non legendo aut non intelligendo. Et si 'legere et non intelligere est negligere,' quanto magis libros scribere aut magno labore colligere et eos nunquam legere est negligere? Et sepe contingit, ut collectis multis libris et minime perlectis, repetatur per mortem anima colligentis; et, que tunc paravit, cuius erunt? Si paucos habueris libros et scienciam modicam, eo facilius reddes racionem. Principaliter enim aquirende sunt virtutes et bona opera, quibus nemo potest male uti, per quas primo queratur regnum Dei; et omnia predicta adicientur tibi [Mt 6:33]—non quantum inordinata quandoque appetis, sed quantum tibi pro salute anime tue sufficit." See also *Disticha Catonis*, ed. Boas (1952), 4.

reading in the light of the Carthusian practice of assembling large libraries, a trait noted already by twelfth-century observers. Kempf's point, however, was to underscore the spirituality of well-digested *lectio divina*: God ultimately exceeds human grasp but quality is more important than quantity in the pursuit of the love of God.[18]

But Kempf's purpose extends beyond warning of the snares set by the academic life and the pursuit of honor and riches. He has a positive program for the student of theology. Its foundation is the text of scripture and the writings of the doctors and saints of the church. This base must never be abandoned for dependence on one's own wits in disputations or discourses. To acquire that foundation, Kempf recommends eager reading and rereading ("foraging": *lectitare*) amid the complete text of the Bible together with the *Postillae* of Nicholas of Lyra ("who is the most profitable and masterful"). The writings, collections of *sententiae*, and the *summae* of the scholastics ("St. Thomas and others"), should supplement the study of scripture. And, alongside Aquinas, Kempf singles out two "modern" theologians for special mention: Heinrich of Langenstein and the chancellor of the University of Paris, Jean Gerson—precisely because they deal best with concrete matters.[19]

Any pursuit of knowledge must be carefully balanced by the acquisition of virtues. Kempf counsels discretion, warning against imbalance in any direction, against an overly zealous pursuit of virtues that hinders academic progress and against an inordinate desire for knowledge.

> Don't think I desire that you spend as much or more time in prayer and devotional exercises as in studying; rather, this I desire: that you pursue your studies ultimately for the sake of virtue, the fear of the Lord, and love of your neighbor, studying as much and as long as is necessary to acquire the above [II.4].

---

[18] See *Ost*, 53 (G1, 39v, 9-27): God is found better by a penitent *affectus* than an investigating *intellectus* (Gerson, *De mystica theologia speculativa*, prologue [ed. Combes, (1958), p. 1]); even if one were to read all the books written in the whole world and learn all the knowledge from the beginning of the world to the end of the age, God would still remain hidden, and one would know less of God than a single drop of the sea or a single point of the universe knows of God. See also Burrows, *Gerson*, 135-39.

[19] *Rect*, II. 2 (47r A, 27-47; pp. 294-95): "Expediret eciam, et valde pro fundamento acquirendo valeret textum tocius biblie diligenter lectitare cum postilla Magistri Nicolai de Lira, que utique est magistralis et utilissima; deinde textum sentenciarum et doctorum scripta, et sepe recurrere ad summas doctorum (Sancti Thome et aliorum) et ex illorum scriptis se fundare, et non sic loqui quasi ex propria fantasia sompniando (quod sine errore quandoque damnabili in hac sciencia fieri non [Pez: vix] potest); et duorum modernorum, scilicet Magistri Henrici de Hassia et Domini Cancellarij Parisiensis, Johannis Gerson summe sunt apprecianda, eo quod priorum doctorum scripta magistraliter resolvunt [Pez: resolvant], et magis ad particularia descendunt [Pez: descendant]." Cf. Burrows, *Gerson*, 143-48, regarding Gerson's ability to "get down to specifics."

Just as the intellect is perfected with knowledge, so the *affectus* must be perfected with virtue. Perfecting the will or *affectus* is in fact more difficult because it is corrupted more subtly by original sin than is either the intellect or the body.[20] We have here an illustration of the way monastic discretion functioned: on the surface, the tradition that placed the origins of sin in the sensual powers and corporal concupiscence seems obvious enough. But Kempf is concerned about the more subtle way pride affects the human person—body, soul, and spirit. The monastic tradition placed pride at the head of the capital sins, and Kempf here offers a discerning reading of that tradition, explaining how the obvious initial onset of sin in sensual and corporal weakness is less dangerous than the more hidden perversion of affective motivations.

A further reason why it is more important for Kempf's student of theology to perfect the *affectus* with virtues than to perfect the *intellectus* with knowledge is that virtues must be used continually lest they begin to be destroyed by vices. In contrast, even though an educated man does not use his knowledge, he remains learned.[21]

We have here yet another fundamental monastic assumption, one which, on the surface, seems to contradict the preceding point: the subtle,

---

[20] *Rect*, II.3 (47r B - 47v A; p. 296). Cf. *Ost*, 4 (G1, 2v, 33 - 3r, 9), where Kempf asserts that sin begins in the will rather than in the flesh or sensual *potentiae*. "Et quia in homine est duplex natura—scilicet caro et spiritus, exterior homo et interior, sive sensualitas et liberum arbitrium—ideo illa inclinacio mala et amor proprius est duplex in homine. Prima et principaliter est ad libertatem voluntatis implendam et ad excellenciam propriam, honores, dignitates, laudes, et gloriam et huiusmodi, ex quibus homo vehementissime inclinatur per superbiam et ad sue voluntatis libertatem. Et illa inclinacio est magis in voluntate, ubi incepit peccatum, quam in carne aut sensualitate. Et illa vocatur quandoque superbia, quamvis proprie post baptismum non sit peccatum, sed fomes peccati aut stimulus superbie. Alia est inclinacio in homine in carne, id est, in sensualitate prout includit carnem et animam sensitivam. Et illa est eciam vehemens inclinacio ad carnalia—ut ad cibum, potum, delectaciones carnis, vestes, et amicos, pueros, parentes, et socios carnales—in quantum ex carne sunt sibi coniuncti. Et quamvis prima inclinacio, que est ad honores, propriam excellenciam, et libertatem etcetera, minus curetur, tamen est periculosior, vehemencior, et communior secunda et oculcius et subtilius movet sine impetu carnis." Compare this to *Ost*, ch. 27 (G1, 18v, 19 - 19r, 1), where, citing Augustine and Peter Lombard and his commentators, Kempf follows the more traditional teaching that (venial) sin begins in the sensual appetite. Kempf's imprecise reference to the *Sentences* would seem to apply to dist. 24-25, 30 (PL 192: 702-704, cf. 707-8 regarding the effect of sin on the free will and 722 on the *fomes peccati* as concupiscence, which launches the movement of soul and body that constitutes actual sin. Steven Ozment's argument from silence regarding the incapacitating effects of sin on the affective powers of the soul in Gerson should perhaps be reexamined. Steven E. Ozment, *Homo Spiritualis: . . . the Anthropology of Johannes Tauler, Jean Gerson, and Martin Luther, 1509-1516* (1969), 69-71. Cf. idem, "The University and the Church: Patterns of Reform in Jean Gerson," *Medievalia et Humanistica*, n.s. 1 (1970), 111-26, at 115-16; Burger, *Aedificatio*, 20, n. 63).

[21] *Rect*, II.3 (47v A-B; p. 297).

hidden *affectus* is shaped and formed not by subtle, hidden exercises, but by active, "external" practice under the guidance of the monastic rule. In other words, inner dispositions are shaped by outer exercise. To employ a modern analogy: anyone who has undergone athletic training knows how quickly muscle tone begins to decline if one neglects one's regimen. So it is with the active monastic life of combat against vices by training in virtues—the muscle tone of the *affectus* must continually be reinforced by rule-governed discipline, unlike that of cognitive knowledge, which, in Kempf's view, is less easily lost. How quickly the inner disposition changes, how rapidly the "fire in the belly" that keeps one faithful to the grinding discipline—whether that of physical training or spiritual exercises—begins to fade if neglected! Kempf might be amused at the recent discovery of affective motivation in education or Brian Stock's discovery of "experience" in Bernard of Clairvaux.[22]

2. Theologia Mystica as the Goal of All Knowledge

Thus Kempf's general advice revolves around the realization that the student of theology, or of any discipline, must involve his heart as well as his intellect, being moved from mere cognitive appropriation to heartfelt internalization of the material learned, being taken with the material learned more than taking up topics, being so *affected* by the meaning of the material that he lives it out.[23] The final destination of Kempf's path for the theologian is the summit of affective wisdom, the mountain of "mystical theology," the *finis omnium scientiarum*. Kempf has Dis-

---

[22] "Experience, Praxis, Work." Stock's summary of Bernard rings true, but Bernard does not appear to me to be proto-modern in his use of *experientia* and related terms. Bernard's emphasis on experience and practice is simply solid patristic-monastic theology. I hope to take up Stock's "modern" reading of medieval monasticism (which he offers as an extension of Max Weber's thesis on the *Rationalisierung* exhibited by monasticism) in future studies.

[23] *Rect.*, II.7 (51r; pp. 312-16), a chapter titled "De modo tradendi [Pez: trahendi] in affectum non solum theologicam, sed eciam alias sciencias." Cf. II.9, 11, 14, and Gerson, *De consolatione theologiae*, bk. IV, prosa 4 (*Oeuvres*, 9:237): ". . . ut ea quae per theologiam intelligit, traducat per jugem ruminationem in affectum cordis et executionem operis." Cf. Hugh of Balma, *Viae Sion lugent*, caput 2, part. 3 (Peltier edition, pp. 19b-21a; illuminative way, par. 47-54 in SC edition), for the aspirative method of transferring every word of scripture into the anagogical sense. On *affectus* and *affectio* and *affectus* (related to *amor*) and *effectus* (related to *caritas*), see William of Saint Thierry, *De natura et dignitate amoris*, 13-17 *et passim* (PL 180:379-408, at 388-91; ed. Robert Thomas [1965], 64-76; trans. Thomas X. Davis, CF, 30 [1981], 69-74); Aelred of Rievaulx, *Speculum caritatis*, III.10-20 (CCCM, 1: 118-28); M. Corneille Halflants, introduction to Bernard of Clairvaux, *Sermons on the Song of Songs*, vol. 1, CF 4 (1979), xxii.

cipulus broach the issue by requesting "more particular," "concrete," or "detailed" instruction on how he could pursue his study in Theologia's school "more surely, fruitfully, and meritoriously."[24]

Kempf's Magistra Theologia notes in response that the theology student ought to pursue mystical theology even if he thinks himself unable to attain it, just as a monk should strive for perfection despite the fact that few attain it "these days" (II.5). There are two theologies: one that is intellectual or speculative, and the other that is affectual or affective. The first can be taught and expounded by any person, even by the reprobate, through knowledge of holy scripture. But the second, the affective or mystical theology, is acquired in the *affectus* as the result of supernatural illumination. Its source is *the* Doctor of Theology, Jesus Christ. It is infused into the human intellect by the Holy Spirit, making mystical or affective theology more certain, more clear, and more perfect than intellectual or speculative theology. It is given only to those living a life of good works performed in love—not to those living in sin. Kempf singles out Pseudo-Dionysius as the first to write on mystical theology, mentions the holy fathers and scholastic doctors collectively as authori-

---

[24] Kempf, *MTh*, I.1 (Jellouschek ed., p. 15). Elsewhere, Kempf describes the theologian as having reference to the third and ultimate order, the *perfecti*—in comparison to the *incipientes* and *proficientes*. See *Cantica*, prologue, ch. 10 (*Bibl. ascetica* 11: 37). Apparently Johannes Schlitpacher had also called upon preachers and professors at Vienna to convert to a study of mystical theology. See Vincent of Aggsbach's letter to Schlitpacher in Pez and Hueber, *Cod. dip.-hist.-epist.* (1729), pt. III, p. 329: "Paulo enim ante recepi a vestra tunc fraternitate quaedam folia scripta intus et foris, in quibus post multam allegationem verborum Hugonis de Palma, tandem in vos assumendo personam Dei praeconis prorupistis in haec verba: 'Quid facitis praedicatores divini verbi, et informatores populi Christiani? Cur negligitis? Quare non recurritis ad pauca verba Mysticae Theologiae, ut ipsis intellectis, difficultates veteris et novi testamenti vobis elucescant, et idoneis verbis possitis inflammare cordia audientium?' . . . Miror tamen non parum, quod vocatis Doctoribus et Divinorum librorum lectoribus et expositoribus verbi divini, simulque informatoribus populi Christiani, Religiosos, quorum memoriam saltem *durch des handtwercks willen* habere debebatis, non vocatis. Quidquid de hoc sit, mihi exclamate libet: O vos ter, quaterque, imo centies felicem, si Doctores, lectores, expositores, et informatores praenominatos vestro clamore terrueritis, ut ad studium Theologiae Mysticae se convertant! Si medietatem eorum, si tertiam aut quartam, vel etiam decimam partem ipsorum ad hoc studium induxeritis, vere et absque scrupulo pronunciabo, vos maiorem vestro clamore fructum effecisse, quam B. Iohannes Baptista, praecursor, et praeco Domini, ac Voc Clamantis in deserto, suo clamore procurasse creditur." Vincent continued by pointing out that the "studium mysticae theologiae," like graduate studies in the university, requires "undergraduate" degrees (the *via purgativa*); it cannot be pursued by leaps and bounds (*per saltum*, perhaps an allusion to the "leapfrog" degrees granted by some universities [e.g., to Erasmus by Turin]; in this instance perhaps aimed at Johannes Keck's degree from the conciliar university in Basel). Vincent apparently felt that some of the participants in the Tegernsee "mystics controversy" were attempting to use "mystical theology" as an easy cure-all for problems of the spiritual life without reckoning sufficently with its arduous prerequisites. Cf. Franz Hubalek, "Briefwechsel," 104.

ties on the subject, and cites Jean Gerson as the most prolific recent writer. The Fathers of the Desert and Bernard of Clairvaux are examples of saints illuminated by this highest knowledge from the Holy Spirit.

Mystical theology can be taught only by the Holy Spirit. However, those who have written on the subject have transmitted a certain method by which the human spirit can be prepared for mystical illumination. That method involves the entry of the intellect into a cloud of darkness, or "obscure cognition." Having reached the limit of such "obscure cognition of God" through negation, the soul abandons negations and begins to be carried on the foundation of faith into a "summum bonum" that is incomprehensible to every human intellect, yet completely lovable and desirable. It is a knowledge known or experienced solely by tasting; where the intellect remains outside, the *affectus* may enter (II.5, see appendix B).

Although Kempf does not propose mystical theology as an escape from theological studies, he does speak of understanding the depths of holy scripture "without an external instructor [*absque doctore extrinsecus*]." Yet this understanding of scripture is complementary rather than antithetical to academic studies. The snatching away of the spirit into God, the *raptus mentis*, leads both to a supernaturally infused cognition of God and to an understanding of scripture theretofore impossible for the human spirit. "Such knowledge is called mystical theology." Kempf notes that Bernard of Clairvaux learned almost none of his knowledge by "humanum studium," rather, he received it "a Spiritu Sancto" (II.5, see appendix B). Of the three "mystical" senses of scripture (allegorical, tropological, and anagogical),[25] the anagogical, is

> the main thrust of scripture and is the end and goal of all scriptures, indeed the aim of all creation. Thus it lurks everywhere in all scriptures and, indeed, in all creatures, even if sometimes only in a hidden, obscure, remote, or mediated manner. Hence it would be most absurd if you set yourself in pursuit of theology and remained ignorant of this sense, refusing to direct all that you read or hear to this end, preferring, as it were, to stick to one of the inferior senses and not strive toward the true end.[26]

---

[25] See *MTh*, IV.4 (p. 268), where Kempf includes all four senses of scripture as part of the second of four modes of cognition of God: (a) "per speculum solum," i.e., through the creatures; (b) "per speculum in enigmate," i.e., in scripture with the aid of the study of theology (utilizing the four senses of scripture); (c) "per radium divinum," i.e., cognition of God by direct, prophetic illumination from God; (d) actual mystical union, face-to-face both in heaven and, in the exceptional cases of Moses and Paul, in this life as a foretaste of eternal life. Parallels are found in *Ost*, 1-2, 28, 44, 47, and *Serm. evang.* [appendix A, no. 14b], no. 45 (G2, 190r).

[26] *Rect*, II.7 (51v B, 8-20; p. 315): "Qui est principaliter in scriptura intentus, et quasi

When Discipulus expresses a desire to know how to gain the anagogical understanding of scripture, Theology confesses that it defies
brief explanation. Although it surfaces more explicitly in the Song of
Songs, it lies hidden beneath the surface elsewhere in the Bible. Thus it
can be taught only by the enabling influence of the Holy Spirit in mystical theology—not by the letter.[27]

Taking up Jean Gerson's advice to students at Paris, Kempf admon-
ishes his correspondent at Vienna:

> It is toward this [mystical theology] that you ought to strive, even if you
> presume yourself incapable of attaining it. For the chancellor at Paris, the
> aforementioned Joannes Gerson, speaks on this matter: '. . . Do you wish
> to know that which is hidden? Then move from the theology of the *intel-
> lectus* to theology of the *affectus*, from knowledge to wisdom, from cogni-
> tion to devotion. This is that theology of which the great Arsenius, a man
> learned in Greek and Latin, confessed himself ignorant; indeed he admitted
> that he had not learned so much as its ABCs. Would that this theology
> were as familiar to all of us who call ourselves theologians as, at this mo-
> ment, it is strange and unknown to us.[28]

Although Kempf considers mystical theology the summit of theology and the proper aspiration of all students of theology, he does not insist that only those who have scaled the mystical heights can call
themselves theologians. As Gerson had pointed out, not all are suited, by
their status and responsibilities in life, to pursue the summit of mystical
scientia-sapientia.[29] For Kempf, a "true theologian" is one "who understands holy scriptures, draws them into his *affectus*, and fulfills them in
works," as the title of part two, chapter six, announces. Alluding to

---

finis omnium scripturarum, et eciam omnium creaturarum; et ubique hic latet in
omnibus scripturis et eciam in omnibus creaturis, quamvis quandoque occultissime et
obscure seu [Pez: et] remote et [Pez: seu] mediate. Et ideo valde absurdum est, te in
theologia studere, et hunc sensum ignorare, et non in omni, quod audis aut legis, ad eum
tanquam in finem tendere, sed quasi stare in sensu aliquo inferiori et non tendere ad
verum finem." Cf. Hugh of Balma, *Viae Sion*, caput 2, part. 3 (Peltier ed., p. 19b; *via illuminativa*, par. 45-46 in SC edition).

[27] *Rect*, II.7 (51v A-B; pp. 314-16). Cf. *Cantica*, prologue, ch.4 (G1, 134v-135v; *Bibl.
ascetica* 11: 15-17); prologue, ch. 9 (11: 35); and Book I, ch. 5 (G1, 147v-148v; 11: 69-
74).

[28] *Rect*, II.5 (49r A; pp. 303-4). See appendix B for the full text and details regarding
Gerson's allusion to Arsenius [*Verba Seniorum* (V), translated by Pelagius, ch. 14, par. 7
(PL 73: 953-54)]. Kempf repeats this reference in ch. 28 of *De affectibus formandis in
horis*. See no. 21 in appendix A.

[29] *Rect*, II.6 (49v A, 32-42; p. 307). Cf. Gerson, *De mystica theologia practica*, con-
sid. 3 (Combes ed., pp. 140-43).

Cicero's description of an orator as cited by Gerson, Kempf defines a theologian as

> a good man, learned in sacred letters, but not only by the education of his intellect, rather much more by training the *affectus*. Thus those things that he understands through theology can be carried, in unceasing rumination, into the *affectus* of the heart and realized in works. Insofar as wisdom is a matter of tasting, according to its etymology, so it is sweet and joyful when dealing with good and it is sour and sorrowful when dealing with evil.[30]

In this manner, at Discipulus's request, Theologia expounds a method in which one might avoid the dangers of pride in learning and transfer all learning, whether theological or not, into the *affectus*, implementing it in actions. It is basic twelfth-century monastic theology.

The student who lives solely on an intellectual level from the spiritual food he ingests through reading and hearing receives no nourishment. Digestion is necessary; the food of the soul must be broken down by repeated chewing, i.e., rumination,[31] before it can fortify the *affectus*. Undigested intellectual food not only fails to nourish, but also distends the malnourished belly of the soul, injuring rather than benefiting, killing rather than bringing life. Too much of anything, even the honey of scripture, can make one sick.[32] Digestion takes place in a continual process of self-examination, a process of applying to oneself the material read or heard. For example: when reading of a certain sin, consider how often that vice is present in your own life; where scripture deals with a certain virtue, consider how lax you are in performing such works and plead

---

[30] *Rect*, II.6 (49v A, 42 - B, 11; p. 307). The extended quotation from Gerson is taken from *De consolatione theologiae*, IV.4 (*Oeuvres* 9: 237-38).

[31] This imagery goes back at least as far as Philo of Alexandria. See *De specialibus legibus* IV.107-8 in Philon d'Alexandrie, *Oeuvres*, vol. 24-25, ed. André Mosès (1970), 25: 264-67.

[32] *Rect*, II.8 (53r A, 23-36; p. 321): "Et in omnibus predictis potest quis ascendere usque ad affectum amoris Dei super omnia; qui est maxime meritorius, et finis omnium, ut dictum est. Si eciam predicta non observaveris, eris similis ei, qui multum comedit et nichil digerit, et ita repleto ventre fame moritur: quia sciencia multa sine affectu est cibus anime non digestus calore caritatis; et ita non nutrit, sed inflat; et ita non prodest, sed nocet; non vivificat, sed mortificat." For the source of this commonplace see Prov 25:16, 27 and Gregory the Great, *Moralia*, bk. 20, ch. 8, par. 18 (PL 76: 148AB; CCSL 143A: 1017), dealing with heretics who pursue divine things in vain curiosity and thus starve in sterility (Job 30:3: "egestate et fame steriles"); cf. Peter Abailard, *Sic et Non*, ed. Boyer and McKeon (1976-77), Prologue. See also Gerson, *Oeuvres*, 2:33; William of Saint-Thierry, *Golden Epistle*, I.31; Bernard of Clairvaux, *Sermones in Cantica* 7.5. Leclercq, *Love of Learning*, 73, gives additional citations. A related passage from Kempf's *Ost*, ch. 51, is cited in chapter one, p. 30, above; full text in appendix B.

with God for his grace that you might progress in that virtue.[33] If as a result your progress in learning slows, have no fear, for "it is far better and more secure and meritorious to know little, but to draw that which you know into the *affectus* and fulfill it in good works than to know many things in the intellect alone."[34] Such a learning process can be applied to the liberal arts, canon law, medicine, the observation of created things, or even to the singing of the choir office.

Discipulus remains unconvinced of the practicality of Theologia's affective method:

> If the Holy Fathers such as Augustine, Gregory, Ambrose, Jerome, and others like them had applied themselves in that way to transfer that which they read into the *affectus* and to acquire virtues, they could scarcely have become so advanced in learning, especially the modern scholastic doctors such as St. Thomas, Bonaventure, and others.

Theologia reminds him that carnal men who do not taste the things of the spirit may well consider pious virtue-building to be foolishness,

> but if you do not strive, according to the method mentioned above, to transfer those things that you read, teach, or hear, into the *affectus* and to fulfill them in works, though you may indeed be learned among men, you would be foolish in God's eyes. For you would be learned, yet irreligious [*doctus et indevotus*]; subtle, but not sublime in the eyes of God; great in repute [*fama*] but not in life; knowledgeable [*scientificus*], but not virtuous; illuminated in the intellect by knowledge, but darkened in the conscience. Thus you would be a light of this world, but not of heaven, because you are luminous, but not conscious; great in the church militant, but small indeed in the church triumphant.[35]

Discipulus here anticipates the results of Paul Saenger's research: as silent reading replaced oral, meditative, monastic *lectio*, it facilitated the retention and integration of a greater quantity of more complex cognitive material and prepared the way for scholastic, research-oriented scholarship.[36] Mistress Theology had counted the cost of her affective method

---

[33] *Rect*, II.8 (52r A-B; pp. 317-18).

[34] *Rect*, II.6 (50r B, 41 - 50v A, 1; pp. 309-10).

[35] *Rect*, III.9 and 11 (53r-54r, 54v-55v; pp. 321-25, 328-33), cf. II.14 (57r A-B; pp. 340-41). In the paragraphs that follow (57v A; p. 342), Kempf once more singles out Gerson, along with Heinrich of Langenstein, as famous practioners of this affective theology.

[36] "Silent Reading: Its Impact on Late Medieval Script and Society." *Viator*, 13 (1982), 367-414.

of theologizing. For her, for Nicholas Kempf, the religious reward of monastic, ruminative *lectio* was well worth the price it exacted in intellectual comprehensiveness.

3. Carthusian Solitude

One prerequisite for this process of digestion and transferral into the *affectus* is withdrawal into "solitude of spirit." Kempf is convinced that such solitude of spirit is most accessible in the monastic life, above all in the semi-eremitical life of the Carthusians.[37] The goal is solitude of spirit, not the simple exclusion of all acts of thought and affection, not mere torpidity. What is required is the exclusion of all useless and transitory things in order to fill the spirit with the divine *affectus* of love through meditation and contemplation of divine and spiritual things. The exclusion of human company—solitude of place—is not essential for solitude of spirit, but is an important aid, just as Christ's withdrawal into solitude on the mountain illustrates. In language reminiscent of the Carthusian statutes,[38] Theologia points out that nearly all the great *secreta* of God that have been revealed, were revealed in physical solitude, whether in the Old Testament, the New Testament, or the history of the Church: Jacob, Moses, Jeremiah, John the Baptist, Jesus Christ, John the Evangelist, the fathers of the desert, Jerome, Ambrose, Augustine, and Gregory all sought solitude of place (II.16). And in the tumultuous and iniquitous days of the end of the world, filled with schism and controversy in the church, it is all the more important that those who are called thereto withdraw into the solitude of the religious life.[39]

---

[37] *Rect.*, II.14 (57v B, 47 - 58r A, 7; pp. 343-44): "Quare diligentissime te admoneo, ut frequenter ad solitudinem cordis secedas; et ibi scienciam in affectum trahas, cogitando et te ipsum interrogando: Hodie legisti, disputasti, aut alios informasti de omnipotencia Dei. An igitur eum plus diligis?" [cited according to *Bibl. ascetica*; V1 has ". . . omnipotencia Dei. Plus enim timeas?"]. Cf. II.15 (58r B.33-39; p. 345): "Nam predicta de modo studendi, non solum in scientijs perficiendo intellectum, sed affectibus bonis et virtutibus perficiendo affectum, omni diligencia nocte dieque in scholis monasticis frequentantur: in quibus non tenditur finaliter ad multum scire, sed ad multum diligere. . . ." See also Leclercq, *Love of Learning*, 2-6, 237-59.

[38] Guigo I, *Consuet.*, ch. 80: "De commendatione solitarie vitae" (SC 313: 286-94, cf. PL 153: 755-58). Kempf adds the names of John the Evangelist, Augustine, Jerome, Gregory, and Ambrose; he deletes Hilarion, Antony (both of whom he presumably included under "desert fathers"), and Benedict.

[39] *Rect*, II.16 (59r B, 10-32; pp. 349-50): "Crede ergo michi, si haberes graciam eligendi solitudinem per religionis ingressum, plus quam unquam esset necessarium [cf. Lk 10:42]. Quippe cum nunquam priori tempore tantam legitur fuisse contradictionem et in-

Discipulus introduces various objections to the monastic life. As civic and political beings, humans seem ill-suited to a life of solitude, indeed, to live alone is contrary to nature.[40] Discipulus is concerned above all that the religious seem to be of little benefit to society as a whole or to the church. In response, in full accord with an older, medieval view of a society of the three orders, now fading in the face of sectarian,[41] civic, and humanist social views, Kempf's Theologia stresses the intercessory aspects of the monastic life, the prayers and groanings offered in the cloister for the sins and failures of the rest of society. Moreover, no one can hope to teach and instruct others until he has corrected his own infirmities; this is impossible unless he has recognized his weaknesses and failures. Nothing points out one's infirmities more efficiently than the monastic life. And the corruption and schism in the church as a whole can only be corrected by men who themselves live as virtuously and blamelessly as possible. By their holy example monastics instruct the church and accomplish more good than all those who "cast out devils in Christ's name" only to discover at the day of judgment that Christ had "never known them [Mt 7:22-23]."[42]

Theologia finds it strange that those who scrupulously struggle to discern whether the voice calling them to enter religion is divine or diabolical seldom suffer pangs of conscience when they think they perceive a vocation to ecclesiastical benefices or academic honors. Not everyone receives a monastic vocation—"he who is able to grasp this, let him receive it [Mt. 19:12]" becomes a slogan for Kempf. Those who have been called, like Abraham and Matthew, should not delay.[43] For those who

---

iquitatem in civitate ecclesie militantis, que iam raro diu stat sine schismate, et iam tali, de quo a seculo non est auditum, ita quod nec generalibus concilijs, a quo est tocius ecclesie auctoritas, obeditur. Et causam istius contradictionis propheta subiungit: quia iam in fine seculorum (ubi secundum Apostolum homines seipsos querunt, et se amant, et honores, divicias et dignitates [2 Tim 3:2]) tunc die ac nocte circumdabit eam super muros civitatis [Is 62:6?], prelatos videlicet ecclesie, iniquitas, et labor in medio eius et iniusticia: quia non deficit de plateis eius usura, dolus, et symonia, . . ." Cf. *Discr*, 3 (VS1, 36v B, 4-23; *Bibl. ascetica*, 9: 393-94).

[40] *Rect*, II.16-17 (58v-60r B; pp. 347-54). Cf. *Prop*, I.17/16 (VS1, 12r A, 28 - 12v B, 43).

[41] For a discussion of how Wyclif's "church of the elect" ecclesiology undermined the place of monastic orders, see Renna, "Wyclif's Attacks," esp. 275-79.

[42] Cf. *Discr*, ch. 4 (VS1, 37r B, 11-15; Pez, *Bibl. Ascetica*, 9: 396-97): "Si enim eis qui dicebant, 'Domine merito dabis nobis regnum celorum, quia in nomine tuo eiecimus demonia, et virtutes multas fecimus'; dictum fuit, 'nescio vos'."

[43] *Rect*, II.15 (58r B, 24; p. 345); II.26 (Vienna cvp 3616, 55v; p. 387); *Prop*, I.17/16 (VS1, 12r B, 15-25), cf. *Rect*, II.25 (missing in V1, found in Vienna cvp 3616, 53v, 14-17; p. 384): "Nemo mittens manum ad aratrum, et respiciens retro, aptus est regno Dei [Lk. 9:62]. Ita habens propositum, et respiciens retro per dilacionem, inabilis {erit} [MS: eit] ad consorcium Christi in conversacione regulari." Just such a delay is the root of Discipulus' dissatisfaction and poor progress in his studies. Cf. ibid. (385).

are called, the monastic life offers the most sure means, through the vows of obedience, poverty, and chastity, to fight the three sins that are the cause of the damnation of many (pride, avarice, and intemperance [*luxuria, gula*]).[44] Because a prior act of the will—the vow of obedience—accompanies the monk's specific acts of obedience, his merit is greater than that of people outside the world of monastic obedience.[45] *If* a monk acts in genuine obedience, the superior whom he obeys becomes accountable at the day of judgment for the monk's deeds. (The "if" looms large, of course.) Furthermore, although people in the world often start a good work, they seldom persevere. The monk recognizes this weakness and enters religion to strengthen externally his lack of inner resolve. He abandons the temptations that come with continued striving for academic degrees and greater knowledge; he lives a life of moderation. Above all, the monastic life brings the monk face-to-face with himself and reminds him of his limitations: "a great part of perfection is to recognize one's own weakness"[46] and to seek support from a community and from obedience to its rule—just as a lame man knows he needs a crutch.[47]

---

[44] See especially *Rect*, II.27 (Vienna cvp 3616, 57r-58v; pp. 390-94, esp. 57v, 6-16): "Verumtamen hoc teneas: quod non est [Pez: sit] facilior, securior, et brevior, atque perfeccior via aut status veniendi ad perfeccionem et ad vitam eternam, quam [Pez *add.* status] religionis. Et esto quod alique sint vie perfecciores vel status, ut episcoporum et, secundum alios [Pez: quosdam], omnium praelatorum et eciam simplicium curatorum sacerdotum; nullus tamen est tam securus, facilis, et tam brevis ad vitam eternam [Pez *add.* quam religiosorum]. Quod ex hoc patet: quia magister noster, qui est immensa patris sapientia, istam viam invenit et suasit, et non aliam, et haut dubium, si alia fuisset securior, pocius [Pez *add.* eam] hominibus suasisset." For Kempf's later statements about the "security" of the monastic life apart from the passages in *De recto fine* under discussion here, see the following: *Prop*, I.6/5 (VS1, 5v, A, 18 - 6r B, 13), cf. *Rect*, II.5 (48v A, 16-17, quoted above), and *De confirmatione*, 10/9 (V5, 13v, 18 - 14r, 16), the latter referring to William of Saint-Thierry's comparison of the monastic cell with heaven (*cella* and *coelum* (*Golden Epistle*, bk. 1, ch. 4; PL 184: 314); *De confirmatione*, 19/18 (V5, 28r, 1-10); *Discr*, 3 (VS1, 35v B, 7 - 36v B, 31, Pez, 9: 387-94); *De vera, perfecta, et spirituali caritate*, 4 (V2, 4v, 7 - 6r, 18); *De confirmatione*, 17/16 (V1, 90v-91r); *Ost*, 15 (G1, 10v, 32 - 11r, 4); *Serm. epist.*, no. 51 (G2, 79v-81v).

[45] Note the way Kempf qualifies this statement in *De discretione*, ch. 4, as discussed in chapter four of the present study.

[46] *Rect*, II.27 (Vienna cvp 3616, 58v; p. 394); Kempf's main statement on this theme is found in *Ost*, ch. 51, which is reproduced in appendix B.

[47] *Ost*, 51 (G1, 38v, 18-24): "Claudus per se non potest ambulare, sed innititur aliene virtuti aut adiutorio, ut baculuo, aut portanti se animali, aut homini suscentanti ipsum. Claudus ergo fit qui totaliter in sua virtute se deficere experimenialiter conspicit et se totaliter in Deum proicit, cuius virtuti innititur in ambulando pedibus amoris et gressibus virtutum, et totaliter et perfecte in Deo facit virtutem et non in se. Vocantur ergo et veniunt ad cenam Domini ad gustandum eterne vite dulcedinem, . . ." For the context see appendix B.

Kempf was not necessarily referring to all monastic orders. In Theologia's eyes, the Carthusian order is clearly superior to the others.[48] Not only did it originate in God's miraculous intervention *in fine saeculi* to rescue professors and students at the Paris university from the peril of academic pride, but it has maintained a purity of observance unknown in other monastic and religious orders. Kempf lists many reasons for this preservation of true observance: the "unique" *vita mixta* that combines the best of the eremitic and coenobitic lives; the rural settings far from the temptation and distraction of the cities; the presence of many learned men in the order[49]; the refusal to accept pastoral responsibilities outside the cloister; strict claustration (family visits are limited to absolute necessity, no women are permitted near the cloister, no secular persons can be buried in the cloister, the prior is forbidden to entertain guests privately); priors are not encumbered by the need to maintain a princely court or by pressures from noble relatives; Carthusian communities are free of episcopal jurisdiction; and the vow of stability is carefully safeguarded. Moreover, an important reason for Carthusian purity lies in the institutions of the annual General Chapter and biennial visitations of each charterhouse. Unlike the Benedictines, all Carthusian visitors carry authority to depose unworthy priors. "Above all, I think this Carthusian Order is governed and preserved by holy illiteracy [rusticitas] and simplicity and by God's grace more than by human knowledge and prudence acquired by study."[50]

Before one dismisses Kempf's apologetic as exaggerated propaganda, a look at the hurdles encountered by Benedictine reformers seeking to establish many of the above principles in Benedictine houses and the ultimate failure of the Benedictine observant movement indicates that Kempf knew what he was talking about[51]; it must have been rather self-

---

[48] See, in addition to *Rect*, II.18-31, the treatise *De confirmatione*, which repeats some portions of these chapters of *De recto fine* nearly verbatim.

[49] Cf. *De confirmatione*, 19/18 (V5, 28r-v).

[50] *Rect*, II.18-19 (Vienna cvp 3616, 41r-45v; pp. 355-65), esp. 42v, 3-14; p. 358: "Hec predicta, scilicet generale capitulum, et visitaciones, et priorum deposicio, vel absolucio inydoneorum aut excedencium, et, quantum fieri potest, dignorum et ydoneorum institucio, maxime conserva{n}t observanciam; et plusquam quelibet magna sciencia: quia in hoc ordine, quamvis non vigeat studium scienciarum, tamen observancie regularis et virtutum, quibus plus conservatur observancia quam magna scientia. Et precipue istum cartusiensem ordinem estimo plus regi et conservari sancta rusticitate et simplicitate et Dei gratia, quam humana scientia et prudencia per studium acquisita.

[51] Ibid., fol. 42v, 14-22; p. 358: "In alijs vero ordinibus, ubi non celebratur predicto modo capitulum generale, et non fiunt continue visitaciones, et prelatorum excedencium amoniciones [Pez: amotiones], tam diu durat observancia sicut prelatus vult: et per unum laxum, carnalem, et secularem prelatum tota observancia cadit in nichilum. Nec episcopi, nec papa curant illud, sed potius quandoque reformacioni, quam facere deberent, repug-

evident to an observer in the fifteenth century. The Carthusian approach to visitation shows an acute understanding of interpersonal dynamics in a human community. Monks and lay brethren alike were required to inform on each other, even when not directly asked about a particular type of offense. Yet the visitor was responsible to investigate any such accusations and was to understand his role as comprising both judge and defense attorney for the accused. He was to remind the community that one must always put the best possible construction on one's neighbor's actions—must always assume that even an apparent misdeed may have been done out of justifiable motives. The main purpose of the visitation was to locate and resolve conflict within the community. Surviving protocols show that the most frequent source of contention was liturgical observance—the point at which Carthusian monks had the most contact with each other and the most important means of integration and community-building in contemplative monastic communities. The liturgical and ceremonial life of the monastic microcosm was no round of *mere* ceremony; rather, patterned, repeated ritual was a load-bearing structural component of monastic life, as it was for much of premodern life. In the largely silent Carthusian world, it was especially easy to be irritated by what one read into another's gestures, expressions, or voice inflection, a point to which Kempf returns in his treatise *De suspicionibus* (appendix A, no. 11).[52] Thus, though the visitation system might appear inquisitorial and obtrusive to modern minds, it was carefully designed to nip in the bud the hidden and affective germ of discontent, the formative sources of dissension that seem unobtrusive to modern minds unattuned to the affective impact of (mere) ceremony.

Kempf devotes the third part of his dialogue to the chief threats to spiritual growth that face the theology student while he remains in the world. In counseling his reader on the best methods of combatting these dangers, Kempf again pursues a dual purpose. He wants to help those who study or live in the world avoid sin, but, by portraying the dangers of the world at such length, he also hopes to strengthen the resolve of his reader to enter the religious life.

Although the learned are usually sophisticated enough to avoid the most obvious moral defects—fornication, impurity, enmity, contention, anger, brawling, etc. [Gal 5:19-21]—there are many sins that pass for

---

nant: et ita sub uno prelato quandoque fit talis lapsus, qui nunquam vel diu non reformatur."

[52] See the fine study by Heinrich Rüthing, "'Die Wächter Israels': Ein Beitrag zur Geschichte der Visitationen im Kartäuserorden," in *Die Kartäuser*, ed. Zadnikar and Wienand, 169-83.

virtues and "no one is more diseased than he who thinks himself to be healthy [Augustine]." For the academic it is not carnal concupiscence, but spiritual or intellectual lust, above all pride or spiritual fornication, that leads to damning spiritual sin.[53] Unlike pride in temporal gain, which disappears when one is deprived of possessions, pride in learning continually renews itself and is virtually indestructible.[54] The academic is also susceptible to the vice of pertinacity, a vice that postures as a virtue, as a praiseworthy defense of one's viewpoint. Confidence in one's own prudence can be laudable if coupled with humility and willingness to learn from others. But confidence that has degenerated into pertinacity is the cause of much schism and heresy.[55]

Other dangers threaten: the desire to assume pastoral duties or other offices out of presumption or out of a desire to control others. A clear vocation or the mandate of one's superior to take up pastoral duties is praiseworthy, but the intentional pursuit of such responsibilities is full of peril to one's soul.[56] Indeed, the life of an academic theologian, priest, or prelate in the world, no matter how much he may hope to contribute to the good of church and society, is far more difficult than the monastic life of obedience to a rule and to one's superior. We must take careful note of Kempf's use of the term *cura animarum*. The context in which it is used, invariably referring to benefices, indicates that it does not imply direct pastoral activity so much as an ecclesiastical position. Kempf's intent was apparently not to denigrate such genuine pastoral activity as may have accompanied the holding of a benefice—saying mass, hearing confession—duties often performed by a hired vicar. But he seldom directly discusses pastoral activities, except within the monastic microcosm.

On the surface there would seem to be little that is novel or original either in Kempf's approach to theological studies or in his call to enter the religious life. Scholars appear to agree with this verdict: although Kempf's treatise on the end or purpose of studies has been allocated a niche in one of the survey histories of spirituality,[57] owing to its publica-

---

[53] *Rect*, III.2 (61r A, 33-41; p. 418). Cf. III.9 (67r-v; pp. 447-49).

[54] *Rect*, III.2 (61v A-B; p. 421).

[55] *Rect*, III.3 (62r A; p. 423); III.14 (71v A; p. 466). Cf. *De confirmatione*, 3 (V5, 5r, 12ff). See the letter from Johann of Speyer to Stephan of Spanberg at Melk in 1441 concerning whether it was a sin to desire to surpass others in learning. Pez and Hueber, *Cod. dipl.-hist.-epist.* (1729), pt. III, pp. 198-201.

[56] *Rect*, II.19 (Vienna cvp 3616, 43r-v; p. 360); III.4 (63r-64r A; pp. 427-33); III.13 (69v B - 71r B; pp. 459-65). On this theme see chapter six, below.

[57] See Vandenbroucke in Leclercq, Vandenbroucke, and Bouyer, *Spirituality* (1968), 462. Cf. Oediger, *Bildung* (1953), 14-15.

tion by Bernard Pez, and has been partially translated into modern German, few attempts have been made to fit it into its context in late medieval theology or monastic history.[58] Kempf's dependence on and appreciation for Gerson can scarcely be overestimated and it is most visible in *De recto fine*—a fact that is even more apparent in the manuscripts than in Pez's edition, which omits at least one extensive excerpt from Gerson.[59] Yet it is only when Kempf's program for the renewal of theology (in its dual meaning of academic study and the monastic life) is compared to that of the pre-Constance Jean Gerson that its outlines become clear.

4. The Monastic Crutch: Security rather than Superiority

Gerson and Kempf agree that theology must be lived out. For Kempf it is best lived out *die et noctu*, day and night, in the cloister. Whereas for Gerson, in his Paris renewal efforts, a theologian is essentially a shepherd of the souls of faithful parishioners, students, or of princes, Kempf's ideal is monastic. The *schola monastica* is the best place to be a theologian, to study (i.e., to pursue) *theologia*, to *do* theology. It is there, in that school of virtues, that the best theology results. At the same time, Kempf emphasizes that the *schola monastica* needs learned men. Especially in "these modern times," it is possible for the learned to bear much fruit in the religious life because nearly all the orders have declined, largely because of their poverty of learning. Did not

---

[58] The exception is the 1936 dissertation by Christian Dolfen, *Die Stellung des Erasmus von Rotterdam zur scholastischen Methode*. The terms that Dolfen employs, namely *theologia practica* and *sola scriptura* are not adequate labels under which to group the three figures Dolfen studies: Gerson, Kempf, Erasmus. Although Kempf considered scripture to be the foundation of theology and insisted on a knowledge of scripture as the first qualification of a true theologian, an impulse "back to the Bible" and the slogan "sola scriptura," are not the key to Kempf's program for renewing theology. Scripture had always been the foundation for traditional monastic theology and it continued to play that role for Kempf. The differences between Kempf and Gerson are dealt with below. As far as Kempf and Erasmus are concerned, Erasmus failed to grasp the indispensability of the cloistered and structured element in the monastic ideal, as is evident in his easy talk of the city-as-cloister (in the letter to Paul Volz that precedes Erasmus' *Enchiridion*). Erasmus also placed more hope in education and more blame on ignorance than did Kempf, for whom education's chief value is the acquisition of discretion by humility and obedience rather than by study. Erasmus' ideal, when compared to Kempf's, is universal, transcending the various orders. Kempf's is provincial: precisely because structures are crucial, it is his order's attention to structures that permits it to preserve best the universal ideal transmitted from the desert fathers onward.

[59] Compare V1, 41v A, 44 - 42r A, 16, with *Bibl. ascetica* 4: 271.

Augustine point out that the religious life holds great profit for the learned who wish to use their *scientia* in humility and fear of God? Not only has the presence of a few learned and proven men preserved the observance of a regular life in many monasteries, but the Carthusian order owes its continuous *observantia bona* to the high percentage, indeed, the dominance, of former university members.[60] In a sense Kempf was advocating a Carthusian *ad fontes* movement: he asserted elsewhere that the order had consisted almost exclusively (*pene solum*) of former university men for its first forty years.[61] Kempf understood his call to be a return to primitive Carthusian practice.

Unlike Gerson at Paris (i.e., before his disillusionment and the reorientation of his reform theology in the wake of the Council of Constance), who praised the ambidextrous life of the prelate and parish priest during his efforts at renewal,[62] Kempf offered single-handed contemplative monasticism as the key to renewal. Yet for all his praise and apologetic defense of monastic life, Kempf never fell into a utopianism that would confuse the monastic life with heaven or the kingdom of God. For him, the monastic rule, the structured life, the boundaries of the cloister walls, were a God-given yet human-governed instrument, a means to reach a larger end: love of God. Kempf believed the monastic life was the most secure means for doing theology, and he challenged university theologians to abandon their perilous life in the world, but he did not forget the instrumentality even of the monastic vocation.[63] The monastic life was an "angelic life" and foretaste of heaven that was nonetheless lived out within clearly human boundaries and structures.[64]

---

[60] See *Prop*, I.9/8 (VS1, 7v B - 8r A) and 17/16 (VS1, 12r B, 17 - 12v 20); *De confirmatione*, 6/5 (V1, 82v A, 37-41) and ch. 19/18.

[61] *De confirmatione*, 6/5 (V1, 82v A, 34-37).

[62] As Mark Burrows points out, *Gerson*, 139-43, 256-59, part of the shift undergone by Gerson in the last portion of his life involved a dramatic modification of his former "stubborn advocacy" of the ideal of *viri ambidextri* in favor of contemplative *viri solitarii* whose office was prayer and hope. In this way Gerson's later theology resembles Kempf's monastic theology of repentant weeping to a remarkable degree. Kempf drew from both the early and the late Gerson.

[63] Kempf is simply following on the monastic tradition here, as illustrated by Nicholas of Dinkelsbühl's sermon to a Carthusian community, presumably Gaming, Aggsbach, or Mauerbach, which cites John Cassian (*Conference* I, ch. 7 [SC, 42: 84; trans. Luibheid, p. 42]). See Madre, ed., "Sermo magistri Nicolai," 198, 205 (faithfulness to tradition).

[64] For the angelic metaphor in monastic literature see Karl Suso Frank, *Aggelikos Bios: Begriffsanalytische und begriffsgeschichtliche Untersuchung zum "engelgleichen Leben" im frühen Mönchtum* (1964); Gerhart B. Ladner, *The Idea of Reform* (1959), 326, n. 17; Brown, *Body and Society*, 329-31; Leclercq, *Love of Learning*, esp. 71-72. For the Carthusian context, see the bulls of Urban II (1091) and Innocent II (1133) describing the Carthusians as living the angelic life in the ante-chamber of heaven in Ber-

This, it seems to me, is one of the most significant results of Jean Leclercq's careful study of *otium, se-curitas, vacatio, quies,* and related words in Hebrew, classical, and Christian history. All of these words had and continue to have passive and therefore, for most people, negative connotations in Latin, English, and other languages. Beginning with Cicero and Seneca, but especially in the thought of Augustine and the medieval monastic tradition, this entire cluster of words was given a parallel set of positive connotations.[65] This is what lies behind Kempf's emphasis on *securitas.*[66] Turning a liability into an instrument of perfection, turning weakness into strength was possible because of the "foolishness of the cross" and Christian belief in the Incarnation. Monasticism provided a "foolish" critique of activism and moralism in their various forms: bureaucratic, militaristic, imperialist, speculative, phallic, dynastic. Yet it also managed to institutionalize what was at first a counter-cultural "folly." The office of the monk is to weep in repentance, not to reconstruct and rectify.[67]

---

nard Bligny, ed., *Recueil des plus anciens actes de la Grande-Chartreuse (1086-1196)* (1958), 15-16, 51.

[65] Significantly, for humanists such as Leon Battista Alberti *ozio* once more became a sin, indeed, "the worst of sins." Protestant and sectarian reformers employed "idleness" as a central term of opprobrium in their attack on monasticism. See the comments by Charles Trinkaus, "Luther's Hexameral Anthropology," in *Continuity and Discontinuity in Church History* [G. H. Williams Festschrift] (1979), 150-68 (repr. 1983).

[66] On *securitas* as freedom, perfect rest from *curae,* see Johannes Altenstaig, *Vocabularius theologie* (1517), fol. CCXXXIv-CCXXXIIr. A convenient glimpse of the roots of the Carthusian tradition on *otium,* repose, silence, and withdrawal, is found in Guigo, I, *Letter 1* in *Lettres des premiers chartreux,* vol. 1, SC 88: 111-12; these themes also run through Guigo I's *Meditations.* Cf. André Wilmart, "L'appel a la vie cartusienne suivant Guiges l'ancien," *RAM,* 14 (1933), 337-48, at 346-47, and Mursell, *Theology,* esp. 120-24. On good and bad leisure in Cistercian circles, see William of St. Thierry, *Golden Epistle,* bk. I, ch. XXI, par. 81 (PL 184: 321; SC 223, p. 206; CF 12: 38): "Omnium autem tentationum et cogitationum malorum et inutilem sentina otium est. Summa etenim mentis malitia est otium iners. Nunquam otiosus sit servus Dei, quamvis a Deo feriatus sit." Note also *Regula Benedicti,* ch. 48, verses 1, 7-8, 9, 24-25. Jean Delumeau sees the pursuit of *securitas* as having been central to the emergence of modern *mentalité,* but is apparently unaware of the role this word played in monastic tradition. In many ways Delumeau's book focuses on a worldly foil to monastic *securitas.* See *Rassurer et protéger: Le sentiment de sécurité dans l'Occident d'autrefois* (1989), and two articles Delumeau cites as having helped inspire his book: Jean Halpérin, "La notion de sécurité dans l'histoire économique et sociale," *Revue d'histoire économique et sociale,* 30 (1952), 7-25; Lucien Febvre, "Pour l'histoire d'un sentiment: Le besoin de sécurité," *Annales: Economies, Sociétés, Civilisations,* 11 (1956), 244-47.

[67] See the discussion of George Grant's understanding of "lament" as a response to activism and technology in the Epilogue to the present study. Note also Leclercq, *Love of Learning,* 396, n. 95, on the *officium plangandi* as the central purpose of monastic life, citing the phrase from Jerome that was commonly repeated by monks: "Monachus autem non doctoris habet, sed plangentis officium." Dieter Mertens, "Kartäuser-Professoren," p. 78, cites several more instances of the *topos.*

As John Cassian put it, both the beginning and the end of the monastic life are from God; monks are left with the middle as the arena of
their human efforts.[68] Deeply embedded in the ancient monastic tradition, the practice of discernment (*discretio*) continually reminded monks
of their limits. As taught by John Cassian, John Climacus (d. ca. 649),
and the *Pastoral Rule* of Gregory the Great, "discretion" emphasized the
skill gained from long experience. With this wisdom a spiritual director,
the "abba" ("apa") of the Egyptian and Syrian deserts, shaped and
formed the young monk, adjusting his prescriptions and guidance, his
"modus loquendi," to meet the novice's pastoral needs (see chapter four,
below).

Reacting to the extreme claims of mendicant theologians regarding
the superiority of the monastic life, the early Gerson considered the
evangelical counsels (vows of poverty, chastity, obedience, etc.) to be
merely instruments.[69] Kempf considered them marvelous and secure
means. Gerson insisted that Christ's "gentle yoke" (Mt 11:30) refers to
the minimal requirements of lay Christianity; Kempf insisted that precisely the monastic rule, because it liberates from anxiety and cares and
brings peace (*otium*), because it makes the monk no longer his own master, is Christ's gentle yoke.[70] In John Cassian's view, the yoke of Christ

---

[68] *Conference* II, ch. 11-12 (SC, 42: 155-57; Luibheid trans. pp. 92-94).

[69] See Burger, *Aedificatio*, 176-93, for a summary of Gerson's pre-Constance views
regarding the monastic life, esp. 180-84. In working out his clerical spirituality, Gerson
insisted that bishops not only have the task of perfecting, they also have the lower tasks
of cleansing (purgation) and illuminating. Priests likewise purify, illumine, and perfect
those who are subject to them. In contrast, monks pursue only their own salvation. They
do not vicariously perfect or illumine others. Gerson is reacting to mendicants, but also
to Bernard of Clairvaux, whom he interprets as saying that monks have a special access
to salvation in the second baptism of monastic vows. (That Bernard was arguing thereby
for the superiority of the monastic life in the same manner as the mendicants seems
doubtful—he could be interpreted in a manner similar to Kempf, and at issue is security,
not superiority, as *Rect*, II.27, quoted in n. 44, above, shows. For Bernard see Hugo
Feiss, "St Bernard's Theology of Baptism and the Monastic Life," *CS*, 25 (1990), 79-91,
at 84-85.) The early Gerson insists that monastic life is inferior because monks can become fearful and uneasy through the addition of human traditions and as a result of the
many opportunities for conflict with their superiors. Instead, all Christians should come
to one Abbot, Jesus Christ, whose yoke is easy (Mt 11:30). The early Gerson served as
an authority for the *Augsburg Confession* on this point. See *The Book of Concord*, trans.
Theodore G. Tappert (1959), 80.

[70] For Gerson see Burger, *Aedificatio*, 180-84. In the Carthusian tradition, Bruno used
this verse in his letter to Raoul le Verd, the letter that describes Bruno's own monastic
conversion. See *Lettres des premiers Chartreux*, vol. 1, SC 88: 74. It was incorporated
into the prayer prayed over a novice making his profession. See Guigo I, *Consuet.*, ch.
25.1, SC 313: 218. Guigo de Ponte also made use of it in *De contemplatione*, II.1 (Du-
Pont ed., p. 176). Guigo de Ponte does not cite the portion of Mt 11:28-30 that refers to
Christ's "gentle yoke" but he is making the same point: in order to lay down the burden
of one's sins one must come to Christ, go out of oneself. Louis Leloir, "La sagesse des

seems hard to endure only to those who fight against it and who refuse to give up control over themselves, control which they never really possessed.[71]

Kempf and Gerson might well have agreed that it takes a stronger person to live the Christian life outside the monastery walls; they might have concurred in the insight that functionally, even if not formally, the lay Christian life is the route of supererogation.[72] Yet while the early Gerson condescendingly labeled monks weak and lame because they needed the crutch of monastic vows,[73] Kempf meekly and gladly embraced weakness, lameness, and blindness because all of these remind one of one's need for grace. For Kempf it is pious lay people who are sadly confused: they underestimate the power of sin in their lives and the magnitude of the grace of perseverence required to struggle against sin. It is *possible* to fulfill the counsels of perfection in the world, he would admit, but secular people fail to persevere because of the fragility and instability of the human spirit: people become bored with the pursuit of holiness unless they have help from institutional structures.[74] Monks are

---

ancien moines," *Studia missionalia*, 28 (1979), 61-95, esp. 77-95, repeatedly refers to discretion as authority based on gentleness, mercy, and humility, citing many examples from the Desert Fathers. Cf. the statement of the five Carthusian priors who gathered at the Grande Chartreuse in 1141 at the request of its prior, Anthelm, to establish a formal structure for the emerging order. Obedience to the General Chapter is specifically described as the gentle yoke and light burden; they are willing to bear it without tiring. Bligny, *Recueil*, 57.

[71] See Kempf, *Rect*, II.15 (58r B, 33 - 58v A, 21; p. 345-46), and Cassian, *Conference* 24, ch. 22-25 (SC 64: 193-99; NPNF, ser. 2, 11: 541-43).

[72] Kempf explicitly refers to the monastic life as the life of supererogation in *Ost*, ch. 13 (G1, 9r, 8 - 9v, 18, cited in n. 74, below) and in *Discr*, ch. 3 (VS1, 35v B, 30-34; 9: 388, see chapter four, p. 126, below). But he is equally explicit about the fact that salvation does not depend on fulfilling the evangelical counsels—the evangelical precepts alone suffice.

[73] Burger, *Aedificatio*, 187-90.

[74] *Ost*, ch. 13 (G1, 9r, 8-27, 9v, 7-18). "Si mens perfectius debet purgari, oportet hominem ex humilitate, paciencia, et obediencia non solum precepta sed eciam consilia implere et ita ex perfecciori gradu virtutum predictarum trium purgata mente illuminari et Deo uniri; quorum consiliorum implecionem et virtutes pertinentes ad contemplativos seu vitam contemplativam docet magister noster Dominus Ihesus Matheo 19 capitulo quasi per totum, et non precipit sed consulit, et consulendo aut hortando vocat ad sui imitacionem per consiliorum implecionem. Et quamvis seculares homines possent consilia implere et ea que sunt supererogacionis opera virtutum obediencie, humilitatis, paciencie, et paupertatis exercere, tamen rarissimum et difficillimum est continuare propter humane mentis fragilitatem et instabilitatem; ut quod hodie incipit, cras postponit, et iterum aliud facere temptat, quod statim ex tedio repudiat. Qui enim voluerit perfecte purgari et virtutes perfecciores acquirere, oportet ipsum infatigabiliter et perseveranter continuare opera virtutum, non solum neccessaria ad salutem, sed eciam que sunt supererogacionis: ut humiliare se non solum coram deo et superioribus quando et quantum oportet, sed coram omnibus. . . . Et quia hoc sic continuare in seculari vita est multum difficile et multis

the ones who are realistic about discerning sin. The monastery is a school for recovering, not recovered, sinners; an incessant session of Sinners Anonymous. The monastic structures are marvelous means rather than mere instruments precisely because they are channels of the grace of God, the grace without which no one can be saved.[75]

In short, though the episcopal and pastoral offices may indeed be more perfect paths or states of life, the monastic path is more secure, easier, and shorter. For Kempf, the monastic life is *securior*, not *perfectior*, and only in its greater *securitas* does any sort of *superioritas* reside.[76]

Indeed, Kempf explicitly asserts that the very vocation to the monastic life is by grace alone. Whereas no one lacks first, or prevenient, grace (the damned are those who fail to attend to the stimulus of first grace),[77] the vocation to enter religion is given only to a few.[78] To those who are called God gives a certain *instinctus* to fulfill the evangelical counsels (*Rect*, III.15). Fear of God prepares for prevenient grace; concomitant grace prepares the will to follow and persevere in the stimulus of prevenient grace toward the monastic life (III.17). Kempf leaves no doubt about the nature of prevenient grace and its relation to human effort:

---

impossibile, ideo eterna Dei sapiencia infinita invenit consilium quod dedit hominibus per quod possent predicta perseveranter exercere, et sic purgari perfecte, et illuminari, et Deo perfecte uniri, secundum presentis vite statum, scilicet per religionis ingressum; et votum obligandi se secundum certum vivendi modum a Spiritu Sancto inspiratum et ab ecclesia approbatum, in quo multa tenetur facere ad que ante votum non tenebatur: ut orare, vigilare, ieiunare, cantare; et a multis prius licitis abstinere: ut a colloquio, a carnibus, a lineis vestimentis et alijs multis, que omnia sunt instituta ut virtutes facilius acquirantur et vicia perfeccius extirpentur, ut mens illuminetur et uniatur Deo perfecto amore." Note that the religious state has been instituted as a concession to the needs of this present life in order that virtues may *more easily* (*facilius*) be acquired. It is indeed a gentle yoke.

[75] *Ost*, ch. 24 (G1, 16v, 27 - 17r, line 18), cf. *Cantica*, IV.9 (Pez, *Bibl. ascetica*, 11: 420-25). See chapter four for a detailed exposition of these passages.

[76] See *Rect*, II.27 (Vienna cvp 3616, 57v, 8-10: "Et esto quod alique sint vie perfecciores vel status, ut episcoporum et, secundum alios [Pez: quosdam], omnium praelatorum et eciam simplicium curatorum sacerdotum; nullus tamen est tam securus, facilis, et tam brevis ad vitam eternam [Pez *add*. quam religiosorum]" (quoted with context in note 44, above).

[77] *Rect*, III.20 (V1, 75v B, 26-39; *Bibl. ascetica* 4: 486): "Scio eciam nunc apertissime quod salvacio hominis est primo et principaliter a Deo, sed dampnacio hominis est a seipso. Nam prima disposicio pro salute hominis est gracia preveniens seu instinctus qui nulli deest. Sed quia, cum homines deberent sequi per liberum arbitrium adiuvante gracia concomitante, tunc negligunt, renuunt, aut contempnunt. Et sic sue dampnacionis cause sunt." For Augustine's similar insistence on the special grace of God in monastic vocation, see Adolar Zumkeller, *Augustine's Ideal of the Religious Life* (1986), 260-62.

[78] *Prop*, I.17/16 (VS1, 12r B, 19-21): "Quod paucissimis Deus dat graciam interne vocacionis et inspiracionis pro religionis ingressu."

Prevenient grace . . . is not a *habitus mentis*, but a certain stirring, thinking, or instigating that is commonly called a divine *instinctus*. It stimulates
and stirs up inside the spirit whatever is good for one's own salvation. This
instinctus, or stirring, cannot be had *ex puris naturalibus*, but is by the free
gift of God. [Previenient grace includes,] e.g., the first stirring or first
thought of detesting sin because it offends God; the first stirring or first
thought of doing something good to the honor of God and one's own salvation; the first stirring of fear of God; the inner goad to despise the world
for love of Christ.[79]

Kempf does assume some sort of human *cooperatio* in the grace-inspired *praeparatio* for a vocation to enter religion. Prevenient grace must
be warmed and incubated by the heat of prayer and the moisture of the
fear of God moderated with hope. Ascetic training during the novitiate
weans the soul from the vices of the world. But above all, the *praeparatio* for the grace of vocation to the monastic life consists in begging God
to supply what one *lacks*, it consists in devout prayer and humble peti-
tioning of God to grant his grace, both to enter and persevere in religion.[80]

The *modus loquendi* of the contemplative monastic life suits those
who need to learn the rules of grammar before they can speak the language of mystical union. Kempf would give his blessing to those who
can learn the language of the love of God and neighbor, of mystical *theologia*, directly, without the external structure of the monastic life. But he
would have insisted that such people are few and that most who try to
learn the language of love outside the monastery end up speaking in broken phrases.

Kempf's call to return to a nonscholastic, monastic theology was
also a proposal to meet the needs of the church in his day. It may be ob-

---

[79] *Rect* III.17(V1, 74r B, 4-22; *Bibl. ascetica* 4: 478-79): "Gracia ergo preveniens in
propositio non est habitus mentis, sed quidam motus, cogitacio vel instigacio, qui vocatur communiter instinctus divinus, quasi intus in mente instigans et stimulans ad aliquid,
quod valet ad salutem propriam. Qualis instinctus vel motus non potest haberi ex puris
naturalibus, sed ex dono gratuito Dei, verbi gracia, motus primus vel cogitacio prima de-
stestacionis peccatorum propter Dei offensam; aut motus primus vel cogitacio faciendi
aliquod bonum propter Dei honorem et propriam salutem; motus timoris Dei; stimulacio
interior de contemptu seculi propter amorem Christi."

[80] *Rect*, III.18-21 (V1, 74v-77r; *Bibl. ascetica*, 4: 480-86). See also *Prop*, II.23 (VS1,
34r A, 24-25): ". . . professio facienda sit pro suo [scil. Dei] honore et anime mee salute,
hec humilitatis peticio, ex corde facta, est disposicio previa ad graciam in professione a
Deo infundendam"; ibid., I.5 (VS1, 5r B, 36-40); I.6/5 (VS1, 6r B, 9-11) [quoting William of St. Thierry on those predestined to the monastic cell]; II.1 (VS1, 20v B - 21r B)
on the grace of being clothed as a novice.

jected, as both Discipulus and, in another context, Johann of Eych, the
Bishop of Eichstätt, objected (chapter six, below), that Kempf's call to
the scholar and potential pastor to leave the world and avoid pastoral responsibilities would weaken the cause of reform and impair the renewal
of spiritual life in the church. In the following chapters we shall look in
greater detail at Kempf's understanding of the role of contemplatives and
monastics in the church and his ideal for the pastor within the cloister.
For the present, it is perhaps enough to recall the undercurrent of quiet,
but not bitter, resignation in certain passages in *De recto studiorum
fine*[81]—for *gelassenheit* and *resignatio* are central to his monastic theology of meekness, weakness, lameness, and blindness, a theology we
shall examine in various facets throughout the rest of this book. Kempf
had given up hope for the conciliar approach to reform, and his attitude
is not surprising against the backdrop of the Vienna Concordat. Although
Benedictine observant reform was still flourishing, Kempf had chosen
the option of the Carthusian life instead, because it was not dependent on
pressure from princes, councils, or popes to accomplish *reformatio*.[82]
How often hope for assistance from princes, popes, or councils had
brought only disillusionment. Kempf placed his hope in the *solitudo
mentis* of the Carthusian cottage, in silence and flight from the fray, ultimately in the grace of God, the sole *Reformator* of both interior and exterior Christian life. "*Qui potest capere, capiat* [Mt 19:12]."

---

[81] *Rect*, I.3 (41r-v; pp. 266-70); III.3 (62r A - 63r A; pp. 423-27).

[82] *De ostensione* closes with an explicit affirmation—citing "all the holy fathers" as
its authority—that the poor (the weak, blind, lame) in spirit more often than not are those
who are indeed poor in social status. Kempf is not preaching social revolution here—low
social status does not guarantee poverty of spirit, i.e., meekness, rather meekness is the
fundamental condition upon which the vision of God is granted. Yet poverty of spirit is
rarely found in those of exalted social status. *Ost*, ch. 53 (G1, 40r, 25 - 40v, 4): "Ex
quibus patet quod simplices et indocti in vili statu constituti, tamen humiles et devoti et
in fide divites, facilius possunt proficere ad videndum regni Dei, eciam in presenti vita,
quam multum docti et in sublimioribus constituti; quia predicte condiciones—ut sint pauperes, debiles, ceci, et claudi—frequencius et perfeccius inveniuntur in simplicibus quam
in sublimibus personis. Nam secundum omnes sanctos patres, si debet regnum Dei ostendi et creator per experimentalem suiipsius gustum intrare mentem, oportet prius exire
omnem creaturam, hoc est omnem actum potenciarum, id est omnes cogniciones et omnes appeticiones aut voliciones cessare et omnem speciem intelligibilem aut sensibilem
et talem mentem perfecte humiliari, et ex simplici et firma fide totaliter se in Deum
proicere ut ipse operetur in sua ymagine; quod in doctis et alti status hominibus raro invenitur."

5. Vienna Academics and Kempf's Schola Monastica

Who had ears to hear and receive the hard sayings of Christ as pro-
claimed by Nicholas Kempf? We can assess the impact of Kempf's call
in at least two ways: first, the personal influence of his call, directed especially at university students and masters, to enter the monastery,[83] and
second, the influence of his writings. Because records of the members of
the Carthusian community at Gaming are relatively comprehensive prior
to and including the year 1458 when one of the monks, Wilhelm Hofer,
drew up a list for a visitation delegation,[84] we can draw some conclusions regarding the numbers and sorts of people who heard and acted on
Kempf's call to the *schola monastica* and thereby construct a sort of
prosopographical balance sheet. Its bottom line suggests that charterhouses, not Benedictine abbeys (as argued by Virgil Redlich), deserve—
loosely, to be sure—the rubric "outposts of the University of Vienna."

Analyzing the influence of Kempf's writings is more difficult. Examining the numerous manuscripts containing his Carthusian and Benedictine contemporaries' writings, or the works of the next generation of
monastics in Austrian and Bavarian houses for traces of his influence is
beyond the scope of this study. We can, however, review the pattern of
the dispersal of Kempf's writings and draw tentative conclusions in several isolated cases where we know definitely who read certain works by
Kempf.

The influx of Vienna academics into the monastery at Gaming during Kempf's priorate has been recognized for centuries. B. Baillie, who
completed Pez's edition of Kempf's commentary on the Canticle,[85] referred to five masters and seven *baccalaurei* who entered Gaming during

---

[83] For the context in the Carthusian order, see Mertens, "Kartäuser-Professoren," 80-
81. He notes that twelve of forty-five "viri illustri" in Theodor Petreius, *Bibliotheca Cartusiana sive illustrium sacri cartusiensis ordinis scriptorum catalogus* (1609; repr.
1968), had university educations.

[84] The Hofer list is found, in autograph, in Vienna cvp 12811 and in a copy annotated
by Leopold Wydemann in Steyerer, "Collectanea." The list was published with supplementary annotations in the article by Zeißberg, "Gaming," 572-96. All tables referred to
here are found in appendix C.

[85] *Bibl. ascetica*, 11:5r. Augustine Rösler, *Der Kartäuser Nikolaus Kempf und seine
Schrift über das rechte Ziel und die rechte Ordnung des Unterrichts* (1894), 265, says
that Gaming reached the peak of its five-and-one-half-century existence under Kempf.
Hörmer, "Kempf," also emphasized the influx of Vienna university members, asserting
that Kempf to a large degree was responsible.

the years Kempf was prior (1451-58). These statistics will take on added significance when we consider the careers of the individuals involved, noting the percentage of *magistri regentes* among them and the positions they attained in governing Gaming and other charterhouses.

A comparison of university-trained religious at Gaming with those at Melk, Tegernsee, and other Benedictine houses in the area served by the University of Vienna, make the numbers and descriptions of the Gaming monks all the more impressive. Although the evidence for Kempf's influence remains partly circumstantial, taken in its entirety, it is not inconsequential. The flowering of the monastic community at Gaming coincided with Kempf's presence, and his contemporaries, subsequent generations of monks, and eighteenth-century monastic historians all testified to his role in that flowering.

A study of Wilhelm Hofer's list reveals that seventeen former Vienna masters (eighteen including Kempf) were members of the Gaming community in 1458 (table 1). All but one can be verified in Vienna university records of one sort or another. Eight, plus Kempf, are found in the list of teaching masters, and the others at least appear in the Vienna university matriculation register. None were mentioned in the *Acta* of the theological faculty. All but two entered Gaming between 1440 and 1456. The interval between their promotion to master of arts and entry into religion was short, usually one or two years. This indicates that few began careers as secular priests or schoolmasters before entering the monastery. Five of the seventeen former masters entered the charterhouse at Gaming roughly contemporaneously with Kempf (ca. 1436-43). Whether Kempf was the dominant influence in their decisions or whether all of these, Kempf included, shared a common motivation from some other source, is unclear. That Kempf had an important role to play in the vocations of the twelve who entered Gaming after 1442-43 is quite probable.

In sum, Gaming numbered fifty-two professed members in 1458, although only twenty-four lived there,[86] the others being scattered throughout Austrian, Hungarian, and Moravian charterhouses. At least seventeen of the fifty-two, one-third of the professed members of the Gaming community in 1458, were *magistri artium*. Eight of them served as priors at Gaming or elsewhere during the fifteenth century, and three more held other offices at Gaming.

---

[86] See Hogg, "Gaming" in *DHGE*, 19 (1981), 19: 988-97. Wydemann's statistics for monks, *redditi*, and *conversi* actually living at Gaming show remarkable consistency over the centuries: 36 in 1396; 39 in 1458; 33 in 1480; 29 in 1719. See Steyerer, "Collectanea," 380r. For a definition of the status of *redditus*, see appendix A.

Vienna masters were not the only academics attracted to the charter-house at Gaming. Between 1432 and 1458, fifteen other Vienna students entered religion there (table 2). Nearly all are referred to by Hofer as bachelors of arts; for most of them, their presence at Vienna, if not their degrees, can be verified in the matriculation register. One, Conrad (Bäuerlein?) of Speyer, was a canon regular at St. Pölten before becom-ing a Carthusian. Judging from the dates of their matriculation at Vienna, most appear to have entered Gaming directly from the university. (Chry-sogonus Hebenkrieg [Habenkrieg, Hebemkrieg] of Krems came to Gam-ing in 1473 after professing in 1467 at Tegernsee.[87]) Four of these bachelors of arts became priors of charterhouses, six others held offices at Gaming or at other charterhouses. Clearly the university-educated re-ligious were favored for positions of leadership. Taken together, Vienna masters and bachelors of arts constituted at least one-half of the Gaming monks in 1458.[88]

It may not have been Kempf who convinced all of these Vienna teachers and students to enter the monastery, since Gaming was "the most important charterhouse in German-speaking regions."[89] Long be-fore Kempf's time it had furnished priors for other charterhouses,[90] and was obviously attractive to university members interested in the monas-tic life. But Kempf's apologetic for the Carthusian life in *De recto stu-diorum fine* and *De confirmatione* may well have had much to do with the increasing numbers of university-educated postulants in the 1440s and 1450s. When compared to profession lists for Melk, Mondsee, and Tegernsee, Wilhelm Hofer's list is unique in the attention given to uni-versity backgrounds, indicating that the unusual percentage of former academics at Gaming was noteworthy during Kempf's lifetime.

Kempf's name was known in university circles. When a group of students sought refuge from the plague by retreating to Gaming (1461), it was the hospitality of the former prior, Kempf, that they recalled in a letter to the son of the Augsburg patrician and humanist, Sigismund

---

[87] Großmann, "Frühzeit," 229, numbers Hebenkrieg among the members of the earli-est humanist circle at Vienna.

[88] The former university members at Gaming came from diverse regions: from Brno in Moravia; from Buda in Hungary; from German cities such as Würzburg, Speyer, Pas-sau, and Munich; and from Austrian towns closer to Gaming (Mödling, Krems, Zisters-dorf, Pöchlarn, Scheibbs).

[89] Hogg, "Gaming," in *DHGE*.

[90] See Zeißberg, "Gaming," 581, regarding Johann of Mergentheim, prior of Pleterje and Lövöld; Müller, "Personalien," 166ff, lists the priors at Olomouc. On the Moravian charterhouses see Jaroslav Vanis, "Die Kartäuser in den böhmischen Ländern," *Analecta Cartusiana*, n.s. 1, no. 2 (1989), 105-12.

Gossembrot, passing on Kempf's greetings to him. The copyist of Kempf's *Memoriale primorum principiorum* indicated that Kempf was still known and respected at the university of Vienna in 1491.

To gain a broader perspective, we look next at the situation at Melk. Here former Vienna professors were among the inaugurators of the Melk reform: Nicholas Seyringer of Matzen and Petrus of Rosenheim left the university in 1403 for observant Benedictine houses in Italy. Between 1403 and 1453, ten, possibly eleven, masters of arts are known to have entered Melk (two by way of Subiaco in Italy; table 4).[91] Of these, five can be identified as *magistri regentes*, or teaching masters. Two of them, Stephan of Spanberg and Konrad Mülner of Nürnberg, appear to have entered Melk first and then returned to Vienna for theological studies. Another held an M.A. degree from Heidelberg before he came to Melk (John Wischler of Speyer). Two were members of the theological faculty before entering Melk early in the fifteenth century (Nicholas Seyringer, M.A. 1395; Urban of Melk, D.Th. 1413). One, Stephan Kolb of Weiten, was a close friend of Georg Peuerbach, the proto-humanist astronomer.[92] As at Gaming, these university-trained religious held important offices. Three were abbots at Melk or other Benedictine houses. Most entered Melk directly from the university. Johannes Schlitpacher of Weilheim was employed as a teacher—at Melk!—for a year before he became a postulant.

Data regarding bachelors of arts at Melk are less clear (table 5), since Kropff frequently refers vaguely to those who entered the monastery "ex studente." We know of eleven specifically designated as *baccalaurei*. Among the twenty-one postulants between 1420 and 1460 who may have studied for some time at Vienna, at least nine probably did not acquire the bachelor's degree. Seven of the twenty-one became priors or abbots at Melk or other houses. The monastic community apparently sent two of them, Wolfgang Frischmann of Emerstorff and Johannes of Obernberg, to Vienna for their studies (1434), since they are listed in the

---

[91] The sources for these figures are Kropff, *Bibliotheca Mellicensis*, and Keiblinger, *Melk*. Redlich gave the number of Vienna graduates or former students at a variety of Austrian and Bavarian monasteries, pp. 13-23. After mentioning Kempf as exhibit A in his exordium (p. 9), Redlich omitted information about Carthusian houses, and his statistics show that Cistercian houses had more Vienna academics in their midst than did Benedictine houses. Occasionally Redlich's basis for asserting that a particular person had studied at Vienna was indirect evidence from the person's writings or contacts with known Vienna students. Hubalek, "Briefwechsel Schlitpacher," confirms several of these by references to the unpublished Vienna arts faculty *Acta*.

[92] See Grössing, *"Astronomus Poeta,"* 64-65, where the text of Peuerbach's poem addressed to Kolb is given.

matriculation register as "frater," and Johannes of Obernberg is explicitly identified as from the monastery of Melk (table 7).

At Tegernsee the prosopographical results are more meager. Only four masters of arts and two bachelors of arts entered between 1429 and 1467 (table 6), although some of the five who "studied at Vienna" may also have earned the baccalaureate. The supposed evidence for Tegernsee and Melk as "outposts of the University of Vienna" rests not on sheer numbers but rather on the outstanding contributions of such leaders in the monastic reform as Bernard of Waging, Konrad of Geissenfeld, Johannes Keck, Ulrich Kaeger, Christian Tesenpacher, and Johannes Schlitpacher, in addition to the scientific and literary endeavors of Tegernsee monastic humanists of the later fifteenth and early sixteenth centuries.[93]

One striking feature of our lists of university-related monks from Gaming, Tegernsee, and Melk (tables 1-6) is that only those with a connection to Melk are mentioned in the *Acta* of the theology faculty. The Gaming university masters and baccalaurei came from the arts faculty, not the theological faculty. Some may have begun theological studies but none apparently advanced far enough to take a degree or to be mentioned otherwise in the *Acta*. Moreover, many of the prominent Benedictines with links to the theological faculty had entered monastic life before Nicholas Kempf came on the scene: Nicholas Seyringer of Matzen, Urban of Melk, Konrad of Nürnberg, Stephen of Spanberg. Johannes Keck entered Tegernsee about the same time as Kempf entered Gaming, but he belonged to an earlier student generation at Vienna and entered Tegernsee a number of years after leaving Vienna.

In short, prosopographic research indicates that men trained in the Vienna arts faculty provided leadership but did not dominate the communities at Melk and Tegernsee in a manner comparable to Gaming.[94]

---

[93] Redlich was aware that his argument was vulnerable. Yet this awareness did not prevent him from claiming that Melk had the "allerstärksten Verbindungen zur Wiener Hochschule" (p. 23).

[94] The monastic community at Melk was approximately equal to the number of professsed monks actually living at Gaming, although it was smaller than the total Gaming community scattered throughout charterhouses in the region. Melk numbered 28 monks in 1426; 34 in 1451. See Eduard Katschthaler, "Melk" in *Topographie von Niederösterreich* (1909), 6: 370-508, at 489. In 1458 Gaming numbered 52 professed members with 24 living there. Over a period of forty years, ca. twenty-nine people who *may* have studied at Vienna professed at Melk. Over a period of thirty-six years, thirty-two former Vienna students, most of them clearly attested as such, professed at Gaming. The Melk postulants, however, numbered fewer teaching masters and fewer *baccalaurei*—indeed, a sizeable number of the twenty-nine may have studied only briefly at Vienna. Over a fifty-year period, five teaching masters entered Melk (Nicholas Seyringer, M.A., 1395 [Subiaco, 1403, Melk, 1418]; Urban of Melk, D.Th, 1413; Konrad Mülner of Nürnberg, M.A., 1436 [Melk, 1423]; Stephan of Spanberg, M.A., 1432 [Melk, 1434); Augustin of

By way of further comparison, between 1400 and 1480, only four members of the Benedictine monastery at Kremsmünster had studied at Vienna. Two of them were sent to the university by the monastic community.[95] At St. Peter in Salzburg, only Rupert Keutzl, abbot from 1466 to 1495, is referred to as a *magister regens* of Vienna, and he was sent to the university as a monk.[96] Additional prosopographic work in this area could be helpful.

Beyond sheer numbers, there are other ways to measure the impact of Kempf's call to enter the monastic life. The group of Vienna masters and students who took up the Carthusian life at Gaming in the 1440s and 1450s provided leadership for charterhouses throughout the Austro-Bavarian-Hungarian region for much of the fifteenth century. At Gaming, the monastery was headed by priors with close ties to Kempf until the end of the fifteenth century. Sigismund Phantzagel, from a Vienna

---

Obernalb, M.A., 1450 [Melk, 1453]). Over a twenty-year period, nine teaching masters, including Kempf, entered Gaming. At Tegernsee the percentage was even lower (table 6). Four masters of arts did enter Tegernsee between 1429 and 1454; two, perhaps three, of them are verifiable as *magistri regentes*. Three of them served as priors. There are nearly as many Vienna graduates in the Tegernsee confraternity lists published in Redlich, *Tegernsee*, as there are in the profession lists published by Pirmin Lindner, "Familia S. Quirini in Tegernsee," *Oberbayerisches Archiv für vaterländische Geschichte*, 50 (1897), 18-130, and *Ergänzungsband zum 50. Band* (1898), 1-318. This indicates that many university graduates became parish priests or schoolteachers but established contact with a monastery like Tegernsee, sometimes retiring there at the end of their lives. But none of the Tegernsee Vienna masters, except perhaps Augustin Holzapfler, entered Tegernsee directly from the university. Johannes Keck was a priest in Munich and represented his bishop at the Council of Basel; Ulrich Kaeger of Landau and Wolfgang Kydrer of Salzburg taught school; Christian Tesenpacher and Kydrer were secular priests. Judging from his references to pastoral activity in *Speculum pastorum et animarum rectorum* (see chapter six, below) Bernard of Waging was a priest, but this does not mean that he had served as a secular priest before entering Indersdorf—his pastoral experience could have come as a member of the Indersdorf canonry.

[95] Altman Kellner, *Das Profeßbuch des Stiftes Kremsmünster* (1968). One of them was Abbot Martin II Pollheimer, who studied while holding that office (Redlich, 14). At Mondsee, despite Jerome of Mondsee's ongoing ties to the university, few persons identified as Vienna graduates can be found in the profession lists until late in the fifteenth century. Three Mondsee monks were sent to Vienna to study (Glückert, "Hieronymus von Mondsee," 115). It is possible that when Vienna academics became monks at Mondsee their university background was not thought to merit attention in the profession list. If that is the case, the indifference toward a university background would in itself underscore the care taken at Gaming to record university connections. See also Glückert, "Hieronymus von Mondsee" (1930), 176; Pirmin Lindner, "Das Profeßbuch der Benediktinerabtei Mondsee," *Archiv für die Geschichte der Diözese Linz*, 2 (1905), 133-99.

[96] Pirmin Lindner, "Profeßbuch der Benediktinerabtei St. Peter in Salzburg (1149-1856)," *Mitteilungen der Gesellschaft für Salzburger Landeskunde*, 46 (1906), 1-128. Redlich rather lamely tries to mitigate this paucity of Vienna academics in the monastery by pointing out that all the masters of the monastery school had studied at the university (p. 15).

patrician family, succeeded Kempf as prior in 1458. He had matriculated at the university in 1442. He was *magister regens* in 1450, but could not have taught very long, since he received his novice's habit at Gaming on January 6, 1453. Elected prior at Aggsbach eight days before being chosen for the same office at Gaming, he served twenty-four years and six months (1458-83), longer than any previous head of the Gaming community. Phantzagel was prior during a difficult period in Gaming's history, contending with political instability in Lower Austria. He also served the Carthusian order as *visitator primarius* for the German province.[97] Johannes (Antonius[98]) Lang of Brno was prior, 1485-86. It is unclear when he began studies in Vienna, since entries for "Johannes (Lang) of Brno" appear on the matriculation register in 1435, 1444, and 1447.[99] The promotion to *magister regens* (1449) of this future Gaming prior is beyond doubt.[100] Lang entered Gaming in 1454, became vice-procurator in 1458, and was prior at Olomouc, 1468-80. He died as prior of Brno in 1501. Johannes (Andreas) Taentl, prior of Gaming, 1483-85, and 1491-96, was the son of a Gaming peasant who grew to maturity during Kempf's priorate, matriculated at Vienna in 1462, and entered the monastery in 1466 after earning his baccalaureate degree.[101]

Other Gaming offices were held by monks of university background who entered during Kempf's time at Gaming (1440-47, 1451-ca. 1462). Georg (Jacobus) Stauthamer from Bavarian Swabia, who matriculated at Vienna in 1443 and became a novice at Gaming on June 15 (feast of St. Vitus) in 1452, was vicar at Gaming and later prior at Brno before his death in 1484.[102] Johannes (Paulus) Saechsel of Reichenhall, who ma-

---

[97] *Matrikel* 1: 226, line 27: first semester, Austrian nation, 4 groschen. See also Zeißberg, "Gaming," 575, 582; the list of *magistri regentes* in Aschbach, *Wiener Univ.* (1865) 1: 622; Steyerer, "Collectanea," 377r; Anton Mayer, "Aus dem geistigen Leben Niederösterreichs im 15. Jahrhundert," in *Festgabe zum 100-jährigen Jubiläum des Schottengymnasiums* (1907), 187-201, at 194-95; Roßmann, *Aggsbach* (1976), 218; and Newenstein, *Pandectae* (1732), 57.

[98] Names in religion are given in parenthesis.

[99] Two of these were suffcently well-to-do to pay a four-groschen fee. A Bernard (Paulus) Lang de Brunna," who may be the person referred to as Bernard, the brother of Johannes (Antonius) Lang in Hofer's list, registered in 1449, second semester, 4 groschen (*Matrikel* 1: 273, line 23). The three Johannes Langs from Brno were: Johannes Lang de Brunn, 1447, first semester, Hungarian nation, 4 groschen (*Matrikel* 1: 254, line 12); Johannes Stephani Lang de Brunna, 1444, second semester, Hungarian nation, 4 groschen (*Matrikel* 1: 240, line 17); and Johannes de Brunna, 1435, first semester, Hungarian nation, pauper (*Matrikel* 1: 212, line 53).

[100] Aschbach, *Wiener Univ.*

[101] Zeißberg, "Gaming," 582, 590; *Matrikel* 2: 76, line 20.

[102] Zeißberg, "Gaming," 589; *Matrikel* 1: 233, line 13: "Georius Stauthaimer de Monaco," 1443, first semester, Rhenish nation, 4 groschen.

triculated at Vienna in 1450 and entered Gaming before 1458, served as vicar at Gaming.[103] Wolfgang (Benedictus) Neuböck of Scheibbs entered Gaming in 1446 after his promotion to *magister regens* in 1444. He became procurator in 1458, then vicar the same year, but was transferred to Lechnitz in Hungary as prior in 1459, where he died in 1465.[104] Mathias Schader of Lengwald, who matriculated at Vienna in 1446 and earned a baccalaureate degree, in 1453 entered Gaming, where he served as vicar. Christian of Wasserburg and Petrus of Brno (matriculated 1441) also served as procurators at Gaming (tables 1 and 2).

The charterhouse at Gaming, one of the wealthiest and most influential in German-speaking areas, fell on hard times after the "Kempf-generation" passed from the scene. Beginning in 1525, the community faced heavy levies from the emperor, a siege by Turkish troops (1529), and reduced income because of the devastation of the property of peasants who fled to the monastery for protection, as well as the threat of Turkish attack in 1532, renewed imperial levies for a campaign against the Turks in 1535, and a severe flood in 1538. Many peasants on land subject to Gaming as well as some priests in parishes belonging to the charterhouse became Protestants.[105]

Until these difficulties arose, however, the generation that entered the community during Nicholas Kempf's period of leadership, and perhaps due to his "recruiting" at the Vienna university, led the charterhouse through one of its golden periods.

6. Writings

Although many copies of Kempf's writings are lost, the Wydemann list and fifteenth-century catalogues permit us to gain some idea of the dissemination of his works among Austrian and Hungarian charterhouses in the fifteenth century. Aggsbach and Seitz appear to have had the larg-

---

[103] Zeißberg, "Gaming," 589; *Matrikel* 1: 276, line 52: "Johannes Saegsl de Reychenhal," 1450, first semester, Rhenish nation, 4 groschen.

[104] Aschbach, *Wiener Univ.* (1865) 1: 626; Zeißberg, "Gaming, 573, 587; Steyerer, "Collectanea," 378v. There are three persons named "Wolfgang of Scheibbs" in the matriculation register; their surnames do not make them likely candidates for identification with Wolfgang Neuböck: *Matrikel* 1: 213, line 3: "Wolfgangus Pistoris de Scheibbs," 1439, second semester, Austrian nation, pauper; *Matrikel* 2: 168, line 40: "Wolfgang Carnificis de Scheibs," 1430, first semester, Austrian nation, 1 groschen; *Matrikel* 1: 229, line 23: "Wolfgangus Dachner de Scheibbs," 1442, second semester, Austrian nation, 4 groschen.

[105] Hogg, "Gaming" in *DHGE*, 19 (1981), 991.

est selection. This is not surprising, since they were the charterhouses closest to Gaming and Geirach where Kempf was prior for long periods of time. Both had as priors former Gaming monks who may have been Kempf's disciples. At Aggsbach, Thomas Papler of Zistersdorf was prior, 1448-58. He matriculated at Vienna in 1437, about the time Kempf began his short teaching career. *Magister regens* in 1443, Thomas became a novice at Gaming on November 24, 1444. Within four years he was prior at Aggsbach, replacing Vincent of Aggsbach who had been removed for contumacy.[106] From Aggsbach Thomas Papler went to Hungary, after a period as vicar at Gaming, to preside over the charterhouse of Lethenkow (Lapis refugii).[107]

Thomas Papler of Zistersdorf was followed indirectly at Aggsbach by Johannes (Bartholomaeus) Hölderle of Munich, 1458-73. He may be the "Johannes de Monaco" who registered at the University of Vienna in 1441. In any case, he became a novice at Gaming in July 1452 (Hofer refers to him as a *baccalaureus* of Vienna), was named vicar in 1458, but went to Aggsbach in December of that year to replace Sigismund Phantzagel after his one-month priorate. In 1478 Hölderle was named prior of the young Carthusian foundation at Ittingen in Switzerland. He returned to Gaming in 1482, where he died in 1488.[108]

Only Kempf's writings on the monastic life were copied at Aggsbach. They include *De proponentibus*, *De discretione*, the *De caritate* cycle, and *De capitulo* (all reported in the fifteenth-century catalogue, perhaps referring to the codex we know today as Vienna cvp 4742),[109] as well as *De sollicitudine*, *De confirmatione*, and the *Tractatus de affecti-*

---

[106] Roßmann, *Aggsbach*, 213-14; *Chartae 1447-1456*, 42-43, 66. In a letter to Bernard Pez, April 9, 1718 ("Peziana" in Melk Stiftsarchiv), Wydemann refers to censures of Vincent by the General Chapter in 1420 and 1425, for "linguae vitium" and notes that Vincent was removed as prior in 1448 for that reason. But Wydemann adds that the verbal attacks were related to the conciliar question and the ecclesiastical abuses of Vincent's day, and thus, in Wydemann's eyes, were less blameworthy.

[107] Zeißberg, "Gaming," 587; Steyerer, "Collectanea," 378v; Aschbach, *Wiener Univ.* (1865) 1: 624; *Matrikel* 1: 196, line 48: "Thomas Papler de Cisterstorf," 1437, Austrian nation, pauper; Roßmann, *Aggsbach* (1976), 214. His letter on the struggle with temptations, written in 1445 while a novice at Gaming (Vienna cvp 4736, 274r-276r) shows no obvious signs of Kempf's favorite themes.

[108] Zeißberg, "Gaming," 578, 589; *Matrikel* 1: 224, line 43: Rhenish nation, 4 groschen; Roßmann, *Aggsbach*, 219. Arno Borst places the blame for problems at Ittingen on Hölderle's administrative ineptness. See *Mönche am Bodensee: 610-1525* (1978), 365.

[109] On fol. 53v an eighteenth-century hand has entered a note explaining that the author of the preceding works (the first three parts of the *De caritate* cycle (nos. 8-10 in appendix A) and possibly of the treatise on discretion found later in the codex, was prior at Gaming; his anniversary was to be observed perpetually in the small cloister.

bus formandis in horis sive officio divino. Mauerbach had the four-part *De caritate* cycle, possibly copied from an Aggsbach exemplar and bound with a collection of legends, visions, and tales (see appendix A, 8-11 for details). Two of these codices are dated 1453 and 1451.

No copies of Kempf's mystical writings can be linked to Lower Austrian monasteries, which suggests that they were written during his Pleterje priorate (1462-67) or near the end of his time at Gaming (1451-62). In contrast, they are found in relative abundance at Seitz, along with some of his works on monastic themes. At Seitz, former Gaming monks and Vienna graduates, Heinrich of Eckenfeld (1471-74) and Christoph Stöckl (1474-77), filled the office of prior. During these years Kempf was head of the nearby charterhouse at Geirach, but all of his surviving mystical writings were completed by 1468, since they are found in a Seitz codex of that date.

Heinrich of Eckenfeld was a contemporary and perhaps a teaching colleague of Kempf. Although his matriculation at Vienna ("Heinricus Praentl de Eckenfelden") in 1435 is clear, whether he became a master of arts is less certain.[110] He became a novice at Gaming on November 13, 1442, and served as prior at Olomouc (1450-57) and Prague (1458) and procurator at Ittingen (1468), before becoming prior at Seitz. He died at Gaming in 1481.

Christoph Stöckl matriculated at Vienna in 1444, took the novice's habit at Gaming as a *redditus* in 1447 (Advent season, 1446), and received a dispensation to become a priest while in the status of *redditus* in 1448. He may have been responsible for the transmission of Kempf's *De mystica theologia* to Tegernsee. His family had long patronized the monastery at Tegernsee.[111] Ulrich Stöckl was a prominent member of the Tegernsee Benedictine community. We know of only two places where Kempf's mystical works were copied: Seitz and Tegernsee (the Budapest copy of *De mystica theologia* was very probably copied at Seitz). The Tegernsee copies are dated 1479 and 1481, shortly after Christoph

---

[110] His name does not appear in the list of masters edited by Aschbach, although Hofer twice refesr to him as a *magister Wiennensis*. See *Matrikel* 1: 188, line 12: Rhenish nation, 4 groschen; Zeißberg, "Gaming," 578, 587; Steyerer, "Collectanea," 378v; Müller, "Personalien," 167-68.

[111] "Johannes Stöckl dedit in fine vite 6 fl. r. 1501 (obiit 5 März 1508), . . ." See Redlich, *Tegernsee*, 221 (the confraternity list for Tegernsee). See also the "Excerpta genealogica ex monumentis Tegurinis" in the subsection, "Diplomatarium Miscellum," of the section, "Monumenta Tegernseesia," in volume six of *Monumenta Boica*, (1766; repr. 1964), 339-40, for references to "Hanns Stoeckel," "Joh. Stoeckel, Sen.," and "Johan Stoeckl." On Christoph Stöckl, see Redlich, *Tegernsee*, 46; the letter from Wydemann to Pez, January 22, 1718, in "Peziana"; Lindner, "Familia S. Quirini," 59; and Zeißberg, "Gaming," 588.

Stöckl's priorate at Seitz, and they refer to Kempf as prior "in Gyrigo [Geirach]."

The community at Seitz also possessed copies of Kempf's sermons, the brief work *De tribus essentialibus* (for which Kempf's authorship is uncertain), the *De colloquio / Super Statuta* combination, Kempf's *De ostensione*, and the commentary on the Song of Songs. Curiously, from Wydemann's list and the manuscripts extant today, we know that Seitz had at least two copies of each treatise. Thus, next to Gaming, it constitutes the most important known center for the copying of Kempf's works. Whether some of these were actually copied at neighboring Geirach, cannot be determined.

We can conclude very little about Kempf's impact on the two charterhouses where he served as prior for thirty years: Geirach and Pleterje.[112] Their submersion beneath the political storms of the sixteenth century not only erased possible traces of Kempf's influence, but it may also have destroyed copies of additional works by Kempf.

It is clear that Kempf's works were known in Hungarian charterhouses.[113] Lövöld had copies of *De discretione* and the *De caritate* cycle. Lethenkow (Lapis refugii) had a copy of *De capitulo*. (A professed monk of Gaming, Wolfgang Neuböck of Scheibbs, was prior at neighboring Lechnitz, 1459-65.) According to Wydemann, Brno in Moravia had copies of the *Memoriale primorum principiorum* and Kempf's sermons. This is not surprising, since the first regular prior of the charterhouse there was a monk from Gaming, who established a fraternal prayer covenant in 1384. Gaming continued to supply many of Brno's priors, including one of Kempf's "disciples," Antonius Lang. Kempf manuscripts made their way to Hungary and Moravia largely from the Lower Austrian houses. Budapest National Museum cod. 387 is a Seitz manuscript and should not be included in assessing the Hungarian dissemination of Kempf's works.

Several codices indicate familiarity with Kempf's writings at the university in Vienna, quite apart from the testimony of the anonymous copyist of the *Memoriale primorum principiorum* cited by Wydemann.

---

[112] See Hogg, "Geirach" in *DHGE*, vol. 20 (1984), cols. 258-62, at 260.

[113] On Hungarian Carthusian libraries, see Adrienne Fodor, "Die Bibliothek der Kartause Lechnitz in der Zips vor 1500," *Armarium: Studia ex historia scripturae librorum et ephemeridum* (1977), 1-22, at 2-3; *Cartusiana*, 2: 303-4. On relations between Gaming and Lövöld, see *Chartae . . . 1447-56*, 42, the "ordinationes" for 1448: "Priori domus Vallis Sancti Michaelis in Ungaria non fit misericordia. Et restituat domui Throni Beate Marie libros quos habet de eadem domo. Et cum hoc satisfaciat dicto Priori domus Throni Marie, de tribus talentis et tribus solidis denariorum Wiennensium quos pretendit sibi deberi."

Several copies of *De recto studiorum fine* (one of them, V1, entirely lacking the specifically "Carthusian" section of part II, yet copied in conjunction with *De proponentibus*, *De confirmatione*, and Heinrich Egher of Kalkar's *De ortu et decursu ordinis cartusiensis*) were in the possession of the university library in 1756 when its manuscripts were transferred to the imperial library for lack of space. It is possible that these codices (V1 and cvp 4912) originated in monastic establishments.[114] But their presence in the university library before 1756 rules out the possibility that they were part of the spoils from the dissolution of the charterhouses in the 1780s. Kempf's *De discretione*, together with the letter-treatise on temptation by Thomas Papler of Zistersdorf and works by Benedictines from Melk and Lambach, was included in a codex (cvp 4736) that was owned in the fifteenth century by Thomas Ebendorfer of Haselbach, one of the leading lights of the Vienna university.

In Benedictine circles, the range of Kempf's works copied was much more restricted. Primarily *De proponentibus* / *De discretione* found favor. In Lower Austria, Melk had three copies of each, plus a copy of the rather insignificant *De tribus essentialibus*. From the testimony of Jerome of Mondsee, we know that Mondsee had a copy of *De proponentibus*, in addition to the extensive excerpts from *De discretione*, the nearly complete copy of *De recto studiorum fine*, and the set of *Regulae grammaticales* that are extant in former Mondsee codices today. Alongside Mondsee, in Upper Austria, Seitenstetten had copies of the sermons on the gospels, and Lambach had a copy of *De proponentibus* and *De recto studiorum fine*. In Vienna, the Schottenstift had *De recto studiorum fine*, *De proponentibus* / *De discretione*, and the *Memoriale primorum principiorum*. In the upper valley of the Enns, just inside Styria, Admont had *De sollicitudine*.

The Bavarian Benedictine houses had only the *De proponentibus* / *De discretione*, which may have reached them through Melk or possibly, via Mondsee. Tegernsee copies of *De recto studiorum fine* (according to Pez) and *De mystica theologia*, and the copy of Kempf's disputation on Aristotle's *Posterior Analytics* which Wolfgang Kydrer[115] brought with him from Vienna, are exceptions to the above pattern. The Indersdorf copy of the *Regulae grammaticales* may be connected to Mondsee, which also owned a copy. A possible Salzburg-Indersdorf-Tegernsee

---

[114] A.-Ch. Kogler, "Mémoire sur la composition et l'origine des divers recueils de privilèges généraux de l'ordre des chartreux," *Revue Mabillon*, 19 (1929), 131-60, at 144 and passim, thought that V1 came from Gaming.

[115] On Kydrer, see Redlich, *Tegernsee*, 41-45, and Dennis D. Martin, "Der 'Tractat von der lieb gots und des Nächsten' in cgm 780 und 394," *ZDA*, 108 (1979), 258-66, and idem, "Kydrer, Wolfgang von Salzburg," in *Verfasserlexikon*, rev. ed., 5: 474-77.

connection runs something as follows: By the early- or mid-1440s, Oswald Nott was a regular canon at Indersdorf, transferring to Tegernsee in 1449, where he copied, among other things, Jerome of Mondsee's *De contemplatione* (clm 18565).[116] Wolfgang Kydrer (matriculated 1437) seems to have been taught by Kempf at Vienna, or at least knew of him and valued his work enough to obtain a copy of his disputation on the *Posterior Analytics*. He then become a schoolmaster in Salzburg (ca. 1445-55) and a priest at Mattsee and Frankenmarkt (1456-61). Both villages are close to Mondsee. Christian Tesenpacher, who matriculated at Vienna in 1449, while Johannes of Donauwörth (= Jerome of Mondsee) was still teaching there, was priest at Frankenmarkt (1454-56) and at Attersee and St. Killian in Oberwang, a parish incorporated to the monastery at Mondsee. During this latter pastorate, Tesenpacher lived in Mondsee. That he and Jerome collaborated is evident from clm 18740.[117] Both Tesenpacher and Kydrer were originally from Salzburg. Nott was from Tittmoning on the Salzach, downstream from Salzburg. Kydrer and Tesenpacher entered Tegernsee together in 1462.[118] Whether Mondsee also played a role in the transmission of Kempf's writings to Seitenstetten and Lambach is unclear.

Without further study it is difficult to make generalizations about Kempf's impact among Benedictines in these Bavarian and Austrian monasteries. We do know that Jerome of Mondsee read Kempf's *De recto studiorum fine* and *De proponentibus* while a novice at Mondsee in 1452.[119] But despite the close resemblance of a few lines in the opening of chapter seven of Jerome's *De profectu religiosorum* and the second part of *De tribus essentialibus*, for which Kempf's authorship is less certain, Jerome of Mondsee's *De profectu* owes more to the *devotio mod-*

---

[116] Nott followed Wilhelm Kienberger and Bernard of Waging from Indersdorf to Tegernsee. Whether he is the "Oswaldus" who matriculated in the Austrian nation at the university in Vienna in 1426 is unclear—Tittmoning would normally be included in the Rhenish nation, and this entry is very cryptic, consisting of a single name and no record of any fee paid. An Oswaldus Weidacher de Ditmanning matriculated in 1434, but his surname does not match. The most likely candidate is the Oswaldus de Trösperg who matriculated in 1429—Trostberg is not far from Tittmoning. More than merely an indefatigable copyist, Nott also translated the Old Testament into German (cgm 219, 220, 221). See Redlich, *Tegernsee*, 136, 142, 184, 193.

[117] According to Glückert, "Hieronymus," 200, note 52, clm 18740, fol. 37v, reads "Hec collecta sunt per venerabilem Magistrum Johannem de Werdea et per me Cristannum Tesenpacher eo tempore provisorem ecclesie sancti Kyliani in Oberbang scripta. Anno 1461." Jerome addressed at least one poem to Christian Tesenpacher (cvp 3604, clm 19855; see Glückert, p. 199, for details).

[118] See Redlich, *Tegernsee*, 36, 41, 55ff., and Heldwein, *Klöster Bayerns*, 47, 117, 127. See also table 6.

[119] See appendix A.

erna than to the writings of Kempf.[120] The rest of his corpus of writings invite more detailed study and comparison to Kempf than was possible within the scope of the present work.

It would probably not displease Kempf to know that scholars find it difficult to ascertain the exact parameters of his influence and impact five hundred years later. His purpose in writing was certainly to train both *superiores* and *subditi* in the religious life. He was a self-effacing pedagogue in the *schola monastica*. As we shall see in greater detail in later chapters, he predicated his hopes for a monastic *reformatio* to a large degree on the presence of good leadership in the monastery. To the extent that the Gaming university-Carthusians of his generation were the product of his wooing and training, he left his mark on the Carthusian life in his century.

The judgment of Pez and Wydemann, who devoted more space in the *Bibliotheca Ascetica* to Kempf's writings than to any other single author, is not without consequence in evaluating Kempf's significance, even though the rediscovery of this forgotten Carthusian prior did not survive the reforms of Joseph II. Above all, the roster of university professors and students who left Vienna for Gaming in the 1440s and 1450s and the list of priors of charterhouses from Schnals to Lechnitz in the 1450s to 1480s suggest that Kempf's presence had an effect on spiritual health in Carthusian circles. The size and timing of the university influx into Gaming, when compared with that into Melk or Tegernsee, suggests, as his eighteenth-century biographer asserted, that it was not unconnected to Kempf.

Because this portion of the exodus from the university into the charterhouse occurred in rural Austria, rather than in such cities as Erfurt, Cologne, or Basel, Carthusian life and spirituality developed along different lines in the Austrian charterhouses where Kempf worked. Kempf had a program for reform—for the regeneration of the individual in the monastic life—but it differed significantly from that of Gerson, Denys of Rijkel, or Johannes of Hagen. In chapter seven we shall consider some models for reform in the monastic tradition and in the nonmonastic society of Kempf's day, in order to understand better how *he* might have measured his "impact" on his world.

---

[120] *Bibl. ascetica* 2 (1723), 171-225, at p. 196; cf. Graz UB cod. 973, 234r, 11-16. The work is analyzed by Marcel Viller, "Lectures spirituelles de Jérome de Mondsee," *RAM*, 13 (1932), 374-88. Viller's assertion on p. 382 that Jerome borrowed from Kempf is based on Viller's ascription of the *Alphabetum divini amoris* to Kempf. See appendix A.

CHAPTER FOUR

PASTOR

Jove equipped us with two sacks: one, filled with our own vices, he put on our backs; another, heavy with others' offenses, he hung in front. Prevented thus from seeing our own sins we are quick to censure the sins of others. [Phaedrus, *Fabulae*, 4.10.]

Let each flee his own vices; for another's will not harm him. [Guigo I, *Meditationes*, nr. 230.]

1. Discretio

A. Discernment and Critical Method

The monastic life is a way of life with its own pedagogical and hermeneutic assumptions. Yet the monastic community understood itself as a microcosm of human society and of the church. In Kempf's view the structures, the grammar, of monastic life were paradigmatic for all of society. At the heart of the monastic grammar for Kempf, as it had been for the earliest monastic communities in the deserts of Egypt and Syria, was *discretio*. Discernment is the monastic alternative to the more critical and speculative epistemology and hermeneutic[1] of medieval school philosophy and theology. Jean Leclercq and others have shown us that early medieval monastic culture possessed a full-orbed theology.[2] A study of Kempf's application of *discretio* to the spiritual life of monks illustrates this epistemology and hermeneutic. It is a hermeneutic and epistemology

---

[1] That monastic discretion is indeed a method of "reading" and was so understood by monks may be seen in a passage from Guigo de Ponte, *De contemplatione*, I.8 (Philippe DuPont ed., p. 146): Each of the twelve steps of contemplation has some kind of meditation, affection, desire, devotion, and clinging; to understand them properly, one must take account of the words' characteristics (*proprietates*) and specific import. Otherwise one can easily misread something, especially if the reader lacks spiritual experience adequate to discern what he reads.

[2] Leclercq, *Love of Learning*, and "Naming the Theologies of the Early Twelfth C.," *Mediaeval Studies*, 53 (1991), 327-36; M. Colish, "Systematic Theology and Theological Renewal in the Twelfth C.," *JMRS*, 18 (1988), 135-56; Mursell, *Theology*.

suited to the rhetorical, ritual, role-playing society of the late antique and early medieval period, just as a more speculative and cognitive epistemology and hermeneutic accompanied the rise of the universities in the high Middle Ages[3] and continued to dominate in modern Protestantism, post-Tridentine Catholicism, and the Enlightenment.

Discernment and *critical method* share a common Greek root, namely *krinein*, "to separate, decide." The two modern English nouns both imply making distinctions, separating one thing from another, analyzing, deciding. Yet they differ in underlying assumptions about the authority and purpose for making distinctions. Nothing in the words themselves require these differences in underlying authority and purpose, rather, it is the context in which each arose that makes the difference[4]— in modern culture the authorities for making critical decisions, critiquing, and analyzing have become almost exclusively rational and cognitive and the purpose of the exercise is normally to discredit rather than encourage belief.

Monastic discernment[5] is the product of a community (minimally a community of master and disciple) in which the spiritual father or pastor

---

[3]   See, e.g., Pierre J. Payer, "Prudence and the Principles of Natural Law," *Speculum*, 54 (1979), 55-70, which outlines the shift from early medieval *discretio* to scholastic *prudentia*.

[4]   For example, twelfth-century Carthusians employed textual criticism on the letters of Jerome and in the compilation of their homiliary, but did so to serve monastic, affective spirituality rather than to challenge the authority of patristic teaching (see Mursell, *Theology*, 75-80, 172-74). William of St. Thierry was aware that the trinitarian Johannine "comma" (1 Jn 5:7) was not found in the oldest manuscripts (*Aenigma Fidei* ; PL 180: 409B; par. 25 in CF 9: 57). In modern scholarship the questions of authority come into play most prominently in so-called "higher" criticism (historical criticism), rather than "lower" or textual criticism, although historical criticism obviously has its roots in textual criticism.

[5]   For the history of "discretio" and the entire subject of spiritual direction, manifestation of thoughts, and spiritual fatherhood, see Irénée Hausherr, *Spiritual Direction in the Early Christian East*, CS 116 (1990). Klaus Berg, "Zur Geschichte der Bedeutungsentwicklung des Wortes Bescheidenheit," in *Würzburger Prosastudien, I* (1968), 16-80, has assembled an immense range of Latin and German philological evidence for *discretio* from antiquity to the eighteenth century, with an impressive chart of the "conceptual field" of the Latin terms on p. 33. He suggests a gradual elimination of the cognitive elements associated with the German term *Bescheidung* took place in the early modern period, leaving an ethical remnant. See also Joseph Lienhard, "The 'Discernment of Spirits' in the Early Church," *Theological Studies*, 41 (1980), 505-29; André Cabassut, "Discretion," in *DSAM*, 3: 1311-30; Rosemarie Nürnberg, *Askese als sozialer Impuls* (1988); Eloi Dekkers, "'Discretio' chez Saint Benoît et Saint Grégoire," *Collectanea Cisterciensia*, 46 (1984), 79-88; Margot Schmidt, "'Discretio' bei Hildegard von Bingen als Bildungselement," in *Spiritualität Heute und Gestern* (1983), 2: 73-94; Leloir, "Sagesse," 77-95; Aquinata Böckmann, "Discretio im Sinne der Regel Benedikts und ihrer Tradition," *Erbe und Auftrag*, 52 (1976), 362-73. Note also Peter Brown's comments in *Body and Society*, 129-31, 227-28, 236-39.

decides and discerns on the basis of reason, experience, and divine gift. Although there are principles for the monastic life, set down most concisely in a rule, the collective wisdom of past spiritual directors (tradition[6]), the director's own experience, and the indefinable and inexpressible direct inspiration of the Holy Spirit[7] are the source of authority for monastic discernment. All three of these come from outside the person whose thoughts and deeds are being discerned. The disciple does not and cannot decide or discern. His life is discerned for him by a more experienced and wiser "other." The wisest thing one can do is to discern one's lack of discernment, to refuse to *trust* in one's own wits, to en*trust* one's path to another, who in turn has also been the product of such extrinsic discernment.

Discernment is learned more by patterning, by doing, by being formed, than by ratiocination. This does not mean that it lacks a cognitive dimension, indeed, the cognitive element may at times seem to prevail, yet prevails only in order to lead one to recognize the limits of cognition.[8] For John Cassian discretion was a combination of both *diakrisis* and *metron*, of intellectual-spiritual acuity in making distinctions and of recognizing limits, of taking stock and tempering, measuring, giving order.[9] He underscored his point by having Abba Moses abruptly break off his discussion of discretion, despite the eagerness of his listeners, when he discerned that it was growing late: too much of anything, even too much talk about discretion, can be damaging.[10]

"Learning one's limits" or "taking one's measure" requires a standard of measurement. Thus one must hand over the process, at the outset,

---

[6] See Nürnberg, *Askese*, 51 on the importance of tradition in Cassian's teaching on discretion.

[7] John Cassian says that discretion "is no earthly thing and no slight matter, but [is] the greatest prize of divine grace." *Conference* II, ch. 1 (SC 42: 111; Luibheid trans., p. 60).

[8] This is well illustrated by Guigo de Ponte, *De contemplatione*, I.7 (DuPont ed., 120-26): both cognitive and affective elements are involved in being affected by and adhering to God, but the loving soul knows how to discern between them and to use each according to its *proprietates*: "Et modo ad istum, et modo ad illum modum se facili convertere potest. Quamvis, ut videtur, nec excessus intellectivus possit fieri sine affectivo nec affectivus equidem sine commixtione intellectivi, novit tamen pia mens inter utrumque discernere et utrumque secundum suas proprietates exercere et tenere, cum ascendit sursum praedicto modo; affici in Deum, idem est praesentialiter Deo frui."

[9] See Schmidt, "'Discretio'," 73-77, and the examples from the Desert Fathers given by Leloir, "Sagesse," 90-94. Cassian describes discretion as walking along the royal road, avoiding being puffed up by excesses either on the right hand (excessive zeal) or left hand (laxity). *Conference*, II, ch. 2 (SC 42: 113; Luibheid trans., p. 62), cf. ch. 16-18.

[10] Thus the main discussion of discretion occurs in the second conference of Abba Moses.

to another standard, who in turn, draws on ancient standards he himself
has learned by experience and patterning. One cannot measure something by itself, especially when it is crooked from the start.[11] One needs
a trustworthy Rule. Both the critical method and monastic discernment
involve the use of measure, limits, reason. The difference is that *discretio*
makes the recognition of limits fundamental and delimiting, in order to
open up the limitless and undefined path to the mystery that is beyond
limits. The critical method uses separation and measuring as the means
to reach truth itself, ultimately, in nineteenth- and twentieth-century
positivism, denying that there is a wisdom that cannot be measured or
reasoned.

Discretio was well suited to the mannered, rhetorical culture of late
antiquity. One modulates (again the idea of proper measure, *ratio*) one's
spiritual counsel to suit the occasion, just as the orator chooses his figures of speech and manner of expression to suit the occasion. Formation
as an orator consists in learning rules and principles, to be sure, but the
application of them requires wisdom and an affective, experienced touch
that cannot be learned abstractly. One can write guidebooks for *discretio*
in spiritual formation just as one can write manuals for oratory, and these
may even bear some resemblance to scholastic *Summae*. But manuals of
spiritual direction and oratory are expected to be put into practice with
flexibility, something virtually excluded by the stricter logic and definite
conclusions reached in the scholastic disputation's *determinatio*. Louis
Leloir goes so far as to translate *discretio* with "pedagogical finesse,"
emphasizing the pedagogical patience, tolerance, gentleness, and mercy
used by the Desert Fathers (who so often are portrayed as flinty figures
of unyielding and terrifying ascetic authority).[12]

---

[11] See the summary of the concept of "manifestation of thoughts" (*exagoreusis*) in the
eastern monastic tradition in Tomas Spidlik, *The Spirituality of the Christian East*
(1986), 246-47, including the words of Dorotheus of Gaza: "Being passionate, we should
absolutely not entrust ourselves to our own heart; for a crooked rule makes crooked even
that which is straight."

[12] "Sagesse," 80-81: "La 'discrétion' des Pères se présente donc tout d'abord comme
une finesse pédagogique, s'exprimant surtout dans la longue patience et l'extrême indul-
gence avec lesquelles ils forment les candidats à la vie monastique; elle est, comme dis-
ent les collections arméniennes, un 'discernement de miséricorde.' Cette éducation
spirituelle comportait d'ailleurs un don du coeur, une réelle affection pour le disciple,
toujours appelé, dans la version arménienne, non 'ordi', 'fili', '(mon) fils', mais 'or-
deak', 'filiole', '(mon) petit enfant'." Les exigences des Pères du Désert sont des exigences d'amour." He continues with an allusion to Benedict's admonition to the abbot
not to wear out his sheep (Gen 33:13): "If you overdrive the ewes for a single day, the
entire flock will die." Discretion involves recognizing and respecting the breaking point
of the weakest member of the community. On gentleness as an attribute of God's fatherhood (compared to his zealous judgment as creator), see Bernard of Clairvaux, *Sermones
super Cantica Canticorum*, 16.4-7 (*S. Bernardi Opera*, 1: 91-94; CF 4: 117-20).

In many ways Gregory the Great summarized several centuries of monastic experience of discretion, not only in his *Pastoral Rule*, but in his entire *oeuvre*.[13] Carole Straw has made a "grammar of reconciliation and complementarity" central to her study of Gregory.[14] Drawing on twentieth-century linguistic philosophy and epistemology, she has pointed out both the metaphoric and the metonymic aspects of Gregory's vision—the way in which *discretio* was both polysemous and organic, separating and uniting. These paradoxical formulations indicate how a hermeneutic of *discretio* could be suited both to an ineffable, mystical, ambiguously mimetic method and at the same time offer a certain kind of "hard" or "scientific" epistemological basis.[15]

> Ironically, while waiting anxiously for the world to end, Gregory provided an intellectual framework to integrate all aspects of life with Christianity. While decrying power, he showed how the Church and the Christian could use and benefit from power and earthly achievements. . . . Gregory deals profoundly and sensitively with the ambivalences that plague human life: why tears of love and grief are so closely allied, why sin nips the very heels of virtue, why the loving God must also have the devil as his *exactor*. His works express a quiet regret, a sadness that any resistance lingers in his soul, however unwilled. Like Job, with whom he identifies, Gregory hum-

---

[13] Dekkers, "'Discretio'," contrasts Gregory and Benedict, arguing that the idea of measuredness is not part of Gregory's understanding of discretion, that Gregory emphasizes the cognitive dimension. I think he has incorrectly taken "moderation" or "measuring" to be an alternative to judging, cognitive discernment. For Cassian (and Kempf) both moderation and distinguishing require both cognitive and affective elements. It would be surprising if both did not figure in Gregory's understanding as well—given Gregory's well known emphasis on the complementarity of love and knowledge: "amor etiam notitia est."

[14] Carole Straw, *Gregory the Great: Perfection in Imperfection* (1988).

[15] Straw, *Gregory*, pp. 16-19. Straw summarizes what she means by "metaphoric" / "paratactic" and "metonymic" / "syntagmatic" in note 67: "In metaphoric and paratactic associations, a separation and distance exist between two elements because their association is wholly arbitrary, though conventional. In metonymic and syntagmatic chains, there is an intrinsic connection through the participation and organic interrelation of elements. Gregory often moves between these two ways of thinking, and the distinction should be appreciated. For instance, the vices are a metaphoric disease of the soul, and yet a metonymic relationship is present as well, because the humors of the body can affect the soul. Man is both a metaphoric world in miniature, and he shares in the four elements of the world metonymically. These relations affect causation and the relations between this world and the next. Augustine's signs are paradoxical and metaphoric, for they both reveal and yet conceal hidden truths. Gregory's signs are sacramental and metonymic: carnal signs reveal hidden spiritual truths, at least to those with discretion." Whereas the Apostle Paul is strictly dualistic, working with polarities, Gregory is concerned with complementarity and reciprocity. "Gregory is able to create a complementarity out of the dialectical opposition of spirit and flesh because each pole has become ambivalent."

bly confronts the universe, but he struggles as Job never did to make his
will truly love what God wills.[16]

In John Cassian and Gregory we encounter many of the themes central to Kempf's understanding of the monastic life as founded on *discretio*: human weakness and frailty as necessitating some extrinsic source of
stability and immutability; humility and compunction spurred by suffering and adversity as the gateway to self-knowledge that permits one to
trust in the discerning pastoring of another; indeed, discretion as the
soul's stable point: the *constantia mentis* lies simply in recognizing that
perfection lies in imperfection.[17] Indeed, *discretio* "is the mother, guardian, and the guide of all the virtues."[18]

Discretio was further developed by twelfth-century writers. Bernard
of Clairvaux described it as *ordinatio caritatis*,[19] and Richard of Saint-
Victor made it the key to his speculative trinitarian theology. He distin-
guished five elements of *discretio*:

   A. *diiudicatio* determines, judges forensically between what is per-
       mitted and not permitted;
   B. *deliberatio* discerns what seems best and most helpful;
   C. *dispositio* analyzes, compares, orders, and categorizes;
   D. *dispensatio* decides what best suits the moment and circum-
       stances;
   E. *moderatio* sees to it that nothing is done to excess.

A and C are intellectual, analytical, cognitive undertakings; B and D are
more affective, sensing; E incorporates both the "left brain" and "right
brain."[20] Richard stands on the threshold of scholastic and critical
method. As was characteristic of his teaching on contemplation, Richard
brought a new level of systematization to the ancient practice of monastic discretion, a degree of organization the Desert Fathers would have
found troublesome. They were accustomed to flying by the seat of their

---

[16] Straw, *Gregory*, 22.

[17] Straw, *Gregory*, chapter 12.

[18] John Cassian, *Conferences*, II.4 (SC 42: 116): "Omnium namque virtutum genera-
trix, custos moderatrixque" (translation by Luibheid, p. 64). Cf. Bernard of Clairvaux,
Sermones in Cantica Canticorum, 49.2 (*S. Bernardi Opera*, 75-76).

[19] In addition to Schmidt, "'Discretio' bei Hildegard von Bingen," 74, see Stock, *Implications of Literacy*, 436-37, 450, referring to Bernard, *Sermones in Cantica Canticorum*, 49.

[20] Richard of Saint-Victor, *Adnotationes mysticae in Ps. 143* (PL 196:381D-382A).
In addition to F. Guimet, "*Caritas ordinata* et *amor discretus* dans la théologie trinitaire
de Richard de Saint-Victor," *Revue du Moyen Age Latin*, 4 (1948), 225-36, see the summary in Schmidt, "'Discretio' bei Hildegard von Bingen," 75, as well as Schmidt's exploration of Hildegard's application of the tradition to trinitarian theology, pp. 76-94.

pants (well-greased by the unction of the Holy Spirit, to be sure). Kempf's understanding of discretion is based primarily in John Cassian and Gregory, although he does attempt his own systematic correlation of various aspects of discretion with the cardinal virtues and the gifts of the Holy Spirit in the second chapter of *De discretione* (see below).

Discretion is a form of exegesis of both one's life and the scriptures. John Cassian distinguishes four steps in discerning whether one's thoughts (i.e., all the movements of the soul) are good or bad, true or false. It is not enough to be able to recognize (1) obviously counterfeit coins bearing the head of a false king or usurper (= the pure gold of scripture under the guise of false and heretical meaning), rather, one must also be able to recognize that some coins may bear the image of the true king yet be made of (2) impure or plated gold, or (3) be of a false weight or corroded metal, or (4) may have the rightful king's image improperly stamped. His summary of these four is anything but systematic—he first mentions only three, but later expands the list to four. He moves freely back and forth between questions of scriptural exegesis (for the word of God is the two-edged sword that pierces even to the marrow[21]) and of pious practices,[22] because both are subject to the word of God in its combined manifestation as written scripture, the gifts of the Holy Spirit, and the "word" of the spiritual director.

Monastic *discretio* depends on a fundamental trust growing out of recognition of one's weakness and the limits of one's measuring. Having recognized in a profound way their sinfulness, the desert monks entrusted the healing process to another because their recognition of their own sinfulness was also a recognition of their inability to heal themselves. In the words that John Cassian put into the mouth of Abba Moses:

> True discretion is obtained only when one is really humble. The first evidence of this humility is when everything done or thought of is submitted to the scrutiny of our elders. This is to ensure that one trusts one's own judgment in nothing, that one yields to their authority in everything, that the norms for good and bad must be established in accordance with what they have handed down [tradition]. Not only will this procedure teach the young monk to march directly along the true road of discernment, but it will actually keep him safe from all the deceits and snares of the enemy.

---

[21] *Conference* II.4 (SC 42: 115; Luibheid trans., p. 64), quoting Heb 4:12. Kempf applies Heb 4:12 to *discretio* in *Ost*, 31 (G1, 24r, 6 - 24v, 11), describing roles for Father, Son, and Spirit in the process of distinguishing true virtues from false virtues and the principal intention or affection of the human soul from its secondary intentions. See appendix B for the text.

[22] *Conference* I, ch. 20, 23 (SC 42: 101-3, 107; Luibheid trans., pp. 55-57).

Someone who lives not by his own decisions, but by the example of the
ancients will never be deceived.[23]

Thus monastic discretion involves a hermeneutic of trust. One must
suspend one's own judgment and permit oneself to be discerned or
judged by someone else, by an authority. (When applied to authoritative
texts, the exegete approaches a text in order to be judged by it and spoken to, rather than to judge and critique it.) This trust or suspension of
one's own judgment seems simpleminded or naive to the modern critical
mind.[24] Yet in the shift from naiveness or simplemindedness[25] as the
fundamental starting point for healing and salvation to naiveness as an
impediment to discovering truth lies the *diakrisis* between *discretio* and
critique. The monastic hermeneutic is a naive yielding of one's (false,
weak) self to another in a quest for one's true self created in the image of
God. The truest discretion involves a single movement: discerning that
sin has twisted one's own measuring stick and rendered it incapable of
discerning.[26]

To recognize the limits, to take one's measure at the outset, is to realize that wisdom or truth is always a quest, never a goal already
achieved. This is clearly visible in Heinrich Egher von Kalkar's fourteenth-century retelling of the origins of the Carthusian order. Bruno, a
master of one of the leading schools of his day, abandons his school-
based quest for truth by means of dialectic to enter upon a quest for God,
a hunting or tracking of wisdom. He embarks on the narrow way by the
compelling force of a horrible miracle at "Paris"—the story of the professor who preached repentance from his funeral bier. Bruno is diverted
from joining a regular monastic community by a series of miracles and
happenstances that lead him to Hugh of Grenoble and the eremitical life.
The implication is that once more that the Carthusian Order's unique
semi-eremitical way of life was established by divine leading. They have
discerned their path with the aid of the leading of the Holy Spirit through
both institutional-human instruments and direct visions and miracles.
With the shift from tracking down knowledge in the schools to pursuing

---

[23] *Conference* II, ch. 10 (SC 42: 120; Luibheid trans., pp. 67-68).

[24] Note Stock's comments on this question in *Implications*, e.g. 472, 520-21 (Ro-
dulph Glaber, Odo of Cluny, Otto of Freising).

[25] I.e., John Cassian's *puritas cordis*, the "singleness of eye" referred to in Mt 6:22,
Lk 11:34.

[26] For a discussion of the interrelatedness of *acedia* (spiritual listlessness) and the human tendency to depend on one's own resources, whether money or skills, see Kenneth
C. Russell, "Roots of the Noonday Demon," *Sisters Today*, 56 (1984-85), 417-22.

the path of God underway Heinrich weaves the language of questing, pursuit, and expert investigation into the account.[27]

The Carthusian editor of Guigo I's *Consuetudines* has argued that *discretio* plays a limited role in the earliest recorded Carthusian legislation (early twelfth century). The word itself appears only once in the customs (19.1) and then it is in the context of the Carthusians' limited hospitality to guests: based on the meager resources of their wilderness monastery, they found it necessary to practice sober discretion in this area. They would house guests on occasion but could not provide for their horses! Yet, although the word itself does not appear frequently, the concept of balance and equilibrium, of soberness in the spiritual life, is fully present (ch. 40-44 of the *Consuetudines*). Moreover, the spiritual director's function is intentionally not part of the legislation of the emerging order. Its centrality in the Carthusian life is simply taken for granted; discussion of its practice takes place in the spiritual literature, not the statutes.[28]

Heinrich Egher van Kalkar likewise gave an important role to discretion among the leadership characteristics of the prior. The prior is a "living rule," a living standard or measurement. Discretion is thus the

---

[27] Van Kalkar, *Ortus et decursus*, Vermeer ed., pp. 91-92: "Vir enim venerabilis, Bruno nomine, oriundus de Colonia sancta Teutonie, nobilis genere, theologus egregius et canonista precipuus, tunc presens, animavuertens clamores illos parisienses non illi dampnato ad salutem fuisse, sed sibi et aliis coaudientibus a Deo datos, pro mutacione status atque vite. Concepit tunc spiritu Jhesu Cristi per artam viam, qui ducit ad vitam, post hoc incedere, postergans amplam, que sepius ducit ad mortem; per quam et ipse et dampnatus elle satis legaliter diu videbantur incessisse. Assumptis igitur sibi diversorum statuum viris, eiusdem sancte intencionis: Magistro scilicet Lauduino, magne litterature viro, Hugone, quodam seculari presbitero, duobus canonicis regularibus et duobus honestis laycis, divertit pro inhabitando heremitorium ad sancte fame virum Hugonem Gracianopolitanum Episcopum. Visitato eciam in via quodam devoto heremita, pro via Domini ab eo experiencius indaganda. Episcopus igitur, audito ab eis quod contigit Parisius, sanctoque eorum proposito, perpendens, quod et ipsi septem sunt, ad memoriam revocat, quod sibi proxime per visionem ostensum fuerat: Apparuerunt enim sibi septem stelle ipsum ducentes ad quendam solitudinis locum, inquo et Dominum construere sibi viderat habitaculum. Sicque senciens eos mistice a Deo vocatos et spiritu Dei sibi adductos, ducendosque in locum premonstratum ab angelis."

[28] The editor's summary of the central themes of Carthusian spirituality, with numbers referring to the chapters of the *Consuetudines*, follows: solitude and contemplative life (24-26); Jesus as model for the Carthusian life (26); union with Christ in contemplative rest (27-29); fidelity to solitude (29); fidelity to the cell (29-30); fidelity to the desert and separation from the world (30); superiors and the necessity of obedience (30); the prior (31); the procurator (31); taking counsel of the whole community in cases of great importance (31); obedience—the editor gives cross references to Guigo's sources: John Cassian, Benedict, Peter Damian, Jerome, but notes that these were frequently modified by Guigo (32-33); poverty (33-36); fraternal charity (36-38); life of simplicity (38-39); life of prayer in the cell (39-40); humility (40-41); equilibrium or balance and wisdom (41-44); spiritual soberness (44-45). SC 313, pp. 24-45.

lived out application of the letter of the Rule[29]; through it the prior can prevent excessive, unreasonable (immoderate, unmeasured) asceticism. The prior is Christ's representative to the monks and his purpose is to serve his monks, above all by the forming of their ascetic life. To do this he must know his sheep thoroughly. For these reasons, although priors could be and normally were appointed by the General Chapter, Heinrich urges that the choice fall one of the members of the community itself. He also has secular responsibilities, but van Kalkar thinks these are less important and gives only general information in this area.[30]

With this background in mind, we turn to Nicholas Kempf's pastoral teaching on *discretio*, to its context in the Carthusian and reformed Benedictine circles of his day,[31] and, by means of comparisons to Luther, Lorenzo Valla, and Gasparo Contarini, to the fundamental implications of monastic structures for the "idea of reform" in the Reformation era.

B. Nicholas Kempf on Discretio

As prior Nicholas Kempf had important pastoral responsibilities. As Vincent Gillespie has outlined, the Carthusian refusal to assume secular pastoral responsibility only permitted them to concentrate all the more on pastoral needs within the monastery.[32] The Carthusian prior was particularly responsible for the pastoral care of the lay brethren, since the eremitical life of the choir monks permitted them to pursue spiritual reading privately and the prior could (and later was expected to) delegate responsibility for spiritual direction of the choir monks to senior members of the community.[33] From the mid-twelfth century onward, lay

---

[29] *Epistolae*, as cited by Heinrich Rüthing, *Der Kartäuser Heinrich Egher von Kalkar, 1328-1408* (1967), 243: "Nam prior in ordine est tamquam viva regula, qui auctoritate Dei et ordinis potest, juxta suam discrecionem, pro tempore, necessitate et qualitate ovium, quarum naturam et condiciones sicut verus pastor cognoscere tenetur, omnia moderari, rigorem nimium racionabiliter interdum laxando, laxaque si qua sibi nimium videntur restringendo." A similar passage occurs in van Kalkar, *Ortus et decursus*, ed. Vermeer, p. 137.

[30] Rüthing, *Egher van Kalkar*, pp. 237-49, cf. 147-71.

[31] Although consideration of Gerson's understanding of *discretio*, especially after Constance, would further expand this context, it has not been incorporated here. See the summary in Burrows, *Gerson*, 243-56.

[32] "Cura Pastoralis in Deserto," in *De Cella in Seculum* (1989), 161-81. The existence of this fine survey obviates the need to include many details and references here.

[33] See Gillespie, "Cura Pastoralis," 164, for citations to Carthusian legislation after the *Consuetudines* of Guigo I.

brethren were forbidden to have books at their disposal, which meant that much of the prior's work was done orally.[34] By Kempf's time, however, it was becoming customary, at least in German houses, to provide vernacular written resources for the lay brethren. It is possible that Kempf may have had something to do with the Gaming vernacular translation of the lay brothers' statutes that has survived[35]; his treatise *De ostensione regni Dei* originated as sermons to lay brethren. His other sermons and other parts of his body of writings point to his work as preacher and pastor to the entire community.

In his basic work on the monastic life after the novitiate, *De discretione* (which begins where *De proponentibus* ends),[36] Kempf explicitly concentrated on discretion as "finding one's measure," noting that many treatises have been written on the other meaning of the word, the "discretion of spirits."[37] His explicitly cited sources include Cassian, Benedict, the *Moralia* of Gregory the Great, Aristotle's *Nichomachean Ethics*, John Climacus, William of Saint-Thierry's *Golden Epistle*, and Heinrich of Langenstein's *De discretione spirituum*. He does not cite Nicholas of Dinkelsbühl, but Nicholas's sermon to a Carthusian community offers a good contemporary summary of the prominent attention given to discretion as a monastic virtue within Vienna university circles.[38]

Kempf opens with a straightforward assertion that discretion is the highest necessity in religious life.[39] When seasoned, indeed "pickled,"[40]

---

[34] Gillespie, "Cura Pastoralis," 165-66.

[35] Wolfram D. Sexauer, *Frühneuhochdeutsche Schriften in Kartäuserbibliotheken* (1978). Sexauer dates the translation of the lay brothers' statutes into German (Vienna cvp 2731, 12r-43r) at Gaming to mid-fifteenth century, i.e., during or close to Kempf's period as prior. A copy of the original translation was made in 1493 or later, at which point cvp 2731 was given to Aggsbach.

[36] Pez, *Bibl. ascetica*, vol. 9, pp. 381-532. For the manuscripts, see appendix A, no. 6. Numbers in parenthesis in the following pages refer to the chapters in the Pez edition.

[37] See Rüthing, *Egher von Kalkar*, 147-71, for a parallel to Kempf within the Carthusian tradition.

[38] See Madre, "Sermo magistri Nicolai," pp. 207-10.

[39] *Discr*, 1 (VS1, 34v B, 1-12; Pez, *Bibl. ascetica*, 9:381-82): "'Bonum est sal' Lucae 14 [Pez: 13]. Sal discrecionem significat. Nam nulla virtus pascit, sapit, nec valet, neque placet, nisi discrecionis sale fuerit condita. Quod [Pez: Quia], si sal discrecionis virtutibus defuerit, ad nihil amplius sunt utiles: sed mittuntur foras extra rationis recte limites; et quasi cibus animae insipidus, evomuntur, ut a demonibus conculcentur. Sine ergo discrecione nulla potest virtus acquiri, nec acquisita custodiri, nec potest esse vera virtus sine ea."

[40] "Condire" can also carry the meaning of "seasoned" as well as "preserved," or "pickled". Although we tend to translate this scripture as "seasoned," in Kempf's context monastic discretion's role in preserving one from sudden failure was central. It is that aspect which made it the most important of all virtues—one might have made a good start and be most zealous in fasting, vigils, hospitality, charity etc., then suddenly slip or fall

with the salt of discretion (Lk 14:34), all acts, all virtues, lead to a good
end, but without the salt of discretion, they lead beyond the limits of
right reason and are useless, or, more precisely, are useful only to be
trampled under the feet of demons. Discretion, prudence, and wisdom,
all virtually synonymous in Kempf's view, have been praised by Solomon and Christ in the scriptures and by the holy fathers and "*even* by the
scholastic doctors"[41] as more to be desired than all possessions and more
necessary than all other virtues. Although necessary for all people, discernment, or prudence, is most important for monastics because they
face more intense, astute, and cunning temptations of the devil (ch. 1).
Only discernment can keep the monk's feet on the narrow way, between
the limits necessary to a following of Christ. This was the conclusion of
the Fathers of the Desert, led by Antony: "it is only discretion that can
lead the monk by firm steps to God."[42] In short, "I know of nothing that
is needed so much, by everyone, to be sure, but especially by the juniors,
as to know how to hold onto the measure of discretion."[43]

Initially Kempf makes some distinctions between prudence and *discretio*, describing two methods of acquiring discernment. One is through
the power of knowing, discerning, and judging intellectually: between
good and evil, between truth and falsehood in speculative as well as
practical matters, between what one should and should not believe. This
is an intellectual power that includes both affective and cognitive elements and is broader than prudence, for discretion involves four of the
gifts of the Holy Spirit: wisdom, understanding, counsel, and knowledge,
whereas prudence is only one of the four cardinal virtues.[44] In another,
ethical, sense discretion is identical to prudence as a cardinal virtue. In

---

from the path. It is lack of discernment that leads to such failures. See John Cassian, *Conference* II, ch. 2, 4; IV, ch. 12 (SC 42: 114, 115-16, 176-78; Luibheid trans., p.
62, 64). Cf. Robert Holcot's application of the "seasoning salt of discretion" to leadership and the fruits of virtues and vices in *Super libros sapientiae* (1494), at the end of
lectio 46.

[41] *Discr*, 1 (VS1, 34v B, 12-14; 9: 382): "Et id patet multiplici sacrae scripture auctoritate et sanctorum patrum et eciam doctorum scholasticorum."

[42] *Discr*, 1 (VS1, 35r A, 9: 383-84), citing Gregory the Great and summarizing his
unnamed source—Cassian, *Conference* II, 2, on perseverance.

[43] *Discr*, 1 (VS1, 35r B, 16-20; 9: 384-85): "Praesertim cum nihil scio adeo necessarium in ordine nostro, quamvis in omnibus, precipue tamen in iunioribus sicut scire discretionis mensuram tenere." Note the combination of "scire" and "tenere mensuram" in
this instance.

[44] Pez lists the four as wisdom, understanding, counsel, and prudence. VS1 originally
had "[donum] prudencie" here; a different hand corrected it to "sciencie" (VS1, 35v B,
10). The Melk manuscript Pez used presumably lacked the correction, although it should
have raised questions in his mind, since prudence is not one of the seven gifts of the
Holy Spirit.

this second sense it is the ability to know, discern, and judge morally between good and evil, between what should be done and what should be
omitted. In this sense it corresponds to two gifts of the Holy Spirit: counsel and knowledge. The narrower sense, for which Kempf uses the term
prudentia, comes from *pro-videntia*, the ability to foresee all circumstances. The broader sense, to which Kempf applies the term *discretio*,
comes from *dis-cerno*, the ability to distinguish between two different
things, especially between the greater and the lesser good or evil. To act
with indiscretion is to exceed or depart from the center of right reason.[45]
In this sense, discretion itself is a gift of the Spirit, for the "discernment
of spirits" is listed in 1 Corinthians 12 under the various charisms of the
Spirit.[46]

For the rest of the treatise, however, Kempf tends to use prudence
and discretion virtually as synonyms. Discretion has three parts, or acts,
and one needs all three to acquire and keep discretion. "Reveal to the
Lord your way and hope in him and he himself will act" (Ps 36:5
[37:5]).[47] God's "acting" consists in setting forth your righteousness and
your judgment (discernment) as a light that is as bright as noonday (Ps
36:6 [37:6]).[48] The first act of discretion is to take counsel—to consult
with, reveal oneself to, the Lord (in the guise of one's spiritual director:
"revela Domino viam tuam"). The second act is to judge what has been
revealed. Significantly enough, Kempf does not dwell on condemnation
of sin, for judgment leads in the same breath to hope in the Lord ("spera
in eo"), indeed, to judge is to hope.[49] The third act is to prescribe what
should be done, not merely by the human penitent, but principally by the
One of whom it is said "et ipse faciet."[50] We should note here that the

---

[45] *Discr*, 2 (VS1, 35v A, 25-27; 9: 386): "Quia dicitur indiscrete agere, qui excedit,
notabiliter autem deficit a medio racionis recte."

[46] Ibid., lines 30-33; 9: 386.

[47] Ch. 3 (VS1, 35v B, 14-22; 9: 387-88). Kempf notes that Benedict offered this same
prooftext in his discussion of the fifth degree of humility, which consists in revealing all
[evil thoughts or deeds]. See ch. 7 of Benedict's Rule.

[48] Cf. *Ost*, ch. 45 (G1, 34r, 13-19), where Kempf asserts that memory, reason, and
will in a human person are acts of God: "Inclina affectum ad eius amorem, et sic venit
Spiritus Sanctus, et sic iam invenis vite ymaginem Trinitatis. Cogita consequenter quod
illa in mente iam dicta, scilicet actus memorandi, actus intelligendi, actus amandi, omnino non sunt actus anime tue; que tales actus non potest ex se habere sed solum a Deo;
sicut corpus ex se non potest aliquos actus habere nisi ab anima. Et sic ex illis actibus
cogita et considera certitudinaliter et perceptibiliter esse Deum in corde tuo, qui est omnia in omnibus et operatur omnia in omnibus." The rest of this chapter is given in appendix B.

[49] This confirms Leloir's point about the large role given to mercy, gentleness, and
patience in discretion as taught by the Desert Fathers.

[50] Ch. 3 (VS1, 35v B, 25-29; 9: 388): "Primus actus est consiliari, de quo dicitur

entire process involves elements external to the person confessing. The initial act is to have enough discretion to reveal oneself to another. The concluding act involves the monk in doing something but that doing remains *principally* the action of God. These three acts correspond to three special abilities: prudence (as described in Aristotle's *Ethics*) and two gifts of the Holy Spirit: knowledge and counsel. Together, these not only teach one to find good and healthful means, but they also make one follow what was divinely considered or inspired, even if it is hard or "beyond the normal" (*supererogative*).[51] The counsel of others is thus of utmost necessity for discretion—both as a starting point and conclusion, as any number of "twelve-step programs" recognize: by entrusting knowledge of one's addictive behavior to someone else, one finally gains knowledge of it and thereby acquires the inner fortitude to resist it; as long as one denies, hides, or ignores the addiction it continues to dominate.

These principles are stated by many "holy fathers and teachers," but the one Kempf cites *in extenso* is Heinrich of Langenstein, in his commentary *Super Genesim*,[52] who in turn cites Aristotle on various types of fallacies—those that deceive the intellect in the acquisition of knowledge of truth and falsehood; those that deceive the *affectus* regarding good and evil in the operation of virtues. From the pagan Philosopher, Kempf moves to two gifts of the Holy Spirit, counsel and knowledge, which necessarily accompany the infused charity given in baptism. They are what move a person on the right path and help one avoid falling into indiscretion in finding the right means and right judging of oneself. Kempf apparently found Heinrich of Langenstein's list of "fallacies" better suited to his own monastic context than Aristotle's. He cites at length the fifteen apparent causes by which men are deceived in judging when they have sinned: *consuetudo, infirmitas, status vel dignitatis excellentia, dispensatio, deceptio, zelum, bona intentio, timor, violentia, ignorantia, passionis vehementia, exemplum ex scripturis.* All of these can be reduced to one type, namely *quod homines ratiocinantur vel iudicant, secundum quod sunt affectionati*—people are influenced in their self-judgment by their own inclinations and attractions. From this root come rationalizations and excuses, blindness to one's own sin, and the

---

'revela domino'. Secundus est iudicare de consiliatis, de quo sequitur, 'et spera in eo'. Tercius actus est precipere et exequi, qui est principalis actus eius de quo dicitur 'et ipse faciet'."

[51] Ibid., lines 30-34; 9: 388.

[52] On Kempf's borrowings from Heinrich of Langenstein, see Hohmann, *"Unterscheidung der Geister"*, 45. None are extensive or central to Kempf's treatise.

tendency to confuse good and evil, vices and virtues, and *iniquitatem* and *aequitatem*. To overcome this self-deception, external counsel is necessary. Not to resort to it is to risk dying in sin while thinking that one is absolved of all things. "There is a way that appears right unto a man but that leads to destruction" (Pr 14:12; 16:25). Christ himself said that some at the last judgment will protest their damnation by insisting they had cast out demons in Christ's name—he will nonetheless dismiss them with the words "I never knew you" (Mt 7:23).[53]

For Kempf, self-examination is inextricably tied to extrinsic counsel, to extrinsic spiritual direction. Whoever places confidence in his own judgment or persuasion, even if he is already wise, is foolish. He will only confuse good with evil, virtues with vices, and truth with error. "One should prudently turn for help to those who are wiser than oneself, authentic, and unaffected in their pursuit of truth and righteousness. Therein lies assurance for one's conscience." Assurance, *securitas*, rests upon external counsel.[54] To reinforce this quotation from Gregory, Kempf cites Gerson's *De consolatione theologiae*: "This is the trap into which many great men fall, for, being great, they are not humble in their own eyes and lean more on their own than on another's prudence."[55] Kempf returns to this theme in chapter five, citing examples from scripture[56] as expounded by Abba Moses in Cassian's second *Conference* (chapter fourteeen) to illustrate the absolute necessity of external counsel for achieving perfection in the spiritual life.

Kempf leaves no doubt that this is the fundamental purpose of the monastic life:

---

[53] Ibid. (VS1, 35v B - 36r B; 9: 388-91), repeated in ch. 4 (VS1, 37r B, 11-15; 9: 396-97).

[54] Ibid. (VS1, 36r B, 44 - 36v A, 11; Pez 9: 392): "Nullus utique sapiens hoc faciet animadversis tot errorum precipicijs et sophisticis viciorum apparencijs; quibus apparet malum bonum, vicium virtus, et error veritas. Sed potius pro assecuratione sue consciencie quisque prudens recurrat ad sapienciores se, veritatis et iusticie sinceros sine affectione zelatores" (lines 4-11), Kempf attributes this to Gregory the Great.

[55] Ibid. (VS1, 36v A, 12-16; Pez 9: 392): "Hic est laqueus magnorum virorum, dum magni, non humiles sunt in oculis suis; dum magis proprie quam aliene innituntur prudencie." The citation is to Gerson, *De consolatione*, bk. IV, prosa 1 (*Oeuvres*, 9: 229). Kempf adds quotations from Proverbs: "Ne innitaris prudentiae tuae" (Pr 3:5); Paul: "dicentes se sapientes stulti facti sunt" (Rom 1:22); and the "gospel" (actually Is 5:21 combined with Jn 9:41): "Vae, qui estis sapientes in oculis vestris, et apud vosmetipsos prudentes. Et iterum, 'Quia dicitis, "Videmus, peccatum vestrum manet. Si autem ceci essetis peccatum non haberetis"' (lines 17-25). The imagery here is that which Kempf uses in *Ost*, ch. 51: leaning on an external crutch for support.

[56] E.g., Samuel's need for Eli's interpretation of God's call (1 Sam 4).

Why should one doubt that the religious life, especially in its vow of
obedience, is inspired and instituted by the moving of the Holy Spirit to
avoid this danger, since within this vow, entirely lacking confidence in
one's own prudence, discernment, and direction, one subjects oneself to
another's judgment? And this is the central reason why this status is more
free from anxiety for those who do not follow their own mind and prudence and why it is more dangerous for those who have forgotten their
vow and are walking according to their own mind and discernment.[57]

We have here a precise statement of what Kempf means when he
says the monastic life is *securior*. It is more free of anxiety to those who
do not follow their own counsel, who *do* obey their vows; at the same
time it is all the more perilous for those who forget their vows. He is
aware that it is possible to fall into error, to follow one's own counsel,
even within the monastery.[58] The cowl and the vow by themselves do
not save—indeed, the very thought that there is something automatically
meritorious about the monastic life is one of the biggest traps a monk
faces—still, the monastic life is institutionally predisposed to make possible a more *Angst*-free existence.[59] Kempf leaves no doubt that the monastic vow has both external and internal dimensions, but insists that
once made, the vow carries an important extrinsic safeguard against the
inevitable self-doubt that a novice faces.[60] As Kempf continues to reinforce his point by citing examples of those who trusted in their own prudence, including Job's friends and the "professor from whose damnation
our Order took its origin," he insists that "examples of many monks of
this sort are found in the writings of the [Desert] Fathers."[61]

But he saves his biggest guns for contemporary church politics:

How much evil grows from this root in the church today. . . . For from
the year 1432 until now a schism continues in the church, a schism between the general council of Basel and Pope Eugenius IV, the like of

---

[57] Ibid. (VS1, 36v A, 26-36; 9: 392-93).

[58] See chapter 4: "Religiosi sue prudencie innitentes possunt in multis casibus pericli-
tari, quando putant se recte ambulare."

[59] Ch. 4 (VS1, 36v B, 35 - 37r A, 2; 9: 394-95).

[60] Ch. 4 (VS1, 37r A; 9: 395), citing canon law and Bernard of Clairvaux on whether
a monk who has entered with firm resolve can be permitted to leave when he doubts the
genuineness of his vocation. Cf. *Prop*, I.30, II.1. See also Aelred of Rievaulx, *Speculum
caritatis*, CCCM, 1: 144-45: monastic vows are freely made but once made cannot be
easily abandoned; yet this by no means means that the monastic life is coerced.

[61] *Discr*, ch. 3 (VS1, 36v A, 39 - B, 4; 9: 393), cf. ch. 5-6 (VS1, 38v A. - 40v A; 9:
404-15).

which has never been heard. For the pope and his adherents, indeed, are holding their own council, a council against a council, as it were. In this schism it is not unlearned men of the world but the much-blinded leading lights of the Church who adhere pertinaciously to one side, as unjust as it may seem, or who insist on holding on to a pestiferous neutrality. What is this if not God the Father hiding his light of true wisdom and withholding his ray of truth from those who fearlessly and foolishly trust in their own opinions, so that many little ones might know what the luminaries blindly ignore?[62]

Within the monastery the possibilities for trusting in one's own prudence while appearing to obey the judgment of others are endless: spiritual pride under the guise of humility (hidden self-congratulation); feigned obedience; secret attachment to objects one has been given special permission to use; envy or hatred of one's neighbor; sins of the tongue (backbiting and denigration of others); hidden suspicions or unspoken rash judgments about others' motives (ch. 4). All of these are examples of trusting more in one's own judgment than in another's discretion. The monastic life has its own special temptations growing out of living in close community—a fertile soil for nursing almost unnoticeable tensions and minor personal affronts into mortal sins of anger and envy.[63]

In the remainder of this treatise, Kempf considers the relation between spiritual director and individual monk, discussing what should be revealed under which circumstances (ch. 6ff.) and the attitude in which it is to be done.[64] "The least anxiety-causing (securior) way to conquer temptations is through revealing them, for this is the most certain sign of

---

[62] Ch. 3 (VS1, 36v B, 4-31; 9: 393-94). Kempf concludes with another quotation from Gerson. "Confido in Domino, quod apud ydiotas solicitos de salute sua, in quibus est simplex fides, certa spes, et suavis caritas, insidebunt fructuosius in animo theologice [Gerson: catholicae] sententie. Et ideo non frustra sunt, sicut apud repletos literis, gignentibus scientiam illam, quam inflare dicit Apostolus. Oculum vero quis nesciat, quantum turbat et excecat inflatio?" Gerson, De consolatione, bk. IV, prosa 4 (Oeuvres, 9: 238).

[63] Ch. 4 (VS1, 38r A, 36 - B, 41; 9: 402-3). In lines 30-41 Kempf cites Heinrich of Langenstein, De discretione spirituum: "Viri spirituales, singulariter religiose viventes, praecipue peccare videntur in temerarijs iudicijs, in aliorum condemnacionibus, et sui ostentacionibus, in nisibus, id est, adhaerencia vel [Pez: et] confidencia sue prudencie, im pulsibus sue impatiencie, in fatuis de se estimacionibus, confidencijs, desiderijs, et murmuracionibus; et super omnia deficere consueverunt in indiscrecionibus." Cf. Ost, ch. 21 (G-1, 14r, 2-10) and ch. 22 (G-1, 15v, 20-30), for brief statements about the "little" things in communal life that easily turn into bigger sins.

[64] On confession in Carthusian practice, see the Statuta Antiqua, II.11 (choir monks), and III.30 (lay brethren). Statuta ordinis cartusiensis (1510), k2 and p5r (repr. AC 99.2, pp 187-89, 262-63).

true humility, by which one traverses the pitfalls of all temptations" (ch. 8). "Through revelation temptation ceases most quickly, or if it continues, it is not a danger but is a profit and merit [to one's soul], especially in humility" (ch. 9). It is pride that hinders one from revealing one's temptations—Pride disputes with Humility, trying to convince the soul to hold something back with the clever argument that, after all, one cannot really reveal everything anyway (ch. 11). To this Humility responds that failure to reveal everything chokes one up, making even short aspirative prayer impossible—a sort of spiritual constipation (ch. 13). Pride comes back: it seems so unnecessary to run to one's director with every little thing between confessions; after all, can't one help oneself a bit? (ch. 14). Sometimes Pride simply has to be told forcefully to shut up (ch. 15), leading to another exhortation about the importance of opening up to one's director (ch. 16).[65]

Not everyone who is advanced in years is fit to be a director of souls.[66] With the desert tradition, Kempf insists on choosing one's director carefully (ch. 18). But having chosen and having revealed one's inner life, one dare not second-guess the person to whom that inner life has been entrusted (ch. 17).[67] An unshakeable confidence in one's spiritual father is essential for a variety of reasons (ch. 19). It is through this con-*fidence* that the monk makes rapid progress; through dif*fidence* toward his spiritual director, he will quickly stumble into the worst evils (ch. 20-21). The issue here is trust, trust above all in the fatherly charity of senior monastics who mirror God's fatherly love in Christ (ch. 23, citing John Climacus).

Yet the battle is not yet won. The Devil comes back in the guise of Pride armed with a chain of relentless logic: how it can be that a mere man, who, we have just learned, is unable to direct himself, can direct others (ch. 24-25)? Sometimes a director is harsh and scolding, inspiring

---

[65] Part of this dialogue was transmitted as a separate treatise. See appendix A. It is based in large part on John Cassian. The theme is common in monastic tradition; one evidence of its ubiquity is found in its application in "semi-monastic" Devotio Moderna circles: "Be open in your confession. Do not be embarrassed to say all you thought or did that is evil and avoidable because you can drive out the devil in no better way than to reveal his whole counsel. Natural modesty and shyness, at a time when a man ought to be open, has destroyed many." "On the Life and Passion of Our Lord Jesus Christ and Other Devotional Exercises," trans. by John Van Engen in *Devotio Moderna* (1988), 189, cf. p. 221 ("Gerlach Peter's First Letter to His Sister Lubbe").

[66] See John Cassian, *Conference* II, ch. 13: Not all grey-haired men have discretion; "grey hair" has to do with wisdom, not chronological age.

[67] This theme is found in John Climacus, *The Ladder of Monks* under step 4: "On Obedience." See John Climacus, *The Ladder of Divine Ascent*, trans. Colm Luibheid and Norman Russell (1982), 92-93.

despair rather than trust (ch. 26). Moreover, Pride asks, what kind of discretion or prudence is this that proceeds by paradox rather than by reason, that must be learned through acquiring virtues rather than cognitive study? Humility concedes the point: it is indeed a foolish prudence—but that is exactly the paradox of humility: by not trusting in one's own prudence, one's own knowledge, by being foolish toward oneself, one is wise through the strength of another (ch. 27-28).[68] Kempf's practice here confirms the claim that monastic theology sets limits to logical argument.

De discretione is not the only work in which Kempf discusses these issues. He returns to them again and again in such works as De capitulo, De suspicionibus, and De sollicitudine. References to a number of passages are listed in appendix A.

It remains for us to look at this theme in Benedictine circles in Kempf's day before we address more directly the implications it may have for late medieval concern with religious anxiety and Anfechtung.

C. Discretion in Reformed Benedictine Circles

Among Kempf's Benedictine contemporaries, we see discretion in operation in a treatise on the role of the abbot[69] written by Johannes Rode (1385-1439), formerly a Carthusian at St. Alban's Charterhouse in Trier, but active in the last portion of his life as head of the Abbey of St. Matthias in Trier (1421-39) and a highly visible Benedictine reformer in Germany. In public prayer, according to Rode, the abbot should act with confidence as an intercessor and leader of his community. But in his chamber he should pray for his own shortcomings and weaknesses, together with those of his brethren, that both he and they might not fall but rather grow steadily, supported on the crutch of heavenly grace. The abbot must play many roles. An attitude or form of behavior appropriate to one group of people or to one setting would be inappropriate in another setting. In public worship the abbot should "model humble devotion and devout humility, . . . singing psalms devoutly with the brethren . . . and

---

[68] The treatise continues with a warning to superiors not to become proud because their junior monks confide in them (ch. 29; VS1, 264r A - 264v B; 9: 505-9). The work concludes with a discussion of the nature of genuine confidence (ch. 30-32; VS1, 264v B-267v A; 9: 510-23) and the vices that make discretion difficult: precipitousness, inconstancy, unreflectiveness (ch. 33-36; VS1, 267v A - 269v A; 9: 523-32).

[69] Liber de bono regimine abbatis, ca. 1435, in Pez, Bibl. ascetica, 1 (1723), 158-204. For a list of manuscripts see Petrus Becker, Das monastische Reformprogramm des Johannes Rode(1970), 34-37. The following discussion summarizes chapters 2-4.

doing nothing to make himself stand out, . . . in everything conforming
to the community." Outside the monastery church, in the cloister, when
the community's discipline needs to be enforced, he is to exhibit a som-
ber decency as befits a prelate, observing all the rules fully, without lev-
ity, but also without visible anger or grouchiness. He is to mask his inner
feelings if something has upset him. As head disciplinarian, as judge, he
must take account of the gravity of the sin and the exact circumstances in
each case. Those who sin frequently and deliberately require handling
different from those who sin inadvertantly, who are quick to admit their
error and are tractable under discipline. At times the abbot's discretion
borders on deviousness: if the offense at hand was directed at the person
of the abbot he should turn the matter over to the wisest of the seniors:
"Then the seniors, at the direction of the abbot but giving the impression
that they are acting on their own, not at his direction, should bow the
spirit of the offender," leaving the abbot free to grant mercy when the of-
fending monk asks for it. Had the abbot played the role of judge in such
an instance, he would be less free to grant genuine forgiveness on a personal basis, an act of reconciliation that is crucial to restore harmony in a
community of sin-prone people.

Another example comes from the reforming Benedictine prior at
Tegernsee, Bernard of Waging. In his debate with the bishop of Eichstätt, Johann of Eych, regarding the reasons why Bernard would not
abandon his contemplative life for pastoral responsibility (see chapter
six, below), he discusses the role of discretion by citing Adam of
Perseigne, a twelfth-century Cistercian whose writings were read in
community at Tegernsee about the time Bernard of Waging composed
his *Speculum pastorum* and *Defensorium speculi pastorum*.[70] In order
not to lose any of his sheep, a faithful shepherd should have bread in his
wallet, a dog on a leash, a walking staff with rod, a horn and a reed pipe.
The bread is the word of God and the bag is the prelate's memory. The
dog is a zealous pastor to fight off the wolves and to console the sheep,
and the rope on which the dog is held is discretion, which keeps zeal in
check by a spirit of piety and knowledge. The pastor's walking staff is
his pious exhortation for consolation, his rod is his authority of power to
correct the restless and those audaciously presumptuous. His horn's terrible sound calls knights to war's conflict—here it represents the terrible

---

[70] See Jean Bouvet, "Le 'Soliloquium' d'Adam de Perseigne," *Collectanea Cisterciensia*, 50 (1988), 113-71, at 113. As prior, Bernard would have been in charge of choosing materials for community reading. The *Soliloquium* attributed to Adam of Perseigne
is found in clm 18610, a manuscript dated 1462 and containing Johann of Eych's correspondence with the Carthusian Jacob of Tückelhausen on the same issues Johann debated with Bernard of Waging.

threatenings of hell by which the knights of Christ are girded with the spirit of fortitude against vices (one of the gifts of the spirit). His reed pipe sings sweetly of eternal delight and comfort. The pairings are pedagogically and pastorally inspired: word contained in memory, a zealous dog contained by the leash of discretion; a consoling staff accompanied by a chastising rod; a bellicose horn together with a sweet pipe—all are metaphors to teach that firmness must always be tempered with consolation or gentleness, that even the sheer word of God requires its container or instrument (the memory of the prelate-pastor), if it is to be of use to the sheep.[71]

D. Leadership and Discretion: Monastic Consolation

Most of Kempf's writings revolve around pastoral questions. One of the large problems of his day was the question of assurance of salvation[72] that eventually led to Martin Luther's crisis of soul and a way of

---

[71] Bernard of Waging, *Defensorium speculi pastorum*, ch. 7 (clm 4403, 54v [62v], 23 - 55r [63r], 8) [the manuscript has both a fifteenth-century and modern foliation]: "Ut ergo fidelis pastor nullam de ovibus perdat, debet secundum Adam de Persensis habere in pera panem, in fune canem, baculum cum virga, cornu cum fistula. Panis est verbum Dei; pera est memoria verbi Dei; canis est zelus pastoris, quo pastor bonus zelare debet pro domo Domini sui et deterrere lupos et consolari agnos, id est subditos, pijs latratibus sancte predicacionis et indefesse oracionis. Funis quo canis tenetur moderamen est zelantis et discretio, quia zelus spiritu pietatis et sciencie temperatur, ne forte sicut ait Apostolus: 'zelum Dei habeat sed non secundum scienciam' [Rom 10:2]. Baculus est pie consolacionis exhortacio, qua sustentet et consoletur pusillanimes, ne in tempore tribulacionis deficiant. Virga est potestatis auctoritas, qua corripit inquietos, ne de impuritate audaciam sumant. Cornu, cuius sono terribili ad belli conflictum milites animantur, est terribilis iehenne comminacio, qua Christi milites in vitiorum mollicie spiritu fortitudinis accinguntur. Fistula, que dulciter canit, eterne dulcedinis suavitatem designat, quam subditorum auribus fidelis pastor dulciter et frequenter intubat. Talis pastor haut dubium non timebit luporum occursum nec ovium morsum, ne aliquam earum perdat; dicens illud veri pastoris 'Omne quod dedit mihi pater non perdam ex eo' [cf. Jn 17:2, 12], quia non divertam ab ovium collegio nec pervertam magisterio nec evertam consilio nec subvertam flagello, sed convertam pio solacio et pascam temporali subsidio, sed et necessariam medelam infirmantibus sollicite impendere curabo." The passage does not appear in Adam's published writings in PL 211 or SC 66, nor is it to be found in the "Soliloquium" published by Bouvet. It may come from unpublished writings by Adam found in clm 18643, fol. 147-63, and Vienna cvp 4485, fol. 147-189. See Bouvet, 113-14.

[72] The literature on this question is vast. In addition to Jean Delumeau as cited in chapter three, above, see Berndt Hamm, *Frömmigkeitstheologie am Anfang des 16. Jahrhunderts: Studien zu Johannes von Paltz und seinem Umkreis* (1982), 5-6, 223-26, 237-50; David C. Steinmetz, *Misericordia Dei: The Theology of Johannes von Staupitz in its Late Medieval Setting* (1968), 122-31; Steven E. Ozment, *The Reformation in the Cities* (1975), 11-13; Oberman, *Werden und Wertung*, esp. 116; Lawrence G. Duggan, "Fear and Confession on the Eve of the Reformation," *ARG*, 75 (1984), 153-75; Thomas N.

understanding God's salvation and human response to it that purportedly
differ completely from medieval "works righteousness." Both Kempf's
theology of leadership, which we shall explore in greater detail in chapter six, and his theology of salvation, which, with its implications for understanding the Reformation era, is addressed in the remainder of this
chapter, are pastoral theologies. He is convinced that the failings of the
church of his day stem from human *hubris*, from the failure to assess
one's own weaknesses with a clear and steady eye. The entire monastic
enterprise rests on this utterly realistic assessment of human sinfulness
and weakness, on an excruciating consciousness of sin.[73] Even more significant for this study is the way monks responded to their profound
awareness of sin: they sought the external aid of a counselor, a spiritual
director, who in turn was a living embodiment of the monastic Rule. To
be a monk is not to trust one's own ability to heal oneself. It is to enter
into a framework of extrinsic aid, to pledge obedience to a Rule. The
Abba of the Desert Fathers and the prior of the Carthusian community
were vicars of both Rule and Christ. Precisely in external counsel from
them lay the monk's hope of recovery from the addictive power of sin.
Like an alcoholic who finally admits his inability to conquer alcohol and
leans on the "rule" of the Twelve Steps and the "community" of his local
Alcoholics Anonymous chapter as a crutch, the monk recognizes the utter necessity of the salt of extrinsic discretion in the spiritual life of the
monastic microcosm and in the church as a whole. Then, and only then,
after taking counsel with someone outside himself, is he able to let God
himself accomplish it (Ps 36:5 [37:5]).

2. Trust in Him Who Justifies the Unrighteous

A monastic commentary on the Song of Songs might be the last
place we would look for teaching on justification by faith alone and extrinsic righteousness.[74] Yet that is where Kempf's doctrine on discretion

---

Tentler, *Sin and Confession on the Eve of the Reformation* (1977); Gerard Zerbolt
in *De spiritualibus ascensionibus*, ch. 17, ed. Martène and Durand (1677), 26: 258-89, at
264, trans. Van Engen, *Devotio Moderna*, 261, cf. ch. 25 on signs of love. For a broader
and later view, see the thought-provoking discussion in William Bouwsma, *John Calvin:
A Sixteenth-Century Portrait* (1988), pp. 32-48: "Calvin's Anxiety."

[73] H. Dörries, "The Place of Confession in Early Monasticism," in *Studia Patristica*,
vol. 5, pt. 3 (1962), 284-311.

[74] We should not be surprised: this short book of love poetry was used throughout the
Middle Ages as a basis for commenting on the most central tenets of doctrine. See Jean
Leclercq's comments in his introduction to *Bernard of Clairvaux: Selected Works*, trans.

as a refusal to trust in one's own prudence leads. In his discussion of Canticle 4:7 we come across a firm assertion of a *sola fide* theology.

Kempf was no proto-Protestant "Reformer before the Reformation," nor can he be fitted here or there on the spectrum of medieval teachings on justification by grace,[75] because he wrote no scholastic *summa* or commentary on Lombard's *Sentences*. Our concern here is with the implications of his Carthusian and monastic *context* for what might otherwise be dismissed as typical medieval *"cooperatio"* soteriology. It is his monastic context that places his statements, imprecise as they may be by scholastic standards, within a theology of extrinsic righteousness grounded in sacramental and institutional mediation.[76] Ironically, Protestant Reformers of various persuasions considered restrictive, pelagian, human, and anxiety-causing precisely the same structures of monastic rule and obedience that monks like Kempf considered freeing, grace-inspired, divine, and consoling.[77]

G. R. Evans (1987), 22. See also Helmut Riedlinger, *Die Makellosigkeit der Kirche in den lateinischen Hoheliedkommentaren des Mittelalters* (1958), and Friedrich Ohly, *Hohelied-Studien: Grundzüge einer Geschichte der Hoheliedauslegung des Abendlandes bis um 1200* (1958). Burrows, *Gerson*, 191-93, shows that the post-Constance Gerson also used the Canticle as a vehicle for his *sola gratia* soteriology.

[75] See Berndt Hamm, *Promissio, Pactum, Ordinatio: Freiheit und Selbstbindung Gottes in der scholastischen Gnadenlehre* (1977), with references to earlier literature on this subject. See also Alister E. McGrath, *Iustitia Dei*, 2 vols. (1986). Hamm argues that virtually all medieval theologians taught that salvation was by God's grace and mercy, yet nearly all differed from Luther on the issue of whether *human* works *merit* eternal life in any sense at all. A comparison of Kempf with the pre-Tridentine Catholic theologians who put forth various theologies of "double justification" (Gropper, Contarini, Seripando) might be very illuminating but cannot be undertaken here. See Edward Yarnold, *"Duplex Iustitia,"* in *Christian Authority* [Chadwick Festschrift] (1988), 204-23.

[76] This is not unlike Gérard Vallée's brief comments in "Luther and Monastic Theology," *ARG*, 75 (1984), 290-97. Vallée notes that the continuity between medieval culture and Luther "is not to be found in a kind of thinking, especially if one considers the type of thinking practised in the schools. The continuity is rather provided by a certain quality of the experience of God which expresses itself either as *compunctio* or as *Anfechtung*. That type of experience emphasizes the passive element in man's relation to God and underlines the fact that man is being acted upon from the outside; correlatively, God's action predominates, disconcerting man and spurring him on. In both contexts God is experienced as a God who disturbs, afflicts, and fills with consternation." For a Carthusian context, note Guigo I, *Meditationes*, no. 76b: "Nusquam ergo secura anima Christiana, nisi in adversis" (SC 308: 126).

[77] Although this entire area needs much more study before we can understand why such opposing conclusions could be reached, it seems fitting to suggest that a crucial paradigm shift lies in the Reformers' interiorizing understanding of the human self and its freedom, compared to the ancient and monastic exteriorizing understanding of the self and of freedom. For a sensitive study of the early Luther from a Catholic perspective of spiritual theology see Jared Wicks, *Man Yearning for Grace: Luther's Early Spiritual Teaching* (1968); idem, "Luther" in *DSAM* 9 (1976), 1206-43; and idem, *Luther and His Spiritual Legacy* (1983). Taken together with Burrows, *Jean Gerson*, a path for reassess-

To call attention to the implications of the monastic context of Kempf's medieval Catholic soteriology is not intended to obscure real differences between Protestant and Catholic views of justification. Yet despite those real differences, comparing Kempf to various Reformation-era figures is neither anachronistic nor arbitrary. Precisely the attention given to the soteriological implications of monastic life by people as different as Lorenzo Valla, Martin Luther, Gasparo Contarini, and Desiderius Erasmus sets the agenda for our analysis here. Only the hegemony enjoyed by nonmonastic, scholastic theologies in studies of both Protestant and Catholic soteriologies has kept us from seeing trajectories that fifteenth- and sixteenth-century theologians saw clearly.

A. Sola Fide: Canticle 4:7

Scholars have have asserted that the soteriology of Luther's Psalm lectures of 1513-15 represents a reinterpretation of the medieval *stercus* and *cloaca* images for human works in combination with a revised understanding of medieval covenant theology. Put briefly, this interpretation argues that Luther applied the traditional phrase, *facientibus quod in se est, Deus non denegat gratiam*, not to what people do but to their faith. For Luther, in the Psalm lectures, faith consisted in recognizing that one is a pauper, humbled [*humiliatus*], emptyhanded, standing "up to the ears" in excrement. *Humilitas* in the Psalm lectures no longer meant humility as "a medieval monkish virtue," rather the concept of *humilitas* at this stage carried the same freight as the expression *extra nos* a few years later—it meant the recognition that we find *in nobis* nothing but *stercora*. The human covenant partner is a pauper, a mendicant, who can do nothing but wail (*clamare*). The doing of the one with faith is to groan and sob because he can only find salvation *extra se* in Christ. The *humilitas* demanded by this covenant is not some kind of virtue, "it is far more the admission of human helplessness and need."[78]

---

ing Luther's relationship to his late medieval context has begun to be cleared. Even Wicks, however, failed to draw on the monastic context assumed by the present study.

[78] Oberman, "Wir sein pettler. Hoc est verum: Bund und Gnade in der Theologie des Mittelalters und der Reformation," in *ZKG*, 78 (1967), 232-52 (repr. 1986). Oberman's interpretation is echoed by that of Ozment, *Homo Spiritualis*, 151-58, 176-78. These interpretations, recapitulated by Alister McGrath, *Luther's Theology of the Cross* (1985), 95-136, must be read together with Jared Wicks, Otto Pesch, and others. See Wicks, *Man Yearning for Grace* (1968), "Luther (Martin)," in *DSAM* (1983), and *Luther and His Spiritual Legacy* (1983). Gerson also used this image, in his late work, *De consolatione theologiae*, bk. I, prosa IV (Gerson, *Oeuvres*, 9:197-98).

Nicholas Kempf also made use of the principle: *facientibus quod in se est, Deus non denegat gratiam*, applying it to the regular sacramental life of the church, while explicitly excluding it from the highest reaches of mystical union.[79] Our concern here is with his application of it to repentance, the essential foundation for mystical union. His "facere quod"—the "monkish virtue," if we follow the conventional interpretation—was simply an admission of one's "poverty, mutilation, lameness, and blindness." The pejorative term "monkish virtue," grounded in Luther's own rejection of his mendicant past, might fit medicant scholastic theology, but it does not fit Kempf.[80]

Kempf employed the passage under discussion here in all three of his writings on mystical theology: his commentary on the Canticle and the treatises *De ostensione regni Dei*, and *De mystica theologia* (see appendix A, nos. 18-20).[81] In *De ostensione*, the passage is set in the con-

---

[79] Kempf, *Cantica*, Prologue, ch. 8 (G1, 138r, 30 - 138v, 5; Pez, *Bibl. ascetica*, 11: 29): "Nec iste gradus amoris in ymagine mentis cum cantico ita acquiritur, sicut gracie gratum faciens, seu caritas cum donis Spiritus Sancti, que ex pacto Christi cum ecclesia, faciente homine quod in se est, infallibiliter infundantur, ut in baptizato parvulo aut adulto non ponente obicem, aut in vere penitente; et in actu seu exercicio caritatis infuse cooperatur ipsum liberum arbitrium. Sed in infusione illius amoris Deus omnino est illimitabilis; quia, quando homo facit omnia quae potest, adhuc dilectus liberrime potest venire aut non venire ad cantandum hoc canticum amoris in mente; et actus illius amoris solummodo causantur a Deo absque libero arbitrio coagente." Cf. ibid., bk. I, ch. 2, 14 [God's grace draws us, but gently, rather than violently; drawn by God's grace we run in imitation of Christ's works (Ca 1:2)], 27. In the prologue, ch. 8, Kempf asserts that justifying grace is granted *infallibiliter* to those who do their best and that the human free will cooperates with God's grace. Cf., *Rect*, III.20, as quoted in chapter three, above—salvation is by grace, not by one's own free will, but damnation comes by the freely willed failure to attend to the stirrings of previenient grace. Kempf thus rejects any sort of double-predestination. However he does not address the crucial issues of whether the rewarding of one's "best" occurs in the context of predestination *ante praevisa merita* and whether one does one's best *ex puris naturalibus*. Cf. Kempf, *MTh*, I.3 (Jellouschek ed., pp. 24-25); *Ost*, ch. 29, 38-39, and *Rect*, II.5 (Schottenstift cod. 336 (296), 48v: Pez, 4: 302). As described in chapter three, above, Kempf explicitly denied that the stirrings to pursue a monastic vocation can be had *ex puris naturalibus* (although a certain human "preparation" and "cooperation" in the form of prayerful, deep yearning may accompany it [*Rect*, III.15-17, Pez 4: 472-79; *Prop*, I.17/16; Schottenstift 336 (296), fol. 12r, 19-21]). In the monastic realm, where God works solely by grace, lies the greater freedom from anxiety. Taking account of the monastic context thus introduces a new complexity into the debates over "Pelagianism" in late medieval and Reformation theology that will need to be sorted out. (Graham White has recently argued that failure to take pastoral dimensions into account has led to a distortions in claims that late medieval scholastic theologians were "semi-Pelagian." See White's "Pelagianisms," *Viator*, 20 [1989], 233-54.)

[80] See Kempf, *MTh*, I.15 (Jellouschek ed., p. 87), for an example of the way he uses such terms as "infused love."

[81] *Cantica*, IV.9 (G1, 233r, 16 - 234v, 2); *Ost*, ch. 24 (G1, 16v, 27 - 17r, 18). It is briefly summarized in *MTh*, II.3 (G1, 60r, 16-25; Jellouscheck ed., pp. 101-2). The full texts of the passages from *Cantica* and *Ost* are given in appendix B.

text of the cleansing that a monk must pursue in order to prepare for contemplative union. This cleansing begins with sacramental penance and
continues with daily, indeed, continual, self-examination and repentance.
Kempf wonders, though, whether this is realistic—is it possible to
cleanse oneself, through genuine contrition and repentance, of every
mortal and venial sin? In Job, Ecclesiastes, 1 John, and elsewhere, the
scriptures clearly say that no one can live without sin. Pseudo-Gregory
the Great (actually an eleventh-century Benedictine from Mont St.
Michel, Robert of Tombelaine[82]), had already examined this question.
Pseudo-Gregory's response, as quoted by Kempf, was

> As long as the holy soul cleanses herself from daily sins through peni-
> tence, as long as daily she washes minor sins away with tears and keeps
> herself from major sins, though she sin repeatedly, she still constantly pre-
> serves her purity through assiduous penitence. Hence it is enjoined else-
> where, "Let your garments always be sparkling white" [Ecclesiastes 9:8];
> and, "the just man lives by faith" (Rom 1:17). Even though immediately
> upon sinning she strays from righteousness, nevertheless, so long as she
> continues to believe in him who justifies the ungodly (Rom 4:5; Gal 3:8;
> cf. Pr 17:15) and singlemindedly weeps for her sins [sua peccata] under
> her/his faith [sub eius fide], she retains her righteousness [iustitiam suam]
> through assiduous ablutions.[83]

The close juxtaposition of "*suam* iustitiam retinet" and "*sua* peccata
deflet" with "sub *eius* fide" might seem to require a referent other than

---

[82] PL 79: 493-548, at 510B-C. Little is known about Robert of Tombelaine, who died
ca. 1090 at Rome. He left Mont St. Michel to become a hermit in Tombelaine, but later
became abbot of St. Vigor near Bayeux (1066). He accompanied Gregory VII to Rome.
Closely bound up with monastic developments in Normandy, he was a friend of Anselm
of Canterbury and is mentioned several times by Ordericus Vitalis. His commentary is
normally described as heavily dependent on Bede's commentary on the Song of Songs;
as we shall see, he contributed at least one original twist. See Guibert Michiels, "Robert
de Tombelaine," in *DSAM*, 13 (1987), 828-31; Paul Quivy and Joseph Thiron, "Robert
de Tombelaine et son commentaire sur le Cantique des Cantiques," in *Le millénaire
monastique du Mont-Saint-Michel* (1967), 2: 347-56.

[83] *Ost*, 24 (G1, 17r, 3-11): "Dum sancta anima a peccatis cottidianis se per penitenciam mundat, dum cottidie peccata minuta cum lacrimis abluit et a maioribus se observat, quamvis frequenter peccet, per assiduam tamen penitenciam mundiciam suam
assidue servat. Hinc enim alibi precipitur 'Semper sint vestimenta tua candida' [Ecclesi-
astes 9:8]. Et illud 'iustus ex fide vivit' [Rom 1:17]. Quamvis enim mox ut peccat a iusticia deviet, tamen dum semper credit in eum qui iustificat impium et assidue sub eius
fide peccata sua deflet, per assiduas abluciones iusticiam suam retinet." Kempf's quotation is letter-for-letter identical with Robert of Tombelaine's text in the Migne edition
[PL 79:510].

the ungodly.[84] But medieval writers were notoriously casual about the distinction between *eius* and *suus*. Yet, even though the faith spoken of here may be the soul's faith, the rest of the passage (and the context of Romans 4:1-5) emphasizes that the only sense in which the human soul can be said to be "completely beautiful" and totally cleansed is that the purity and beauty is God's doing, not the soul's. That Kempf and his monastic sources had Romans 4 in mind when they used the phrase "eius fide" seems probable.

Alongside Pseudo-Gregory (Robert of Tombelaine), Kempf also cites Bede,[85] although Bede makes only an oblique allusion to Rom 1:17 ("live justly through grace")—it is Robert of Tombelaine who adds the idea of "believing in him who justifies the ungodly." Here we have an epitome of early medieval religion: penitence, weeping for one's sins, "retaining one's righteousness through assiduous penance and tears." Although all this seems to be "monkish virtue," Kempf insists it is all the gift of God's grace and that all the monk, or anyone, can do is to recognize one's dis-ability.

However, Kempf was not simply dependent on Robert of Tombelaine and Bede. In the Carthusian Order the entire process of clothing a novice and receiving his profession, as outlined in chapter one, section one, above, emphasized God's extrinsic activity in the "path of rule-bound observance."[86] And the very phrase, "God, who justifies the impious" was part of the psalmody chanted as the new novice was led to his cell.[87] As we have seen, the very center of the monastic life for Kempf is an extrinsic trust in the structure of the monastic rule and in the role of the pastoral confessor or spiritual director, a greater confidence in the prayers of others than in one's own.[88] Over and over Kempf emphasized that recognition of one's own weakness, blindness, lameness, and poverty is the crucial factor in being invited to the heavenly banquet (both

---

[84] Guigo de Ponte did use an extrinsic referent in a similar context, referring to the confidence of the soul being God's confidence. See the discussion of Guigo in chapter five, below. Kempf does the same in *Ost*, ch. 45 (G1, 34v, lines 2-5: "Qui frequenter considerat presenciam Dei in corde, predicto modo recto corde eum querendo, faceret sibi Deum valde familiarem et frequenter presentem et, valde mens sua prius purgata, illuminaretur *per eius cognicionem* et sibi uniretur per amorem, ut diceret Deus 'illuminacio mea' [Ps 138:11; 27:1]" (emphasis added). We shall return to this chapter of *De ostensione* below. Its full text is found in appendix B. See also Burrow's discussion of this issue in Gerson's *De consolatione theologiae: Gerson,* esp. pp. 177-79.

[85] *In Cantica canticorum allegorica expositio* in PL 91: 1065-1235, at 1137-38.

[86] Guigo I, *Consuet.,* 25.1.

[87] *Statuta antiqua,* II.23.14, quoted in chapter one, above.

[88] See the quotation, full of baptismal imagery, from *Prop,* II.23 (VS1, 34 A, 7-31), in chapter one, above.

the eschatological banquet in heaven and mystical union and the Eucharist on earth).[89] This is the "judgment and justification" that the soul applies to herself daily.[90]

That faith is the central concept for Kempf is evident from his juxtaposition of Bede and Ps.-Gregory, who are unusual, if not unique, among medieval commentators on this verse in their mention of faith here.[91] Kempf called the words of Bede and especially those of Robert of Tombelaine "words of consolation,"[92] thereby pointing to the key concern of the entire late Middle Ages: assurance of salvation.

B. Extrinsic Righteousness

The debate over "Pelagianism" and "works-righteousness" in the late Middle Ages as a background for the Protestant Reformation has continued ever since that Reformation. Following the polemics of Ren-

---

[89] Kempf, Ost, ch. 51 (G1, 38r, 25 - 39r, 3), text in appendix B.

[90] Ost, ch. 24 (G1, 17r, 10-17): "Behold how briefly and fundamentally Blessed Gregory effectively presents this step of purgation . . . for whoever keeps himself from the more grave sins, yet occasionally, even frequently, falls into lighter sins, nonetheless through the judgment and justification which he applies to himself daily is always cleansed and is said to preserve his innocence. He is thus made totally beautiful and no flaw is found in him, because, even if for the moment he is dirtied, nevertheless it does not last a long time" (original text in appendix B).

[91] Indeed, I have found no similar reference in other printed medieval Canticle commentaries, although my research has depended heavily on Riedlinger's summaries for those still in manuscript. Since Riedlinger did not take note of this "sola fide" aspect in Kempf or Robert of Tombelaine's commentaries, it is possible he has missed it in others. A comparison to the roughly contemporaneous commentary on Canticles by John of Mantua highlights the way Bede and Robert of Tombelaine deal with this passage. John of Mantua refers only to the role of the church's sacraments, without the crucial "ex fide" that Kempf adds. Iohannis Mantuani in Cantica Canticorum et de Sancta Maria Tractatus ad Comitissam Matildam, ed. Bernhard Bischoff and Burkhard Taeger (1973), 89. For a discussion of the background of this commentary in ecclesial and lay politics see Silvia Cantelli, "Il commento al Cantico dei Cantici di Giovanni da Mantova," Studi medievali, ser. 3, vol. 26 (1985), 101-84, with citations to other literature.

[92] Cantica, IV.9 (G1, 233v, 5-16; Pez, 11: 422): "Hec sunt consolatoria verba, in quibus Beatus Gregorius aperte declarat, que in presenti vita requirantur ad hoc, quod anima sancta, Christi sponsa, dicatur totaliter aut perfecte pulchra et sine macula. Et dicit hic Beda: 'Nemo est super terram sine peccato, nec infans unius diei, sed ideo fides perfecta et celeste desiderium omnem maculam abstergit levioris peccati. Tota ergo est pulchra ecclesia, in quantum se castam et immunem ab omni peccato custodit. Si quando autem levi peccato fuscatur, cita penitudine et recta fide ad celeste desiderium in ea pristina pulchritudo recuperatur.' Hec Beda inter caetera. Est ergo anima dilecti sponsa tunc, tota pulchra, quando nec in opere, nec in verbo, nec in aliqua animae potencia diu perseverat peccatum; quando per penitentiam, aut lachrimas, aut sacramenta ecclesie ex fide deleatur [Pez: deletur]." For context see appendix B.

aissance humanists and Protestant theologians, scholars have conventionally assumed that monks were notoriously guilty of trusting in works righteousness.[93] In the present, purportedly ecumenical age, some scholars have attempted to rehabilitate various scholastic theologians.[94] Bengt Hägglund has even attempted to vindicate the soteriology of the German mystics (largely mendicants) and, to some degree the "romance" mystics (largely contemplative monks) writing in Latin.[95] For the most part, however, medieval contemplative monastics remain soteriologically suspect, and, apart from modern Catholic and monastic scholarship, centuries-old stereotypes survive.

On the one hand, Kempf directly applied the "facere quod in se est" principle to mystical union. In chapter thirty-nine of *De ostensione*, Kempf compared the influence of divine prevenient grace to the effect of the planets on the earth. No one can escape this influence, and through it one can do what is in oneself, *ex suis naturalibus*, to come to the knowledge of God with the aid of concomitant grace. If you do what is in you to know God, i.e., if you are attentive, waiting for the influence of the Trinity, then you will come to faith. No human having full use of his reason can ignore the prevenient grace of the *influxus Dei* in his soul; what the human can do beyond grace, *ex puris naturalibus*, is attend to or resist that *influxus Dei*. One cannot ignore it; but one can reject it. No one should be surprised that Jews and infidels do resist; what will be a surprise is when many apparently faithful Christians, especially the learned and those trained in knowledge of scriptures, even many religious and spiritual people, are exposed at the Last Judgment as having failed to attend to the *influxus Dei* of grace.[96] Kempf expanded on this theme in

---

[93] Bernhard Lohse, *Mönchtum und Reformation: Luthers Auseinandersetzung mit dem Mönchsideal des Mittelalters* (1963), based largely on Johann von Paltz, for whom see Hamm, *Frömmigkeitstheologie*; Lorenzo Valla, *De professione religiosorum*, which attacks the assertion that good works performed by monks carry greater merit. See the discussion by Charles Trinkaus in "Humanist Treatises," and *In Our Image*, 651-82.

[94] For summaries see O. H. Pesch and A. Peters, *Einführung in die Lehre von Gnade und Rechtfertigung* (1981); McGrath, *Iustitia Dei*; and Karlfried Froehlich, "Justification Language and Grace: The Charge of Pelagianism in the Middle Ages," in *Probing the Reformed Tradition* [Dowey Festschrift] (1989), 21-47.

[95] Bengt Hägglund, "The Background of Luther's Doctrine of Justification in Late Medieval Theology," *Lutheran World*, 8 (1961), 24-46 (repr. 1971). See also the fine study of these issues in Eckhart by Alessandro Klein, *Meister Eckhart: La dottrina mistica della giustificazione* (1978), esp. pp. 74-78: "'Christus pro nobis' e 'Christus in nobis'," and pp. 97-108: "La giustificazione come deificazione: 'iustitia aliena, non extranea'."

[96] *Ost*, 39 (G1, 29v, 10 - 30r, 2): "Ita nullus homo habens completum racionis usum potest ignorare influxum Dei in animam per graciam prevenientem, si quantum posset ex naturalibus ad talem influxum attenderet in se, quem nullus alius homo potest scire sicut

chapter forty-five, where he noted that God is always present, always revealed in the hearts of those who are attentive to the influx of his grace;
God is always to be found in one's heart if one seeks him with a right
heart—a heart that is devout and sincere in its *affectus* and humble in its
intellectus; an *affectus* that is not curved in on itself but turned toward
love of God by infused love (*caritas*).

Kempf was well aware of the overtones of self-salvation here. He
took pains to make clear that a simpler way was possible—God is present in the human heart, in the *imago Dei*, in the image of the Trinity, in
which God alone acts in the soul's acts of memory, understanding and
will. Kempf thus outlined a sort of *cogito, ergo non ego sed Deus est*
doctrine.[97]

Where Kempf wrote of doing one's best *ex suis naturalibus*, he insisted that grace is ever present.[98] In his commentary on the Canticle,

---

ipsemet homo in se, quia talis gracia preveniens est multiplex et valde diversa in
diversis hominibus. Ita quod nemo potest scire in quolibet particulari homine sicut ipsemet homo, si attenderet. Et ex tali gracie influxu possit consurgere in Dei cognicionem et
amorem, et sic faciendo quod in se est, ille tandem illuminaretur gracia supernaturali et
gratuita, qua paratus est Deus illuminare omnem hominem venientem in hunc mundum
et facientem quod in se est. Et hunc est quod nullus homo paganus aut iudeus aut
quicumque alius quantumcunque indoctus excusatur de sua dampnacione, quia quilibet
habet influxum spiritualem in animam a sole divinitatis et a celo celorum benedicte trinitatis, quam si attenderet et sequeretur faciendo quod in se est, Deum cognosceret et consequenter ad fidem veniret. Sed qualis sit ille influxus in quolibet homine omnino est in
presenti vita occultum, sed in finali iudicio, quando aperiuntur libri, tunc omnibus erit
manifestum quali influxu gracie quilibet homo sit preventus. Nec mirum si pagani et infideles non advertunt aut non secuntur talem influxum, cum multi fideles, non solum
simplices sed quandoque multum docti et illuminati sciencijs sacris aut eciam quandoque
religiosi et spirituales viri, non advertunt illum influxum aut non secuntur, peccatis impe-
dientibus. Qualem tamen influxum multi philosophi excellenter et perfecte invenerunt et
in suis scriptis reliquerunt sicut de hoc dictum est in tractatu de ostensione regni Dei
prope finem" [= *MTh*, V.5; Jellouschek ed. pp. 372-77].

[97] *Ost*, ch. 45 (G1, 33v, 14 - 34v, 10, at 34r, lines 29-36): ". . . homo semper cum gracia Dei potest Deum invenire, si solum recto quesierit corde. Quid autem est recto corde
quererere? Hoc est affectu devoto et sincero et humili intellectu, ut affectus seu voluntas
non sit retorta aut tornata per amorem ad creaturas, sed Dei amorem per caritatem infusam. Et intellectus non sit obliquatus ad seipsum, ut putet se posse tales cogitaciones
habere, aut tales cogitaciones seu actus predictos suos esse, aut se aliquid in eis habere
putans se aliquid esse aut posse—cum nichil sit et sine Deo omnino nichil possit et nichil
sit." The full text of the chapter is given in appendix B. Cf. *MTh*, I.15 (Jellouschek ed.,
pp. 86-88) on *caritas infusa* and III.13 (pp. 238-44) regarding God's acts in the human
soul.

[98] One is reminded of Bernard of Clairvaux's *Sermones in Cantica Canticorum*,
3.5—the very confidence one has in approaching God involves God's grace already
given: "Once you have had this twofold experience of God's benevolence in these two
kisses, you need no longer feel abashed in aspiring to a holier intimacy. Growth in grace
brings expansion of confidence. . . . 'The one who knocks will always have the door
opened to him [Lk. 11:10]' It is my belief that to a person so disposed, God will not refuse that most intimate kiss of all, a mystery of supreme generosity and ineffable sweet-

quoting Robert of Tombelaine on Ca. 4:6b as his authority, Kempf asserted that the bride cannot arrive at total cleansing through her own efforts and that the Bridegroom makes up what she lacks. Her very striving is born up and brought to effectiveness by the Bridegroom through his grace, and what the Bridegroom praises in the bride is his own work.[99] Kempf returned to this point to give it special emphasis: "And even though the Bride is unable to attain to this purity through herself and her own effort, nevertheless the Bridegroom, when he deigns to come, supplies what is lacking and, in the moment of his coming or a little before, he will perfectly cleanse her."[100]

Much the same point is made in De ostensione, chapter twenty-seven. "When you fall from grace," he had told his reader in chapter twenty-four, "wash yourself in the grace of Christ." Now he explains that no one can live for very long without committing venial sins. Even the saints and holy men admit that they are black as coals. However, when ignited by alien power (aliena virtus) the heat of the fire burns off the scale and they glow warmly and burn. The aliena virtus that accomplishes this is the Holy Spirit, which consumes scale and rust and purifies gold.[101]

---

ness." Translation by Kilian Walsh in CF 4: 19-20. Cf. Heinrich Arnoldi, Dialogus de modo perveniendi, ch. 32 (Bibl. ascetica, 6: 123-24). The same principle applies in Kempf's discussion of a vocation to the monastic life as he outlined it in Rect, III.15, 17, 20 (VS1, 72v B, 74r A - 74v A, 75v B, 26-39; Pez 4: 472, 478-79, 486); Prop, I.16 (VS1, 12r B, 19-21).

[99] Kempf, Cantica, IV.8 (G1, 232v, 35 - 233r, 4; Pez 11:419): "Hijs quippe virtutibus sancta ecclesia vel unaqueque anima munda efficitur, quia dum per voluptatum mortificationem vicijs reluctatur, et per sanctas oraciones frequenter lacrimis abluitur, sordes lavat, ut sponso placeat, cui pulchra apparere conatur. Cuius conatum ad effectum sponsus per graciam suam ducit, opusque suum in sponsa benigne laudat cum dicit: 'Tota pulchra es etc.'" Cf. Gregory the Great (the genuine Gregory, not Robert of Tombelaine), Expositiones in Canticum Canticorum, par. 39 (CCSL, 144, p. 38): "Nigra sum sed formosa. 'Nigra per me, formosa per donum; nigra de praeterito, formosa ex eo quod facta sum in futuris.' Quomodo nigra? Quomodo formosa? Nigra sicut tabernacula Cedar, formosa sicut pellis Salomonis. Et non est iustum, ut aliquis ex praeterita vita pensetur, et non magis adtendatur quod fuit, sed quod est."

[100] Cantica, IV.9 (G1, 234r, 4-7; Pez 11: 424): "Et quamvis [Pez add. Sponsa] ad hanc mundiciam non possit per se et per suum conatum pertingere, tamen quando dilectus dignatur venire, tunc ipse supplet defectum; et in ipso tempore adventus sui, aut paulo ante, perfecte eam mundabit, 'et totam pulchram' facit [Pez: faciet], ita ut ei dicat: 'tota iam pulchra es amica mea et macula non est in te.'" For context see appendix B. Ozment made much of Luther's references to Christ's coming not on the basis of man's having been cleansed in preparation but on the basis of a "preparation" that is human sinfulness and unrighteousness. This seems to be precisely Kempf's point here. See Ozment, Homo Spiritualis, 176-83.

[101] Ost, 27 (G1, 19v, 11 - 20r, 12): "Ex predicta enim causa peccatorum venialium, quibus sancti omnes, quandoque denigrantur et sua opera bona quasi polluuntur, vocant se nigros sicut corvos et sicut carbones desolatorios [Lamentations 4:8?]. Sicut enim car-

The final step, as in all of Kempf's writings, is to make an affective, personal application. "Now humbly accuse yourself of your negligence and say from the heart, 'O my Beloved, that I am not completely beautiful is because of my own negligence. I have not avoided those occasional major sins to the degree that I am able and ought to do and I have been careless in repenting of the smaller sins. . . .'"[102] Monkish virtue has reappeared, one might think. But the key to all of this is not what one has achieved, but what one lacks; the key is longing for the Beloved, the *desiderium ad Dilectum*.

> This beauty, according to Saint Bernard, is gained through a great loving longing for the Bridegroom. Hence he says in Sermon 31: 'The fire will go before him and burn up his adversaries round about. The fire of holy desire ought to precede his appearance to every soul to whom he is coming, to burn up the rust of vices and thus to prepare a place for the Lord.' But this purity and beauty is not acquired perfectly through that fire of love that precedes, rather through that fire of love which fills, through the Bridegroom himself in his coming.[103]

bones ex sua natura semper nigri sunt, eciam quando sunt igniti, et non habent nisi nigredinem. Ita homo ex se, quantumlibet sanctus, non habet nisi peccatum. Sed virtute aliena, scilicet calore ignis, consumunt, rubiginem calefaciunt, et lucent, ardent, et incendunt. Ita sancti viri virtute aliena, scilicet Spiritus Sancti, consumunt rubiginem peccati et mundant aurum, calefaciunt et incendunt proximos et lucent bonis operibus per ignem scilicet caritatis. Sic terra sine solis radijs est pulvis et lutum, sed per solem facit multiplicem fructum. Sancti ergo viri per huiusmodi peccata non deficiunt sed proficiunt, ita ut caritatis ignis et omnium virtutum habitus augeantur. Iuxta illud, virtus in infirmitate perficitur, quia ex perfecta caritate et suiipsius perfecta consideracione et ex dono discrecionis spirituum statim percipiunt huiusmodi motus inordinatos, quos fortiter reprimendo per actum virtutis, augentur in eis virtutes per tales actus virtutis quos sic formant inresistendo. Et sicut nix cadens in estate statim liquescit, et guttule aque in ignem proiecte consumuntur, et parva pluvia a terra multum siccata absorbetur, ita talia peccata in sanctis viris non manent. Et quedam vasa preciosa purgantur a rubigine aut inmundicia per cineres aspersos aut pulveres seu arenam ut splendeant, sic per venialia talia mundatur perfecte anima. Inperfecti autem et negligentes et tepidi et quasi nichil venialia peccata curantes paciuntur magnum detrimentum, tam in multo acquirendo quam in penis quas sibi accumulant, et impediuntur in acquisicione virtutum et extinguitur fervor caritatis; et sic successsive ipsa caritas tepescit in eis, et quandoque totaliter perditur [fol. 20r] per multiplicacionem venialium. Qui enim non curat minima, paulatim decidet in maxima peccata. Et hec est causa principalis quod pauci proficiunt, quia non ita curant nec advertunt venialia peccata sicuti deberent et ut sancti patres tradunt."

[102] Kempf, *Cantica*, IV.9 (G1, 234r, 20-27; Pez 11: 425): "Hic accusa te humiliter de tua negligencia, et ex corde dicas: 'O mi dilecte, quod non sum totus pulcher, ex mea negligencia est, eo quod peccata eciam quandoque graviora, sicut possem et deberem, non omitto; et de levioribus negligenter peniteo, et quasi ex quadam consuetudine confiteor sine dolore, et iterum reincido eadem sine timore. Et hec est causa, quod non purgor nec mundor. O [Pez *add.* igitur] misericordissime, da mihi fervorem ad cavendam frequentacionem peccatorum, et dolorem [Pez *add.* ea] diluendi.'"

[103] Kempf, *Cantica*, IV.9 (G1, 234r, 27-34; Pez 11: 425): "Hec autem pulchritudo secundum beatum Bernardum acquiritur per magnum amoris desiderium ad dilectum.

The framework for all of this is penitence. *De ostensione* is built around the three levels of purgation, each of which has its own purgation, illumination and union.[104] The first level of purgation is sacramental penance[105]; the second and third levels are more developed, monastic forms of these. All virtues, e.g., humility, patience, obedience, are accessible to all Christians in a degree sufficient for salvation. Beyond that first level, there is humility in a special or perfect sense, patience in a special or perfect sense, etc. Self-love resulting from original sin is destroyed by the church's sacraments, especially baptism, penance and Eucharist. This brings one to the first level of purgation: patience, humility, and obedience in their normal, frequent, devout, and sacramental form. Illumination and union of spirit on this normal, lay level come through love of God and neighbor—the active life. Thus there is a form of purgation, illumination, and union available to the laity in the active life, primarily in the sacraments. Chapters twenty-four and following address the higher, perfect, levels of purgation, illumination and union, beginning with the question whether it is possible to have absolutely perfect purgation.

Thus precisely at the point at which Kempf emphasizes self-judgment, repentance, and complete cleansing from sin by what initially appears to be human effort and ecclesial channels, he introduces his assertion that complete cleansing comes from outside oneself. He is perfectly willing to use the language of habits and virtues but they are virtues perfected in infirmity, and the work is directly the work of God in the soul.

Unde dicit Sermone 31. sic, "'Ignis ante ipsum precedet, et inflammabit in circuitu inimicos eius' [Ps 96:3 Vulg.]. Oportet namque, ut sancti desiderij ardor preveniat faciem eius ad omnem animam, ad quam ipse est venturus; qui omnem consumat rubiginem viciorum; et sic preparet locum domine." Sed illa munditia et pulchritudo non acquiritur perfecte per illum ignem amoris precedentem, sed per [Pez *add.* illum] ignem amoris, qui infunditur, per ipsum dilectum venientem." [*S. Bernardi Opera*, 1: 221.] Guigo de Ponte makes much the same point, quoting the same sermon by Bernard of Clairvaux. See Guigo de Ponte, *De contemplatione*, I.2 (Dupont ed., p. 86).

[104] Outlined in *Ost*, ch. 10 (G1, 6v, 25 - 7v, 32).

[105] Kempf, *Cantica*, IV.9 (G1, 233v, 13-16; Pez 11: 422): "Est ergo anima dilecti sponsa tunc, tota pulchra, quando nec in opere, nec in verbo, nec in aliqua animae potencia diu perseverat peccatum; quando per penitentiam, aut lachrimas, aut sacramenta ecclesie ex fide deleatur [Pez: deletur]."

C. Monastic Texts and Context

To this point Kempf might still appear to be simply one more representative of typical medieval Catholic *cooperatio* soteriology in which
justification depends on an inward disposition which, free gift of God's
grace though it may be, nonetheless becomes the *sine qua non* of eternal
life and permits legitimate talk of meriting salvation.[106] It is important to
reiterate that Kempf is not presented in the present study as a forerunner
of the Reformation. He does use the "disposition language" of medieval
Catholicism. Not so much the texts he wrote as the personal and institutional context in which he wrote them distinguishes, however subtly, his
monastic soteriology from medieval scholastic theologies of grace. In his
writings Kempf insists that the disposition, the *faciendum quod in se est*,
is nothing more and nothing less than recognition of one's blindness,
weakness, helplessness.[107] And he voted both with his feet and *viva voce*
when he vowed obedience to a Rule. Precisely as a monk he understood
the alien character of that disposition of infused righteousness because
the monk is the one who daily knows himself to be completely poor,
blind, weak, maimed, and lame, unable to save himself. In Kempf's
view, monks are those whose deep consciousness of sinfulness, of inability to dispose themselves, drives them to the crutch of a monastic context. In *De discretione* Kempf insists again and again that the monk who
thinks otherwise, who tries to guide himself, who tries to use the monastic life to earn salvation, is sure to fail as a monk. Monastic life requires
the institutionalizing of renunciation, the structured recognition of one's
own weakness and the vowed acceptance of guidance from the Rule and
one's superiors as the sure way of salvation.

That Kempf is following his own Carthusian tradition will become
apparent from the discussion of his mystical theology in chapter five.
Yet the Carthusian tradition is only part of a longer tradition of the desert. Kempf understood the unconditionality of God's grace precisely because the Carthusian order stood in continuity with the tradition of the

---

[106] Berndt Hamm, "Was ist reformatorische Rechtfertigungslehre?" *ZThK*, 83 (1986),
1-38. See also Alister McGrath, *Iustitia Dei*, 1: 182-87. Peter Manns, "Zum Gespräch
zwischen M. Luther und der katholischen Theologie," in *Thesaurus Lutheri* (1987), 63-
154 (repr. 1988), attacks Hamm in unbecoming and intemperate language, arguing that
Hamm makes what is characteristic of catholic soteriology out to be the "system-spren-
gende" anticatholic element in the Reformation (74-75).

[107] *Ost*, ch. 51, as found in appendix B; cf. chapter three, above.

Desert Fathers.[108] The sixth-century abbot, John Climacus, tells of a monk who, having told his Abba he was ready to submit to him like iron to the blacksmith, was commanded to stand at the gate and, each time someone passed by, to kneel and say, "Pray for me, Father, because I am an epileptic." He did this for seven years and "achieved great humility and compunction."[109] Other stories remind one of military boot camp experiences designed deliberately to break the will of raw recruits: When Paul the Simple brought a jar of honey to Antony, Antony said, "Break the jar and pour out the honey." Paul did so. Then he said to him, "Gather up the honey again with a spoon without collecting any dirt with it." Antony also told Paul to weave baskets, then a few days later to unweave them all; to sew up his cloak and then take out the stitches and sew it up all over again.[110]

The Carthusians incorporated this principle of unconditional self-alienation into their statutes, most symbolically in the exhortation given to the newly professed monk: "From this time forward, he who has been received must understand himself to be a stranger to everything which is of the world, to the extent that he has control over absolutely nothing, not even over himself, without the permission of the prior." A concept of 'himself' exists here only to define what he must give up utterly in order to fulfill his vocation and avoid damnation.[111]

---

[108] One example comes from the novitiate of Abba John the Short, who was told by his Abba to water a stick he had planted in the ground. John did this faithfully for a year, although it meant walking all night to fetch water. Finally it blossomed and bore fruit. The Abba picked some of the fruit and took it to church and said to the brothers there, "Take and eat the fruit of obedience." Pelagius the Deacon, *Verba seniorum* (= bk. V of the *Vitae patrum* as edited by Herbert Rosweyde), part 14, paragraph 3 (PL 73: 948B; ET by Owen Chadwick in *Western Asceticism*, 150).

[109] John Climacus, *Ladder of Divine Ascent*, step 4, trans. Luibheid and Russell, pp. 97-98.

[110] *Historia monachorum in Aegypto*, ch. 24, as trans. by Norman Russell in *The Lives of the Desert Fathers* (1980), p. 114; critical edition by A.-J. Festugière, Subsidia Hagiographica, 6 (Brussels, 1961, 1971) [not seen]. The story is told also in Rufinus's Latin version of the *Historia monachorum*, ch. 31 (PL 21: 458C), but mentioning only the baskets and clothing, omitting the honey jar and spoon. In Palladius, *Historia Lausiaca*, ch. 28 (PG 34: 1080/1082CD) only the honey and the clothing are mentioned, not the baskets. For the complex interrelationship between the Greek, Latin, Syriac, Armenian, Coptic, Ethiopic, and Arabic versions of the *Historia Monachorum* see Palladius, *Historia Lausiaca*, ed. E. Cuthbert Butler (1898, 1904), e.g., pp. 28-33 on Paul the Simple.

[111] "Ex hoc tempore, qui susceptus est ita se ab omnibus quae mundi sunt intelligit alienum, ut nullius prorsus rei, nec sui quidem ipsius sine prioris licentia habeat potestatem. Cum enim ab omnibus qui regulariter vivere decreverunt, obedientia magno studio sit servanda, ab his tamen tanto devotius ac sollicitius, quanto districtius asperiusque subiere propositum, ne si quod absit ista defuerit, tanti labores non solum careant premio, sed et supplicium dampnationis incurrant." Guigo I, *Consuet.*, 25.2 (SC 313: 218). The same point is made in ch. 75 regarding the profession of a lay brother.

Modern readers shrink in horror from the "blind obedience" of the monks, from the explicit assertion that the spiritual director, the "apa," stands in Christ's stead vis-à-vis the novice or learner.[112] We are inclined to consider this another example of "monkish virtue"—trusting in another human, not in God's grace.

We must take a closer look, however, or we shall miss the point. Medieval Christian understandings of self began from the outside in order to form the inside. One plays various roles in life—father, husband, wife, student, mother, master, disciple, child. These various roles, not some irreducible inner, personal entity, create identity. The acts of trusting, naive, even blind[113] obedience in the early monks are a symbolic handing over, in a world that knew symbols to be utterly real, of one's misguided efforts at self-construction in order to begin to assume the proper selfhood of a creature created in the image of God.[114] One's distorted will, once curved in upon oneself selfishly, is symbolically handed over to someone else (standing in Christ's stead) as the first step in receiving it back so that one can play one's proper role. The core of the human self comes from outside (as the image of God) and the restoration of that deformed self likewise comes from outside.[115] Yet this same extensive understanding of self permitted human and creaturely things to play roles for God's grace as sacraments without necessarily becoming idolatrous efforts by humans to save themselves.

The Abba plays a role and plays it so well that he becomes the symbolic channel for extrinsic grace. It was the suprahuman, transcendent, larger-than-life role he played that made him an icon, a stylized figure of Christ. This role had never disappeared among the Carthusians, who combined the spirit of the desert and the zeal of the heroic eremitical reformers of the eleventh century with the humane affectivity of Augustine. Again and again Kempf urges his reader to trust his spiritual father, not to hold back, to reveal all his innermost thoughts. Only in

---

[112] Climacus, *Ladder*, step 4, "On Obedience"; ET by Luibheid and Russell, 91-92.

[113] Seeing things crookedly might help us realize that what seems a pejorative attribute to us could be a positive attribute for Kempf.

[114] The "discovery" of the modern inner-directed self has sometimes been traced to Augustine's *Confessions*. This is not the place to evaluate the various interpretations of Augustine's *Confessions* or his understanding of self. See chapter seven, below.

[115] *Outside* and *inside* here are analytical terms. It is self-contradictory to say that one's self is shaped from outside one*self*, unless there is some "inside" self to define what is outside. Yet precisely here lies the paradox of patristic and medieval *imago Dei* anthropology—the assertion that the human self is formed from the outside. Conceptually the language is problematic. However, this understanding of the human self as a congeries of roles, with the role of imago Dei as its basis, is visible in patristic and medieval practice, especially in sacramental practice.

transferring one's interiority to the external shoulders of a role-playing Abba is there security and cleansing, indeed "liberty."[116] Salvation lies outside of the monk in Christ and the symbolic way the monk pursues that is through trusting, repentant confession.

At the risk of redundancy, it must be emphasized once more that drawing attention to Kempf's *sola fide* texts about alien virtue does not make Kempf a forerunner of the Protestant Reformation. Yet it does call attention to monastic *texts* within a monastic *context* that has not yet received its due from students of historical theology. Beginning with the ritual bridal procession and the unconditional self-alienation of the bride outlined in chapter one's description of the Carthusian investiture of a novice and profession of vows, the structural context of monastic life makes the monastic understanding of grace unconditionally opposed to self-salvation.

Kempf's contemporaries sensed this, for it was the monastic *context* that was under attack in his day and in the decades that followed his death in 1497. Not only representatives of the Brethren of the Common Life, but Erasmus, Lorenzo Valla, Luther, and Gasparo Contarini, who differed on many theological issues, all relativized the monastic context. Therefore, to conclude this chapter, we look briefly at the views on monastic vows held by three of these men.

D. Luther, Valla, and Contarini with a View toward Kant

Luther too was concerned about penance and contrition, about perfection in repentance. This is what launched him on his reformation career. He too realized that perfect cleansing through contrition and sacramental penance was impossible. Under Staupitz' tutelage, he turned his gaze to Christ[117] and found Christian liberty. How ironic it is that the

---

[116] See the opening lines of the "Merchant's Tale" in Chaucer's *Canterbury Tales*. "And trewely it sit wel to be so, / That bacheleris have often peyne and wo; / On brotel ground they buylde, and brotelnesse / They fynde whan they wene sikernesse. / They lyve but as a bryd or as a beest, / In libertee and under noon arreest, / Ther as a wedded man in his estaat / Lyveth a lyf blisful and ordinaat / Under this yok of mariage ybounde." [And truly, it is well that it is so, that bachelors often have pain and woe. They build on shifting ground and find shiftiness when they suppose they have security (i.e. freedom from care, *securitas*). They live but as a bird or a beast, in liberty and under no restriction, whereas a wedded man in his estate lives a life blissful and ordered, bound under this yoke of marriage.] Larry D. Benson, general editor, *The Riverside Chaucer*, 3rd ed. (1987), 154.

[117] Oberman, *Werden und Wertung*, 2nd ed. (1979), 112; cf. David C. Steinmetz, *Luther and Staupitz* (1980).

very monastic tradition Luther rejected, because in his view it destroyed liberty,[118] insisted that the context of Rule and obedience could direct one's false self away from itself toward God.

Far from being human efforts to save oneself, Kempf considered obedience to the Rule and spiritual direction to be, admittedly fallible, ways to avoid trying to save oneself.[119] What the monks found consoling, in light of their excruciating consciousness of sin,[120] Luther—in his equally profound consciousness of sin—found unremittingly excruciating.[121] Luther was not opposed to the principle of created things as, ad-

---

[118] Luther, *De votis monasticis* (1521), e.g., ch. 2 (WA 8: 594-96). Luther's inability to see the monastic vow, the Rule, and obedience to a spiritual director as liberating is the key theme of the treatise. He accepts the principle that one can freely commit oneself to celibacy but denies practically that a lifelong commitment is "free." For Luther freedom for obedience to Christ requires the ability to revoke one's commitment to monastic structures. The monks would have said that it is the permanent commitment, the resolve not to revoke obedience once given (which does not preclude dispensation from vows when extrinsically discerned through proper spiritual direction), that sets one free from continually having to resolve to recommit oneself to monastic structures. The commitment to monastic structures sets one free to obey Christ. A preemptive decision not to give in to sin frees one's self (at least in part—monks were very realistic about the limits of this "freedom") from the continual struggle to resist. Such "freedom" takes a long time to develop and few monks achieve it perfectly. But the key to freedom in this system is precisely what Luther attacks as unfree: the preemptive commitment to a rule, to a director etc. and then the resolve, imperfect as it often may be, not to question that commitment. This seems bizarre to the modern mind but a rough parallel can be seen in the athlete embarking on a training program: a firm decision never to skip a workout or a commitment to another person as one's manager frees one from the worst part of the daily struggle to carry through on one's program. As we have noted, the same principle underlies Alcoholics Anonymous and other "twelve-step" programs.

[119] See the discussion of Kempf, *De discretione*, ch. 4, above: the monk who thinks he cannot fail is certain to fall.

[120] Dörries, "Place of Confession"; for the Carthusian tradition, see Mursell, *Theology*, 82-91.

[121] Ironically, when the German translation of Luther's *De votis monasticis* appeared in Basel (Froschauer), the publisher used precisely Mt 11:28-29, as the motto for the title illustration—a picture of Christ bearing his cross. Protestant polemicists were convinced that Christ's gentle yoke had been turned into a heavy burden, an excruciating burden, by monastics. See the description by Hans-Christoph Rublack, "Die Rezeption von Luthers *De votis monasticis iudicium*," in *Reformation und Revolution* [Wohfeil Festschrift] (1989), 224-37, at 231. The history of the use of this verse—from Guigo I, *Consuet.*, 25.1, to Gerson, to Kempf, to the Swiss reformers, thus serves as a window on the various perceptions of monasticism in the late medieval and Reformation era. Luther's comments in his commentary on Galatians show that he knew the monastic language of weakness but failed to find the Rule comforting: "I tried to live according to the Rule with all diligence, and I used to be contrite, to confess and number off my sins, and often repeated my confession, and sedulously performed my allotted penance. And yet my conscience could never give me certainty, but I always doubted and said, 'You did not perform that correctly. You were not contrite enough. You left that out of your confession.' The more I tried to remedy an uncertain, weak and afflicted conscience with the traditions of men, the more each day found it more uncertain, weaker, more troubled."

mittedly fallible, mediators of divine grace; indeed, he insisted on infant baptism and real presence in the Eucharist precisely as buttresses for alien faith.[122] Yet the very principle he recognized in defending infant baptism and real presence against Karlstadt and the Anabaptists[123] escaped his comprehension in considering the monastic rule and the authority of the spiritual father.

Recently scholars have begun to reexamine Luther's relationship to the monastic life.[124] Reinhard Schwarz and Heinz-Meinolf Stamm have argued that Luther preserved the essence of monasticism while rejecting its structures. "Luther separated the genuine meaning of the concept of the spiritual Body of Christ from the monastic way of life and developed it into a general definition of the Christian life."[125] We are indebted to them for their careful analysis of Luther's attitudes toward monastic life; together with the work of Peter Manns[126] and one of Schwarz's students, Hellmut Zschoch,[127] the "monastic theology" delineated by Jean Leclercq is finally beginning to receive its due from students of the Reformation. Schwarz, for example, is very much aware of the role of faith in monastic life and touches on many of the points made here. In the end, both Stamm and Schwarz, however, conclude that, although Luther does

---

WA 40.II.15.15, translated by E Gordon Rupp, *The Righteousness of God* (1953), 104, repeated by David C. Steinmetz, *Luther in Context* (1986), 2.

[122] This theme has been dealt with at various points in the literature. I content myself here with a reference to Heiko Oberman's discussion at various places in *Luther: Mensch zwischen Gott und Teufel* (1983; ET 1989), which repeatedly comes back to the theme of "fremder Glaube," e.g., pp. 243-57 (German edition).

[123] E.g., *Wider die himmlischen Propheten, von den Bildern und Sakrament*, part 2 (1525): "Now when God sends forth his holy Gospel, He deals with us in a twofold manner, the first outwardly, then inwardly. Outwardly he deals with us through the oral word of the Gospel and through material signs, that is, baptism and the sacrament of the altar. Inwardly He deals with us through the Holy Spirit, faith, and other gifts. But whatever their measure or order the outward factors should and must precede. The inward experience follows and is effected by the outward. God has determined to give the inward to no one except through the outward." Translation by Conrad Bergendoff in *Luther's Works*, vol. 40, ed. Helmut T. Lehmann and Jaroslav J. Pelikan (1958), p. 146; cf. *WA* 18: 136, 9-18.

[124] Heinz-Meinolf Stamm, *Luthers Stellung zum Ordensleben* (1980); Reinhard Schwarz, "Luther's Inalienable Inheritance of Monastic Theology," *American Benedictine Review*, 39 (1988), 430-50. Earlier literature includes Lohse, *Mönchtum und Reformation*; H. Bacht, "Luthers 'Urteil über die Mönchsgelübde' in ökumenischer Sicht," *Catholica* 21 (1967), 222-51; and P. Y. Émery, "Luther et le monachisme," *Verbum Caro*, 78 (1966), 82-90; René H. Esnault, *Luther et le monachisme aujourd'hui* (1964).

[125] Schwarz, "Inalienable," 449-50.

[126] Manns, "Gespräch."

[127] *Klosterreform und monastische Spiritualität im 15. Jahrhundert: Conrad von Zenn OESA* (1988). An edition of Conrad Zenn's *Liber de vita monastica* is an important research *desideratum*.

reject monastic vows in *De votis monasticis*, he preserved the principles of monasticism in a nonmonastic context. The same argument has been used to explain a leading Anabaptist who was a former Benedictine.[128] Scholars in many disciplines today emphasize the importance of context and recognize that ideas do not float freely in space and time. Revisionist scholarship on "nominalism" and "humanism" proceed from that same basic assumption. Yet in regard to Luther on monasticism, recent studies have tried to privilege "essence" over context, content over structures. Victors write history, and monastic structures, i.e., the monastic context, clearly lost the public relations battles of the fifteenth and sixteenth centuries.

The developments that led to Luther's and Erasmus's repudiation of monastic context were underway a century earlier, as Nicholas Kempf entered Gaming. In *De professione religiosorum* Lorenzo Valla interpreted the taking of vows as eliminating freedom, as binding the monk under necessity. Valla believed secular religiosity was superior to monastic piety because the lay person acts out of freedom whereas the monk acts out of necessity. An adult person should obey God, not man, although a "tutorial relationship" of obedience legitimately characterizes children. Yet that is exactly what the monks understood themselves to be: children, unable to make decisions on their own, requiring obedience to a tutor's guidance.[129] Valla believed that it was possible for all Christians to outgrow spiritual childhood; the monks thought that this degree

---

[128] C. Arnold Snyder, *The Life and Thought of Michael Sattler* (1984). See my critique in "Anabaptism and Monasticism: Michael Sattler and the Benedictines Reconsidered," *Mennonite Quarterly Review* 60 (1986) 139-64. Snyder's response in "Michael Sattler, Benedictine: Dennis Martin's Objections Reconsidered," *Mennonite Quarterly Review*, 61 (1987), 251-79, has not caused me to modify my viewpoint. See also Sean F. Winter, "Michael Sattler and the Schleitheim Articles," *The Baptist Quarterly*, 34 (1991), 52-66; Eoin de Bhaldraithe, "Michael Sattler, Benedictine and Anabaptist," *Downside Review*, 105 (April 1987), 111-31; and Peter J. A. Nissen, "De Moderne Devotie en het Neder-lands-Westfaalse Doperdom," in *De Doorwerking van de Moderne Devotie: Windesheim 1387-1987* (1988), 95-118, at 102-6.

[129] One example must suffice here. In his *Viae Sion lugent*, caput 3, particula 4 (Peltier ed., 45b; par. 113 in the SC edition), Hugh of Balma calls the purgative way "the childish way" in the course of an appeal to the leveling effect of mystical theology: ". . . ideo cum beato Dionysio, sed quod magis, cum Domino Jesu Christo, rogo illum, quicumque hoc scriptum inspexerit, ne indoctis hujus mundi doctoribus philosophis, carnalem vitam ducentibus, ullatenus manifestet, nisi hac via puerili velint incipere, scilicet purgativa via, et citius quam aliquis esse non tantum in aliqua liberalium artium, sed in arte mechanica industrius operator, in seipsos sola divina inmissione gradatim ascendentes, omnia quae dicta sunt multo melius et multo jucundius experimentali notitia veracissima approbabunt." An even more socially critical statement is found earlier: the childlike path of purgation bows the heads of the proud in keeping with the phrase to that effect in the Magnificat (ibid., p. 43b, *via illuminativa*, par. 103 in the SC edition). Cf. Peltier, pp. 3a, 4a, 5a (Prologue, par. 6 and *via purgativa*, par. 2, 3 in the SC edition).

of maturity was rare, indeed impossible, short of heaven. Did not Christ
say, "Unless you become like little children. . ."? In considering monastic structures, Valla's overriding concern was human freedom of the will
and he called for a religious coming of age in a way that strikingly anticipates Kant's definition of "enlightenment": "Enlightenment is man's re-
lease from his self-incurred *tutelage*. Tutelage is man's inability to make
use of his understanding *without direction from another*. . . . 'Have courage to use your own reason!'—that is the motto of Enlightenment" (emphasis added).[130] Erasmus linked Luther's and Valla's views on
necessity and Luther gladly accepted the linkage. Yet Luther's and
Valla's views on the freedom of the will were actually quite dissimi-
lar,[131] and Luther would have rejected the *hubris* of Valla's idea of human coming of age even as he bitterly opposed Erasmus on the question
of free will—which makes the agreement of all three about the baleful
effects of the bondage of monastic vows all the more ironic.

Perhaps the most interesting comparison, however, is between
Kempf, Luther and Gasparo Contarini. Racked by doubts about being
able to bring forth genuine repentance worthy of justification, Contarini
briefly considered following a friend into the monastic life, then concluded that he could live just as securely (i.e., free of such anxieties) in
the world as in the monastery. Having taken for granted the popular perception that the monastic life was more meritorious, he found liberation
in breaking through that assumption.[132]

---

[130] Immanuel Kant, "Beantwortung der Frage: Was Ist Aufklärung?" in *Berlinische Monatsschrift*, ser. 4, no. 12 (1784), 481-94, transl. Lewis White Beck in Kant, *Founda- tions of the Metaphysics of Morals and What Is Enlightenment?* (1959), 85, as quoted by Colin Brown, *History and Faith: A Personal Exploration* (1987), 13.

[131] Valla and Luther agreed only in rejecting contingency. See the discussion by Harry J. McSorley, *Luther Right or Wrong?* (1969), esp. pp. 325-27, with citations to Eras- mus's diatribe and Luther's *De servo arbitrio*. The differences between Luther and Valla should be apparent from Trinkaus's discussion of Valla in *In Our Image and Likeness* (1970), 103-70.

[132] Hubert Jedin, "Ein 'Turmerlebnis' des jungen Contarinis," in Jedin, *Kirche des Glaubens, Kirche der Geschichte: Ausgewählte Aufsätze und Vorträge* (1966), 167-80 (originally published 1951), with references to Jedin's discovery and publication of Con- tarini's correspondence on this matter in "Contarini und Camaldoli," *Archivio italiano per la storia della pietà*, 2 (1959), 53-117. Additional letters between Tommaso (Paolo) Giustiniani and his friends, including Contarini, were published in *Annales Camaldu- lenses ordinis Sancti Benedicti*, ed. Giovanni Benedetto Mittarelli and Anselmo Costa- doni (1773) (repr. 1970), 9: cols. 446-611. Cf. Yarnold, *"Duplex iustitia,"* 212-13. Jedin noted that the outcome of Luther's "tower experience" was a communion with Christ es- tablished by faith; whereas for Contarini it was faith, hope, and a beginning of love. He also noted that Luther's discovery was the outcome of a professional theologian's exe- getical wrestling with scripture, whereas Contarini was a well-instructed layman seeking vocational direction (171).

Although Jedin's assumption that Contarini seriously considered a monastic vocation has been challenged by a number of scholars,[133] most have addressed the issue out of slight acquaintance with contemplative monasticism.[134] Far from indicating that he never struggled with a monastic vocation, Contarini's awareness that he was socially and temperamentally unsuited to the monastic life may only have heightened his inner turmoil.[135] Even his assertion that "such fine thoughts [of monastic vocation] are not in me" could be read as expressing a sad awareness that he lacked the vocation he thought he ought to have.[136] Neither Contarini

---

[133] Nelson H. Minnich and Elisabeth G. Gleason, "Vocational Choices: An Unknown Letter of Pietro Querini to Gasparo Contarini and Niccolò Tiepolo (April, 1512)," *Catholic Historical Review*, 75 (1989), 1-20, at 2. Among the literature cited there, I have found the following most useful in assessing the question at hand: James Bruce Ross, "Gasparo Contarini and His Friends," *SR*, 17 (1970), 192-232; Felix Gilbert, "Religion and Politics in the Thought of Gasparo Contarini," in *Action and Conviction in Early Modern Europe* [Harbison Festschrift] (1969), 90-116; Heinz Mackensen, "Contarini's Theological Role at Ratisbon in 1541," *ARG*, 51 (1960), 36-57; Gigliola Fragnito, "Cultura umanistica e riforma religiosa: il 'De officio viri boni ac probi episcopi' di Gasparo Contarini," *Studi veneziani*, 11 (1969), 75-189; Innocenzo Cervelli, "Storiografia e problemi intorno alla vita religiosa e spirituale a Venezia nella prima metà del '500," *Studi veneziani*, 8 (1966), 447-76; Giuseppe Alberigo, "Vita attiva e vita contemplativa in un'esperienza del XVI secolo," *Studi Veneziani*, 16 (1974), 177-225.

[134] Ross's appeal to an Aristotelian *philia* tradition to explain Contarini's lack of interest in monasticism would have benefited from some consideration of the Ciceronian tradition on friendship as absorbed and modified by medieval monasticism. Although the most thorough exposition has appeared since Ross wrote (Brian Patrick McGuire, *Friendship and Community: The Monastic Experience, 350-1250* [1988]), the medieval Christian appropriation of Cicero's *De amicitia* was by no means unknown in 1970.

[135] For summaries of the crucial letters of February 1 and April 24, 1511, see Mackensen, 50-54. Gilbert (p. 95) is disingenuous, following a citation of Contarini's assertion in his first letter to Tommaso (Paolo) Giustiniani (1511) with one from 1516, after Contarini's vocational crisis was resolved. Only the assertion in the first letter is significant in regard to the question whether Contarini ever seriously considered becoming a monk, and that first letter was written before Contarini read Giustiniani's letter confiding that he was struggling mightily with sin even in the monastery. Even if Contarini did not seriously entertain a monastic vocation when he wrote the first letter, he may indeed have done so during the vocational crisis described in his second letter, only to find a "sola gratia" resolution of the tension between that consideration and his doubts about having a vocation. Gilbert translates Contarini's reference to the "padre religioso pieno di sanctità" of San Sebastiano who was instrumental in his spiritual breakthrough as a "wise priest" (unlike Mackensen's "a religious" and "pious monk" (pp. 52-53). In this way Gilbert disingenuously downplays the monastic element in Contarini's discernment process. See Jedin, "Contarini und Camaldoli," p. 64 [14].

[136] Like Gilbert, Alberigo cites only the phrase "non è in mi sì boni pensieri" (Alberigo, "Vita attiva," p. 193-94) while Fragnito completes the quotation: "... non è in mi sì boni pensieri, ma solum me dolgio ... de la mia tanto obstinata mente et indurato cor, che, vedendo i miei amici ogni giorno proceder di ben in meglio, al contrario se ne vadi di mal in peio," i.e., Contarini could only grieve that his obstinate and hardened heart was going from bad to worse, even while he observed his friends proceeding daily from good to better. Fragnito, "Cultura umanistica," 100; cf. Jedin, "Contarini und Camal-

nor Luther realized that the same liberating theology of trust in a merciful God who justifies men and women who can never do enough to justify themselves formed the center of the monastic life of penitence from its beginnings in the Egyptian desert.

Still, there is an important difference between Luther and Contarini: Contarini handled his struggles of conscience in what monks would call a process of vocational discernment. Interestingly, his spiritual crisis was sparked when Tommaso (Paolo) Giustiniani confided to him in a letter that even in the monastic life he found himself slipping back again and again into sin—which is the same realization that tormented Luther and which was, as we have seen, the same pastoral premise from which Kempf turned to Romans 4:5 for comfort. Contarini's "breakthrough," however, did not come from long brooding over his own thoughts. Rather, it came on Holy Saturday, in the course of attending worship, and after taking counsel with a mendicant religious, a member of the Poor Hermits of St. Jerome (congregation of St. Peter of Pisa)[137] who served the church of San Sebastiano and who had heard Contarini's confession. Only then did Contarini conclude that his lack of vocation to the monastic life need not damn him—a point Kempf and other monastics freely conceded. Contarini did not reject the legitimacy of monasticism for others who did have vocations.[138] In contrast, Luther entered the monastery hastily and against the counsel of his father. Unable to rescue his monastic vocation, Luther rejected the monastic life more fundamentally than Contarini. The wide reception of that rejection helped ensure that the possibility of a monastic vocation would be lost to Protestants for centuries to come. In this way he more closely resembled Valla than Contarini but was operating out of psychological motives rather than Valla's theological motives.

Hubert Jedin mused about the irony of Contarini's efforts to reach a compromise with the Lutherans at the Regensburg Colloquy in 1541. Contarini and Luther had had similar "reformation breakthroughs" and their theologies were close in many ways. Perhaps the deeper irony is that many of the main actors on the fifteenth- and sixteenth-century stage found *discretio*, the mother of all virtues, the guide to the royal *via media*, the "finesse pédagogique" of the desert Abba, too multifaceted and

---

doli," p. 62 [12]. Gilbert and Alberigo have done little more than pull a prooftext out of context.

[137] See Max Heimbucher, *Die Orden und Kongregationen der katholischen Kirche* (1907), 2: 238.

[138] Jedin, "Turmerlebnis" in *Kirche des Glaubens*, p. 173; cf. Alberigo, "Vita attiva," 196; citing the text in Jedin, "Contarini und Camaldoli," p. 70 [20].

paradoxical to grasp and reduced matters to much simpler, black-or-white, either-or, polemics.[139]

---

[139] As an illustration I offer Luther's caricature of the counsel he received from fellow Augustinians at Erfurt, taken from the *Dictata super Psalterium* on Ps. 99 (LXX), as translated by E. Gordon Rupp, *The Righteousness of God* (1953), 115, and quoted in David C. Steinmetz, *Luther in Context*, pp. 7-8 (WA 3, 447, 30-34): "Ah! (they say) what are you worrying about? It isn't necessary: you have only to be humble and patient. Do you think that God requires such strict conduct from you? He knows all your imaginings and he is good. One groan will please him. Do you think that nobody can be saved unless he behaves so strictly? Where would all the others be, then, in whom you see no such violence? Perish the thought that they should all be lost! It really is necessary to observe '*discretion*,' etc. And so gradually the unhappy soul forgets the fear of the Lord, and that the kingdom of heaven suffers violence" (emphasis added).

CHAPTER FIVE

LOVER

That the Song of Songs is obscure . . . indicates that these songs sung between God and a soul chosen as bride and mated and united to God in the human spirit's chamber, united in the very image of God, are utterly mysterious and completely inexpressible. Not even the bride herself is able to express what she has perceived. . . . When hearts have been moved to jubilation of this sort, the things that result within the spirit cannot be put into conventional and customary words. Just as people drunk with wine lose the ability to talk in a normal fashion, so the bride drunk with sober intoxication speaks in a way intelligible not to anyone and everyone but only to lovers loving in a similar way. So too, after tasting the sweetness of glory, Peter did not know what he was saying. [Kempf, *Cantica*, prologue, ch. 6.]

1. The Two Kingdoms: Here and Hereafter

At first glance one might think that a study of Nicholas Kempf's mystical theology would best begin with his five-part magisterial treatise, *De mystica theologia*. There is, however, much to commend an approach to Kempf's mystical theology through the work we shall refer to as *De ostensione regni Dei*. The confusing relationship between the two is discussed in appendix A. Our concern here is to place Kempf's mystical theology in the context of late medieval affective, contemplative theology,[1] with special attention to the Carthusian tradition. Embedded in a traditional monastic context of compunction and repentance, the *via purgativa* takes on particular importance for the Cistercian and Carthusian contemplative writers. Because the roots of this Latin mystical tradition lie in the monastic centuries of the early Middle Ages, when monastic theology was largely coterminous with Christian theology in the West, we should not be surprised to discover this mystical theology subsumed under sacramental soteriology, offering a foretaste of the union all be-

---

[1] Johann Auer, in "Die *Theologia Mystica* . . . Jakob von Jüterbog," in *Die Kartäuser in Österreich*, vol. 2, AC 83.2 (1981), 19-52, at 23-24, is one of the few scholars to take account of Kempf's mystical theology from a theological standpoint, commenting that Kempf's *De mystica theologia* "shows special theological depth, but remained rather obscure," i.e., not widely known.

lievers will experience in heaven rather than supplying a means to by-
pass sacramental soteriology. And because mystical theology is embedded within the soteriology of the entire church, for Kempf and the
tradition in which he wrote the highest contemplative union is always by
God's grace alone. Kempf's efforts to resolve the debates of his day over
the role of love and knowledge in contemplative union and the age-old
conundrum of grace and free will led him to postulate two kinds of contemplative union, roughly corresponding to the later distinction between
acquired and infused contemplation.

From *De ostensione* it becomes clear that Kempf's mystical theology consists of two interlaced strands. In this he differs from the early
Gerson, who makes a two-level, superior-inferior, distinction between
the sacramental life of all Christians and the contemplative foretaste of
heaven experienced by those who take the mystical route of the penitent
affectus rather than the inquiring *intellectus*. This appears to be the import of Gerson's emphasis on purgation as the first step of the threefold
way, leading on to illumination and union,[2] as well as the import of his
hierarchical ecclesiology. In contrast, Kempf interweaves purgation all
the way through his teaching on contemplation. In *De ostensione regni
Dei*, each of the three steps in the revelation of the kingdom has a stage
of purgation, illumination, and union. The contemplative life is a lifelong
repentance and cleansing, precisely because, as a monk in the tradition of
the desert, Kempf was convinced that one never leaves repentance behind and that tears of repentance are scarcely distinguishable from the
tears of joy in foretaste of heaven.[3] The goal of mystical theology is the
kingdom of God, life eternal, which yields the *scientia sanctorum*, the
knowledge of God experienced by the saints in heaven in the beatific vision and in the nuptial union celebrated by the wedding supper of the
Lamb (Rev 19). The path to this revelation of the kingdom begins with
the sanctifying grace imparted in the sacrament of penance (presuppos-

---

[2]   Burger, *Aedificatio*, 111-12, 123-24, emphasizes the initiatory character of penitence for Gerson. Cf. Pascoe, "Jean Gerson: Mysticism, Conciliarism, and Reform," 140,
146-47: purgation is located primarily in the sacraments of baptism and penance and in
other forms of church discipline; illumination is identified with preaching and doctrinal
teaching; union is found in the other sacraments, especially the Eucharist.

[3]   In this Kempf is once more indebted to the Carthusians' attention to the legacy of
the Desert Fathers and early monasticism. See Irenée Hausherr, *Penthos: The Doctrine
of Compunction in the Christian East* (1982). Kempf knew John Climacus and John Cassian intimately, since they were available in Latin. His teaching on penitence and compunction also owes much to Gregory the Great, and the Carthusian emphasis on lifelong
repentance also has roots in the penitential movements and clerical reforms of the eleventh century. See Heinrich Egher van Kalkar, *Ortus*, ed. Vermeer, pp. 94-95, on parallels
between the Carthusian regimen and the penance assigned a priest who has committed
fornication.

ing, of course, the sanctifying grace of baptism and the presence of genuine contrition). Led by God through paths of righteousness,[4] most *viatores* attain the revelation of the kingdom only after death.[5]

Some, however, are privileged to experience a foretaste of the kingdom in this life.[6] This is the second strand, the specifically mystical
thread. The mystical union is simply a foretaste in this present life of the
eschatological beatific vision. To be sure, it is not identical to the vision
of the saints in heaven. But it is a clearer vision of God than the enigmatic vision of faith that some had postulated was the only vision of God
possible in life on earth (see below, section two). This clear vision, or
foretaste, of the kingdom forms the subject matter of *De mystica theologia* parts III-IV.

In this way Kempf's mystical theology is a monastic path of salvation embedded within and interpenetrated by a general soteriology and
ecclesiology. Although the first degree of cleansing, or purgation, begins
with genuine repentance and the sacrament of penance available to all
Christians, the second degree of the traditional *via purgativa* for Kempf
is the monastic life in which perfection is supported by the structures of
Rule and spiritual direction.[7] In keeping with a tradition extending back

---

[4]   *Ost*, ch. 1, referring to Wis 10:10, found in Graz UB 262 (G1), 1r, lines 4-11; cf.
MTh I.14-15, pp. 80-88. Citations to *Ost* will be to chapter, folio, and line in Graz UB
262. References to *MTh* will be to part and chapter; on occasion specific page numbers
in the Jellouschek, Barbet, Ruello critical edition are added. Where only a chapter reference is found in parenthesis it refers to *De ostensione*.

[5]   See the chart of Thomas Gallus' coordination of the nine choirs of angels with the
journey from nature to grace, i.e., with the process of salvation in Walsh, "Thomas Gallus et l'effort contemplatif," 24. The same chart appears in Walsh, "'Sapientia Christianorum': The Doctrine of Thomas Gallus Abbot of Vercelli on Contemplation"
(dissertation, 1957), 82. For Thomas, mystical union in its highest level is solely by
grace. However he lacks Kempf's emphasis on a *sola fide* approach to the lower stages,
the process of repentance and purgation, as outlined in chapter four above.

[6]   *Ost*, ch. 1 (G1, 1r, 1-19); ch. 19 (G1, 13r, 14-16); ch. 52 (G1, 39r, 5-11).

[7]   *Ost*, ch. 10 (G1, 7v, lines 10-32): "Et sic patet solucio dubij. Est eciam hic adver-
tendum quod predicte virtutes habent tres gradus, sive capiantur generaliter sive speciali-
ter. Nam quedam est humilitas necessaria et sufficiens ad salutem; similiter quedam
paciencia et obediencia necessaria et sufficiens, et sic capiuntur in predicto primo modo
purgacionis. Alia est humilitas perfecta; similiter paciencia et obediencia. Et illa est pro-
ficiencium, et pertinet ad secundum gradum purgacionis. Alia est perfectissima humilitas; similiter paciencia et obediencia. Et ille sunt perfectissimorum et pertinent ad
tercium gradum purgacionis, illuminacionis, et unicionis. Et de illis postea erit dicen-
dum. Et sic iam patet quod sicut ex originali peccato causatur in homine amor malus
hominis ad seipsum et ad creaturas, per quem fortissime inclinatur ad avertendum se a
Deo et ad convertendum se ad seipsum tam in corpore quam in spiritu, et ex hoc inclinatur ad transgrediendum mandata Dei et implendo propriam voluntatem et libertatem a
Deo, ut post mandatum difficilius sit implere preceptum aut obmittere prohibita quam
prius, ut ostendit *Apostolus ad romanos* [ch. 7]. Sic predicte virtutes destruunt illum
amorem per pacienciam et avertunt hominem ab amore predicto ad se et ad creaturas et

at least as far as Jerome, Kempf refers to the monastic profession as a second baptism that cleanses from all sins (ch. 14-15).[8] The reform and renewal of the human image of God disfigured by sin begins for all Christians in baptism and penance (ch. 7, 11), but further cleansing is necessary to remove the stubborn spot left by sin. This can occur most thoroughly with the aid of monastic structures—to which, as we have seen, one is called by grace alone. A discussion of the three degrees of the *via purgativa* (cf. *MTh* II.1-6) constitutes the longest section of *De ostensione* (ch. 4-21), and much of the rest of *De ostensione* is given over to lengthy digressions preparatory to the third degree of union and the *ostensio regni Dei*.

The emphasis on the three degrees of purgation in part reflects the circumstances that gave rise to the work. It originated in a series of sermons preached to the lay brethren, presumably at Gaming or Pleterje. [*Ost*, ch. 3 (G1, 2v, 17-19)]. Apparently only after both *De mystica theologia* and the commentary on the Canticle had been completed did Kempf, at the insistence of his auditors, transform these sermons into a treatise. An emphasis on practicality and simplicity pervades the work,[9] and even the long digression (ch. 31-45) on various paths to knowledge of God eventually yields to the description of a simpler way (ch. 46). In contrast, the express purpose of *De mystica theologia* was to reconcile seemingly contradictory teachings about mystical theology,[10] and a more speculative and systematic approach dominates that work.

---

convertunt hominem ad Deum et inclinant mentem ad implendum mandata et obmittendum prohibita. Et ad hoc cooperantur omnia sacramenta ecclesie, precipue penitencie et eucharistie. Et sic prima purgacio consistit in predictis virtutibus per usum et frequentacionem sacramentorum ecclesie rite et digne susceptorum, ac devotam et frequentem eorum usum. Et illa purgacio, ad quam sequitur illuminacio mentis et unicio eius per caritatem proximi ex amore Dei, pertinet ad vitam activam."

[8] On this theme see Edward E. Malone, "Martyrdom and Monastic Profession as a Second Baptism," in *Vom christlichen Mysterium* [Casel Festschrift] (1951), 115-34; idem, *The Monk and the Martyr* (1950); Placide Deseille, "Théologie de la vie monastique selon saint Bernard," in *Vie Monastique* (1961), 503-25, at 515-19; Hugh Feiss, "St. Bernard's Theology of Baptism and the Monastic Life," *CS*, 25 (1990), 79-91; Bernard of Clairvaux, *Sermones de diversis*, no. 11, in *S. Bernardi Opera*, 6: 124-26 (PL 183: 570-71), and idem, *De praecepto et dispensatione*, 17.54, in *S. Bernardi Opera*, 3: 288-89 (PL 182: 889-90); Lohse, *Mönchtum*; and Thomas Aquinas, *STh*, IIa, IIae, q. 189, art 3.

[9] *Ost*, ch. 17 (G1, 11v, 6-10): "Qualiter autem et quomodo et quantum quociensve tales post illum purgacionis gradum illuminentur, et quomodo sepe Deo per amorem uniantur, quis explicare posset cum tot modis fiant et tam diversis graduum differencijs, quod est inexplicabile; quamvis et de hoc sint multe scripture. Aliqui tamen modi magis conveniens et pro simplicibus utiliores sunt hic explicandi." See also ch. 29 (G1, 21v, 28 - 22r, 1) and 30 (G1, 22r, 8-10) in appendix B.

[10] *MTh*, I.2; *Cantica*, I.1. Kempf describes the difference between the more "scholas-

2. Paths of Righteousness in "De ostensione"

De ostensione is organized around the traditional threefold path of purgation, illumination, and union. Each of the three is further divided into three degrees, producing a ninefold structure that corresponds to the Pseudo-Dionysian hierarchy of angels.[11] Kempf begins with three chapters outlining Adam's and Eve's fall into sin by free choice and the resulting twofold inclination toward evil: (a) the attraction to the sensual and temporal and (b) the inclination to pride and self-deception. The effects of sin can be overcome through humility, patience, and, inseparable from both, obedience.[12] The starting point is the sacrament of penance, in which genuine contrition stimulates patience, confession requires humility (since one submits to another human being for God's sake), and *satisfactio* demonstrates obedience (ch. 7).[13] Full and complete penitence is the absolutely essential foundation for all subsequent cleansing. It marks the beginning of the conversion to God that undoes the original sin of aversion from God and conversion to the creaturely.

The first degree of illumination and union follow upon this sacramental cleansing (ch. 8). *Gratia gratum faciens* and the gifts of the Holy Spirit illumine a man so that he knows himself and recognizes his inordinate love of self. This self-knowledge leads to an admittedly incomplete love of God and neighbor, i.e., union in the first degree (ch. 9). The first

---

tic" *MTh* and the more affective tone and purpose of his commentary on the Canticle in *Cantica* I.1.

[11] *Ost*, ch. 2 (G1, 1v, 26 - 2r, 12); cf. *MTh*, II.1, pp. 89-94. The correlation to the hierarchy of angels is more detailed in *MTh*, which, however, lacks the other imagery used in *Ost*, ch. 2 (G1, 2r, 9-15), regarding the four senses of scripture: the moral or tropological corresponds to the purgative way, the allegorical or mystical to the illuminative way, and the anagogical to the unitive way. The historical sense applies to all three. Both *MTh* and *Ost* have the dawn, morning, and midday metaphor for the three ways (*Ost*, ch. 2 [G1, 2r, 15-23]; *MTh*, II.1, p. 91).

[12] *Ost*, ch. 6; cf. *MTh*, II.3, 6.

[13] *Ost*, ch. 7 (G1, 4v, 28-38): "Primus ergo gradus purgacionis seu vite purgative omnibus neccessarius fit per sacramentum poenitencia et eius tres partes quibus completur penitencia, scilicet contricionem, confessionem, et satisfaccionem; quorum primum ex radice paciencie procedit, qua extirpatur amor proprius hominis ad se et ad suos, sive ad quascumque creaturas. Secundum ex humilitate, quo homo in hijs que ad solum Deum pertinent, scilicet scire occulta cordis sui, subicit se homini propter Deum. Tercium ex obediencia perficitur, qua homo implet iniunctum sibi ab homine. Pro quo intelligendo est sciendum quod, sicut in arbore que evertitur principalis causa eversionis est in radice non bene profundata aut putrefacta in terra, tamen eversio ipsius arboris, et casus seu ruina, incipit a supremis ramis se inclinantibus versus radices ad terram.

degrees of purgation, illumination, and union suffice for salvation, but they are most incomplete and require daily renewal. They can lead to a revelation of the kingdom of God only after death and after further cleansing in purgatory. Yet they do belong to "mystical theology," broadly speaking.

The virtues of patience, humility, and obedience can be understood in two ways (ch. 10). In a general sense they are associated with sacramental penance and the first degree of purgation, illumination, and union. In a strict sense, however, they pertain to the second and third degree of each of the three ways. To advance to these higher levels, one must undertake to remove sin's discoloration of the *imago Dei*, a stain that remains even after the eternal penalty has been remitted through sacramental grace.[14] That the venial sins which settle like dust on the *imago Dei* must also be removed, scarcely needs underscoring. The means to the removal of the residual stain and the flecks of venial sin is the monastic life. To be sure, a path of supererogation (cf. *MTh*, II.2), of observance of the three evangelical counsels, is possible for those remaining in the world. Rarely, however, do people in the world persevere—human frailty, procrastination, and instability usually defeat such attempts (ch. 13). The three monastic vows[15] help overcome human weakness (ch. 14) and make one an imitator of Christ, who himself lived this life of self-denial, patience, humility, and obedience. [16] The vows constitute a second baptism, a second degree of purgation.[17] The monastic life sets the stage for the second degree of illumination and union by opening one's eyes, by illumining one to the pitfalls of sin, and by removing the deafness caused by sin, until one recognizes the transitoriness of temporal things and rises in profound, loving gratitude to union with God in the second degree (ch. 17). It is noteworthy that illumination here is primarily recognition of one's own blindness, a self-awareness, an awareness of one's lack of illumination, rather than an overpowering, ecstatic outpouring of God's brightness. Union in this stage is likewise the nonecstatic

---

[14] *Ost*, ch. 11; cf. *MTh*, IV.14, p. 310.

[15] *Ost*, ch. 14 (G1, 10r, 24-30), explains why the three vows are poverty, chastity, and obedience and not patience, humility, and obedience: the latter refer to the interior spirit, of which God alone is judge. Poverty, continence, and obedience are subject to external observation and discipline. The Carthusian statutes, chapter 23, list as a formula of profession the same three promises as are found in chapter 58 of Benedict's rule: stability, obedience, and *conversio morum*. Cf. *RB 1980: The Rule of St. Benedict in Latin and English with Notes*, ed. Timothy Fry et al. (1981), 457-66. For the controversy over Carthusian indebtedness to the Benedictine rule, see Hogg, "Carthusians and the 'Rule of St. Benedict'," with references to other literature.

[16] *Ost*, ch. 15; cf. *MTh*, II.19.

[17] *Ost*, ch. 14 (G1, 10r, 1-18); ch. 15 (G1, 10v, 26 - 11r, 4).

result of recognizing who one is—a recognition that makes one more closely united to God for having realized one's distance from God.

Thus two of the three degrees of purgation, illumination, and union are rather "mundane" by the standards most modern scholars have set for mystical theology. We should not be surprised by this nonecstatic, mundane mysticism, for it reminds us that we tend to underestimate the importance of the hard-slogging, ascetic "active life" of combat with sin to medieval monastics and mystics, something they never underestimated. Like an athlete who feels exhilarated after a hard session of training, the monk living the active ascetic life already partakes of illumination and union. The tingling sense of vigor and healthfulness that an athlete feels is probably a better metaphor for mystical illumination and union than are the ecstatic images scholars customarily present. This "mundaneness" of mystical theology in the two lower degrees is not without significance for the highest levels, as we shall see.

Even the third degree of the spiritual life begins with purgation—the active life of struggle against vices is integrated with the "contemplative life" at all levels, much as an athlete never stops training. One does not leave purgation behind after attaining illumination or union. Kempf discusses this third degree of purgation at length, with frequent digressions, in chapters 18-28. If the first degree is a sprinkling with hyssop and the second degree is a complete washing, the third degree is a bleaching until the *imago Dei* is as white as snow (Ps 50 [51]:9). Kempf employs a textile analogy: the soul is like linen that is first washed in lye made from the ashes of penitence combined with the blood and water of Christ's passion, then spread out in the sun to bleach with all the hidden corners exposed so that no stain of sin is missed (ch. 18).[18] The cleansing effi-

---

[18] *Ost*, ch. 18 (G1, 12r, lines 29 - 12v, 17): "Ita mens aut anima, coniuncta et contexta cum carne, oportet primo lavari per lixivium quod fluit de Christi corpore. Christi enim humanitas fuit, sicut ceteri homines, cinis in sacco, de quo dicitur 'Concidisti saccum meum' [Ps 29:12; *conscidisti* in Vulgate]. De quo sacco cinerum multipliciter conciso fluxit lixivium, sanguis scilicet et aqua de latere, quod recte dicitur lixivium, quia ex igne caritatis in camino passionis contraxit caliditatem et virtutum [G1, fol. 12v] mundandi omnes pannos lineos a vetustate originalis peccati et a maculis peccatorum actualium. Ex hoc enim lixivio de illo sacco cinerum fluente receperunt efficaciam mundandi omnia sacramenta ecclesie. Et ita omnes tres purgaciones indigent illo lixivio, tamquam primo neccessario, sine quo non potest fieri purgacio. Et hinc est quod ad omnes purgaciones valde utile est quod mens sepe aspergatur aut lavetur illo cinere per meditacionem passionis Christi, et devota sacramentorum frequentam sumpcionem, precipue eukaristie et penitencie. Nam sic illo lixivio aspersa aut bene lota, et facilius lavatur aquis lacrimarum et cicius dealbatur. Tercia igitur purgacio consistit in hoc, quod mens sic lota expandatur sicut pannus in radijs solis per omnimodam simplicitatem et puritatem—in nullo servans plicam aliquam duplicitatis occultacionis peccatorum aut excusacionis, et sic expansa cottidie ymmo sepe uno die perfundatur aqua lacrimarum mentalium aut eciam corporalium, donec ipsi solis radij divine, scilicet gracie, omnem terrestitatem et

cacy of all the church's sacraments flows from this lye, and all three kinds of purgation depend on it. The key to the third and most perfect cleansing is daily self-judgment (ch. 19), for, as Gregory the Great pointed out, if we judge ourselves, we have nothing to fear from the Last Judgment.[19]

This third purgation of self-judgment is the essential, complete predisposition for receiving the revelation of the kingdom of God (ch. 20). Only a few accomplish such daily self-examination and humble self-judgment,[20] but those who do so not only are cleansed of all sins and their penalties, but also experience growth in all virtues, because they have pulled up the root of sin and planted the root of all virtues by developing patience, humility, and obedience. Divine light and grace now illumine a soul that is a spotless mirror. The soul experiences peace, and the yoke of obedience and the burden of patience grow light. Furthermore, sometimes the vision of the kingdom of God is granted in the present life to those who can handle it without becoming bloated by spiritual pride as they feed on the sweetness of the foretaste of the heavenly banquet.[21] The benefits after death that follow from daily self-judgment and cleansing include immunity from the devil's accusation, bypassing purgatory to see God immediately after the soul leaves the body, receiving a crown of glory with the martyrs, and taking part with Christ and the apostles in the Last Judgment.[22]

It is at this juncture that Kempf stops to ask if such perfect cleansing is indeed possible. Up to this point his exposition has sounded like one more example of supposed "monkish virtue": i.e., the revelation of the kingdom, the heavenly bliss of salvation and healing, is granted to those who struggle hard enough in the active, ascetic life. However, as we

---

vetustatem consumant et omnem maculam contractam penitus extrahant et exsiccent, ut mens fiat sicut byssus omnino super nivem dealbata, candida, et munda, ut sic ad templum Dei apta." [Much of this material is repeated from or parallel to, chapter eleven.] One might also note Kempf's reference to Christ's humanity, like that of other humans, being a bag of ashes. One certainly could not accuse him of docetic tendencies.

[19] Cf. *MTh*, II.3, pp. 100-102, where the editors cite *Moralia*, bk. 25, ch. 7, no. 14 (PL 76: 327B-328A).

[20] *Ost*, ch. 19 (G1, 13r, 13-21): "Quod iudicium quia paucissimi perfecte de se faciunt, et ideo rarissimi sunt qui perfecte purgentur et super nivem dealbentur, et hunc est quod paucissimis ostenditur regnum celorum in presenti vita sed post longam purgacionem et locionem per purgatorij penas. Istius tamen iudicij purgacione et iusticiam est perutile scire, ut qui non vult aut forte non faciliter potest sic purgari et iustificari, tamen ex hoc humilietur ut iudicem futurum magis timeat, qui eo districtius iudicabit et diucius ac gravius puniet, quanto homo se hic iudicare aut punire negligencius egit, et quanto plus sibi ipsi in presenti vita pepercit."

[21] *Ost*, ch. 23 (G1, 15v, 33 - 16r, 22).

[22] *Ost*, ch. 23 (G1, 16r, 22 - 16v, 7).

have seen in chapter four, above, in *De ostensione*, chapter twenty-four, Kempf proceeds to explain that such perfect, spotless cleansing is impossible except by faith in Christ's alien power through the Holy Spirit. "Monkish virtue" and mystical union are thus integrated into an extrinsic, *sola gratia* spirituality. We should not be surprised. After all, for Kempf the active life to a large part consists in recognizing one's weakness. Illumination, as we have seen, is recognition of one's blindness. Union is knowledge of one's distance from God. The active life itself is a curiously (by modern standards) "passive" matter of recognizing what one is not. Yet, this recognition comes about within a disciplined monastic life fully worthy of the term *ascesis*, i.e., athletic training. All of these elements were already present in the first centuries of desert monasticism.

In short, it is the word *monkish*, not the word *virtue*, that is misplaced in Reformation and post-Reformation attacks on "pelagian" "monkish virtue." Kempf's *De ostensione* reveals that precisely the *monastic* life (the two higher degrees of purgation, illumination, and union) is a life of meekly acknowledged dependence on God's grace alone. Kempf applies the "disposition" and *facere quod in se est* language of the much pilloried "medieval Catholic soteriology" to the "lower," sacramental stages, which monks have in common with lay people in the world. Yet "stages," for Kempf and other monastic mystics, tend to run in circles, not sequentially.

The illumination (and implicitly, the union) that follows this third degree of cleansing by faith and the extrinsic power of the Holy Spirit is described in chapters 28-30, beginning with a review of all three degrees of illumination. This is accomplished with the aid of the imagery of dawn (= tropological sense of scripture), morning (= allegorical), and midday sunshine (= anagogical) which gradually dissipates the fog of sin (ch. 28). Kempf often cites Hugh of Balma as the best authority on the third degree of illumination and union in which one is taught by the anagogic sense of scripture to free oneself for God alone, to know his complete will, to cling to him, and to carry out his will.[23]

Kempf thought it important to clarify the relation of this third degree of illumination (knowledge) to the way God is experienced (ch. 29) in the beatific vision. The vision of God experienced at the third degree of illumination is superior to that of Adam before the fall, but only because Adam did not have the benefit of sanctifying grace.[24] On the other

---

[23] *Ost*, ch. 28 (G1, 20v, 21-30).

[24] See Ladner, *Idea of Reform*, 159-60, on Augustine, sanctifying grace, and the return to and transcendence of paradisiacal innocence through Christ. See appendix B.

hand, although the mirror of the soul, the image of God, has been cleansed, it is never perfectly spotless—the *fomes peccati* remains to cloud it in a manner unknown before the fall. Above all, the vision granted in this life, no matter how clear and complete, is still like a dark night compared to the beatific vision in heaven. As developed more fully in *De mystica theologia*, III-IV, the more one progresses in mystical cognition, the more deeply one enters the cloud of darkness and blindness in which one walks by faith, not by sight.

These matters are not Kempf's concern in *De ostensione*. He has neither time nor space to enter into a discussion of the various modes of illumination and union in the third degree,[25] nor can he take up the question of union by love alone,[26] i.e., the question that animated the Tegernsee mystics controversy[27] and stimulated, in part, Kempf's first mystical treatise, *De mystica theologia*[28]. Kempf's purpose in *De ostensione* is to remain on the practical level, to encourage his listeners and readers to strive for more complete purgation, to let Christ's lyesoap scrub the soul clean and let it bleach in God's sun until it is ready for illumination and union. That is far more important than poring over the countless books written on mystical illumination and union.[29]

Still, Kempf cannot resist a digression to discuss the various paths to cognition of God: knowledge arising from reverence at the realization that God's spirit pervades and fills all things (ch. 31); cognition of the invisible gained through contemplation of all visible things as traces and footprints of God (ch. 32-33, 42, 44); cognition gained through the natural desire for God that is the mark of the *imago Dei* (ch. 34-35, 40); cognition resulting from consideration of the angels as insignia (*signacula*, *sigilla*) of the likeness of God (ch. 36); cognition arising from consideration of the powers of the soul which govern the body as God governs the

---

[25] *Ost*, ch. 29 (G1, 21v, 11 - 22r, 5); cf. *MTh*, II.5-16, 20.

[26] *Ost*, ch. 30 (G1, 23r, 5-13); cf. *MTh*, II.12-16, 20-21, IV.8-10.

[27] The standard account remains Edmond Vansteenberghe, *Autour de la docte ignorance* (1915), which includes some of the important texts. The most recent survey is by Margot Schmidt, "Nikolaus von Kues im Gespräch mit den Tegernseer Mönchen über Wesen und Sinn der Mystik," in *Das Sehen Gottes nach Nikolaus von Kues* (1989), 25-49. Heribert Roßmann has studied the roles played by Johannes Keck, Marquard Sprenger, and Vincent of Aggsbach in a series of articles listed under his name in the Bibliography, notably "Die Stellungnahme des Kartäusers Vinzenz von Aggsbach zur mystischen Theologie des Johannes Gerson," in *Kartäusermystik und -mystiker*, vol. 3 (1982), 5-30. See also Haas, "Schools of Late Medieval Mysticism," 165-73. The course of the controversy was also outlined, based largely on Vansteenberghe, in Hubalek, "Briefwechsel Schlitpacher," 93-120. Many of the letters referred to by Hubalek, pp. 151ff. were published in Pez and Hueber, *Cod. dipl.-hist.-epist.* (1729).

[28] For Kempf's pastoral role in the controversy, see p. 175, below.

[29] *Ost*, ch. 29 (G1, 22r, 1-5).

world (ch. 37, 41); cognition and even union with God through the invisible working of grace, much as the heavenly bodies influence life on earth (ch. 38-39). There are some for whom these paths of cognition will be too lofty and perplexing (cf. *MTh*, II.17-19). For them it suffices to descend within themselves, to find God in his image and similitude in the human soul, to seek him with a righteous heart (ch. 45). An even simpler approach is suitable for youth: learning to know God as a distant yet loving Father who sends gifts and letters (scripture) from afar (ch. 46). All of this, in a broad sense, is part of the revelation of God's kingdom.

After a recapitulation of the threefold cleansing (ch. 47), we are on the threshold of the *ostensio regni Dei* in a strict sense,[30] where all previous cognitions and unions cease. "For even if God is known with certainty through faith, in the aforementioned ways, nevertheless, when he makes himself present in the *imago* through experience, then all the previous cognitions will become darkness and ignorance, as if man formerly had known nothing of God."[31] This is a path that ascends above the setting sun (Ps 67 [68]: 5). When it is frequently followed, it becomes the final preparation for the *ostensio*, the superintellectual light that dawns in the soul. Here Kempf leaves the matter, for he has dealt with these lofty subjects elsewhere.[32] He adds a warning about the chief impediments to the revelation of the kingdom[33] and repeats his basic theme about the prerequisites for the *ostensio regni Dei*.[34]

All are invited to the *cena domini*, another of Kempf's favorite metaphors for mystical union and the *ostensio regni Dei*. All are invited

---

[30] *Ost*, ch. 47 (G1, 36r, 16-30).

[31] *Ost*, ch. 48 (G1, 35v, 16-23): " Nam occasus ille dicitur cessacio omnium cognicionum intellectualium et omnium actuum amoris Dei ex potencijs anime procedentibus cum caritate infusa; que cessacio recte dicitur occasus, quia occidunt cogniciones et erunt tenebre in potencijs anime. Sed Dominus ascendit super occasum illum per lumen superintellectuale, hoc est per cogniciones et amores sui, qui sunt super omnem intellectum et omnem facultatem omnium virium anime et potenciarum. Et de illis latissime est dictum in tractatu de ostensione regni Dei [= *MTh*]." The full text of ch. 48 is found in appendix B.

[32] *Ost*, ch. 48 (G1, 36v, 28-32): "Sed pro omni illa materia iam scripta et eciam pro tractatu de ostensione regni Dei [= *MTh*] et exposicione super cantica que omnia finaliter tendunt ad unum finem, ut scilicet mens disponatur et per vias rectas deducatur [Wis 10:10] ut detur sibi gustare et videre in presenti vita regnum Dei."

[33] *Ost*, ch. 48 (G1, 36v, 32 - 37r, 4).

[34] *Ost*, ch. 49-50, 52. For monks this includes the observance of the rule; obedience to superiors; respect for superiors, even when they are in error or carnally inclined; daily self-judgment; and above all, triumph over self-love. For nonmonastics, it requires some work of supererogation, some abstinence from a licit thing. Kempf considers the possibilities for nonmonastics in this regard to be too varied for enumeration here.

to the banquet *after* death, but those who are most perfectly cleansed may be permitted a foretaste on earth. Since the time of Adam and Eve, however, self-love has intervened and threatens to keep some from the banquet altogether (ch. 50). Those who attend, whether for a foretaste in this life or the full repast in the next, are the poor, the weak, the blind, and the lame—those who are poor in true humility; those weak ones who patiently endure infirmity; the blind who may lack the light of great learning but have love; and the maimed or lame who are unable to walk without the support of others, but who realize this and throw themselves upon God as upon a crutch. Such "blindness" is what is called in the vernacular *Abgeschiedenheit*; such lameness, i.e., dependence on *aliena virtus* of Christ, is called *Gelassenheit*. We see here how Kempf draws the language of German mysticism into his very traditional Latin and monastic theology of mystical union.[35]

The treatise ends with a chapter emphasizing the priority of a penitent *affectus* over an inquiring *intellectus*, the priority of devout desire over empty erudition. All that one knows, hears, and reads must be drawn into the *affectus* and carried out in deeds.[36] In practice, the kingdom of God is revealed more often to the simple and unlettered than to the learned: *Sinite parvulos . . . ad me venire: talium est enim regnum caelorum* (Mt 19:13).[37]

---

[35] *Ost*, ch. 51 (G1, 38v, 30 - 39r, 3); full text in appendix B.

[36] This is clearly reminiscent of Gerson, e.g., his letter of April 29, 1400, to the masters of the Collège de Navarre, or *De consolatione*, bk. IV., prosa 4 (*Oeuvres*, 9: 237). See Gerson, *Oeuvres*, 2:33. However, as we have also seen, it recalls Kempf's earlier *Rect*, e.g., II.6 (Pez 4: 307, 309-10), II.8 (317-18); II.9 (321-25), II.11 (328-33), II.14 (340-41, 343-44).

[37] *Ost*, ch. 53 (G1, 40r, 30 - 40v, 30 passim; Kempf draws here on Augustine's *Enchiridion* and Bonaventura's *Itinerarium mentis in Deum* for his affective theology of union): "Nam secundum omnes sanctos patres, si debet regnum Dei ostendi et creator per experimentalem suiipsius gustum intrare mentem, oportet prius exire omnem creaturam, hoc est omnem actum potenciarum (id est omnes cogniciones et omnes appeticiones aut voliciones cessare et omnem speciem intelligibilem aut sensibilem), et talem mentem perfecte humiliari, et ex simplici et *firma fide totaliter se in Deum proicere ut ipse operetur in sua ymagine*, quod in doctis et alti in status hominibus raro invenitur, . . . quia tales simplices communiter sunt devociores quam literati. Et fides talium est magis simplex et minus inquieta per fantasias contrarium opinionum et disputacionum quas audiunt aut legunt. . . . Et habent maiorem curam de sua salute, et quanto minus occupantur circa intellectum per scienciam multam, tanto liberius circa affectum per actus virtutum et Dei amorem. . . . Et tales facilius possunt fieri ceci ut regnum Dei videant de quibus dixit Christus, 'Sinite parvulos venire ad me; talium est enim regnum celorum' [Mt 19:13-15; Mk 10:14-16; Lk 18:15-17]. Per hunc modum Apostolus Paulus inducere conatus est ipsos Athenienses phylosophos ad cognoscendum Deum, ex ipsorum scripturis hoc probans, ut patet actuum xvii [Acts 17:15-34]. Ad huius sciencie plenitudinem, ut dicit beatus Augustinus in fine manualis opus, est intima pocius compunccione quam profunda investigacione; suspirijs quam argumentis; crebris gemitibus quam copiosis ar-

3. The Two Mystical Unions

Kempf's *De ostensione regni Dei* sets forth a twofold mystical union: first, the "unitive way" that, strictly speaking, is not mystical yet
corresponds to much of what modern scholars would include under that
label, and second, the *unio sanctissima cum Sancte Trinitate in imagine*,[38] which corresponds to the *ostensio regni Dei*.[39] *De ostensione* has
to do with the preparation for and the experience of the "unitive way,"
even though it makes only passing reference to the *unio sanctissima*.

De mystica theologia begins with an outline of the structures of the
human soul, her original righteousness, the fall into sin, and redemption
(part I). We learn that man consists of lower, middle, and upper aspects.[40] The lower man is that of the senses, both interior and exterior;
his life is that of activity, of moral virtues and their corresponding
knowledge, the life of Leah and Martha. The middle man consists of the
three powers of the soul (*voluntas, intellectus, memoria*) which constitute similitude with God; his life is that of acts of contemplation, of the
theological virtues and the gifts of the Holy Spirit, the life of Rachel and
Mary Magdalene. The upper man is the image of God (although the similitude of the middle man can also be considered an *imago Dei* in an
inferior degree); his life is that of the sweetness of the celestial home.[41]
Kempf consistently links the *imago Dei* to the essence of the soul and the
similitudo Dei to the powers of the soul, referring to *doctores modernio-
res* and especially those writing on mystical theology.[42] But he insists

---

gumentacionibus; lacrimis quam sentencijs; oracione quam leccione; gracia lacrimarum quam sciencia litterarum; celestium pocius contemplacione quam terrestrium oc-
cupacione. Et dominus Bonaventura in fine Itinerarij mentis in Deum sic ait, 'Si queris
quomodo hec fiant et quomodo scilicet hec sciencia acquiritur, interroga graciam, non
doctrinam; desiderium, non intellectum; gemitum oracionis non studium lectionis; spon-
sum non magistrum; Deum non hominem; caliginem non claritatem; non lucem sed
ignem totaliter inflammantem et in Deum excessivis unicionibus et ardentissimis affec-
cionibus transferentem'" (emphasis added).

[38] Of the numerous references to this phrase cited in the index to the critical edition,
one might consult first *MTh*, II.7, pp. 117-18. Cf. *Cantica*, prologue, ch. 2 (*Bibl. ascetica*, 11: 7).

[39] *Ost*, ch. 3 (G1, 2r, 31-33).

[40] *MTh*, I.4, based on a combination of Peter Lombard and Hugh of St. Victor.

[41] A good summary of Kempf's theological anthropology and psychology is found in
MTh, I.10, pp. 67-68.

[42] *MTh* I.5-8, III.3-5 etc. Francis Ruello lists Ruusbroec, Gerson, and Hendrik Herp
here. See the Jellouschek edition, p. 430. Herp can only be considered a parallel to, not

that one dare not view the analytical distinction between the powers of the soul and the essence of the soul, or between the powers themselves, as in any way detracting from the soul's unity.[43]

The description of the human soul and its three aspects, together with the discussion of the *imago* and *similitudo Dei* leads to a brief soteriological outline (ch. 11-15) of man's multiple affinity for God, of man's original righteousness and the difference between it and *caritas infusa*, and of the difference between the old man of original sin and man renewed in Christ. This soteriological outline is important because it sets the stage both for the discussion of the three degrees of purgation that follows (II.1-6) and because Kempf's teaching on mystical union is so closely intertwined with his understanding of the path of salvation.[44]

The outline of the three degrees of purgation that opens part II contains in a nutshell the contents of the main part of the treatise *De ostensione*. At several points in *De mystica theologia* Kempf notes that it is not his purpose to deal with the three degrees of purgation, illumination, or union in detail. His purpose is to discuss the *unio sanctissima in imagine*. He must, however, begin with an explanation of what the lower union, the *vita unitiva* of the three degrees, is, and how it differs from the mystical union strictly speaking, the *unio sanctissima*. This he undertakes in *De mystica theologia*, II.7-21.

The *via unitiva* is a union in actual love. Kempf uses *amor* or *dilectio* to describe the active love and distinguish it from *caritas*, which is an infused *habitus*. Actual love differs also from natural love (*MTh*, II.8) because the latter lacks the *gratia gratum faciens* that is linked to both *caritas* and actual love. There is a sense in which the *unio sanctissima* is

---

an influence on, Kempf, since Kempf probably had no direct access to the writings of his contemporary.

[43] *MTh*, I.5, pp. 41-42. Kempf is repeating a theme dear to twelfth-century monastics like Aelred of Rievaulx. See the discussion in Amédée Hallier, *The Monastic Theology of Aelred of Rievaulx* (1969), 6-9; Bernard McGinn, *The Golden Chain: A Study in the Theological Anthropology of Isaac of Stella* (1972), 141-43; and Endre von Ivánka, "La Structure de l'âme selon S. Bernard," in *Saint Bernard Théologien* (1955), 202-8. Cf. Wilhelm Hiss, *Die Anthropologie Bernhards von Clairvaux* (1964), 88-90.

[44] See, for example, the summary passage in *MTh*, I.15, p. 87: "Quibus virtutibus et donis [faith to believe and know God; hope to obtain and retain salvation; and charity to love God above all creatures; together with the gifts of the Holy Spirit] homo iustificatur, ut sit iustus iusticia fidei, que per dilectionem operatur. Et illa iusticia sufficit ad hoc quod homo possit deduci per vias rectas, ut tandem ostendatur illi regnum Dei, quamvis in tali iusto amor predictus [in margin: scilicet naturalis malus, or, as mentioned infra, fomes peccati] non sit deletus sed manet in homine maxima contrarietas et pugna inter amorem a Dei infusam et amores naturales (sinderesim et conscienciam et racionem) et inter amorem predictum pestiferum, quem oportet quotidie et incessanter reprimere et occidere et crucifigare, ut possit vetus homo mortificari et novus renovari de die in diem, exuere veterem hominem et induere novum [Eph 4:24] qui secundum Deum creatus est."

also a union in actual love, since, as we shall see, actions in the human soul do exist in the higher union. They are not, however, *actus proprios*, rather, they are infused from God. As a union in actual love between God and man, the *via unitiva* differs from the other unions of God with man: the general union of God with all creatures and the hypostatic union of God and man in Christ.[45]

The *via unitiva* takes two forms.[46] One is an affirmative union in the *synderesis*, in which love is caused "concomitantly and conservantly" by intellectual cognition.[47] The second is also in the synderesis, but with cessation of all actual cognition in favor of a loving ascent.[48] The affective path, however, seems to dominate the *via unitiva*, and Kempf consistently identifies the *via unitiva* with the mystical theology of Hugh of Balma. At this point (II.9), Kempf briefly mentions the *unio sanctissima*, or *unio proprie . . . sine aliquo medio creato*, as integrally following upon the affective *via unitiva*, since the *unio sanctissima* presupposes the cessation of all of the soul's acts and powers, both cognitive and affective.

An extensive excursus in chapters twenty and twenty-one offers a scholastic *dubium* on the question that stimulated the Tegernsee controversy: whether one can ascend to God solely by love without prevenient or concomitant cognition. True to his desire to reconcile seemingly contradictory viewpoints, Kempf proposes an interpretation of the movement of the will, through a *habitum perfectum acquisitum vel infusum*, from cognition of one thing to love of another thing without any actual previous or concomitant cognition of the latter object, a sort of aspirative, anagogical leap of love that essentially represents Hugh of Balma's position, though not in the interpretation of Hugh favored by Vincent of Aggsbach.[49]

Some might consider this effort to reconcile the various views to be a piece of sophistry, and Kempf admits that it is impossible *de communi lege*, but he also warns that too much zeal in disputing over these issues

---

[45] *MTh*, II.7, esp. p. 117.

[46] *MTh*, II.9, p. 126.

[47] *MTh*, II.9, 10, 12-15.

[48] *MTh*, II.9, 11, 16, 20-21.

[49] *MTh*, II.21, p. 174: "Nam in hoc credo omnes concordare quod voluntas, sine omni cognicione actuali, cuiuscumque rei, de communi lege, non moveantur ad actum suum elicitum aut liberum. Nec hoc pretendunt loquentes de amore predicto [advocates of affective ascent without cognition], sed, habita cognicione actuali de aliqua re, potest voluntas per habitum perfectum acquisitum vel infusum surgere in amorem alterius rei absque actuali cognicione illius, iuxta modum predictum [the affective path of cessation of all cognitive acts outlined as the second part of the *via unitiva*]." Cf. pp. 172-73, 175.

can only lead one farther away from the love one claims to be seeking, an admonition probably aimed at Vincent of Aggsbach. Learned men may laugh at the affective approach of Hugh of Balma, but the simple peasant or old woman understands. The peasant or old woman may not be able to read or write, but can tell his or her experience orally.[50] Kempf therefore describes a number of simpler ways to union.[51] The path of humility is particularly suited to simple folk; once more Hugh of Balma has dealt with this way.[52] Another method makes use of meditation on Christ's passion, on God's creation, and various prayers, an approach reminiscent of the digressions in *De ostensione*, chapters thirty-one to thirty-four, but also referring to Guigo de Ponte's *De contemplatione* and Hugh of Balma's *Viae Sion lugent*. Finally, he commends a life of imitation of Christ, especially of Christ's passion, a life of thankful acceptance of adversity for Christ's sake. All of these are forms of the *via unitiva*.

The third and fourth parts of *De mystica theologia*, which constitute nearly half of the work, deal with the ultimate union, the only union that should be called "mystical union" in the strict sense. Whereas the *via unitiva*, even in its affective form where actual love replaces cognitions, was located in the *potentiae animae*, or *similitudo Dei*, the ultimate union is a union in the essence of the soul, in the *imago Dei*. Even the *actus amoris* by which one loves God *ignote* in the affective portion of the *via unitiva* ceases, or, put in a different way, it ceases to be a human *actus* and is instead produced or infused by God alone. All the sacraments, because they require the use of the powers of the soul, are briefly relinquished. One must be completely free from attachment to anything creaturely, a state, Kempf notes, that is referred to in the vernacular as *Abgeschiedenheit*. Although *de potentia ordinata*[53] the theological virtues of faith, hope, and charity are still essential to union with God, *de potentia absoluta* even these in a certain sense may be said to cease, yet, Kempf hastens to add, they are also prerequired in their most complete degree, since perfect *abnegatio*, or *Abgeschiedenheit* is itself a perfect form of hope and trust in God and as such it requires humility and patience.[54]

---

[50] *MTh*, II.21, pp. 176-77. Again, this echoes the concluding paragraph of Hugh of Balma's supposedly absolutely affective *quaestio difficilis*, although the contrast between orality and literacy is Kempf's addition.

[51] *MTh*, II.17-19; cf. *Ost*, ch. 45-46.

[52] *Viae Sion lugent*, caput 3, particula 1-2 (*via unitiva*, par. 1-57 in SC edition).

[53] Kempf's phrase is *de communi lege*.

[54] *MTh*, III.1, pp. 179-81; IV.17, 324-27; *Ost*, ch. 51.

There are places in *De mystica theologia* (e.g., II.3), where the two-fold distinction between *via unitiva* and *unio sanctissima* seems to give way to a threefold schematization: affirmative, or cataphatic union of love caused by cognition; a negative, or apophatic, union by love alone (both of these are active unions); and a passive union without created medium.[55] Although Kempf often refers to the ultimate union as the "third union," which follows upon the affirmative and the negative unions of the *via unitiva*, the key distinction is that between passive and active unions, between unions that involve human *actus proprios* and the union that consists solely in infused activity (III.13). This infused *actus imaginis Dei* is produced by God without any created medium, is instantaneous, and involves a taste and experience of its object, rather than an enigmatic vision in a mirror darkly (III.15). It is more complete than the hypostatic union of God and man in Christ because the mystical union is a union with the entire Trinity (III.11).[56]

Although chapters six through eight of part III deal with ways of knowing and loving God in this mystical union, the overarching emphasis of part III is on the affective nature of the union. Much of part IV deals with the *scientia sanctorum* that accompanies the ultimate union, in the *imago Dei*, although here again the reciprocity between knowledge and love is emphasized. Kempf specifically sets forth four ways of knowing God: the *speculum creaturarum*,[57] the *speculum in aenigmate scripturarum*,[58] the *radium divinum* in which the *mens* is illuminated to know God but not through study or knowledge of scripture,[59] and knowledge of God face-to-face either in heaven or in the present life *per praesentiam Dei in unione sanctissima*.[60]

Yet even this *unio sanctissima* does not occur entirely in this present life. It falls short of the eschatological beatific vision, yet it is partially already beyond this present life. Kempf tries to reconcile the divergent views of Augustine, Gregory, and Bernard on the possibility of the beatific vision in life on earth.[61] A *visio Dei sicuti est* is not possible, *de communi lege*, in the present life.[62] But an experiential vision which ex-

---

[55] Cf. *MTh*, IV.9.

[56] Kempf bases himself here on the scholastic commentators on Lombard's *Sentences*. See the Jellouschek edition, pp. 228, 451, for references.

[57] *MTh*, IV.3; *Ost*, 32-33.

[58] *MTh*, IV.4a; *Ost*, 44.

[59] *MTh*, IV.4b; *Ost*, 38.

[60] *MTh*, IV.5-6.

[61] *Ost*, ch. 1 and 48; *MTh*, III.10.

[62] *Ost*, ch. 1 (G1, 1r, 14 - 1v, 26); *Cantica*, I.27-28 (*Bibl. ascetica*, 11: 172, 178, the latter on Ex 33:20); *MTh*, IV.4-7, esp. ch. 5.

ceeds the enigmatic vision (1 Cor 13:12) is possible by grace this side of heaven.[63] Kempf implies that Bernard and Gregory approached the question from the viewpoint of a *viator* possessing sanctifying grace when they denied the possibility of a face-to-face vision on earth. In contrast, Augustine's letter *De videndo Deo* took the viewpoint of Moses, Paul, and the Virgin Mary, who received special grace and were granted some sort of vision of God as he is. Kempf suggests that the clear vision as understood by Augustine is granted to people who are not purely in the wayfarer's state and not in full control of their human senses, but who have been raised above human senses in ecstasy. After all, did not Paul say that he did not know whether he was in the body or out of it (2 Cor 12:2-3)? Thus, those to whom the *clara visio*, or *ostensio regni Dei*, is given find themselves in a *status medius* between heaven and earth. They are neither simply *viatores* nor are they on a level with the beatified in heaven. In this way the clear vision exceeds Bernard's and Gregory's enigmatic vision.[64] Of course this clear vision is extremely rare, and Kempf's discussion of it is essentially hypothetical, not experiential.

Apart from the technical question of the beatific vision,[65] Kempf's main concern is with the vision of God that is accessible to earnest Christians, both within and, occasionally, outside of the monastery. As we have seen above, by complete cleansing, which is impossible apart from trust in Christ's alien *virtus* grounded in Christ's sacrifice on the cross, it is possible to return to and even exceed the vision enjoyed by Adam before the fall, a contemplation of God's presence by means of a "certain inner inspiration in an unclouded mirror."[66]

---

[63] *Ost*, ch. 1 (G1, 1r, 19 - 1v, 26); text in appendix B.

[64] *Cantica*, I.28 (*Bibl. ascetica*, 11: 179); I.29 (11: 183); V.4 (12: 128). Cf. *Ost*, ch. 1 (G1, 1v, 4-25, as quoted in appendix B). See also *Ost*, ch. 3 (G1, 2r, 20 - 2v, 35), and 30 (22r, 17 - 23r, 13, quoted in appendix B), where Stephen's vision of God (Acts 7:55-56) is added as a second example; *MTh*, I.3, p. 25; III.9-10; IV.5-6. See also Ladner, *Idea of Reform*, 190-92, on Augustine.

[65] E. Cuthbert Butler, *Western Mysticism* (1924; repr. 1967), 78, 88, 125-33, 175-76. On Augustine see Frederick Van Fleteren, "Augustine and the Possibility of the Vision of God in this Life," *Studies in Medieval Culture*, vol. 11 (1977), 9-16; Augustine, *Letter 147 (De videndo Deum, Epistola ad Paulinam), Letter 148* (PL 33: 596-630). On Gregory see Joseph P. McClain, *The Doctrine of Heaven in the Writings of St. Gregory the Great* (1956), 27-52, esp. 27-29. See also William of Saint-Thierry, *Epistola ad Fratres de Monte Dei*, bk. II. par. 25 (PL 184: 354 [= par. 296-300 in SC 223: 382, 384), and especially the opening paragraphs of his *Aenigma Fidei* (PL 180: 397-400); Bernard of Clairvaux, Sermon 31 on Canticles in *S. Bernardi Opera*, 1: 219-26; Thomas Aquinas, *STh*, Ia. q. 12 and IIa.IIae, qu. 180. Cf. H.-F. Dondaine, "L'objet et le 'medium' de la vision béatifique chez les théologiens du XIIIe siècle," *RTAM*, 19 (1952), 60-130. See also Hugh of Balma, *Viae Sion lugent*, cap. 2, part. 1 (Peltier ed., p. 9a [= *via illuminativa*, par. 6-7, in SC edition]).

[66] Peter Lombard in *Ost*, 29 (G1, 21r, 4-10, 19-35; 21v, 19-23); see appendix B.

Kempf was familiar with an affective mystical theology that he identified with Hugh of Balma and Pseudo-Dionysius and his commentators. This affective mystical theology loomed large on Kempf's horizon, not so much because it was the climax of a long process of assimilation of the influence of Origen and Proclus via Thomas Gallus (Endre von Ivánka),[67] but because Vincent of Aggsbach had made Hugh of Balma his champion against Gerson and Cusanus. Kempf was probably a close bystander, since Vincent of Aggsbach's prior during the 1450s was a professed monk of Gaming and one of Kempf's "disciples," who seems to have turned to Kempf for help in dealing with his obstreperous *subditus*. Once more we find Kempf functioning as a pastor, even in matters of mystical theology.[68]

---

[67] Analyses of trends in medieval mysticism are many and confusing, given the many points of departure offered by the complex language of contemplative writers. Several studies that span the centuries and consider the development of the affective mysticism of Hugh of Balma or the relationship of twelfth-century Cistercians and Victorines to fourteenth-century German Dominicans are the following: Haas, "Schools of Late Medieval Mysticism"; Endre von Ivánka, "Der 'Apex Mentis'," *ZKTh*, 72 (1950), 147-66 (repr. 1964, 1969); idem, "Zur Überwindung des Neuplatonischen Intellektualismus in der Deutung der Mystik: Intelligentia oder Principalis Affectio," *Scholastik*, 30 (1955), 185-94 (repr. 1964, 1969), but note the critique of Ivánka's thesis by Bernard McGinn, *Golden Chain*, 150-51, and in James J. Walsh, S. J., "'Sapientia Christianorum': . . . Thomas Gallus . . . on Contemplation" (diss., 1957), esp. 208-11; David Knowles, "The Influence of Pseudo-Dionysius on Western Mysticism," in *Christian Spirituality* [Rupp Festschrift] (1975), 79-94; idem, *The English Mystical Tradition* (1964), 21-38; F. Edward Cranz, "Cusanus, Luther, and the Mystical Tradition," in *The Pursuit of Holiness in Late Medieval and Renaissance Religion* (1974), 93-102.

[68] We have a letter from Thomas Papler of Zistersdorf, prior at Aggsbach (1448-58), to Johannes Schlitpacher at Melk, written during the controversy, and referring to Vincent's having sent many inquiries on mystical theology to Schlitpacher, requiring much time and effort from Schlitpacher in response. Thomas, who thinks Vincent's preoccupation is *minus utilis* and "bears only modest fruit or no fruit at all," asks Schlitpacher whether it would be wise to permit Vincent to pursue these matters. Then he comments that "an outstanding and religious prelate in our land" has admonished him that Vincent's preoccupations run the risk of succumbing to the sin of pride, urging that Thomas communicate this to Vincent as his pastoral duty: "Admonuit me quidam nobilis et religiosus Praelatus in terra nostra dicens: 'Pater, ego dico vobis, quod frater iste in periculo stat, quia in spiritu meridiano, id est, superbiae, laborat, et vos tenemini sibi dicere tanquam pastor.'" (Pez and Hueber, *Cod. dipl.-hist.-epist.* [1729], letter 20, p. 357). The "outstanding and religious prelate" most certainly was Nicholas Kempf, who was still prior at Gaming during these years—Thomas specifies that this prelate was from Lower Austria (*terra nostra*), and, as a professed monk of Gaming, Thomas naturally would have turned to Kempf for counsel on how to handle a difficult pastoral case. As noted in chapter three, p. 107, above, Leopold Wydemann pointed out that Vincent's sharp tongue was related to his extreme position on conciliar politics. See his letter to Schlitpacher in Pez and Hueber, p. 328, where he excoriates Nicholas Cusanus and denounces Cusanus's efforts at monastic reform, because Cusanus had abandoned the conciliar cause at Basel; in the same letter Vincent fulminates against those who use mystical theology as a catch-all cure for ecclesial woes.

Kempf affirms the value of this affective *via unitiva*; indeed, it is in many ways the center of his interest, as *De ostensione* makes clear. He does indeed postulate a highest level of mystical theology that has both cognitive and affective elements, or, more precisely, is at once both superintellectual and superaffective, thus relativizing Vincent's extreme affectivity. Yet Kempf's highest union, the *union sanctissima*, is extremely rare and already partly out of this world.[69] Thus, de facto, the *via unitiva* remains more important for Kempf. It is accessible only to those who are adequately purified, although, as we have seen, purification rests on God's grace and on a simple recognition of one's own weakness, lameness, and blindness, which relativizes the elitism that might otherwise seem implied. At points Kempf even links this *via unitiva* to the general union of the Church with God as the mystical body of Christ,[70] suggesting something of a "democratized mysticism."[71] Moreover, the mystical theology described in *De recto fine* is quite accessible—Magistra Theologia obliged Discipulus when he asked for an easier way to mystical theology.[72]

Thus the question of the accessibility of the two mystical unions is related to the problem of grace and free will we have explored in the preceding chapter. Kempf is even more emphatic about the *sola gratia* nature of the most perfect union (the *unio sanctissima*). It cannot be acquired in the same way as *gratia gratum faciens* and the seven gifts of the Holy Spirit—to those who do their best, God is bound by his *pactum cum ecclesia* to grant sanctifying grace. In the case of the *unio sanctissima*,

---

[69] In *MTh*, V.3, pp. 365-66, citing Gregory the Great. Kempf notes that only a very few friends of God receive the special grace of union *by faith* in the image of God. Elsewhere he reminds his readers that only with great labor are a very few able to obtain a taste of the banquet that was easily available to Adam and Eve before the fall. See *Ost*, ch. 50 (G1, 37v, 7-10), cf. *Cantica*, I.10 (*Bibl. ascetica*, 11: 97), and II.8 (*Bibl. ascetica*, 11: 320).

[70] *MTh*, III.12. See also *Cantica*, Prologue, ch. 8 (*Bibl. ascetica*, 11: 29).

[71] Heiko A. Oberman, "Simul Gemitus et Raptus: Luther und die Mystik," in *Kirche, Mystik, Heiligung, und das Natürliche bei Luther* (1967), 24-59, at 38; English version (1971), 237; Burrows, *Gerson*, 34-36, 143-48. See also Steinmetz, *Misericordia Dei* (1968), 160-64, and idem, "Religious Ecstasy in Staupitz and the Young Luther," *Sixteenth Century Journal*, 11 (1980), 23-37.

[72] *Rect*, II.6 (V1, 49v A; *Bibl. ascetica*, 4: 306). See the summary in chapter three above.

. . . when one has done all he can, the Beloved can freely come or not come to him to sing this song of love [namely, the Canticle of Canticles] in the human spirit. The action of that love is *caused by God alone without any accompanying action of the free will* [emphasis added].[73]

For the *via unitiva*, a sort of *facere quod in se est* approach applies: the exercise of humility and patience, if done *perfecte et perseveranter*, prepares one for the revelation of the kingdom,[74] yet, even this perfect and persistent cleansing consists in recognizing one's inability to repent perfectly and persistently. Chapter two of the prologue to the commentary on the Song of Songs provides one of the clearest statements on the two forms of union:

Moreover, this union, or mating, of the human mind in the present life is by carried out by two means: One means is through the action of infused love, out of which man is able by his free will to ascend to a love of God known in faith. This form of loving and knowing union is carried out in a mirror darkly. It has many stages of perfection and all scripture is filled with this manner of union. In the second manner of union the human spirit is united with God far more excellently through God's very presence. Uniting himself in his image in man in an ineffable way, he produces there, without any mediation, a cognition of himself and a love of his experiential presence.[75]

---

[73] *Cantica*, Prologue, ch. 8 (G1, 138r, 30 - 138v, 5; *Bibl. ascetica*, 11: 29): "Nec iste gradus amoris in ymagine mentis cum cantico ita acquiritur, sicut gracia gratum faciens, seu caritas cum donis spiritus sancti, que ex pacto Christo cum ecclesia, faciente homine quod in se est, infallibiliter infunduntur, ut in baptizato parvulo aut adulto non ponente obicem, aut in vere penitente: et in actu seu exercicio caritatis infuse cooperatur ipsum liberum arbitrium. Sed in infusione illius amoris Deo omnino est illimitabilis; quia, quando homo facit omnia, quae potest, adhuc dilectus liberrime potest venire aut non venire ad cantandum hoc canticum amoris in mente: et actus illius amoris solummodo causantur a Deo absque libero arbitrio coagente." Cf. ibid., I.27 (*Bibl. ascetica*, 11: 171-75); *MTh*, I.3, pp. 24-25.

[74] See especially *Ost*, ch. 29 (G1, 21v, 20-22). Cf. *Rect*, II.5 (V1, 48v A-B; *Bibl. ascetica*, 4: 302), and *Ost*, ch. 38-39, where Kempf expands on his references to the "cooperation of free will" in the first or lower mystical union, outlining a means whereby cognition of God is granted to all who "do their very best."

[75] *Cantica*, prologue, ch. 2 (G1, 132v, 34 - 133r, 10; *Bibl. ascetica*, 11: 7): "Hec autem unio seu coniunctio mentis humane in presenti vita fit duobus modis [133r]: unomodo per actum caritatis infuse, ex qua cum libero arbitrio homo consurgere potest in amorem Dei cognitum per fidem. Et illa unio amoris et cognicionis fit per speculum in enigmate et habet multos gradus perfectionis, et tota scriptura est plena de illo modo unionis. Secundo modo unitur mens humana Deo multo excellencius per presenciam ipsius Dei, se unientis in ymagine hominis modo ineffabili, et ibi sine medio, producendo cognicionem sui et amorem de sua presencia experimentali. Qui amor et cognicio sunt super omnes anime vires et potencias, et vocantur superintellectuales et superaffectuales. Nec

A *facere quod in se est* yet *sola gratia* approach to mystical union was not unique to Nicholas Kempf. The contemporary Carthusian prior at Basel (1449-87), Heinrich Arnoldi of Alfeld, put the following words into Christ's mouth: "if the devout soul does what she can, namely, if she desires me with all her innermost heart and spares no labor for love of me. . . . then *at the time and place I choose*, I will snatch her away in spiritual ecstasy" (emphasis added).[76] Arnoldi's handbook of mystical theology was translated into German within a few years of its composition and into French in the next century. For Arnoldi, like Kempf, doing what one can consists in "humility, knocking on the door, and seeking refuge under the saints' protection, leaving the rest to Christ, namely, the time and the mode of answering the soul's yearning."[77]

Heiko Oberman has outlined a "nominalist," covenantal, penitential mysticism in Gerson and other late medieval theologians.[78] Steven Ozment has pointed to the doctrine of the powers of the soul and the *Grund* of the soul in Gerson and Tauler, arguing that they assumed a *terminus ad quem* for human beatitude (vision of God) in this life and that Luther was reacting precisely to this ontological faculty within the human person with his "stercus" and "clamare" theology of humility: the only faculty or ability humans possess is to cry out in recognition of their dissimilarity to God.[79] Kempf and Arnoldi should cause us to reexamine Tauler and Gerson on these matters. Although both the Carthusians integrate the "covenantal" language of "doing one's best" into their mystical theology, we have seen how their idea of "doing one's best" is indeed a recognition of one's lameness and blindness and a longing that God's

---

ex caritate infusa, que respicit liberum arbitrium, producitur ille amor, nec cognicio ex specie intellectuali aut ex fanthasmate, sed immediate a Deo."

[76] Arnoldi, *De modo perveniendi ad veram et perfectam Dei et proximi dilectionem*, ch. 32 (*Bibl. ascetica*, 6: 2-214, at 123-24).

[77] Ibid., p. 123: "Verumtamen, quemadmodum etiam superius te avisavi, sic iterum aviso te, ut tu facias id quod in te est, te humiliando, pulsando, et sanctorum patrocinia saepe quaerendo, et reliquum mihi committas, scilicet modum et tempus exaudiendi. Si ita feceris, confide, quod cum minus putas, mirabilia experieris." On Arnoldi, see Eugen Hillenbrand, "Arnoldi, von Alfeld, Heinrich," in *Verfasserlexikon*, rev. ed., vol. 1, cols. 487-89; L. Ray, in *DSAM*, vol. 1 (1937), 892; Martin, "'Tractat von der lieb gots und des Nächsten'"; and Kent Emery, Jr. "Lovers of the World and Lovers of God and Neighbor: Spiritual Commonplaces and the Problem of Authorship in the Fifteenth Century," in *Historia et spiritualitas Cartusiensis* (1983), 177-219. To Emery's summary should be added that the Tegernsee abridged translation (1477-78) was made from Melk cod. 1002, which was directly dependent on the Basel incunabulum. The work was translated into French at Paris in 1570.

[78] Oberman, *The Harvest of Medieval Theology* (1963, 1967. 1983), 323-60; idem, "Gabriel Biel and Late Medieval Mysticism," *CH*, 30 (1961), 259-87.

[79] Ozment, *Homo Spiritualis*, 151-58, 176-78.

grace might make one what one is not. Kempf talks of the *image of God*, of affective and intellective powers of the soul, of synderesis. Yet it is clear that this fits within a context of lameness and blindness, of human inability to cleanse oneself perfectly, of dependence on alien virtue and the crutch of the monastic rule and abbot. Union with God ultimately surpasses all human powers, both affective and cognitive, and it is neither within nor without this present life, rather, it partakes of both this life and the next. Ozment is too quick to dismiss the possibility that similar, apparently contradictory, statements by Tauler may be the result of Tauler's pastoral context, seeking instead a "more theoretically conditioned" explanation.[80]

Ozment's analysis of Gerson is based on a narrow range of Gerson's writings, his academic mystical writings of the pre-Constance period. In Gerson's post-Constance work, *De consolatione theologiae* (1418) we find a context of questing, yearning trust in God's overwhelming providence and predestination, coupled with an emphasis on the absolute priority of grace. It is noteworthy that Kempf draws heavily on this late work by Gerson, as well as on his early reform writings at Paris. In *De consolatione* Gerson approaches more closely to the monastic context he had critiqued as a secular master at Paris.[81] After his sojourn at Melk in 1418, the Paris chancellor took up close contact with the Celestines and Carthusians during his retirement in Lyon.

The question of Tauler's understanding of the ground of the soul and the existence of a mystical *terminus ad quem* within this present life is complex. For the sake of brevity, I refer to his own explanation of the misunderstandings that arose over Eckhart's teaching: "Moreover, one dear teacher taught you and spoke on this subject [unitive prayer in Jn. 17:21], and you did not understand him. He spoke from the point of view of eternity, and you understood him from the point of view of time."[82] This may be the sort of confusion underlying Ozment's claim that mysticism was a "commonsense science of the presently active *potentia Dei absoluta*."[83] If there is one thing Kempf strives to make clear, it is that

---

[80] *Homo Spiritualis*, 30-34. The synergistic "business deal" aspects of mystical theology for Tauler, Ozment suggests, stem from Tauler's lack of clarity about the "line between divine and human being." This itself is a pastoral issue of great significance.

[81] Burrows, *Gerson*, 139-43, 256-63, on Gerson's new appreciation for monasticism; cf. pp. 163-95 regarding his "seeking" soteriology.

[82] Edmund Colledge, "Meister Eckhart, His Times and His Writings," *The Thomist*, 42 (1978), 240-58, at 255. See "Clarifica me pater claritate quam habui prius," sermon 15 in *Die Predigten Taulers*, ed. Ferdinand Vetter, (1910), 69, lines 26-28.

[83] Ozment, "Mysticism, Nominalism, and Dissent," in *Pursuit of Holiness* (1974), 67-92; idem, *Mysticism and Dissent (1973)*, 1-13.

the distinction between heaven and earth, between the eschaton and the temporal present, is never fully overcome. It may be briefly blurred in the case of a very select few: Moses, the Virgin Mary, and the Apostle Paul, perhaps a few "friends of God." But even they are in a *status medius* between heaven and earth. There is no genuine *terminus ad quem* in this life, only a questing and yearning clinging to the threshold of heaven without ever setting foot across that threshold.[84]

Kempf probably knew at least some of Tauler's writings. We know that he attempted to obtain copies of them from the Dominicans at Vienna (appendix A, sect. 5). Although Leonard Huntpichler's ignorance of the existence of Tauler frustrated that attempt, Kempf may well have attained his object through the library at Melk or Tegernsee, where Tauler's and Eckhart's writings were known. His interest in German mystical writings is evident from his effort to correlate his traditional, Latin, affective teaching with the key terms of the German mystical tradition: *Abgeschiedenheit* and *Gelassenheit*.[85] His heavy use of Gerson is obvious. These interconnections, which deserve a full-scale study, and the way Kempf deals with grace and free will, the powers of the soul, and the temporal/eternal distinction in setting forth his teaching on mystical theology should give us pause in assessing Gerson and Tauler.

As Eckhart ceases to be studied as *the* mystic *par excellence*, even Eckhart can be brought back down to earth, as Tauler insisted he should be. Perhaps we can begin to appreciate the mendicant pastoral context in which he worked, even as Kempf's monastic and pastoral context is so crucial to understanding his theology of grace and free will, of heaven and earth. Richard Kieckhefer has pointed the way: "Eckhart did not view ecstatic or abstractive union with God as integral to the life of the soul or even as a goal to be sought or particularly treasured. The state to which he invites his reader is habitual and nonabstractive union. . . ."[86]

---

[84] *Cantica*, Prologue, ch. 4 (Pez 11: 17), where the highest canticle of union within this life is explicitly described as inferior to the song of praise sung in heaven. Cf. *MTh*, III.1, p. 180, regarding *potentia ordinata* and *potentia absoluta* in mystical union.

[85] Graz UB 910 contains copies of a number of Latin and German mystics—Hugh of Balma, Johann of Kastl (Ps.-Albertus Magnus), Nicholas Cusanus, Bonaventure, Thomas Gallus, Heinrich Seuse, Meister Eckhart, alongside Kempf's *De capitulo*. The codex comes from Seitz, and parts of it were copied in 1492 and 1501. It is tempting to speculate that it might be a compilation designed to supplement Kempf's *De mystica theologia* and other mystical writings, which survive primarily in Seitz copies. Whether Kempf had anything to do with its compilation is difficult to say; closer analysis of the contemporary marginal annotation of some of its contents (only the Latin texts are annotated) might be instructive.

[86] Kieckhefer, "Meister Eckhart's Conception of Union with God," *Harvard Theological Review*, 71 (1978), 203-25, at 224. Cf. Dietmar Mieth, *Die Einheit von vita activa und vita contemplativa* (1969), esp. 323-30 (Tauler), and 154 (Eckhart); Alois M.

That is what Kempf's *via unitiva* most closely approximates. The Latin, affective tradition, grounded in Augustine's theology of a questing, yearning will on the pilgrimage from unlikeness back to a renewed image and likeness of God[87] is indeed the dominant tradition from which Eckhart, Tauler, and Ruusbroec should be interpreted. Nicholas Kempf's synthetic and systematic teaching, *when studied within its monastic context*, is an important interpretive tool for examining this tradition.

4. The Carthusian Tradition on Mystical Theology

As pointed out in chapter two above, modern readers are often mystified and put off by the repetitiveness and convolutedness of treatises on contemplative or mystical theology. This is particularly true of the Carthusian tradition. In his *De contemplatione*[88] Guigo de Ponte (d. 1297) moves rapidly through eight of twelve steps in his first three chapters, dwells on the next four steps in seven chapters, then concludes the first book by returning to preparatory material. In his second book he deals with mystical union, dividing it into speculative and anagogical unions, each with parallel subdivisions, only to move back to the basic division between active and contemplative lives in book three, beginning, however, with the contemplative life and concluding with "mundane" discussion of the active life of virtues. From a linear perspective the "climax" of the entire treatise occurs in the middle of book two, turning the last

---

Haas, "Die deutsche Mystik im Spannungsbereich von Theologie und Spiritualität," in *Literatur und Laienbildung im Spätmittelalter und in der Reformationszeit* (1984), 604-42; and Georg Steer, "Die Stellung des 'Laien' im Schrifttum des Straßburger Gottesfreundes Rulman Merswin und der deutschen Dominikanermystiker des 14. Jahrhunderts," ibid., 643-60, esp. p. 651. See also Herbert Grundmann, "Neue Beiträge zur Geschichte der religiösen Bewegungen im Mittelalter," *Archiv für Kulturgeschichte*, 37 (1955), 129-82, at 171; and idem, "Die geschichtliche Grundlagen der deutschen Mystik," *DVfLG*, 12 (1934), 400-29 (repr. 1964), all of which emphasize the pastoral context for Eckhart's mysticism. The normative character of Eckhart's mysticism was challenged by Günter Müller as early as 1926. See "Zur Bestimmung des Begriffs 'altdeutsche Mystik'," *DVfLG*, 4 (1926), 97-127 (repr. 1964). Compare this to the effusiveness of Richard K. Weber, "The Search for Identity and Community in the Fourteenth Century," *The Thomist*, 42 (1978), 182-96, at 195: "Meister Eckhart was at the center of this mystical revolution. He was its greatest figure. . . . More and more historians have come to recognize his greatness."

[87] See, for example, David Bell's exposition of these themes in William of Saint-Thierry, *The Image and Likeness: The Augustinian Spirituality of William of Saint Thierry* (1984).

[88] Edited by Philippe DuPont, AC, 72 (1985). See DuPont's valiant efforts at distilling a system out of Guigo's treatise in his introduction, pp. 11-20.

book into something of an anticlimax in the eyes of a modern reader. The organization of Hugh of Balma's *Viae Sion lugent* is somewhat more straightforward but is also not without its repetitions and redoublings.[89]

From a monastic perspective, however, there is method in this circularity: the external, literal aspect of active combat against virtues is integrated into the entire process of "lofty" mystical union and thus a return to the preparatory, active life at the end of the treatise is a climax in its own way. Mystical life consists of multiple climaxes, not of simple linear progression. Above all, it is fully embedded in the sacramental life of the church and, even more so, in the monastic life. Herein may lie one of the more significant differences between the affective Franciscan mystics of the late Middle Ages (Rudolf of Biberach, Hendrik Herp) and the Carthusians.[90]

For Guigo de Ponte, the first of twelve steps of contemplation is the sinner's justification (i.e., baptism), which continues in the sacrament of penance, the second plank that God gives the sinner after the shipwreck of innocence. The second step is diligent imploring of God for anointing with grace, the third step is compunction, the fourth is suffering with and rejoicing with one's neighbor, the fifth is suffering with Christ (via

---

[89] A full discussion of the late medieval Carthusian mystical tradition is not possible in the present study. Some of the more important literature includes Francis Ruello, "Statut et rôle de l'*intellectus* et de l'*affectus* dans la *Theologie mystique* de Hughes de Balma," in *Kartäusermystik und -mystiker* (1981), 1: 1-46, and the introduction to Ruello's forthcoming critical edition of the same work; Philippe Dupont, "L'ascension mystique chez Guiges du Pont," ibid., 47-80, and DuPont's introduction to his critical edition; James Hogg, "Hugh of Balma and Guigo du Pont," in *Kartäuserregel und Kartäuserleben* (1984), 1: 61-88; Faustino de Pablo Maroto, "Amor y conocimiento en la vida mística, según Hugo de Balma," *Revista de espiritualidad*, 24 (1965), 399-447. The unpublished dissertation by Patricia A. Guinan, "Carthusian Prayer and Hugh of Balma's *Viae Sion Lugent*" (1985) offers a useful biographical and historiographical summary but does not probe theological issues deeply. Older studies include Jean Krynen, "La pratique de la theorie de l'amour sans conaissance dans le *Viae Sion lugent* d'Hughes de Balma," *RAM*, 40 (1964), 161-83, and J. P. Grausem, "Le *De contemplatione* du chartreux Guiges du Pont," *RAM*, 10 (1929), 259-89. An English translation of these two works is forthcoming in the CWS series.

[90] Note Thomas Renna's perceptive comments about thirteenth-century changes that prepared the way for attacks by secular masters like Wycliff (and Gerson): many thirteenth-century spiritual writers "discuss contemplation apart from the monastic life. By avoiding references to the cloister St. Bonaventure implies that the mystical ascent is attainable by anyone, assuming sufficient grace. The Belgian women mystics often dissociate their ecstasies from the *vita monastica* as such. They stress the role of divine grace, not the practices of their contents. . . . The scholastic treatments of the *status perfectionis* . . . often include traditional monastic virtues within other nonmonastic states of perfection. So too, the monastic state was judged inferior to the mixed life. . . . The monk was losing his distinctive qualities and his place in the church's charismatic hierarchy, as well as in its organizational structure." Renna, "Wyclif's Attacks," 272.

meditation on his passion), the sixth step is the flamelet of burning desire. Only in the seventh step does the Bridegroom, the Word of God, penetratingly descend into the thirsty soul, followed by the eighth step of upwardly striving contemplation. The ninth step is constant meditation on scripture, the tenth is the overshadowing cloud in the heart's inner chamber, the eleventh is the overpowering of the spirit (*excessus mentis*) in which the soul anticipates eternal beatitude while yet on earth. The twelfth step is the falling away of the flesh, i.e., death. Thus baptism-penance and death (i.e., all of life) bracket the contemplative ascent from begging for grace to the *excessus mentis*.[91]

The Carthusian tradition of mystical theology, as exemplified by Hugh of Balma and Guigo de Ponte,[92] also emphasizes the same fundamental role of painfully penitent humility that we have found in Kempf,[93] a humility that recognizes one's own inability to merit mystical union. Hugh of Balma admits a role for both nature and grace in the first stage of the third path, the way of unitive love, but actual experiential and direct knowledge of divine things is by grace alone. His prooftext depends on the grammatical distinction between the active and passive voice in the Latin translations of Pseudo-Dionysius:

---

[91] Guigo recapitulates this in *De contemplatione*, bk I, ch. 11; Dupont edition, pp. 160-64.

[92] To speak of a "Carthusian tradition," is, of course, misleading to some degree, since Carthusians permitted great latitude in spiritual development. Still, Hugh of Balma's affective mystical theology was influential in the late Middle Ages, especially, though not exclusively, among Carthusians. Guigo de Ponte knew it and many lesser-known late medieval Carthusians also used Hugh's work. It clearly set the stage for the Tegernsee controversy, since Hugh is one of Vincent of Aggsbach's main authorities. I have deliberately chosen not to include Denys of Rijckel in the purview of this chapter. Although he shares with Hugh a special veneration for Pseudo-Dionysius, he interprets his namesake through a scholastic and speculative filter that owes much to Albert the Great, Thomas Aquinas, Henry of Ghent, and others. See Kent Emery, Jr., "Twofold Wisdom and Contemplation in Denys of Ryckel," *JMRS*, 18 (1988), 99-134, and Mertens, "Jakob von Paradies . . . über die mystische Theologie," 39-40, quoting Denys's definition: "mystica theologia non est formaliter seu essentialiter amor aut fervor, sed cognitio." (*De contemplatione*, bk. III, art. 14, in *Dionysii Cartusiensis Opera Omnia*, vol. 41: 270B). Although Emery describes the Tegernsee controversy (erroneously turning Johann Schlitpacher into a monk of Tegernsee), he admits that there is no real reason to link Denys the Carthusian to the controversy. That my decision not to include him in the "Carthusian tradition" is not arbitrary gains support from the fact that Denys was apparently criticized by his fellow Carthusians for his "uncarthusian" scholastic and speculative interests. See Emery's discussion of Denys's self-defense, his *Protestatio ad superiorem suum*, and its probable context in "Twofold Wisdom," 101-3.

[93] Balma, *Viae Sion lugent*, caput 1, particula 1 (Peltier ed., 4b-5a [*via purgativa*, par. 2-3 in SC edition]).

In the third path, when through insatiable longing the human spirit sighs for complete union with her Beloved, she is more acted upon than acting as she is divinely raised up to be irradiated by the third ray. The Beloved then says to the one who has longed so long, *Friend, go up higher* (Lk 14:10). In this regard Denys said in the *Mystical Theology*, "Strive upward [*consurge*] unknowingly to that union and knowledge which is above the spirit," [*De mystica theologia*, ch. 1] where the practice of unitive love is handed on, where the *affectus* rises up to the unspeakable mystery unknown to the understanding. Then he adds these words, speaking to Timothy: "Removing from yourself all things, and freed from trappings, you will be brought up on high in purity to the radiance of divine darkness" [ibid.] In speaking of the uplifting of unitive love he says "Strive upward" [*consurge*], for grace and nature are at work here. After that he says, "You will be brought up on high" [*sursum ageris*], since grace, not nature, lifts the human spirit to experiential and direct knowledge of divine things, and through grace the human mind is made ready for such experiential and direct knowledge.[94]

But it is not only in the highest level of mystical union that a *sola gratia* theology operates for Hugh. The same is true of the most fundamental levels. Hugh presents an analogy between God's predestination (which chooses some to enjoy eternal beatitude and leaves others in eternal damnation), and the calling of some to monastic[95] and mystical life. Just as we have observed with Kempf, Hugh embeds his teaching on mystical union firmly in the context of genuine contrition and sacramental penitence. The prerequisites for mystical union are contrition, humility, and complete prostration.[96] It is indeed "enough for the Creator if a man does what he can," yet "these things cannot be accomplished without special grace," and "contrition for sins is granted from on high." In

---

[94] *Viae Sion lugent*, caput 2, particula 1 (Peltier ed., p. 9a-b [= *via illuminativa*, par. 6-7, in SC edition]). Cf. cap. 3, pt. 4 (Peltier, p. 45b [= *via unitiva*, par. 108, in SC edition]), where his interpretation also turns on the shift from active to passive voice in the Sarracenus translation of Pseudo-Dionysius.

[95] And not just any religious life at that, but specifically to the most austere and holy of the monastic orders. Interpolations in the 1495 Straßburg edition substituted "Franciscan" for "Carthusian" in an earlier paragraph (6a top [= *via purgativa*, par. 6 in SC edition]) and, in the passage referred to here (Peltier, p. 6a bottom [= *via purgativa*, par. 7 in SC edition]), added a reference to "preaching poverty throughout the whole world" that was clearly intended to imply the Hugh favored the Franciscans. But even with the interpolations, the references to the desert and to John the Baptist unmistakeably point to the Carthusians, quite apart from the exposure of the interpolations by the editor of the 1588 Vatican edition. See Hogg, "Hugh of Balma and Guigo du Pont," 72-73; Pablo Maroto, "Amor y conocimiento," 406.

[96] *Viae Sion lugent*, ch. 1, part. 1; Peltier ed., pp. 4b-5a (= *via purgativa*, par. 2-3, in SC edition).

other words, Hugh uses the traditional *facere quod in se est* language and, at first seems to endorse the view that "doing one's best" by prostrating and deprecating oneself involves "monkish virtue" and binds God to grant "congruent" merit. Yet he concludes by insisting that even the minimal sorrow over one's inability to sorrow is possible only by virtue of special grace.[97] In Hugh's mystical theology we find the same yearning affectivity we have already observed in Nicholas Kempf's writings— in the end, doing one's best consists in sighing and weeping over what one cannot do:

> The soul should humble herself in the following manner: First she should revisit her sins in some sort of hidden place, especially in the hidden silence of the night. She should review the main ones succinctly, lest the devil lead her to delight in them. Against this she ought to apply the following remedy: with her face turned toward the heavens, let her enumerate her main sins, up to about ten or twelve, in God's sight, as if she were speaking to him. As she names them, let her sigh, exalting God in everything and putting herself down in everything, as far as possible, saying "Lord Jesus Christ (or whatever form seems best to her), I am that most wicked sinner, wretched, and more unhappy, more abominable than the most wicked. For I have offended against your majesty in so many ways and to such a degree that I am unable to list them any more than one can number the multitudinous sands of the sea. She should sigh and groan there as best she can, because, just as a file applied to iron pushes away a bit of the iron's rust with each grating stroke, so too any sort of sigh or groan removes something of the rust of sin, even that which remains after the inpouring of grace. Thus cleansing herself more and more, the soul *is raised by divine aid, or yearning*, to the perception of things which reason does not research and understanding does not catch sight of.[98]

Guigo de Ponte also underscores the *sola gratia* nature of mystical contemplation. In his key chapter on the method of ascending to God in affective love, it is God who "cracks open the cloud a little bit for the seeking soul," it is God's "hidden means involving his own countenance" that "moves and advances, attracts and restores the soul."[99] All the soul can do is thirstily cling, holding on tight as she is raised above herself.[100] Her candle is kindled by being placed next to God's, and even

---

[97] *Viae Sion lugent*, cap. 1, part. 2; Peltier, pp. 6a-b (= *via purgativa*, par. 9, in SC edition).

[98] "Et sic magis ac magis anima se purgans, ad percipienda quae ratio non investigat, vel intellectus speculatur, divino subsidio, vel desiderio elevetur." *Viae Sion lugent*, cap. 1, part. 2 (Peltier, p. 5a [= *via purgativa*, par. 3, in SC edition]), emphasis added.

[99] *De contemplatione*, II.8 (Dupont ed., p. 222-24).

[100] Ibid., III.4 (p. 274).

her clinging consists in God's faithfulness. All she really "does" is to close her eyes and lean more eagerly on God's own faithfulness.[101] Even the prayer by which one begs for the special grace needed for contemplation, which is the office of the angels, must occur out of "yearning for the Creator and out of the restoration of the inner man, rather than confidence in merits."[102]

Nor does Guigo's *sola gratia* theology apply solely to the upper reaches of contemplation. His most explicit statement comes, as it does for Kempf, at the outset of the process, in his discussion of the fundamental repentance and cleansing needed for spiritual growth:

> Let the faithful sinner wisely beware lest, no matter what state he finds himself in, he place his confidence in his own merits. Rather, let him approach emptyhanded, like a little pauper, stripped of everything, begging alms from his Lord. And let him not do this out of false humility, hiding his confidence in merits [cf. Mt 25:18 etc.], rather, let him know without a doubt that "no living person shall be justified in the Lord's eyes" [Ps 142:2b (143:2b)], indeed, we are not even able to render an account of our thoughts, should the Lord wish to enter into judgment with us. [Ps 142:2a (143:2a), cf. Job 9:3]. In this way, even the one who presses forward urgently toward the good Lord who calls sinners [Mt 9:13] will not be thought presumptuous. In the world, when beggars step forward to beg alms of the rich, they are considered more wretched, not more worthy, in proportion to their neediness; far from being considered presumptuous or proud, the greater their need, the greater is the pity with which goodhearted rich folk view them.[103]

---

[101] Ibid., II.13 (p. 250): "Credo quod quando bonus Dominus tibi utrumque modum contemplandi dederit, saepius et libentius te exercitabis per modum anagogicum, qui nec videt nec intelligit, sed clausis oculis et velata facie a facie Domini certis tamen intensionibus seu extensionibus humilium desideriorum creatoris praesentiam videt et nititur *in ipsius fiducia* avidius amplexari quasi adhaerendo eius pedibus ad fruendum quam per alium modum qui, sicut supradictum est, videre non potest id quod videt" (emphasis added). The external reference of "in ipsius fiducia" cannot be questioned, for the soul is being addressed in the second person. "Ipsius" can only refer to God. DuPont's translation evades the issue by simply omitting the pronoun. Cf. chapter four, p. 138, above.

[102] Ibid., II.6: "Tertius vero gradus est contemplatio summae deitatis. Aspiranti autem ad contemplationem summi boni non ex confidentia meritorum sed ex desiderio creatoris cum reformatione interioris hominis, tria sunt necessaria, scilicet oratio, materia, et modus exercitandi. Cum enim officium contemplandi, quod est angelorum, sit supra humanam scientiam et virtutem ad quod nemo potest pertingere nisi abundantiori gratia favente et faciente, patet manifeste quod valde est necessaria continua oratio ad continuam gratiam impetrandam, sine qua nihil possumus facere. Ioanne. Haec oratio non debet esse vocalis in multiloquio, sed spiritualiter mentalis quae mentem teneat et erigat ad Deum, . . ." See also II.2 (p. 180) and II.4 (pp. 194, 196).

[103] Ibid., II.5. Cf. Guigo I, *Meditationes*, nos. 16, 19, SC, 308: 108: "Hoc solo iustus es, si ob peccata tua, damnandum te agnoscas et dicas. Si iustum te dicis, mendax es [1 Jn 2:4], et a Domino veritate damnaris, sicut contrarius ei. Dic te peccatorem, ut verax Domino veritati convenias, liberandus [Jn 8:32]. . . . Cum laudatori blandus es, non iam

Although we have critical editions for three Carthusian mystics (Hugh, Guigo, and Kempf) and transcriptions and editions of others (Jacob de Paradiso,[104] Richard Furth of Methley),[105] much more study will need to be undertaken before a synthetic overview of late medieval affective spiritual theology can be written, for such an overview will need to take account of late medieval Franciscan spiritual writers, notably Rudolf of Biberach[106] and Hendrik Herp,[107] who resemble yet differ from our four Carthusians, as well as the pervasive influence of Bonaventure, whom Kempf cites at a number of places.

---

tuo laudatori blandus es. Non enim iam tu laudaris. Quippe, tu vanus. Cum dicitur: 'Quam bonus, quam iustus', qui hoc est laudatur, non tu, qui non es. Imo etiam vituperaris non parum. Quippe tam malus tamque iniustus. Laus enim iusti, iniusti est vituperatio. Ergo tua, ut iniusti. Cum ergo laudatori iusti applaudis, tuo verissimo vituperatori applaudis, quia iniustus es. Non est enim iustus, qui se putat iustum. Nec unius diei infans [Job 25:4, cf. Job 15:14, 14:5 (*Vetus Latina*)]." Note also the editor's note regarding Guigo I's understanding of liberty, pp. 312-14.

[104] Jacob de Paradiso's two-part treatise *De actionibus humanis et de mystica theologia* and *De theologia mystica* (1451) has been edited in Jakub z Paradyza, *Opuscula inedita*, ed. Stanislaw Andrzej Porebski (1978), pp. 175-247, 249-312. Although called a critical edition, it is based on a single manuscript (fifteen are known) and the critical apparatus is restricted to documenting the editor's emendations and identifying scriptural sources and Jacob's explicit references to his authorities. The edition was not widely distributed and was apparently unknown to Johann Auer and Dieter Mertens. See Auer, "Die *Theologia mystica* des Kartäusers Jakob von Jüterbog," in *Die Kartäuser in Österreich* (1981), 2: 19-52, which includes the text of chapters 1-3 and 8-10; Mertens, "Jakob von Paradies" (1982). Jacob's second part, on mystical theology, is very much in the affective tradition and is heavily dependent on Gerson and Hugh of Balma. The issues of grace and merit raised by Mertens, "Jakob von Paradies," p. 39-41, require more study in relation to changes in Jacob's own thinking after 1452. See ch. 6, below.

[105] On Richard Furth of Methley see James Hogg, "Mount Grace Charterhouse and Late Medieval English Spirituality," in *Collectanea Cartusiana* (1980), 3: 1-43, at 25-39, which is a more detailed version of Hogg's article on Richard in *DSAM*, 10 (1979), 1100-1103. See also Hogg's other articles on Methley as listed in the Bibliography; Michael G. Sargent, "The Self-Verification of Visionary Phenomena: Richard Methley's *Experimentum veritatis*," *Kartäusermystik und -Mystiker* (1981), 2: 121-37; and James Walsh, "Introduction" to *The Cloud of Unknowing*, CWS (1981), 15-19. Professor Hogg has announced that a critical edition of Methley's works is underway. Methley was born in 1451 or 1452 and was prior of the London Charterhouse just before the Reformation.

[106] His *Septem itineribus aeternitatis* is found in *Bonaventurae opera omnia*, ed. A. C. Peltier (1866), 8: 393-482. Cf. Margot Schmidt's corrigenda in her edition of *De septem itineribus aeternitatis* (1985).

[107] See Georgette Epiney-Burgard, ed., *Henri Herp: De Processu humani profectus: Sermones de diversis materiis vitae contemplativae* (1982), and the compendium of contemplative tracts that was printed under the title *Theologiae mystica libri tres* by M. Novesianus at Cologne in 1538 (reprinted Farnborough: Gregg Press, 1966). Later sixteenth-century editions and the 1611 edition by A. Quentel at Cologne contain a text expurgated by Vatican censors. See *DSAM*, 7 (1969), cols. 341-66, and Lucidus Verschueren, *Hendrik Herp O.F.M., Spieghel der volcomenheit*, 2 vols. (1931). I have seen only volume one of Verschueren's edition and have relied on the 1538 edition for the text.

But comparisons to the Franciscans are only part of the picture. A full description and interpretation of the Carthusian place in late medieval mysticism must also take account of Thomas Gallus, Gerson, and Ruusbroec, to say nothing of the impact of Carthusian contemplative writers on the Spanish and French schools of the sixteenth century. If the present study has at least drawn attention to the presence of a thoroughgoing theology of grace underlying a mystical theology that is fully embedded in the sacramental and ecclesial path of salvation, it will have served its admittedly interim purpose. For the present, we must turn our attention in the remaining two chapters to a theme that accompanies Kempf's emphasis on meekness, weakness and humble dependence on God's grace: leadership by way of contemplative *otium*, strength through the monastic wall of renunciation, reform by way of retreat.

CHAPTER SIX

PRELATE

Not only do I not forbid those whose purer minds can grasp things more sublime than I present, I greatly rejoice with them—though they should then put up with me as I serve simpler things to simpler souls. If only everyone were able to interpret scripture! I would not have to busy myself with these expositions! . . . and I would have leisure to see how lovely God is (Ps 45:11 Vulg.). Now however, I must confess it is not permitted me to seek after God, to contemplate him, . . . in . . . the form in which the angels long to view him forever, God with God. And I, a man, describe him as a man to men, . . . as gentle rather than sublime; anointed rather than lofty, . . . commissioned "to preach good news to the poor, to heal those broken in heart, to proclaim forgiveness to the captives and openness to those who are closed off; to proclaim a year pleasing to the Lord" (Is 61:1-2). [Bernard of Clairvaux, *Sermones super Cantica canticorum*, 22.3]

1. The Church and Her Orders: Monastic Microcosm

Nicholas Kempf left no systematic treatise on the structure of the church. As a monk, he focused his attention more on the observance of the rule, the government of his monastery, and the pursuit of contemplation than on the government of the church. Yet his program for the proper pursuit of theology, the love of God, centered as it was on the *schola monastica*, made necessary some consideration of the justification for choosing the religious life in a time when the church was confronted with schism and corruption. For Kempf himself, the religious life needed no defense. To a contemplative whose religious vocation has been clearly discerned, the contribution of the religious life to the life of the church is obvious. However, Kempf wrote to convince and encourage others. Scattered through his writings on contemplation and mystical theology are references to the purpose he envisioned for the religious life within the structure of the church.

Fundamental to Kempf's defense of the monastic life is the realization that the monastery is the church in microcosm.[1] If only the church

---

[1]   See *Serm. evang.*, no. 34 (G2, 171v A, 26 - 172r B, 7), where Kempf describes the monastery as Christ's sheepfold and the church as a larger fold protecting all souls—with Christ (not the pope) as the shepherd. Cf. *Cantica*, VIII.22 (G1, 326v, 37 - 327r, 10;

outside the monastery were more like that inside the cloister! Kempf implicitly recognizes the need for preachers and prelates outside the cloister, but insists that their preaching and administration is in vain without the prayer and devotion of monks. He recommends the religious life both for the salvation of one's soul and the salvation of the church. Given these axioms, he devotes his writing and his energy to the needs of sheep and shepherds in the monastic microcosm.[2]

In the present chapter we attend to Kempf's scattered, unsystematic comments about the role of monastics within the church and the way in which monastic prelates mirror leadership roles of the church as a whole. Our purpose here is not so much to systematize and reconcile all his illustrative metaphors, but rather to develop a sense of the scope and inspiration for Kempf's monastic ecclesiology. Only then can we turn to the question of his attitude toward reform and renewal of church and society and fit it into its contemporary context: Benedictine and Carthusian monasticism, urban and rural society, active and contemplative ideals, noble and bourgeois culture.[3]

In his commentary on the Canticle Kempf harbors no illusions about a pure, unblemished church, or even an unblemished monastic microcosm, on earth. Only heaven will be populated solely by "good" people.[4]

12: 389-90): "Dicit ergo primo: 'Vinea fuit pacifico in ea, scilicet vinea, que habet populos' [Ca 8:11]. Vinea hic capitur pro qualibet congregacione monastica, aut eciam pro quolibet homine perfecte vite, in religione constituto, quorum mentes debent esse sicut vinea, proferentes vinum spiritualis dulcedinis quod Deum letificat, angelos et homines. Hec vinea monastice vite fuit pacifico, scilicet Christo domino, qui pacem veram attulit mundo. Sed iam pro maiori parte non est vinea, sed spinetum, in qua crescunt spine, tribuli, urtice, et omnes herbe nocive et inutiles omnium viciorum et peccatorum: quia singularis ferus depastus est eam [Ps 79:14 (80:13)], quia materia observancie est destructa, et patefacta omnibus transeuntibus. Hec est in ea, que habet populos. Si capitur pro congregacione monastica, tunc est in vinea illa magna, que est tota ecclesia, que habet populos. Si cura pro congregacione monastica, tunc est in vinea illa magna, que est tota eclesia que habet multos populos diversorum statuum et condicionum, et non solum religiosos."

[2] For the roots of this theme in the pre-Benedictine *Rule of the Master*, see Karl Suso Frank, "Kloster als scola dominici servitii," p. 84.

[3] In the present chapter Kempf's *Explanatio in Cantica Canticorum* (see appendix A, no. 20) will be cited by folio and line numbers in Graz UB, cod. 262 (G1) and by volume and page numbers in *Bibl. ascetica*. Where divergent, chapter citations are given according to the numbering of both the *Bibl. ascetica* edition and G1.

[4] *Prop*, II.14 (VS1, 30v A, 32-34): "Tribulacionem vero in dorso nostro Deus posuit cum hostem quem non videmus, quasi a dorso percucientem nos temptare permittit, qui tanto liberius nos percutit in dorso, quanto eius verbera non videntes sentimus. Istius inimici argumenta sunt frequenter sophistica. Et scripturarum auctoritates false allegat, aut male exponit, sicuti et Christo facere presumpsit. Homines quoque super capitibus nostris ambulant, cum nos iniuste conculcant et molestant, hij in nullo loco desinunt. Ubique enim mali mixti sunt bonis in terris. Et nusquam soli boni nisi in celo." Cf. *Cantica*,

What kinds of people, which orders, which members, make up the church militant on earth?

Kempf uses several sets of figurative images to illustrate the various orders in the church.[5] One, borrowed from Bernard of Clairvaux, describes four *status*: (1) major prelates (represented by the cedar beams of Canticle 1:16); (2) inferior prelates and clergy (the rafters of pine); (3) the *populus*, which includes prelates, clerics, princes, kings, and "powers" as well as all people (the house supported by the rafters and beams); and (4) the religious, or monks (the couch, which, alas, *in tempore praesenti*, is not always a place of repose).[6] Although Kempf stresses the key role of the prelates who support the entire house (yet are also part of the house that they themselves support), he accords the place of favor and delight to the couch of the religious life. In his exposition of Canticle 3:5, the bride represents the contemplative soul, and the daughters of Jerusalem are the faithful of the church who have made little or no progress in contemplation. The roes represent the greater prelates; the hinds, the lesser prelates and *doctores*.[7]

We must pause at this point to consider what Kempf means by the word *prelate*. Like Gregory the Great and spiritual writers of the Middle Ages, indeed, like Clement of Rome in the subapostolic period,[8] Kempf

---

VIII.22 (G1, 327r, 16-20; 12: 390-91): "Qui ergo ad religionem venerit, cogitet, quod non solum inveniet perfectos, sed eciam populos: et pacienter discat eos portare, si ipse vult perfectus esse, et non per inpacienciam a perfectione cadere. Nam et tales sunt, de quibus dilectus paulo ante dixit: Soror nostra parvula est, et ubera non habet [Ca 8:8]. Et tales sunt pingendi [*compingendi*, Vulgate] tabulis cedrinis [Ca 8:9]. . . ." Cf. the discussion of the temptations to self-deception within the monastic life in chapter four, pp. 127-28, above.

[5] On *ordines* in the church, see Yves Congar, "Les laics et l'ecclésiologie des 'ordines' chez les théologiens des XIe et XIIe siècles," in *I laici nella societas cristiana dei secoli XI e XII*, (1968), 83-117, dealing with, among others, Honorius of Autun's commentary on the Song, with its ten orders corresponding to the head, eyes, cheeks, lips, hands, etc. of the bride, the church.

[6] *Cantica*, I.33 (ch. 34 in G1, 181r-v; 11: 206-08). Kempf gives more ecclesiological significance to this passage than does either Bernard of Clairvaux in his sermon 46 on the Canticle (which Kempf cites as his source for the inspiration to apply Ca 1:15-16 to the states of life in the church) or Origen (*Homiliae in Cantica Canticorum*, II.4, SC 37: 86-89.) Kempf adds to Bernard's exposition a lament about the decline of religious life; Origen applied the beams and the rafters to priests and bishops but assigned the figure of the couch to the human body.

[7] *Cantica*, III.6 (G1, 220v; 11: 370).

[8] *1 Clement*, I.3, XXI.6, XLII.4-5, XLIV.4-5; Gregory the Great, *Regula pastoralis* passim; John Chrysostom, *De sacerdotio*, SC 272; Gregory of Nazianzus, "In Defense of His Flight to Pontus and His Return," (= *Oration* II), ed. J. Bernardi, SC, 247 (1978), 84-240, trans. Charles G. Browne and James E. Swallow, NPNF, ser. 2, vol. 7 (1893, 1955), 204-27. On the twelfth century, see Congar, "Laics," 97-98; on the late medieval period see Leopold Lentner, "'Stella clericorum': Ein Pastoralbuch des späten Mittelalters," in

equates the role of pastor, or shepherd, with that of prelate, ruler, rector. Shepherding souls involves governing, directing, and ruling. Indeed, "pastor," "superior," "praelatus," "vicarius," and "praepositus novitiorum" are named in one breath in one of Kempf's sermons.[9] Kempf may warn urgently of the abuses of the prelate's office outside the cloister, but his very demanding pastoral ideal is applied just as relentlessly to the role of the head of a monastic community. In every sense the monastic prelate is both shepherd, pastor, and ruler.

In effect, Kempf is applying to the monastic microcosm the concern for clerical reform that is so evident in the writings of Nikolaus of Dinkelsbühl, Thomas Ebendorfer, and other members of the "Vienna School."[10] The same efforts to establish what would now be called a professional approach to clerical training were characteristic of other areas of late medieval Europe.[11] Among the numerous handbooks that Denys of Rijkel wrote for all manner of topics, states of life, and professions were manuals for both secular *and* regular clergy: *De vita et regimine praesulum, De regimine praelatorum, De vita et regimine archidiaconorum, De vita canonicorum, De vita et regimine curatorum* (*Opera*, vol. 37). Applied to monastic pastoral questions,[12] Kempf's treatises *De ca-*

Dienst an der Lehre [Cardinal König Festschrift] (1965), 263-74, at 266. For Jacob de Paradiso, citing Bernard of Clairvaux, *praelati* are all those who have the *cura animarum. Subditi* are all those who do not. See Mertens, *Iacobus Carthusiensis*, 98-99.

[9] *Serm. evang.*, no. 34 (G2, 171r A, 18-22): "Prelatus vel pastor pro subditis spopondit quando eorum regimen assumpsit et illaqueatus est pro eis respondere in finali iudicio. . . ." and (173r B, 4-10): "Et quamvis predicta reciproca cognicio pastoris seu superioris [Jn 10:14-15] sive sit prelatus, vicarius, aut noviciorum prepositus, et ovium seu subditorum omnium, precipue novellorum, sit summe necessaria et cadat sub precepto ex parte utraque [the reference is to 172v B., 10, above: 'Iuxta illud scripture "Agnosce vultum pecoris tui"' (Ez 34:17, 22?)]." Elsewhere Kempf uses *rectores* as an equivalent for prelate and pastor. See François Vandenbroucke in Bouyer, et al., *Christian Spirituality* (1968), 2: 8, for similar usage by Gregory the Great. Cf. Kempf, *Cantica*, I.28 (ch. 29 in G1, 174r, 31-32; *Bibl. ascetica*, 11: 178): "Pastores vero sunt angeli et prophete, apostoli et doctores et prelati ecclesie, quibus est commissum tabernaculum sacre scripture."

[10] In addition to the *Stella clericorum*, another typical example is Ebendorfer's *De regimine animarum* (Vienna cvp 3780, 30v-64v), a manual on sacramental confession written for parish clergy.

[11] Although this trend goes back to the thirteenth century, inspired in large part by the Fourth Lateran Council and by developments in the late twelfth-century at the emerging university of Paris, it flourished especially in the fourteenth and fifteenth centuries. See John W. Baldwin, *Masters, Princes, and Merchants: The Social Views of Peter the Chanter and His Circle*, 2 vols. (1970); Leonard E. Boyle, *Pastoral Care, Clerical Education, and Canon Law, 1200-1400* (1981); R. M. Ball, "Thomas Cyrcetur, a Fifteenth-Century Theologian and Preacher," *JEH*, 37 (1986), 205-39, for an orientation.

[12] For the sometimes unclear boundaries between Carthusian pastoral care of lay brethren, lay employees, and secular people in England, see Gillespie, "Cura Pastoralis," esp. 166-72.

pitulo, De discretione, and *De suspicionibus* represent the same general concern with pastoral care and leadership.

Kempf apparently found a typology partly based on spiritual and intellectual qualities more illuminating than one based solely on temporal or external states of life, although we learn something about his views of social order in the process.[13] He offers a threefold spiritual division of the church. First there are the unlearned, simple but devout faithful (*laboratores, rustici, mechanici, mulieres simplices*) who correspond to the young maidens (*adulescentiae*) of Canticle 6:6-7 as well as the beginners (*incipientes*) of the traditional threefold mystical path. Second, there are people with special intellectual talent or acquired learning who use their natural and God-given gifts and learning solely for teaching, preaching, or directing others. They correspond to the concubines of Canticle 6:6-7 and the *proficientes* of the mystical way. Finally there are the contemplatives who, by the grace of God freely given, cling in love and perfect charity to the king. They correspond to the queen of Canticle 6:6-7 and the *perfecti* of mystical union. The same framework appears elsewhere with the addition of an inferior order, the *anima peccatrix*. The two lower orders (young maidens and concubines; *incipientes* and *proficientes*) should minister to the contemplatives (queen, *perfecti*) so that the entire church may move closer to her goal of union with God.[14]

With these outlines of the orders or states of life in the church in mind, we can now consider the relationship between the two groups Kempf is most concerned with: prelates (pastors, *doctores*) and contemplatives (religious). Some contemplatives, of course, function as prelates and pastors—a problematic situation that will occupy us for much of this chapter. For the sake of analysis, however, we shall first consider the two separately.

Kempf asserts that the religious and the *doctores* (often used by Kempf as a collective term to include preachers, teachers, pastors, and prelates[15]) are the two primary orders in the church. The church is like the tents of Canticle 1:4. Like the tents of Kedar, on the outside she is rough and swarthy from facing the adversities and persecutions of sin.

---

[13] Congar argues that *ordines* with reference to the functions in the church took on an additional meaning denoting social classes from the eighth century onward. See "Laics," 91, and Georges Duby, *The Three Orders* (1980); note the review essay by Elizabeth A. R. Brown, "Georges Duby and the Three Orders," *Viator,* 17 (1986), 51-64.

[14] *Cantica,* VI.9-10 (G1, 276v-278r; 12: 147-55) gives the threefold typology. The fourfold variation is found in chapter one of the brief commentary on the first chapter of the Canticle that is appended to *MTh* (Jellouschek edition, pp. 390-91).

[15] On the meaning of *doctores* see *Cantica,* IV.13 (G1, 237v-23r; 11: 439-42); VII.13 (G1, 296r; 12: 241); VIII.16 (G1, 322r; 12:365-66).

On the inside, the church's concealed beauty can be seen—like the curtains of Solomon. But there are primary and secondary curtains of Solomon. The primary ones are the most interior curtains, shielding the ark of the covenant. These are the contemplatives, the martyrs of the church who castigate their bodies or shed their blood.[16] The secondary curtains are the confessors, pastors, and prelates who live the active life and protect the spiritual vessels of the temple, namely the souls committed to their care.[17]

In the last of his eight books of commentary on the Canticle, Kempf devotes two chapters to the relationship between contemplatives and prelates and their role in the church (VIII. 19-20). Both contemplatives and prelates are walls, supporting the church (Ca 8:9). Prelates and pastors must be ambidextrous, living both the active and contemplative lives. In contrast, not all contemplatives must live the active life—only those who have been charged with the care of souls, i.e., with administrative and pastoral office in the monastery. By implication, most contemplatives fall into the category of *subditi*—they are sheep needing shepherds. They grow in love by obedience to their superiors who are walls and silver bulwarks lifting up their eyes to seek the foe advancing from great distance. The superiors owe their position as prelates to gifts of knowledge, understanding of scripture, discernment of spirits, discretion, and good intention in their acts. The *subditi, inferiores,* or *minores* (who may live the active life as simple faithful or the contemplative life as simple monks) are walls in the church, to be sure. But they are the weakest portion of the wall, the *ostium,* or gate, the most easily penetrated portion of the house above which the bulwark of prelates and pastors towers for defense.[18] (Thus the theme of humble meekness, blindness, lameness, and poverty that we found to be central in *De ostensione* and *De mystica theologia* is also fundamental to Kempf's allegorical ecclesiology and his pastoral ideal.) In his comments on Canticle 1:9 and 4:4 Kempf refers to the *doctores* as the neck of the church, describing the neck as the tower of David, countering the self-will, self-love, and fleshly concupiscence of the tower of Babel. He interprets the *doctores,* prelates, or pastors as the neck connecting the body of Christ, the

---

[16] In keeping with ancient monastic tradition, Kempf thus conflates "red martyrs" and "white martyrs"—those who physically died for the faith and those who disciplined their bodies in the desert hermitages. See Malone, "Martyrdom and Monastic Profession."

[17] *Cantica,* I.15-17 (ch. 16 in G1, 158v-162r; 11: 115-29).

[18] *Cantica,* VIII. 16 (G1, 322r-v; 12: 365-68). See also *Serm. evang.,* no. 34 (G2, 172r B, 12-16) for the pastor or shepherd as a defender against wolves.

faithful, with the head of the church, Christ himself.[19] Although on one occasion he refers to the *doctores*, prelates, and pastors as the eyes of the Beloved, because of their keener vision for truth and teaching,[20] the dominant image is that of the tower, neck, or bulwark.

The role of the contemplatives in the church, although it is not one of defense and protection, is nevertheless an exalted one.[21] The contemplatives are the cheeks of the church, as lovely as the cheeks of the turtledove (Ca 1:9). Down these cheeks flow the tears of intercession. When healthy, they are red with the abundant holy love of God and neighbor, with the passion of act and will, and with compassion for all mankind. They reveal the disposition and complexion of the person (church); they indicate whether that disposition is modest, honest, timorous, humble, meek, and chaste. Below the cheeks the beard begins: the solicitude of temporal or intellectual thoughts and acts. The cheeks are higher and nearer to the eyes (which represent the gifts of the Holy Spirit) than is any other part of the body. The cheeks end where the neck (which apparently includes the chin and beard) begins, i.e., the contemplatives encounter the *doctores ecclesiae*. Adorned with the necklace of scripture (the golden chain of the exposition of scripture),[22] the neck and cheeks should meet as in the primitive church when the apostles, disciples, and teachers (*doctores*) joined the saints at Jerusalem (Acts 15). Together, the cheeks and neck are ornaments for the church.[23]

Thus, as cheeks,

> religious and contemplatives are the highest states of life, those states of life that are the most familiar and closest to God. They are often admitted to the chamber of the king to receive the kiss of peace for the salvation and consolation of the entire church. . . . Just as a physical kiss is usually given on the cheeks, the most beautiful part of the face, hairless and pure, so the religious ought to be lovely and pure so that the Church's Bridegroom may find in the religious a place undefiled and suited for the embrace.[24]

---

[19] *Cantica*, IV. 6 (G1, 230v-232r; 11: 410-15).

[20] *Cantica*, V.16 (G1, 258r; 12: 66). Elsewhere Kempf portrays prelates and superiors as the "mouth" (V.13) or "lips" (IV.13) of the body of Christ.

[21] The following summary is taken from *Cantica*, I.31 (ch. 32 in G1, 179v; 11: 198-99).

[22] Kempf plays on *monile* and *monere* in referring to the "collum, id est, doctores sancti . . . sicut monilia." *Cantica*, I.31 (ch. 32 in G1, 179r, 9-10; *Bibl. ascetica*, 11: 196).

[23] Elsewhere Kempf refers to the religious as the *mammae* of virgins or maidens and to the *doctores* as the *ubera* full of the milk of doctrine. *Cantica*, IV.12 (G1, 236v-237v; 11: 435-38).

[24] *Cantica*, I.31 (ch. 32 in G1, 179v, 18-27; 11: 199-200).

But alas, how few are found who are as lovely as turtledoves!

In his more systematic work on the life of contemplation, the *De mystica theologia*, Kempf also explains the position occupied by religious and contemplatives in the church.[25] In general, religious are the highest *status* in the church, but those rare religious who reach union with God in the *imago Dei* have an even more important role to play. They are the pillars that support the church, the *columnae ecclesiae* (cf. Gal 2:9). They are like the anchor that keeps a ship from running aground in a storm; they are the special friends of God who gain from God the mercy without which the entire world would perish.[26] They are like Abraham, who interceded for the few righteous who might be left in Sodom and Gomorrah (Gen 18:32); like Moses, who obtained mercy for the people of Israel (Ex 32:10); like the Virgin Mary (and Judith and Esther who prefigured her as liberators of their people), "who, while walking this earth, obtained by her prayers the healing salvation of the faithful, the conversion of the peoples, and the preservation of apostles and preachers"; like Paul, whose prayers saved the lives of all on board his ship (Acts 27:27-44). More than that, these pillars of the church intercede for mercy to save the spiritual, not merely the physical, lives of their people.[27] There are very few of these special friends of God because (a) few cleanse themselves adequately in the *via purgativa*; (b) few would be humble enough to avoid the trap of spiritual pride if they were given this great grace—even Paul had his thorn in the flesh (2 Cor 12:17)[28]; (c) God hides his sweetness so that men seek it more eagerly and, when they obtain it, gain greater merit *by faith* than they would have gained by sight and taste[29]; and (d) God gives the good wine last, unlike men, who serve the best wine first (Jn 2:10).

Kempf does not disparage the pastoral or governing office in the church. He considers its protection essential for the flowering of the inte-

---

[25] *MTh*, V.3, pp. 362-66.

[26] On "friends of God" in the desert monastic tradition, see John Climacus, *Ladder of Monks*, step 1; trans. Luibheid and Russell, p. 73-74, where the term is applied both to angels and to human beings.

[27] *MTh*, V.3, p. 363: "Unicus enim homo, eciam si inter centum milia aut plures invenitur, cui Deo sic unitur in ymagine et speciali amicicia sibi conjungitur, cum quo suas habet delicias, totam Ecclesiam sicut Moyses potest sustentare ne pereat et obtinere misericordiam et reconciliacionem longe efficacius quam ipse Moyses," because of the assistance of the merits of Christ's passion and the prayers of the saints, martyrs, and devout faithful. Other examples include Stephen (Acts 7) and the martyrs and confessors.

[28] Cf. Guigo I, *Meditationes*, no. 263, SC 308: 184.

[29] *MTh*, V.3, p. 365: "Tercia causa, quia Deus abscondit suam dulcedinem, ut homo anxius querat et maius meritum recipiat per fidem quam si hic videret et gustaret."

rior, contemplative life. The sheep need shepherds and gates need towers of defense. The church as a bride is adorned by the exposition of holy scripture through her *doctores* and preachers. But at the heart of the structure are the contemplatives, especially those who reach full union. The latter are few, but their pleas and prayers are able to save the entire people of God from destruction fifteen centuries after Christ just as the intercession of Esther or the courageous cunning of Judith saved their people centuries before Christ. In Esther and other Old and New Testament figures, Kempf finds his model for the monastic life in the perilous times that face the church in his century. As we shall see, by including contemplative worship and intercession within the function of defense, women and meekly womanish monks can be considered full participants in the leadership of the church and can be viewed as part of its system of loadbearing columns.

2. The Perils of Pastoring

Why is the church beset by so many troubles? Why are the times so dangerous? Kempf does not consider his *saeculum* to be the worst of all possible *saecula*. For the most part his is not an apocalyptic frame of mind. The present state of the church is no worse than it was in the days of Augustine, Ambrose, or Gregory,[30] who faced serious challenges. Kempf is not minimizing the ecclesial problems of his day.[31] But he is deliberately resisting apocalyptic panic. There is much that needs correction and reform, and Kempf is convinced that the root of the problem is pride and a spirit of ambition and presumption—human qualities that are not at all novel. Kempf's understanding of history is not so much based on a linear crescendo toward the end as on a steady and profound consciousness of human sin and an equally steady and profound confidence in God's provident mercy. He decries the learned members of the body of Christ who think that the church cannot be governed without them and who seek to rule even though Christ has not committed his flock to them. These are the men who assume that it is more fruitful to read sophistries

---

[30] *Rect*, III.4 (V1, 63v B; *Bibl. ascetica* 4: 431). Kempf argues here that it is useless to use the perilous state of the church as a rationale for seeking pastoral office. Ambrose, Augustine, and Gregory did not seek the *cura animarum* but were called to it, indeed, forced into it. Kempf asserts that the same applies in his day.

[31] See ibid., II.16 (V1, 59r. B, 10-32; *Bibl. ascetica*, 4: 349-50)—never before has such contradiction (i.e., backbiting) and evil existed in the "civitate ecclesie militantis," a situation that confirms the prophecies about the evil conditions of the last days.

than to pray psalms. He believes that the assumption of pastoral office rarely takes place without direct or indirect simony.[32] Yet despite such sweeping accusations of errant leadership in the church, Kempf resists any inclination to declare the church apostate. If people who have no calling to rule are ruling for selfish and illegitimate reasons, his response is to encourage those who have legitimate callings not to shirk that task.

On the other hand, although Kempf insists that the condition of the church is not worse than in the days of Augustine or Gregory, he does think it is much worse than it was in the *primitive* church. With Jerome, Kempf believed in a "Constantinian fall" of the church.[33] Using the same arguments drawn from Gregory the Great that were employed by Bernard of Waging in his debate with Johann of Eych (see below), Kempf insists that there was a time when the office of bishop was praiseworthy and good, one to be desired (1 Tim 3:1). It was a time when bishops were the first to be dragged to the palm of martyrdom (*ad martirii palmam trahebatur*—note the use of the passive voice).[34] It was also a time when the church was not so exalted with temporal riches and honors as it has been since the time of Constantine.[35] In the primitive and youthful church, apostles, martyrs, confessors, and hermits relinquished all they had, even body and soul, counting all things as nothing for love of God and neighbor, because their love was founded on the Rock, Christ. But "today" rarely does anyone enter the desert and abandon all things of this world in order to seek spiritual gain.[36] Rather than using a "restitutionist" view of church history to question the legitimacy of church offices,

---

[32] *Prop*, I.4 (VS1, 4v A, 15-29) and I.16/15 (VS1, 11v A, 27-43). Cf. *Rect*, III.4 (63r; *Bibl. ascetica*, 4: 428) and III.12 (4: 457) on plural benefices, and *De confirmatione*, 4 (V1, 81v B, 13-14). *Prop*, I.16/15, offers the most detailed catalogue of Kempf's objections to the pastoral office. Cf. Vincent of Aggsbach's polemics against the failings of pastors in Pez and Hueber, *Cod. dipl.-hist.-epist.*, pt. III, p. 336.

[33] Gerson too believed in a decline of the church at the time of Constantine—which gave rise to a need for canon lawyers! See Burrows, *Gerson*, 128, note 67, with references to discussions in Pascoe and Burger.

[34] The text is given, in context, in the following note. In Kempf's view, one of the prime requirements for a pastor is that he be willing to give his life for his sheep, in imitation of Christ, the good shepherd (Jn 10:11). See *Serm. evang.*, no. 34 (G2, 168-73), as discussed in the present chapter under the rubric, "Bonus Pastor."

[35] *Prop*, I.17/16 (VS1, 12v A, 13-20): "Tunc enim ut exponit Gregorius laudabile [MS laudale] et bonum fuerat episcopatum desiderare, quando is [MS hijs], qui episcopatus erat primus ad martirii palmam trahebatur. Necdum ecclesia tantis temporalium diviciis et honoribus erat sublimata sicut posterius tempore Constantini." The same ideas appear nearly verbatim in *Rect*, III.4 (63v B; *Bibl. ascetica*, 4: 431).

[36] *Cantica*, VIII.6 (G1, 311v; 12: 316-17). Cf. Jerome, *Vita Malchi* (PL 23: 55): "Ecclesia nata sit, et adulta, persecutionibus creverit, et martyriis coronata sit; et postquam ad Christianos principes venerit, potentia quidem et divitiis major, sed virtutibus minor facta sit."

Kempf (and Bernard of Waging with him) argues that the pristine early church possessed officeholders who were true servant martyrs, true pastors who gave their lives for their sheep.

Part of the trouble is the failure of the pope to listen to Theology's pleas and to defend her against the impertinence of Canon Law.[37] But leadership has also failed at other levels. The prelates of the church must admit that they have been darkened by the sun while sleeping instead of guarding the vineyard committed to their care (Ca 1:5). Their lives are *defectuosa*, stained by incautious decisions in correcting and judging those placed under them. The task of caring for the vines is indeed a difficult one. No matter how diligently prelates of the church watch and guard their vines, there are always visible and invisible foes who destroy them. Unless the Lord himself joins them in their task, the vineyard's keepers labor in vain. These foes are the demons, infidels and pagans, Jews, heretics and schismatics, evil Christians, and especially the "false brethren," members of the monastic community who fall into self-deception and error. Yes, even the stirrings of the sin-corrupted human body, which we have from our mother, war against the mother herself.[38] All of these are the "sons of the mother," or sons of Mother Church, who fight against the bride: even the demons, as created spirits, however apostate, are "sons of Mother Church"; likewise the pagans, who are descended from Adam and Eve and thus belong to the church in the broad sense, and the Jews, who are sons of the church by the faith which they once had and in which they "conceived us" (*nos genuerunt*). All of these oppose the church and all the faithful who wish to live devoutly and will continue to do so until the end of the world. But they attack especially pastors and prelates, who, more concerned with tending the vines of the spiritual lives of others people, neglect their own vines. Indeed one can put these words into the mouth of Mother Church herself: "They put me in charge of the vineyard; I have not kept up my own vineyard."[39]

By putting the words of Canticle 1:5 into the mouth of Mother Church he suggests that the church as a whole has "not kept up her vineyard." In this sense the church is subject to error. But he does not move

---

[37] See chapter three, pp. 73-75, above.

[38] They are not so much to be hated or despised as to be resisted—for who hates his own flesh? Kempf does not fall into a Gnostic dualism, whether in regard to the body or in regard to heretics and Jews, or even with regard to demons. All of God's creation, including human flesh, as corrupted by sin as it may be, is in some sense part of Christ's body, the church. Evil is a perversion of a good that should have been. It has no ontological status of its own.

[39] *Cantica*, I.16-18 (ch. 17-19 in G1, 159v-162r; 11: 115-31), esp. I.16 ([17 in the MS], G1, 159v, 33 - 160r, 15; 11: 121-22).

from that suggestion to assert or imply the total apostasy and irreformability of the church as did some of the apocalyptic sectarians of the late Middle Ages and Reformation era (Waldenses, Wycliffites, Hussites, Anabaptists). Impatience with the church's imperfection is itself a fall from perfection—in a sense Kempf uses the very language and assumptions of the radicals to point out their error.[40] Even his decision to withdraw to the monastery, a radical step to be sure, does not mean that he considers office illegitimate or the institutional church irreformable. As we shall see in subsequent pages and chapters, Kempf is convinced that withdrawal is the best way to reform church leadership. Although he has not given up on reform of human and ecclesial power and authority, his path to reform is one of strategic retreat, meekness, voluntary renunciation, and attendance upon God's reforming will.

Because of the failure of pastoral and ecclesiastical leadership, those who follow, whether contemplative monks or active faithful, must be cautious. False pastors of the flock try to convince their sheep to take false paths, relying on their power and prestige to lead the flock astray. Indeed, such false shepherds make up the majority of prelates and pastors—the true path is a narrow one and leads through persecution.[41] The sheep must be alert. Often the elect (and not merely the simple faithful among the elect) are unsure which side to choose in the midst of schism and heresy. They must ask the Beloved himself where he pastures his sheep in the heat of the day of persecution (Ca 1:6),[42] rather than trusting

---

[40] *Cantica*, VIII.22 (G1, 327r, 16-26; 12: 391): "Qui ergo ad religionem venerit, cogitet, quod non solum inveniet perfectos, sed eciam populos: et pacienter discat eos portare, si ipse vult perfectus esse, et non per inpacienciam a perfectione cadere. Nam et tales sunt, de quibus dilectus paulo ante dixit: 'Soror nostra parvula est, et ubera non habet' [Ca 8:8]. Et tales sunt pingendi [Vulg.: *compingendi*] tabulis cedrinis [Ca 8:9], aut si nimis duri sunt et asperi, ut depingi nequant, tunc prius planandi sunt dolabris, ac quandoque mollificandi virgis aut disciplinis. Et hoc concernit prelatos, de quibus dixit: 'tradidit eam custodibus' [Ca 8:11]. Sed prochdolor multi prelati scilicet et pastores, monastice vite custodes, pessime et negligentissime custodiunt, et per se vineam dissipant et destruunt, in transgressione regularis observancie primi, et eo liberiores, quo irreprehensibiliores et incorrigibiliores." See also *Serm. evang.*, no 34 (G2, 173r A, 21 - B, 4), where Kempf takes up the lament of Ez 34:8-12, much as Gregory of Nazianzus ("Flight to Pontus, par. 64-66 [SC 247: 176-80, NPNF, ser. 2, vol. 7, pp. 218-19]) and many others had done. See also John of Speyer's comments as cited in Kropff, *Bibliotheca mellicensis*, 273-77.

[41] *Cantica*, I.20 (I.21 in MS; 11: 141; G1, 165r, 1-8): "In quacunque ergo congregatione fueris constitutus, si vis esse pulchra inter mulieres, et ut in sponsam elegi possis, non ignores, te oportet sustinere persecuciones a filijs matris tue, si non volueris 'vagari post vestigia gregum' illorum. 'Arcta,' inquit dilectus, 'est via que ducit ad vite' perfectionem, et arctissima, que ducit ad cellaria regis. Et ideo paucissimi ambulant per eam; quos oportet sequi, et non multitudinem popularem."

[42] *Cantica*, I.20 (ch. 21 in G1, 163v-165r; 11: 135-41).

the prelates, *rectores*, or pastors, who, like Aaron, are fashioning golden
calves in the absence of the contemplative Moses, who is alone on the
mountain with God.[43] Where human leadership seems to have failed,
there Christ is present, watching over his own vineyard. [44]

The evils in the church are not merely the result of a failure of leadership. As we have seen, few religious can be found who are pure and
lovely enough for the kiss of the Beloved. Far from being like the turtledove, they are as rapacious as hawks, as voracious as wolves, and as avaricious as impudent dogs.[45] All the states of life in the church have fallen
to such depths that the Beloved is rarely found in the *domus ecclesiae*.
(Kempf adds a warning against being quick to judge others when one's
own house is not in order.)[46] Both leaders and followers refuse to follow
the counsel of others, preferring to trust in their own inadequate prudence.[47] Indeed, it is because of the sinfulness of the entire people that
the Beloved permits so many hypocrites to govern souls.[48]

In the face of sin and evil on every hand, can Kempf with a good
conscience recommend the religious life? Should not the dangers of the
age call the best minds and most devout souls to the care of souls and the
government of the church? The question betrays an inability to enter
fully into the monastic world where the validity of the *solitudo mentis*
and the contemplative life is evident. We are the ones who must see
things crookedly in order to grasp Kempf's point. Yet even in Kempf's
day, some in the world looked askance at monastic voluntary renunciation. Kempf was thus compelled to defend contemplatives, especially the
Carthusians, against the charge that they were not useful to society because they did not preach or undertake other work beneficial to the

---

[43] *Cantica*, VI.16-17 (G1, 284r-v; 12: 182-85). Kempf also compares false prelates to
those who trample the vineyard with their chariots (Ca 6:11).

[44] See *Cantica*, VIII.22 (G1, 327r, 27-29; 12: 391), where Kempf consoles the contemplative with the promise of the Beloved: "'Vinea mea coram me est' [Ca 8:12]; ac si
dicat patenter: 'Si custodes male custodiunt, tamen ego sum semper vobis religiosis presens, et in medio vestrum: et estis sicut vinea coram me'."

[45] *Cantica*, I.31 (ch. 32 in G1, 179v, 29-37; 11: 199-200).

[46] *Cantica*, I.33 (ch. 34 in G1, 182r, 21-26; 11: 209): "In qua tamen consideracione,
ne quis superbiat et alios iudicare incipiat, primo suam propriam domum et lectulum cordis consideret, qualia tigna virtutum et laquearia donorum habeat. Et primo de se
ingemiscat, et suam domum reformare studeat, et lectulum suum floribus odoriferis on-
arare, et tunc potest postea secure pro alijs ingemiscere." See also *Serm. evang.*, no. 34
(G2, 173r B, 10-20).

[47] *Discr*, 3 (VS1, 36v B, 4-23; *Bibl. ascetica*, 9: 393).

[48] *Cantica*, V.5 (G1, 247v, 19-21; 12: 21): "Dum autem moderno tempore rarissime
vocentur tales perfecti viri ad aliorum curam, sed magis ipse dilectus facit regnare yp-
pocritas propter peccata populi."

church. Citing Aristotle and Aquinas, he asserted the greater perfection
and nobility of the contemplative life and reminded the proponents of
preaching that preaching benefits others not by its own merits but because righteous men pray and live in contemplation with unceasing at-
tentiveness, interceding for the preachers of the church:

> Whoever lives well preaches good works more effectively than one who
> cries out in the crowd with great eloquence but lacks a good life. More-
> over, a monk who devoutly obeys and humbly keeps silence catches more
> fish in the net of a good life [bonae conversationis] than a person who dis-
> putes much, preaches subtly, or speaks floridly.[49]

Citing Robert of Tombelaine (Pseudo-Gregory the Great), Kempf
insists that there must be freedom for some to follow the "voice of the
Beloved" (Ca 2:8) to the holy leisure of busily loving God. In so doing
they experience the embrace of the Beloved and see how great is his love
for the church.[50] Let the sheep follow the Good Shepherd away from the
wolves of the world and the snares of the hunter to the richest pasture of
all, the desert of the monastic life, which never lacks for spiritual re-
pasts.[51] Not all are called, indeed, only a few are able to handle the hard

---

[49] Serm. evang., no. 51 (G2, 206v A, 8-16): "Quis ergo bene vivit, efficacius per bona
opera predicat quam qui in populo absque bona vita cum magna facundia clamat. Religiosus eciam devotus, obediens, et humilis tacens, plures capit pisces sue bone conver-
sacionis rethe, quam qui multum disputat, subtiliter predicat, et loquitur ornate." See also
De confirmatione, 2 (V1, 79v B, 37-39) and 17/16-18/17; Rect, II.30 (Vienna cvp 3616,
63r-66r; Bibl. ascetica, 4: 406-9) and II.17 (Vienna cvp 3616, 60r A, 42 - 60r B, 22;
Bibl. ascetica, 4: 354): "Veluti multum reputat se ecclesie Dei prodesse, cum legit,
predicat, aut quandoque solum sophismata disputat; quamvis illa non possint prodesse,
nisi ex bona vita, oracione, et caritate, quibus ipsa presumptuosa mens sepe caret, et
aliorum precibus et meritis fructum facit in alijs, quamvis non sibi, licet glorietur, tanquam ipsa ecclesie Dei tanta bona conferat. . . . et finaliter dicere audeo, quod valde stultum est et presumptuosum, propter alijs proficere manere in seculo, profecto cum
predicantes verbo reperiantur in quolibet angulo, sed predicantes bona et sancta vita raro
reperiantur in ecclesia. Solitarius eciam qui bene et religiose vivit quod multi verbis
predicant, ipse ostendit exemplis, et ita bene vivendo nunquam cessat predicando." See
also Cantica, IV.12 (G1, 236v-237v; 11: 435-37).
[50] Cantica, II.8 (G1, 208v, 1-8; 11: 318): "Hanc vacandi Deo licenciam libentissime
sponsa suscipit, statimque verbum sponsi amplectitur et dicit quod sequitur: 'Vox dilecti
mei.' Ac si dicat, 'hanc vocem predictam sic prohybentis me suscitari a suo amore, dilecti mei esse cognosco; hanc ab eius ore desidero audire, quia in hoc video quantum me
diligat cum me ab amplexibus eius desiderabilibus impediri prohybeat.' Ex quibus patet
quam utile sit Deo vacare per amorem et quantum tales Deo placeant, quamque utiles
sint ecclesie, tam vivis quam defunctis. . . ."
[51] Serm. evang., no. 34 (G2, 168r B, 8-23): "O quam bonus pastor est Christus nobis,
fratres karissimi, qui non solum a luporum faucibus et inferni claustris nos liberavit, sed
eciam ab hoc seculo nequam, luporum insidijs et venatorum laqueis ocultis pleno, nos
abduxit; et a veteri fermento non solum in baptismatis fonte purgatos, sed eciam in ordi-

words of Christ (Mt 19:11-12), but never does society suffer because Christ calls some to the desert.[52] The preaching, pastoring, and administration of those outside the monastic microcosm depends upon the prayers and devotion of monks for its efficacy, and thus the religious life serves both the salvation of one's soul and the salvation of the church.

Is it right for someone called to serve the church with his prayers in the desert of contemplation to turn around and *accept* the pastoral care of souls? Would one not thereby leave the "more secure" path to salvation that one began to follow when one entered religion and deprive the church of an essential service?[53] In answering the question Kempf relies heavily on Gregory the Great as a model for the contemplative who reluctantly but properly accepts the call to pastoral duties.[54]

Kempf's answers,[55] however, are also fully within the Carthusian tradition. For Heinrich Egher of Kalkar, one of the most profound dangers in the life of a Carthusian is administering an office in the order.[56] Carrying out one's office can easily alienate a monk from his calling. If leadership is assumed with inner affirmation and if one finds satisfaction in exercising pastoral office, one risks destroying one's monastic nature. Thus a good monk should never desire an office for its own sake or out of inner agreement (*naturaliter vel de per se*), rather, only under compulsion and incidentally (*violenter et accidentaliter*). Heinrich insists that many Carthusians are no longer recognizable after exercising an office.[57]

---

nis professione mundatos ad uberrime pascue loca, scilicet monastice vite deserta, nos perduxit et ibi nos pascere quottidie spiritualibus epulis paratus est; non solum pascere sed eciam nobiscum epulari. . . ."

[52] *Prop*, I.17/16 (VS1, 12r B, 17-35): "Non omnes capiunt verbum hoc, sed qui potest capere, capiat. Unde certissimum est, quod paucissimis Deus dat graciam interne vocacionis et inspiracionis pro religionis ingressu; ymmo inter decem milia hominum, vix uni, et eciam inter decem quos Deus sic vocat, vix unus sequitur! Iuxta salvatoris vocem, 'multi sunt vocati, pauci vero electi' [Mt 20:16]. Et satis mirabile est, quod tales timent quod Deus suos electos perire permittat, nisi ipsi propria voluntate et presumpcione in seculo remanerent. Cum tamen ipse per prophetam promiserit se suum gregem in necessitate per seipsum visitare et pascere. Nec considerant quod nullus est status religionis in toto mundo a Deo contrarius profectui proximorum, quin si Deus vult ipsum preesse, et si ipsum elegerit, eciam velit nolit ipsum alijs proficit."

[53] *Rect*, II.30 (Vienna, cvp 3616, 66v; *Bibl. ascetica*, 4: 410).

[54] See *Registrum epistolarum*, bk. I, letter 5 (Monumenta Germaniae Historica, Epistolae, 1: 5-7; trans. NPNF, ser. 2, vol. 12: 74-76). For a discussion of the way Gregory drew upon the monastery for the service of the church see Karl Suso Frank, "Kloster als scola dominici servitii," 86-89.

[55] *Prop*, I.17/16 (VS1, 12r B, 37 - 12v A, 6), quoted in chapter one, n. 45, above.

[56] My source for the following discussion is Rüthing, *Heinrich Egher von Kalkar*, 235-49.

[57] "Contigit autem aliquando, quod quidam satis religiose se habentes sine officio mirabiliter mutant mores, intentionem et vitam adepto officio. Iam enim sue reclusionis

Other monks become so involved in their tasks that, when they return to being simple monks, they are unable to let go of their office and start to meddle in tasks that are no longer their responsibility.

For Heinrich Egher van Kalkar, the prior's significance is beyond question: he is a representative of Christ to the monks, but his purpose is to see to their salvation. One of his most important responsiblities is to support the monks by the forming of their ascetic life, to which end he must know his sheep—through their "manifestation of thoughts." A related task is to prevent excessive, unreasonable asceticism. The prior also has secular responsibilities, but Heinrich thinks these are less important and gives only general information in this area. In no case dare the prior forget his responsibility to show compassion toward the poor.[58] For his external responsiblities, the prior needs a certain kind of serenity, but he must also not be lax or neglect anything necessary for the good financial health of the house. His greatest danger is the risk that he will neglect his monastic calling, which alone offers the strength to overcome the dangers. Other problems, e.g., subjects who lack charity or are contrary or disobedient, who insist on having their own way against their superiors, are less significant. Economic problems come at the end of the list.

For both Heinrich Egher of Kalkar and Nicholas Kempf, the propriety of *accepting* pastoral duties is not at issue. The question is whether anyone, above all a contemplative, should *seek* pastoral office.[59] Here Kempf differs from Gregory the Great,[60] who suggested that some men laudably seek the preaching office, but only if they are blameless in their own lives. Kempf insists that no monk and few, if any, nonmonastics should ever seek the *cura animarum*. He warns repeatedly that the desire to assume pastoral office or to preside over others as head of a monastic community covers with a veneer of good zeal an inward, secret presumptuousness and pride in one's own knowledge and abilities.[61] Why else

---

obliti amicos foraneos visitant et patrias nativas honorari volunt, carnales norunt quasi fiunt et seculares, laute comedentes et bibentes, vestiti splendide, equitantes gloriose et commitentes Deo spiritualia, penitus se dant ad temporalia." (*Pro eligendo priore*, fol. 148r, as cited in Rüthing, *Egher von Kalkar*, 236.)

[58] *Epistolae*, as cited in Rüthing, 242: "Quando aliqua occurrunt scilicet solvendo pauperibus mercedem suam et alia iustitialia et pietalia vel misericordialia, ut semper facias proximo tuo sicut Domino Iesu Christo—si apud te esset—faceres, qui docuit: 'Quod uni ex meis minimis feceritis, mihi fecisti' [Mt 25:40]."

[59] See Philip Rousseau, *Acetics, Authority, and the Church in the Age of Jerome and Cassian* (1978), 58-59, who makes this same distinction regarding Pachomius, and Noel Molloy, "Hierarchy and Holiness: Aquinas on the Holiness of the Episcopal State," *The Thomist*, 39 (1975), 1-55, at 7, regarding Aquinas (*STh*, IIa, IIae. q. 185. art. 1).

[60] *Regula pastoralis*, I.7-8.

[61] See *Rect*, I.8 (V1, 44r B; *Bibl. ascetica*, 4: 281); II.19 (Vienna cvp 3616, 43r-v;

should parishes with onerous duties find no one interested in them unless as an absentee paying a vicar to do the hard work. Surely if those seeking pastoral positions were truly interested in the salvation of the souls of the faithful they would not turn from such positions.[62]

No, the pastoral office is to be viewed with healthy respect, indeed, with awe bordering on fear.[63] If the voice of the Beloved comes to the contemplative, if the church calls a contemplative to pastoral office (Kempf is referring here to the pastoral office within the monastery), that soul protests that she has washed her feet and undressed to rest from all exterior concerns (Ca 5:2-3). If she must answer the call, then she should take care not to soil her hands and head in addition to her feet.[64] She should bear the pastoral care of souls humbly and patiently rather than reject it out of a preference for contemplative quiet or out of excessive scrupulosity. Indeed, there is at least one positive aspect to pastoral duties: the pastor will notice that some of the souls entrusted to his care are more perfect than he is. A humble and perfect superior puts those placed in his care ahead of himself and considers himself unworthy to govern them. A pastor discovers his own lack of progress in the contemplative life and his shortcomings in cultivating the vineyard of his interior life; he thus approaches the care of the vines of other souls with greater humility.[65] Awareness of their dis-abledness is precisely what leaders need if they are to lead ably.

The contemplative called to the care of others can take comfort in the fact that the Beloved, through the chorus of young maidens, is careful to call the Shulamite, or bride, back from the care of the vineyard (Ca 6:10-12).[66] The contemplative soul can be consoled by the realization that prelates, or pastors, are essential to the life of the monastery. They

---

4:360); III.4-5 (63r-64v; 4: 427-44); III.13 (69v B - 71r B; 4: 459-65); chapter 3 of the short commentary on the Canticle appended to *MTh* (Jellouschek ed., p. 401); *Prop*, I.3 (VS1, 4r B, 2-5); and *Serm. evang.*, no. 11 (G2, 135r).

[62] *Rect*, III.4 (V1, 63r A - 4v B; 4: 429).

[63] See *Prop*, I.18/17 (VS1, 12v B - 13r A), a chapter titled "Pastoralis cura est formidanda propter racionem in finali iudicio districtissimi reddenda." Cf. Bernard of Clairvaux, *Sermones in Cantica Canticorum*, 12.9: "Respect the bishop but fear his job," quoted by Bernard of Waging, as discussed below, under the rubric, "Too Much for Womanish Shoulders."

[64] *Cantica*, V.4 (G1, 246v-247v; 12: 16-21). But Kempf sarcastically assures his contemplative readers that "today" the church rarely calls such mature or perfected men to pastoral offices, preferring to give such positions to hypocrites.

[65] *Cantica*, I.22 (ch. 23 in G1, 165v-167r; 11: 145-49). See also I.16 (ch. 17, G1, 160r; 11: 122), and VIII.22 (G1, 326v-327r; 12: 389-91).

[66] *Cantica*, VI.16-17 (G1, 284v-284v; 12: 182-90). The Shulamite had been sent out to look over the nut orchard. The nut trees are the tallest, most fruitful, and most perfect trees, and they thus represent contemplatives.

defend, nourish, and instruct those who have made little progress (the "sister who is small and has no breasts" in Ca 8:8).[67] They also aid the contemplatives who have made great progress by ensuring that they are not wakened or "stirred up" until they please, i.e., until the hour of contemplation is complete (Ca 2:7; 3:5). The superior or prelate must discern when "cogent necessity" permits disturbing contemplative rest. Indeed, Kempf suggests that monks who miss the canonical hours during periods of contemplation should not necessarily be penalized. After all, Moses would not have been required to repeat the canonical hours he might have missed during the time he spent on the mountain alone with God![68]

3. Bonus Pastor

Kempf sets high standards for the pastor-prelate. His pastoral ideal is set forth most completely in a sermon on John 10 that was probably delivered to fellow Carthusians at Geirach or Pleterje.[69] Kempf tells us that a good shepherd gives his soul or lays down his life for his sheep (Jn 10:11).[70] A hireling, caring little for his sheep, runs away (168v B, 6-15). Many Christian prelates are hirelings who pursue wealth more than the salvation of souls ("magis student avaricie quam animarum saluti"). A good shepherd gives his life for his sheep by being prepared to suffer willingly anything that appears expedient for the spiritual health of those committed to his care. Neither hatred nor honors, neither slander nor praise, nor any other prospect of good or adverse fortunes dare distract him from his care for their souls (169r A, 6-16). He must live *exemplariter* in regard to food, clothing, vigils, or labors (citing Bernard of Clairvaux, 169r B, 5-9). He must not govern tyrannically, for if he does, he is worse than a hireling, having become a wolf as well (169v B, 1-9). He dare not be too timid in correcting or disciplining errant monks (169v B, 16 - 170r A, 3). He must not fail his charges when they face temptation—any shepherd who does not console, exhort, and instruct in compassion when his sheep are invaded by the wolf of temptation is

---

[67] *Cantica*, VIII.15 (G1, 320v; 12: 359-60), and VIII.18 (G1, 323r-324r; 12: 372-77).

[68] *Cantica*, II.8 (G1, 208r-v; 11: 317-19). See also III.6 (G1, 220v; 11: 370).

[69] *Serm. evang.*, no. 34. Citations in brackets refer to folia, column, and line numbers from Graz cod. 559 (G2).

[70] Cf. Robert Grosseteste on this theme as summarized by Leonard E. Boyle, "Robert Grosseteste and the Pastoral Care," in *Medieval and Renaissance Studies*, 8 (1979), 15 (repr. 1981).

unwilling to give his life for his sheep. He should not neglect to visit
them in their cells (170r A, 3-16). Like Christ, who fed five thousand
followers in their hour of need, the prelate is to break and distribute the
consoling word of God, lest his charges starve in their struggle against
temptation.[71] Finally, the good shepherd lays down his life for his sheep
in incessant prayer and intercession for his sheep, thus following Paul's
example (170v A, 15-21).[72]

A good pastor must also know his sheep perfectly, knowing which
are more prone to evil.[73] According to Gregory, to know is to love, and
love cannot exist without knowledge; according to Aristotle, the will
cannot accept that which is unknown. Thus it is essential that both sheep
and shepherd have love for each other. The shepherd dare not remain
aloof or elevated in his estimation of himself, but must come down (submit) to his sheep and visit among them. For their part, the sheep must
purely and sincerely reveal the state of their spiritual health (170v B, 10-
20; 171v B, 13-19). This insight leads to an exposition on the monastic
prelate's role as confessor. The confession required annually by canon
law is obviously not enough. Both monk and *pater monasticus* must
make an effort to ensure that the prelate knows the state of the con-
sciences of his pastoral charges.[74] Indeed, Kempf is so convinced of the
awesome responsibility carried by the prelate-pastor for the souls of his
monks (the superior is responsible to account for them at the last judgment[75]) that he suggests procedures for observing and ascertaining the
state of their spiritual health that would seem unjustifiably meddlesome
to modern religious, to say nothing of modern nonmonastics.

Kempf's polemic against hypocritical prelates and preachers in *De
recto studiorum fine* and his emphatic warnings against seeking pastoral
office should not obscure his carefully developed teaching on the monas-

---

[71] This is the theme of sermon 53 (G2, 208r-209v).

[72] E.g., Rom 1:9-10; Eph 1:15-16; Phil 1:3-4; Col 1:3; 1 Thess 1:2-3.

[73] G2, 170v B, 3-10; 171 A, 18-24. Cf. the summary of Heinrich Egher of Kalkar's
views above and the Rule of St. Benedict, ch. 2, verses 31-32.

[74] 172r A, 28 - 173r A, 6. See also chapter four, above. Kempf points out in the sermon (173r A, 29 - B.4) that the lack of discretion on the part of monks who try to pasture
themselves in pursuing their own studies, reading, prayer, solitude, and labor, leads them
astray. On confession in the monastic context, see the Rule of St. Benedict, ch. 7. step 5.

[75] 171r A, 18-22, quoted in n. 9, above. On this long tradition, see Basil, *Long Rules*,
question 25, trans. by Sr. M. Monica Wagner (1950), p. 287, citing Ez. 3:20. Note the
following passage from the *Life of St. Mary the Hermit*: when in her naiveness she asks
"Uncle Abraham" why he did not tell her that the sexual relations he had with her were
sinful, his response was: "It is is I that shall answer for thee to God at the Day of Judgment. It is I that shall give satisfaction to God for this sin." *Verba Seniorum*, bk. 1 (PL
73: 657BC), translation by Helen Waddell, *Desert Fathers*, 198.

tic prelate as a pastor of monks. His teaching shows little originality—
much comes from Gregory the Great, Bernard, and the Desert Fathers.
But his teaching also bears the mark of his own experience as a pastor-
prelate and his compassionate determination to direct souls. As modern
people we are inclined to dismiss treatises on the pastoral *ideal* as ivory
tower ruminations. After all, the conviction that the late medieval clergy,
both secular and regular, was riddled with corruption and laxity was
widespread then and remains well-entrenched today, at least in popular
perception. And Kempf agrees. His own polemics seem to condemn him
when he sets forth a positive pastoral ideal. Yet the charge of "idealism"
or "ivory tower daydreaming" is a most unrealistic way to respond to
Kempf's writings on the pastorate. The monastic life is a highly developed product of centuries of experience. No community of adult men or
women can live together for very long on the basis of ideals alone. It is
far more likely that strangers to monastic life carry an idealized and unrealistic image, whether positive or negative, of what goes on behind
cloister walls, as visitors to monastic communities soon discover.

4. *"Too Much for Womanish Shoulders"*

    Nicholas Kempf reluctantly accepted the high calling of pastoral of-
fice within the monastery. A contemporary reformist Benedictine at Tegernsee was confronted with a call to pastoral leadership outside his own
monastery, a call from a reform-minded, humanist-inspired bishop
whose arguments would readily convince modern readers. By exploring
the Benedictine's response we may understand better Kempf's insistence, despite a reorientation toward the world by some of his contemporaries in urban charterhouses, on "cowardly" monastic withdrawal as the
best means to reform the church.
    In April 1461 the bishop of Eichstätt wrote to the abbot of the Bene-
dictine monastery of Tegernsee requesting that Tegernsee's prior be released to assist in the reform of monasteries within the diocese of
Eichstätt. The bishop, Johann of Eych, was born ca. 1404 at Aich near
Heilbronn, studied arts at Vienna (1423ff[76]), and became a member of
the Eichstätt Cathedral chapter before 1429. Johann studied canon law at
Padua (1429-33), one of the important channels for the transmission of
Italian humanism to south Germany. He taught canon law at Vienna during Kempf's time at the university (1434-38) and also served as chancel-

---

[76] *Matrikel*, vol. 1, p. 140, Rhenish nation, April, 1423, paid 8 groschen.

lor for the Austrian Duke Albrecht V and as his representative at the
Council of Basel. He was a friend of Aeneas Silvius Piccolomini and Nicolaus Cusanus. As bishop of Eichstätt (1445-64), he assembled a group
of humanist-oriented associates,[77] contributed to plans for the University
of Ingolstadt, and encouraged church reform.[78]

The man whose services he requested, Bernard of Waging, was born
ca. 1400, apparently in Waging, northwest of Salzburg,[79] studied at Vienna in the 1420s, entered the house of Austin canons at Indersdorf ca.
1430, transferred to Tegernsee in 1446,[80] and became prior in 1452.[81]
He wrote a number of works on spiritual direction,[82] mystical theology,[83] and monastic reform. He was no stranger to the sort of work Johann of Eych had in mind, having helped Nicholas Cusanus in the

---

[77] Reimann, *Pirckheimer*, 97-98, citing Max Herrmann, *Die Rezeption des Humanismus in Nürnberg* (1898), 21; Joachimsohn, *Hermann Schedels Briefwechsel*, letters 1, 7,
14. For Johann's ties to early Vienna humanists see Großmann, "Frühzeit," 226-29.

[78] See Ernst Reiter in *NDB*, 10: 483-85; and *Verfasserlexikon*, rev. ed., 4: 590-92; idem,
"Rezeption und Beachtung von Basler Dekreten in der Diözese Eichstätt unter Bischof Johann von Eych (1445-1464)," in *Von Konstanz nach Trient* [Franzen Festschrift] (1972),
215-32.

[79] Virtually all biographical information on Bernard of Waging's life before he became a Austin canon at Indersdorf rests on Pez's comments in *Bibl. ascetica*, 7: fol. b2-
b3. Bernard is not a very common name in the *Matrikel* at this period. A "Bernhardus de
Arnsdorff" matriculated as a pauper at Vienna in April 1423 in the Rhenish nation (*Matrikel*, vol. 1, p. 139), the same year as Johann von Eych. The index identifies Arnsdorfs
located in Niederbayern and in the Oberpfalz, but there is also an Arnsdorf just across
the Salzach River, north of Salzburg, much closer to Waging. The possibility that Bernard and Johann of Eych were fellow students at Vienna is intriquing but difficult to establish definitively. Pez quotes from several Tegernsee manuscript colophons that assert
that Bernard was born in Waging. The only student from Waging listed in the *Matrikel* is
a "Mauricius Grublinger de Baging," who matriculated in October 1423 in the Rhenish
nation, paying 2 groschen. It is conceivable that "Bernard" was a monastic name adopted
when he entered in religion, in which case Mauricius Grublinger could be our Bernard of
Waging. It is also possible that the man we know as Bernard of Waging was not listed at
all in the *Matrikel*.

[80] Redlich, *Tegernsee*, 138-42.

[81] Werner Höver in *Verfasserlexikon*, rev. ed., vol. 1 (1977-78), 779-89; Virgil
Redlich, *Tegernsee*; Vansteenberghe, *Docte ignorance*; Paul Wilpert, "Bernhard von
Waging, Reformer vor der Reformation," in *Festgabe für seine königliche Hoheit Kron-
prinz Rupert von Bayern* (1954), 260-75.

[82] E.g., *Remediarius contra pusillanimes et scrupulosos*, in *Bibl. ascetica*, 7: 447-525.

[83] Various writings are listed in Höver's *Verfasserlexikon* article and discussed in
Vansteenberghe, *Docte ignorance*. Note that the *Strictilogium de mystica theologia* at-
tributed by Wilpert to Bernard is probably by Konrad of Geissenfeld (Höver in *Verfas-
serlexikon*, col. 788, citing Roßmann). See also Martin Grabmann, "Die Erklärung des
Bernhard von Waging O.S.B. zum Schlußkapitel von Bonaventuras Itinerarium mentis in
Deum," *Franziskanische Studien*, 8 (1921), 125-35, and idem, "Bernhard von Waging . . .
ein bayerischer Benediktinermystiker des 15. Jahrhunderts," *SMGB*, n.F. 60 (1946), 82-98;
Werner Höver, *Theologia Mystica in altbairischer Übertragung* (1971).

abortive reform of monasteries in the diocese of Brixen.[84] He undertook
a variety of responsibilities within the Melk Benedictine reform.[85]

Bernard traveled to Eichstätt to confer briefly with the bishop.[86] In
the course of their conversation, Johann of Eych apparently made some
disparaging comments about the self-centeredness of monks who enjoy
leisure instead of serving the church. When he returned to Tegernsee
Bernard lost little time responding to the bishop. We are fortunate to
have several manuscript copies of Bernard's response, the bishop's
counter-response, and Bernard's reply to the bishop's response.[87]

Despite many similarities between these two reformers, in the exchange between Bernard of Waging and Johann of Eych we glimpse a
confrontation between two mentalities: Johann of Eych speaks from an
urban, humanist, activist concern for the commonweal of the church and
society, doing so with a "masculine" appeal to *virilitas* and virtue; Bernard of Waging defends the value and utility of the traditional contemplative monastic culture in which the "idea of reform" is still that of the
patristic *reformatio imaginis Dei* described by Gerhart Ladner and Jean
Leclercq. In the process he articulates a courtly ideal of strength through
meek renunciation, of courage through cowardice.

In his initial response to Johann of Eych, the *Speculum pastorum et
animarum rectorum* (early 1462),[88] Bernard offers some of the standard
arguments for the *securitas* of the monastic life when compared to the
risks inherent in ecclesial leadership. It is clear that Bernard uses the
term "pastoral office" to refer primarily to the bishop's office, although it
also includes abbots, parish rectors, and special assistants to the bishop

---

[84] See Wilhelm Baum, *Nikolaus Cusanus in Tirol* (1983), esp. 142-49, 174-80, with
references to other literature and to manuscript sources. As a friend of Cusanus, Johann
of Eych knew of Bernard's efforts in the Tyrol.

[85] See Redlich, *Tegernsee*, 101-13; Pez, *Bibl. ascetica*, 7: b3-b5.

[86] He did speak to the nuns at Bergen and he later drew up, at the bishop's request, a
set of psalmody guidelines for the Eichstätt cathedral canons. See Pez, *Bibl. ascetica*, 7:
b5.

[87] The following will be based on Munich, SB, clm 4403, from the monastery of St.
Ulrich and Afra in Augsburg, which contains all three parts of the exchange. Parts are
also found in clm 7007, 29v-47r (*Speculum Pastorum* only, from Indersdorf); clm
18548b, 111v-124v, 192r-219v (*Speculum pastorum, Defensorium speculi pastorum*,
from Tegernsee); and clm 18596, 214r-226v (*Inpugnatorium speculi pastorum*, from Tegernsee). See Paul Wilpert, "Vita Contemplativa und Vita Activa: Eine Kontroverse des
15. Jahrhunderts," *Passauer-Studien: Festschrift für Bischof Dr. Dr. Konrad Landers-
dorfer O.S.B.* (1953), 209-27.

[88] Clm 4403, 1r/9r-23v/31v. This codex has a dual foliation and will normally be
cited with both numbers. The lower numbers represent the original, fifteenth-century foliation; the higher numbers represent a modern pencil foliation.

in work such as Johann of Eych had in mind for Bernard.[89] In the third and fourth chapters of the *Speculum pastorum*,[90] Bernard sets forth the dangers inherent in pastoral office, especially lust for domination (chapter four), the need on occasion to exercise coercion against heresy and error (chapter four), and the pastor's responsibility before God's judgment seat for the souls entrusted to him.[91]

We also catch a glimpse of the wide range of responsibilities he thinks a pastor should shoulder. There are the obvious things: seeing that divine worship is carried out properly and with suitable flourish; feeding people with the word of God so that they do not starve spiritually; correcting and keeping in order the moral life of the community by word and example; seeing that Sundays and holy days are properly observed (that markets and merchants sell only absolute necessities on such days). A bishop must keep his clergy disciplined and tonsured, keep them out of taverns, free of gluttony, and away from concubines. He must not neglect to hold synods and visitations. Serious moral lapses, e.g., adultery and incest, require stiff penalties, including, if necessary, assistance from the secular arm. But there are legal and economic responsibilities too: he must watch for cases of false oaths and perjury in both secular and ecclesiastical courts and for harsh sentences by which avaricious judges in both types of courts eat up the substance of the poor and working folk. He must see to it that fraudulent pilgrimage shrines are uprooted;[92] ferret out commercial fraud and usury;[93] guard against simony, fraudulent abbatial elections, and the misuse of indulgences;[94] control superstitions;[95] and monitor trades and business—watching for tailors who cut off pieces of their customers' precious cloth for private gain, or vendors who use false weights and measures.[96] To prove his point about the dangers of pastoral office, Bernard offers a list of dozens of bishops or abbots who resigned their office to pursue contemplation, a list culled from the lives of the desert fathers and medieval hagiography (chapter two)[97] and of

---

[89] Ch. 3; clm 4403, 7v/15v-10v/18v.

[90] Clm 4403, 7v/15v-10v/18v.

[91] Ch. 6; cf. ch. 4, clm 4403, 43v/51v, 11 - 44r/52r, 5.

[92] While engaged in the abortive effort to reform the St. Georgenberg canonry Bernard would have encountered the issue of the authenticity of a bleeding host miracle; in Bavaria, the chapel at Andechs, another major site of bleeding host pilgrimage, was reformed under the auspices of Tegernsee.

[93] Clm 4403, 8v/16v, 20-37.

[94] Clm 4403, 8v/16, 37 - 9r, 14.

[95] Clm 4403, 9r/16v, 14-20.

[96] Clm 4403, 9r/17r, 20 - 9v/17v, 1.

[97] The issue was a live one at Tegernsee, since Nicolaus Cusanus told the monks of

great Christian saints who preferred solitude but still courageously embarked upon the more risky path.[98]

His exegesis of 1 Tim. 3:1: "He who desires the bishop's office desires a good thing," is worth noting: citing Aquinas, Bernard asserted that only the principal or final cause of the bishop's office, namely serving the good of one's neighbor, is a good thing to desire; the other aspects of episcopal office, its high status and its temporal honors, should not be desired.[99] One must balance the risk of temptation to desire it for false reasons against the reality of pastoral needs. For monks, the risks loom large: they know their weakness in the face of temptation, and the price of losing the struggle against temptation is nothing less than eternal damnation. Like a scorpion, the pastoral office licks with its tongue and stings with its tail (chapter seven).

Bernard also knew how hard it was, even in the face of compelling necessity, to be a good pastor. His pastoral ideal could be characterized as "servant leadership." For Bernard, quoting Gerson, hierarchy is an inverted pyramid. The pope is truly, not hypocritically, the servant of the servants of God; he carries, as it were, all men on his head.[100] Citing Hugh [of Saint-Victor? St. Cher?], Bernard comments: "He is a true pastor who is delighted by responsibility, not honor; charity, not power; and service given to others, not received from others."[101] This applies to secular as well as spiritual leaders (ch. 4, clm 4403, 43v 11-44r 5).

---

his desire to resign from from his office as bishop and retire to contemplation, asking counsel of Bernard. See the letters between Cusanus and Bernard of Waging, February 12, 1454, August 16, 1454, September 9, 1454, in Vansteenberghe, *Docte Ignorance*, 121-22, 139-40, 143-50.

[98] Ch. 1 (clm 4403, fol. 1v/9v, line 26 - 2r/10r, line 4).

[99] Ch. 6; clm 4403, 16v/24v, 18-34: "Verum ad principale obiectum quo dicitur 'qui episcopatum desiderat' etc. Sanctus Thomas plenius et clarius respondet. Dicit enim quod in episcopatu tria possunt considerari, quorum unum est principale et finale, scilicet episcopalis operatio, per quam utilitati proximorum intendit. Aliud est altitudo gradus, qui episcopus super alios constituitur. Tertium autem communiter se ad ista habet, scilicet reverentia et honor et sufficientia temporalium. Appetere igitur episcopatum ratione huius circumstantie tertiae malum est et illicitum et pertinet ad cupiditatem et ambitionem. Quantum vero ad secundum, scilicet ad celsitudinem gradus, appetere episcopatum est presumptuosum; sed appetere proximis prodesse est secundum se laudabile et virtuosum. Attamen prout episcopalis actus habet annexam gradus celsitudinem, presumptuosum esse videtur quod aliquis preesse appetat ad hoc quod subditis prosit, nisi manifesta imminente necessitate. Haec ille." Cf. Aquinas, *STh*, IIa IIae, qu. 185, art. 1.

[100] Ch. 6, clm 4403, 16v/24v, 13-18: "Nempe ut ait doctor insignis et emeritus Johannis de Gersona pretactus, 'Omnis dominatio primatus et prelatio est verissime servitus; nec frustra nec ficte nec mendose dicit se summus pontifex servum servorum, tamquam, habens omnes homines impositos super caput suum, redditurus de omnibus rationem.'"

[101] Ch. 3; clm 4403, 8r/16r, 8-10: "Et [Venerabilis Hugo] subdit, 'Verus prelatus est, quem delectat onus non honor; caritas, non potestas; servitus alijs inpensa, non ab alijs suscepta.'"

Furthermore, pastors are not the only ones who serve genuine needs. Monks also aid the church by their intercession and liturgical worship (chapter six). Indeed, Bernard's defense of the contemplative life boils down to an assertion that what Christ meant by saying that "Mary has chosen the better part" was that worship is the best part of the Christian life, that worship is better than activity in the world, and that worshipers do benefit their neighbors.[102] He concluded with a word of consolation for those who once held the episcopal dignity but resigned it to pursue a monastic or eremitic life (chapter seven).

Johann of Eych's response was a treatise written as a single epistle and titled in the manuscripts, *Inpugnatorium speculi pastorum et animarum rectorum*.[103] It was written in a simple Latin rather than in the elegant style of contemporary humanist epistolography. This may have been a concession to Bernard of Waging's more pedestrian latinity.[104] Johann of Eych began by lauding the contemplative life in language reminiscent of Petrarch, but soon unloaded both barrels against Bernard's apology for monastic withdrawal. When the young man asked Christ what he should do to merit eternal life, Christ did not tell him to go to a monastery, rather, he told him to obey the commandments and to sell all and follow him. The latter can be done by remaining in the world and observing the commandments with a charity that suffers all, believes all, hopes all (1 Cor 13).[105] Virginity and withdrawal are legitimate but

---

[102] Ch. 7; clm 4403, 18v/26v-19r/27r. Cloistered religious benefit their neighbors by giving a good example of the Christian life, by loving God above all else, by preaching with their deeds (deeds are more likely to be free from falsity than are words), by praying devoutly for others (the devout prayer of a contemplative united to God is worth that of two hundred or a thousand active, less devoted, people), by serving as the eyes which illuminate the entire body and focus all the body's deeds and works; by worship and intercession without ceasing, day and night.

[103] Clm 4403, 24r/32r - 32r/40r.

[104] Both at the beginning and end of his response to Johann's response Bernard apologized for not writing in eloquent epistolary form. Because he has so much to say he will divide his work into chapters and call it a *libellus*. He will turn his back on both the rhetorical and the scholastic style and write in a "stilo grossiori proprio mihi et accomodo," responding simply point by point to the order of Johann's letter. *Defensorium*, prologue (clm 4403, fol. 33r/41r, 37 - 33v/41v, 12 and ch. 10, clm 4403, fol. 69r/78r, 33-34. Yet Bernard could not resist tossing in a few rhetorical flourishes in the course of his treatise. In ch. 7 he makes use of word plays from Adam of Perseigne (*animabus* and *avibus* and the extended pastoral imagery described in chapter four, p. 132, above). See clm 4403, fol. 53v/61v, 34 - 54r/62r, 7; 54v/62v, 23 - 55r/63r, 8. At the end of the work he notes that it is now approaching the hour for the great silence and he must stop; tomorrow he will finish up with a fresh stylus—thus making a wordplay on the *stilus grossior* with which he had begun. See ch. 10, clm 4403, fol. 66r/74r, 4-5.

[105] Clm 4403, fol. 25r/33r, 14 - 25v/33v, 11.

only as counsels of perfection. Observing the commandments is equally
legitimate.

Thus monks are perfectionists[106] who desire an impossibly pure
church instead of realizing that the impossibility of guarding all parishioners from error, of teaching them well, guiding their lives, protecting
them from economic and social fraud, dare not deter one from taking on
pastoral care. Even in your own monastery, Johann reminds Bernard
(who, as prior, needed no reminding), you have an abbot whose task it is
to amend the lives of others. You cannot be serious when you say that
pastoral care of others leads to neglect of one's own spiritual life and
risks damnation. Furthermore, even if there is risk involved, you should
have courage to enter cautiously into that arena. Like cherubim (*pennata
animalia*) with eyes in front and back, prelates must look to all sides and
be wary of danger, but should not flee risk. This is what Christ meant
when he talked about a faithful and prudent servant, about being wise as
serpents. What kind of soldier would run from battle because he was
afraid of being wounded? True soldiers show their scars as proof of their
courage. Merchants take risks for the sake of temporal gain—how can
you be so timid for the sake of an eternal crown?[107] Johann continues,
citing Cicero on civic responsibility: no matter how lofty one's scholarly
and literary contemplation may be, if the fatherland is threatened, if a fire
breaks out in the city, if a flood comes, if enemies are storming the walls,
you will break off your contemplation to help save the city or land.[108]
Bernard had said that one of the reasons he would not take on pastoral
responsibility was that in these last days the world is declining rapidly
and there are too many incorrigible people impossible to pastor. For Johann that is the ecclesial equivalent of the enemy storming the wall, of a
fire breaking out in the city. The church desperately needs help. In short,
the bishop's reply boils down to calling Bernard a coward. Merchants,
soldiers, or citizens of a town endangered by fire take risks for the sake
of reward. Why should not Bernard?

Bernard explains why at the end of his *Defensorium speculi pastorum* (December 1462).[109] He points out that Johann has raised two distinct questions: first, should those who have not yet accepted the *cura*

---

[106] Bernard had explicitly affirmed a "wheat and tares" ecclesiology and denied the
possibility of a pure and perfect church this side of heaven. See *Speculum Pastorum*, ch.
4 (clm 4403, fol. 12v/20v, 5-27).

[107] Clm 4403, fol. 26v/34v, 16 - 27r/35r, 6.

[108] Clm 4403, fol. 28r/36r, 26 - 28v/36v, 2.

[109] Clm 4403, 33r/41r - 69r/78r. The full text of the relevant chapter is found in appendix B.

animarum choose a better life instead, namely the contemplative life, and second, should those who already carry the burden of pastoral care on their shoulders leave it to pursue the contemplative life. The second question is not in doubt, having been decided (negatively) by the pope. Therefore he will deal with the first question. He cannot disagree with Johann of Eych's praise of pastoral care because it is so well written and compelling. (And, we should recall, Bernard himself set forth a positive pastoral ideal in his *Speculum*.) But Bernard is ready to respond to Johann of Eych's charge that contemplatives are cowards.

The way he responds is classically monastic: he simply concedes the bishop's strongest point. Monks *are* cowards. They are womanish. It was Johann's scorn that was misplaced, not his description. Instead of sarcastically saying, "It's fine for women to sit at the feet of Christ and do nothing while men bravely shoulder risks," Bernard insists that it is fine for womanish men, contemplatives, to sit at Christ's feet and "do nothing." Bernard's authority is his Cistercian namesake, in his twelfth sermon on the Song of Songs:

> My brothers, let us give due honor to bishops but have a wholesome fear of their jobs, for if we comprehend the nature of their jobs we shall not hanker after the honor. Let us admit that our powers are unequal to the task, that our soft effeminate shoulders cannot be happy in supporting burdens made for men. It is not for us to pry into their business but to pay them due respect. For it is surely churlish to censure their doings if you shun their responsibilities; you are no better than the woman at home spinning, who foolishly reprimands her husband returning from the battle. And I add: if a monk happens to notice that a prelate working in his diocese lives with less constraint than he, and with less circumspection; that he speaks more freely, eats as he pleases, sleeps when he will, laughs spontaneously, gives rein to anger, passes judgment readily, let him not rush precipitately to wrong conclusions, but rather call to mind the Scripture: 'Better is the wickedness of a man than a woman who does good [Sir. 42:14].'[110]

---

[110] Sermon 12.9, in *S. Bernardi Opera*, 1: 66; translation by Kilian Walsh, CF 4: 84-85. A parallel is found in Bernard's letter to Aelred of Rievaulx, in which he brushes aside Aelred's insistence that the burden of writing what we know as the *Speculum Caritatis* was too much for his (Aelred's) "girlish" shoulders. See Bernard's letter no. 523 in *S. Bernardi Opera*, 8, pt. 2: 486. The passage from Bernard's sermon nine continues as follows: "For you do well in keeping a vigilant eye on your own behavior, but the man who helps many [people] acts with more virile purpose fulfilling a higher duty. And if in the performance of this duty he is guilty of some imperfection, if his life and behavior are less than regular, remember that love covers a multitude of sins [1 Pet 4:8]. I want this to be a warning against that twofold temptation with which the devil assails men in religious life; to covet the fame of a bishop's status, and to pass rash judgment on his excesses."

Johann of Eych had blithely quoted the passage from Ecclesiasticus
that Bernard of Clairvaux cited: "better the sins of men than the virtues
of women." In Johann's view, with risk and the bravery needed to face
it, come some errors. But society can tolerate these better than it can survive timidity on the part of its best minds and hearts. Bernard of Clairvaux, Bernard of Waging, and Johann of Eych drew on the commentary
by Rabanus Maurus that found its way into the *Glossa Ordinaria*.[111] Unlike Johann of Eych, the two Bernards read it with monastic eyes. Conventional worldly wisdom assumed that men have more discretion than
women, but the monastic commentators immediately added the reminder
that even men of discretion fall into sin. What matters is whether they
become proud in their sin or whether they repent of it—whether a second, monastic, discretion comes into play. A man's "sin" is only "good"
if it leads to repentance, whereas a man[112] is weak and indiscrete if he
lets his good deeds make him proud and impenitent. Although Rabanus's
concluding explication of the aphorism from Ecclesiasticus lacks gender-
specific tags ("the sin of the strong sometimes is an occasion of virtue
while the virtue of the weak is an occasion of sin" ["quia nonnumquam
etiam culpa fortium, occasio virtutis fit, et virtus infirmorum, occasio
peccati"]), the context makes it clear that men are normally the strong
and women are the weak who go away confounded for having confused
the two.

Bernard of Waging does not quote the full passage, omitting the
quotations from Job and the explanation of the eternal opprobrium borne

---

[111] PL 109: 1067CD. "'Melior est iniquitas viri quam benefaciens mulier, et mulier
confundens in opprobrium.' In sacro eloquio mulier aut pro sexu ponitur, aut pro infirmitate: pro sexu quippe, sicut scriptum est: 'Misit Deus Filium suum, factum ex muliere,
factum sub lege' (Gal 4); pro infirmitate vero, sicut in Job legitur: 'Homo natus de muliere, brevi vivens tempore' (Job 4). Et hic per hunc sapientem dicitur. 'Melior est iniquitas viri, quam benefaciens mulier.' Vir etenim fortis quilibet et discretus vocatur; mulier
vero mens infirma, vel indiscreta accipitur. Et saepe contingit ut etiam discretus quisque
subito labatur in culpam, atque indiscretus alius et infirmus bonam exhibeat operacio-
nem; sed is qui indiscretus atque infirmus est, nonnumquam de eo quod bene egerit amplius elevatur, atque gravius in culpam cadit. Discretus vero quisque, etiam ex eo quod
male se egisse intelligit, ad discretionis regulam arctius reducit, et inde altius ad justitiam
proficit, unde ad tempus a justitia cecedisse videbatur, quia in re recte dicitur: 'Melior est
iniquitas viri, quam benefaciens mulier.' Quia nonnumquam etiam culpa fortium, occasio virtutis fit, et virtus infirmorum, occasio peccati. Haec mulier confundit in opprobrium, quia hic res confusione dignas gerens pro hoc opprobrium sustinebit in
aeternum." Citing Rabanus's sermon "De studio bono et discretione semper habenda"
(PL 110: 123D-124A), Dekkers has argued that Rabanus reduced discretion to a purely
human prudence which must itself be employed with discretion. See Dekkers, "'Discretio' chez S. Benoît et S. Grégoire," 87-88.

[112] Rabanus utilizes adjectives expressing "feminine" qualities but puts them in grammatically masculine forms: "Is qui indiscretus atque infirmus est."

by women. In the context of his debate with Johann of Eych and his quotation from Bernard of Clairvaux regarding womanish weakness, Bernard of Waging uses the passage from the *Gloss* to make a different
point: The very *virilitas* of men, which makes them more discrete in a rational sense, also inclines them to pride and impenitence. Sitting at home
and meekly doing "nothing" is "virile", i.e, has discretion, in the monastic sense (the repentant discretion of humility), while the virile courage
and risk-taking to which Johann challenged him, if done without the discretion of humility, can be womanishly devoid of discretion, i.e., devoid
of the truest, monastic, penitent discretion. Instead of proudly showing
off one's scars (errors), a monk's discretion teaches him to lament the
wounds incurred in the battles of leadership. The two Bernards thus employed a *monastic* form of *discretio* to counter the simplistic gender-spe-
cific categories of the "world" (men have, women lack, discretion). It is
the bishop whose understanding of *virtus* and *discretio* is one-dimen-
sional and androcentric.

Bernard of Waging's reading is reinforced by Bernard of Clairvaux's comments in the paragraph preceding the above quotation (Sermon 12, par. 8).

> There have been times, . . . when . . . I could hear people saying: 'Why
> this waste?' [Mt 26:8]. They complained that I thought only of myself. . . .
> In effect they said: 'This could have been sold at a high price and the
> money given to the poor' [Mt 26:9]. But what a poor transaction for me, to
> forfeit my own life and procure my own destruction, even if I should gain
> the whole world [Mt 16:26]! . . . But . . . the Lord . . . takes my part with
> the query: 'Why are you upsetting this woman?' [Mt 26:10]. . . . This is not
> a man, as you think, who can handle great enterprises, but a woman [Prov
> 31:19]. . . . The work that he performs for me is good [Mk 14:6], let him be
> satisfied with this good until he finds strength to do better. . . .[113]

Although the Cistercian drew on commercial imagery from the New
Testament, he used it to show that a "bad bargain" may actually be the
best investment. Here virtue is disguised as a vice, rather than vice versa,
as we have encountered the theme in Nicholas Kempf. But the point is
the same: what you see is not necessarily what you get; deeper, hidden
meanings and implications must be diligently pursued. Where Johann of
Eych called for calculated risk-taking, both Bernards were interested in
blue-chip stocks that were "safe" investments precisely because the real

---

[113] Sermon 12.8, pp. 83-84; translation by Kilian Walsh.

spiritual risks were incalculable and only God can guarantee a solid return on one's capital.[114]

In a world in which entrepreneurial activity[115] could begin to com-
pete with prowess as a warrior in defining manliness, both Bernard of
Waging and Bernard of Clairvaux preferred contemplative meekness's
lower "yield" here and now in order to lay up treasure in heaven.[116] In
the monastic context, virility is expressed in the ancient sense of the "active life" of struggle against vices and formation in virtues: by offering
oneself up as a sacrifice through disciplining the body, one becomes
truly virile, fit for womanish contemplation. The thirteenth-century Carthusian Guigo de Ponte put it succinctly:

---

[114] *Speculum pastorum*, ch. 3 (clm 4403, 9v/17v, 41 - 10r/18r, 13): "Confidat [10r/18r]
igitur fidelis et prudens ac sollicitus pastor in eo qui incrementum tribuat, scilicet Deo—
et quando et quomodo voluerit. Ipse plantans, ipse rigans, Deo incrementum commitens
[1 Cor 3:6-7]; neque enim ultra habens quid faciat et securus prommissa Domini expec-
tet. 'Euge,' inquientis, 'serve bone et fidelis' etc. [Mt 25:21, 23]. Ecce recommendatur
de bonitate et fidelitate, non de fructum ubertate, reputans fructum ubi reperit fidelita-
tem, et servi bonitatem fraude et dolo sublatis. Nichil ergo dampnacionis est hijs qui fideles fuerint in commissis; Domino secure possunt dicere: 'Iusticiam tuam et veritatem
tuam non abscondi [Ps 39:11 (40:10)], ipsi autem contempnentes spreverunt me' [cf. Is
1:2]. Et respondebit Christus, 'Non es servus maior domino suo [Jn 13:16, cf. Mt 10:24];
ipsi nolebant audire te, quia nolebant audire me [Lk 10:16].'" Note Bernard's application
of the parable of the talents [Mt 25]: for Bernard a faithful and prudent pastor looks to
God, not to his own financial talents, to increase his capital; even though, in the parable,
the faithful servant was the one who invested his money rather than burying it. Bernard
is not necessarily saying that the faithful pastor does nothing, but he is reminding Johann
that profit comes from God, not from human skill alone, and that the servant was praised
not for having made a profit but for having been faithful. Although Bernard did not explicitly cite it, Ps 39 (40) concludes, "Ego autem mendicus sum et pauper; Dominus sollicitus est mei" (vs. 18).

[115] Cf. *Speculum pastorum*, ch. 1 (clm 4403, fol. 2v/10v, 13-31): don't be like a merchant who gathers much profit but puts it in a sack with holes in it [Hag 1:6]; don't be
like a bell on a church that rings to call people to church but which never enters the
church itself; don't be someone who shows the way to others but never enters on it himself—these kinds of people lose what they have gained—and, unfortunately, there are
many of them. For similar use of a commercial metaphor with a negative connotation,
see the Carthusian Guigo I, *Meditationes*, no. 182, SC 308: 158.

[116] See *Speculum pastorum*, ch. 7 (clm 4403, 22v/30v, 23-29): "Ex quibus omnibus
premissis mentis oculo adverte, an tibi expediat pericula prelature in monasterio delites-
cendo evasisse et solius unius, videlicet pro te, sollicitum esse debere, in pacis tranquilli-
tate vivere, mente Deo adherere, ac portum maris huius fluctuantis attingisse. Licet enim
forte cum minori lucro, tamen magis secure." Note the recurring use of variants of *securus* in this and in the preceding quotations, combined with the allusions to commerce and
risk-taking (*pericula, minori lucro, magis secure*). Bernard also addresses the question
of the security of the monastic life in the introduction and in chapter two of his *Defensorium speculi pastorum*. The monastic life is a school of *virtues* and its ordered, structured, path makes it more secure, more effective, and quicker. All of this is a response to
Johann of Eych's insistence that the most secure path lay in the active life (clm 4403, 34r
[42r], 30 - 34v/42v, 7; 37r/45r - 40v/48v). Cf. ch. 10 (clm 4403, fol. 65v/73v, 27), where
Bernard of Waging defines *securus* as *seorsum a cura*.

[Entry into the joyous wine-cellar by grace of sapiential contemplation]
. . . applies to a soul of long-standing ascendant experience, who knows
how to offer herself to God . . . as a burnt offering of holy ascents in a
crackling fire, who has offered her body in virile and austere repentance
and in earnest discipline. For whoever pursues contemplation but does not
sacrifice his own body, . . . cannot compare himself to those active men
who constantly mortify the flesh with sacrifice and martyrdom. Thus it is
said in Ecclesiasticus, "Better the wickedness of a man than the good deeds
of a woman." Such a contemplative is no man but would be better called a
woman, who nonetheless does a good work in the Savior. Just as many
worldlings are better than many monks, so the perfect active life is better
and more powerful than a contemplative life lived lazily.[117]

Although Guigo scornfully dismisses half-hearted, undisciplined
contemplatives as wimpish women, as a womanish, affective monastic
writer he is quick to assert that even the weakest and most inadequate
human works are "good works in the Savior." As we have seen (chapter
five, above) he repeatedly reminds his readers that mystical contemplation at its highest levels is entirely by God's grace,[118] and he describes it
in thoroughly erotic, feminine terms: a loving, yearning, longing clinging
to God for dear life, an opening up of oneself in order to be penetrated by
the Spirit.

The exercise of anagogical contemplation has three steps. The first is the
godly spirit's imaginative clinging to Christ's humanity through devout affection, . . . The second step is the godly spirit's clinging of discernment . . . in
godly love to the divinity clothed with humanity, . . . The third step is the human spirit's yearning, unitive clinging in which she gently burns for God,
knowing experientially that one who clings to God in this way is one spirit
with him. In this step, as the godly spirit leaves behind mental and anagogical prayers and, inflamed with divine longing, pants for the face of her
own Author, she is joined to heavenly things and separated from earthly
things. With love growing from her own fervor she opens herself to receive
and in receiving is set on fire. Then with great longing she gazes wide-
mouthed at celestial things and in some wondrous way tastes what she
seeks to have. This tasting, moreover, is the clinging, the union, through
which the pious spirit enjoys God, in whom she blissfully reposes.[119]

---

[117] Guigo, *De contemplatione*, III.11 (Dupont ed., pp. 322, 324).

[118] "In hoc quidem mentis excessu ipsa mens non per se sed trahente Dei gratia cuius
bona voluntas non prima est sed pedissequa, secedit ac abstrahitur actualiter ab omnibus
exterioribus, sensibilibus et visibilibus, quadam levi et tranquilla dulcedine tota se con-
vertens, prout potest, ad divinas et interiores infusiones, . . ." ibid. III.7 (pp. 300, 302).

[119] Ibid. II.10 (pp. 230, 232).

Johann of Eych's program had two main sources. He was drawing on the Vienna pastoral theology inspired by the writings of Heinrich of Langenstein, Nicholas of Dinkelsbühl, Thomas Ebendorfer, Johannes Geuß and others. This circle of university theologians and court preachers wrote manuals for parish priests, supervised monastic reform, and generally sought to improve the education and discipline of the parish clergy.[120] Indeed, Johann of Eych had some significant success in implementing this Vienna program.[121] And Bernard of Waging wholeheartedly agreed with these reforms.[122] But Johann was also drawing on the humanist ideals of the urban patriciate. His examples were taken from military and commercial-urban settings favored by contemporary neo-Ciceronian Italian "civic humanists." Bernard of Waging, notably, uses pastoral and agricultural imagery, as well as military and urban metaphors.[123] He belonged—at least since his monastic formation, if not before—to a different world, to one that preferred to take a more placid and long-term view based on the assumption that the outcome of any venture is determined by forces beyond human control, a world in which peasants, aristocrats, and monks play their assigned roles obediently and leave the outcome, for better or worse, to the providence of God. Reform ultimately is a matter for the true *Reformator*, the Lord of history.

---

[120] See chapter two, p. 59, above, for literature.

[121] A most interesting visitation protocol from the diocese of Eichstätt in 1480 indicates a diocese that was certainly not free from clerical concubinage and clerics who frequented taverns, but which, on the whole was in a remarkable state of institutional and spiritual health. This visitation protocol is all the more significant for the fact that the episcopal visitor who carried it out took his task extremely seriously and went to great lengths to ferret out the least offense. It is anything but an official, laundered, report card. Peter Thaddäus Lang, "Wurfel, Wein und Wettersegen: Klerus und Gläubige im Bistum Eichstätt am Vorabend der Reformation," in *Martin Luther: Probleme seiner Zeit* (1986), 219-43. How much the state of health of the diocese of Eichstätt in 1480 owed to Johann of Eych, who had died sixteen years earlier, is difficult to say. Some evidence of his procedure is visible in a description of proceedings against a group of Hussite-Waldensians in 1460. Here the approach taken seems to be cautious and careful, with an overarching concern to reintegrate the heretics into the church and to instruct laity regarding their errors. Franz Machilek, "Ein Eichstätter Inquisitionsverfahren aus dem Jahre 1460," in *Jahrbuch für fränkische Landesforschung*, 34/35 (1974/75), 417-46.

[122] One concrete example comes from Thomas Ebendorfer's excoriation of the "libido dominandi" that he sees dominating the church everywhere. The lust for domination was high on Bernard of Waging's list of risks inherent in pastoral office, as noted above. See the summary of Ebendorfer in Harald Zimmermann, "Romkritik und Reform in Ebendorfers Papstchronik," in *Reformatio Ecclesiae* [Iserloh Festschrift] (1980), 169-80, at 175-76.

[123] The three circles of "sense-perceptible" metaphors that Hugh of Balma uses to illustrate the rhetorical reasons for pursuing union with God are drawn precisely from agriculture, commerce, and warfare. See *Viae Sion lugent*, cap. 3, part. 2 (Peltier ed., pp. 28b-29a [= *via unitiva*, par. 35-37, in SC edition).

Scholars are only beginning to explore the reasons for rising misogyny in late medieval urban culture.[124] Humanists, including one associated with Eichstätt, Albrecht of Eyb,[125] did write treatises in defense of marriage and against the supposed unnatural, monastic praise of virginity. Yet in the present instance, it is the urban, humanist, activist reforming bishop who quotes the line from Ecclesiasticus, "better the sins of men than the virtues of women," with misogynist overtones. And it is Bernard of Waging who insists that both men and women are subject to sin and that feminine qualities may indeed be helpful, not in preventing sin, which is impossible, but in dealing with sin repentantly.

Monastic discretion was a way to temper and curb confidence in reason. The affective, loving, womanish clinging to God pursued by monastics was an implicit critique of the excesses of rational cleverness, of the machismo that lay behind both the rise of scholasticism (Abelard is paradigmatic here) and the rise of commerce and trade: both depend on a shrewdness and sharpness of analytical ability that the Wisdom literature of the Old Testament continually criticizes. Bravery and bluster may have their place but machismo is also dangerous, since pride in one's cleverness can blind one to faults and block repentance.[126] Awareness of precisely these pitfalls is what drew the monks to the cloister. It should not surprise us to learn that Bernard of Waging, Vincent of Aggsbach, Jacob de Paradiso, and others writing on mystical theology eagerly explored the *Vitae* of renowned medieval women saints in order to understand better why God granted them a disproportionate share of genuine visions and revelations.[127]

---

[124] Charles Muscatine, *The Old French Fabliaux* (1986), pp. 24-46; Mary Jane Stearns Schenck, *The Fabliaux* (1987), esp. 109-11, 120.

[125] William Melczer, "Albrecht von Eyb (1420-1475) et les racines italiennes du premier humanisme allemand," in *L'Humanisme allemand (1480-1540)* (1979), pp. 31-44, with references to additional literature. See also G. Zippel, "Gli inizi dell'Umanesimo tedesco e l'Umanesimo italiano, nel XV secolo," *Bollettino dell'Istituto storico italiano per il medio evo e archivio muratoriano*, 75 (1963), 345-89, at 379-83.

[126] The way crusading warrior virility could be combined with rules of Quixotically "useless" courtesy under the miraculous providence of God, is fully visible in Odo of Cluny's portrait of saintly Gerald of Aurillac, a tenth-century warrior who fought for justice using human weakness in order to show how the ultimate victory rests with God: his men fought with swords held by the point rather than the hilt, yet triumphed nonetheless. See Barbara H. Rosenwein, *Rhinoceros Bound: Cluny in the Tenth Century* (1982), p. 75; Rosenwein and Lester K. Little, "Social Meaning in the Monastic and Mendicant Spiritualities," *Past and Present*, no. 63 (1974), 4-32; and Georges Duby, *The Chivalrous Society* (1977), 166-67.

[127] See the introduction to the present study. In the course of asserting the same primacy of "feminine" contemplation, Kempf ascribes to prayer itself precisely the warrior and leadership qualities that Johann is looking for in the flesh. In a long list of biblical heroes who led their people successfully through national crises and obtained mercy

As he concluded the chapter under discussion here (chapter nine)[128]
Bernard of Waging said to the bishop: "You agreed with me in bemoan-
ing the sad state of the church, lamenting how rebellious and insolent so
many are. You are right—you need men to speak to insolent men, the
virtuous must correct the errors of the virile. I'm a woman, I'm not the
kind of person you need for your reform. By your own criteria, you
should be looking elsewhere." Bernard did not dispute the need for courage, risk-taking, and self-sacrifice on the part of pastors; had he not earlier cited Gregory to the effect that bishops were on the front lines of
martyrdom in the bloody war faced by the primitive church?[129] He
merely knew that it was not his calling.

Many of the same "womanish" virtues that combined with "virile"
ones to produce Bernard of Waging's contemplative cowardice are the
qualities that, according to Stephen Jaeger, created courtliness in the
tenth and early eleventh centuries[130]: in courtly culture, alongside the
"virile" virtues of gravity tempered with affability, foresighted judgment,
and mastery of action (= the monastic *vita activa* as combat against
vices), we find humility, compassion, gentle yet grave authority, patient
amiability (combined with "manly" zeal in exacting vengeance), and,
perhaps most significantly, *mansuetudo* (gentleness of spirit, benevolent
passivity shown to friends and enemies alike, associated with patience,
humility and modesty): in short, the *vir mansuetus* suffers abuse without
murmuring, knows no anger or resentment. In combination these produce *moderamen, moderatio,* and *mensura,* i.e., the discretion we have
encountered throughout the present study. Although Jaeger cannot completely ignore the obvious parallels in monastic culture, he arbitrarily
credits the rise of courtliness to the influence of Cicero and secular classical antiquity.[131]

When Bernard of Waging called on his twelfth-century namesake in
support of his side of the debate, he was not defending a narrow *con-
temptus mundi* but an entire mentality of social salvation that rested on
individual, "passive" regeneration—the reformation of the image of God

---

from God so that their people would not perish, he names not only Abraham
(whose intercession saved the few righteous who lived in Sodom and Gomorrah), Moses,
and Paul (whose prayers on board ship saved the entire company from death), but also
the Virgin Mary, Judith, and Esther as "liberators of their people." *MTh,* V.3, pp. 362-63.

[128] Clm 4403, 64v - 65r.

[129] *Speculum Pastorum,* ch. 5 (clm 4403, fol. 15v/23v, 28-36).

[130] C. Stephen Jaeger, *The Origins of Courtliness. . . 939-1210* (1985), pp. 17-48.

[131] The work of Jean Leclercq is notably absent from Jaeger's book. See Leclercq,
Monks and Love in Twelfth-Century France (1979); *Monks on Marriage: A Twelfth-Century View* (1982).

in the soul and the reformation of the commonweal, with both of these assured by prayer and intercession, ultimately by trust in a mysterious yet provident God, rather than trust in military combat, codified canon law, emergent bureaucracies, scholastic systems, encyclopedic natural science, or civic activism.[132] Reform monasticism in the fifteenth century was indeed responding to changes in both city and countryside—as Schreiner and others have insisted, monastic reform is not static traditionalism but is a dynamic response, a form of *Zeitanpassung*.[133] But response to contemporary trends can be either approving or disapproving. Current scholarship on late medieval monasticism invariably looks at the ways in which monastic reform cooperated with new trends in education, politics, or social structures. Bernard of Waging was employing his twelfth-century sources to critique (he might say, "to discern") the overtones of the neo-Ciceronian concept of *virtù*, which, for Johann of Eych and his sources (Petrarch, Salutati, Bruni) was still altruistic but which could also lead to Machiavelli's machismo.[134] Discerning critique does not necessarily make one an ostrich-like reactionary: Bernard of Waging reached for twelfth-century *auctoritates* not out of timidity in the face of late medieval urban-scholastic culture, but out of a poised and long-established cultural tradition that maintained a positive role for disciplined contemplative renunciation. Discretion, in his eyes, was indeed the better part of valor.

In the end, discretion also caused the monk to "capitulate" to the bishop, revealing how much they shared in their zeal for reform. Yet Bernard was careful to express his concession in traditional monastic terms: if God called the monk to pastoral care, whether within or outside the monastery, the monk must obey. At the end of his treatise Bernard announced that, if it was God's clear leading, for the salvation of souls, correction of morals, freeing of people from the snares of the devil and returning them to their creator, for reform of the regular monastic life, he would cheerfully and of his own free will, *temporarily* leave his monastic repose.[135]

Ten years later, in 1472, Bernard died while serving as confessor to nuns in the Benedictine monastery of Bergen near Eichstätt.

---

[132] See Albert Rabil, Jr.'s, discussion of this last-mentioned, very controversial, term in "The Significance of 'Civic Humanism' in the Interpretation of the Italian Renaissance," in *Renaissance Humanism* (1988), 1: 141-74.

[133] Schreiner, "Benediktinische Klosterreform."

[134] See the summary by Maristella Lorch, "Petrarch, Cicero, and the Classical Pagan Tradition," in *Renaissance Humanism* 1: 71-94, at 74-76.

[135] Ch. 7; Clm 4403, fol. 52v/60v, 14-28.

5. Noblesse Oblige

Like Bernard of Waging, Kempf based his disinclination toward
pastoral office on the fathers of monasticism, whom he knew well
through the Latin versions of the writings of John Cassian, John Climacus, the Sayings of the Desert Fathers (*Vitae/Vitas Patrum*; *Verba
Seniorum*[136]), and Basil of Caesarea, as well as letters and tracts by
Jerome. In *De confirmatione*, Kempf's basic work on Carthusian history,
he located the origins of the Carthusian order in the life of the desert fathers of Egypt, citing as his authority Bernard (William of Saint-Thierry)
in the *Golden Epistle*. He offered the Carthusian order as the fount of
twelfth-century monastic renewal and the godparent of the Cistercian
and Praemonstratensian orders—both of which originated in the "miracle
of Paris" that gave birth to the Carthusians. The mendicant orders,
Kempf noted laconically, came along much later.[137]

The primacy of the contemplative life had been assumed by advocates of monasticism from Basil of Caesarea and Gregory of Nazianzus
through John Cassian and Bernard of Clairvaux. Even Thomas Aquinas,
a mendicant, defended, with qualifications, the superiority of the *vita
contemplativa* in a much-quoted formulation.[138] Yet not all monastic
apologists from the contemplative monastic tradition had the same attitude as Kempf had toward the office of pastor and prelate.

During two of the outstanding "monastic centuries" that preceded
Kempf's own not particularly monastic century, namely the fourth-fifth
century and the twelfth century, monastic leaders professed the ideal of
withdrawal and asserted the priority of the contemplative life. Yet precisely these same monastic leaders functioned as leaders in the church as

---

[136] For a study of the manuscript tradition, see Columba M. Batlle, *Die "Adhortationes sanctorum patrum" ("Verba seniorum") im lateinischen Mittelalter* (1971).

[137] *De confirmatione*, ch. 9/10 (V5, 12v, 14 - 14r, 27). The chapter is titled: "Ordo cartusiensis incepit in Egypto a sanctis patribus in heremo ut Anthonio et Paulo." Cf. William of Saint-Thierry, *Epistola ad Fratres de Monte Dei*, I.1, I.4 (PL 184:309-11 [= par.
1, 13 in SC 223: 144]). See also Kempf, *De confirmatione*, 16/15 (V5, 23r, 4-21).

[138] *STh*, IIa. IIae. q. 182. As a mendicant, Aquinas placed more value on the active life
than did Kempf. Both religious and prelates are *in statu perfectionis* (q. 184, art. 5-6),
but "semper agens praestantius est patiente [Augustine]" and the "status perfectionis po-
tior est in episcopis quam in religionis [art. 7]." Because the duties of a pastor are more
difficult, the *status* of a priest excells that of a *nonordained* religious [art. 8]. See also
qq. 185-86. For Jean Gerson's discussion of this during his Paris career, see Burger, *Aedificatio*, 158-93.

a whole. Many of them, however reluctantly, developed a theological justification and high regard for the role of pastor and prelate, for the "ruler of souls," in the church at large.[139]

In the mid-fourth century Hilary of Poitiers described ecclesiastical office by combining the language of aristocratic *otium* and *securitas* with the Roman sense of public service, language fully familiar to us from our study of monastic attitudes toward contemplation and leadership: "In a state of leisure which is aware of its security, the happy spirit relaxes in its anticipation . . . it likewise speaks out to others through the service of an imposed priesthood, expending its favors in its responsibility for public salvation."[140] In the turbulent provincial politics of fifth-century Gaul aristocratic "monk-bishops" were common.[141] Peter Brown has suggested that a "highly articulate, but narrow section of the aristocracy," found the monastic life compatible with the traditional life of the country gentleman.[142] This "nobility" theme can be traced throughout medieval

---

[139] Rousseau, *Ascetics*; idem, "The Spiritual Authority of the 'Monk-Bishop': Eastern Elements in Some Western Historiography of the Fourth and Fifth Centuries," *JTS*, n.s. 22 (1971), 380-419; Peter Brown, "The Rise and Function of the Holy Man in Late Antiquity," *Journal of Roman Studies*, 61 (1971), 80-101; idem, *The Making of Late Antiquity*; Rosemarie Nürnberg, *Askese*; Ladner, *Idea of Reform*. For the twelfth century see John R. Sommerfeldt, "Consistency of Thought in the Works of Bernard of Clairvaux," (PhD diss, University of Michigan, 1960), and idem, "Social Theory of Bernard of Clairvaux," in *Studies in Medieval Cistercian History* (1971), 35-48. See also Placide Deseille, "Théologie de la vie monastique selon Saint Bernard," in *Vie monastique*, 503-25.

[140] "In hoc igitur conscio securitatis suae otio mens spebus suis laeta requieverat . . . tamen per ministerium impositi sacerdotii etiam ceteris praedicabat, munus suum ad officium publicae salutis extendens. . . ." (*De trinitate*, 1.14; CCSL, 62:15). My attention was drawn to this by Ralph W. Mathisen in *Ecclesiastical Factionalism and Religious Controversy in Fifth-Century Gaul* (1989), 7.

[141] E.g., Paulinus of Nola (ca. 363-431), Honoratus of Arles (bishop ca. 427-29), Hilary of Arles (bishop ca. 429-49), Faustus of Riez (ca. 408-490, bishop of Riez from ca. 455). Nürnberg, *Askese*, 206-69; Rousseau, *Ascetics*. Cf. Rousseau, *Pachomius: The Making of a Community in Fourth-Century Egypt* (1985); Raymond van Dam, *Leadership and Community in Late Antique Gaul* (1985), 119-56; Mathisen, *Ecclesiastical Factionalism*; Brown has dealt with the countercultural aspects of celibacy in *The Body and Society* (1988); Joseph T. Lienhard, *Paulinus of Nola and Early Western Monasticism* (1977).

[142] Brown, *The World of Late Antiquity* (1971, 1974), 109-10; cf. Brown, "Patrons of Pelagius: The Roman Aristocracy between East and West," *JTS*, n.s. 21 (1970), 56-72; Elizabeth A. Clark, *Jerome, Chrysostom and Friends: Essays and Translation* (1979); and Anne Yarborough, "Christianization in the Fourth Century: The Example of Roman Women," *CH*, 45 (1976), 149-65; Dennis E. Trout, "Augustine at Cassiciacum: *Otium honestum* and the Social Dimensions of Conversion," *Vigiliae Christianae*, 42 (1988), 132-46. Cf. Jacques Fontaine, "Valeurs antiques et valeurs chrétiennes dans la spiritualité des grands propriétaires terriens à la fin du IVe siècle occidental," *Epektasis* [Daniélou Festschrift] (1972), 571-95; Patrick J. Geary, *Before France and Germany: The Creation and Transformation of the Merovingian World* (1988), 143-49; Mathisen, *Ecclesiastical Factionalism*, 69-140, et passim. See also the study by Martin Heinzel-

contemplative monasticism[143] and was restated under the label "spiritual nobility" when bourgeois monks were admitted to ancient abbeys as part of the Melk Reform.[144]

The outstanding example of monastic *noblesse oblige* in the West, of course, is Gregory the Great: descended from the Roman nobility, founder of Roman monasteries, yet pressed reluctantly into ecclesial service at a crucial juncture in the history of the western empire, author of *the* manual for episcopal pastoral office throughout the Middle Ages and of the sole source for the life of St. Benedict.[145] Gregory's *Regula Pastoralis* transmitted to the western Middle Ages the "awesome" conception of the priesthood developed against a monastic and contemplative backdrop by Gregory of Nazianzus, who entered pastoral service in large part out of the sense of duty common to the provincial gentry,[146] and by John Chrysostom,[147] whose sense of calling as a preacher resembled Augustine's efforts to integrate the bishop's and preacher's office into life in an ascetic community.[148] The issues raised by Gregory of Nazianzus and Chrysostom were well known to medieval monastics: in a

---

mann, *Bischofsherrschaft in Gallien: Zur Kontinuität römischer Führungsschichten vom 4. bis zum 7. Jahrhundert* (1976), esp. 185-246.

[143] Friedrich Prinz, *Frühes Mönchtum im Frankenreich . . . (4. bis 8. Jahrhundert* (1965), esp. 449-61, 489-548, argues, among other things, that monastic hagiography played a central role in integrating the Graeco-Roman ideal of leisured nobility with the work ethic of early Christianity.

[144] See Schreiner, "Mönchsein in der Adelsgesellschaft," citing, among others, Johannes Keck at Tegernsee. For the late-medieval debate over spiritual nobility, see Volker Honemann, "Aspekte des 'Tugendadels' im europäischen Spätmittelalter," in *Literatur und Laienbildung* (1984), 274-86, discussion, 287-88. The theme of spiritual nobility is ancient—see the statement by Eucherius of Lerins, quoted by Nürnberg, *Askese*, 115: "The highest dignity of nobility is to be counted among the sons of God." *Vita Honorati*, pt. 1, ch. 4, lines 13-14 (SC, 235, p. 78).

[145] Gregory's authorship has been challenged by Francis Clark, *The Pseudo-Gregorian Dialogues* (1987). His thesis has not been widely accepted. Responses are listed in the bibliography under Meyvaert, Clark, Engelbert, Cremascoli, and Verbraken; note also the review by Carole Straw in *Speculum*, 64 (1989), 397-99.

[146] "Oration on His Flight to Pontus and His Return" (SC, 247: 84-240; NPNF, ser. 2, vol. 7, pp. 204-27): Gregory had fled to the wilds of Pontus because he longed for solitude and was ashamed of those who were unfit for pastoral office yet nonetheless pushed their way to the altar of the Lord. He had an overwhelming sense of unworthiness for the difficult task of shepherding souls ("it is harder to learn to rule than to submit to being ruled"—Kempf's renunciation-weakness theme in a nutshell) and was convinced that he was "too weak for war"—precisely the sentiments of Bernard of Waging. He returned out of consideration for the age and frailty of his father, out of longing for his "friends and brothers" among the flock, and out of the conviction gained from a study of scripture, especially the story of Jonah, that flight was wrong.

[147] Louis Bouyer, *History of Christian Spirituality* (1963), 1: 440-44; Jean-Marie Leroux, "Monachisme et communauté chrétienne d'après Saint Jean Chrysostome," in *Vie Monastique*, 143-90.

letter to the Carthusians and his old friend, Guigo I, Peter the Venerable discussed precisely these writings.[149]

Drawing on earlier resources, Gregory the Great exalted the mixed life of the pastor-prelate-preacher who finds strength for his task in contemplation yet also considered the *opus Dei* of the monk to have a pastoral effect on the church: in their prayers, the religious not only intercede and weep for the church, but they also teach by example and word.[150] Gregory was an important source for Kempf, yet he was no proto-Carthusian. His reluctant but genuine appreciation for the mixed life sets him apart from Kempf. Bred for the cloth, like Basil of Caesarea and Gregory of Nazianzus, Gregory's sense of duty was too strong for him to take the path of fighting by yearning *otium* that we have seen in Bernard of Waging and Nicholas Kempf.

Bernard of Clairvaux followed the pattern we have observed in the lives of these patristic figures. One of the great lovers of contemplation in the history of the church yet carrying from his knightly upbringing a sense of sociability and *noblesse oblige*, he took an active role in church and theological politics of his day: from the election of Innocent III through his lobbying at the Council of Etampes, to his pastoring of bishops, nobles, kings, and popes in his letters and travels. He called on the nobles of Europe to join the Second Crusade and helped set up the regency for the king of France while absent on crusade.[151] Although he re-

---

[148] See Frederik van der Meer, *Augustine the Bishop* (1961); Luc Verheijen, *Nouvelle approche de la Règle de Saint Augustin* (1980, 1988); Adolar Zumkeller, *Augustine's Ideal of the Religious Life* (1986); George Lawless, *Augustine and His Monastic Rule* (1987), and idem, "Psalm 132 and Augustine's Monastic Ideal," *Angelicum*, 59 (1982), 526-39.

[149] Giles Constable, ed., *Letters of Peter the Venerable*, (1967), 1: 44-47.

[150] See Gregory, *Regula Pastoralis*; Jean Leclercq in Bouyer, et al., *History of Spirituality*, 2: 3-12; Leclercq, *Love of Learning*, 31-44; Robert Gillet, "Spiritualité et place du moine dans l'église selon saint Grégoire le Grand," in *Vie monastique*, 323-52; Butler, *Western Mysticism*, 221-41; Carole Straw, *Gregory the Great*. Even in his *Dialogues* Gregory gives an active role to Benedict as an urban noble who abandoned his studies to live as a "holy man" and miracle-worker, converting the countryside even while living in the strictest asceticism. Gregory thus transfers the term "vita activa," previously applied to the monastic struggle against vices, to the apostolic life of pastoral ministry. See Charles Dumont, "Saint Aelred: The Balanced Life of the Monk," *Monastic Studies*, 1 (1963), 25-38, at 26, n. 1.

[151] Sommerfeldt, "Consistency," esp. 1-3, 124; idem, "Social Theory," 36; Deseille, "Théologie de la vie monastique," 520-23; Yves Congar, "Die Ekklesiologie des Hl. Bernhards," in *Bernhard von Clairvaux: Mönch und Mystiker*, 79-97; Jean Leclercq, *Saint Bernard mystique* (1948), esp. ch. 13ff; Elizabeth Kennan, introduction to Bernard, *Five Books on Consideration: Advice to a Pope*, trans. Anderson and Kennan (1976), 1-18. See Bernard's *Sermones de diversis*, no. 22, in *S. Bernardi Opera*, 6: 170-71 (= PL 183: 595) on the priority of contemplative life but not to the exclusion of the active life, and on the monastic life as the quickest, most secure path. Cf. Hallier, *Aelred*, 66-78.

mained an advocate of monastic withdrawal from society, Bernard answered, in the spirit of monastic obedience, the call of bishop and pope
for advice and leadership. In Jean Leclercq's view, his famed sermons on
the Song of Songs were not written solely for the edification of the community at Clairvaux, but to combat heresy at Cologne, to teach contemplation to a wide audience, and to refute the errors of Gilbert of
Poitiers.[152] Yet he insisted that pastoral leadership can only be exercised
by those who have first experienced the grace of contemplative union.[153]

Bernard had genuine respect for each of the three orders in society:
married people, prelates and clergy, monks. He did not invariably urge
clerics to leave the world and become monks, rather he sought to encourage those who showed evidence of a genuine monastic vocation.[154] To
prelates and priests he preached the necessity of developing spiritual virtues to equip them for the tasks of governing souls.[155] He counseled William of Saint-Thierry to remain in his office as abbot, although he
recognized William's longing for contemplation and solitude. Even
when Bernard intervened in the schism of 1130 he did not advocate personal holiness at the expense of canonicity of election in choosing between the two contenders.[156] Bernard could respect and appreciate the
life of each of the orders of society and maintain a high view of the office of pastor alongside that of the monk, as long as his society and its
components were intact. Where the lines between the orders were
blurred, as in the case of some of the itinerant advocates of the apostolic

---

[152] Leclercq, "Introduction" to Bernard, *On the Song of Songs*, vol. 2 (1976), xii-xiii.

[153] *Sermones in Cantica Canticorum*, 23.7 (*S. Bernardi Opera*, 1: 143, lines 4-14;
trans. in CF, 7: 31). Cf. sermon, 18.6 (*Opera*, 1: 107, line 23 - 108, line 9; CF 4: 138-39).

[154] *Sermo ad clericos de conversione* [ca. 1140; delivered to student clerics at Paris] in
S. Bernardi Opera, 4: 69-116 (PL 182: 834-56). Sommerfeldt, "Consistency," 175-95,
argues that the sermon is an attempt to convince students and clerics of the limits of reason and the need for a "mystical epistemology" in the life of the secular priest as well as
the religious for whom Bernard made "mystical epistemology" of paramount importance. Cf. Deseille, "Théologie de la vie monastique," 521, and Renna, "Wyclif's Attacks on the Monks," p. 271.

[155] Bernard's ideal for a secular cleric can perhaps best be seen in his *Vita et rebus S.
Malachiae* in *S. Bernardi Opera*, 3: 297-378 (PL 182: 1073-1110), trans. by Robert T.
Meyer (1978). Cf. Bernard's letter no. 42, *Ad Henricum Senonensem Archiepiscopum* in
S. Bernardi Opera, 7: 100-131 (PL 182: 809-34).

[156] See Sommerfeldt, "Consistency," 253-60; Hayden White, "The Gregorian Ideal
and Bernard of Clairvaux," *JHI*, 21 (1960), 321-48; and Sommerfeldt's response in
"Charismatic and Gregorian Leadership in the Thought of Bernard of Clairvaux," in *Bernard of Clairvaux* [Leclercq Festschrift] (1973), 73-90. Elizabeth Kennan expressed
similar reservations about White's arguments in "The *De consideratione* of St. Bernard
of Clairvaux and the Papacy in the Mid-twelfth Century: A Review of Scholarship," *Traditio*, 23 (1967), 73-115.

life, Bernard became critical.[157] This respect for the orders of society differed from Joachim of Fiore's vision of a totally monaticized society in which all orders are subsumed within one contemplative *civitas* or *monasterium*.[158]

The Benedictine tradition, and, in a modified form, the Cistercian tradition, like the pre-Benedictine monastic communities in both the East and the West, had always remained open to active involvement in affairs of church and society. Some have even questioned whether Benedictine monasticism should be described as "contemplative."[159] No one would deny that label to the Carthusians. Perhaps it is false to compare Kempf to Gregory the pope or Bernard, counselor of popes. Was Kempf merely being true to his Carthusian calling?

In a broad sense he was. Although Bruno was called to Rome soon after establishing himself and his colleagues in the "desert" of the Grande Chartreuse, he obeyed unwillingly, and his colleagues were sure that it meant the end of the new foundation. The *Vita antiquior* (mid-thirteenth century) says little about Bruno's accomplishments in Rome. In contrast, the *Vita altera* (1515), while retaining the protestations about the tragic effect of Bruno's departure that are characteristic of the *Vita antiquior* as well as Heinrich Egher of Kalkar's *Ortus et decursus* and most other Carthusian chronicles before the sixteenth century, adds a paragraph about Bruno's contribution to the government of the church, a church that was "in turbatione maxima propter persecutiones Henrici quarti imperatoris." Heinrich Egher of Kalkar, writing in the midst of the Great Schism, was just as concerned about the ecclesiopolitical setting in which Bruno found himself, but locates Bruno's contribution in his withdrawal into the penitential life prescribed for repentant priests who had committed fornication, not in his role as consultant to the pope at Rome. The regimen prescribed for a repentant priest began with the priest's complete seclusion from public view, since as a priest he had played a

---

[157] See especially Chenu, *Nature, Man, Society*, and Thomas J. Renna, "Bernard versus Abelard," in *Simplicity and Ordinariness* (1980), 94-138, at 108-14. See also Duby, *Three Orders*, esp. 222-27.

[158] See the description of the "Dispositio novi ordinis pertinens ad tercium statum" in Marjorie Reeves and Beatrice Hirsch-Reich, *The "Figurae of Joachim of Fiore* (Oxford: Clarendon, 1972), 232-48, and Edith Pasztor, "Ideale del monachesimo ed età dello Spirito come realtà spirituale e forma d'Utopia," in *L'età dello Spirito e la fine dei tempi in Gioacchino da Fiore e nell Gioachimismo medievale* (1986), 55-124. Cf. Reeves, "The Originality and Influence of Joachim of Fiore," *Traditio*, 36 (1980), 269-316; Sandra Zimdars-Swartz, "Joachim of Fiore and the Cistercian Order: A Study of *De vita sancti Benedicti*," in *Simplicity and Ordinariness* (1980), 293-309.

[159] Compare Cuthbert Butler's additions to his *Benedictine Monachism* (1961/1962), 400-403, 410-13, to chapters 18 and 19 of the original as published in 1924.

public role and his sin had public implications.[160] When Kempf retells
the story of Bruno,[161] he does not embellish the incident negatively or
positively, but recounts the event in one terse line and then proceeds immediately to the story of Hugh of Lincoln, the reluctant yet saintly Carthusian bishop of Lincoln.[162] Kempf largely ignores the other examples
of Carthusians who became bishops (Boniface of Savoy, who was Archbishop of Canterbury in the thirteenth century, and a series of bishops of
Grenoble in the twelfth century),[163] and he does so with some justification, for they are exceptions that only prove the rule: Carthusians did
shun the kind of secular apostolic and pastoral work that other monastics
accepted with differing degrees of enthusiasm.

In Kempf's own day, however, the Carthusian order was changing.
Within many urban charterhouses a definite turning toward the world,
described by Jedin as a "Copernican change"[164] was underway. Kempf's
contemporary, Denys of Rijkel, played an active role in church affairs,
accompanying[165] Nicolaus Cusanus during his monastic reform legation
through the Low Countries and writing manuals on nearly every con-

---

[160] *Ortus*, ed. Vermeer, pp. 94-95.

[161] *De confirmatione*, 9/8 (V5, 11v, 29-30).

[162] *De confirmatione*, 9/8 (V5, 12r, 27 - 12v, 14).

[163] For the rather unedifying controversy between the Carthusians and Eugenius III
over the ordination of a Carthusian as bishop of Grenoble, 1149-51, see the summary by
Mursell, *Theology*, 48, drawing on unpublished studies by the archivist at the Grande
Chartreuse. See also Mursell's broader discussion of Carthusian involvement in church
politics, 48-52, 238-45.

[164] Jedin, *Konzil von Trient*, 1: 115. The reference to a "Copernican change" was not
carried over into the English translation. See also Mertens, *Iacobus Carthusiensis*, 13,
233; Rüthing, *Egher von Kalkar*, 262-68; James Hogg, "Everyday Life," 127-28, where
the transformation is explained by the attraction the order held for wealthy patrons, who
in turn endowed Carthusian monasteries near large cities (Paris, Dijon, Straßburg, Cologne, Mainz, Koblenz, Trier, Nürnberg, Florence, Lucca, Pisa, Naples, London, Siena—
which had three charterhouses close to its walls) rather than in remote mountain valleys.
At Nürnberg the crowds at the newly-erected Carthusian church caused the patron of the
charterhouse, Marquard Mendel, to provide for the construction of a separate chapel far
enough from the monastery church to restore the latter to the quiet that was essential for
the Carthusian life. See Heinrich Heerwagen, "Die Kartause in Nürnberg, 1380—1525,"
Mitteilungen des Vereins für Geschichte der Stadt Nürnberg, 15 (1902), 88-132, at 103.
See also Baier, *Untersuchungen . . . Ludolf von Sachsen*, 1: 28-29, who misleadingly asserts that the new urbanized identity must be assumed for all study of late medieval Carthusians, and Paulus, "Kempf" (1928), 22-23.

[165] Heinrich Rüthing, "Die Kartäuser und die spätmittelalterlichen Ordensreformen,"
in *Reformbemühungen und Observanzbestrebungen*, ed. Kaspar Elm (1989), 35-58, at
49, points out that Josef Koch, *Nikolaus von Kues und seine Umwelt* (Heidelberg, 1948),
134, says merely that the two men met at Roermond. That Denys actually accompanied
Cusanus is evident from the prefatory letter to Denys's *Enarrationes in septem Epistolas
Catholicas, Dionysii Opera Omnia*, 13: 539-40, cited by Karel Swenden, "Dionysius van
Rijkel—Biografische Nota," *Ons geestelijk Erf*, 24 (1950), 170-81, at 177.

ceivable topic of interest to lay and religious readers from all walks of life: from princes and soldiers, archdeacons and bishops to parish priests and widows. His entire ecclesiology reveals a much more positive evaluation of the secular clergy and episcopacy than do Kempf's writings.[166] Largely self-taught, Denys sought to apply the scholastic theology of the Cologne Thomists and Albertists to the Carthusian mystical tradition, and thus represents a scholastic version of the urban, humanist opening to the world found in charterhouses at Basel, Erfurt, Nürnberg and elsewhere. Not surprisingly, Denys seems to have been attacked from within the order for being "un-Carthusian."[167]

The most important aspect of the "Copernican shift" involved manuscripts and books, a straightforward development from the Carthusian interest in copying manuscripts that caught the eye of outsiders as early as the twelfth century. In the late fifteenth and early sixteenth century, the Basel charterhouse[168] regularly loaned its books to nonmonastics. Indeed, the librarians Georg Carpentarius (d. 1531) and Ludwig Moser (d. 1510) kept a record of approximately five hundred books loaned between 1482 to 1528: among the borrowers were the printers Johannes Amerbach and Hieronymus Froben in search of classical texts, but also secular priests, university students and professors, and schoolmasters.[169] Heinrich Vullenho's foreword to a codex containing treatises on the nature of the Carthusian life explained that it had been assembled so it could be loaned for the edification of interested outsiders. A special abridgement of William of St.-Thierry's *Golden Epistle*, made for the same purpose, has survived in multiple copies.[170] The lay brothers' library, consisting largely of books in German, was likewise extensive, both in number of volumes and range of material. It was not unique

---

[166] Eugen Ewig, *Die Anschaungen des Kartäusers Dionysius von Roermond über den christlichen Ordo in Staat und Kirche* (1936).

[167] See Kent Emery, Jr.'s discussion of Denys's *De contemplatione*, in which he blurred the distinction between the active and contemplative lives, in Emery, "Twofold Wisdom." Denys defended himself against his unknown attacker in his *Protestatio ad superiorem suum, Opera*, 41: 625-26.

[168] On the Basel charterhouse in general, see the chronicle of the monastery edited by Wilhelm Vischer and Alfred Stern in *Basler Chroniken*, vol. 1 (1872), 233-548, and *Cartusiana*, 2: 236-37.

[169] Mertens, *Iacobus Carthusiensis*, 63-65, referring to Basel UB cod. A I 4. Max Burckhardt, "Bibliotheksaufbau," has provided a more detailed analysis of the catalogues and the use of the library. Cf. Carl Christoph Bernoulli, "Über unsere alten Klosterbibliotheken," *Basler Jahrbuch* (1895), 79-91, at 83-86; Hubert Elie, *Les Editions des statuts de l'Ordre des Chartreux* (1943), 16-25.

[170] Volker Honemann, "The Reception of William of Saint-Thierry's *Epistola ad fratres de Monte Dei* during the Middle Ages," in *Cistercians in the Late Middle Ages* (1981), 5-18, at 14-15. The reference is to Basel, UB, cod. A VII 20 and A IX 14.

among charterhouses: the urban Carthusian communities at Mainz and
Cologne also had large vernacular libraries, as did the rural charterhouse
at Schnals in South Tyrol.[171]

Perhaps the most interesting aspect of the "lending library" in the
Basel charterhouse is the justification given by Vullenho for the copying
of books that were intended for loan[172]:

> We Carthusians have written in our statutes: "Because we are not able to
> preach with our mouth the word of God, at least let us preach it with our
> hands, namely, in the copying of books of edification, exhortation, and de-
> votion."

This passage, from Guigo's *Consuetudines*, chapter twenty-eight,[173]
had already served generations of Carthusians as a justification for their
own work of copying manuscripts primarily for internal use.[174] Here it
finds an expanded application: not only do Carthusians copy works of

---

[171] Sexauer, *FrühneuhochdeutscheSchriften*, has reconstructed the Basel lay brothers'
catalogue. See also Burckhardt, 40-41, with citations to additional secondary literature.
Sexauer, who has edited two vernacular translations of lay brothers' statutes, including
the Gaming translation that may have been carried out under Kempf's supervision (see
appendix A), suggests that vernacular manuscripts in Carthusian libraries may have been
used by persons outside the monastery in addition to use by lay brothers for whom they
were primarily intended. Sexauer's findings also make it clear that some Carthusian lay
brethren were literate, even though earlier Carthusian legislation, reaffirmed as late as
1432, forbade lay brethren to learn to read. See the summary in Gillespie, "Cura Pastoralis," 166. For Mainz, where the lay brothers' library catalogue has not survived, see
Heinrich Schreiber, *Die Bibliothek der ehemaligen Mainzer Kartause, die Handschriften
und ihre Geschichte* (1927), 20-24.

[172] Carthusian booklending began early. One of the anecdotes most frequently retold
by college lecturers involves precisely this sort of commerce between Cluny and the
Grande Chartreuse. In letter 24 Peter the Venerable not only sighs over the burdens of
office but points out that he cannot send one of the books requested by the Carthusians,
since much of it had been eaten by a bear in one of Cluny's dependent granges. Giles
Constable, ed., *Letters of Peter the Venerable* (1967), 1: 47.

[173] The chapter is titled, "De utensilibus cellae." See also Erich Kleineidam, "Die
theologische Richtung der Erfurter Kartäuser am Ende des 15. Jahrhundert," in *Miscellanea Erfordiana* (1962), 247-71, at 249 (repr. 1983). "Manibus praedicare" was quoted
and credited to Cassiodorus in the Carthusian chronicle, *Laudemus* (ca. 1260). See Wilmart, "Chronique," 117, cf. P. J. Gumbert, *Die Utrechter Kartäuser und ihre Bücher im
frühenfünfzehntenJahrhundert* (1974), 308-12. Peter the Venerable also used the phrase
in letter 20. Note also Gillespie's application of the phrase to issues of external pastoral
care, "Cura Pastoralis," 172-81.

[174] Carthusian libraries, like all monastic libraries, had always loaned books, but primarily to other charterhouses or to monasteries of other orders. Already in the twelfth
century Guibert of Nogent remarked upon the fine library the Grande Chartreuse had assembled. See Guibert de Nogent, *Autobiographie*, I.11, ed. Edmond-René Labande,
(1981), p. 68. Cf. Giles Constable, ed., *Letters of Peter the Venerable*, vol. 1, pp. 45-47,
vol. 2, p. 112.

edification and exhortation, but the immense libraries[175] they accumulate through copying are now made accessible to people from all literate walks of life.[176] Alluding to the opening of Gregory the Great's *Regula pastoralis* (which in turn alludes to Gregory of Nazianzus), the north German Carthusian, Werner Rolevinck went so far as to describe printing as the *ars artium*, a new means of pastoral care.[177]

At Nürnberg and Paris Carthusian libraries were also the source of texts for some of the first printed books.[178] At Erfurt the library catalogue was intended more for internal use, but its very comprehensiveness and systematization indicate the trend toward research utility that characterized the urban Carthusian setting.[179]

The Carthusians at Cologne, with their splendid library and vigorous spiritual and intellectual life, took a leading role in inspiring the re-

---

[175] On Carthusian libraries in general, see Paul J. G. Lehmann, "Bücherliebe und Bücherpflege bei den Kartäusern," in *Miscellanea Francesco Ehrle*, vol. 4 (1924), 364-89 (repr. 1960), including the text of a treatise by Oswald of the Grande Chartreuse, a friend of Jean Gerson, on how to copy, collate, and emend manuscripts; J. de Ghellinck, "Les catalogues de bibliothèques médiévales chez les chartreux et un guide de lectures spirituelles," *RAM*, 25 (1949), 284-98. Cf. Kleineidam, "Theologische Richtung"; Heinrich Schreiber, *Die Bibliothek der ehemaligen Mainzer Kartause* (1927); Gumbert, *Utrechter Kartäuser*; Thompson, *Carthusian Order*, 313-34; Richard B. Marks, *The Medieval Manuscript Library of the Charterhouse of St. Barbara in Cologne* (1974).

[176] Indeed, before long, the Carthusian lending libraries had become too successful for their own good—at Cologne, the librarian's code of 1558 placed strict limits on borrowing of books by outsiders, forbidding them to browse in the library, because "many poor monks and students in great numbers steal our books by putting them up their sleeves or in their pockets." Marks, *Library*, 32.

[177] Dieter Mertens, "Früher Buchdruck und Historiographie," in *Studien zum städtischen Bildungswesen* (1983), 83-111, at 85, n. 9, with reference to additional literature.

[178] At Nürnberg the works of Thomas a Kempis, Denys of Rijkel, and William of Paris came from the Charterhouse. See Machilek, "Klosterhumanismus," 14, 16, 25-27; Reimann, *Pirckheimer*, 161-96; Gerhard Pfeiffer, ed., *Nürnberg—Geschichte einer europäischen Stadt* (1971), 102, 131; F. Eichler, "Groß, Erhart," in *Verfasserlexikon*, rev. ed., 2: 102-6. Peter Danhauser's dedicatory epistle to [Ps.-] Denys of Rijkel (actually Jacob van Gruitrode), *Specula omnis status humane vitae* (Nürnberg: Peter Wagner, 1495) mentions plans to hold a Platonic symposium in the Nürnberg Charterhouse. See Emil Reicke, *Willibald Pirckheimers Briefwechsel* (1940), vol. 1, p. 25, n. 41. At Paris, the nearby charterhouse of Vauvert furnished Lefèvre d'Etaples with manuscripts of works by Ramon Lull and possibly of Jan Ruusbroec, Hildegard of Bingen, and Mechthild of Hackeborn. See Augustin Renaudet, *Préréforme et humanisme à Paris . . . (1494-1517)*, 2nd ed. (1953), 482-83, 512-13, 597, 621-22, 635-37; cf. H. Bernard-Maitre, "Un théoricien de la contemplation à la chartreuse parisienne de Vauvert: Pierre Cousturier dit Sutor (c. 1480-18 juin 1537)," *RAM*, 32 (1956), 174-95, at 175, citing Renaudet; Eugene F. Rice, Jr., "Jacques Lefèvre d'Etaples and the Medieval Christian Mystics," in *Florilegium Historiale* [Ferguson Festschrift] (1971), 90-124.

[179] Kleineidam, "Theologische Richtung," analyzes the theological presuppositions on which the Erfurt charterhouse's library catalogue was based. See *Mittelalterliche Bibliothekskataloge Deutschlands und der Schweiz*, ed. Paul Lehmann (1928), 2: 232-593.

newal of Catholic spirituality in the sixteenth century.[180] They also sought to transform preaching by hand into preaching through publishing, including, for a time, a press in the cloister itself (something not unknown in Benedictine[181] or mendicant houses, but unusual for Carthusians, even for the urban houses).[182] Carthusians also played important roles in the translation of devotional classics into the vernacular (Ludwig Moser and Georg Carpentarius at Basel[183]).

Nor was the Carthusian "apostolate" outside the cloister walls limited to the lending of manuscripts and printing of books. In the late fifteenth century Geiler of Kaysersberg (1445-1510), Jacob Wimpfeling (1450-1528), Johannes Heynlin of Stein (1430/33-96),[184] and Erasmus all placed much of their hope for reform in a program of education for the clergy.[185] Heynlin himself became a Carthusian and Wimpfeling's clerical reform efforts were assisted by Carthusians.[186]

---

[180] See *Cartusiana*, 2: 267-69; Gérard Chaix, *Réforme et Contre-Réforme*; idem, "Les traductions de la Chartreuse de Cologne au XVIe siecle," in *Kartäusermystik und -mystiker* (1982), 5: 67-78; idem, "Sainte-Barbe, Cologne et l'empire au XVIe siecle," in *Die Kartäuser in Österreich* (1981), 3: 96-111; Alois Winklhofer, "Johannes vom Kreuz und die Surius-Übersetzung der Werke Taulers," *Theologie in Geschichte und Gegenwart* [Schmaus Festschrift] (1957), 317-48; Joseph Grevin, *Kölner Kartause*; Matthäus Bernards, "Zur Kartäusertheologie des 16. Jahrhunderts: Der Kölner Prior Petrus Blomevenna," in *Von Konstanz nach Trient* [Franzen Festschrift] (1972), 44-79; Marks, *Library*, 131-35.

[181] See, for example, Josef Bellot, "Das Benediktinerstift St. Ulrich und Afra in Augsburg und der Humanismus," *SMGB*, 84 (1973), 394-406, at 398-99.

[182] On the Cologne printing press, see Zadnikar and Wienand, *Die Kartäuser*, pp. 232-33.

[183] On Moser and Carpentarius, see Sexauer, *Frühneuhochdeutsche Schriften*, ch. 3; *Cartusiana*, 1: 138; Herman Gumbel, "Moser, Ludwig," in *Verfasserlexikon*, vol. 3: 434-37; Walter H. Haller, *Studien zur Ludwig Moser, Kartäusermönch in Basel* (1967).

[184] Heynlin wrote an *Epistola de qualitate sacerdotis*. He entered the Basel charterhouse in 1487. While prior of the Sorbonne, 1467-1473, he, together with Guillaume Fichet, helped recruit from Germany the first printers in the city. See Beat Matthias von Scarpatetti, "Heynlin, Johannes, de Lapide," *Verfasserlexikon*, rev. ed., (1981), 3: 1213-19. Heynlin was a professor at Basel, Tübingen, and Paris; a preacher at Basel; and a friend of the Upper Rhein circle of humanists. See Max Hossfeld, "Johannes Heynlin aus Stein," *Basler Zeitschrift für Geschichte und Altertumskunde*, 6 (1907), 309-56, and 7 (1908), 79-219, 235-398; Manfred Lemmer, "Brant, Sebastian," *Verfasserlexikon*, rev. ed., 1: 992-1005.

[185] See Friedrich Oediger, "Über die Klerusbildung im Spätmittelalter," *HJ*, 50 (1930), 145-88.

[186] Paulus, "Kempf" (1928), 22-23, notes that Sebastian Brant exempted the Straßburg Carthusians from his acerbic attacks on religious orders. Brant's "Carmen sapphicum" to the Carthusians is well known. See Adam Wienand, "Ein Loblied auf die Kartäuser von Sebastian Brant, Basel," in *Die Kartäuser*, ed. Zadnikar and Wienand, 238-41. See also Walter Baier, "Johannes Nicolai," 155-79, and *Cartusiana*, 2: 365-66. For the Straßburg Charterhouse in general, see Francis Rapp, "Chartreux et ville dans l'Empire: le cas de Strasbourg," in *La naissance des chartreuses* (1986), 237-58, esp. 249-51.

Gregor Reisch (ca. 1470-1525) entered the Freiburg Charterhouse but maintained contact with a wide circle of friends, including Erasmus, Wimpfeling, Beatus Rhenanus, Ulrich Zasius, and Geiler von Kaysersberg. A former teacher of the Catholic reformer Johannes Eck, he also advised Emperor Maximilian and helped edit Erasmus's Jerome edition, even as he served the Carthusian order by helping with the 1510 Amerbach edition of the Carthusian statutes.[187]

At Basel, Georg Carpentarius, who studied at the university in Basel at the same time as Ulrich Zwingli (1503-4), translated Erasmus's anti-Reformation writings and chronicled the Reformation in Basel, 1521-28.[188] At Cologne and at one of the Yorkshire charterhouses Carthusians wrote world chronicles.[189] The impact of English Carthusians on lay spirituality and the role of the London Charterhouse has only begun to be explored.[190] Especially in the larger German cities the Carthusians seemed to be retracing at a distance the mendicant, Benedictine, and Camaldolensian path toward becoming pious *litterati* suited for the salons of the urban elites.[191]

---

[187] Contrary to the conventional interpretations, Mertens, "Kartäuser-Professoren," 76, insists that Reisch did not continue to teach at the University of Freiburg after entering the charterhouse. See also Petreius, *Bibliotheca Cartusiana*, 109-12; *ADB*, 28: 117; *Cartusiana*, 1: 153-54; Rowan, "Chronicle," 154-59; Robert Ritter von Srbik, *Maximilian I und Gregor Reisch* (1961). For his role in compiling and publishing the Carthusian statutes see Elie, *Les éditions*. One of Reisch's students, Otto Brunfels, was described by Linnaeus as the "father of botany." Brunfels left the charterhouse in 1521 for a career as a pastor, teacher, and author of a popular *Flugschrift* against tithes. See *NDB*, 2: 677, and *Vom Pfaffenzehnten* in *Flugschriften der Bauernkriegszeit*, ed. Adolf Laube and Hans Werner Seiffert (1978), 158-77.

[188] For these aspects of Carpentarius's activity, see Sexauer, *Frühneuhochdeutsche Schriften*, 193-99, with citations to additional literature.

[189] See James Hogg, "The Ways of God to Man: The Carthusian Chronicle of Universal History in Oxford Bodleian Library MS. E. Museo 160," in *Kartäuserliturgie und Kartäuserschrifttum* (1989), 152-63, with citations to further literature. This sort of activity parallels Reisch's involvement with Hartmann Schedel's *Nürnberg Chronicle* and early cartography as described by Rowan, "Chronicle." The Cologne chronicle, Werner Rolevinck's *Fasciculus Temporum*, was published in 1474.

[190] For the *Cloud of Unknowing* and its circle, see James Walsh's introduction to the CWS edition. A devotional anthology written on the eve of the Reformation, *The Pomander of Prayer* was the subject of an essay by Robert A. Horsfield, "*The Pomander of Prayer*: Aspects of Late Medieval English Carthusian Spirituality and Its Lay Audience," in *De Cella in Seculum* (1989), 205-13. For London see David Knowles and W. F. Grimes, *Charterhouse* (1954), 13, and Thompson, *Carthusian Order* (1930), 167-98.

[191] Mertens, "Kartäuser-Professoren," 82: "Es scheint so, daß die zu Kartäusern gewordenen Akademiker die Praxis des Ordens in litteris verändert haben. Im 15. und 16. Jahrhundert—das wollen die Gelehrtengeschichten der Welt apologetisch beweisen—besitzen die Mönche des hl. Bruno etwas, das Bruno als Mönch nicht mehr gesucht hat: literarische und wissenschaftlich-gelehrte Bedeutung." See also Elm, "Mendikanten und Humanisten," and Stinger, *Humanism*.

But this portrait of a Carthusian "Copernican shift" is deceptive, since these developments were limited to the urban charterhouses, most of which were relatively recent foundations. And even there we find parallels to Kempf's more traditionally Carthusian attitude opposed to involvement outside the monastery. The most striking parallel is found in Jacob Kunike de Paradiso (d. 1465).

Jacob de Paradiso (Jacobus de Clusa, Jakob of Jüterbog)[192] matriculated at the University of Cracow in 1420 as a forty-year-old Cistercian from the monastery of Paradyz (near Meseritz in Poland). He abandoned a career as a professor of theology and preacher at the university to become a Carthusian at Erfurt in 1443. Toward the end of his life Jacob defended a doctrine of flight from the world that is even more radical than Kempf's, a complete rejection of pastoral work outside the monastery, including involvement in monastic reform.

Jacob de Paradiso had not always held an apocalyptic view that the times were too perilous for monastic involvement of any sort outside the cloister. Whereas in writings from 1452 to 1456 he clearly placed the pursuit of the *salus propria* ahead of the *salus aliorum*, his *De dignitate pastorum et cura pastorali* of 1442 had stressed the high calling of the pastoral office (citing Chrysostom, Gregory, Augustine, Ambrose, and Bernard) and referred to pastors and prelates as the *columnae ecclesiae*. Although he cautioned against seeking the "honors" rather than the "onerousness" of the pastoral office, and emphasized that the apostles were compelled (*coacti*) into the *cura animarum*, this pre-Carthusian treatise lacked the pessimistic, radical flight from the pastoral office that is evident in Jacob's *Ars moriendi* (1452).[193]

Even after becoming a Carthusian, Jacob initially remained active in monastic reform. At the request of leaders in the Bursfeld reform, he wrote a *Formula reformanda religiones* (1444), and he delivered conferences to provincial chapters of the Bursfeld congregation in 1452 and 1455. His works were widely copied in reformed Benedictine houses and he corresponded with the Bursfeld reformer, Johannes Busch. Jacob's concern for general church reform is most visible in his *Avisamenta ad*

---

[192] See Ludger Meier, *Die Werke des Erfurter Kartäusers Jakob von Jüterbog in ihrer handschriftlichenÜberlieferung* (1955), and Mertens, *Iacobus Cartusiensis* (cf. *DSAM*, 7: 52-53), for a summary of the literature. Several of Jacob's works were published in the eighteenth century, including one in Pez's *Bibliotheca ascetica*, vol. 7. Many more are found in fifteenth- and sixteenth-century editions, but apart from Porebksi's edition of the *Opuscula inedita*, no modern editions exist. See also Petreius, *Bibliotheca Cartusiana*, 151-56.

[193] I have used a copy of the *De dignitate pastorum et cura pastorali* found in Innsbruck, UB, cod. 633, 174r-192v (Charterhouse of Schnals in South Tyrol). Jacob also wrote *De negligentia prelatorum*, a work I have not seen. See Meier, *Werke*, no. 65.

papam pro reformatione ecclesiae, sent to Nicholas V in 1449. Resolution of these ambiguities and of the development in Jacob's viewpoint between 1442 and 1452 require study of the manuscript record, for which Meier, Mertens, and others have provided an introduction.

Jacob's later statements *against* the pastoral office for religious in his *Ars moriendi* did not go unchallenged. His fellow Carthusian at Erfurt, Johannes Brewer of Hagen,[194] prior at Eisenach, 1454-56, and at Erfurt, 1457-60, and also a consultant in Benedictine reform,[195] contentiously[196] disputed Jacob's claim that the best way to avoid sin and thereby to avoid damnation is to spurn all offices and all contact with officeholders.[197]

In Johannes of Hagen's view, the *cura animarum* does not lead to sin for all but a few, virtually unapproachable, *viri heroici*, as Jacob had argued.[198] Rather, the *cura animarum* is an obligation for all who are fit (*idonei*) for it. Far from a rare exception, an active life in the pastorate can be lived without falling into sin, if one avoids placing oneself in situations where the stimulus to sin becomes overpowering. Johannes of Hagen's concern lies as much with an *ars bene vivendi* as with *ars moriendi*. True to his concern with the art of living rightly, Johannes cites

---

[194] From Hagen (between Minden and Hildesheim), b. 1415, Johannes may have studied arts at Cologne and began law studies at Erfurt in 1439. He abandoned his university career in January 1440 to become a novice at the Erfurt charterhouse, Mons S. Salvatoris. See Joseph Klapper, *Der Erfurter Kartäuser Johannes Hagen, ein Reformtheologe des 15. Jahrhunderts* (1961), 266-71; H. Rüthing, "Jean Hagen" in *DSAM* 8: 543-52; Erich Kleineidam, "Theologische Richtung,", 266-71; Mertens, *Iacobus Carthusiensis*, 206; Petreius, *BibliothecaCartusiensia*, 162-94; *Cartusiana*, 1: 112-13. Many of the Erfurt Charterhouse codices containing his works are now found at Parkminster Charterhouse, Sussex, England, although one of his commonplace books is in the Newberry Library in Chicago, MS 67.3 (Erfurt Charterhouse C142, cf. Klapper, *Hagen*, 2: 428-29). The Parkminster codices are available on microfilm at Hill Monastic Manuscript Library, Collegeville, Minn.

[195] Klapper, *Hagen*, 113-17.

[196] *Chartae . . .1457-65*, 94, *1466-74*, 125. The entry for 1460 refers to an earlier disciplinary action, giving 1454 as the date. The Chartae for 1454 contain no reference to Johannes of Hagen, a fact that puzzled a seventeenth-century reader, who made a note to that effect in the margin. Klapper notes that he was overly critical of the Erfurt Charterhouse's use of *donati* to staff an incorporated parish while using the income from the parish's tithes, apart from a small stipend for the vicar, for the monastery. See Josef Klapper, *Hagen*, 1: 28-30.

[197] The entire debate, including Jacob de Paradiso's reaction to Johannes of Hagen's criticisms, is discussed at length with copious excerpts from the writings of both men in Mertens, *Iacobus Carthusiensis*, 206-42. I am dependent on this account.

[198] In *De vera, perfecta, et spirituali caritate*, ch. 4 (V2, 5r, 34 - 5v, 4), Kempf cites Aristotle's [*Nichomachean*] *Ethics*, VII.1, to the effect that not all are capable of heroic virtues or divine perfection. He couples this with Mt. 19:11: "Non omnes capiunt verbum istud, sed quibus datum est."

concrete examples of how merchants and others active in the world can reduce their exposure to temptation by ethical choices in business practice or other aspects of daily living. To follow Christ, Johannes insists, is to be active in preaching, ministry, and in good works. He not only denies that the *cura animarum* is an inevitable temptation to sin and threatens one's salvation; he insists that the pastorate is fruitful and has potential for merit. *Perfectio* is not limited to a certain status, and the monastic life, rather than being *the* embodiment of *perfectio* and *religio*, is merely a refuge for those who are not suited (*idoneus*) for the pastorate.[199] Kempf, Bernard of Waging, and Jacob de Paradiso would agree with this last point—and meekly concede their unsuitedness, weakness, lameness, and blindness.[200]

Who represents the Carthusian tradition here? Jacob de Paradiso's world-denying *Ars moriendi* far surpassed the works of Johannes of Hagen in popularity.[201] Yet, within the cities that had become the centers of culture in the late Middle Ages, Jedin's "Copernican shift" held sway among Carthusians—until the more powerful currents of the urban Reformation swept through, overwhelming charterhouses in Nürnberg, Erfurt, London, and elsewhere.

Living on the periphery of the Holy Roman Empire, far from any sizeable city and probably coming from a *petite bourgeoise* background one generation removed from the village, Kempf had a variety of reasons for narrowing his vision to the monastic microcosm and thus siding with the "old" Carthusian tradition, even though he outlived Jacob de Paradiso by thirty years. Although Kempf quoted Gregory, Bernard, and Augustine on the necessity for monks to answer the pastoral call when it comes from God and not from their own presumption, he restricted that pastoral activity to the cloister. He recognized that someone has to take up the care of souls outside the monastery, but he left the call to that task to God's providence. Indeed, he went to some length to woo clerics from the care of souls and from ecclesiastical careers to the *schola monastica*, although he seems not to have wanted to dissuade anyone who had a

---

[199] Ironically, a parish incorporated into the Erfurt Charterhouse became a main point of contention during the sixteenth-century Reformation in Erfurt. See Robert W. Scribner, "Civic Unity and the Reformation in Erfurt," *Past and Present*, 66 (1975), 29-60, and Joachim Kurt, "Die Reformation und ihre Auswirkung auf die Erfurter Kartause zur Zeit von 1517-1555," in *Die Kartäuser und die Reformation* (1984), 92-118, at 103-10.

[200] For debates over pastoral involvement outside the monastery among English Carthusians, see Gillespie, "Cura Pastoralis," 168-72.

[201] Jacob's *Ars moriendi* is found in fifty manuscript copies and two printed editions, mostly from Carthusian and reformed Benedictine circles, while Johannes of Hagen's polemic against Jacob was scarcely noticed. Mertens, *Iacobus Carthusiensis*, 232.

genuine call to the secular priesthood. His concern lay with those who sought pastoral office for the wrong reasons and his concern was for what they would do to the church and their own souls if they became pastors. Even within the monastery he did not make a virtue of necessity when the Bride is awakened from contemplative slumber to answer the knock at the door. It must be answered, to be sure, but only for a time; mercifully, before long, the contemplative will be able to return to proper repose.

Kempf had a high standard for the pastor, in keeping with the Vienna school, but he applied it only to the monastic microcosm. Yet, with Gregory the Great, he believed firmly that monks fulfill an essential pastoral role for the entire church precisely by their contemplation. Like Moses, Judith, Esther, and the Virgin Mary, these noble and "solitary friends of God" may yet obtain mercy from God for his errant people. They are indeed "liberators of their people." Kempf's vision of freedom is an ancient, biblical and contemplative one that runs fully counter to the growing drive for communal, territorial, and individual freedom in the Renaissance and Reformation. His monastic love for *otium*, while it seems similar to Petrarch's and other humanists' longing for leisured solitude, was based on a social vision that was disappearing in the wake of the urban and commercial growth. His reform vision looked "back" to earlier monastic centuries when each order in society had its legitimate place and when a type of perfection was thought to be possible for all, each in his own state of life.[202] To explore both the similarities and differences between Kempf's vision of solitude and social responsibility on the one hand, and that of Petrarch on the other, is the task of the following chapter.

---

[202] See Gerhart B. Ladner, "Homo Viator: Medieval Ideas on Alienation and Order," *Speculum*, 42 (1967), 233-59.

CHAPTER SEVEN

LEADING THE RETREAT

One day a Lover approached the home of his Beloved. He knocked on the door. A Voice within responded to the knocking: 'Who is there?' The Lover answered: 'It is I'. The Voice within spoke, almost sadly: 'There is no room here for me and thee'. The Lover went away and spent much time trying to learn the meaning of the words of his Beloved. Then one day, some time later, he once again approached the home of his Beloved and, as before, knocked on the door. Once again, as had happened earlier, the Voice within asked: 'Who is there?' This time the Lover answered: 'It is Thou'. And the door opened and he entered the home of his beloved. [Sufi story retold by William H. Shannon in "The Spirituality of Thomas Merton," *Cistercian Studies*, 25 (1990), 233-45, at 233. Used by permission.]

1. The Idea of Reform

Can one legitimately refer to Nicholas Kempf's vision of reform and renewal through renunciation and retreat as a reform program? Or, if that much is indeed granted, must one not conclude that it is a quietistic, self-defeating reform program that represents an aberration of little consequence in the broad stream of late medieval and early modern history? Do not contemplative religious, by the very nature of the life they have been called to live, relinquish their claim to affect the larger church and society? Are they not perhaps even to be viewed as counter-cultural and sectarian in their attitude toward society and the church? Herbert Workman offers the classic sectarian Protestant interpretation of monasticism: "from the first Monasticism lay over against the Catholic Church, . . ." and "has rarely attempted to reform the Church, much less the State."[1] Yet Gerhart B. Ladner has made the monastic vision central to the patristic and medieval vision of reform.[2] The present chapter seeks to clarify

---

[1] Herbert B. Workman, *The Evolution of the Monastic Ideal*, 2nd ed. (1927; repr. 1962), 11-20. Cf. Owen Chadwick, *John Cassian*, 63-64.

[2] Ladner, *The Idea of Reform*, and "Die mittelalterliche Reform-Idee und ihr Verhältnis zur Idee der Renaissance," *MIÖG*, 60 (1952), 31-59, are perhaps most directly relevant to the themes of the present chapter. Cf. John Van Engen, "Images and Ideas: The Achievements of Gerhart Burian Ladner, with a Bibliography of his Published Works," *Viator*, 20 (1989), 85-115; see also Lewis W. Spitz and Charles Trinkaus in

Kempf's understanding of reform, using Petrarch's flirtation with solitude and the monastic life as a foil. For all his fascination with and longing for contemplative withdrawal, the poet laureate of fourteenth-century
Italy could not embrace the reform through renunciation presented by
classic contemplative monastic theology. In the end, he could not abandon his own drive to fashion himself in the image of God instead of permitting his self to be re-formed from the outside.

In Ladner's view, in the late Middle Ages, the Christian idea of reform took three main forms: the *imitatio Christi* of the *devotio moderna*
and Franciscan writers,[3] the *perfectio* idea as distilled from the monastic
tradition and defined scholastically by Aquinas (*STh.*, IIa, IIae. q. 184),
and the *reformatio* of the conciliar movement. The roots of the monastic
reformatio-perfectio ideal lie in the first centuries of monasticism. Seeking personal salvation, the monks of the Egyptian and Syrian deserts entered solitude in order to lead on earth the life of the angels and saints in
heaven, to find an answer to the question of the rich young ruler, "What
shall I do to be saved?" (Mt 19:16-22). Theirs was a personal *reformatio*
under the guidance of spiritual directors—the *seniores* who preceded
them into the desert. The monastic profession was a second baptism, a
second cleansing from sin, a washing that regenerates and renews. In its
permutations into communal, coenobitic monasticism and its application
to the church as whole, especially through the efforts of Basil the Great
in the East and Augustine in the West, this monastic *reformatio* provided
the foundation for ecclesial reform.[4]

Dictionary of the History of Ideas, ed. Philip P. Wiener and others (1973), 4: 69,
146; J. Leclercq, "The Bible and the Gregorian Reform," *Concilium*, 17 (1966), 63-67;
Konrad Repgen, "'Reform' als Leitgedanke kirchlicher Vergangenheit und Gegenwart,"
RQ, 84 (1989), 5-30.

[3]   The distinctiveness of this form of spirituality is underscored in an article by Ewert
Cousins, "Francis of Assisi: Christian Mysticism at the Crossroads," in *Mysticism and
Religious Traditions* (1983), 163-90. See also Stanislaus Grünewald, *Franziskanische
Mystik: Versuch einer Darstellung mit besonderer Berücksichtigung Bonaventura*
(1936); Kurt Ruh, "Zur Grundlegung einer Geschichte der Franziskanischen Mystik," in
Altdeutsche und altniederländische Mystik (1964), 240-74, and Richard W. Southern,
The Making of the Middle Ages (1953), 219-57.

[4]   Although for Augustine everything on earth has some similitude to God, Christ is
the only perfect image of God; humans reflect that image imperfectly. See Ladner, *Idea
of Reform*, 185-97. But cf. John Edward Sullivan, *The Image of God: The Doctrine of St.
Augustine and Its Influence* (1963), esp. 21-22, 39-41, and Gerald Bonner, "Augustine's
Doctrine of Man: Image of God and Sinner," *Augustinianum*, 24 (1984), 495-514. The
Greek theologians' pursuit of assimilation to God becomes in Augustine a union with the
Trinity in the psychological *imago Dei*, and Augustine's principal vehicle for carrying
into effect his idea of reform was his "ideal of a monastic or quasi-monastic life for cler-
ics and laymen." Ladner, "Reform-Idee," 48-52. Zumkeller, *Augustine's Ideal*, 103-44,
provides a narrative index to Augustine's ideas about the monastic life, drawing on his

In the western Middle Ages the monastic ideal as *the* way of *reformatio imaginis Dei* remained strong. Aelred of Rievaulx's *Mirror of Charity* will serve paradigmatically here.[5] Fundamental to his understanding of the monastic life is Aelred's teaching on the image of God in the very essence of the human being, making humans *capax Dei*. Having lost through sin the likeness, but not the image, of God, the human problem is to recover that likeness, to return like the prodigal son from the land of unlikeness.

> Aelred's monastic doctrine . . . is primarily a doctrine of salvation. The Christian flies from the world and withdraws into solitude with a high end in view, that of securing his salvation. . . . Far from savoring of selfishness, this withdrawal from the world proclaimed the primacy of the spiritual over the temporal and the monk's strong conviction of the one thing necessary. . . . The monastic life was regarded primarily as a means, the most excellent of all means, to lead fallen man back to God. The Abbot of Rievaulx explicitly pointed out the difficulty confronting all men of effecting this necessary return and the relative ease offered by the cloister to those who desired to fix themselves deliberately on the way to God. (Hallier, 68)

The pilgrimage of this restoration involves primarily the *affectus* (defined as an inclination or sudden, unpremeditated liking), yet does not occur without the *intellectus*. The journey back is cast in terms of *eruditio* and *disciplina*, an ascetic process of individual formation that occurs in the monastic community. One cannot read Aelred's *Mirror of Charity* without being struck by his powerful social and communal vision. The reformation of the image of God in the soul is inextricably bound up with the reform of the community. In part III of his *Mirror* he expounds the seven Sabbaths of social love, concentric circles of love of self, friends and family, all Christians, Jews and heretics, and enemies. Rather than gloss over or deny the variety that exists in human relationship— from family and friends to bitter enemies—he affirms that the same yearning for and love of God that drives one along the path from unlikeness to likeness, from sin to salvation, also undergirds a healthy society.[6]

---

entire corpus. See especially 172-87 on the restoration of the image of God, which is recognizable through contemplation.

[5] As masterfully described by Amédée Hallier, Aelred was above all a teacher and his monastery a school. The French title of Hallier's book, *Un éducateur monastique: Aelred de Rievaulx*, captures this conviction better than the title of the English version: *The Monastic Theology of Aelred of Rievaulx*.

[6] *Mirror*, III.1-6 (CCCM, 1: 105-14); ET by Elizabeth Connor, annotated by Charles Dumont, CF 17 (1990).

By withdrawing to the monastic microcosm for the sake of giving one-self completely to love of God one nonetheless contributes to, indeed makes possible, the healing for all of society—Christian and non-Christian alike.

2. Petrarch and Monasticism

The Christian monastic-perfection-*reformatio* tradition is not the only western approach to renewal. Gerhart Ladner also notes the existence of a classical, vitalistic rebirth and renaissance tradition. In nineteenth-century scholarship, thirteenth- and fourteenth-century Renaissance humanism was described as a conscious reappropriation of classical models. Since the twentieth-century "revolt of the medievalists," the continuities between the Renaissance and the Christian Middle Ages have been emphasized.[7] It should surprise no one that the question of an interrelationship between Renaissance humanism and medieval monasticism has been raised.[8] A closer examination of Petrarch's love-hate relationship with the monastic life may permit us to glimpse better the process of transition from a monastic-led medieval world to the early modern urban-commercial society.

Giles Constable, Anna Maria Voci, and Jean Leclercq have recently examined Petrarch's attitudes toward monastic life.[9] Constable notes that the writings in which Petrarch deals with monasticism were among his most popular works during his lifetime: *De otio religioso, De vita solitaria*, his letters to his brother Gerard the Carthusian, his meditations on the Penitential Psalms. In these writings he never criticizes monasticism and frequently praises it lavishly. The central period of his monastic enthusiasm was 1343 to 1353[10]; during his last twenty years, he made

---

[7] See the collection of essays edited by Albert Rabil, Jr., *Renaissance Humanism*, 3 vols. (1988), especially volume 1, for a summary of scholarship updating Wallace Ferguson's classic work, *The Renaissance in Historical Thought* (1948).

[8] See chapter two, nn. 106-108, above, for literature.

[9] Giles Constable, "Petrarch and Monasticism," in *Francesco Petrarca: Citizen of the World* (1980), 53-99 (repr. 1988); Anna Maria Voci, *Petrarca e la vita religiosa* (1983); Jean Leclercq, "Temi monastici nell'opera del Petrarca," *Lettere italiane*, 43 (1991), 42-54. Voci views Petrarch's "monastic writings" as secular transpositions of the *eremitic* monastic ideal.

[10] Hans Baron has furthered reduced the significance of Petrarch's flirtation with monasticism, describing it as an untypical interlude: "For about six years in the middle of his humanistic career, his thinking differed both from the humanism of his youth and from the mature thought of his last two decades; it is an interlude for which no other

fewer references to monasticism but maintained contacts with many monks and monasteries—Benedictines, Camaldolese, Carthusians, Celestines, Cistercians, Dominicans, Franciscans, Vallombrosans. Leclercq's study took account of recent evidence that a second brother of Petrarch was a Benedictine of the Olivetan congregation.[11] In other words, despite Voci's strictures, Constable and Leclercq have shown that Petrarch knew monks and their way of life well and was known by them.

Petrarch's interest in monasticism was reciprocated from the monastic side. In Northern Europe, Carthusians played an important role in the transmission of his writings,[12] beginnning with Arnold the Carthusian (d. 1411) in the Low Countries,[13] who, however, carefully removed the lengthy digressions and numberless allusions to classical literature from his version of *De remediis*.

Although Constable says Petrarch had no coherent view of the nature of the monastic life,[14] it seems fair to say that he genuinely admired monks[15] and did understand what their life involved at its core—submis-

---

writing of Petrarch's is more informative than the *Secretum*." *Petrarch's Secretum: Its Making and Its Meaning* (1985), vii.

[11] Giuseppe Billanovich, "Un ignoto fratello del Petrarca," *Italia medioevale e umanistica*, 25 (1982), 375-80; I have not seen the article by Mauro Tagliabue and Antonio Rigon, "Fra Giovannino fratello del Petrarca e monaco olivetano," *Studi petrarcheschi*, n.s., 6 (1989), 225-55, announced by Leclercq in "Temi Monastici," p. 44.

[12] My survey of surviving manuscripts from Germany, Switzerland, and England, for copies of Petrarch's *De vita solitaria*, *De otio religioso*, and the *Secretum*, yielded the following results: unknown provenance (19); nonmonastic private provenance (13); monastic provenance (17). Six of seventeen monastic copies were Carthusian (but three of the six came from a single charterhouse—Mainz), three were Cistercian, and two were Benedictine. See the various volumes of the Censimento dei codici petrarcheschi, listed under "Manuscript Catalogues" in the Bibliography, as well as Michael Jansenas, ed., *Petrarch in America: A Survey of Petrarchan Manuscripts* (1974). The situation in France was different, probably reflecting in part the fate of Carthusian libraries there. The Censimento volume by Elisabeth Pellegrin, reports the following: unknown provenance (5); nonmonastic private provenance (9); monastic provenance (11). The monastic copies came from Benedictine (6), Victorine (3), Williamite (1), and Cistercian (1) houses. None came from charterhouses. Of course, any statistical analysis based on surviving manuscripts is of limited significance. Voci offers a survey of monastic copies of *De vita solitaria* in Germany, France, and Italy, *Petrarca*, 132-35.

[13] Nicholas Mann, "Recherches sur l'influence et la diffusion du 'De remediis' de Pétrarque aux Pays-Bas," in *The Late Middle Ages and the Dawn of Humanism Outside Italy* (1972), 78-88, and M. A. Nauwelaerts, "Rodolphe Agricola et le Pétrarquisme aux Pays-Bas," ibid., 171-81. Cf. George W. McClure, "Healing Eloquence: Petrarch, Salutati, and the Physicians," *JMRS*, 15 (1985), 317-46, at 332-33. Petrarch's most popular Latin work in Low Countries was *De remediis utriusque fortunae*, but in the abridged form produced by Arnold ca. 1400 (published 1470).

[14] "Petrarch and Monasticism," p. 72.

[15] Some have doubted this; Constable affirms it, "Petrarch and Monasticism," pp. 67-69.

sion to the rule, to the yoke of obedience—although he tended to focus on other aspects.[16] Indeed, it was precisely obedience that proved the stumbling block for him, as we will see in our examination of his struggle with *acedia*. He simply could not bring himself to submit to a rule and regarded himself as constitutionally unable to make a full commitment. His "monastic theology" reached its climax in *De otio religioso*, written for and influenced by Carthusians. But he remained outside the monastic life, and that makes all the difference. Petrarch's struggle throughout his life was with himself. He was well aware of the pitfall of trusting in his own strength for salvation. But the very strength of his consciousness of self kept him from the kind of self-abandonment required by a monastic rule.

We see this in *De vita solitaria*, where a key element of his "retired man's" good life is independence—the worst type of "busy man" is one who is at others' beck and call in order to make a living: "Perhaps you will think the condition of those persons happier who are taken up with other people's business. They, however, are ruled by the power of another man's nod and learn what they must do from another man's look. *They can claim nothing as their own.*" As we have seen in·chapters one and four above, this is exactly the opposite of the Carthusian statutes, in which the novice is exhorted to claim nothing as his own, not even himself. Petrarch continues:

> Between these men and such as are condemned to pass their lives in the dungeons of rulers and kings I know not what difference there is except that the former are bound with chains of gold, the latter with iron. The chain is fairer, the servitude equal, the blame greater, because they do of their own accord what the others are compelled to do by force.[17]

The distance between this and the ancient monastic concept of servitude, voluntary bondage, of being prisoners (desert fathers) should be clear.

Petrarch made an effort to incorporate monastic elements into his life in the world.[18] *De vita solitaria*, I.2.1-2, outlines some of these ele-

---

[16] Significantly, obedience is missing in Petrarch's list of the things he admired in the Carthusian way of life: poverty, repose, brethren, silence, solitude, forests, nocturnal chants, celestial peace, friendship with God, eternal life—contrasted with life in the world (Constable, "Petrarch and Monasticism," p. 68). Constable notes Petrarch's awareness of the role of obedience later (p. 85).

[17] Petrarch, *De vita solitaria*, Bk. I, tract. 3, ch. 1, ed. Antonio Altamura (1943), 30; translated by Jacob Zeitlin, *The Life of Solitude by Francis Petrarch* (1924), 122-23.

[18] Constable, "Petrarch and Monasticism," 75.

ments. The retired man rises early, goes to a flower-filled spot on a "salubrious hill" and

> breaks joyously with pious lips into the daily praises of the Lord, the
> more delightedly if with his devout breath are harmonized the gentle mur-
> mur of the downrushing stream and the sweet plaints of the birds. He first
> prays for innocence, a bridle for his tongue to make it ignorant of conten-
> tion, a shield for his eyes to protect them from vain sights, purity of heart,
> freedom from delusion, and continence which tames the flesh. Soon after,
> during the third set of praises, he worships the third person in the Trinity,
> and prays for the visitation of the Holy Spirit, for a tongue and a mind that
> sound forth saving confession, and for charity burning with a heavenly
> flame for the enkindling of one's neighbors.[19]

There is much that is monastic here—e.g., the clear allusions to the
contents of the daily office. But there is also much that is not, notably, an
inappropriate *context* for the *opus Dei*. Petrarch's description is idealized, with little awareness of the sort of discipline needed to counter distraction in the day-in, day-out cycle of canonical hours. In the light of the
treatises written about the perennial monastic struggle to discipline wan-
dering minds in choir, it would most difficult to maintain regular recitation of all seven hours in the sort of romanticized setting that he offers as
a helpful context, as a structural element of his quasi-monastic retirement
(note how he pairs the "salubrious" hill to "salvific," healing, "confession" [*saluberrimem collem*; *salutifera confessio*]). Moreover, the very
freedom of movement that the retired man enjoys, in contrast to the busy
man thronged about by clients and lawsuits, conflicts with the fundamental principle of monastic claustration and *stabilitas*.

Petrarch's *De vita solitaria* is also unmonastic in its advocacy of total solitude and directness. The retired man pursues Christ alone, without
any human mediation.[20] Even the solitary Carthusians for whom he
wrote *De otio religioso* reserved a significant role for the community and
for spiritual direction. There is little room for the latter in Petrarch—its
place is taken by the pursuit of literature. Generally one can say that *De
vita solitaria* and *De otio religioso* are not written from long experience
in solitude or even the quasi-monastic life. That Petrarch was unsuccess-

---

[19] Altamura ed., I.2.1-2., pp. 23-24; Zeitlin translation, pp. 111-12, slightly modified.
Boccaccio uses similar language, with explicit reference to the Desert Fathers as his
model, in bk. 14, ch. 11 of his *Genealogiae Deorum*. See Giovanni Boccaccio, *Genealogie Deorum gentilium*, ed. Vincenzo Romano (1951), 2: 712. I owe this reference to
Carol A. N. Martin.

[20] Altamura, I.5.3., p. 46-47; Zeitlin, I.4.8, pp. 146-47.

ful in living even the quasi-monastic life he embarked upon is evident from the *Secretum*, where the problem is *acedia*, a purportedly urban vice that Petrarch claimed the well-regulated solitary life would eliminate.[21] Petrarch's inner strength permitted him greater confidence in his ability to achieve solitude of spirit even in the absence of solitude of space, as when necessity forced him into the city.[22] He credits the ability to do this to the wise counsel of Quintilian, which he had memorized and which he quotes here at length. Although Kempf agreed that one could have solitude of spirit even in the absence of solitude of place,[23] a traditionalist Carthusian like Kempf took the easy way out and tried mightily to ensure that no necessity ever drove him into the city. Solitude of place may not be necessary, but the whole point of *De recto fine* was to underscore how much solitude of place can help achieve solitude of spirit.[24]

As Constable rightly notes, Petrarch's flirtation with the monastic life was largely a response to his brother's entry into religion. Reacting more than following a clear sense of vocation, he wavered back and forth. And he knew that he was wavering and indecisive: "Petrarch was keenly aware of these weaknesses and depressed by his inability to overcome them."[25] This may be the key to understanding what Petrarch was experiencing. As we have seen from Kempf's writings, monks know their weaknesses only too well—it is the recognition of weakness, of one's inability to discipline one's own will, that brings them to seek the assistance of a rule and spiritual direction. Refusing to be overconfident in his ability to discipline himself, yet refusing to become depressed by his inability to overcome that weakness, the monk lets the rule overcome

---

[21] Altamura, I.9.4 - I.10.1; Zeitlin I.6.4-6.

[22] Altamura, 1.4.2, p. 38; Zeitlin 1.4.3, pp. 135-36: "Apud me, inquam, cui ut verum fatear, non tam proprio studio, aliove monitu, ut ita sentirem, quam naturae ipsius persuasione consultam est, vita proculdubio singularis ac solitaria, non modo tranquillior, sed altior est atque securior. . . . Sed ita, ut si qua me necessitas in urbem cogat, solitudinem in populo, atque in medio tempestatis portum mihi conflare didicerim, artificio non omnibus noto, sensibus imperitandi, ut quod sentiunt non sentiant."

[23] See chapter three, p. 85, above.

[24] See Guigo, *Consuet.*, ch. 41, 50, 64. Obviously these restrictions applied best to the Grande Chartreuse, but it is in the spirit of these that so many charterhouses were located in isolated valleys, and it is obvious that Kempf wished to minimize contacts with the outside world as much as possible. These are the issues that were at stake in the controversies carried on in fifteenth-century urban charterhouses. See chapter six, above.

[25] Constable, "Petrarch and Monasticism," 76-81; cf. Davy A. Carozza and H. James Shey, "Introduction" in *Petrarch's Secretum*, trans. Carozza and Shey (1989), 22: "If Petrarch never achieved peace of mind, it was surely for the same reason that Francesco would never achieve it. The entire dramatic logic and energy of the *Secretum* brings Francesco to a point where he should abandon his secular studies; but he cannot, precisely because Petrarch himself could never abandon them."

his weakness, gratefully accepting the rule as a crutch. Petrarch was trying to overcome his will's wavering weakness without a crutch, by main
force. Unable to do so, he suffered from depression and *acedia*.

Constable is correct to point out, echoing Trinkaus, that Petrarch
had no blindly optimistic *theology* of human nature, yet equally important is the realization that in *practice* he was still trying to get by without
a crutch. Constable puts a good face on it all: "In fact, his failure to follow this course [right course of life, moral rightness] or to become a
monk was not owing simply to weakness of will. His pride, sensuality,
melancholy, and love of fame, which he saw as sins, were also positive
qualities feeding his creative genius."[26]

Monks enter a monastery not so much by willpower as by recognition of their lack of it. If Petrarch lacked weakness of will, i.e, had a
strong will (creative genius), that is precisely why he could never be a
monk and to his credit, he realized it—something modern scholars have
not noticed. With Wilkins, Constable asserts that Petrarch's quasi-monastic austerities and practices "were a matter rather of personal piety
than of formal obedience, [which] shows all the more clearly the influence of Gerard's monastic practices on his brother's life. . . . Certainly
Petrarch lived more like a monk than most clerics, and I dare say many
monks, of his time."[27]

This is not exactly untrue, but it still misses the point that, without
crossing the threshold of obedience, these personal pious practices were,
despite all their similarities to monastic life, quite different. In effect,
Constable suggests that Petrarch retained the substance of monasticism
while rejecting its form, especially obedience.

Yet form cannot be so easily separated from substance. One can be
a sincere onlooker who has only good things to say about monasticism
(unlike many of Petrarch's contemporaries), yet still be separated by a
wide gulf from the monastic life. Indeed, the very fact that Petrarch attempted to transfer traditional contemplative life outside the cloister
walls, far from indicating his quasi-monastic orientation, could indicate
how little he and his contemporaries really understood about the essence
of monasticism. What was once the solution—the wall of the Rule and
the self-alienating obedience to a superior that is central to the monastic
vision—has become the problem.

If this book's analysis of Kempf, Luther, and Contarini is correct,
the difference between Petrarch and Kempf lies in a different understanding of the self. The roots of the modern interiorized self should

---

[26] Constable, "Petrarch," 85.
[27] Constable, "Petrarch," 85-86.

probably be sought in the urban and commercial growth of the eleventh and twelfth centuries, but its budding begins only in the Renaissance and its blossoming comes in the eighteenth and nineteenth centuries. In two published articles and in a series of unpublished articles, F. Edward Cranz has offered an interpretation of Augustine and the medieval tradition similar to the one outlined here. The anthropology of Christian antiquity assumed an external source for the human self that was nonetheless "within" the human self: the *imago Dei*. In the wake of the epistemological changes of the twelfth century (the first "nominalism" of Abelard in which the mind legislates or creates concepts), a new understanding of the human person emerges with profound implications for understanding God and the Trinity, as well as contemplative union. Cranz locates the crucial changes, the emergence of a new understanding of an intensive rather than extensive self, precisely with Petrarch and Nicolaus Cusanus[28] rather than with Augustine, at whose feet the discovery of modern or quasi-modern interiority is often laid. Augustine "turned inward," to be sure, but what he found inwardly was an extensive image of an "Other"—the Trinity.[29] Sin's distortion of this image of God caused it to curve in upon itself instead of letting it extend itself toward God as it was intended to do.

Both Petrarch's strong will and his love of unmediated solitude are aspects of his intensive rather than extensive understanding of the self. In the opening of book two of the *Secretum* Franciscus announces, "I have no hope from within myself, my hope is from God." Augustinus proceeds to show how much he does trust in himself. Franciscus disputes it,

---

[28] Professor Cranz graciously supplied copies of his four unpublished talks. They are partially summarized and applied to a contemporary secular educational vision by Robert E. Procter in *Education's Great Amnesia: Reconsidering the Humanities from Petrarch to Freud* (1988), arguing that Cicero also held an extensive understanding of the self. Cf. idem, "The *Studia Humanitatis*: Contemporary Scholarship and Renaissance Ideals," *Renaissance Quarterly*, 43 (1990), 813-18. The main outlines of Cranz's interpretation are found in F. Edward Cranz, "Cusanus, Luther, and the Mystical Tradition" in *The Pursuit of Holiness* (1974) 93-102, and "The Transmutation of Platonism in the Development of Nicolaus Cusanus and of Martin Luther," in *Nicolo Cusano agli inizi del mondo moderno* (1970) pp. 73-102. Cranz asserts that the ancients identified the human self with the eternal *nous* within the human self.

[29] In this regard I find the interpretation of Augustine offered by Charles Taylor, *Sources of the Self: The Making of the Modern Identity* (1989), 127-39, problematic. Taylor emphasizes the importance of Augustine having found God's image when he "turned inward," but does not adequately wrestle with the "otherness" of a Creator-God. Instead of this being a "turn to radical reflexivity" (131), I would consider it a turn to extensivity. That one can discover an extrinsic, alien Person at the very core of one's self underscores the remarkable paradox of Christian insistence on a personal Creator become incarnate. This, it seems to me, is the point of *Confessions*, X.24-26: God dwells in the human memory yet finding God there leads the creature to the Creator, not to itself.

and Augustine says he could argue the point but will let Franciscus's own conscience convict him.[30]

Petrarch was aware of how much he was departing from the extensive tradition. He knew that hope and help must come from outside himself in the manner we have seen Kempf describe. Yet he could not escape loving himself, loving "his prison house" (484). That is what placed him close to despair. He knew all about Augustinus's extrinsic answer—that help comes from outside oneself—but it did not seem to work for him and he seemed to end up with Pelagian self-salvation (pp. 498-502). Petrarch opens *De vita solitaria* with the following *credo*: "I believe that a noble spirit will never find repose apart from God, in whom is our end, *or* in himself and his secret thoughts, *or* in some intellect united by a close likeness with his own."[31] Note that he gives three options, one of which is oneself. He continues: "But whether we are intent upon God or upon ourselves and our worthy pursuits—by which we pursue both [God and ourselves]—or whether we are seeking for a mind like our own, we ought to withdraw as far as may be from crowds of people and bustling cities" (I.1.1).

To this point our analysis has drawn on *De vita solitaria* and the *Secretum*. As we shall see, *De otio religioso* modifies some of these elements. It forms an important element of Charles Trinkaus's examination of Petrarch's anthropology and theology, of his understanding of the human will, the human condition, and divine salvation.

Trinkaus's description of Petrarch rings true. But his conclusion that Petrarch's views were "centrally Christian", as much as it may appear to be supported by *De otio religioso*, rests on an intensive-self reading of the medieval tradition and especially of Augustine. The present study's conclusions support an extensive reading of Augustine's understanding of self. The very text with which Trinkaus opens his book,[32] from *De trinitate*, bk. 12, ch. 11, seems to point the *imago Dei* anthropology more toward the Creator than the human self (obviously both referents are possible; the issue here is relative emphasis).

> For the true honor of man is the image and likeness of God, which is not preserved except it be in relation to Him by whom it is impressed. The less therefore that one loves what is one's own, the more one cleaves to God.

---

[30] Ponte edition, p. 474, 482.

[31] Cranz, "Luther, Cusanus," cites precisely this "parody of Augustine" as his main example of the new definition of the self found in Petrarch.

[32] Trinkaus, *Image*, 1: xiii.

But through the desire of making trial of his own power, man by his own bidding, falls down to himself as to a sort of intermediate grade.

Trinkaus explains: "It will be our thesis that the new vision of man in this period found its inspiration in a revival of the *patristic* exegesis of the Genesis passage: 'And He said: "Let us make man in our own image, after our likeness.""[33] Trinkaus would agree that Petrarch used Augustinian voluntaristic *imago dei* anthropology to create a proto-modern intensive self,[34] as his detailed explication of Petrarch in the opening chapter of his book makes clear. Yet this intensive self seems to me to be foreign to, not faithful to, Augustine[35] and the medieval monastic tradition, as outlined by Ladner. There is a difference between a theology in which the image of God consists in an emulation of the Creator by means of man's "trial of his own powers" and the monastic theology of meekness, weakness, lameness, and blindness in which even the trial of man's own powers is an act of God.[36] Even if the Augustine passages cited above permitted the sort of interiorizing interpretation given them

---

[33] Ibid. Cf. Trinkaus, *The Poet as Philosopher* (1979), esp. ch. 2, and "Italian Humanism and the Problem of 'Structures of Consciousness'," *JMRS*, 2 (1972), 19-33.

[34] "The central conclusion of this book is that the Italian Renaissance, conceived essentially along Burckhardtian lines, was accompanied by a powerful assertion of a philosophy of will by leading representatives of Italian humanism and among philosophical circles influenced by them. . . . Moreover, some of its leading proponents found inspiration in the prescholastic Christian theological tradition, drawing the full eudemonist and voluntarist implications from the theology of St. Augustine for the first time. . . . The assertion of an energetic, individualist drive for fulfilment as a major motif of Renaissance culture by Burckhardt thus found its theoretical statement and justification among the humanists. But it found it . . . in a plea for a renewal of a theology of grace as the acceptance that divine force alone was capable of restructuring the naturally egotistical motivations of mankind towards higher ethical and religious goals. Moreover the capacity and drive of man to command and shape his world was regarded as an emulation of divinity, since it was in this respect that man was created in the image and likeness of God" (xx-xxi, cf. xiii-xiv).

[35] I find corroboration for my reading of Augustine in A. M. Neiman, "The Arguments of Augustine's 'Contra Academicos'," *Modern Schoolman*, 59 (1982), 255-78 and idem, "Augustine's Philosophizing Person: The View at Cassiciacum," *New Scholasticism*, 58 (1984), 236-55. That medieval Carthusians read (Pseudo-) Augustine this way is indicated by Guigo de Ponte, *De contemplatione*, III.2 (Dupont ed., p. 260), where, speaking of contemplative life as "peaceful and suitably ordered [*decora*, gentle and loveable, hidden and yearning. It seeks God, thirsts for God, and clings to God. As Augustine says, 'I owe myself more to myself than to others, yet I owe myself to God much more than to myself.'" The purported citation from Augustine has not yet been verified in his writings, but Guigo reveals that he understood Augustine to have set forth an inward search for an orientation beyond oneself toward God.

[36] Kempf, *Ost*, ch. 45 (G1, 34r, 13-19). The entire chapter is reproduced in appendix B.

by Trinkaus and Taylor, Nicholas Kempf is clear on the point: the image of God in man points primarily toward the Creator.

In contrast to the psychological paralysis so characteristic of Petrarch,[37] the monks, as we have seen, dumped their sins on the shoulders of another, indeed, an Other. Erich Loos[38] and Siegfried Wenzel[39] have explored Petrarch's struggle with *acedia* in considerable detail, concluding that Petrarch departed significantly from the medieval tradition. The root meaning of *acedia* is indifference, or freedom from concern, and it came to be used as equivalent to the hermits' noonday demon of listlessness, restlessness, and flagging commitment. John Cassian defines *acedia* as *anxietas sive taedium cordis*. He added the parallel vice of *tristitia*, from which come irritability, pusillanimity, bitterness or bearing grudge, despair (*rancor, pusillanimitas, amaritudo, desperatio*). As Jean Leclercq has noted in his *Otia Monastica* the line between good *otium* and bad *otium*, good "freedom from cares" and bad "restlessness," is a narrow one. For Kempf and the monastic tradition, the rule creates *otium* but also creates structures to combat *acedia*, since the ego is at the root of both *acedia* and the excess *sollicitudo* that prevents good *otium*. Loos and Wenzel emphasize that Petrarch's *acedia* is not so much spiritual restlessness[40] as solicitude over the harsh blows of fortune.[41]

Our purpose here is not to disparage Petrarch's deep Christian piety, but simply to insist on the nonmonastic character of that piety. His writings, even those that laud the monastic life, are a tapestry woven from ancient classical sources rather than a plaited carpet of scriptural allusions characteristic of such great monastic masters of Latinity as Bernard of Clairvaux. With all due respect for Petrarch's many admirers, a humble monastic simplicity simply is missing from his writings.[42] The differ-

---

[37] Trinkaus, *Image*, 15-17, 29-30.

[38] "Die Hauptsünde der *acedia* in Dantes *Commedia* und in Petrarcas *Secretum*: Zum Problem der italienischen Renaissance," in *Petrarca, 1304-1374: Beiträge zu Werk und Wirkung* (1975), 156-83.

[39] "Petrarch's Accidia," *SR*, 8 (1961), 36-48, and *The Sin of Sloth: 'Acedia' in Medieval Thought and Literature* (1967).

[40] See Russell, "Noonday Demon"; idem, "Acedia—The Dark Side of Commitment," *Review for Religious*, 47 (1988), 730-37.

[41] Trinkaus agrees with Wenzel insofar as the Petrarch of the *Secretum* is concerned but argues that *De otio religioso* follows the medieval, religious, understanding of *acedia*.

[42] E.g., *De otio religioso*, 750-54, 758-772, where long lists of classical authorities follow the disclaimer that time fails him to cite them. Cf. pp. 702, 704, 706, 728, 730, 734, and his concluding chapter in *De vita solitaria*, where he humbly claims he can not hold a candle to the ancients, even though they lacked the truth available only through Christ's humility—yet concludes with the best flourish of classical eloquence he can manage. "As it is, the original source of eloquence [i.e., the ancients, esp. Cicero] allures

ence was obvious to the monks who did so much to popularize Petrarch's monastic writings in northern Europe—with the classical "fillers" removed.

If these differences are kept in mind, a comparison of Petrarch and the monastic tradition can be fruitful. The monks did have much in common with the early humanists, but submission to a rule out of recognition of one's weakness and need for a crutch (submission not in theory or intent but as a lived reality) separates Petrarch from those behind the wall of the rule. Trinkaus has suggested that humanist rhetoric and language served as a rule, as the structure of the humanists' lives.[43] The parallel is valid, but once more the difference lies in the fact that language is not extrinsic to man in the same way that the monk's rule is. How could this tool which the humanists crafted and shaped so fondly and fulsomely be a standard for them? At best they would be measuring themselves by themselves—by a crooked rule that makes everything it measures crooked—to quote Dorotheus of Gaza.[44]

Yet Petrarch comes so very close to the monastic vision at points. Trinkaus devotes a major portion of his discussion of Petrarch to his views on assurance of salvation, justification, and faith in Christ's work as enunciated in book I of *De otio religioso*.[45] Petrarch asks how there can be any proportion between God's majestic perfection and human weakness. His inner turmoil is caused by the combination of a realization that God is powerful to save and the fear that he [Petrarch] is un-able to be saved. God's mercy may be great but it certainly cannot exclude justice. Such considerations seem to lead to despair. But God's mercy transcends human misery, and even if it does not extinguish justice, it tempers it and restrains it. He places his hope in Christ's work and clings to hope.

---

us by clear brilliance of style, but it is without the true light of doctrine. It soothes the ear but it does not give repose to the mind nor lead it to that highest and securest enjoyment, that peace of the intellect to which, though wicked and headstrong men despise it, there is no approach save through the humility of Christ. These things I have addressed to you with such affection of mind that every rustle of the branches breathed upon by the wind and every ripple of the waters gushing from the ground about me seems to say a single thing: 'You argue well, you counsel uprightly, you speak the truth." Note that the imagery here is the same as that used in describing the setting of his morning prayers in I.2.2. *De vita solitaria*, II.10.10; Altamura, 154-55; translation from Zeitlin, pp. 315-16.

[43] *Image*, xxv.

[44] See chapter four, p. 116, n. 11, above.

[45] Rotondi/Bufano ed., 624-30.

This, therefore, is the sum of it: cling to hope, let no one take that away from you; and if what we hope for may well be large, they are large matters to us; to God nothing is large before Whom "our substance is as if nothing," and before Whose eyes "a thousand years are as yesterday when it passes." They are great things, I admit, indeed immense if compared to human merits. Elevate your minds to the Giver: everything will seem very small and not only possible but easy. For what is it, I ask, which makes hope waver and souls shake? We seem worthy of punishment, unworthy of mercy, and in both we are not mistaken: for it is our part to be afflicted, His to be merciful. And it is a worthy thing for His dignity to swallow up our lack of dignity, which certainly could not happen if the sin of man could impede the mercy of God. So be it, therefore, that we are worthy of hatred: He is worthy of mildness and mercy: He is worthy to spare, worthy to hate nothing of all the things which He made, worthy to abandon no one of those whom the Father delivered unto Him.

Trinkaus comments that Petrarch expressed a quasi-Pelagian view of free will in the *Secretum* but that his real struggle was with despair, which he countered by placing an exhortation to trust in grace in the mouth of Augustinus.

> . . . in the *De otio*, grace is fully affirmed, but again desperation is the great danger. For him the foundations of religion are psychological, and not epistemological. If one can have assurance, can feel confident that one's inevitable human actions will not lead to perdition if mercy is desired because of the infinity of divine benevolence, if one believes that one has been *saved* or can be *saved* from the almost infinite mass of self-centredness and affective responsiveness to the external world, then the epistemological problem becomes insignificant. In comparison to this absolute contrast of human sin and weakness with divine benevolence and power, anything can be believed. Faith for Petrarch springs from hope, disbelief from despair.[46]

In Petrarch's own words:

> Thinking over these matters, since all works of God towards humankind seem miracles and full of ineffable grace, nothing seems impossible, nothing incredible; since this foundation stands that God is omnipotent and all-benevolent, nothing can be imagined so magnificent that He cannot do it, so beneficent that He does not wish it. . . . God has come among men borne of a virgin and dwelt among us, taught us the way of life; having been crucified, He suffered and died, descended to the lower regions, de-

---

[46] Trinkaus, *Image*, 1: 31-32.

spoiled Hell, ascended to heaven and is awaited for judgement. These are great things, I admit, but what of all these is impossible to God?[47]

Thus Trinkaus concludes that Petrarch's solution was a psychological movement "from subjective pathos to faith, . . . to a posture of confidence and trust in saving grace."[48] Both Nicholas Kempf and Petrarch struggled with despair, with the very possibility that a just God could save sinners. Both were deeply conscious of sin. The difference between them—superficially slight but actually deep—is that Kempf's *securitas*, his solution to inner turmoil and despair, was the monastic *life*, the structure of the rule and obedience to a third person, to a spiritual director.

Especially toward the end of *De otio religioso*, Petrarch affirms strongly the necessity of help from outside oneself, of trust in God's mercy.[49] Without the assistance of grace one is unable to master the body. The meekness-weakness language of monastic renunciation is present: Christ tells us to learn of him for he is meek and lowly of heart. Christ is father, lord, master, and our God and he wants us not to learn of him virtues that we could not imitate anyway, rather, he wants us to learn what is most appropriate for men—meekness and humbleness of heart.[50] Do not trust in human strength, in horses or bows, for God is our salvation, our strength, our *securitas*. There is only one remedy for God's wrath: be still, fear, hope and pray that he will have mercy.[51] Stand back, be available for God, and taste and see his goodness; know yourself and find yourself in God.[52]

---

[47] Rotondi/Bufano ed., pp. 628, 630; quoted and translated by Trinkaus, *Image*, 1: 32.

[48] Ibid.

[49] E.g., Rotondi/Bufano ed., pp. 716, 720, 740, 744, 798-90. See also Klaus Heitmann's remarkable study of the tension between human and divine resources in Petrarch's struggle to understand fortune, fate, and Christian providence: *Fortuna und Virtus: Eine Studie zu Petrarcas Lebensweisheit* (1958).

[50] Rotondi/Bufano ed., 740-42.

[51] "Quod est autem beneplacitum regis nostri, quo salvari nostra possit infirmitas? Certe illud etiam scimus: 'Beneplacitum est Domino super timentibus eum et in eis qui sperant super misericordia eius' [Ps 146:11]. Hic est rectissimus trames ad salutem, hic sequendus est nobis; 'non in arcu nostro sperabimus et gladius noster non salvabit nos' [Ps 43:7], sed 'dextera Dei et brachium eius et illuminatio vultus eius' [Ps 43:4]. . . . Hec est, non alia, salus nostra; hec nostra virtus, hec nostra securitas, hoc remedium unicum contra iram Domini: vacare, timere, sperare et orare 'ne in furore suo arguat nos neque in ira sua corripiat nos' [Ps 6:2 = 37:2], sed eam longe faciat a nobis 'amoveatque plagas suas' [Ps 38:11]; et interim ita vivere ut audientiam et misericordiam mereamur. Amanda nempe misericordia, tremenda iustitia; hanc bonis actibus mitigemus, illam piis precibus imploremus." Rotondi/Bufano, p. 744.

[52] Rotondi/Bufano, 798, 800.

Petrarch caught much of the monastic vision. Indeed, nearly all the elements are in place—recognition of human inadequacy, recognition that only God can save. It would be easy to conclude that he shared the monastic vision outside the monastery's walls. Yet precisely therein lies the difference. A genuinely monastic vision includes the realization that without the wall of the rule there is no monastery, that without formation extrinsically through obedience to another no monastic *persona* can take shape. Without an extrinsic crutch, a person's *own* mighty efforts to surrender him*self* to simple trust in God's grace almost invariably end up as attempts at self-salvation.

Petrarch was a complex person. As Constable rightly notes, the tension within which he lived contributed to his creative genius. It will not do simply to subsume *De vita solitaria* and the *Secretum* under *De otio religioso*. Nor can we talk about a progressive development, since *De otio religioso* is far from his last work and he continually revised and rewrote most of his works. Indeed, if Baron is right, already with the *Secretum* he began to return to the more "secular" orientation of his early years and abandoned the "singular preoccupation with medieval values" that characterized *De otio religioso*, and *De vita solitaria*, having realized "that in solitude he was not able to experience God as fully as he was experiencing the two secular components of the solitudinarian life."[53] Instead we must recognize the tensions with which he lived, for they were the tensions of a changing world in which the crutch of the monastic wall and rule had become more and more a question mark.[54] The Petrarch of the *Secretum* and of *De vita solitaria* is as much the "real" Petrarch as the Petrarch of *De otio religioso*. In the last-mentioned work he comes extremely close to the monastic vision and it is no acci-

---

[53] Baron, *Petrarch's "Secretum"*, 246-47.

[54] Note Thomas Merton's comments in response to Pope Paul VI's request for a "message of contemplatives to the world," quoted in M. Basil Pennington, ed., *Monastery: Prayer, Work, Community* (San Francisco: Harper and Row, 1983), p. 13: "My dear Brother, first of all, I apologize for addressing you when you have not addressed me and have not really asked me anything. And I apologize for being behind a high wall which you do not understand. The high wall is to you a problem, and perhaps it is also a problem to me. Perhaps you ask me why I stay behind it out of obedience? Perhaps you are no longer satisfied with the reply that if I stay behind this wall I have quiet, recollection, tranquility of heart. . . . My flight from the world is not a reproach to you who remain in the world, and I have no right to repudiate the world in a purely negative fashion, because if I do that my flight will have taken me not to truth and to God but to a private, though doubtless pious, illusion. Can I tell you that I have found answers to the questions that torment the man of our time? I do not know if I have found answers. When I first became a monk, yes, I was more sure of 'answers'. But as I grow old in the monastic life and advance further into solitude, I become aware that I have only begun to seek the questions."

dent that, purged of its classical "fillers," the work was read with profit
by monastics, including the Carthusians to whom it was addressed.

Our purpose here is by no means to dismiss as superficial or misguided Petrarch's wrestling with the central issues of Christian faith.
Rather, the present study seeks to point out the way in which his intro-
spective and wavering yet powerful will is paradigmatic for an emerging
modern world. All of this Trinkaus has captured well. Yet, as Cranz insists, Petrarch faces more toward the modern inner-directed, intensive
self and away from the role-playing, rule-bound, extensive self that characterized much of the ancient and medieval world, a role-playing, rule-
bound self which, in the late Middle Ages, was most deeply rooted in
traditional monasticism. Petrarch did indeed perceive acutely the anxiety,
insecurity, and alienation created by the inner-directed self that came
with urbanization and the growth of entrepreneurial society. His genius
was to be acutely sensitive to it before it had really triumphed. Yet, until
we recognize the psychological and social dynamics involved in monastic vows and monastic claustration, we will find it all to easy to minimize
the "high wall" and disparage the crutch that separates monastic from
quasi-monastic life. Petrarch illustrates how one can be "so near, yet so
far away."

In the early seventeenth century, Jacob Bidermann took this theme
and combined it with one of Nicholas Kempf's favorite themes (vices
that masquerade as virtues) to create a dramatic retelling of Carthusian
origins in the damnation of an apparently pious, learned, and upright
man, a man who was so close yet so far away from genuine discernment.
The present study ends where it began: with an alien voice from outside
this present life. Instead of silencing a voice from the grave, in this story
the voice miraculously resisted burial. As our epi*logue*, it calls for an attentive ear.

DEAN OF LIBERAL ARTS IN HELL

In the year of our Lord's Incarnation 1082 or thereabouts, when the famous school flourished at Paris, especially in the customary disciplines of liberal arts, theology, and canon law, a great marvel is said to have taken place there. A certain outstanding professor, one who was, so it seems, honored above the other teachers for his renown, teaching, and knowledge, and marvelously well liked, suddenly was seized by a grave and mortal illness, and shortly after taking to his bed, breathed his last.

After a day of lying in state in the university's hall while the divine office was chanted continuously, according to custom at Paris, the entire university, students as well as professors, gathered the next morning to carry out solemn funeral rites worthy of such a man. When the honored pallbearers tried to lift the bier on which the dead man lay so that they could carry him to the church, suddenly he who seemed to be—and was— dead raised his head and sat up on the bier. To the utter amazement of all present, he cried out 'By the just judgment of God I have been accused.' Having said this, he hung his head and lay down again as before. Terrified and astonished by this voice, everyone considered the matter and concluded that there was no way to finish the burial that day. They put it off until the next morning.

A great crowd assembled the next morning. When they tried to carry the corpse to the church, the dead man, just as on the preceding day, raised his head and intoned with a mournful and terrifying voice: 'By the just judgment of God I have been judged.' The great multitude, hearing and comprehending clearly what the voice said, was more confounded than before. Consulting each other, they once more decided to wait until the next day to bury the man.

On the third day the whole city, having heard of the wonder, assembled. Having made all the preparations, they were ready to carry the corpse away when the dead man, just as before, filled the air with a loud and most sorrowful cry: 'By the just judgment of God I have been condemned.'

Nearly all who heard these horrifying words, shaken with immense fear and trembling, were certain the man had been damned, a man who had seemed to lead an upright life of brilliant renown, outstanding honor, and manifold knowledge and wisdom surpassing all others. At that time Master Bruno was at Paris. He was a German from Cologne, of no mean parentage, and was then a canon of the Cathedral Church at Reims, and a master of theology in the schools there. Shocked by the three declamations into a hearty repentance, he said something like the following to certain of his colleagues who were present: 'Dear friends, what in the world shall we do? We shall all perish together and never be saved unless we flee. If these things happen in a lush meadow, what will happen in a desert? If a man of such worthiness and such erudition, who seems to have led such an upright life, who was so renowned and famous, if such a man beyond a shadow of a doubt has been damned, what shall we wretched little men do? If the mournful voice of one human being shakes us with such horrible and stupefying fear and trembling, what shall we do when the roaring of the lion, when the trumpets of the last judgment, strike our ears? Together with everyone else we shall hear: "Arise O Dead and come to judgment." In that hour, whereto shall we flee? How shall we be able to appear at this fearful judgment where the pillars of heaven tremble and the angels are terrified and the fearful are purged? Where shall we then hide? It will be impossible to conceal ourselves yet unbearable to appear. Let us therefore flee from the face of the sword of the Lord, let us seek out his face beforehand in confession, let us come and adore and throw ourselves down before God, let us weep in the presence of the Lord who made us. Having heard today this astonishing voice, let us not harden our hearts but let us depart from the midst of Babylon, let us exit the five cities already burning with fire and brimstone and, following the example of Paul the hermit, Saint Antony, Arsenius, Evagrius and other saints together with blessed John the Baptist, seek out the caverns of the wilderness. Let us make ourselves safe in the mountains that we might escape—in the ark of Noah and the bark of Peter in which Christ commands the winds and the tempest to stop—the wrath of the eternal Judge, the sentence of eternal damnation, and the drowning of sinners. That is, let us escape in the ship of penitence and arrive at the haven of rest of eternal salvation.'[1]

Bruno led his friends from "Paris"to the Grande Chartreuse.

Discretio from the Edge of the Grave

Our study opened with the story of the prior of the Grande Chartreuse commanding his predecessor to cease and desist, under monastic obedience, from working miracles. It concludes with the often retold story of the "miracle of Paris" that inspired Bruno and his six companions to seek out the wilderness of the Chartreuse mountains. Nicholas Kempf made the story central to his interpretation of Carthusian history

---

[1]   The story first appears in *Laudemus*, a portion of which forms part of the *Vita antiquior auctore primorum quinque Cartusiae Priorum chronologo anonymo*, from which my translation is made. See André Wilmart, "La chronique des premiers chartreux," *Revue Mabillon*, 16 (1926), 77-142, at 130-31, and *Acta Sanctorum*, vol. 51, Octobris III (1770; repr. 1868), 703-7, cf. PL 152: 481-92. Lengthy discussions of its authenticity are found in the aforementioned *Acta Sanctorum* volume and in Le Couteulx, *Annales*, 1: XLV-CVI. Nicholas Kempf cites it in *De confirmatione*, ch. 9/8 (cvp 13904, 11v, 7-10) and 10/9 (14r, 24-25). Cf. *Rect*, e.g. III.2 (V1, 61r A; *Bibl. ascetica*, 4: 418); *Prop*, I.12/11 (VS1, 8v B, 4-30), and *Discr*, 3 (VS1, 36v B, 1-4). A variation on the story appears in *De confirmatione*, 19/18 (cvp 13904, 31r, 6 - 31v, 19), derived apparently from Peter the Chanter.

because it offered a paradigm for the order's mission: to rescue those swollen with pride of learning, pride of accomplishment, pride of making, pride of technique,[2] from damnation.

Ever since the tower of Babel, ever since *homo artifex* fired up his forge and began to ply the arts—"making trial of his powers"—he has struggled with the temptation to idolatry, the temptation to confuse his derivative artistry with God's archetypical artistry (Rom 1). The monastic theology of meek "powerlessness" is best understood in this light: if the human temptation is to pride in technique, to idolatry of artifice, then the solution is a repentance which recognizes that, since the Fall, humans have been better at making sins than making anything else. This deep consciousness of sinfulness is but another side of the patristic and medieval sacramental conviction that the things God made were made good and are thus potentially instruments of grace. To keep technique (language, sexuality and reproduction, scholarship, theology, politics, i.e., all human powers) in its place[3] as a tool and not an idol, the monks fled to the shelter of radical renunciation, yet renunciation made possible by the structures and techniques of the Rule and by spiritual direction. They institutionalized the renunciation of their technique, renouncing even the effort to renounce technique, through the practice of dumping all such efforts onto someone else's shoulders (the shoulders of a spiritual director) and onto the framework of the Rule. This was their best hope for keeping technique in its place.

Of course, even this institutionalization of renunciation ultimately fails. When it does, all one can do is to "trust in him who justifies the unrighteous" (chapter four). But insofar as any structure can work, this structured renunciation, this crutch for one's lameness, has the best chance

---

[2] I am using this word here in the sense employed by Jacques Ellul, *La Technique ou l'enjeu du siècle* (1954), translated by John Wilkinson as *The Technological Society* (1964). One can note striking parallels (minus Ellul's strident appeal to personalist iconoclasm) in the writings of the Canadian political philosopher, George Grant. Convinced of the superiority of a classical, traditionalist worldview that was replaced in Canada by the "universal homogenizing liberal state" as recently as the 1950s, Grant nonetheless insists that politically activist efforts to recover a traditionalist society are impossible. If activism (Ellul's *technique*) is the problem, one cannot solve that problem with more *technique* or activism. One can only lament what has been lost *tendebantque manus ripae ulterioris amore*—and stretch one's arms toward the farther shore in love (Grant, *Lament for a Nation* [1965; repr. 1978], 97, quoting Virgil, *Aeneid*, VI.314. See also Grant, *Technology and Empire* (1969). Neither Grant nor Ellul have addressed the monastic office of lament, repentance, and weeping in this light.

[3] On monasticism as a source of Christian humanism, see Albert Deblaere, "Humanisme chrétien et vocation monastique." *Studia missionalia*, 28 (1979), 97-132.

of success.[4] Truly this is theology "by grace alone" that belongs firmly within the medieval and patristic world.

Monastic *discretio* is a hermeneutic and an epistemology—of concreteness rather than abstraction, of orality rather than literateness, of the ad hoc and flexible.[5] Peter Brown has captured this well, drawing on a story from the Desert Fathers that Jean Gerson retold and Nicholas Kempf inserted into his *De recto fine*:

> Such movements [of the heart] were best conveyed orally to a spiritual father. It was a situation which tended to give priority to the languages closest to the heart, that is, the vernaculars of Egypt and the Near East—Coptic, Syriac, and demotic Greek. The deepest relief of the soul came now, not from the written page, but from the tap of the Old Man's fingers on his disciple's chest, which assuaged the heart beneath. The shift from a culture of the book to a *cultura Dei*[6] based largely on the nonliterate, verbal interchange of a monastic "art of thought", was rightly hailed as the greatest and the most peculiar achievement of the Old Men of Egypt: it amounted to nothing less than the discovery of a new alphabet of the heart.[7]

Brown refers to Abba Arsenius's response when asked why he, a man of culture from the imperial court, a man learned in Greek and Latin, was taking counsel, i.e., manifesting his thoughts, to an Egyptian peasant. Arsenius owned up to his erudite training and cultivated background but pointed out that he had not even learned the ABC's of the language spoken by this peasant monk, namely, the language of toiling at

---

[4] This is precisely the difference between Ellul and the monks: Ellul cannot make instrumental use of any structure, even a structure of institutionalized renunciation, a language of silence. He can only call to radical, inner-directed revolution in obedience to a Kierkegaardian-Barthian Wholly Other. For a glimpse of a contemporary Catholic "structured radical renunciation" fundamentally compatible with the monastic "meekness theology" outlined here, one might turn to Hans Urs von Balthasar, who drew from the same Barthian iconoclasm as Ellul but combines it with a Catholic sacramental, incarnational faith in the instrumentality of form. The best introduction to his thought is now David Schindler, ed., *Hans Urs von Balthasar: His Life and Work* (1991).

[5] In the introduction to his *Institutiones*, SC 109, John Cassian emphasizes that he had long resisted requests to write down and codify what he knew about the way of life of the desert monks. He thought it simply unnecessary. Much the same appears in the dedicatory letter of Guigo I's *Consuetudines*, which may well have been modeled on John Cassian's. Note also Kempf, *Prop*, II.23, quoted in chapter one, p. 21, above, regarding the written profession as an aid to memory, which is clearly Kempf's primary concern—a piece of paper cannot automatically keep a monk on the right track, but his memory can use all the help it can get.

[6] Brown points out that this term was used by the earliest Latin translation of the *Life of Anthony* to translate *ascesis*.

[7] Peter Brown, *Body and Society*, 227-28.

right living, of possessing virtues.[8] Brown contrasts this monastic "alphabet of the heart" with the erudite urban study circles around Origen, Justin Martyr, and others. Of course, one can ask whether this "alphabet of the heart" in early monasticism did not revert to a hermeneutic of the book in medieval monasticism, as Brian Stock insists. The fact that Gerson and Kempf cite precisely this story to buttress their claims for the difference between scholastic and mystical theology suggests that the "alphabet of the heart" had not been unlearned entirely.[9]

The voice of monastic meekness is a powerfully arresting voice from the edge of the grave. It is a nearly buried but irrepressible voice from the past. Time and again Western intellectuals have formed its funeral cortege and carried it out to the cemetery: from Lorenzo Valla, Martin Luther, and Henry VIII to the enlightened Joseph II and on to the utilitarians and liberationists of the last two centuries—untold numbers of modern men and women have convinced themselves of the uselessness of monastic life. Yet they never fully succeeded in burying it. Again and again the contemplative religious life has sat up on its bier and warned the world of judgment for sin: initially in the nineteenth-century renewal of Benedictine monasticism (both Roman Catholic and Anglican), which was responsible in large part for the Liturgical Movement and, by extension, for much of Vatican II; most recently in the post-World-War-II monastic renewal symbolized by, but by no means limited to, the personage of Thomas Merton.

Seen in the waning light of the Modern Project, the monastic life symbolizes something larger than itself: a traditional world in which self-identity is formed by role-playing rather than romantic authenticity, a world of symbol, liturgy, and gesture rather than literality and textuality.

---

[8] *Apophthegmata Patrum, Appendix ad Palladium,* "De Abbate Arsenius," par. 4-6 (PG 65: 89-90), cf. *Verba Seniorum* by Pelagius the Deacon (PL 73: 953-54). For the use of this passage by Gerson and Kempf, see chapter three, p. 82, above, and appendix B (*Rect,* II.5). For the same story in the Armenian tradition, see Leloir, "Sagesse," 66, citing his edition of the Armenian version. Cf. the translation by Helen Waddell, *The Desert Fathers* (1957), 117, cf. p. 59, and the translation by Owen Chadwick, *Western Asceticism* (1958), 156-57. Cf. Vincent of Aggsbach as cited in Gerson, *Oeuvres,* 10: 570, art. 3.

[9] The implications of Brown's comments for Stock's *Implications of Literacy,* in which the monks are assigned more to the textual than the oral side of the spectrum, are considerable. For a discussion of mouth, brain, heart, ears, and eyes as organs of reading and prayer, see Saenger, "Books of Hours, 247-53. For monks, oral recitation of the canonical hours, even if done privately as was the case for much of the Carthusian *horarium,* remained central. Note Kempf's preference for the simple and illiterate over the learned and literate in *MTh,* II.21, pp. 176-77, chapter five, p. 172, above.

2. Dean of Liberal Arts in Hell

Jacob Bidermann (1578-1639) is often described as the most significant German Jesuit author of the sixteenth and seventeenth centuries. His
teacher, Matthäus Rader (1561-1634), described by one historian as the
"spiritual center of late humanist circles in Bavaria,"[10] singled out Bidermann as the best among the thirteen hundred students Rader had taught
and, with typical humanist hyperbole, put him on par with Aquinas,
Aristotle, Cicero, and Virgil.[11] *Cenodoxus*, Bidermann's school-drama
based on the "Doctor of Paris" story, has been performed several times
during the twentieth century, primarily in variations on the German
translation by Joachim Meichel (1635), but also in a musical theater ad-
aptation set in the idiom of African-American gospel music.[12]

When the play was performed at Munich in 1609 the audience included leading citizens of Munich and a variety of Bavarian court nota-
bles for whom students from the Jesuit gymnasium performed
Cenodoxus as part of the normal program of school dramas. (In Munich
these performances doubled as court theater.) Although presented in neo-
Latin as a pedagogical device, the lengthy play made a powerful impact
on the packed hall—if some of the reports are to be believed. Initially the
audience laughed at the slapstick comedy of the opening scenes. However, the audience's mood turned to seriousness, shock, and then horror
"as the spectators realised the enormity of the sins portrayed and became
aware of the power of hell; and by the end of the play the members of the
audience, trembling at the sight of a soul eternally damned, were reflecting in stunned silence on the punishment their own sins merited."[13]

---

[10] Richard van Dülmen, "Die Gesellschaft Jesu und der Bayerische Späthumanismus:
Ein Überblick mit dem Briefwechsel von J. Bidermann," *Zeitschrift für Bayerische Landesgeschichte*, 37 (1974), 358-415, at 372.

[11] Ibid., 373: "Tres ego discipulos memini de mille trecenti, Stengelium doctum,
Drexeliumque pium, Atque Bidermannum, qui nunc est alter Aquinas, Atque Stagirites,
Tullius atque Maro." The other two were Jeremias Drexel and Georg Stengel.

[12] Written and produced by John Walsh, S.J., and Thomas Kavenaugh as part of the
Ignatian Year celebrations of 1991 at St. Louis University. See the description by Michael Isaacson, "Passion Play," *Universitas* (St. Louis University public relations department), 16, no. 3 (Spring 1991), 10-12. John Patrick Donnelly, S.J., drew my attention to
this production.

[13] Description from "Praemonitio ad lectorem" in Jacob Bidermann, *Ludi theatrales*
(1666; repr. 1967), as translated in Denys G. Dyer's preface to Jacob Bidermann, *Cenodoxus* (1974), introduction by Dyer, pp. 1-2.

Fourteen members of the audience are said to have gone into retreat to do Loyola's *Spiritual Exercises*, and the student who portrayed Cenodoxus is said to have entered the Society of Jesus, where he lived in holiness ever after (*pluribus annis adeo innocenter ac sancte vixit*).[14]

Critics have virtually ignored the possibility of Carthusian influence on Bidermann.[15] We do know that the Cologne Charterhouse, in many ways at its height during the sixteenth century, had a significant impact on the Jesuit apostle to Germany, Peter Canisius, who in turn assisted the Cologne Carthusian Laurentius Surius in his editorial work.[16] In the Latin-German playbill distributed for the 1617 Ingolstadt performance of *Cenodoxus* Bidermann cites Surius's biography of Bruno[17] as his main source for the Bruno legend.[18] Bidermann certainly had many other sources for his knowledge of the monastic tradition, including the Desert Fathers. Reading his play with that tradition in mind opens entirely new interpretive possibilities, totally missed by previous interpreters who have read it as a Jesuit response to Neo-Stoicism and a contribution to the Roman Catholic debate on grace and free will in France and Spain. The two leading interpreters, Tarot and Dyer, both use the Neo-Stoic philosophy of Justus Lipsius as their main interpretive tool, since Bidermann's letters reveal initial fascination followed by sharp rejection of Lipsius's philosophy. Tarot is aware of John Cassian's theology of the cardinal sins, but follows them through the medieval scholastic rather than monastic tradition.[19] In discussing the classic prooftext for the Neo-

---

[14] See the analysis by Günter Hess and Ursula Hess, "Spektator-Lector-Actor: Zum Publikum von Jacob Bidermann's *Cenodoxus*," *Internationales Archiv für Sozialgeschichte der deutschen Literatur*, 1 (1976), 30-106 (the Latin text from the "Praemonitio ad Lectorem" is found on p. 88-89). Although Günter Hess disputes the "historicity" of statements in the posthumous edition of Bidermann's plays (1666) to the effect that "spectacular" conversions occurred, he admits that the play had a "significant" impact. The article offers a remarkable analysis of the interconnections between students in Bidermann's rhetoric classes—which included sons of the Bavarian civil service, bourgeoisie, and court circle. The Hesses reprint all the relevant primary texts surrounding the play's three performances (1602 in Augsburg, 1609 in Munich, 1617 in Ingolstadt) and describe the process by which the two surviving manuscripts were copied, thus providing considerable information beyond that available in the critical edition by Rolf Tarot (see below).

[15] At least two other Jesuit dramas of the sixteenth century were based on the story of St. Bruno: Mathäus Rader's *Theophilus* and Jakob Gretser's, *Udo*. See van Dülmen, "Gesellschaft Jesu," 584.

[16] See Greven, *Kölner Kartause* (1935); Chaix, *Recherches*, 1: 397-300, 303, and index; Zadnikar and Wienand, *Die Kartäuser*, e.g., 252-55.

[17] I.e., the *Vita tertia* found in the *Acta sanctorum* collection.

[18] The playbills for 1609 and 1617 are reprinted in the critical edition: Jakob Bidermann, *Cenodoxus*, ed. Rolf Tarot (1963), pp. 135-64.

[19] How little progress has been made in thirty years is evident from Jean-Marie Val-

Stoic interpretation of *Cenodoxus*, the deathbed scene in act IV, scenes 1 and 3, Tarot and Dyer miss a potential source in the medieval *ars moriendi* tradition; likewise they interpret the theme of patience solely from the Stoic tradition, ignoring the long monastic tradition on *patientia*. Finally, for a potential source for the theme of hypocrisy, Tarot turns to Luther rather than the monastic tradition on pseudo-virtues.[20]

James A. Parente, Jr.,[21] explains *Cenodoxus* as a parody of Erasmus "whose feigned ironic humility doubtless troubled the earnest pedagogical sensibilities of Bidermann." Parente claims that Cenodoxus's "confidence about his intelligence and reason had led him to ignore God" and that "his apparently sincere works of charity and Stoic forbearance of death had further convinced his followers of his wisdom and sanctity. But this pursuit of learning was subsequently revealed as vain and hypocritical, for Cenodoxus had not been inspired by piety." Familiarity with the monastic tradition on pseudo-virtues, on vices disguised as virtues, might have helped him here—the whole point of the play is that seemingly genuine and sincere piety can in fact be hypocritical, misdirected, and therefore damnable. Parente seems not to have considered the Bruno-legend that lay behind the play, for he comments: "In a grisly scene typical of the Jesuits' belief in the pedagogical utility of visual images, the soul of Cenodoxus was dragged into hell as his corpse announced the punishment to the terrified mourners."

Indeed, all of the important themes that Bidermann worked into his drama are present in the spiritual teaching of Nicholas Kempf. Ceno-

---

entin, *Le théatre des Jesuites dans les pays de langue allemande (1554-1680)* (1978), 552-53. Valentin cites the use of the term *cenodoxus* in the Pauline writings and its Latin translation in the Vulgate before moving directly to Thomas Aquinas. John Cassian and the desert tradition are not even mentioned.

[20] Denys G. Dyer wrote a dissertation on Bidermann's *Cenodoxus* in 1950. Rolf Tarot has produced both a dissertation, "Jakob Bidermanns *Cenodoxus* (Cologne, 1960; published Düsseldorf: Triltsch, 1960), and the critical edition mentioned above. A comparison of the two reveals that most of the material in the dissertation was incorporated into the introduction to the 1963 critical edition; for the issues at hand, see particularly p. XX-XXVI of the latter. I have not seen Dyer's unpublished dissertation and my comments are based on the introduction to his 1974 translation of *Cenodoxus*. One of the few literary critics to take account of the ascetic tradition in Bidermann's work is Günter Müller, *Deutsche Dichtung von der Renaissance bis zum Ausgang des Barock* (1927, 1957), 136-37, 192-93. Aware of the Cologne Carthusians and their impact on reformed Catholic lay and clerical circles, Müller suggested that Bidermann combined the medieval ascetic tradition with humanist *Bildung* to produce a penetrating dramatic incarnation of what baroque intellectualism had made out of divine revelation and the church's teaching on the human condition in the world and in eternity. The condescending and dismissive treatment of all of Bidermann's work by Thomas W. Best, *Jacob Bidermann* (1975), can be dispensed with here.

[21] *Religious Drama and the Humanist Tradition* (1987), 47-48.

doxus, the famed teacher and civic counselor, magnanimous to the poor
when others are watching but callous toward suffering when alone,
seems to do everything right. Even on his deathbed he endures his inex-
plicable suffering piously and patiently, confesses his sins, and dies
trusting in God's providence and grace. Unfortunately, as the denoue-
ment of the play shows, he was sincerely going through the motions, not
actually living out, the medieval *ars moriendi* and ascetic tradition. Un-
derneath it all lies a layer missed by the critics: the root problem for
Cenodoxus is lack of discretion, the governor, the *moderatrix* of all the
virtues.[22] He cannot distinguish true virtues from false ones, true *securitas* from false *securitas*, true visions from false visions. When his guardian angel forces the demons of hell against their will to show Cenodoxus
a true vision of hell, his lack of discretion leads him to declare it a mere
dream and to take seriously a false (i.e., a truly demonically inspired)
foretaste of heaven. Throughout his life he thought he was trusting in
God's mercy and providence when in fact he was trusting in his own
trust, in his own false discretion,[23] that highly lauded discretion that he
employed to counsel the city's government and teach piety to his students. Cenodoxus is a paradigm of the temptations of leadership that
John Cassian,[24] Bernard of Waging, and Nicholas Kempf warned about:
in teaching others, leading others, pastoring others, counseling others—
in doing much good—one runs the risk of being damned for having ap-
propriated what was an office, a gift, a tool, and having tried to integrate
it into one's own spiritual goods.[25]

Dyer makes much of fact that the Cenodoxus's sin was not named
in the original legend and was added by Bidermann (vainglory = *cenodoxus* in Greek).[26] Technically this is true, and Bidermann's own preface
to the play makes a point of this "invention." But, as we have seen in
Kempf's writings, pride is *the* sin peculiar to the learned and was the obvious source of damnation for a Paris professor.[27] Kempf's university-

---

[22] John Cassian, *Conference*, II, ch. 4 (SC 42: 116; trans. Luibheid, p. 64).

[23] See particularly Kempf's quotations from Pr 14:12; 16:25, and Mt 7:23 in *De dis-
cretione*, ch. 3, discussed in ch. 4, p. 127, above. Kempf himself includes the Doctor of
Paris in his catalogue of those who lacked discretion. See *Discr* ch. 3 (VS1, 36v A, 39 -
B, 4; 9: 393).

[24] *Conferences*, II.1 (SC 42: 112; trans. Luibheid, p. 61): Unless one pursues discretion with all zeal, one is sure to go wrong, take the wrong turn, and end up in hell. Cf.
II.3-4 (SC 42: 114-15; trans. Luibheid, p. 63-64), which deal with the temptations of
leadership and giving counsel.

[25] Hausherr, *Spiritual Direction*, 36, points out that attaining a nonproprietary attitude
marks the highest degree of *diakrisis* for Origen.

[26] Pp. 10, 202, referring to lines 2090ff and 2166ff.

[27] Kempf points out that God "voluit in excellentissimo doctore illud ostendere quod

oriented interpretation of Carthusian history, when combined with the patristic and medieval insistence that pride is the chief of all the cardinal sins,[28] suggests that Bidermann's "invention" was not, as Dyer implies, mere coincidence or happenstance:

> *Cenodoxus* is the drama of the individual without grace, caught in the web of his individuality, the tragedy of the unqualified assertion of man's identity and its consequences for his soul. Cenodoxus is eternally damned, and the reason for his damnation is his spiritual pride. . . . But it must be stressed that this is not conscious hypocrisy on his part. He is no Tartuffe. He is an unconscious hypocrite; and even when he appears to be consciously hypocritical, as in the Navegus scene (II.VI), he is quite unaware that he is thereby sinning, just as the Pharisee in St. Luke, chapter 18, is not aware of any fault in his conduct.[29]

Dyer is fascinated by what he sees as a sudden twist in the story: the man who thinks he is righteous ends up being damned; if such a one can't be saved, who can be? On the surface, this is what the legend said. But if one looks at the monastic tradition on discretion, on vices masquerading as virtues, on how easy it is to be proud of being humble, it would be obvious that this hiddenness of sin is the fundamental problem of human existence. The monks are those who recognize the pervasiveness, hiddenness, and seriousness of sin in the depths of their being and thus serve as a living reminder to those who are more nonchalant. Not to be conscious of one's own hypocrisy points less to the hiddenness of sin than to one's lack of spiritual discretion. Cenodoxus is Everyman and all can identify with him if they only stop to reflect on their motives and intentions. And that is what the funereal "marvel" of Paris is supposed to accomplish: to make onlookers stop and examine themselves. Cenodoxus is no helpless victim of an arbitrary God who enjoys surprise endings; Cenodoxus is the personification of every human heart.

Bruno and his companions did not know what Cenodoxus's sin was, but all they really needed to know was that the judgment was just—the key words in the entire play are "Justa judicia Dei. Pereat scelestus."

---

nullus deberet de sua scientia presumere, et in universitate solemnissima, in omnium membrorum universitatis presentia, ut nullum possit latere dampnationis causa, et ut eadem per totum mundum omnibus doctis et in scientia divitibus fieri manifestissima et usque ad finem seculi predicanda." *De confirmatione*, 5 (Vienna, ÖNB cvp 13904, fol. 7r, 17-24). Unlike Dyer, Kempf finds everything to be perfectly obvious.

[28] Lester K. Little, "Pride Goeth before Avarice: Social Change and the Vices in Latin Christianity." *AHR*, 76 (1971), 16-49. Dyer is aware of Cassian's teaching on the cardinal sins. See the introduction to his translation, p. 12.

[29] Dyer, introduction to his translation, pp. 12-13.

["Just are the judgments of God. Let the sinner perish."], spoken by the entire heavenly court of judges ("omnes judices"; line 2057), and "Justo Dei judicio damnatus sum" ["I am damned by God's righteous judgment"], spoken by Cenodoxus (2072).[30] If an apparently pious man is justly condemned, then the only possible sin is pseudo-virtues, hypocrisy, lack of discretion. One does not need to know the exact crimes, for he obviously had to have been putting on some sort of false front.

This is underscored by act V, scene 7, the scene immediately following the judgment. Bidermann drives his point home here in a series of tragicomic inversions as the demons receive Cenodoxus's condemned spirit in hell[31]:

> Demon: "Why are you making strange? Don't you know you are among friends? You act as if we are strangers."[32]
> Cenodoxus: "You are my enemies [hostes]."
> Demon: "No, we are your hosts [hospites]. Why are you so frightened? Yesterday you were calmer."

When he was calm he was mistaken; now that he really knows the truth, he is afraid. He accuses them of being deceivers and impostors. They admit it, saying in effect, "Yes we are, but you *knew* that long ago and chose to ignore (not to know) it, now you simply know what you always knew but can no longer ignore." Cenodoxus now has the discretion he lacked earlier and his knowledge is bitter.

> Demon: "Why did you trust us back then? If we were your friends then, why treat us as strangers now?"
> Cenodoxus: "I won't trust you any more."[33]

The last phrase is full of irony, since he is here to stay and will be a mistrustful stranger, alienated from those to whom he really was attached during his life, when he should have used discretion to separate himself

---

[30] On p. 199, notes to lines 175-188, and 204-205, Dyer asserts that even Cenodoxus is unaware of his sin, of his hypocrisy—he thinks his sin is really virtue. If that is true, God's judgment cannot be just. Bidermann has the heavenly court go to great lengths to make sure that Cenodoxus in the end knows his condemnation is a just sentence, which means that he was, at least in some small way, aware of his hypocrisy during his life, as the opening chapters of the Epistle to the Romans and with it the medieval theological tradition, insisted.

[31] Even this scene can find an antecedent in at least one Carthusian source, although in citing it I do not intend to imply any direct influence on Bidermann. Chapter 3 of *De sollicitudine*, the treatise on pedagogy attributed by Wydemann to Kempf, discusses what those who spurn the *words* of the gospel will have to *say* in hell.

[32] Translations are by Dyer, occasionally slightly modified.

[33] Panurgus: Ha ha; quid horres? inter alienos tibi videris esse? noster es; tui sumus. / Spiritus [of Cenodoxus]: Hostes mei estis. / Asteroth: Hospites imo tui. / Asempholoth: Quid jam feroces? placidior fueras heri. / Spiritus: Impostor es. / Asempholoth: Pridem sciebas; cur fidem tamen habuisti? / Spiritu: Non habebo in posterum. (2097-2102)

from them. Having been attached to the false ones during life he brings eternal alienation, unattachedness, *krisis*, upon himself—separated from the God to whom he should have been attached (*affectus*) yet also alienated from the demons he undiscerningly trusted during his life.

As the demons receive Cenodoxus the masquerader, the impostor, in hell (2098-2102) they continue to disguise and falsify hell, just as they had done during his life (with the one exception forced on them by his guardian angel). They greet him with a diabolical salute to his health:

> Demons: Hail Cenodoxus.
> Cenodoxus: I am hale no longer. I'm lost.[34]

They make him dean of liberal arts in hell:

> Demons: "He was the ablest, wisest, cleverest of men. The very heart [*corculum*] of wisdom and learning. Why, then, we'll make him Dean of Liberal Studies in fiery hell."[35]

Famed as an advisor, famed for his (false and inadequate) discretion, Cenodoxus's skills and counsels will now serve the Devil, as indeed they always had (2125-26). They tell him how beatific a place he is in (2128-37), how *blessed* he is.

> Demon: "How blessed you are."
> Cenodoxus: "How wretched."
> Demon: "Your problem is that you simply don't know your blessedness."
> Cenodoxus: "Wretch that I am, I don't, I don't."[36]

Once more the irony is palpable. For once he *knows* something for sure, he knows he is not blessed. He knows, admits, truly knows for the first time that he is wretched, not happy. For once he can agree with the demons' statement—"You don't know your blessedness"—wholeheartedly. What he knows is his unblessedness, his lack of heavenly *beatitude*; what the demons call blessedness is his lot for eternity because he lacked the discretion during earthly life to distinguish a foretaste of heaven from a foretaste of hell.

But Bidermann is not finished. He has yet to portray the response of the onlookers (act V, scene 8, lines 2163-2204). Cenodoxus's lack of discretion during life, and his clear vision and loud voice after death make it possible for Bruno and his companions to gain true discretion,

---

[34] Omnes: "Cenodoxe salve." / Spiritus: "Salvus esse desij. Perij." (2103-4)

[35] Philautia: "Potissimus fuit, nempe, omnium et prudentium et sapientium."/ Hypocrisis: Quasi corculum et prudentiae et sapientiae. / Panurgus: Antistes ergo litteris creabitur Phlegethonticis." (Phlegethonticis means "fiery hell") (2119-21)

[36] Philautia: "Quam tu beatus?" / Spiritus: "Quam miser?" / Philautia: "Nescis tuam beatitatem." / Spiritus: "Heu, nescio miser, nescio." (2128-30)

the insight that sin is so pervasive that what appears to be virtuous may actually be sinful. Once that insight has dawned, once one becomes radically conscious of sin, a dedication of one's entire life to repentant service of God is the only hope. That is the conclusion Bruno and his companions draw from the story. Instead of accenting their confusion and surprise at the hiddenness of Cenodoxus's sin as modern critics have done, the point Bidermann's Bruno makes is that he has discerned exactly what to do.

Paraphrased, Bruno's speech runs as follows: If only he had told us the cause of his condemnation more clearly, then we could flee from it. But he did not. By his silence he tells the cause more clearly, by not telling us he tells us better (2163-68).

Bidermann's Bruno is drawing on the monastic tradition of silence. Discretion, true knowledge about life and death, heaven and hell, grows out of silence. Language is inadequate to address the deepest matters. Not in active, virtuous living, not in technique, but in withdrawal lies hope.

Bruno continues: Had he told us one particular sin, e.g., hate or arrogance, we would fall into other sins while trying to avoid that one. It is better that he not be specific and that we flee to avoid all sins (2168-75). To name one aspect of hell is as futile as to name one sin—all aspects of hell are interconnected. I would rather shut up than to give only a hint. Anything I might say would be too little, would be nothing. ("Malo contiscere, quam pauca dicere. Quicquid enim disero, parum erit, nihil erit.") To talk about hell's torments is to describe happiness in comparison to the reality of these torments. ("Imo quicquid dixero, suave erit, amoenum erit, beatum erit; inferis si conferas cum suppliciis.") Because human language is inadequate to describe hell, one could *talk* about it forever and no one would believe it. Silence is better ("Hoc unice dicam; idque milliesque dicam millies, interrogatus de inferorum miseria; *non creditur, non creditur, non creditur*" (2186-92).[37] Far from illustrating a Jesuit proclivity for the use of graphic visual imagery, Bidermann's *Cenodoxus* delimits language and vision in order to empower silence and withdrawal. Bidermann knew precisely what the Carthusian life meant and he fills the stage with it: Bruno's concluding soliloquy is an eloquent testimony to silence's triumph over words.

Three times and more we have tried to carry monastic *discretio* out to burial. And now the postmodernists have assembled a funeral cortege

---

[37] The clear allusion to Luke 16 has been missed by Bidermann's modern editors. Generally the critics have put more effort into finding Bidermann's allusions to Terence and Plautus than to his biblical and medieval sources.

for modernity, a curious cortege of impenetrable verbiage by which to deconstruct all language. Where is the *clara tuba* sounding from the judgment seat of history to awaken womanish, repentant, weeping discretion at the threshing floor of modernity's harvest? Are we ready to employ the history and theology of monastic silence and withdrawal to winnow what is left of modern confidence in critical literality? If the present study has permitted the monastic *corpus* to speak from its funeral bier, to shout over the cacophanous dirge of technicized scholastic philosophy and theology, *studia humanitatis*, urbanization, commercialization, and Enlightenment; if it has shed light on a premodern *homo clamans plangensque* as an alternative to a structuralist *homo faber* and poststructuralist *homo ludens*, it will have begun to achieve its aim. *Qui potest capere, capiat*!

OPERA

We are fortunate to possess a list of more than thirty works attributed to Nicholas Kempf by Leopold Wydemann (1668-1752), the vicar and librarian at Gaming who collaborated with Bernard Pez at Melk in the early eighteenth century.[1] Wydemann had not seen all of the treatises he listed. As a Carthusian he was unable to undertake the library travels that the Benedictine brothers Bernard Pez (1683-1735) and Hieronymus Pez (1685-1762) at Melk undertook in imitation of the French Maurists. Even if the legwork was beyond his capability, Wydemann did much of the handwork for the Carthusian texts that formed a large part of Pez's *Bibliotheca ascetica*. He copied manuscripts, offered his opinions on questions of authorship, and furnished biographical and historical details to Pez.

Wydemann's work is important above all because in most instances he listed the *initia*, the number of chapters and subdivisions within the texts, and the size of the codices he had seen at Seitz, Aggsbach, and Gaming. In view of the dispersal and destruction of the Austrian Carthusian libraries under Joseph II a half-century later,[2] Wydemann's data permit the otherwise nearly impossible task of identifying in modern manuscript collections the extant copies of Kempf's often anonymously transmitted writings. It also makes possible a more complete estimation of the transmission of Kempf's works in the fifteenth century, since Wydemann cited copies in Aggsbach, Gaming, Olomouc, and Seitz that

---

[1] The handwritten list is found in Melk, Stiftsbibliothek cod. 683 (766), 1r-3r. It was published in the preface to volume 4 of *Bibl. ascetica*. See also Wydemann's letters to Pez in "Peziana": January 22, 1718, May 29, 1720, and May 6, 1721, for Wydemann's comments on specific works by Kempf. On the Pez brothers see Ludwig Hammermayer, "Die Forschungszentren der deutschen Benediktiner und ihre Vorhaben," in *Historische Forschung im 18. Jahrhundert* (1976), 122-91; Eduard Katschthaler, *Über Bernhard Pez und dessen Briefnachlaß* in *39. Jahresbericht des k. k. Obergymnasiums der Benediktiner zu Melk* (1889), 5-106; P. Séjourné, "Pez (Bernard)," in *DThC*, 12 (1933), 1356-64; and "Pez (Jérôme)," ibid., 1564-65; *ADB*, 25: 569-73 (Bernard), 573-75 (Hieronymus); Hugo Hantsch, "Bernhard Pez und Abt Berthold Dietmayr," *MIÖG*, 71 (1963), 128-39; Martin Kropff, *BibliothecaMellicensis* (1747), 546-608, 677-82; and H. Rumpler in *New Catholic Encyclopedia* (1967), 11: 248. Stanislaus Autore's article in *DThC*, 15 (1950), 3614-16, catalogues only the texts that Wydemann helped Bernard Pez edit.

[2] See especially Hoffmann, "Aufhebung Gaming," 67ff, 126-29, and Winner, *Klosteraufhebungen*, 110ff.

have been lost. All the modern summaries of Kempf's writings have been based on Wydemann's list. Kempf's writings can be divided into four subject areas that also correspond roughly to the chronological order of their composition:

1. Academic and Pedagogical Writings
2. The Monastic Life
   A. Vocation, Novitiate, and Profession
   B. After Profession, including sermons to monks
3. The Carthusian life
4. Mystical spirituality
5. Liturgica, Sermons, Letters, Catechetica, Vernacular Writings
6. Dubia et Spuria

1.Academic and Pedagogical Writings

Two works survive from Kempf's arts faculty teaching.[3]

1. *Regulae grammaticales* (before 1442). R 1

> Inc. "Prima regula grammaticalis est ista utrum cuiuslibet construccionis suppositionalis suppositum et appositum debent in numero persona et rectitudine convenire In ista questione erunt tercius articuli principales In primo videbitur {de} coniunccione quelibet et quot modis capiamur secundus quelibet suppositionalis et que sit suppositum et appositum tertius an semper debet aut convenire in numero quartus an semper in persona quintus an semper in rectitudine"
>
> Expl. "Et que quandoque coniunctiones et sive sint adverba sive coniunctiones quando coniungunt dicciones casuales tunc debent coniungere consimiles casus Deo gracias"
>
> Vienna, ÖNB, cod. 4966 (Mondsee), 245r-279v; Munich, SB, clm 7649 (Indersdorf), 108r-132v.

Both the Mondsee and Indersdorf copies are attributed to Kempf in their colophons[4] and dated 1442 after Kempf had entered the charter-

---

[3] In the following pages "R" refers to the list by H. Rüthing in *DSAM*, 8: 1699-1703, and "W" refers to Wydemann's list in Melk 683 and the preface to *Bibl. ascetica*, vol. 4.

[4] Mondsee: "Expliciunt regule gramaticales reverendi magistri kemph de argentina et finite sub anno domini m cccc xlii"; Indersdorf: "Expliciunt regule grammaticales reverendi M. Nycolai kempf de argentina collecte in studio wienne a.d. 1442."

house at Gaming. The Mondsee copy also contains the third part of Jerome of Mondsee's commentary on Alexander de Villa Dei's *Doctrinale*, dated in 1453 after Jerome left Vienna to enter Mondsee. The two parts of the codex were originally separate, leading to the probable conclusion that the second half containing Kempf's treatise originated in university circles in Vienna and was Jerome's personal copy. The Indersdorf copy makes a direct reference to having been made at the university; it contains part two of the *Doctrinale*.

Based on a misreading of the incipit in the Mondsee copy, G. L. Bursill-Hall attributed a number of other sets of grammar rules to Kempf[5] but denied Kempf's authorship of the Indersdorf set, since its incipit seemed to be different from the Mondsee copy. In actuality, these two copies follow each other closely. None of the other sets of rules were attributed to Kempf by their copyists, and none of them contains the text found in the Mondsee and Indersdorf copies.

2. *Disputata super libros posteriorum Aristotelis* (1439) R 2

> Inc. "Circa primum librum posteriorum aristotelis movet Albertus primo questionem istam utrum sciencie de demonstracione sint quatuor cause"
>
> Expl. (Munich) "11. Utrum eiusdem demonstracionis possunt esse plura media causalia non subordinate in eodem genere cause" (no text follows this title for an eleventh *quaestio*).
>
> Expl. (Karlsruhe, *quaestio* twelve) "ad huius libri posteriorum finem nos salubriter perduxerit Pro quo grates sibi referamus uni in trinitate In seculorum secula benedicto Amen Et sic est finis huius operis Anno domini 1449"
>
> > Munich, SB, clm 19677 (Tegernsee), 156r-221v; Karlsruhe, Badische Landesbibliothek, cod. aug. 130 (Reichenau), 121r-187r.

---

5   Basel, UB, cod. F VII 8, 1r-46r; Berlin (West), SB Preußischer Kulturbesitz, cod. Lat. Q. 926, fol. 32-52; Cracov, Bibliotheca Jagiellonska, cod. 1944 (BB. XXVI. 12), pp. 261-308; Leipzig, UB, cod. 1235, fol. 308r-357v; Munich, SB, clm 3131 (Andechs), 173-180v; Munich, SB, clm 5942 (Ebersberg), 161v-78v; Munich, SB, clm 6725 (Freising), 204-215v; Munich, SB, clm 18998 (Tegernsee), 13-50; Munich, SB, clm 19656A (Tegernsee), 148r-175r; Wolfenbüttel, Herzog-August Bibliothek, cod. Helm 576 (Kloster Brunshausen near Gandersheim), 204v, 220r (fragments); Wolfenbüttel, Herzog-August Bibliothek, cod. Helm 692, 192v-196 (fragments). See Bursill-Hall, pp. 31, 36, 99, 104, 144, 147, 148, 157, 158, 274, 280, 281. Vienna, cvp 3820, 161r-189r, has the same text as several of the above. It was not associated with them in Bursill-Hall's census because the incipit given in the Vienna catalogue is incomplete.

Clm 19677 was copied by Wolfgang Kydrer in 1439 while he was a student at Vienna and was brought with him when he entered Tegernsee in 1462. The disputation was apparently copied again in 1449 in Vienna by a student named Vincent Kunst of Cottbus[6] (indicating that additional copies circulated in the university). It was brought to Reichenau by Johannes Pfuser of Nordstetten, librarian and later abbot (1464-92) of Reichenau.[7] The order of the questions follows that of the commentary on the *Posterior Analytics* found in manuscripts in Cracow, Munich, and Leipzig which Michalski attributed to Buridan but which Markowski has argued was in fact written by Albert of Saxony. Kempf certainly thought the commentary was by Albert.[8]

3. *Tractatus de sollicitudine superiorum habenda erga subditorum et innocentiam custodiam* (before 1456) R 27, W 19

Inc. "Super alios dei ordinacionem a quo paulo testante"
Expl. "et postea in eternam et in seculorum seculo habitant in celestibus per graciam superfluentem."
Admont, Stiftsbibliothek, cod. 103, 391r-405r. Aggsbach owned a copy from the fifteenth to the eighteenth century.[9]

This work could not have been written later than 1456, judging from the colophon of the preceding treatise in Admont 103, which ends in the same gathering and was written in the same hand as *De sollicitudine*. The colophon reads, "finiti in die agapiti [August 18] Anno etc. 56 (fol.

---

[6] Kunst matriculated in 1449, April 14, Hungarian nation. See *Matrikel*, 1: 269.

[7] See *Die Handschriften der Landesbibliothek Karlsruhe*, VII.2 (1914; repr. 1971), 287-88. On Pfuser, who was an excellent librarian but a less than outstanding abbot, see Hermann Baier, "Von der Reform des Abtes Friedrich von Wartenburg bis zur Säkularisation (1427-1803)," in *Die Kultur des Abtei Reichenau* [1200th Anniversary Festschrift] (1925; repr. 1974), 1: 213-62, at 216, 224-27; and S. K. Padover, "German Libraries in the Fourteenth and Fifteenth Centuries," in *The Medieval Library* (1939), 454. Pfuser professed at Reichenau in 1447 and was sent to Vienna for studies. He appears in the matriculation register in 1458 (first semester) as "Johannes Pawser de Norstetten." He paid a six-groschen fee.

[8] See Mieczyslaw Markowski, "Jean Buridan est-il l'auteur des questions sur les 'Seconds analytiques'?" *Mediaevalia philosophica polonorum*, 12 (1966), 16-30; cf. idem, *Buridanica quae in codicibus manu scriptis bibliothecarum Monacensium asservantur* (1981), 17-19, 144-45; idem, "Johannes Buridans Kommentar zu Aristoteles' Organon in Mitteleuropas Bibliotheken," in *The Logic of Jean Buridan* (1976), 9-20, at 14-16.

[9] See Theodor Gottlieb, ed., *Mittelalterliche Bibliothekskataloge Österreichs*, 1: 523-611, at 607, lines 17-19. I have also used the detailed summary in Roßmann, *Aggsbach*, 342-69, at 362. Cf. Pez, *Bibl. ascetica*, 4: 6vv, no. xxi, for Wydemann's reference to this codex in the eighteenth century.

391r, cf. 387v). The work was apparently written for schoolteachers, and
its purpose is as much pastoral as pedagogical: chapter one notes that
school rectors are not free of a domestic obligation to pastoral care, even
though in a strict sense they are not charged with a sacerdotal *cura animarum*.[10] The treatise deals with the upbringing of children in the fear of
God and in flight from vices, especially from *luxuria*. Two themes characteristic of Kempf's other writings support Wydemann's ascription of
this treatise to Kempf: the responsibilities and cares of those entrusted
with leadership and the problem of recognizing vices that masquerade as
virtues.[11] Although, in the absence of solid external evidence, the work
cannot with complete certainty be assigned to Kempf, internal evidence
and Wydemann's attribution make Kempf's authorship credible.

2. The Monastic Life

A. Vocation, Novitiate, Profession

4. *Dialogus de recto studiorum fine ac ordine et fugiendis vitae
saecularis vanitatibus* (1447) R 3, W 20

Inc. (prologue) "Voluntatis mee fuit atque consilij"; (chapter 1)
"Stultum et periculosum est diu fluctuare"
Expl. "Deus time et mandata eius observa . . . sive bonum, sive
malum sit. Amen."
Vienna, ÖNB, cvp 4259 [V1], 39r-77r; cvp 3616 (Mondsee),
1r-95r; cvp 4912, 291r-386v; Vienna, Schottenstift, cod. 143
(64), 179r-265v; Lambach, Stiftsbibliothek, MS chartac. 259,
74r-139v. All copies are incomplete. V1 lacks part II, ch. 18-

---

[10] Admont Stiftsbibliothek, cod. 103, 391r B, 17-35: "Nec arbitretur rectores scolarium se ad hanc sollicitudinem non esse obligatos, quia et si non habet animarum curam
proprie dictam, ut videlicet per sacramentorum medicamina curare debeant vulnera subditorum, quod concernit curatores in ecclesia, habent tamen curam circa eorum salutem
mores et vitam sicut paterfamilias ad suos domesticos et familiam—quorum qui curam
non gerit infidelibus deterior erit, dicente *Apostolus primo ad Thymotheum quinto* [1
Tim 5:8]: 'Si quis suorum maxime domesticorum curam non habet, fidem negavit et est
infideli deterior.' Quia infideles racione naturali domesticos suos ad bonos mores
dirigunt, plus eciam tenentur predicti scolarium et domorum studentium rectores ad
curam predictorum quam paterfamilias stipendium et nutrimentum obligatur."

[11] *De sollicitudine*, ch. 8. Cf. *Discr*, ch. 1 (*Bibl. ascetica*, 9: 382) and ch. 3 (9: 390);
Ost, ch. 31; *Serm. epist.*, sermon no. 65; *De vera et falsa caritate*, esp. ch. 1.

21; the other four lack part III, ch. 15-21; the Schottenstift copy also lacks Part II, ch. 14-19, the final paragraph of ch. 30, and all of ch. 31.

Gaming and Tegernsee owned copies in the early eighteenth century, since Wydemann referred to a Gaming copy in quarto and Pez made his edition (*Bibl. ascetica* 4: 258-492) from a Gaming manuscript. Pez mentioned a Tegernsee copy in the preface to that edition.[12] Portions of the treatise (I, II.1-16, III.18-21) were translated into German by Augustin Rösler, *Der Kartäuser Nikolaus Kempf und seine Schrift über das rechte Ziel und die rechte Ordnung des Unterrichts*, Bibliothek der katholischen Pädagogik, 7 (1894).

The five copies show few variant readings. The missing chapters described above make it unlikely that any, except possibly cvp 4912 and 3616, are directly dependent on each other. Jerome of Mondsee read this work during his novitiate; he may have brought it with him to Mondsee from the university. Both V1 and cvp 4912 belonged to the university library at Vienna in 1756,[13] although A.-Ch. Kogler has speculated that V1 may have originally come from Gaming. *De recto fine* has been interpreted from both pedagogical and ascetic perspectives.[14] Both perspectives are correct—all interpretations have failed to take account adequately of the interrelatedness of pedagogy and ascetic and mystical theology for Kempf.

5. *Tractatus de proponentibus religionis ingressum de anno probacionis usque ad professionem inclusive* (ca. 1440-51) R 24, W 2

Inc. "Convertimini ad me et salvi eritis ysaye 45o Quamvis divina miseracio multis varijsque modis in scripturis sanctis"
Expl. "iterum declinas post veteres mores tuos et consuetudines."

---

[12] On the Gaming and Tegernsee copies see also Melk 683, fol. 3r, and *Bibl. ascetica*, 4: b3.

[13] They are listed in the catalogue of the university library compiled by Benedikt Joseph Heyrenbach in 1777 and 1778 (cvp series nova cod. 2194, fol. 266r-268r, and cod. 2196, 348r-v). Their former shelf numbers were 534 and 176. Information from Professor Otto Mazal in a letter of May 9, 1981.

[14] Pedagogical: Paulus, "Kartäuser Nikolaus Kempf" (1928); Rösler; Dolfen, *Stellung Erasmus*, 27-30; ascetic: Hörmer. Rösler's translation, which appeared in a series on education, omits the sections on monastic life.

Under the title *De proponentibus religionis ingressum*:

Fulda, Hessische Landesbibliothek Aa 114, 114r-146r	F
Parkminster, St. Hugh's Chrtrhse, D150 (b 16 b), 1r-38v	Pk
Melk, Stiftsbibliothek, cod. 1093 (423), pp. 2-118	Mk1
Melk, cod. 878 (722), 178r-224r	Mk2
Melk, cod. 1562 (614), 143r-172r	Mk3
Rein, Zisterzienserstift, cod. 6, 3r-116r	R
St. Pölten, Bischöfl. Alumnatsbibl., cod. 77, 16r-61r	S
Vienna, ÖNB, cvp 4259, 14-38r	V1
Vienna, Schottenstift, cod. 336 (296), 3r-34v	VS1
Rimini, Biblioteca Gambalunga, 71, 42r-101v	Ri
Munich, SB, clm 16196 (St. Nikolaus, Passau), 6r-28v	M6

Under the title *De religionis ingressu*:

Munich, SB, clm 21625 (Weihenstephan), 265r-298v	M7
Lambach, Stiftsbibliothek, MS chartac. 259, 2r-72v	La

Under the title *De triplici statu religionem ingredientium*:

Munich, SB, clm 18555b (Tegernsee), 103r-163v	T1
Munich, SB, clm 18563 (Andechs/Tegernsee), 1r-74v	T2
Munich, SB, clm 4728 (Benediktbeuren), 36r-61v	M2a
Munich, SB, clm 5827 (Ebersberg), 42r-81r	M2b
Munich, SB, clm 7531 (Indersdorf), 235r-271r	M4

The Weihenstephan copy lacks a few lines in the final chapter. The charterhouse at Aggsbach owned a copy in the fifteenth century, and the Gaming library held one in the early eighteenth century. The Melk Stiftsarchiv possesses an eighteenth-century copy (MkA), sewn loosely in gatherings and, lacking a shelfmark, identified on the front only by the title and author: "De proponentibus religionis ingressum magistri Nicolai Kemph prioris in Gemnico." This undoubtedly was prepared as part of Pez's projected but never completed publication of the work.[15]

---

[15] *Bibl. ascetica* 4: 4r; Roßmann, *Aggsbach*, 362; Gottlieb, *Mittelalterliche BibliothekskatalogeÖsterreichs*, 1: 233, line 32; 239, line 33; 595, lines 18-19. The text of the eighteenth-century copy held today by the Melk Stiftsarchiv follows the Melk text family. It may have been made in Gaming from a Melk manuscript, for we know from Wydemann's letters that Pez sent Melk copies of Kempf's writings to Gaming (letter of May 6, 1721). It is hard to imagine, however, that Gaming did not have a copy of this work in the eighteenth century and the copies sent from Melk may have been other works by Kempf or, if they included *De proponentibus*, it might have served the purpose of colla-

This work could not have been written later than 1451, when both Mk1 and S were copied.[16] Jerome of Mondsee read the treatise as a novice in 1452. Both Johannes and Jerome ascribed the work to "Master Nicholas Kempf." Because internal evidence indicates that De discretione (no. 6 below), often transmitted as the "third part" mentioned in De proponentibus,[17] was begun before 1449 (ch. 3), one might also date the composition of De proponentibus before 1449. But Leopold Wydemann speculated that De discretione was written before De proponentibus,[18] questioning whether it was indeed the third part mentioned by Kempf at the beginning and end of De proponentibus. Although clearly related in content, the two works were not initially transmitted together. One of the earliest copies of De proponentibus, made at Melk, lacked at first the De discretione, although the copyist noted the author's mention of a third part. The same is true of La. This, of course, does not mean that De discretione had not yet been written, merely that the copyist did not have a copy of De discretione at hand when he copied De proponentibus. The other early copy (S), possibly of Carthusian origin, lacks any title or ascription and carries no copyist's mention of a third part to follow.[19] The earliest Vienna copies of De discretione are also independent of De proponentibus. It is possible that De proponentibus was written at Geirach, ca. 1447-49, while De discretione was begun in 1449 but not finished until after 1451. Parts of Ri were copied in 1438 (fol. 251v), but the Kempf treatise was not.[20]

---

tion. Part I, ch. 6, in the Melk Stiftsarchiv copy shows evidence of having been compared to the Vienna text family.

[16] Kropff, Bibliotheca Mellicensis (1747), 246 and Mk1, p. 118: "Explicit secunda pars huius tractatus magistri nicolai chemph de argentina. Anno domini millesimo quadringentesimo 51o in dedicacione ecclesie mellicensis [February 27] per fratrem Johannem de Spitz finitus. Tercia vero pars de qua supra nondum erat compilata." I am indebted P. Gottfried Glaßner of the Melk Stiftsbibliothek for information on the date of the anniversary of the dedication of the fifteenth century "ecclesie mellicensis." St. Pölten, Bischöfliche Alumnatsbibliothek, cod. 77, fol. 61r, reads: "Et sic est finis huius operis Amen Deo gracias 1451 Anno domini etc. quinquagesimo primo in vigilia Tyburcy [August 11?] etc." The St. Pölten manuscript also contains a series of questions related specifically to the Carthusian order (fol. 1-16) and various sermons by Vienna theologians. It is mentioned briefly by Gerhard Winner, "Zur Bibliotheksgeschichte des ehemaligen Augustiner-Chorherrenstiftes St. Pölten," in Translatio Studii [Kapsner Festschrift] (1973), 48-74, at 62, 64. La has a note of 1449 at the end of Ebendorfer, De confessione. I have seen only a microfilm copy of La and thus could not study the gatherings to assess whether the entire codex was copied in 1449.

[17] De proponentibus, I.2 (VS1, 3r B, 35-39), and II.22 (VS1, 33v B, 1).

[18] Wydemann to Pez, May 6, 1721, "Peziana," fol. 2r.

[19] De proponentibus, I.28 (VS1, 18v B, 39-41); I.11 (VS1, 27v B, 22ff.).

[20] Donatella Frioli, I Codici del Cardinale Garampi nella Biblioteca Gambalunghi-

We can distinguish two text families among the copies of *De proponentibus*. The first (X1) consists of the three Melk fifteenth-century copies, whose texts follow each other very closely, and the
eighteenth-century Melk Stiftsarchiv copy. The Vienna, St. Pölten, Rein,
Fulda (Blaubeuren), Parkminster,[21] and Bavarian copies all belong to
one family (X2). VS1 (copied 1464-65) offers an interesting mediation
between both families, having been copied from an X2 exemplar but corrected with marginal additions according to the Melk family. The Fulda
copy, from Blaubeuren by way of Weingarten,[22] lacks the corrections incorporated into some of the Melk copies and added in the margins of
VS1 but seems not to have been copied from any of the Bavarian cluster.
The tentative *stemma codicum* found in appendix C is based on the colla-
tion of sample chapters.

The prologue found in V1 and R appears in the Melk, Fulda, Parkminster, Rimini, and Schottenstift manuscripts as chapter one. Because
of the resulting discrepancy in chapter numbering, citations to Part I are
given in this study in dual form, e.g., "ch. 5/6," where 5 refers to the
numbering of V1/R and most of the Bavarian manuscripts, and 6 refers
to the numbering of the Mk/VS/F/Pk/R copies. The St. Pölten copy and
most Bavarian manuscripts do not title chapter one as a prologue but
they still correspond to the lower V1/R numbering because they combine
what are chapters one and two in the Mk/VS/F/Pk/Ri numbering into a
single chapter one. Wydemann indicated in a letter of May 6, 1721, that
the Gaming copy he used did the same.

How the treatise reached the Bavarian monasteries is not clear. All
Bavarian copies lack the more complete readings of the Melk family that
were entered on VS1, and most are titled differently than the Austrian
copies. The earliest among the extant Bavarian copies is T1, but, judging
from its colophon, it was copied after the *De discretione* of T3, both being the work of Oswald Nott of Tittmoning. A further reference in a different hand is found after Nott's colophon in T1 and refers to the
combination *De proponentibus/De discretione* in T2. Nott copied other

---

ana (1986), 24, 81-84, and eadem, *Biblioteca civica Gambalunghiana* in *Catalogo
di manoscritti filosofici nelle Biblioteche italiane* (1980), 1: 131-34. I would like to
thank Dr. Paola Delbianco of the Biblioteca Gambalunga for supplying additional details.

[21] The text transmitted in F and Pk is very closely related. An eyeskip in chapter 1
suggests that Parkminster could have been copied from F, but F could not have been copied from Pk.

[22] See Schreiner, "Klosterreform," 139. A detailed description of this codex by Re-
gina Hausmann of the Württembergische Landesbibliothek is forthcoming. I am grateful
to Dr. Hausmann for providing photocopies of the opening chapters of *De proponentibus*
in this codex, permitting me to place it approximately on the *stemma*.

portions of T2. Had T2 been finished before T1, one could reasonably expect Nott's colophon in T1 to have referred to T2. Instead he pointed only to T3 and it remained for a different, certainly later scribe, to call the attention of the reader of T1 to the Kempf writings in T2.

We may thus conclude tentatively that the *De proponentibus* of T1 preceded the *De proponentibus* and *De discretione* of T2 (made at Andechs in 1458).[23] *De discretione* clearly arrived in Bavaria before *De proponentibus*—arriving first in T3 (undated) or in the 1457 Andechs copy found in M1 (copied by Sigmund Schröttinger of Seebach).[24] All early Bavarian copies of these two treatises were made either at Tegernsee or its newly acquired daughter house at Andechs. Three other copies of *De proponentibus/De discretione* (M2a and M2b, which are directly dependent on each other, and M4) stand in close relationship to the 1458 Andechs copy (T2). Variants in M7 indicate that it may have been copied in conjunction with the Tegernsee/Andechs cluster, but M6 clearly was transmitted independently.[25] Based on Dr. Hausmann's assessment of the watermarks, the Blaubeuren copy (F) was made sometime between 1453 and 1469. A tabulation of the Bavarian cluster follows:

M1	3034	*De discretione*	1457	Andechs
T3	18211	*De discretione*	?	Tegernsee
T1	18555b	*De proponentibus*	?	Tegernsee
T2	18563	*De prop./De discr.*	1458	Andechs
M2a	4728	*De prop./De discr.*	1462	Benediktbeuren
M2b	5827	*De prop./De discr.*	?	Ebersberg
M4	7531	*De prop./De discr.*	?	Indersdorf

In *De proponentibus* Kempf sought to counsel and encourage postulants and novices in the religious life, a *status* that is more perfect, more secure from anxiety about one's soul, and more meritorious (by virtue of the rule as crutch) than other states of life. In part I Kempf cautioned against delaying too long in order to deliberate or seek advice (ch. 5/6). He then discussed some of the commonly, often devilishly, raised objec-

---

[23] Nott copied fol. 145r-189r in T2 (see the colophons fol. 170r, 189r). The colophon in T1, fol. 163v, reads (in Nott's hand, apparently written at the same time as the text that precedes it): "Tercia pars huius tractatus habetur in libro epistolarum beati bernardi abbattis d 31 [T3/clm 18211]." A different hand added: "Quere hos tractatus magistri nicolai kempf in libro h 45 [T2/clm 18563] et est in meliori forma."

[24] On Schröttinger (d. 1471), see Redlich, *Tegernsee* (1931), 146-50, 194; Pirmin Lindner, "Familia S. Quirini," 67; Johannes Heldwein, *Die Klöster Bayerns*, 128.

[25] Unlike the Austrian copies and M6/M7, most of the Bavarian copies do not divide *De proponentibus* into two parts. M7 was apparently copied from a manuscript that was not subdivided but M7's copyist added a two-part division.

tions to entering religion: fear of the rigor of Carthusian solitude or the desire to acquire academic degrees or greater learning stemming from perilous pride in academic achievements (ch. 7/8-13/14). As with pastoral duties (ch. 15/16-17/18), so with studies: to whom much is given, of him much will be demanded at the last judgment. Kempf continued part I with a discussion of which order one should enter, of the necessity to leave parents and home, and of the time required to adjust to solitude and an austere life. Part I closes with a description of how a postulant should seek admission as a novice and an explanation of the difference between the status of monk and *redditus*. (*Redditi* were lay brothers who handled the external affairs and extraneous field work of the Carthusian community, freeing the *conversi*, or lay brothers in a strict sense, for work closer to the main monastery, where they could live more separated from the world. The *redditi* were gradually replaced by the *donati*, who signed a civil contract rather than taking even the simple vows of the *conversi* and *redditi*. The distinctions between these categories, however, soon became blurred.[26])

In Part II Kempf discussed whether and in which circumstances one may leave the novitiate to return to the world, or postpone one's intended profession (ch. 1-5). Exhortations to patience and humility as the most effective means against vices follow, together with an explanation of the symbolism of the Carthusian vestments (ch. 6-7). Another of Kempf's most prominent themes appears in chapters 8, 9, and 14-16: no monk should trust too far his own prudence and discretion, but should rather entrust himself to a spiritual director. In addition to advice on day-to-day life in the cell and during divine office, with a characteristic warning against indiscretion in spiritual exercises, Kempf turned to another theme that occurs in his other works: the displeasure, dislikes, and suspicions that may arise toward fellow monks, superiors, or spiritual directors (ch. 16-19; cf. *De capitulo* and *De suspicionibus*). After chapters on silence and on moderation in food and drink, the concluding chapter (23) deals with the profession itself ("De professione et modo se preparandi ad eam"). In this way Kempf's *De proponentibus* offers insight into the Carthusian novitiate that is not commonly found in Carthusian writings of the preceding century.[27]

---

[26] See Jacques Dubois, "L'institution des convers au XIIe siècle, forme de la vie monastique propre aux laïcs," in *I laici nella "societas cristiana" dei secoli XI e XII* (1968), 183-261, abridged and translated as "The Laybrothers' Life in the Twelfth Century: A Form of Lay Monasticism," *CS*, 7 (1972), 161-213, here *CS*, 7 (1972), 188; and E. Margaret Thompson, *The Carthusian Order in England*, 123-34.

[27] See Rüthing, *Egher von Kalkar*, 12-13, regarding the problems encountered in gaining knowledge about Carthusian spiritual formation and novitiate in the fourteenth

6. *De discretione* (begun before 1449) R 34, W 4

Inc. "Bonum est sal Luce XII [Lk 14:34] Sal discrecionem significat"
Expl. "quam quis vovet expresse de qua tamen posterius lacius dicetur."

Vienna, ÖNB, cvp 4742, 139r-170v	V2
Vienna, ÖNB, cvp 4736, 49r-107r	V3
Vienna, Schottnstft, cod. 336 (296), 34v-51v, 260r-269v	VS1
Melk, cod. 1093 (423), pp. 119-338	Mk1
Melk, cod. 878 (722), 225r-296v	Mk2
Melk, cod. 1562 (614), 172r-205r	Mk3
Budapest, UL, cod. 72 (charterhouse Lövöld), 97v-154v	B1

Under the title *De religiosorum profectibus et perfectione*:

Munich, SB, clm 3034 (Andechs), 159v-202r	M1
Munich, SB, clm 18211 (Tegernsee), 165v-188v	T3
Munich, SB, clm 18563 (Andechs/Tegernsee), 75r-136v	T2
Munich, SB, clm 4728 (Benediktbeuren), 62r-87r	M2a
Munich, SB, clm 5827 (Ebersberg), 82r-124v	M2b
Munich, SB, clm 7531 (Indersdorf), 203r-234v	M4

Excerpts in Vienna, ÖNB, cvp 4789, cvp 4121; Melk 683; published in *Bibl. ascetica*, 9: 380-532

V2 is incomplete, lacking ch. 25b-36. V3 may have been owned by Thomas Ebendorfer of Haselbach. Aggsbach owned a copy in the fifteenth century, and the Gaming library held one in the eighteenth century.[28]

The Austrian and Hungarian copies of *De discretione* show a number of generally minor text variations, indicating that each was copied independently from exemplars belonging to a common text family. The Bavarian copies, transmitted under a distinct title, fall into two groups: (A) T3 and M1 and (B) T2, M2a, M2b, and M4. As discussed above in

---

century. In Kempf's century, writings by Denys of Rijkel and others removed some of the obscurity.

[28] On V3 see Lhotsky, *Thomas Ebendorfer* (1957), 64. For the Aggsbach and Gaming copies see *Bibl. ascetica*, 4: 4r; Roßmann, *Aggsbach* (1976), 362. The Aggsbach copy may be identical with V2.

conjunction with *De proponentibus*, the first Bavarian copy of *De discretione* was either T3 (Nott) or M1, the latter dated 1457 and copied at Andechs. In 1458 a third copy, T2, was made at Andechs in close cooperation with Oswald Nott (see fol. 145r-189r in Nott's hand). Its variant readings, largely omissions, indicate that it was probably copied from either T3 or M1 rather than from one of the Austrian copies. Nott took this codex (T2) with him when he returned to Tegernsee from Andechs. The remaining three Bavarian copies (M2a, M2b, and M4) follow T2 closely.

De discretione was begun before the Basel schism ended in 1449. Wydemann assigned it a date of ca. 1446.[29] For its contents see chapter four, section 1.B, above. A portion (ch. 11-14) of the dialogue between *Humilitas* and *Superbia*, between a spiritual director and a monk whose pride makes him unwilling to reveal all, was excerpted in a Mondsee manuscript (cvp 4121, 181r-189r) under the title, "Disputacio superbie cum humilitate quod non omnia sunt revelanda, ex dictis M. N. K."[30] [Incipit: "Incumbit modo argumenti dissolvere"; Explicit: "pure revelare sicut enim teste sapiencie abscondens scelere sua non dirigetur ita quando" breaking off in mid-sentence; cf. Pez 9: 448.]. Extensive excerpts and summaries from chapters 4 through 30 of *De discretione*, including parts of the dialogue between Humility and Pride, are found in a Mondsee notebook, Vienna cvp 4789, 89r-108v. They range back and forth, not necessarily following the order of the original treatise. They may have been made by Jerome of Mondsee. Wydemann also reported the existence at Gaming of a German version of *De discretione*.[31]

---

[29] Ch. 3 (VS1, 36v B, 4-19; *Bibl. ascetica*, 9: 393). References to the neutral party in the schism might suggest a date before the Vienna concordat of 1447-48. Wydemann to Pez, May 20, 1720, fol. 2rv; May 6, 1721, fol. 1v-3r.

[30] The eighteenth-century excerpts, "De revelatione," in Melk cod. 683, 7r-17v, are not extracted word-for-word, but represent summaries of sections from ch. 11-19 (cvp 4121 excerpts word-for-word) of *De discretione*. They were probably made by Wydemann, who mentioned such an undertaking in a letter to Pez, May 6, 1721, fol. 3r.

[31] "Tractatum de discretione spirituum ejusdem Nicolai, qui alias tam in vulgari quam in latino habetur separatus." Wydemann to Pez, May 29, 1720.

B. After Profession

7. *De tribus essentialibus omnium religiosorum* R 25, W 18

Inc. "Tria sunt omnis religionis fundamenta ad que quilibet tenetur religiosus"
Expl. "homines castos faciliarius diligunt. Amen."
  Melk, Stiftsbibliothek, cod. 1381 (280), pp. 597-604; Graz, UB, cod. 973 (Seitz), 232v-235v.

The relatively commonplace subject matter of this short treatise, which cites scripture, Bernard of Clairvaux, Gregory, and Jerome on obedience, voluntary poverty, and chastity, offers little internal evidence for its date of composition or for testing its ascription to Kempf by Wydemann. It contains nothing that would make Kempf's authorship questionable.

[8-11. *De caritate et vitiis* (ca. 1449-51)]

The following four treatises were transmitted as a unit and constitute a four-part work to which I have given the collective title, *De caritate et vitiis*. The works are found in three manuscripts, Vienna, cvp 4742 (V2), Budapest, UL, cod. 72 (B1), and Bibliothèque Nationale, Latin 3619 [P] (Mauerbach). P is dated 1453; the other two were probably copied in the early 1450s.[32] An eyeskip in B1 (3v, 28-30) corresponds with the vertical alignment of two occurrences of *hermon* in P, suggesting that B1 was copied directly from P. Both B1 and P are clearly textually superior to the hastily copied V2. Between the fifteenth and eighteenth centuries the Aggsbach library owned a copy dated 1451.[33] The Mauerbach copy made its way to Paris by way of Buxheim (seventeenth century). Since half of P's contents[34] correspond to Vienna cvp

---

[32] The Budapest manuscript can be dated to 1467. Wydemann reported an Aggsbach copy that was dated "in die S. Agapiti martyris [August 18] anno 1451." Watermarks in Vienna cvp 4742 point to a date between, or in any case not before, the years 1449-1453. See Gerhard Piccard, *Findbuch der Wasserzeichenkartei im Hauptstaatsarchiv Stuttgart*, vol. 2, pt. 3 (1966), watermark series XI, nos. 211-12.

[33] *Bibl. ascetica*, 4: 4r-v; Roßmann, *Aggsbach*, 362. The Aggsbach copy may be identical with Vienna, cvp 4742.

[34] P is a most interesting manuscript, made up of two distinct parts, yet rubricated by the same hand throughout. The first part, dated 1453, contains Kempf's four-part trea-

4739,[35] presumably an Aggsbach manuscript, it is possible that the other half, consisting of Kempf's four treatises, was made from the 1451 Aggsbach copy, with V2 representing a second, hasty copy, from the same 1451 Aggsbach exemplar.

Although not expressly attributed to Kempf in any manuscript, the treatises reflect his characteristic themes and these support Wydemann's ascription to Kempf. Again and again the reader is reminded that great care must be taken to discern between true and false virtues and vices. Great stress is laid on concord within the cloister as expressed in the opening of Ps 132 [133]: "Ecce quam bonum et quam iocundum habitare fratres in unum."[36]

8. *De vera, perfecta, et spirituali caritate* (Wydemann: *De tendentia ad perfectionem*) R 9, W 9

Inc. "Ecce quam bonum et quam iocundum . . . Contraria iuxta se posita dicente Aristotelis clarius se declarant"
Expl. (Vienna) "videbimus quam bonum et iocundum erit nos habitare in unum hic et in futuro debet [quod ? Paris] nobis concedat christus dominus cum patre et spiritu sancto unus deus benedictus." (Budapest) "antequam scrupuli in eo fuerint radicati."

Budapest, UL, cod. 72 [B1], 1r-18v; Vienna, ÖNB, cvp 4742 [V2], 1r-13r (incomplete); Paris, Bibliothèque Nationale, Latin 3619 [P], 2r-16r (incomplete).

9. *De vera et falsa caritate inter fratres in unum habitantes* R 15, W 5

---

tise. The second part was copied at Mauerbach (fol. 194) in a single hand by a "brother Jerome" (fol. 138), and consists of a series of legends and tales, including Johannes de Alta Silva's *Dolopathos*, Petrarch's Latin version of the Griselda story, the story of Karlomann and Pepin, and the *Visio Tnugdalis*. See the detailed description (unaware of Kempf's authorship) in *Bibliothèque Nationale, Catalogue général des manuscrits latins* (1975), 6: 367-70.

[35] See Adolf Mussafia, "Über die Quelle des altfranzösischen 'Dolopathos'," *Sitzungsberichte der kaiserlichen Akademie der Wissenschaften* [Vienna], Phil.-hist. Cl., 48 (1864), 246-67.

[36] Cf. *De proponentibus*, I.5/6 (VS1, 6r A, 23-25); II.14 (30v B, 4); *Serm. epist.*, no. 48 (G2, 74r-76v) and no. 61 (G2, 97r-98v); *De capitulo*, 1 (V2, 54r, 2-3). The theme is a prominent one in Augustine, who is cited in *De vera, perfecta, et spirituali caritate*, ch. 1. See Augustine, *Enarrationes in Psalmos*, CCSL, 40 (1956), 1926-35.

Inc. "Omnibus nostris virtutibus et bonis aliqua sunt vitia et mala adeo vicinia et similia"

Expl. "tali pestiferi magistri discipulus efficiatur. Quod non omnibus [Paris: quod nobis concedere dignetur]"

Budapest, UL, cod. 72 [B1], 19r-32r; Vienna, ÖNB, cvp 4742 [V2], 13r-23r; Paris, Bibliothèque Nationale, Latin 3619 [P], 16v-31r.

To a discussion of true and false charity Kempf added three chapters on the fruits of true and false charity, which are true and false peace, the latter giving rise to a detestable vice of *conspiratio*.

10. *De peccatis caritati contrariis scilicet inpatientia, ira, invidia, et odio et suis filiabus et nepotatibus* R 16, W 6

Inc. "Visum est aliquantulum de vera proximi amicicia"

Expl. "in nobis acquirere caritatem et pacem perpetuam quam nobis donare dignetur auctor pacis et caritatis" [Paris: caritatis, Christus dominus, qui cum Patre]

Budapest, UL, cod. 72 [B1], 33v-75v; Vienna, ÖNB, cvp 4742 [V2], 23r-53r (incomplete); Paris, Bibliothèque Nationale, Latin 3619 [P], 31r-74r.

The final portion of this treatise in both manuscripts is a series of patristic excerpts under the heading, "Documenta sanctorum patrum contra predicta peccata tradita et in proposiciones redacta." This was listed as a separate work by Wydemann and Rüthing (R 17, W 7), since, in V2 these thirteen *propositiones* were added as an appendix, fol. 49v-53r, whereas in B1 they were numbered consecutively with the earlier chapters.

11. *De suspicionibus* R 18, W 8

Inc. "In predictorum quatuor viciorum scilicet inpaciencie, ire, invidie, et odij expugnacione"

Expl. "et ita decipiam Achab id est serenitatem [Paris: fraternitatem], quod nobis donare [Paris: prestare] dignetur"

Budapest, UL, cod. 72 [B1], 76r-97v; Vienna, ÖNB, cvp 4742 [V2], 221r-235r; Paris, Bibliothèque Nationale, Latin 3619 [P], 74r-96r.

According to Wydemann (*Bibl. ascetica*, 4: b 4v), an incomplete copy found at Seitz in the eighteenth century contained further reference to a Pleterje copy.

The treatise takes as its point of departure the story in 3 Kings 22 and 2 Paral. [2 Chron] 18 of Kings Ahab and Jehoshaphat at war with the Syrians. Ahab, disguised to avoid becoming a special royal target, was killed by a stray Syrian arrow. Jehoshaphat, under attack because he made no attempt to disguise the fact that he was a king, called upon God and was saved. In the same way, according to Kempf, the stray arrows of suspicions destroy the fraternal concord, or *serenitas*, represented by Ahab. The need for careful judgment and discretion on the part of both followers and leaders (subjects and superiors) once more appears as a characteristic concern of Kempf. These themes are even more prominent in the following work:

12. *Tractatus de capitulo religiosorum* (1450-65) R 29, W 13

> Inc. "Quamvis in omni loco et tempore sit bonum et iocundum habitare fratres in unum"
> Expl. "per graciam humilitatis et predictorum principiorum et omnium virtutum perducat nos ad gloriam eternam."

> Budapest, UL, cod. 77 (charterhouse Lapis refugii, i.e., Lethenkow), 76r-157v; Vienna, ÖNB, cvp 4742 [V2], 54r-132v; Graz, UB, 910 (Seitz), 82r-117v (incomplete).
> An Aggsbach and a Seitz copy existed in the early eighteenth century; these may be identical with V2 and Graz, UB, 910.[37]

The transmission of this bulky work (ninety-two chapters in four parts), together with the cycle *De caritate et vitiis* in V2 and thematic similarities with that work make a date of composition in the 1450s or early 1460s probable. A Gaming monk, Wolfgang (Benedict) Neuböck of Scheibbs (entered Gaming in 1446) was sent in 1459 as prior to the charterhouse of Lechnitz, a neighboring, quasi-daughter foundation of Lethenkow [Lapis refugii], near Menédekszirt on the Slovakian/Polish border. He died in 1465. He may have had something to do with the transmission of the Kempf treatise in Budapest, UL, cod. 77. But it is also possible that the manuscript was copied from a Lövöld codex.

---

[37] *Bibl. ascetica*, 4: 5r-v; Roßmann, *Aggsbach*, 362.

Kempf's works were known there (B1), and Prior Gabriel of Lethenkow (1463-71) was a former monk of Lövöld.[38] Furthermore, the Hungarian charterhouses generally had close ties to the Lower Austrian houses.

The three surviving copies of *De capitulo* show only minor textual variations but none appears to be directly dependent on the another. The Graz copy, bound with texts copied between 1484 and 1492, breaks off in mid-sentence near the end of chapter fourteen of part three.[39] Kempf's authorship can scarcely be questioned on the basis of internal evidence, and the first attribution to Kempf occurred in a note added to the Budapest copy only short after his death.[40]

The work discusses various issues arising out of the weekly Carthusian chapter of faults: the proper attitude of patience and humility required of the person confessing his fault; the proper role for fraternal correction; the situations calling for accusation of one monk by another and the witnesses required in such cases; the rare situations when the accused may legitimately defend or excuse himself; the justice, patience, and humility required of a superior and of the others attending. Kempf insists on the importance and necessity of authority and reminds those in positions of authority of the complexity, responsibility, and difficulty of their task.

Wydemann reported the existence of a vernacular version of this work (R 30, W 14), made for the benefit of the lay brothers at Gaming. It does not appear to have survived the dispersal of the Gaming library. Wydemann gave as the *incipit*: "In dem puech Job am funffzehende capital stet geschriben was ist der mensch das er will sein unvermailigt" Although Wydemann had not seen this version, he suggested that it was actually a distinct treatise with a different number of chapters. The fifteenth-century Aggsbach catalogue also describes a work by Kempf written for lay brethren.[41]

---

[38] See chapter three, section 5, above, regarding Neuböck. Three Gaming monks spent some time at Lövöld in the mid-fifteenth century. They were Johannes of Mergentheim, a monk of Gaming who was prior at Lövöld before his election as prior at Gaming in 1443 [he died before he could make the trip to Gaming]; Wolfgang of Wolkersdorf, who entered Gaming from Melk in 1440 and died at Lövöld in 1474; and Johannes Velber of Passau, who entered Gaming in 1441. Dissatisfied, Velber returned to Gaming. Information on Prior Gabriel of Lethenkow (Lapis refugii) was supplied by Adrienne Fodor of the Budapest University Library.

[39] On the Graz codez see Maria Mairold, "Zur Bibliotheksgeschichte der Kartause Seitz," in *Die Kartäuser in Österreich* (1980), 1: 23-47, at 32, 39, 47.

[40] Budapest, UB, cod. 77, 157v (fifteenth- or early sixteenth-century hand).

[41] Roßmann, *Aggsbach*, 362; Gottlieb, *Mittelalterliche Bibliothekskataloge Österreichs*, 1: 607, lines 14-15: "Tractatus de ordine cartusiensi ad convertendos et conversos, quomodo se habere debeant magistri Nicolai Kempf."

13. *Memoriale primorum principiorum in scolis virtutum*, or *Modus vivendi in ordine, praecipue cartusiensi* (1441-62) R 26, W 3

> Inc. "In scolis scienciarum teste Aristotele eciam"
> Expl. "ad pacem cordis et caritatem per finem et in futura vita ad eterna premia a primo principio deo taliter perseverantibus usque in finem reservata et in seculorum secula duratura Amen."

> Vienna, Schottenstift, cod. 137 (58), 187r-200r.
> Gaming owned two copies and the charterhouse at Olomouc in Moravia had one copy in the eighteenth century.[42]

Paulus dated the composition of this treatise in 1441 on the basis of a colophon (1491) reported by Wydemann, that referred to the writing of the work "ante quinquaginta annos" and informed the reader that the author's works and his reputation were still highly regarded in Vienna university circles.[43] The same anonymous scribe, however, comments that the author drew on his experience, the best teacher, rather than on citations from the Fathers. Kempf was not a particularly experienced monk in 1441, but the scribe may have been referring to Kempf's spiritual experience gained while a teacher. The work's obvious point of reference is the university as a foil for the charterhouse, and it apparently circulated in university circles.

The thirty short chapters of the *Memoriale* share much material in common with nos. 6-12 above. Chapter 25 on secular *amor* recalls chapter 2 of *De vera et falsa caritate*; chapter 17 corresponds to chapter 7 of *De vera, perfecta, et spirituali caritate*; chapter 30 repeats the characteristic caution against vices masquerading as virtues and the necessity of following the discretion of others more experienced in the spiritual life; and chapters 6-8 deal with revelation and obedience to one's spiritual director in a manner reminiscent of *De discretione*.

Because several of the previously described works on the monastic life originated as sermons, it is not out of place to introduce here two sermon cycles that are in effect series of miniature treatises on monastic themes.

---

[42] *Bibl. ascetica* 4: 4r.

[43] *Bibl. ascetica*, 4: 1v; cf. Melk, Stiftsbibliothek, cod. 683, 2v.

14a. *Sermones super epistolas et evangelia de tempore per totum annum* R 5, W 29-30

Super epistolas:

Inc. (prologue) "Sermo generalis secundum Aristotelem minus utilis (sermon one) Incipit dominica prima in adventum domini: Quomodo religiosus debeat seipsum cognoscere . . . Apostolice leccionis que in hoc sacro dominicali adventus tempore in missarum sompniis leguntur"

Expl. "Consistit felicitas summa in cognicione et amore ineffabilibus ad quam nos perducere dignetur christus dominus cum patre et spiritu sancto in secula benedictus Amen."

Graz, UB, cod. 559 [G2] (Seitz), 1r-114v.

14b. *Super evangelia*:

Inc. (prologue) "Sicut panis bene masticatus et contritus facilius deglutitur digeritur meliusque suscipientem nutrit . . . (sermon one) Quomodo ante iudicium finale erint signa in sole luna et stellis spiritualibus id est ecclesiasticis personis precipue sancta ewangelia lectio docet nos de adventu iudici et finali iudicio et signis"

Expl. "et superbis maioris culpe ocasio quia sicut electis omnia in bonum ita reprobis omnia in malum cooperantur."

Graz, UB, cod. 559 [G2] (Seitz), 115r-248v; Graz, UB, cod. 973 (Seitz), 1r-212r; Melk, cod. 953 (352), pp. 3-339.

A copy was held by the charterhouse at Olomouc in the eighteenth century.[44]

The copy in Graz, UB, cod. 973, omits major sections within many sermons and has frequent variations in word order to provide smooth transitions. It was more hurriedly copied and lacks rubrics, but its marginal annotations indicate heavier use than G2. Wydemann's attribution to Kempf is supported by transmission in two nearly identical Seitz codices, each containing two other Kempf treatises (nos. 7, 16-17). Graz 973 fits the description given by Wydemann of a Seitz quarto with "Sermones in evangelia dominicalia totius anni ad religiosos eorumque reformandos mores." The other codex, G2, may well be the Seitz folio referred to by Wydemann as a *Liber sermonum super epistolas et evangelia totius anni*—Wydemann had not compared these and assumed that

---

[44] *Bibl. ascetica*, 4: 7r.

they were different sets of sermons. The Melk copy is attributed to "a Carthusian" in a fifteenth-century hand; an eighteenth-century hand (Pez?) added a specific name that was later so thoroughly blotted out as to be indecipherable from microfilm. The opening reference to Aristotle's maxim, "Sermo generalis . . . minus utilis" is also found in *De recto fine*, II.5.

These sermons demonstrate an ability to find applications for the lectionary that reached into the most practical aspects of life in the cloister. Kempf's concern with *discretio*, with false or pseudo-virtues, and with the role of leaders in the monastery recur in these sermons.[45] Their transmission in Seitz codices provides only a tenuous indication of their date of origin—perhaps after 1462 during Kempf's Pleterje or Geirach priorates.

3. The Carthusian Life

15. *De confirmatione et regula approbata ordinis cartusiensis* (1452-60) R 22, W 21

> Inc. "Legitur Apokal. 12. quod postquam draco traxit terciam partem stellarum celi tunc mulier amicta sole et lunam"
> Expl. "et aput districtum iudicere premia eterne pacis inveniant."
> Vienna, ÖNB, cvp 4259 [V1], 78r-94v; Vienna, ÖNB, cvp 13904 [V5], 1r-33r.
> Aggsbach owned a copy from the fifteenth to the eighteenth centuries; the Gaming library held one in the eighteenth century.[46]

The claim that Kempf wrote this treatise rests on Wydemann's authority and the work's treatment of Carthusian origins as a flight from the university, which corresponds to Kempf's *De recto fine* and his life experience. Exactly when *De confirmatione* was written is a bit obscure, since chronological data within the treatise appears to be inconsistent. At one point the authors says that 368 years have elapsed since the founding of the Carthusian order (1083-84) and 254 years since Innocent III's

---

[45] On pseudo-virtues, compare *Rect*, III.1 (V1, 60v-61r; *Bibl. ascetica*, 4: 415-17), and *Discr*, esp. ch. 4, with *Serm. epist.*, nos. 23, 63, and 65. On leadership and authority in the monastery, see *Serm. epist.*, nos. 3, 51-52, 54-55, and *Serm. evang.*, nos. 10-11, 29, 49, and 67.

[46] *Bibl. ascetica*, 4: 6r; Roßmann, *Aggsbach*, 362.

pontificate began (1198), the year in which he placed the beginning of the Dominican order (ch. 15/16; V5, 23r). Both these dates would yield 1451-52. But an earlier chapter (7/6, V5, 9) tells us that 298 years had elapsed since the order was confirmed by Alexander III, 78 years after its founding (1161-62). This would mean that 376 years had elapsed since the founding of the order, yielding 1459-60 as the date at which *De confirmatione* was being written. It is possible that the treatise was written over a period of time and Kempf saw no reason to bring the chronological references into conformity; perhaps he made an arithmetical error or was assuming different dates for historical events than those employed by modern historians.

Although cvp 13904 (V5) has been claimed as coming from the Roermond charterhouse near today's Dutch-German-Belgian border,[47] its script and binding suggest an Austrian origin, and it may even be a Gaming codex.[48] It shows scarcely any variants when compared to V1, although the latter divides chapter 4 into two chapters. (This accounts for the dual citation in this study; lower numbers refer to V5, higher numbers to V1.)

De confirmatione contains most features of Kempf's theological, ascetic/mystical program in concise form. His purpose was to defend the Carthusian order from the rumors and scurrilous tales current outside the houses of the order. He sought to disprove the charge that the order had never received papal approval and to discredit accounts of the purported dire consequences of the order's ascetic practices, notably total abstention from eating flesh foods. His purpose was not unusual, but Kempf's treatment differs somewhat from that of other contemporary defenses of the order.[49] In telling the apocryphal story of the "Professor of Paris"

---

[47] E. Persoons claimed that it came to Vienna after Roermond was dissolved under Joseph II. E. Persoons, "Handschriften uit Kloosters in de Nederlanden in Wenen," *Archives et bibliothèques de Belgique*, 38 (1967), 59-107, at 85. Although Persoons referred to Lucidus Verschueren, *De Bibliotheek der Kartuizers van Roermond* (1941), nos. 164-66, this seems to be incorrect. The treatises contained in V5 are not listed anywhere in Verschueren's work, nor is this codex included in the list of extant manuscripts on p. 100. Österreichische Nationalbibliothek records indicate that the codex was purchased from a private collector in 1854. Letter from Professor Otto Mazal, May 9, 1981.

[48] A.-Ch. Kogler, "Mémoire," 134

[49] E.g. Denys of Rijkel's *De praeconio sive laude ordinis cartusiensis* in *Opera omnia*, vol. 38 [= *Opera minora*, vol. 6] (1909), 413-35. According to Trithemius, Denys of Ryckel also wrote a *De institutione et regula ordinis cartusiensis*, but his Montreuil editors could not locate such a work. A perusal of Heinrich Egher of Kalkar's *De ortu et decursu ordinis cartusiensis*, found in V1, 128r-136v, indicates that Egher of Kalkar had little interest in the academic connections of Saint Bruno, apart from retelling the famous "Professor of Paris" story. Comparison with Jacob de Paradiso (Jüterbog), *De approbatione et confirmatione statutorum ordinis cartusiensis*, might be enlightening.

(see the Epilogue, above) Kempf stresses that this divine miracle was granted in the last days to rescue professors and students from the perils of academic pride and office-seeking (ch. 3-6/5).

16-17. *Tractatus/Sermones de colloquio* and *Super statuta ordinis cartusiensis* (before 1467) R28/23, W 15-16

> Inc. "Nullus in communi colloquio aliquod loqui debet quod nolit ab omnibus intelligi vel audiri"
> Expl. "et vos in eam in eternum confirmabo."
> Graz, UB, cod. 559 [G2] (Seitz), 249r-260v; Graz, UB, cod. 973 (Seitz), 213r-232v.

Although titled as sermons and originally delivered as such (indicated by the form of address: *Amabiles in christo patres et fratres*), the six chapters *De colloquio* more closely resemble a treatise on the "sins of the tongue" theme that occurs elsewhere in Kempf's writings.[50] *Super statuta ordinis cartusiensis* follows *De colloquio* in both codices. The two copies reveal only a very few, mostly orthographical, variations, and are undoubtedly directly related. A date of origin is hard to establish. A passage in *De peccatis caritati contrariis* (no. 10, above) might be taken to indicate that *De colloquio* was written before the four-part cycle *De caritate et vitiis* (which originated before 1467, probably as early as 1450-55). On the other hand, the transmission of *De colloquio* and *Super statuta* exclusively in Seitz manuscripts could be seen as implying a later origin, after Kempf began his Slovenian priorates in 1462.

---

[50] On the *peccata linguae* in Kempf's writings, see *De vera, perfecta, et spirituali caritate*, ch. 1 (V2, 1r); *Discr*, e.g., ch. 4; *Serm. epist.*, no. 38 (G2, 58r-59v) and 48 (74r-76v); *Serm. evang.*, no. 40 (G2, 182v-184r). The topic, of course, was a common one for monastic writers. Cf., e.g., Thomas Ebendorfer of Haselbach, *De peccato linguae* in clm 5623, 1085, and clm 7510, 60-148, and the treatise by the same title ascribed both to Ebendorfer and Nicholas of Dinkelsbühl in Vienna, ÖNB, cvp 4838, 312v-356v. Alois Madre attributes the work to Ebendorfer. See *Nikolaus von Dinkelsbühl*, 328, regarding a copy in Munich clm 16172, 254r-313v. Johannes Geuß also wrote a treatise on the topic that was popular enough to appear in an *incunabulum* edition. See also Carla Casagrande and Silvana Vecchio, *I peccati della lingua: Disciplina ed etica della parola nella cultura medievale* (1987).

4. Mystical Spirituality

The fourth main area of Nicholas Kempf's literary efforts is that of mystical spirituality and related ascetic spiritual exercises. Only three works are extant on these themes, but they are some of Kempf's longest and most studiously composed writings. All were written before 1468, since they are found copied in one hand in a Graz codex dated 1468. They were thus composed either at Gaming, perhaps in the four years between the end of Kempf's priorate there (1458) and his move to Pleterje (1462), or, at Pleterje itself between 1462 and 1467. Assuming their composition at Pleterje would help explain the absence of copies at Melk or Aggsbach.

18. *De ostensione regni Dei* (ca. 1462-68) R 31, W 23

Inc. "Regnum Dei per claram visionem videbitur quibusdam ostensum in presenti vita . . . Iustum deduxit dominus per vias rectas . . . [Wisdom 10:10]."
Expl. "dicamus cum Philippo sufficit nobis."
Graz, UB, cod. 262 (Seitz), 1r-41r [G1]; Budapest, Széchényi National Library, cod. 387 (Seitz), 136r-173v (*lacunae*) [= B3]; Melk, Stiftsbibliothek, cod. 683 (766), 23r-95v (eighteenth-century, final chapters bound in incorrect order) [= MkP2].

The three manuscripts show only minor text variations. The copyist of the Budapest codex (dated 1486-88), Mathias Maselhart of Alzey, also copied Graz cod. 1006, and Vienna cvp 4744 (both are Seitz manuscripts). Maria Mairold has identified the blind stamps of the binding on B3 as products of the Seitz workshop.[51] Maselhart took the liberty of omitting sections in chapters 29, 38, 39, 41, and 48; a defect noted in the margin in an eighteenth-century hand. But G1 also shows evidence of having been examined by an eighteenth-century reader who added the missing final paragraph and ascribed the work to Kempf. Both codices contain notations in an eighteenth-century hand that may be that of the copyist who prepared the copy in MkP2 for Wydemann or Pez; the hand

---

[51] Maria Mairold, "Bibliotheksgeschichte Seitz," 27-29, 32, 34, 37-38.

is not that of Wydemann himself.[52] Kempf's authorship of the work can scarcely be questioned: a fifteenth-century hand ascribes the treatise to Kempf in the Budapest manuscript, and, as we shall see, its contents are closely interconnected with Kempf's other writings on mystical spirituality. (For a summary of its contents, see chapter five, above.)

Kempf referred to two treatises with confusingly similar contents and titles. He called one a *Tractatus de ostensione regni Dei* and left the other untitled. It is to the latter that we turn our attention first. Wydemann labeled it *De regno Dei*, claiming to know of a Seitz copy. The copy in MkP2 bears that title and follows G1 closely; all evidence points to the assumption that G1 served as a text for the copyist of MkP2. It seems likely that Wydemann knew the G1 copy and gave it the title *De regno Dei* perhaps to distinguish it from the *De ostensione regni Dei* mentioned by Kempf himself in the work under discussion here (ch. 3, 28, 39, 48) and in ch. 2 of the prologue of his commentary on the Canticle. Matthias Maselhart calls it *De ostensione regni Dei* (fol. 173v). The contents of our no. 18 would be well summarized under the title *De ostensione regni Dei*, and one would not hesitate to give it that title, if it did not itself point the reader to another, distinct treatise by that title. When Kempf refers to his treatise *De ostensione regni Dei* in his commentary on the Canticle and in our treatise number 18, he is referring to the work known to us as Kempf's *De mystica theologia* (no. 19, below). The index to the critical edition of the latter lists eight direct references to the *ostensio regni Dei* theme and additional references to related topics. *De mystica theologia* I.4, which follows directly upon the work's introduction, refers to Wisdom 10:10, the theme verse of our treatise no. 18. A second reference appears in *De mystica theologia*, V.1. Perhaps the most telling cross reference is in *De mystica theologia*, II.7, where the highest mystical union, the *unio proprie dicta*, is called the "ostensione regni Dei," with the comment that "de qua ostensione est principale propositum in hac materia."

In chapter 39 of our treatise no. 18, we are referred to a discussion "near the end" of "my treatise *De ostensione regni Dei*" (= *De mystica theologia*, V.5). The Canticle commentary, prologue, chapter 2 refers in the past tense to a "more detailed discussion" in "my treatise *De ostensione regni Dei*," which fits the themes discussed in *De mystica theologia*, II.7.[53] Much of Part IV of *De mystica theologia* corresponds to ch.

---

[52] Letter from Hofrat Dr. Mairold, April 11, 1980.

[53] *De ostensione*, ch. 3 (G1, 2r, 34-37): " "Et de illis tribus ultimis gradibus purgacionis, illuminacionis, et unionis, et in hijs que prerequiruntur ad ostensionem regni Dei et scienciam Dei, que datur in ipsam ostensionem regni, extat specialis tractatus, qui di-

30-37 of *De ostensione* on various means of knowing God. Large portions of Part I of *De mystica theologia* follow *De ostensione* closely in their coverage of the subject of purgation.[54]

Our treatise no. 18 was not only preceded by Kempf's *De mystica theologia*, but also by the commentary on the Canticle. Chapter 3 of *De ostensione* describes both the *De ostensione regni Dei* [i.e. *De mystica theologia*] and a certain *Expositio prolixa super cantica canticorum*.[55]

To summarize: Kempf first wrote the lengthy treatise we know as *De mystica theologia*, titling it *De ostensione regni Dei*. It would appear that he had no intention, at this point, of writing a detailed commentary on the Canticle, rather, he appended a brief four-part commentary on that book to this initial treatise on mystical theology. Perhaps the latter stimulated his interest and led to the prolix *Expositio super cantica canticorum*. Next, or perhaps concurrently, he began a series of conferences for the lay brethren—presumably preached in German—on the subject of mystical theology and ascetic preparation for it. At the request of his auditors, he rewrote this material into the treatise we know as *De ostensione regni Dei* (no. 18). Thus his *De ostensione* is a summary, a recapitulation of the other two works on mystical theology, a summary

---

citur de ostensione regni Dei pergustum in presenti vita." Cf. ch. 28 (20v, 25-30): "Et de illa illuminacione mentis et modo vivendi Deo per sensum anagogicum tractat Hugo de Palma, latissime declarando quod ex omni scriptura potest mens illuminari per sensum anagogicum et per viam unitivam Deo appropinquare, de quo eciam in alio loco aliquid est dictum scilicet in tractatu de ostensione regni Dei. Et de illo modo illuminacionis et unicionis hic est aliquid superaddendum." See also ch. 39 (29v, 35 - 30r.2): ". . . qualem tamen influxum multi philosophij excellenter et perfecte invenerunt et in suis scriptis reliquerunt, sicut de hoc dictum est in tractatu de ostensione regni Dei prope finem" (cf. *De mystica theologia*, V.5 [372-77 in Jellouschek edition], and *Expositio in cantica canticorum*, prologue, 2 (G1, 133v, 6-7; *Bibl. ascetica*, 11: 9): "De ista unione sanctissima, et actibus cognicionis et amoris excellentissimis, lacius dixi in tractatu de ostensione regni Dei, que hic presupponens replicare non debui." Another statement is found in *De ostensione*, 48 (G1, 36v, 23 - 37r, 2): "In qua ostensione cognoscitur et amatur Deus intime et ineffabiliter ex sua presencia experimentali in anima et tunc sibi mutuo locuntur Deus et anima. . . . De quibus principaliter locuntur cantica canticorum sicut ibidem eciam satis extense est dictum exponendo cantica, et ideo hic transeundum. Sed pro omni illa materia iam scripta et eciam pro tractatu de ostensione regni Dei et exposicione super cantica que omnia finaliter tendunt ad unum finem, ut scilicet mens disponatur et per vias rectas deducatur ut detur sibi gustare et videre in presenti vita regnum Dei. . . . De quibus tamen in alijs locis sparsi et est lacius dictum, sed hic breviter repetendum et compendiose ac succincte brevissima indoctis illiteratis." Another statement is found in ch. 30, referring both to *MTh* and *Cantica*. See appendix B.

[54] E.g., *De mystica theologia*, II.2 (p. 96): "Et de illis duobus modis seu gradis [purgationis] est dictum in prima parte huius, de quibus hic non est principalis intencio, quia requiritur longe melior et perfectior purgacio mentis cui debet ostendi regnum Dei in presenti vita per gustum quam communiter per illos duos modos solet fieri, ideo de illis hic est transeundum."

[55] G1, 2r, lines 37-38.

probably aimed at an audience of lay brethren and begun with the aim of concentrating on purgation.[56]

I have chosen not to restore Kempf's own title, *De ostensione regni Dei* to what was known as his *De mystica theologia* in manuscripts copied during his own lifetime. *De ostensione regni Dei* would fit both treatises well, and the confusion that would result from renaming no. 19 "De ostensione regni Dei" and referring to no. 18 as "De regno Dei" (Wydemann), "De triplici via," or "De via unitiva" seems unnecessary.[57] Although *De ostensione* (our no. 18) was written later than nos. 19 and 20, we have considered it first because its story sheds light on the other two treatises.

De ostensione concentrates for half its length on ascetic themes (ch. 1-28).[58] Kempf modified his intention to give only cursory attention to the third degree of each *via*: nearly a third of the work (ch. 29-46) deals with the threshold of the those third degrees. Chapter 47 is a recapitulation of the preceding chapters. Chapters 48-53 cover themes that, strictly speaking, belong to the *ostensio regni Dei* or *scientia sanctorum in praesenti vita* that he had covered more extensively elsewhere, i.e., in *De mystica theologia*. Although it is the last of his three works on mystical themes, in combining ascetic and mystical theology *De ostensione* constructs a bridge from Kempf's earlier ascetic and monastic writings to his works dealing specifically with the higher reaches of mystical spirituality.

---

[56] Chapter 3 (G1, 2v, 10-24): "Et ita cantica canticorum sunt precise de ultima perfeccione et fine principalissimo et nobilissimo in hac vita possibili, quia de amore perfectissimo et unione Dei cum anima et ostensione regni Dei et cantico mentali, quod tunc mutuo cantant per affectionem et amorem, Deus et anima. Nec imputet, qui legerit hanc materiam et 'tractatum de ostensione regni Dei' et consequenter 'exposicionem super cantica', quia idem sepe in diversis locis scribitur; quia tunc, quando de ostensione regni Dei scripsi, non fuit cogitacio aliqua de scribendo super cantica, et sic ultimo hanc materiam in ordine predictorum presencia fratribus laicis pro maiori parte predicavi, et ad plurimorum instanciam postea opusculum hoc collegi. Et hoc enim contigit eadem sepe repetita, et eciam quia sepe materia exigebat repeticionem, ut quod in uno loco brevius, obscurius, aut incidentaliter fuit dictum; in alio planius et lacius et clarius declaratum. Omnes enim de hac re scribentes sepe idem dictum replicant, ut patet diligenter advertenti aliorum scripta sicut eciam sic in ipsis cantica canticorum, ut patet intuenti et legenti ea."

[57] The two last-mentioned titles would be based on Kempf's distinction between mystical theology "strictly speaking" and the threefold "via unitiva." See chapter 5 of the present study.

[58] See the detailed summary in chapter 5 above.

19. *Tractatus de mystica theologia* (ca. 1458-65) R 11, W 25 [= R 14, W 22]

> Inc. "Mistica theologia que est finis tocius theologiae ab igno-
> rantibus vilipenditur. Capitulum primum. Cum sciencia non
> habe[a]t inimicum nisi ignorantes, tanto plures habebit inimicos
> aut vilipensores quanto a paucioribus scitur"
> Expl. "et alijs virtutibus amplis et latis."
>> Graz, UB, cod. 262 (Seitz), 43r-128v [G1]; Budapest, National
>> Library, cod. 387 (Seitz), 174r-252r (*lacunae*) [B3]; Munich,
>> SB, clm 18587 (Tegernsee), 169r-318v; Munich, SB, clm 5828
>> (Ebersberg), 1r-118r; Melk, Stiftsbibliothek, cod. 682 (765)
>> (eighteenth century).
>> Gaming owned a copy in the early eighteenth century. See also
>> "Excerpts" below.
>> Critical edition: Nicolas Kempf, *Tractatus de mystica theolo-
>> gia*, edited by Karl Jellouschek, Jeanne Barbet, and Francis
>> Ruello, AC 9 (1973).

Jeanne Barbet discussed the relationship between the four fifteenth-century copies in the introduction to the 1973 edition. The variations she noted between the Budapest and Graz copies probably stem from Matthias Maselhart's practice of "correcting" and omitting freely, as we have already observed in the case of *De ostensione*.

We have seen that this work, the phantom "De ostensione" that so puzzled Wydemann, was the first of Kempf's writings on mystical theology. This means that it probably was written during Kempf's second period at Gaming, placing it in close proximity geographically and chronologically to the Tegernsee mystics' controversy. As we have seen in chapter five above, it is probably to Kempf that Aggsbach's prior, Thomas Papler of Zistersdorf, turned for counsel about how to deal with Vincent of Aggsbach. Between 1448 and 1473 Aggsbach's priors came from the Gaming community. Kempf's writings were known at Tegernsee; a letter of 1466 from Kempf's successor as prior at Gaming, Sigismund Phantzagel, to Prior Bernard of Waging at Tegernsee is known.[59]

De mystica theologia could not have been written before 1454, since it quotes Nicolaus Cusanus's *De visione Dei* (completed October 1453) in III.13.[60] The date for writing *De mystica theologia* should probably be

---

[59] Redlich, *Tegernsee*, 100. On Phantzagel and Papler, see chapter three, section 5, above.

[60] Vansteenberghe, *Autour de la docte ignorance*, 38.

placed in the late 1450s or early 1460s rather than "around 1450" as the introduction to the Analecta Cartusiana edition suggests. Kempf's interest in questions of mystical theology during the years between his Gaming and Geirach priorates (1458-62) is evident from a response by Leonard Huntpichler of the Dominican convent in Vienna to Kempf's request for information on copies of Tauler's writings that Kempf thought might be available in the convent library. Huntpichler knew nothing of the existence of a person by the name of Tauler![61] One puzzling aspect, however, is the absence of copies of *De mystica theologia* at Melk or Aggsbach. Perhaps it was not finished when Kempf left Gaming for Geirach in 1462.

A short excerpt from *De mystica theologia*, II.3 (Jellouschek edition, pp. 99-101), is found in Munich, SB, clm 9082, 63v-64r. This manuscript came from Oberalteich, where Christian Tesenpacher became abbot in 1484. On Tesenpacher's connections to Kempf and Jerome of Mondsee, see chapter three, section 6, above. The excerpt deals with the "purgatio mentis ab omnibus peccatis."

20. *Explanatio in cantica canticorum* (1458-68) R 4, W 26

> Inc. (prologue) "Egregius psaltes et prophetarum eximius et rex"
> Expl. "videamus, laudemus, et diligamus quod ipse nobis prestare dignetur (etc.)."
> Graz, UB, cod. 262 (Seitz), 132r-332r [G1].
> Published in *Bibl. ascetica*, vols. 11-12 (1735, 1740).

This massive eight-part work of four hundred handwritten pages in folio format reveals Kempf's thorough acquaintance with the main authorities on the interpretation of what Kempf considered to be the most mystical of scriptural writings (*De recto fine*, II.7), especially Origen, Bernard of Clairvaux, and Pseudo-Gregory the Great (Robert of Tombelaine). Yet it is not limited to subjects related to mystical psychology, mystical union, or the "clara visio Dei in praesenti vita" of the *De ostensione regni Dei*, as we have seen in the discussion of ecclesial leadership in chapter six, above.

Two additional works on mystical subjects were included in the Wydemann list. *Tres gradus ascendendi in triplici triclinis mentis* is, as suggested by H. Rüthing (R 12), identical with part of *De mystica theo-*

---

[61] J. Gabler, ed., "Ein Brief des Wiener Dominikaners und Universitätsprofessors Leonhard Huntpichler an den Kartäuser Nikolaus Kempf von Straßburg," *AEKG*, 9 (1934), 135-36.

logia (II.1). The confusion arose because B3 has a colophon at the end of part I, followed by a blank space, before part II begins. The rubricator gave the title *Tres gradus* to part II on that basis.

Wydemann also recorded the titles of a series of *Collationes breves super evangelia dominicali de sensu anagogico perducente ad unionem cum Deo* in an appendix to his list (MkP2, 5v-6r), referring to a copy at Seitz. Nothing fitting this description has yet been located in modern manuscript collections.

5. *Liturgica, Sermons, Letters, Catechetica, Vernacular Writings*

A. *Liturgica*

21. *Tractatus de affectibus formandis in horis sive in officio divino*
R 10, W 11

Inc. [Cum omnis creatura et omnis scriptura et omnis laus divina" (Wydemann)]
Expl. "delectacione et gaudiis eternis omnes electos suos. Amen."
Rimini, Biblioteca Civica Gambalunga, ms. 76, 1r-11r [ch. 21-29 only].
Surviving fragment published in Frioli, "Il 'Tractatus', pp. 391-404.

22. *Expositio canonis totius missae* R 8, W 12

Inc. "Signa ornatus et verba sunt instituta ad hauriendam devocionem. Capitulum primum divine miseracionis etc. Divine miseracionis clemencia ac immenseque bonitatis inscrutabilis sapiencia non solum verbis sed eciam signis"
Expl. "O quantum humanum genus dilexisti ut ad redimendum ipsum caro fieri voluisti, utinam te amarem sicut dignum esset nunc et semper teque laudarem in secula seculorum benedictum dominum et gloriosum."[62]
Rimini, Biblioteca Civica Gambalunga, ms. 76, 11r-75r.

---

[62] Information on incipit and explicit was supplied by Dr. Paola Delbianco of the Biblioteca Civica Gambalunga and Dr. Donatella Frioli of the University of Padua.

Leopold Wydemann mentioned a *Tractatus de affectibus formandis in horis sive officio divino* (Inc. "Cum omnis creatura et omnis scriptura et omnis laus divina"; Expl. "gaudiis eternis omnes electos suos"), extant at Seitz and Gaming. This is probably identical to the treatise on the Carthusian choir office mentioned in the fifteenth-century Aggsbach catalogue: *Expositio divini officii secundum modum Carthusiensium magistri Nicolai Kempf.*[63] Pez reported that a German version of *De affectibus* had once existed. Wydemann also listed a work under the title *Expositio canonis totius missae* (Inc.: "Divina miserationis clementia"; no explicit given; W 12, R 8). In Graz, UB, cod. 1563, which has been missing since World War II, a brief *Expositio canonis, immo totius missae* (fol. 121-24v) was expressly attributed to Kempf. It was preceded by *quomodo quis debeat se praeparare ad missam* (fol. 83v-117; = R 9) with the incipit, "De preparacione ad missam, quomodo quis debeat se preparare et quando" and explicit, "valde indigent iustorum intercessione," which was ascribed to Kempf in a later hand. Preceding these two works was a *Tractatus de affectibus formandis in horis* (fol. 37-83).[64]

An *Expositio canonis totius missae* found in B3 was attributed to Kempf in a seventeenth- or eighteenth-century hand. It is a series of brief glosses on the words of the canon of the mass, beginning "Te igitur. Igitur est certe sacerdos enim credens divina miserationis." A similar incipit is given in the Graz catalogue for this work in the missing cod. 1563 ("Te igitur. Igitur est certe sacerdos enim credens deum sacris misteriis adesse"), although Wydemann's incipit and the length of the *Expositio* do not correspond to the work under that title in the Graz and Budapest codices.

Donatella Frioli discovered a portion of a treatise that corresponds to Wydemann's and Pez's description of *De affectibus formandis*, together with an apparently full copy (thirty-seven chapters) of an *Expositio canonis totius missae* in a codex in the Biblioteca Civica Gambalunga that formerly belonged to Cardinal Giuseppe Garampi (1725-1792), the prefect of the Vatican Library. She has published the eight surviving chapters of the first treatise.[65] Both treatises were copied by a Johannes Müldorf, about whom nothing further is known.[66] The codex also con-

---

[63] Gottlieb, *Mittelalterliche Bibliothekskataloge Österreichs*, 1: 582, lines 11-12.

[64] Anton Kern, ed., *Die Handschriften der Universitäts-bibliothek Graz* (1956), 2: 358-59.

[65] Donatella Frioli, "Il 'Tractatus de affectibus formandis' di Nicola Kempf, un'opera che si riteneva perduta," *Studi Medievali*, ser. 3, vol. 30 (1989), 367-404.

[66] Colophon (Dr. Delbianco) "Explicit liber per manus Ioannis Muldorff. Heu male finivi quia scribere non bene scivi. Deus sit propicius anime ipsius. Amen. Ave Maria gratia plena Dominus tecum. Explicit liber iste. Laus sit tibi, Ihesu Christe. Amen.

tains a brief *De praeparatione ad missam* by Bonaventure and a work on the seven Penitential Psalms by Pierre d'Ailly. This configuration of treatises points to the Rimini codex being identical with a codex mentioned in the fifteenth-century Aggsbach catalogue. Although neither Kempf work has a title in the Rimini manuscript and one follows the other with no break, the number of chapters in the *Expositio* (37) corresponds to Wydemann's description and the content of chapter twenty-eight of *De affectibus*, a "commendacio theologie mistice" repeats nearly verbatim Kempf's quotation of Gerson's description of the characteristics of a true theologian and the Arsenius passage on mystical ABCs in *De recto fine*. The copy in the Rimini codex was finished on the vigil of the second Sunday of Advent, 1452.[67] This would fit the work into the context of Kempf's monastic writings in the late 1440s and early 1450s, yet also reinforces Kempf's university connections.[68]

Both *De affectibus* and the *Expositio* put into practice Kempf's method for transferring all things into the *affectus*. The first twelve chapters of the *Expositio* outline methods of preparing to celebrate mass. Chapters 13-23 discuss the spiritual significance of the liturgy up to the preface of the canon. The remaining chapters then not only give the spiritual ("mystical") sense of the parts of the canon, but also correlate them with the seven canonical hours of the monastic *opus Dei*. Thus there is considerable overlap between the two works.[69]

Apparently no longer extant is a treatise *De modo confitendi peccata venialia* (R 33, W 10), with the incipit as given by Wydemann, "Quamvis mentis meae oculis" A copy was found in the Aggsbach library from the fifteenth to the eighteenth centuries.[70]

---

[67] Fol. 75r: "Explicit liber per manus Iohannis Muldorff"; item, fol. 108r; cf. fol. 85v: "1452 in vigilia secunde dominice adventus Domini." Quotations from Frioli, p. 371-72. No fewer than five Johannes de Müldorf are listed by Aschbach as *magistri regentes* at Vienna. Even though two of them became regent masters only in 1456 and 1462, either of them could be the person in question, since the various colophons give the name merely as "Iohannes Müldorf," whereas the reference to "Magister Johannes Müldorf" is an owner's mark and could have been added long after the copy was made. It is thus possible that the work was copied by a Vienna student in 1452.

[68] Frioli, "Tractatus," 374-75, suggests that *De affectibus* might be the earliest of Kempf's writings, since it amplifies themes found in *De recto fine*. The most one can safely say is that it belongs between 1445 and 1452, since it is difficult to determine priority based merely on material common to both works.

[69] The preceding summary is based on the chapter titles of the *Expositio*, which were graciously supplied by Dr. Frioli.

[70] *Bibl. ascetica*, 4: 5r; Roßmann, *Aggsbach*, 362.

B. Sermons (cf. no. 14, above)

The sermons in Admont, Stiftsbibliothek, cod. 350 and 358, which were attributed to a "Nicolaus de Argentina" by the Admont cataloguer and were mentioned by Rüthing (R 5), like those in Vienna, ÖNB 3766 and 3767,[71] are not from Kempf but from another Nicholas of Gaming. The two codices now found at Vienna were copied in 1412 at Mondsee and had been attributed to Kempf by Pez. A *Sermo de tota passione Christi* in Basel, UB, cod. A VIII 32 (R 6) is not by Kempf but is the work of a "Iohannes Nicolaus de Argentina doctor utriusque iuris" of the Straßburg charterhouse.[72] In *De ostensione*, ch. 9 (G1, 6v, line 24), Kempf mentioned a sermon on the Feast of St. John the Evangelist and one for lay brethren on Pentecost (ch. 38). These may have been part of a cycle of *Sermones sanctorum dies et festis* that Wydemann listed (W 30) but had not seen. The incipit Wydemann gives (W 32) for a series of "Sermones seu postilla in Dominicas" (Inc.: "Adventum Domini recolentes, scientes eum venisse in carne pro salute vestra") belongs to the widely disseminated sermons of Conrad of Waldhausen (1330-69) in Vienna Schottenstift cod. 90, 183; Graz UB 648, 680; Munich clm 19452; Salzburg St. Peter b VIII 6; St. Pölten 9; Herzogenburg 39 and 52; Kremsmünster 217; Seitenstetten 110, 157 (where the handwritten catalogues attribute it to Kempf on the strength of Wydemann's incipit); Klosterneuburg 233, 428; Admont 327.

C. Letters

No letter from Kempf is known to have survived. The response to him from Leonard Huntpichler of the Vienna Dominican convent is found in Munich, SB, clm 18606, 53r-v, in a copy made by Oswald Nott in 1470 (published by Gabler). In addition, Kempf's letter to the abbot of Admont in 1458, mentioned in chapter one of this study, appears to have been extant in the nineteenth century and may still be somewhere in the Admont Stiftsarchiv.

---

[71] See S. Autore in *DThC*, 8, pt. 2, cols. 2337-39.

[72] Walter Baier, "Des Johannes Nicolai OCart (+ 1475) Passionstraktat, der fälschlich Nikolaus Kempf zugeschrieben wurde," in *Die Kartäuser in Österreich* (1980), 1: 155-79.

D. Catechetica

Pez and Wydemann reported that Kempf wrote treatises on the *Our Father, Apostles' Creed*, and the *Decalogue* for Albrecht V's wife, Elizabeth, but "where these may be found today, we were unable to learn from anyone."[73]

E. Vernacular Writings

From various sources we have reports of the translation of writings by Kempf into the vernacular, in some instances by his own hand. In addition to translations of *De discretione* and *De capitulo*, Pez and Wydemann reported having searched for but having failed to find a copy of Kempf's supposed German translations of *De affectibus formandis in horis sive officio divino*.[74] Pez also listed translations by Kempf of sermons by Pseudo-Augustine, the Pseudo-Origen homily *Maria stabat ad monumentum*,[75] Heinrich of Langenstein, *Tractatus de proprietate monachorum*, and "various works" by Gerson. He thought that copies of translations of the four last-mentioned authors could be found at Gaming in the early eighteenth century. Based on Pez and Wydemann, Hans Rupprich included Kempf among the Vienna school of translating; based on Rupprich, Kempf's name continues to appear in the secondary literature as a significant vernacular writer.[76] Diligent searching may eventually discover some of those most readily identifiable as Kempf's, e.g.,

---

[73] Pez, *Bibl. ascetica*, vol. 4, preface, fol. b8.

[74] *Bibl. ascetica*, 4: b8. Although this information does not appear in the Wydemann list in Melk 683, Pez was undoubtedly drawing on information supplied by Wydemann.

[75] The homilies have been attributed to Odo of Morimond. For German translations see Kurt Ruh, *Bonaventura Deutsch*, 224. A translation of the "Homilia in feria quinta post pascha secundum Iohannem Cap. XX," with the incipit: Ir prüder, wir haben gehört, das maria magdalena gestanden ist aussen pey dem grab. . . , and the explicit: "Ich han gesehen den herren und dye ding, dye hat er mir gesagt. Das ist das endt" is found in Innsbruck UB 979, 81vb-90va. The translation is the work of Heinrich Haller. See Nigel Palmer, "Ein Handschriftenfund zum Übersetzungswerk Heinrich Hallers und die Bibliothek des Grafen Karl Mohr," *ZdA*, 102 (1974), 49-66, at 53.

[76] E.g., Christoph Cormeau, "Wiens Universität"; Nikolaus Henkel, "Leipzig als Übersetzungszentrum am Ende des 15. und Anfang des 16. Jahrhundert," in *Literatur und Laienbildung* (1984), 559-78, at 573; Sexauer, *FrühneuhochdeutscheSchriften*, 24-25, 182, cf. p. 185 on Kempf as the author of the *Alphabetum divini amoris*.

the German version of *De discretione*. *De ostensione* apparently originated in German as sermons to the lay brethren, and Kempf occasionally
used German phrases in that work as well as in his commentary on the
Canticle (e.g. II.19), and elswhere. The German version of the Carthusian lay brothers' statutes from the *Statuta Antiqua* (Vienna cvp 2731,
12r-43r) and *Nova Statuta* (cvp 2731, 52r-54r), made at Gaming in the
middle of the fifteenth-century, may have been made under Kempf's supervision.[77]

6. Spuria and Dubia

Kempf has been erroneously claimed as the author of several widely
distributed late medieval spiritual writings. Leopold Wydemann, Nikolaus Paulus, Marcel Viller, Yves Gourdel, and Engelbert Krebs all
claimed the *Alphabetum divini amoris* for Kempf. The arguments in favor of Kempf's authorship go back to Wydemann who pointed to little
more than a possible Carthusian origin for the treatise and to changes in
a Gaming copy of the *Alphabetum* that Wydemann took as an indication
he had located the autograph of the work. As Rüthing indicated, the
manuscript distribution of the *Alphabetum* makes Kempf an unlikely
author.[78] A tentative survey of the Austrian manuscripts points to a date
of composition before 1434.[79] The question of Kempf's authorship can-

---

[77] Edited, together with a parallel translation from the Basel charterhouse, in Sexauer,
FrühneuhochdeutscheSchriften, 215-80. Cvp 2731 is from Aggsbach, but was produced
at Gaming. Apparently a second copy was made at Gaming later in the fifteenth century
and the original was then given to Aggsbach. See Sexauer, p. 209-12.

[78] Wydemann to Pez, January 22, 1718, f. 3v-4v. Paulus, "Kempf" (1928), 29-30, and
idem, "Wer ist der Verfasser des Alphabetum divini amoris?" *ZAM*, 3 (1928), 157-60,
based his claims for Kempf on Pez and Wydemann; Krebs (*Verfasserlexikon*, 2: 785)
cited Paulus. Viller's arguments against Nider's authorship, which were based on incorrect readings and false assumptions, are found in "Nider est-il l'auteur de l'alphabetum
divini amoris?" *RAM*, 4 (1923), 367-78. Paulus took issue, not entirely convincingly,
with Viller's arguments in "Wer ist der Verfasser," drawing on James Connolly's refutation of Viller in Connolly, *John Gerson* (1928), 372. But Paulus went on, not to argue
for Nider, but to propose Kempf against Connolly's arguments for Nider. By 1932, in
"Lectures spirituelles de Jérôme de Mondsee," 382, Viller had accepted Paulus's candidate, Kempf. The *Alphabetum* was attributed to Kempf at numerous points in the initial
volumes of *DSAM* (1: 353 [Viller]; 1: 203; 2: 749, 915-916). Rüthing, in *DSAM*, 8: 1703,
was the first to challenge the attribution to Kempf since S. Autore in *DThC* 8: 2339
(1925).

[79] Salzburg, St. Peter, cod. b III 2 is dated 1434, and Kremsmünster, cod. 268, was
probably copied before 1440, according to data in the handwritten catalogues. Pez referred to a note in a Salzburg codex that ascribed the work to Martin of Zips, a member
of the Vienna Schottenstift community, and placed its composition in the year 1433.

not yet be considered absolutely closed, but it seems most doubtful. A critical edition of this work would be most helpful.

Kempf has also been claimed as the translator of the sermons of Nicholas of Dinkelsbühl that became known as the *Büchlein von der Liebhabung Gottes*.[80] Although Paulus argued for Kempf as the translator[81] Hermann Maschek and, most recently, Bernhard Schnell have convincingly argued for Thomas Peuntner.[82] Nor is Kempf a likely candidate for the author of the anonymous Carthusian prefatory letter found in many manuscripts of the *Büchlein*.[83]

The *Dialogus de modo perveniendi ad veram et perfectam Dei et proximi dilectionem*, written by the prior of the Basel charterhouse, Heinrich Arnoldi of Alfeld (d. 1487), has been falsely attributed to both Kempf and Denys of Rijkel.[84] The treatise *Von der abgeschiedenhayt* in

---

Both Pez and Paulus assumed that Martin was merely the copyist. See Bernard Pez, ed., *Thesaurus anecdotorum*, (1721), 1: vi-vii, and Paulus, "Kempf" (1928), 30. Pez noted that a Melk copy of the *Alphabetum* was made by Johannes of Spitz, the member of the Melk community who copied Kempf's *De proponentibus* in 1451. Wydemann may well have been correct in assuming a Carthusian author. The colophon in Vienna, Schottenstift, cod. 64 (252), 288v, reads, ". . . explicit alphabetum divini amoris ex fonte et dono Dei pro institutione ordinis carthusiensis in solitudine degencium." A similar colophon appears in Seitenstetten 223, along with an explanation why the work should be called "Alphabetum divini amoris" (because its chapters were arranged mnemonically—"ut facilius retineri possit clausule in memore") and because it deals with the love of God. It bears the date 1449—whether that represents the date of this particular copy or simply repeats a date given in the copyist's exemplar, is unclear.

[80] This claim was still being made as late as 1969. See Rainer Rudolf, ed., *Heinrich von Langenstein, Erchantnuzz der Sund*, 14-15, based on Hans Rupprich, *Wiener Schrifttum*, 149, 162.

[81] Paulus, "Kempf" (1928), 42-46, and idem, "Ein mittelalterliches Büchlein von der Liebe Gottes," *ZAM*, 3 (1928), 69-72.

[82] Maschek, "Der Verfasser des Büchleins von der Liebhabung Gottes," *Zentralblatt für Bibliothekswesen*, 53 (1936), 361-68; Schnell, *Thomas Peuntner, "Büchlein von der Liebhabung Gottes"*, esp. 2, 48 on Kempf.

[83] Schnell notes that the "Carthusian's Letter" lacks the characteristics of the Austrian dialect found in Peutner's text. Contrary to Schnell's implication, this would not exclude Kempf as a possible author of the letter, since he was of Alsatian origin. The author of the preface claims to have known Nicholas of Dinkelsbühl while a student at Vienna—as we have seen, it is doubtful that Kempf was at Vienna before Nicholas of Dinkelsbühl died (Schnell repeats the conventional assumption that Kempf was a student of Nicholas of Dinkelsbühl.) Kempf must, however, be excluded from consideration, since a comment by the copyist of cgm 4590 clearly identifies the Carthusian as a member of the Christgarten Carthusian community (near Nördlingen).

[84] Pez corrected this ascription to Kempf when he published the *Dialogus* in *Bibl. ascetica*, vol. 6: 2-214. Cf. ibid., 4: 6v, no. xxvii, for Pez's original ascription to Kempf. Trithemius had assigned the work to Arnoldi—an attribution against which Rösler compiled arguments in *Der Kartäuser Nikolaus Kempf*, 274. Autore argued in favor of Arnoldi in *DThC*, 8: 2339. For the most extensive discussion of the issues, see Emery, "Lovers of the World," 191-203. See also Martin, "Der 'tractat von der lieb gots'." The

Budapest, NL, cod. 387, attributed to Kempf in a seventeenth- or eight-eenth-century hand, is actually the well-known work of the same title by Meister Eckhart. Stanislaus Autore cited a collection "Ex Nic. de Argentina dictis excerpta de praesagiis futurorum" in Basel, UB, cod. A V 39, which I have not seen, and a "De adventu Christi" at Straßburg, which was destroyed in 1870. The latter was probably the well-known four-teenth-century work by Nicholas of Straßburg, O.P. The Basel work may also consist of excerpts from Nicholas of Straßburg, O.P.[85]

work (Hain, 11491) has been published among the writings of Denys of Rijkel at Cologne (1534), Munich (1603), and in the Montreuil *Opera Omnia*, vol. 41 (Tournai, 1912).

[85] Autore in *DThC*.

APPENDIX B

TEXTS

Kempf, *De recto fine*, II.5 (V1, 48v A.8 - 49r A.19; Pez, 4: 301-4).[1]

Secunda, scilicet mistica, {theologia} acquiritur per affectus solo
Deo illustrante inmediate intellectum humanum ex affectu seu amore in-
tenso previo in voluntate. Ita quod solus Magister noster Christus Dominus inmediate est illius scientie auctor et doctor per Spiritum Sanctum
intellectui humano infundens modo supernaturali. Et illa est certior,
clarior, et perfectior quam prima {theologia}, et solis bonis in caritate
existentibus concessa et non malis, de qua multipliciter loquitur scriptura. Unde propheta dixit "Gustate," scilicet per affectum, et tunc
"videte," per intellectum. Et iterum "accedite ad eum," per affectum et
"illuminanimi" secundum intellectum. De ista theologia primus scripsit
Beatus Dyonisius Ariopagita, et post eum multi sancti patres et scolastici
doctores; inter quos ille modernus Johannes Gerson plures scripsit tractatus. Et per istam scientiam fuerunt instructi sancti patres a Spiritu
Sancto, scilicet Anthonius et alij in Egipto, et sanctus Bernhardus, quasi
totam suam scientiam non humano studio, sed predicto modo a Spiritu
Sancto hausit. . . . Omnes de ea scribentes dicunt quod nullus potest intelligere nisi expertus, et nullus potest eius intellectum capere ab homine
docente nisi a solo Spiritu Sancto. Tradunt tamen modum aliquem dispo-
nentem mentem hominis ad eam, videlicet, quod quando quis quantum
potest elevat se ad cognoscendum Deum, tamen solum cognoscit per
speculum in enigmate et est in cognitione obscura et privativa. Unde dicunt
quod semper quantum intellectum noster conatur se elevare ad cognoscendum Deum, tamen semper fertur in caliginem, id est obscuram cognitionem. Et Augustinus in quadam omelia declarat quod quidquid homo
cogitat esse Deum vel in Deo, si resolvendo se apprehendit, illud [Pez:
id] esse finitum, tunc non est [Pez: sit] Deus.

---

[1] Questions by Discipulus have been omitted. In the following texts v and u and c
and t have been normalized (including wlt/vult), as have w and b; ÿ has been normalized
to ij; capitalization and punctuation have been modernized and normalized. Editorial additions are enclosed in { }. For texts that were published by Pez, variants in the published
version have been noted. In other texts, significant variants have occasionally been
noted, but all texts are essentially presented here as slightly modified transcriptions.
Their purpose is to give the reader access to a few of the central unpublished texts discussed in the present study. All references to the Psalms employ the Vulgate numbering.

Et ita tunc oportet secundum scribentes de eadem theologia mistica, primo obmittere affirmationes et procedere per negationes et privationes: ut quod Deus sit infinitus sine fine absque initio, incircumscriptibilis, incomprehensibilis. (Nec curo hic disputare, an possit haberi conceptus simplex singularis vel communis, incomplexus [Pez: inconnexus] de Deo, quod communiter conceditur, quamvis difficulter in corde percipitur [Pez: percipiatur], ita esse sicut sepe ore loquimur.) Postquam autem homo per huiusmodi privationes et negationes quantum potest se elevat ad cognoscendum Deum et non potest ultra pervenire. Tunc dimissis illis per fundamentum fidei, incipit affective ferri in aliquod summum bonum, solum fide creditum et omnino intellectu humano incomprehensibile, sed totum amabile et desiderabile, hoc incipit ferventissime amare et affectum in ipsum extendere, quamvis eo modo intellectus non potest nec potuit capere sicut affectus ipsum diligit. Et hoc est quod dicunt istius scientie experti "per gustum," quod ubi intellectus foris stat, affectus intrat [Pez: intret]. Ex tali autem affectu continuato, quandoque sequitur raptus mentis humane in Deum. Et post huiusmodi affectus Spiritus Sanctus quandoque ex sua gratia infundit homini supernaturaliter cognitionem de Deo, et intellectum divinarum scripturarum, eo modo quo prius habere nequivit. Et talis tunc notitia vocatur mistica theologia. Et in huiusmodi affectibus intensis, et in dilectionibus, quae secuntur ex cognitione, que infunditur, consistit secundum veritatem fidei felicitas humana. Sicut etiam satis propinque ad hoc videtur tendere Aristoteles in 10. Methaphysice, quantum ex naturali ratione concludere potuit; sed, ubi ipse defecit, theologia supplet.

Ad hanc, ut dixi, debes tendere, etiam si nunquam presumas posse pervenire; de qua dicit Cancellarius predictus Johannes Gerson: "Sic preparet homo ad hanc capienda mentis puritatem, non oris loquacitatem. Exspectet, quoniam solus Spiritus Sanctus eius est doctor et operator. Vis ergo secretum cognoscere, transfer te a theologia intellectus ad theologiam affectus, de scientia ad sapientiam, de cognitione ad devotionem." "Hec est," inquit idem, "theologia illa quam magnus Arsenius, vir grecis et latinis litteris tunc eruditus, fatebatur se nescire, ymmo nec primam litteram alphabeti in ea didicisse."[2] "Que theologia," inquit, "utinam nobis omnibus qui theologi nominamur, tam familiaris esset quam extranea et ignota."[3]

---

[2] *Apophthegmata Patrum, Appendix ad Palladium*, "De Abbate Arsenius," par. 4-6 (PG 65: 89-90), cf. *Verba Seniorum* by Pelagius the Deacon (PL 73: 953-54). Additional references are found in the Epilogue, above.

[3] Gerson, *De vita spirituali animae*, near the end of the lectio prima; *Oeuvres*, 3: 127.

Kempf, *De ostensione*, excerpts from chapter 1 (G1, 1r, 19 - 1v, 26).

Sed de ostensione regni Dei in presenti vita et de scientia sanctorum quam dat sanctis suis, de quibus est principale intentum in presenti materia, maior est difficultas, que et qualis sit illa ostensio regni et [MkP2 *add.* quae] scientia sanctorum, de qua Christus dixit apostolis quibusdam "Quod non gustarent mortem nisi prius viderent regnum Dei" [Mt 16:28; Mk 9:1; Lk 9:27], et de qua dixit, "regnum Dei intra vos est" [Lk 17:21[4]]. De quo dixit Beatus Augustinus ad Paulinam in libro de videndo deum, quod Moysi, quia doctor Iudeorum, et Paulo, quia doctor gentium, fuit concessum clare sicut sanctis in patria videre Deum. Quia de Moyse dixit Deus numeri xii [Num 12:8]: "Ore ad os loquor ei, et non per enigmata et figuras Dominum videt." Et ita videtur secundum Beatum Augustinum et eum sequentes quod hec clara Dei visio saltem ad momentum sit possibilis viatoribus, et aliquibus concessa; et si Moysi et Paulo, tunc a fortiori Virgini Marie, et etiam Iohanni Baptiste, quo maior inter natos nemo surrexit [Mt 11:11; Lk 7:28], et aliqui etiam affirmant idipsum de Sancto Steffano [Acts 7]. Et sic iustis deductis per vias rectas ostenderetur regnum Dei in presenti vita per talem visionem claram quod etiam fuit figuratum in transfiguratione Christi coram discipulis,[5] quamvis secundum doctores communiter solum viderunt humanitatem Christi in forma gloriosa et non clare divinitatem. Sed Beatus Gregorius quinto moralium dicit quod talis visio non concedatur [G-1, 1v] mortalibus unde sic inter cetera dicit: Nos igitur quousque carnis corruptione premimur nullomodo claritatem divine potentie, sicut in se incommutabilis manet, videmus, quia acies infirmitatis nostre non sustinet quod de eius eternitatis radio super nos intolleribiliter fulgat [MkP2: *fulget*; B3: *fulgent*]. Et Beatus Bernhardus sequens Beatum Gregorium in sermone 31 et sequentibus, super illo verbo "Indica mihi ubi cubas in meridie" [Ca 1:7], idem dicit, et latissime ostendendo quod predicta clara Dei visio non fiat viatoribus [MkP2: *sed*] solum sanctis in patria et angelis. Et fundamentum Beati Augustini est quia omnis visio, que non est enigmatica et per figuras, est clara Dei visio, aliunde Moyses non excessisset cognitionem et visionem aliorum prophetarum. Sed Beatus Bernhardus et Beatus Gregorius et alij communiter ponunt aliam visionem, que excedit enigmaticam longe, et tamen multum est inferior visione patrie; et tali visione cognoscitur experimentaliter presentia Dei, non tamen clare videtur taliter sicut sancti in patri [MkP2: *vident*], nec solum proprie per figuras et enigmata, sed per realem et experimentalem sui presentiam. Et in hac

---

[4]   Cf. Kempf, *Cantica*, I.28 (pp. 178-79); I.29 (pp. 181ff).
[5]   Mt 17:1-13; Mk 9:2-13; Lk 9:28-36, cf. *MTh*, III.15.

cognitione dicunt ostendi regnum Dei in presenti vita, perquam datur etiam scientiam sanctorum. Possunt tamen concordari faciliter Augustinus et alij sancti patres: Quia illa visio clara non datur puris viatoribus, adhuc sensibus humanis utentibus, quod etiam Beatus Augustinus concederet. Per hec tamen non volunt negare, quin Deus ex speciali gratia potu{er}it [MkP2] aliquibus dare, et verosimiliter dederit, sed tunc eos super usum humanorum sensuum ymo omnium actuum potentiarum anime sublevaverit. Et ideo Paulus dixit "sive in corpore sive extra corpus nescio, Deus scit" [2 Cor. 12:2-3]. Et sic tales non sunt, in statu tali, puri viatores, sed in quodam statu medio. Sed quamvis Christus habuit usum omnium sensuum humanorum et anime virium, tamen semper a sua conceptione habuit claram visionem illam, quia fuit viator et comprehensor, et hec fuit in Christo singulare, quia fuit Deus et homo, sed alijs potuit concedere per momentum cessante in eis usu sensuum.

Kempf, *De ostensione regni Dei*, ch. 24 (G1, 16v, 27 - 17r, 18).

Quomodo mens potest purgari ut sit sine macula, cum nullus possit hic vivere sine culpa. Capitulum XXIIII. Sed occurrit hic merito dubium quomodo sit possibile aliquem hominem in presenti vita sic perfecte purgari ut statim post mortem videat aut quandoque etiam in presenti vita gustet regnum Dei; cum multipliciter scriptura testetur nullum hominem posse vivere sine peccato: quia non est homo qui vivat super terram qui non peccet [3 Kings 8:46; 2 Chr 6:36; Ecl 7:21]; et omnes declinaverunt ad peccatum [cf. Is 56:11; Ps 52:4; Rom 3:12]; ita quod nec infans unius diei dicatur esse sine peccato [cf. Job 14:4; 25:4][6]; et qui dixerit se peccatum non habere mendax est [1 Jn 1:8-10]; et multe alie scripture sunt [G1, 17r] de hoc. Quomodo ergo poterit anima sic purgari ut fiat tota pulchra et macula nullius peccati sit in ea, Beatus Gregorius super illo verbo in canticis, "Tota pulchra es etc." [Ca 4:7a], movens hoc dubium, sic respondet: "Dum sancta anima a peccatis cottidianis se per penitentiam mundat, dum cottidie peccata minuta cum lacrimis abluit et a maioribus se observat, quamvis frequenter peccet, per assiduam tamen penitentiam munditiam suam assidue servat. Hunc enim alibi precipitur, "Semper sint vestimenta tua candida"; et illud "iustus ex fide vivit" [Rom 1:17]. Quamvis enim mox ut peccat, a iustitia deviet, tamen dum semper credit in eum qui iustificat impium et assidue sub eius fide peccata sua deflet per assiduas ablutiones, iustitiam suam retinet. Ecce quam

---

[6]   Kempf seems to be drawing on both Bede (PL 91: 1137-38), whom he acknowledges by name in the parallel passage in Kempf's Canticle commentary (see below) and Haimo of Auxerre (PL 117: 319AB). The conflation occurs already in Robert of Tombelaine (PL 79: 510BC).

breviter et fundamentaliter ponit Beatus Gregorius istum purgationis gradum efficacius et modum prius diffuse declaratum, quia qui se custodit a gravioribus et, si quandoque ymmo sepe in leviora peccata cadit, tamen per iudicium et iustitiam quam facit de seipso cottidie semper mundatur, ut innocentiam servare dicatur et tota fit pulchra in qua non est macula [Ca 4:7b] dicatur; quia et si aliquando ad momentum maculatur, tamen quia non manet diu, et sic quod modicum est nichil reputatur, et ita dicitur manere tota pulchra et sine macula.

Kempf, *De ostensione regni Dei*, ch. 29-31 (G1, fol. 20v, 31 - 24v, 11).

Tertius modus purgationis disponit mentem ut sibi ostendatur regnum Dei. Capitulum 29. Unde sciendum est quod per illum purgationis gradum tertium et ultimum, qui sit per cottidianum sui ipsius iudicium, mens disponitur ut illuminetur divino lumine ad cognoscendum Deum et ea que Dei sunt, secundum modum in hac vita possibilem per communem modum videndi Deum per speculum in enigmate . per potentias anime [G1, 21r] et eorum actus, et ad amandum Deum secundum caritatem infusam in supremo gradu contemplative vite. Tamen enigmatice disponitur, etiam quod Deus possit venire ad ymaginem et ibi velut in throno sedere, iuxta illud: iudicium et iustitia preparatio sedis tue [cf. Ps 9:5,8; Pr 16:12].

Pro quo est sciendum sicut dicit Magister in secundo Sententiarum distinctione 23 prope finem: Adam post creationem et ante lapsum habuit cognitionem Dei et consequenter amorem ipsius non ita excellenter sicut sancti in patria qui vident eum immediate in sua substantia sine obscuritate, nec ita enigmatice, id est obscure, sicut nos in hac vita qui videmus per speculum obscuratum per peccatum, sed quadam inspiratione interiori qua Dei presentiam contemplabitur per speculum clarum, in quo nulla erat peccati nebula sicut post peccatum [MkP2: est] in qualibet anima, ut patet ex predictis.[7] Et sic patet quod quamvis Adam ante lapsum cognovit naturali cognitione et amavit naturali amore Deum sibi presentem esse, tamen per quodam medium, tamquam per speculum clarum. Sic anima sancta, si fuerit perfecte purgata, ut saltem ad tempus nulla sit in ea peccati nebula, ut cognoscere possit Dei presentiam et eum amare et sibi uniri, tamen de communi lege solum sit ad huc in presenti vita obscure et non clare, precipue quando cognoscitur per potentias anime et amatur per voluntatem ex caritate infusa—quia de cognitione et amore Dei in ymagine potest secus esse, ut alibi est declaratum. Post hanc ergo tertiam purgationem pervenit mens ad excellentissimam Dei

---

[7] Lombard, *Sent*, II, dist. 23.4 (PL 192: 701).

cognitionem consimilem aut perfectiorem sicut habuit Adam ante lapsum in statum innocentie. Et puto quod perfectiorem propter gratiam gratum facientem sive caritatem infusam, quam Adam non habuit. Sed ex
alia parte semper in homine manet aliquid de fomite originalis peccati, a
quo sola Beatissima Virgo Maria totaliter purgata fuit, qui fomes peccati
originalis, sicut fumus aut nebula aut rubigo, potest impedire ne tam perfecta Dei visio fiat in speculo mentis sicut in primis parentibus. Et etiam
molestia corporis quod corrumpitur aggravat animam post lapsum, quod
ante non impedivit, et venialia peccata que faciliter committuntur. Sed
Adam nullum habuit impedimentum nec difficultatem nec resistentiam
convertendi se ad Deum per cognitionem et amorem quotienscunque voluit. Perfecta tamen caritas potest illa, ad tempus saltem, impedimenta
aufferre.

Hec illuminatio mentis, quantumcunque fuerit in hac vita clara et
perfecta, tamen erit sicut nox tenebrosissima respectu clare visionis
minime in patria—dicente Christo de Iohanne Bptista [Lk 7:28]: "qui
minimo fuerit in regno celorum maior est illo." De qua etiam maximus
propheta David dixit: "Illuminatio mea [G1, 21v] in delicijs meis in presenti vita est solum nox" [cf. Ps 138:11].[8] O sancte David! O prophetarum propheta! Si tua illuminatio tanta, tamquam perfecta ut esses in
delicijs, fuit solum nox, quid de nostris illuminationibus inperfectissimis
non in delicijs sed in peccatis? Numquid erunt clare nequaquam si nox
obscurissima in presenti vita erit illuminatio nostra et consequenter amor
qui sequitur erit inperfectus raro generans delicias? Quanto enim magis
conamur illuminari per cognitionem Dei, tanto plus intramus noctis
caliginem, et nostra illuminatio semper terminatur in quadam ignorantia
et cecitate et caligine, qui per fidem ambulamus non per speciem [2 Cor
5:7], et nubes tenebrosa recipit nobis Deum nostrum ab oculis mentis
nostre, et lumen cognitionis eius sit sicut tenebre eius.

Quot autem sunt modi species et differentie sive gradus in illa illuminatione mentis cum affectu amoris, qui dicuntur contemplatio, et exer-
citia sive actus proprii vite contemplative ex lectione, oratione,
meditatione, et similibus dispositionibus previjs (purgata prius mente)
procedentes—quis possit enumerare aut verbo aut scripto explicare?
Nam sicut a tempore aurore usque ad claram [sic MS] diem aut meri-
diem infiniti sunt radij solis sibi succedentes, ita in mente diverse illuminationes et amoris affectiones, secundum quod fuerit mens melius
purgata et purificata et pro eorum receptione disposita. Quanto enim

---

[8] For Hugh of Balma's use of this verse, which may have influenced Kempf, see
Viae Sion, prologue par. 6 in SC edition (Peltier, p. 3a); via illuminativa par. 9 (Peltier,
p. 9b), via unitiva, par. 68 (Peltier p. 35b).

mens fuerit mundior et clarior ac purior a peccatis, vitijs, et radicibus
peccatorum, tanto illuminatio erit maior et calor amoris unitivi intensior
et fortior. Et quia pauci sic perfecte se purgant, ideo pauci illuminantur
perfecte et Deo uniuntur; nam secundum gradum purgationis sequitur
claritas illuminationis et fervor amoris.

Et de illis modis et gradibus contemplationis et illuminationis et unitivi amoris et modis ascendendi et proficiendi in eisdem sunt innumer-
abilia scripta sanctorum patrum et doctorum diversorum, quorum multi
scripserunt non solum ex scientia speculativa ex auctoritate aliorum sed,
quod efficacius est et securius, ex propria experientia. Nam heu multi
scribunt multa que in seipsis nunquam experti sunt, quia nunquam pur-
gati perfecte a peccatis fuerunt. Quid prodesset, ymmo temerarium
videretur [G1: videtur], aliquid superaddere scribendo de modis contemplationis, illuminationis mentis, et unitivi amoris scriptis sanctorum patrum et doctorum? Sed magis utile esset [G1: est] et necessarium ut
unusquisque studeat mentem et conscientiam perfecte purgare, iuxta modos predictos, ut possit consequi effectualiter illuminationem, et tandem,
per vias rectas pura mente et mundo corde incedendo, possit Deum
videre (iuxta illud: "Beati mundo corde quoniam ipsi Deum [G1, 22r]
videbunt" [Mt 5:8]), et ita mereri ut sibi regnum Dei ostenderetur. Unusquisque ergo principaliter et pre omnibus studeat mentem purgare,
magis quam multos libros perlustrare et multum disputare de contemplatione, per que non potest mens illuminari nisi prius purgata sed sepe con-
tenebrari ex peccatis curiositatis aut vanitatis aut alterius vitij se
huiusmodi studio conmiscentibus.

*Deus ostendere se potest clare in presenti vita menti perfecte pur-
gate a pena et culpa. Capitulum 30m.* Ut autem aliqui modi pro simplicibus et devotis possint haberi, quibus possent se ex fide elevare in
Dei cognitionem et amorem per purgationem mentis predictam, est
primo sciendum quod divina essentia penitus a nulla creatura in celo aut
in terra totaliter et perfecte est cognoscibilis et comprehensibilis sicut est,
quia hoc solius Dei est proprium (iuxta illud: "nemo cognoscit Patrem
nisi Filius, nec Filium quis cognoscit nisi Pater" [Mt 11:27]); nec anima
Christi potest videre taliter deitatem, ut communiter dicunt doctores.
Quia sic cognoscere est terminos rei cognite comprehendere; Deus autem
infinitus est, qui non habet terminos, et sic non potest cognosci comprehensive, nisi a virtute infinita, que est in solo Deo.

Secundo sciendum, quamvis essentie divine lux inaccessibilis sit [1
Tim 6:16], tamen sanctis in patria et angelis et hominibus sanctis in pre-

senti vita est sicut speculum voluntarium ostendens unicuique, quantum
vult et dat scire et cognoscere seipsum, et ea que fiunt in creaturis aut futura sunt, que qualia et quantum vult, secundum dispositionem mentium
et merita singulorum; et hoc sive per claram visionem sui sicut in patria
sive per enigmaticam sicut in presenti vita. Et hinc est quod non omnes
videntes clare Deum equaliter sunt beati et equaliter cognoscunt et sci-
unt, nec omnes hic in caritate existentes equaliter Deum contemplantur:
et hoc est quod dixit "in domo Patris mei mansiones multe sunt" [Jn
14:2].

Tertio est sciendum quod secundum multos doctores et sanctos patres, ut Gregorium, Bernhardum, et alios, Deus in presenti vita non
videtur nec de communi lege nec videri potest ab aliquo homine clare
sicut ipsum vident sancti in patria; sicut videntur de hoc multe scripture
sonare. Sed solus Christus ab instante sue conceptionis sic videt divinam
essentiam secundum supremam anime virtutem seu portionem. Sed Beatus Augustinus in libro De videndo Deum tenet quod talis visio sit possibilis in vita presenti, et sic facta Moysi et Paulo in raptu, et sic a maiori
Beate Virgini Marie frequenter. Et de hoc in alijs locis, scilicet super
cantica et in tractatu de ostensione regni Dei [*MTh*, IV.5 (271-76); *Cantica*, I.29 (11: 181-85)], latius est dictum; ideo hic transeundum. Unde
secundum aliquos talis visio conceditur ex speciali gratia multis, quamvis [G1, 22v] de paucis sit scriptum. Quia quando mens alicuius hominis
perfecte esset purgata, ut veniret ad suum originalem innocentiam ut nec
mortale nec veniale peccatum in se maneret nec habitus vitiosus nec rubigo peccati nec macula nec aliqua pena pro peccatis solvenda, tunc sibi
in presenti vita ostenderetur regnum Dei; quia tunc nichil impediret si
saltem pro utilitate et salute talis hominis prodesset ut postea non super-
biret sed humilior fieret. Et ita quibusdam ostenditur in vita presenti, ut
creditur Paulo et Moyse secundum Beatum Augustinum; quibusdam
mortis articulo, ut aliqui putant de sancto Stephano; alijs stanti post mortem, ut latroni et multis alijs. Maior vero parti ostenditur post purgatorij
penam, quia oportet prius mentem purgari ab omni culpa et liberari ab
omni pena. Quia si post mortem salvandis non ostenditur regnum Dei
nisi prius solvant novissimum quadrantem in purgatorio, multo minus in
hac vita. Et ita paucissimi solvunt dum sani sunt, aliqui per infirmitates
diutinas ante mortem, alij per penam mortis, ultimi per penas purgatorij.
De quibus dixit Beatus Gregorius 24 Moralium: "Iustorum anime a levi-
bus contagijs ipso sepe mortis pavore purgantur, et eterne retributionis
gaudia iam ab ipsa carnis solutione percipiunt, plerumque vero contemplatione, quadam retributionis eterne [PL *internae*], etiam prius quam
carne spolientur, hylarescunt et dum vetustatis debitum solvunt, novi iam
muneris letitia perfruuntur. Recte dicitur 'videbit faciem eius in iubilo'

[Job 33:26],[9] vel, 'liberabit animam suam, ne pergeret in interitum sed vivens lucem videret' [Job 33:28]."[10] Hec ille inter alia plura videndo ibidem. Est tamen verum quod Deus per suam specialem gratiam in suo adventu ad mentem per regni Dei ostensionem, ut tamquam ignis inmensus, supplere defectum potest purgationis et pene solutionis. Nam ante suum adventum nescio si possibile sit aliquod sic fieri preparatum. Sicut enim ipsius minime est ostendere, ita etiam est ipsius potentie mentem preparare per ostensionem. De hac illuminatione et amore qui sequitur, hic pertranseo extensius scribere, ex eo quod in alij predictis scriptis recolo me, quantum Deus donaverat, plura dixisse.

Est etiam alius illuminationis istius gradus, qui etiam sit in ymagine; citra tamen claram Dei visionem, qua mens illuminatur ad experiendum Dei presentiam et experimentaliter cognoscit ipsum, non posse cognosci perfecte. Et illa illuminatio sequitur amorem et vocatur superintellectualis, quia tunc in mente cessant omnes alie cognitiones intellectuales et omnes actus [G1, 23r] potentiarum. Est adhuc alius illuminationis gradus per revelationes internas et inspirationes, per species aut similitudines rerum aut inmissionem cognitionum intellectualium, aut alijs multis modis, quibus illustratus fuit intellectus prophetarum et sanctorum ad cognoscendum secreta Dei aut futura. Et quandoque fuit secuta unio per actum amoris, quandoque non—ut in Balaam. Et de illis, precipue de prima illarum, tractat Beatus Bernhardus in sermone 31 super Cantica et in alijs sermonibus ibidem sepe. Et Beatus Gregorius dat exemplum quod tunc Deus cognoscitur presens, sicut quando quis clausis oculis percipit lumen excellens sibi presentatum ante oculos corporis. Quia in illa illuminatione in ymagine secundum eos ostenditur regnum Dei quantum est in hac vita possibile, tamen diversis diversimode secundum diversos illius illuminationis gradus, ut dicit Beatus Bernhardus in predicto sermone 31mo. Et de illis etiam est in alijs supra nominatis dictum, ideo similiter hic transeundum.

Quomodo Deus potest cognosci, quia est spiritus omnia penetrans, omnia replens, et per infinitum omnia excedens. Capitulum 31m. Ad intelligendum autem modos cognoscendi Deum et illuminandi mentem ut sequatur unio amoris secundum communem viam vite contemplative per intellectum et voluntatem in speculo et enigmate, hoc est per intellectum scripturarum et vestigium creaturarum, est sciendum, ut dicitur Iohannis quarto, "Deus est spiritus" [Jn 4:24]. Et quamvis spiritus capitur multipliciter et valde generaliter pro flatu hominis, aut etiam pro vento corpo-

---

[9] Cf. ch. 23 (G1, 16v, line 20), which has other parallels to this section.
[10] *Moralia in Job*, bk. 24, ch. 11, par. 34 (PL 76:306C).

rali, aut aere, aut etiam pro anima brutorum—ut dicit Beatus Bernhardus
sermone quinto super Cantica—tamen hic debet capi proprie solum pro
spirituali substantia indivisibili ac insensibili seu invisibili, quales sunt
Deus, angeli, anima humana, et dyaboli. Sic loquendo de spiritu, tunc
eius natura est quod sit omnino indivisibilis, quod non habet partes nec
quantitatem nec figuram, sed ubicumque est ibi totus est, quia nichil est
ipsius quando sit ibi. Exemplum: anima humana tota est in qualibet parte
corporis viventis et in toto simul, et non est maior aut plus in toto quam
in minima, etiam indivisibili parte, si puncta indivisibilia sunt ponenda.
Et illa natura convenit spiritui ex sua nobilitate, quia quanto res habet
partes magis distantes ab invicem, tanto habet minorem virtutem suam,
quia virtus unita fortior est seipsa dispersa, et inperfectionis est habere
virtutem dispersam in partibus distantibus quam habere in omni parte totam virtutem simul. Sic etiam angeli, quamvis sint in aliquo determinato
loco circumscriptive, tamen sunt in qualibet parte illius loci toti et in toto
simul. Sic ymaginati sunt phylosophi de intelligencijs et motoribus celorum et orbium, quod non adhererent ipsis [G1, 23v] faciendo unum, sicut
anima hominis cum corpore facit unum hominem, sed coasisterent sibi,
ita quod unus angelus coasisteret uni toti celo et cuilibet eius parti, et in
qualibet parte esset totus et simul in toto esset totus. Et quanto est in minori parte totum et etiam in maiori, tanto maioris virtutis et perfectionis.
Et quia Deus est infinitus, tanto magis est infinite virtutis et perfectionis,
quanto in quolibet puncto indivisibili est totus et simul in omnibus [est
B3] totus et super omnia in infinitum.

Secundo est sciendum quod Deus est spiritus immensus, infinitus,
incircumscriptibilis, incomprehensibilis, omnia penetrans et nulli adherens, et per infinitum omnia excedens, inmobilis, incommutabilis, omnia
replens (iuxta illud: "Spiritus Domini repletit orbem terrarum" [Wis 1:7];
et, "ego celum et terram impleo" [Jer 23:24] dicit Dominus per Ysaiam).
Et potest aliqualiter ymaginari: si lumen solis omnes creaturas penetraret
sicut aerem serenum, et si lumen solis esset proprie spiritus quod non
haberet partes sed ubique esset totum simul (sicut anima humana est in
toto corpore et in qualibet parte), et si idem lumen solis penetrando omnes creaturas ultra eas per infinitum spatium ex omni parte diffunderetur
et maneret semper inmobilis in se et inpermutabilis et invariabilis, tunc
aliquomodo possit cogitari de spiritu qui est Deus, qui est lumen divinum
omnia penetrans, omnia replens, ubique totum, et super omnia infinitum.
Et illud pulchre et breviter quidam Atheniensis philosophus expressit[11]

---

[11] Cf. Nicolaus Cusanus, *De docta ignorantia*, I.23, cf. I.12, II.11 (Hoffmann-Kliban-
sky ed., pp. 46-47); *De coniecturis*, ch. 16. This phrase is quoted by Meister Eckhart and
a wide variety of medieval and early modern authors. For its origins see Clemens Baeumker, "Das pseudo-hermetische 'Buch der vierundzwanzig Meister' (Liber XXIV phi-

cum dixit, "Deus est spera cuius centrum est ubique et circumferentia nusquam." Qui intelligit quid sit spera, clare habet similitudinem descriptionis de natura divina, quod Deus est ubique totus et tamen incircumscriptibilis et omnia per infinitum excedens et omnia includens et replens et nusquam inclusus; quia hoc esset spera cuius centrum esset ubique et circumferentia nusquam. Ut patet bene consideranti per illum modum Iohannes evangelista voluit docere Deum cognoscere, quando dixit "Deus spiritus est, et qui volunt adorare oportet in spiritu adorare" [Jn 4:24]. Quasi dicat, qui vult Deum cognoscere et amare et ex amore adorare, consideret et sciat quod Deus est spiritus, et quia est spiritus immensus, incircumscriptibilis, infinitus etc., oportet mentem se elevare ad cognoscendum Deum ut spiritum talem incomprehensibilem et inmutabilem et indivisiblem ubique totum.

Istis notatis et bene consideratis, aliqualiter potest mens illuminari ad cognoscendum Deum, quomodo sit spiritus, ubique totus, omnia penetrans, omnia replens, omnia movens, omnia vivificans, et omnia infinitum excedens; et tamen in se omnino inmobilis, inpermutabilis, incircumscriptibilis. Ut sicut athomi moventur in radijs solis incessanter, ita creature moventur in Deo; et tamen sicut radij solis non videntur mutari secundum motum [G1, 24r] athomorum in eis voltantium. Ita ipsum lumen divinum in nullo mutatur qualitercumque creature in eo [ea G1] existentes mutentur per generationem aut corruptionem aut alio motu. Sic etiam creature omnes sunt sicut vitrum clarum in radijs solis positum et penetratum ab eis; quod si frangitur in mille partes, radij solis quasi fixe manentes et inmobiles penetrant partes, sicut prius totum, in se non mutati secundum hominum apparentiam. Et ita tunc mens hominis potest cogitare quomodo Deus, qui est spiritus, sit sibi presens, omnia sua interiora penetrans, et plus intimus sibi et suis interioribus cogitationibus [et B3] motibus (intentioni, volitioni, et proposito suo) et inclinationibus quam ipsa mens sit sibi intima.

Et ex hac cogitatione aliqualiter illuminata, {mens potest} consurgere ad timorem, reverentiam, et amorem Dei, sicut presentis sibi et omnia millesies acutius quam gladius penetrantis. Et omnia nuda sunt et aperta oculis eius, pertingens usque ad divisionem anime et spiritus compagum quoque et medullarum et discretor cogitationum et intentionum cordis [Heb 4:12]. Pertingit enim usque ad divisionem anime et spiritus distinctius: quomodo homo, cognoscens quid sit sensualitatis et quid rationis in eo, et qui motus, actus, et cogitationes fiant ex sensualitate et

---

losophorum): Ein Beitrag zur Geschichte des Neupythagoreismus und Neuplatonismus im Mittelalter" (1927), 208. A new edition of the work with a reinterpretation of its significance is found in Françoise Hudry, ed., *Le livre des XXIV philosophes* (1989).

qui ex voluntate et ratione. Pertingit ad divisionem compagum, id est verarum et falsarum virtutum quibus interior homo compaginatur, ad quorum divisionem Deus pertingit, quia distinctissime et clarissime cognoscit quando sunt vere virtutes et quando ficte et false, quod sepe homo ignorat. Pertingit etiam usque ad divisionem medullarum: medulla mentis est intentio principalis in operatione, aut potius ipse amor aut affectio ex qua procedit intentio, ex qua sicut ex medulla vivificantur ossa, id est potentie anime et earum actus et operationes. Hec medulla quandoque est infecta et mala, quando intentio hominis principalis occulte est perversa et tegitur in ossibus, id est potencijs anime, sicut medulla; ut quandoque homini videtur quod aliquid recta intentione agat (ut ex zelo iustitie, aut ex pietate misericordie, aut similimodo), et tamen primaria medulla intentionis est displicentia, invidia, avaritia, aut vana gloria, aut aliud huiusmodi—tunc est medulla intentionis infecta, sicut de hoc dicit Beatus Augustinus in Soliloquio. Et ad divisionem illarum medullarum Deus pertingit penetrando. Et hoc est quod subditur: et discretor cogitationum et intentionum cordis. Et hanc divisionum faciet in finali iudicio in conspectu omnium hominum bonorum et malorum et omnium angelorum.

Et ex hac consideratione presentie Dei sic cor [B3 *add.* hominis] penetrantis, homo deberet consurgere in cognitionem Dei timorem, [G1, 24v] reverentiam, et amorem, et sibi facere consuetudinem in hoc, quia tunc consequeretur mentis illuminationem et disponeretur ad perfectam humilitatem et Dei amorem post mentis purgationem per iudicium et iustitiam de seipso factam iuxta predicta.[12] Pertingit ergo penetrando Dei spiritus et Dei verbum, scilicet Filius, ymmo ipsa tota Trinitas, usque ad divisionem anime et spiritus, discernendo actus spirituales et motus eius ab actibus intellectus et voluntatis. Dividit etiam compages virtutum et potentiarum anime inter omnes virtutes veras et falsas, discernendo et virtutem potentiarum anime [13] et virium discernendo. Dividit medullam amoris et dilectionis, ac omnium affectionum anime, que valde occulte sunt, quandoque male et inordinate. Discretor est omnium cogitationum et intentionum occultarum, quas clarius cognoscit et discernit quales sint, ex qua radice pullulant, quam ipsemet homo. Ecce qualiter omnia penetrat.

---

[12] Ch. 19-22.

[13] inter . . . anime *add. in marg. manu alia.*

Kempf, *De ostensione regni Dei*, ch. 45 (G1, 33v, 14 - 34v, 10).

Quomodo quilibet homo potest Deum semper invenire in corde suo.
Capitulum 45. Si autem quis tam modice fuerit intelligentie quod non
potest ascendere in celum ad cognoscendum Deum, nec ad abyssum
creaturarum ut illuminetur mens sua in Dei cognitione et amoris vinculo
sibi constringatur, est adhuc alius modus inveniendi ipsum semper et
quotienscunque quis voluerit in corde suo. De quo dicit Apostolus ad
Romanos x. [Rom 10:6b-8] ex verbis Moysi, "ne dixeris in corde tuo,
'Quis ascendet in celum aut quis descendet in abyssum,' ad cognoscendum scilicet Deum, quia prope est in corde tuo," si tantum recto
quesieris ipsum corde. Videndum est ergo quomodo recto corde sit quer-
endus ut inveniatur semper quotienscunque homo vult in corde suo; inventus cognoscatur et ametur. Pro quo est sciendum quod anima in sua
natura et essentia, et ipsius ymago, qua est ad Dei similitudinem facta,
est invisiblis ymmo nec perfecte intelligibilis, precipue quo ad naturam
ymaginis Dei in ipsa anima cognoscitur, tamen et percipitur certitudinaliter ex actibus suis, quia homo percipit se habere memoria rerum intelligi-
bilium, etiam de Deo percipit se habere intellectionem aut actum per
quem intelligit rem de qua habet memoriam; percipit etiam se habere
voluntatem, id est actum volendi aut non volendi, amandi aut audiendi
rem cognitam per intellectum, et ex illis certitudinaliter scit in se habere
animam intellectivam nobiliorem quam sunt anime brutorum animalium
et quod anima sua habet illas tres virtutes in se, quod potest memorari,
intelligere, et velle; ut dictum est.[14]

Secundo est sciendum [G1, 34r] quod sicut anima est vita corporis
vivificans corpus et producens omnes actus corporis per quos scitur certitudinaliter quod anima est in corpore et cognoscitur, ita Deus est vita
anime ipsam vivificans et omnes actus anime producens longe excellen-
tius quam anima producit actus corporis, quia Deus est principalis causa
omnium actuum anime, scilicet memorandi, cogitandi, volendi aut no-
lendi, in quantum actus sunt, et precipue in quantum sunt actus anime
unientis per caritatem et meritorij, dicente Apostolo. Non sumus suffi-
cientes cogitare aliquid ex nobis quasi ex nobis, sed sufficientia nostra ex
Deo est. Et sicut de cogitatione, ita a fortiori de volitione aut memorati-
one est intelligendum quod a Deo sunt.

Istis notatis, si vis invenire Deum in corde tuo, convertas mentem ad
habendum memoriam de Deo, et sic invenisti Patrem, et coneris habere
bonas cogitationes et intellectiones aut meditationes de Deo aut spiritualibus rebus, et sic iam natus est in te Filius. Inclina affectum ad eius

---

[14] Chapter 34 (G1, 26r, 29-26v, 20).

amorem, et sic venit Spiritus Sanctus, et sic iam invenis vite ymaginem Trinitatis. Cogita consequenter quod illa in mente iam dicta, scilicet actus memorandi, actus intelligendi, actus amandi, omnino non sunt actus anime tue; que tales actus non potest ex se habere sed solum a Deo; sicut corpus ex se non potest aliquos actus habere nisi ab anima. Et sic ex illis actibus cogita et considera certitudinaliter et perceptibiliter esse Deum in corde tuo, qui est omnia in omnibus et operatur omnia in omnibus. Et ita in omnibus alijs actibus anime cogita, ut quod Deus est in intentione tua, in omni cogitatione tua, in omni voluntate, in omni proposito tuo, ymmo in medulla voluntatis et intentionis et in radice qui omnia illa operatur in me; et quamvis ipsum non possum videre, sicut nec animam meam, que est vita corporis, tamen ex illis actibus ego percipio ipsum esse in me, ymmo sanctam Trinitatem esse in ymagine mentis mee, quam cognosco et diligo ac magis cognoscere et diligere cupio.

Certissime autem quandocunque vult et quotienscunque vult homo semper cum gratia Dei potest Deum invenire, si solum recto quesierit corde. Quid autem est recto corde querere? Hoc est affectu devoto et sincero et humili intellectu, ut affectus seu voluntas non sit retorta aut tornata per amorem ad creaturas, sed Dei amorem per caritatem infusam. Et intellectus non sit obliquatus ad seipsum, ut putet se posse tales cogitationes habere, aut tales cogitationes seu actus predictos suos esse, aut se aliquid in eis habere putans se aliquid esse aut posse—cum nichil sit et sine Deo omnino nichil possit et nichil sit; et sic tunc non queritur [G1, 34v] recto corde et ideo non invenitur ut cognoscatur et ametur modo predicto. Qui frequenter considerat presentiam Dei in corde, predicto modo recto corde eum querendo, faceret sibi Deum valde familiarem et frequenter presentem et, valde mens sua prius purgata, illuminaretur per eius cognitionem et sibi uniretur per amorem, ut diceret Deus "illuminatio mea" [Ps 138:11; 27:1]. Et illi sunt qui dicere possunt regnum Dei intra nos est [Cf. Lk 17:21], quia ipse fecit nos sibi regnum et sacerdotes [Rev 1:6], quia invenimus eum in templo sancto suo [Ps 10:5], in corde scilicet nostro et in ore. Iam non est nos necesse ad celum ascendere per altissimas contemplationes de divinitate eius, nec ad abyssum per scripturarum profunditatem aut creaturarum cognitionem, quia prope invenimus eum in corde etc.

Kempf, *De ostensione regni Dei*, ch. 48 (G1, 36r, 31 - 37r, 5).

Ultimum iter faciendum Deo ut ascendat super occasum et regnum Dei ostendatur quid sit. Capitulum 48. Omnis sacre scripture et omnium katholicarum scripturarum et omnium creaturarum finis principalis circa predicta tria versatur, ut scilicet mens purgetur per sensum moralem, illuminetur per sensum [G1, 36v] allegoricum, et inflammetur per sensum anagogicum.[15] Et quid philosophorum studia aliud finaliter quesiverunt, nisi ut contempnantur presentia et insistatur studio veritatis et anheletur ad vitam meliorem, quamvis multi ex eis per rectas vias non ambulaverunt aut verum finem non quesiverunt. Est autem preter predictas vias ad ostensionem regni adhuc unum iter necessarium, de quo dicit propheta: "Iter facite ei qui ascendit super occasum" [Ps 67:5]; et illud: "Iter non est aliud nisi actus perfectissimus amoris Dei in supprema et nobilissima potentia anime, scilicet in synderesi, post omnes predictas illuminationes et unitivos amores; qui actus potest formari secundum quosdam sine cognitione previa aut concomitante, aut ad minus potest manere cessante omni cognitione actuali."

Et illius actus frequentatio est ultimum iter et suppremus gradus mentis et ultima preparatio ante ostensione regni Dei, per que preparatur iter illi qui solet "ascendere super occasum, cui Dominus est nomen" [Ps 67:5], qui postquam dignatur venire et se menti ostendere tunc videtur regnum Dei. Et ipse ascendit super occasum, id est longe altius quam fiat occasus. Nam occasus ille dicitur cessatio omnium cognitionum intellectualium et omnium actuum amoris Dei ex potencijs anime procedentibus cum caritate infusa; que cessatio recte dicitur occasus, quia occidunt cogniciones et erunt tenebre in potencijs anime. Sed Dominus ascendit super occasum illum per lumen superintellectuale, hoc est per cognitiones et amores sui, qui sunt super omnem intellectum et omnem facultatem omnium virium anime et potentiarum. Et de illis latissime est dictum in tractatu de ostensione regni Dei.[16]

In qua ostensione cognoscitur et amatur Deus intime et ineffabiliter ex sua presentia experimentali in anima, et tunc sibi mutuo locuntur Deus et anima per affectus et per iubilum et per mutuum gaudium et letitiam et per huiusmodi; de quibus principaliter locuntur cantica canticorum sicut ibidem etiam satis extense est dictum exponendo cantica[17] et ideo hic transeundum. Sed pro omni illa materia iam scripta et etiam pro tractatu de ostensione regni Dei et expositione super cantica, que omnia finaliter tendunt ad unum finem, ut scilicet mens disponatur et per vias rectas deducatur ut detur sibi gustare et videre in presenti vita regnum Dei, sunt hic adhuc aliqui cautele breviter avertende, quibus ostenditur que impediant mentem et que promoveant; de quibus tamen in alijs locis sparsi et est latius dictum, sed hic breviter repetendum [G1, 37r] et compendiose ac succincte brevissima via ostendenda, que potest omnibus

---

[15] allegoricum *del.*, anagogicum *add. alia manu* G1.

[16] I.e., Kempf, *Tractatus de mystica theologia.*

[17] I.e., Kempf, *Expositiones in Cantica Canticorum.*

competere, etiam simplicibus, indoctis, illiteratis, et quamcumque parvi
fuerint ingenij, dummodo tamen sint fervidi ac devoti, diligentes ac per-
severantes in studio amoris Dei.

Kempf, *De ostensione regni Dei*, ch. 51 (G1, 38r, 25 - 39r, 3).

*Per quatuor virtutes designatas—per pauperes, debiles, cecos, et
claudos—gustatur regnum Dei in cena eterne vite. Capitulum 51m.* Cum
autem omnes predicti tamquam inabiles et indigni repellantur et audiant
quod nemo illorum gustabit cenam regni celorum, nunc videndum est qui
admittantur; de quibus subditur: "voca pauperes, debiles, cecos, et claudos" [Lk 14:13, 22]; de quibus dicitur quod "erant introducti et sic gus-
taverunt cenam" [Lk 14:24]; in quibus designantur quatuor virtutes aut
conditiones que requiruntur ad hoc ut regnum Dei ostendatur per gustum
cene.

Prima est paupertas, id est vera humilitas, non solum intellectualis,
que fit per cognitionem veram suorum defectuum, sed affectionalis aut
voluntatis. Et de hac alibi latius dictum est.

Secundo, quod fit debilis in corpore sufferende patienter [G1, 38v]
omnes molestias corporales inmediate recipiendo a Deo,[18] de qua debili-
tate dixit Apostolus: "cum infirmior tunc potens sum" [2 Cor 12:10]. Et
rursum quod fit debilis in resistendo iniurijs aut quibuscunque malis a
quocunque illatis, sed recipiat patienter et gaudenter in mente a Deo,
sicut "apostoli qui ibant gaudentes de consilio, eo quod digni inventi es-
sent pro nomine Christi contumelia pati" [Acts 5:41].

Deinde tertio quod fit cecus ut viderat, de quibus dixit Christus,
"Ego veni in mundum ut qui ceci sunt videant, ut qui vident ceci fiant"
[Jn 9:39]. Fiat, inquam, cecus a nimio studio intellectuali quo impeditur
affectus ab amore, sed recedat quantum potest ab omnibus intellectuali-
bus cognitionibus et per affectum simplicem extendit se in Dei amorem.
Qui enim comedit nimium de melle non sibi prodest, cum non digerit sed
evomit, et sic vertitur sibi in amaritudinem evomendo. Sic qui nimium
comedit de scientia intellectuali, etiam sacre scripture (que per mel designatur) quando non digerit eam in affectum per amorem trahendo, tunc
evomit per vanitatem alios docendo et in se vacuus remanendo. Comedat
ergo unusquisque de melle, id est scientia sacre scripture, quantum sibi
sufficit pro amore Dei, ut in eo plus crescat quam in scientia, quia "scientia inflat, amor ad vitam eternam edificat et perducit" [1 Cor 8:1].

Postremo quartus fiat claudus. Claudus per se non potest ambulare,
sed innititur aliene virtuti aut adiutorio, ut baculo, aut portanti se animali,

---

[18] Cf. ch. 13, 17, 26.

aut homini suscentanti ipsum. Claudus ergo fit qui totaliter in sua virtute se deficere experimentaliter conspicit et se totaliter in Deum proicit, cuius virtuti innititur in ambulando pedibus amoris et gressibus virtutum, et totaliter et perfecte in Deo facit virtutem et non in se.

Vocantur ergo et veniunt ad cenam Domini ad gustandum eterne vite dulcedinem, qui predictas quatuor habent virtutes, scilicet humilitatem sicut pauperes, patientiam veram sicut debiles, simplicitatem bonam (magis scientes amare quam disputare, Deum diligere quam multam scientiam habere), qui dicuntur ceci, et qui seipsos perfecte abnegant in spiritu et in carne, Deo committendo, qui vocantur claudi etc. Pauperes enim sunt qui sunt humiles spiritu. Sed debiles {sunt} qui seipsos abnegaverunt et animas suas perdunt ut inveniant eas [Mt 10:39; 16:25; Mk 8:35; Lk 9:24-25; Jn 12:25]. Sed ceci sunt qui mentem suam ab omnibus cogitationibus, fanthasijs, et cognitionibus et intelligibilibus proposse abstrahunt, et sic absoluti ab omnibus creaturis et speciebus sensibilibus et fanthasmatibus, Deo per amorem inherent, que virtus vulgariter vocatur abgeschaidenhait. Nam si scientia etiam sacra sepe impedit, quanto magis cogitationes inutiles aut nocive et fanthasie sensuales aut intellectuales. [G1, 39r] Claudi vero sunt qui, iam in se deficientes, aliena virtute reguntur, de quibus dixit Apostolus: "Qui spiritu Dei reguntur hij filij Dei sunt" [Rom 8:14]. Et vocatur hec virtus relictio aut resignatio sui ipsius, vulgariter gelassenhait.

Kempf, *Explanatio in Cantica Canticorum*, bk. IV, ch. 9 (G1, 233r, 16 - 234v, 2; Pez, *Bibl. Ascetica*, 11: 420-25: commentary on Ca 4:7).

Quomodo sponsa dicitur a dilecto tota pulchra, cum nemo sit sine peccato [Pez: vitio] *et de modo per quem potest fieri tota pulchra.* Predicta faciendo impletur in sponsa secundum Beatum Gregorium, quod sequitur in littera qua ei a dilecto dicitur: "Tota pulchra es, amica mea, et macula non est in te" [Ca 4:7]; quod de ecclesia sancta et etiam qualibet anima perfecte mundata potest intelligi. Nam de ecclesia dicitur, quod sit "sine ruga et macula"; et de anima sancta, "templum Dei sanctum est" [Eph 5:27; 1 Cor 3: 17]; et, "vos mundi estis," inquit dilectus discipulis suis, "sed non omnes" [Jn. 13:10]. Que verba, sive de ecclesia sive de quantumlibet perfecta et sancta anima accipiantur, non invenitur sic pulchra ut sit sine omni macula mortalis aut venialis delicti, sed solum in capite ipso sponso Ihesu Christo, et matre eius virgine gloriosa ex singularis gratie privilegio invenitur hec [Pez *add.* tota] pulchritudo.

Sed quia totum tantum valet sicut perfectum, et perfectio status presentis vite post lapsum humani generis non requirit hanc munditiam ab omni peccato tam mortali quam veniali (qui status conclusit secundum scripturam omnia sub peccato, ut non glorietur in conspectu Dei omnis caro, sed ut omni misereatur [Pez: sed . . . misereatur *om.*]). Et ideo hic Beatus Gregorius movens dubium, quomodo dicitur "sponsa tota pulchra es et sine macula" cum tamen multipliciter scriptura testetur neminem esse sine peccato, nec unius diei infantem; solvendo sic dicit: "dum sancta anima a peccatis cottidianis se per penitentiam mundat; dum cottidie peccata minuta cum lacrimis abluit, et a majoribus se observat; quamvis frequenter peccet, per assiduam tamen penitentiam, munditiam suam assidue servat. [233v] Hinc est, quod precipitur, 'sint vestimenta tua semper candida' [Ecclesiastes 9:8]. Et illud, 'Iustus autem ex fide vivit' [Rom 1:17]. Quamvis enim mox ut peccat, a iustitia deviet, tamen dum semper credit in eum qui iustificat impium et assidue sub eius fide peccata sua deflet, et [Pez: et *om.*] per assiduas ablutiones iustitiam suam retinet."

Hec sunt consolatoria verba, in quibus Beatus Gregorius aperte declarat, que in presenti vita requirantur ad hoc, quod anima sancta, Christi sponsa, dicatur totaliter aut perfecte pulchra et sine macula. Et dicit hic Beda: "Nemo est super terram sine peccato, nec infans unius diei, sed ideo fides perfecta et celeste desiderium omnem maculam abstergit levioris peccati. Tota ergo est pulchra ecclesia, in quantum se castam et immunem ab omni peccato custodit. Si quando autem levi peccato fuscatur, cita penitudine et recta fide ad celeste desiderium in ea pristina pulchritudo recuperatur." Hec Beda inter caetera.[19]

Est ergo anima, dilecti sponsa, tunc, tota pulchra, quando nec in opere, nec in verbo, nec in aliqua animae potentia diu perseverat peccatum; quando per penitentiam, aut lachrimas, aut sacramenta ecclesie ex fide deleatur [Pez: deletur].

Nam ubi principaliter et frequenter solet sponsa peccare, scilicet in capillis, id est cogitationibus; in labijs, in dentibus, in genis, in collo; prius laudavit eam tanquam mundam. Hic nunc generaliter subjungit "eam totam mundam"; quod tunc sit secundum Beatum Gregorium, quando "ad montem Myrrha" secundum modum predictum et "ad collem thuris" frequenter "vadit." Et ita hac clausula debet sic intelligi: "tota pulchra es," id est, perfecte pulchra es, quantum pertinet ad presentem vitam; "et macula" peccati cuiuscunque "non est in te" scienter [Pez *add.* in culpa] perseverando, et ex negligentia [Pez *add.* in ea] crescendo; nec manet, quin diluatur modo predicto.

Nec tamen putandum credo, quod nullus, quantumlibet sanctus, possit stare in hac vita aliquo parvo tempore aut momento sine peccato, sic

---

[19] This seems to be a combination of quotations from Bede (PL 91: 1137-38), Haimo (PL 117: 319AB), and Robert of Tombelaine (PL 79:510BC).

quod non actualiter peccet veniali peccato, aut in veniali perpetrato maneat. Quia sanctus Iohannes Baptista, apostoli, et prophetae, et multi sancti verosimiliter quandoque aliquo tempore venialiter non peccaverunt, nec in veniali preterito [Pez: peccato] permanserunt, que sicut gutte aque in igne caritatis consumabantur [Pez: consumebantur], omnes tamen habuerunt possibilitatem propinquam peccandi et aliquando venialiter peccaverunt. Nec credendum est Moysem peccasse, quamdiu fuit in monte; nec paulum, quamdiu fuit in tertio celo; et sic nec alios sanctos tempore quo erant cum Deo.

Oportet ergo, ut aiunt sancti patres, sponsa mundari perfecte ab omni peccato, mortali et veniali, ymmo ab omni habitu vitioso, et ab omni poena pro peccata debita, antequam introducatur in thalamum regis, ubi eum [134r] presentem in suo videat dyademate, et sibi [Pez: ei] copuletur et uniatur in ymagine; quia hec munditia et pulchritudo requiritur in sanctis animabus post hanc vitam ad videndum Deum in sua gloria, ergo multo magis in presenti vita feculenta et turbida.

Et quamvis [Pez add. Sponsa] ad hanc munditiam non possit per se et per suum conatum pertingere, tamen quando dilectus dignatur venire, tunc ipse supplet defectum; et in ipso tempore adventus sui, aut paulo ante, perfecte eam mundabit, "et totam pulchram" facit [Pez: faciet], ita ut ei dicat: "tota iam pulchra es amica mea et macula non est in te." Quando enim Dominus Ihesus intrat Egyptum, tunc cadent [Pez: cadunt] omnia ydola peccatorum et vitiorum. Sed hoc non fuit [Pez: erit] tuum [Pez add. sponsa] opus, nec ex tua diligentia, sed ex mea gratia [Pez add. dicet dilectus].

Et hoc est, quod Beatus Gregorius in praedictis verbis in fine dixit: "cuius conatum," scilicet sponse, "pro sua pulchritudine ad effectum sponsus per gratiam suam ducit, opusque suum in sponsa benigne laudat, cum dicit, "tota pulchra es amica mea et macula non est in te."

Ex predictis colligitur, quod volens perfecte mundari, et totus pulcher fieri, necesse erit [Pez add. illi] ut se a levioribus etiam minimis peccatis diligenter custodiat et cottidie pro eisdem, quia cavere omnino non potest, peniteat, lacrimas effundat, et se castiget. Alioquin nunquam proficiet ut sponso placere valeat taliter, ut audire mereatur, "tota pulchra es amica mea."

Hic accusa te humiliter de tua negligentia, et ex corde dicas: "O mi dilecte, quod non sum totus pulcher ex mea negligentia est, eo quod peccata etiam quandoque graviora, sicut possem et deberem, non omitto; et de levioribus negligenter peniteo, et quasi ex quadam consuetudine confiteor sine dolore, et iterum reincido eadem sine timore. Et hec est causa, quod non purgor nec mundor. O [Pez add. igitur] misericordissime, da mihi fervorem ad cavendam frequentationem peccatorum et dolorem [Pez *add.* ea] diluendi.

Hec autem pulchritudo secundum Beatum Bernardum acquiritur per magnum amoris desiderium ad dilectum. Unde dicit Sermone 31 sic, "'Ignis ante ipsum precedet, et inflammabit in circuitu inimicos eius' [Ps 96:3]. Oportet namque, ut sancti desiderij ardor preveniat faciem eius ad omnem animam ad quam ipse est venturus; qui omnem consumat rubiginem vitiorum; et sic preparet locum Domine." Sed illa munditia et pulchritudo non acquiritur perfecte per illum ignem amoris precedentem, sed per [Pez *add.* illum] ignem amoris, qui infunditur, per ipsum dilectum venientem. De quo subjungit Beatus Bernardus, "Tunc scit omnino, quod iuxta est Dominus, cum senserit se illo igne [134v] succensam, et dixit [Pez: dixerit] cum propheta, 'de excelso misit ignem in ossibus meis, et erudivit me' [Lam 1:13]." Hec Bernardus.[20]

Bernard of Waging, *Defensorium speculi pastorum*, ch. 9 (clm 4403, fol. 63v [71v], 37 - 65r [73r], 6).

Sequitur ulterius in epistola de ipsa questione proposita quam tua illustrata sapientia dividendam censuit, et recte quidem, ut videlicet primo queratur de hijs qui nondum prelationem adepti aut alicui animarum cure sunt prepositi: an eisdem magis expediat religionem ingredi vel pro lucrandis animabus plebis curam suscipere. Nam qui iam pastorali cure humeros summiserunt, utrum eisdem contemplationis causa ob vite melioris [fol. 64r (72r)] frugem liceat episcopale onus abicere, dubium esse non videtur, cum sit res ista auctoritate apostolica dudum determinata. De primis questio agit, non de secundis, prout ex supradictis ymmo ex infradicendis evidenter elici potest. Deinde plurima per ordinem in ipsa epistola de zelo animarum earumque regimine et cura sunt parte doctissime subtiliter utiliterque congesta, in quibus calamum latius extendendo, sentencijs gravissimis et doctrinis suavissimis ad inserviendum saluti animarum Christique oviculas pascendum, quemque magis communia quam propria amantem, plusque aliorum multorum quam suam solam beatitudinem zelantem, pulcherrime disserendo nedum rationabiliter persuadere, quin etiam efficaciter inducere conaris. Sed neque, ais, metu periculi onus pastorale quempiam debere recusare, quinymmo cum apostolis in cunctis periculis edoces gloriari; nec militem Christi in pugna pro eterna gloria pusillanimem inveniri, quin potius

---

[20] Bernard of Clairvaux, *Sermones super Cantica Canticorum*, 31.4 (*S. Bernardi Opera*, 1: 221-22).

multis adversitatibus et periculis voluntarie subdi. Quibus quidem omnibus, ut aestimo, ceteris paribus, mea scripta dissona non sunt.

Post multa disputando dissertissime, arguis contra me de milite qui suam fortitudinem cicatricum probat ostensione; sic quoque prelati casum esse quandoque humilitatis patientieque clipeum, neque statim post culpam commissam Dominum peccantem deicere, sed patienter tempus penitendi expectare. Quodque si vires debeant probari, necesse sit quandoque virtutem debilitari. Probas hec ipsa per autentica exempla, ac tandem adducis verbum sapientis: "Quod melior sit iniquitas viri quam benefaciens mulier." "Non sic ego de me," subinfers, "qui in antro latito neque adversis probor, unde nec scio cuius virtutis existo quia periculis non temptor." Verum est utique: Ego mulier quia fragilis et mollis, cui convenit in domo sedere, nere et flere. Virum, quod est nomen virtutis, condecent opera fortiora: ut puta foras exire, contra hostes dimicare, cedere, et superare, constantemque in acie pugne perstare. Qui si quandoque et raro ceciderit, aut quippiam non eque egerit, adiciet ut mox iterum resurgat curabitque, ut postea virilius agat. Non sic de muliere, quae citius et facilius cadit, tardius tamen ac difficilius resurgit; maneat ergo necesse est in domo et operetur bona quae potest, quamvis minora, et viri iniquitati [MS *inequitati*] minus valitura, neque se eis presumat [fol. 64v (72v)] aliquatenus comparare, nec eis consedere, quorum labores non prevalet portare nec opera exercere. Hinc Beatus Bernhardus[21]: "Fratres," inquit, "revereamur pontifices, sed vereamur eorum labores. Si enim pensamus labores, non affectamus honores. Agnoscamus impares vires nostras, nec delectet molles et femineos humeros virorum supponere sarcinis. Non observemus eos, sed honoremus. Inhumane nempe eorum redarguis opera, quorum onera refugis. Temerarie obiurgat virum de prelio revertentem mulier manens[22] in domo. Dico enim: si quis de claustro est,[23] eum qui versatur in populo et interdum minus bene minusve circumspecte sese agere deprehenderit, verbi gratia in verbo, in cibo, in somno, in risu, in ira, in iudicio, non ad iudicandum confestim prosiliat, sed meminerit scriptum: 'melior est iniquitas viri quam benefaciens mulier' [Ecclus 42:14]. Nam qui in tua custodia[24] vigilas bene facis; sed qui iuvat multos melius facit et viriliter agit.[25] Quod si implere non sufficit absque aliqua iniquitate, id est absque

---

[21] Bernard of Clairvaux, *Sermones super Cantica*, 12.9 (*S. Bernardi Opera*, 1: 66; cf. also 12.8 (ibid., pp. 65-66), hereafter abbreviated as *Opera*].

[22] nens *Opera*.

[23] si is, qui de claustro est *Opera*.

[24] Nam quidem in tui custodia *Opera*.

[25] multos, et melius facit et, virilius [agit *om.*] *Opera*.

quadam inequalitate vite et conversationis sue, memento 'quia caritas
operit multitudinem peccatorum' [1 Pet. 4:8]. Hec dicta sint contra gemi-
nam temptationem, quia[26] sepe viri religiosi episcoporum vel ambire
gloriam, vel excessus temere iudicare, dyabolicis instigationibus incitan-
tur." Hec Bernardus. Aliter sed non contrarie exponit glosa ordinaria[27]:
Melior inquit (id est utilior) est iniquitas (id est lapsus viri, supple per
discretionem postmodum humiliter resurgentis) quam mulier benefaciens
(id est quam minus prudens benefaciens, et benefaciendo indiscrete pre-
sumens). Ubi consequenter glosa dicit: Vir in hoc loco fortis et discretus
vocatur; mulier mens infirma et indiscreta. Et sepe contingit ut discretus
labatur in culpam, {atque} infirmus exhibeat operationem bonam. Sed
indiscretus de bonis suis superbiens gravius cadit; discretus penitens ad
discretionis regulam redit, et de cetero fortius et cautius agit. Sepe enim
culpa fortium fit occasio virtutis et virtus infirmorum occasio peccati.
Hec ibi.

Rursum ea que secuntur in epistola omnia sunt plana, ubi inter alia
lamentaris, O pater sanctissime una mecum, status ecclesiastici miser-
abilem collapsum, paucitatem in ecclesia Dei bonorum presidentium, vitia publica et enormitates maximas ipsorum prelatorum, et exorbitantias
quam plurimas animarum rectorum, denique malitiam temporum et per-
versitatem, insolentiam [fol. 65r (73r)] ac rebellionem subditorum. Af-
fers nichilominus de tua sapientia contra hec singula antidota salutaria et
sana, que utique sanis intellectibus, non animis femineis et mollibus, sed
viris virtutum et fortibus sapida et efficacia existunt. Nam et viris vir lo-
queris, virtuosus virtuosis, robustus robustis—mulieribus infirmis me
michique similibus prorsus exclusis.

---

[26] qua *Opera*.

[27] For the full text from PL 109, see chapter six, above. Bernard of Waging cites the
Gloss in an abbreviated, "telegram" form. I have placed his own interpolating glosses in
parenthesis.

TABLES

Stemma Codicum: De proponentibus and De discretione

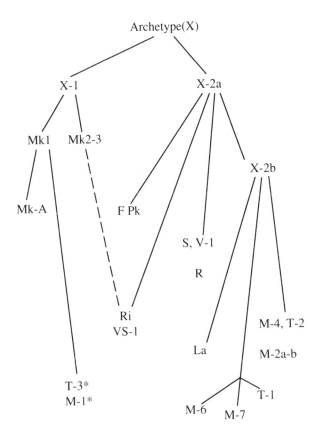

* De discretione only

Table 1: Vienna Masters of Arts at Gaming

Name	Matr.	Degr.	Date	Rel.	Death	Offices Held	Auth.
Caspar (Antonius) of Berchtldsdrf		MA	1435				H/A
Nicholas Kempf	1433	MA	1437	1440	1497	see chapter 1	H/A
Leonhard of Schlüsselfeld	1429	MA	1435	1440	1474		H/A
Gregorius de Zesma	1434	MA	1439	1440	1462		H/A
Johannes Velber of Passau	1431	MA	1440	1441	1471		H/A C6:135
Heinrich Praentl of Eckenfeld	1435	MA		1442	1481	P Olom (1453), Prag (1458) Ittngn (1468), Stz (1471-74)	H
Thomas Papler of Zistersdorf	1437	MA	1443	1444	1474?	P Aggsbach (1448-58), Leth-enkow (1458-64); V Gaming	H/A C6:178
Wolfgang (Bene-dictus) Neuböck	1442?	MA	1444	1446	1465	V Gaming; P Lechnitz (1459-65)	H/A C5:205
Georg Pernhei-ßel of Munich	1442	MA?		1450	1478	P Pleterje	H
Johannes (Ambrosius) of Issenau				1450	1469		H
Andreas Pisca-toris of Pöchlarn	1444	MA?		1450			H
Sigismnd Phantza-gel of Vienna	1442	MA	1450	1453	1483	P Aggsbach (1458), Gaming (1458-83)	H/A
Johannes (Anto-nius) Lang	?	MA	1449	1454	1501	P Olomouc (1468-80), Gaming 1485-86), Brno	H/A
Bernard (Paulus?) Lang of Brno	1449?	MA?		1454	1483	P Brno (1481ff.)	H
Christian of Wasserburg	1443?	MA?		1455	1486	Pr Gaming	H
Johannes (Kilian) of Würzburg	?*	MA?		1456	1483	Sacr, Vp, V Gaming	H
Karolus**		MA?					H
Wolfgang of Klosterneuburg		MA	1474				H

Key: In the first column, names in religion are given in parentheses. The date of matriculation is from the Vienna University *Matrikel*; a question mark indicates that several identifications are possible. The third column gives the date of the dgree; the fourth column the date of entry into monastic life, usually, the beginning of the novitiate.

Authorities: H - List of Gaming monks by William Hofer, in Zeißberg, "Gaming" (1880), some data added by Wydemann; A - List of *magistri regentes* in Aschbach, *Wiener Universität* (1865), 1: 596-627; C3 - *The Chartae of the Carthusian General Chapter, Paris, Bibliothèque Nationale MS Latin 10887*, Part I: *1438-46 (Ff. 1-144)*, ed. Michael Sargent and James Hogg, Analecta Cartusiana, 100.3 (Salzburg, 1984); C4 - *The Chartae of the Carthusian General Chapter, Paris, Bibliothèque Nationale MS Latin 10887*, Part II: *1447-56 (Ff. 145-333v)*, ed. Michael Sargent and James Hogg, Analecta Cartusiana, 100.4 (Salzburg, 1984); C5 - *The Chartae of the Carthusian General Chapter, Paris, Bibliothèque Nationale MS Latin 10888*, Part I: *1457-65 (Ff. 1-157v)*, ed. Michael Sargent and James Hogg, Analecta Cartusiana, 100.5 (Salzburg, 1985); C6 - *The Chartae of the Carthusian General Chapter, Paris, Bibliothèque Nationale MS Latin 10888*, Part II: *1466-74 (Ff. 159-307)*, ed. Michael Sargent and James Hogg, Analecta Cartusiana, 100.6 (Salzburg, 1985).

Key to Offices Abbreviation: Ab - Abbot (Benedictine); P - Prior (Benedictine and Carthusian, with Carthusian Prior being equivalent to Benedictine Abbot); V - Vicar; Pr - Procurator; Vp - Viceprocurator; Sacr - Sacristan; RegCan - Regular Canon; Pst - secular priest; Rel - religious, religion (monastic).

*No fewer than eleven Johannes or Killians of Würzburg appear in the *Matrikel*, 1449-53.

**The Hofer list has "Karolus, Magister Wiennensis."

Table 2: Vienna Baccalaurei at Gaming

Name	Matr.	Degr.	Rel.	Death	Offices Held	Auth.
Conrad (Bauelein?) of Speyer-	1432	BA	1440*	1472		C4-C6*
Ulrich Thonhauser of Amberg	1435?	BA	1432/6	1473		C6:211
Simon Misnensis		BA	1442	1473	Pr Gaming	C6:211
Johannes (Paulus) Wagner of Baden		BA	1443	1474	Sacr, V Gaming; P. Brno	C6:211
Christoph Stöckl of Tegernsee	1444		1447	1477	P Seitz (1474-77)	
Balthasar		BA	1448**	1466		C6:32
Simon (Gabriel)		BA	1451	1495		
Johannes (Bartholomaeus) Hölderle of Munich	1441	BA	1452	1488	P Aggsbach (1458-73), Ittingen (1478-82)	
Georg (Jacobus) Stauthamer of Munich	1443	BA	1452	1482	V Gaming, P Brno	
Johannes Saechsl of Reichenhall	1450	BA	1453	1500	V Gaming	
Mathias Schader of Lengwald	1446	BA	1453	1507	V Gaming	
Michael Wildendorfer of Vienna		BA	1456***	1477		
Petrus of Brno	1441	BA	1457	1510	Pr and V Gaming	
Martin Turnaer of Mödling+	1450	BA			Cantor, V Schnals	
Albertus Franco		BA++				
Andreas Taentl of Gaming	1462	BA	1466	1510	P Gaming (1483-85, 1491-96)	
Paul (Chrysogonus) Hebenkrieg+++	1447	BA	1473	1513	P Olomouc (1490-92) Gaming (1502-10)	

Note: Except where otherwise noted, all data in this table based on Hofer list in Zeißberg, "Gaming."

*Conrad of Speyer was already a canon at St. Pölten. References to his stormy Carthusian career are C4:65, 91, 139, 160, 183, 184; C5:165; C6:135.

**"Balthasar" [Walthasar] entered sometime before 1448. Zeißberg cites the copy of excerpts from the *Chartae* of the General Chapter, according to which Balthasar was to return to Geirach where he had become a monk; apparently he entered Gaming as *clericus redditus*; this entry is not found in the *Chartae* edited by Hogg and Sargent. At his death in 1467 he was described as a monk professed of Geirach in the Paris manuscript edited by Hogg; in the one consulted by Zeißberg (cod. 86 of the Haus-, Hof-, und Staatsarchiv in Vienna), as a monk professed of Gaming.

***Wildendorfer remained a *redditus* all his life.

+Martin Turnaer taught school at St. Leonhard

++Albertus Franco is mentioned in H as "Baccalaureus Wiennensis."

+++Chrysogonus Hebenkrieg first professed at Tegernsee in 1467; the Hofer list gives his death date as 1513; a letter from Wydemann to Pez, Jan. 22, 1718, says 1515.

Table 3: Benedictines Entering Gaming

Name	Prof.Ben.	Gaming	Death	Offices Held
Sigismund Phelzberger of St. Pölten	Melk		1452	
Jodocus	Seitenst.	1440	1450	P Olomouc (1448)
Wolfgang of Wolkersdorf	Melk	1440	1474*	
Konrad (Anselm)	Tegernsee	1443	1488	P Schnals
Paul (Chrysogonus) of Krems	Tegernsee	1473		

Sources: Hofer list in Zeißberg, "Gaming"; summary by Wydemann in a letter to Pez, Jan. 22, 1718. Wydemann added the name of Christoph Stöckl, but questioned whether he was a monk at Tegernsee or whether 'de Tegernsee' refers to his family home. The latter supposition is correct. Two former Cistercians are mentioned in Müller, "Personalien," 167, as professed monks of Gaming who later served as priors of Olomouc. A Johannes of Spangenberg left Heiligenkreuz for Gaming in 1441; a Mathias entered Gaming sometime before 1444 when he became prior at Brno.

*Wolfgang of Wolkersdorf died at the Hungarian charterhouse of Lövöld.

Table 4: Vienna Masters at Melk

Name	Matr	Degr.	Date	Rel.	Offices Held	Auth.
Nicholas Seyringer of Matzen	1389	MA Bth	1395 1399?	1403	Ab Melk (1418-23) P in Italy	AFT:5, 6, 52, 120
Petrus of Rosenheim	1398	MA?	1398-	1403	P Melk (1418-25)	T:101
Urban of Melk	1409	DTh	1413			A; AFT index
Johann Wischler of Freinsheim (John of Speyer)		MA		1418	P Melk (1433)	MA at Heidelb.; Pst then monk
Konrad (Mülner? Wagner?) of Nürnberg	1429?	MA DTh	1433 1448	1423	Unsuccessful reform Ab Obernburg, 1426	Hu:79-80; AFT index
Konrad of Geißenfeld	1426a	MA	1431	1433	P Melk + Tegernsee	R
Johannes of Spiz	1430?	BTh		1434		Kr:245
Stephan of Spanberg	1423? 1426?	MA BTh	1431 1438	1434	P Melk (1443-51), Ab Melk (1451-53)	A; Kr:248; AFT 79, 117, 700
Johannes Schitpacher of Weilheim	1424*	MA	1429	1436	P Melk (1451-55, 1460-63), P Mariazl	Taught Vienna 1429-34
Laurenz of Graz	1432	MA		1438	Ab Mariazell (1448), Göttweig (1462)	Kr:442
Johannes of Isny	1445-50	MA		1450		
Augustine of Obernalb		MA	1450	1453	P Melk (1472-75)	A; Kr:377,446
Ludwig Schanzl of Krems	1443	MA		1453	Ab Melk (1474-80)	
Konrad of Würzburg	1441?	Dlur	1457**	1470		K

Authorities: Where no specific authority is cited, Kropff, *Bibliotheca Mellicensis* (1747) [= Kr] or Keiblinger, *Melk* (1867-68) [K], is the source. Redlich, *Tegernsee* (1931), offers information on most people listed here [= R]; T = Franz X. Thoma, "Petrus von Rosenheim" (1927); A = list of *magistri regentes* in Aschbach, *Wiener Univ.*, 1:596-627; AFT = Uiblein, *Die Akten der Theologischen Fakultät der Universität Wien* (*Acta Facultatis Theologicae*); Hu = Hubalek, "Briefwechsel Schlitpacher," 79-80; all matriculation dates are based on the *Matrikel*; where a range of dates is given (e.g., Johannes of Isny, 1445-50), several entries from the *Matrikel* might apply—see the list in Table 7.

*Schlitpacher does not appear in the matriculation register. See Hu 34-37.

**Konrad of Würzburg entertained Martin of Senging in Nürnberg in 1457; degree prior to that date?

Table 5: *Vienna Baccalaurei at Melk*

Name	Matr.	Degr.	Rel.	Offices Held	Auth./Comments
Leonard Peuger	1385?		1420		Kr:200 "lib. arts"
Heinrich of Krain			1425		K:254, 533 "arts"
Wolfgang of Steyer			1426	P Salzbrg, Mariazll, Melk	R
Martin of Senging			1427	Basel Cncl; Pst then Melk	R "studied at Vienna"
Christian Eibensteiner	1415?		1428	Ab Melk (1435-51)	K
Wolfgang Frischmann of Emerstorf	1434?		1432		Hu "studied Schlit." Kr:357, 368
Wolfgang of Neuburg	1428?	BA	1433		Kr
Thomas of Laa	1429	BA?	1434		Hu; Kr:246
Johann Hausheimer of Welbling		BA	1434	Ab Melk (1453-74)	Hu; K
Thomas of Baden	1429	BA	1435	P Melk (1455-60, 1475-78)	Kr:363; K
Johann Schlect of Haching	1430	BA	1435		K "d. leprosy" Kr:363
Johannes of Obernberg	1434		1435		Kr:217-18; Hu
Melchior of Stammheim		BA	1435	Ab Ulr. and Afra (Augsbg)	Hu; Kr:340
Andreas of Melk		BA?			Hu
Johannes of Ulm	1424?	BA?	1436		Hu
Michael of Pfarrkirchen	1421?	BA?	1436		Hu
Theobald of Emersdorf		BA?	1436		Hu
Stephan Kolb of Weiten*	1436		1441	Ab Vienna Schot. (1479-82)	Kr:444 "ex studente"
Nicholas of Görlitz	1450		1453		Kr:337 "ex studente"
Johann of Megies (Transylvania)	1438?	BA	1460	P Melk (1483)	Kr:484; K 644n
Leonard of Felddorf	1475		1478		Kr:467 "iuvenis scholaris"

Table 6: Masters and Baccalaurei at Tegernsee

Name	Matr.	Degr.	Date	Interim	Rel.	Offices	Auth
Johannes Keck of Giengen	1426	Bth DTh	1429 1441	Pst (Munich) Basel Council	1445	P 1445	A; AFT 657
Ulrich Kaeger of Landau	1444	MA	1449	Schoolteacher	1457	P 1465	A?
Wolfgang Kydrer of Salzburg	1437	MA	1441	Teacher/Pst Salzbg area	1462		A
Christian Tesen-pacher of Salzbrg	1449	MA	1452-54	Pst Salz-burg area	1462	P 1476-82	
Augustine Holz-apfler of St. Veit		MA?			1472	P 1482-1504	L "AA LL bacca-laurius et doctor"
Bernard of Waging	1423?	BA		RegCan Inders. ca. 1436-47	1447	P 1452-65	
Konrad Airim-schmalz of Weilh.	1440	BA	1445		1447	Ab 1461-92	
Benedict Heimfelder			1440?	Pst 1440-42	1453		R "studied Vienna"
Oswald Nott of Tittmoning	1426-34?			RegCan Inders.	1449		
Paulus Steger of Munich	1441				1447		R "studied Vienna"
Ambrosius Schwerzenbeck					1456		R "studied Vienna"
Chrysogonus (Paulus) Hebenkrieg	1447				1467	P Gaming (1502-10)	
Petrus Rueger of Hofkirchen	1469			Pst nr Munich	1493	Subprior	
Thomas Leitner of Schliersee					1497?		R "studied Vienna"

Note: To this list should be added Konrad Geissenfeld, who came to Tegernsee from Melk in 1445. See Table 4.

Authorities: Redlich, *Tegernsee*, is assumed; others as above, Tables 1 and 4; L = Lindner, "Fa-milia S. Quirini."

Table 7: Vienna Matrikel Entries Related to Table 4 (Melk Magistri)

Name	Matr.	Sem.	Nation	Fee
Nicolaus Saüriger de Maczen	1389	II	Austr	2 gr (also rector, 1401 I)
Petrus de Rosenhaim	1398	I	Rhen	2 gr
Urbanus de Melk	1409	I	Austr	2 gr (also rector 1427 I, 1435 I)
Cunradus Müllnär de Nürnberga	1429	I	Rhen	4 gr (identification uncertain)
Conradus Funificis de Geysenueld	1426	II	Rhen	pauper
Johannes Höffel de Spicz	1425	II	Austr	27 denarii
Johannes Pinttenschüch de Spitz	1430	I	Austr	4 gr
Stephanus Pawr de Spanberg	1423	II	Austr	4 gr
Stephanus Franch de Spannberg	1426	I	Austr	1 gr
Laurencius Friderici de Grecz	1432	I	Austr	4 gr
Laurentius Carnificis de Grätz	1444	I	Austr	pauper
Johannes Ellnhofen de Ysnin	1445	II	Rhen	2 gr
Johannes Huber de Isnin	1445	I	Rhen	2 gr
Johannes Lieb de Ysnin	1445	II	Rhen	2 gr
Johannes Scholss de Ysnin	1445	II	Rhen	pauper
Johannes Sieber de Isnin	1445	I	Rhen	2 gr
Johannes Strasser de Ysen	1447	II	Rhen	pauper
Johannes Fuchsöder de Ysni	1450	II	Rhen	4 gr
Ludwicus Schänczl de Krembs	1443	II	Austr	4 gr
Conradus Schörg de Herbipoli	1441	II	Rhen	4 gr

*Citations to the *Matrikel* for the Gaming monks listed in Tables 1-3 are given in the footnotes to chapter three, above. The purpose of the present list is to indicate the degree of precision or lack thereof in giving matriculation dates for Benedictines in Tables 4-6. In many instances the identification of a particular monk with a particular matriculation date must be considered uncertain.

Table 8: Vienna Matrikel Entries Related to Table 5 (Melk Baccaluarei)

Name	Matr.	Sem.	Nation	Fee
Leonardus Payger	1385	II	Austr	4 gr [directly followed by Stephanus Payger, 4 gr]
Christannus Eybenstainer de Rauespach	1415	I	Austr	4 gr
Frater Wolfgangus de Emerstorff	1434	I	Austr	4 gr [directly followed by Johanne of Obernberg]
Wolfgangus Schoppel de Neuburga Forensi (Korneuburg)	1428	I	Austr	4 gr [identification very uncertain]
Thomas Wölfl de Laa	1429	I	Austr	tenetur [admitted on credit]
Thomas Piscatoris de Paden	1429	II	Austr	2 gr
Johannes Slecht de Hechingen*	1430	II	Rhen	4 gr
Johannes de Oberburg monasterii Mellicensis	1434	I	Austr	4 gr
Johannes Cholly de Vlma	1424	I	Rhen	pauper
Johannes Hofleich de Vlma	1424	I	Rhen	4 gr
Johannes Kemmer de Vlma	1426	I	Rhen	4 gr
Johannes Petz de Vlma	1426	I	Rhen	4 gr
Johannes Jäger de Vlma	1429	I	Rhen	8 gr
Johannes Ruderbawm de Vlma	1433	I	Rhen	8 gr [". . . plebanus in Dürnkam"]
Johannes Wissinger de Vlma	1437	I	Rhen	4 gr
Johannes Funck de Vlma	1437	I	Rhen	4 gr
Johannes Valb de Vlma	1438	I	Rhen	4 gr
Michael Sweckerberger de Pfarrkirchen	1421	II	Rhen	4 gr
Stephanus Kolb de Mellico	1436	II	Austr	4 gr
Nicolaus Prem de Gurlicz	1421	I	Hng	4 gr
Nicolaus Lindener de Görlicz	1421	II	Hng	pauper
Nicolaus Weinreich de Görlicz	1438	II	Hng	pauper
Nicolaus Schönfelder de Gorlicz	1440	I	Hng	pauper
Nicolaus Judicis de Gorlitz	1450	I	Hng	2 gr
Johannes Funificis de Megies	1438	II	Hng	2 gr
Johannes Molitoris de Megies	1438	II	Hng	1 gr
Leonardus Harman de Feldorff	1475	I	Rhen	2 gr

*The entry for Johannes Slecht de Haching in 1420, second semester, Rhenish nation, 4 groschen was crossed out with the marginal notation: "Johannes Slecht de Haching exclusus in consistorio de mandato universitatis, et non inventus est nullus propinquius nisi presens."

Table 9: Vienna Matrikel Entries Related to Table 6 (Tegernsee Academics)

Name	Matr.	Sem.	Nation	Fee
Johannes Chechk de Gienging	1426	I	Rhen	4 gr
Ulricus Pellificis de Landaw	1444	I	Rhen	3 gr
Wolfgangus Chydrer de Salczburga	1437	I	Rhen	4 gr
Cristannus Tässempacher de Salczburga	1449	I	Rhen	4 gr
Bernhardus de Arnsdorff	1423	I	Rhen	pauper [identification uncertain]
Conradus Ayrimsmalcz de Weilhaim	1440	II	Rhen	4 gr
Oswaldus	1426	I	Austr	—
Oswaldus de Trösperg*	1429	I	Rhen	pauper
Oswaldus Weidacher of Ditmanning	1434	I	Rhen	4 gr
Paulus Steger de Monaco	1441	I	Rhen	4 gr
Paulus de Krembs	1447	I	Austr	3 gr
Petrus Rueger de Hofkirchen	1469	II	Rhen	4 gr

*For discussion of possible identifications for Oswald Nott, see chapter three above; for Bernard of Waging (de Arnsdorff), see chapter six, above.

BIBLIOGRAPHY

Primary Sources

Abelard. See Peter Abailard, below.

Aelred of Rievaulx. *Speculum Caritatis*. In *Aelredi Rievallensis Opera Omnia*. Vol. 1: *Opera Ascetica*. Edited by A. Hoste and C. H. Talbot. CCCM, 1. Turnhout: Brepols, 1971.

Albert of Saxony [Albertus de Saxonia]. *Questiones subtilissime super libros posteriorum*. Venice, 1497. Reprinted Hildesheim: Georg Olms, 1986.

Altenstaig, Johannes. *Vocabularius theologie*. Hagenau: Heinrich Gran, 1517.

Ancelet-Hustache, Jeanne, ed. *Traité sur l'amour de Dieu, composé vers 1430 par un clerc anonyme de l'université de Vienne*. Paris: Honoré Champion, 1926.

Angerer, Joachim, ed. *Die Bräuche der Abtei Tegernsee unter Abt Kaspar Ayndorffer (1426-1461), verbunden mit einer textkritischer Edition der Consuetudines Tegernseenses*. SMGB, *Ergänzungsband*, 18. Ottobeuren: Bayerische Benediktinerakademie in Kommission beim Verlag Winfried-Werk, Augsburg, 1968.

Annales Camaldulenses ordinis Sancti Benedicti. Ed. Giovanni Benedetto Mittarelli and Anselmo Costadoni, 9 vols. Venice: Io. Baptista Pasquali, 1755-73. Reprinted Farnborough, Hampshire: Gregg Press, 1970. Correspondence between Tommaso (Paolo) Giustiniani and others in volume 9 (1773), cols. 446-611.

"Anonymi benedictini anno MCCC epistola de consuetudine et modo vivendi coenobitarum monasterii Sublacensis." In *Bibl. ascetica*, 8: 492-502.

Anthelme, prior of the Grande Chartreuse. See *Lettres des premiers chartreux*, below.

Apophthegmata patrum. See *Historia monachorum*, Palladius, Pelagius the Deacon, Rufinus, below.

Heinrich Arnoldi of Alfeld. *Dialogus de modo perveniendi ad veram et perfectam Dei et proximi dilectionem*. In *Bibl. ascetica*, 6: 2-214.

Augustine of Hippo. *Confessiones*. Edited by Luc Verheijen. CCSL, 27. Turnhout: Brepols, 1981. Various translations.

___. *De doctrina Christiana*. Ed. J. Martin. CCSL, 32. Turnhout: Brepols, 1962. Various translations.

___. *Sancti Aurelii Augustini Enarrationes in Psalmos, CI-CL*. CCSL, 40. Edited by E. Dekkers and Joannes Fraipont. Turnhout: Brepols, 1956.

___. *Letter 147* (*De videndo Deum, Epistola ad Paulinam*); *Letter 148*. PL 33: 596-630. CSEL 44: 274-347. Translated by Sister Wilfrid Parsons in *Saint Augustine, Letters*. Vol. 3. Fathers of the Church, 20. New York: Fathers of the Church, 1953, 170-238.

[Basel Charterhouse, Chronicle]. Edited by Wilhelm Vischer and Alfred Stern. In *Basler Chroniken*. Vol. 1. Leipzig: S. Hirzel, 1872, pp. 233-548.

Basil of Caesearea. *Long Rules*. PG 31: 889-1052. Translated by M. Monica Wagner. FC, 9. Washington, D.C.: Catholic Univ. of America Press, 1950.

Bede. *In Cantica canticorum allegorica expositio*. PL 91: 1065-1235.

Bernard of Clairvaux. *Ad Henricum Senonensem Archiepiscopum*. PL 182: 809-834. *S. Bernardi Opera*, 7: 100-131.

___. *De praecepto et dispensatione.* In *S. Bernardi Opera*, 3: 253-94 (PL 182: 859-94). Translated by Conrad Greenia. CF, 1. Shannon, Ireland: Irish Univ. Press for Cistercian Publications, 1970, pp. 103-50.

___. *Sermo ad clericos de conversione.* In *S. Bernardi Opera*, 4: 69-116 (PL 182: 834-56). Translated by Marie-Bernard Saïd. CF, 25. Kalamazoo: Cistercian Publications, 1981, pp. 11-79.

___. *Sermones de diversis*, no. 11, 22. In *S. Bernardi Opera*, 6, pt. 1: 124-26, 170-78 (PL 183: 569-71, 595-600).

___. *Sermones super Cantica Canticorum.* PL 183. *Sancti Bernardi Opera*, vols. 1-2. Edited by Jean Leclercq, C. H. Talbot, H. M. Rochais. Rome: Editiones Cistercienses, 1957-58. Translated by Killian Walsh and Irene M. Edmonds. CF, 4, 7, 31, 40. Kalamazoo: Cistercian Publications, 1971, 1976, 1979, 1980.

___. *Vita et rebus S. Malachiae.* In *S. Bernardi Opera*, 3: 297-378 (PL 182: 1073-1110). Translated by Robert T. Meyer as *Life and Death of Saint Malachy the Irishman*. CF, 10. Kalamazoo: Cistercian Publications, 1978.

___. *Selected Works.* Translated by G. R. Evans. CWS. New York: Paulist Press, 1987.

Bernard of Waging. *Speculum pastorum et animarum rectorum* and *Defensorium speculi pastorum*. Clm 4403, fol. 1r (9r) - 23v (31v); 33r (41r) -69r (78r). Cf. Johann of Eych.

Bidermann, Jacob. *Cenodoxus.* Edited by Rolf Tarot. Neudrucke deutscher Literaturwerke, n.F., 6. Tübingen: Max Niemeyer, 1963.

___. *Cenodoxus.* Translated by Denys G. Dyer with Cecily Longrigg. Edinburgh Bilingual Library, 9. Austin: Univ. of Texas Press, 1974.

___. *Ludi theatrales* (1666). Reprinted in Deutsche Neudrucke, Reihe Barock, 6-7. Edited by Rolf Tarot. Tübingen: Max Niemeyer, 1967.

Bligny, Bernard, ed. *Recueil des plus anciens actes de la Grande-Chartreuse (1086-1196).* Grenoble: Imprimerie Allier, 1958.

Boccaccio, Giovanni. *Genealogie Deorum gentilium.* Edited by Vincenzo Romano. Scrittori d'Italia, 201 (= Boccaccio, *Opere*, 11). Bari: Giuseppe Laterza e Figlio, 1951.

Book of Concord, The. Translated by Theodore G. Tappert. Philadelphia: Muhlenberg, 1959.

Bruno the Carthusian. See *Sancti Brunonis Vita antiquior*; *Lettres des premiers chartreux*, below.

Cassian. See John Cassian.

Chadwick, Owen, translator. *Western Asceticism.* Library of Christian Classics, 12. Philadelphia: Westminster, 1958.

The Chartae of the Carthusian General Chapter, Paris, Bibliothèque Nationale MS Latin 10887. Part I: *1438-46 (Ff. 1-144).* Edited by Michael Sargent and James Hogg. AC, 100.3. 1984.

The Chartae of the Carthusian General Chapter: Paris, Bibliothèque Nationale MS Latin 10887. Part II: *1447-56 (Ff. 145-333v.* Edited by Michael Sargent and James Hogg. AC, 100.4. 1984.

The Chartae of the Carthusian General Chapter, Paris, Bibliothèque Nationale MS Latin 10888. Part I: *1457-65 (Ff. 1-157v).* Edited by Michael Sargent and James Hogg. AC, 100.5. 1985.

The Chartae of the Carthusian General Chapter, Paris, Bibliothèque Nationale MS Latin 10888. Part II: *1466-74 (Ff. 159-307).* Edited by Michael Sargent and James Hogg. AC, 100.6. 1985.

Chaucer, Geoffrey. *Canterbury Tales.* In *The Riverside Chaucer.* 3rd ed. Edited by Larry D. Benson and others. Boston: Houghton Mifflin, 1987.

Chevallier, Philippe. See Pseudo-Dionysius, below.

Chrysostom. See John Chrysostom.

Clement of Rome. *First Letter to the Corinthians.* Translated by Kirsopp Lake. Loeb Classical Library, 24. Cambridge, Mass.: Harvard Univ. Press, 1912.

Climacus. See John Climacus.

Conrad of Eberbach. *Exordium magnum cisterciense.* Edited by Bruno Griesser. Series Scriptorum Sancti Ordinis Cisterciensis, 2. Rome: Editiones Cistercienses, 1961.

Cusanus, Nicolaus. *De docta ignorantia.* Edited by Ernst Hoffmann and Raymond Klibansky. Nicolai de Cusa *Opera Omnia,* vol. 1. Leipzig: Felix Meiner, 1932.

Damerau. See Nicholas Prünzlein von Dinkelsbühl.

Denifle, Heinrich, ed. *Chartularium Universitatis Parisiensis.* Vol. 4. Paris: Fratres Delalain, 1891.

Denys of Rijkel [the Carthusian]. *Doctoris ecstaticis Dionysii Cartusiensis Opera omnia.* 44 volumes. Montreuil, Tournai, Parkminster: Charterhouse of Notre Dame de Près, 1896-1913.

___. *De contemplatione.* In *Opera omnia,* vol. 41 [= *Opera minora,* vol. 9]. Tournai, 1912, pp. 135-289.

___. "Difficultatem praecipuarum praecedentium librorum absolutiones breves ac necessarias." In E. M. Vos de Wael. *De mystica theologia van Dionysius Mysticus in de Werken van Dionysius Cartusianus.* Nijmegen: N. V. Centrale Drukkerij, 1942, pp. 229-58.

___. *De praeconio sive laude ordinis cartusiensis.* In *Opera omnia,* vol. 38 [= *Opera minora,* vol. 6]. Tournai, 1909, pp. 413-35.

___. *De vita et regimine praesulum, De regimine praelatorum, De vita et regimine archidiaconorum, De vita canicorum, De vita et regimine curatorum.* In *Opera omnia,* vol. 37 [= *Opera minora,* vol. 5]. Tournai, 1909, pp. 63-110.

Devotio Moderna: Selected Writings. Translated and edited by John H. Van Engen. CWS. New York and Mahwah: Paulist Press, 1988.

Dionysius the Pseudo-Areopagite. See Pseudo-Dionysius, below.

Disticha catonis. Edited by Marcus Boas. Posthumously edited by Hendrik Johann Botschuyver. Amsterdam: North-Holland, 1952.

Ebendorfer of Haselbach, Thomas. *Chronica Austriae.* In *Scriptores rerum Austriacarum.* Vol. 2. Edited by Hieronymus Pez. Leipzig and Regensburg, 1725, pp. 682-987. New edition Alphons Lhotsky in Monumenta Germaniae Historica, Scriptores rerum Germanicarum, nova series, 13. Berlin: Weidmann, 1967.

Desiderius Erasmus. *De libero arbitrio.* Edited by Johannes von Walter. In *Quellenschriften zur Geschichte des Protestantismus,* Heft 8. Leipzig, 1910. ET in *Luther and Erasmus: Free Will and Salvation.* Translated by E. Gordon Rupp and A. N. Marlow. Library of Christian Classics, 17. Philadelphia: Westminster, 1969, pp. 35-97.

"Excerpta genealogica ex monumentis Tegurinis" in the subsection "Diplomatarium Miscellum" of the section, "Monumenta Tegernseesia." In *Monumenta Boica*, vol. 6. Edited by the Bayerische Akademie der Wissenschaften. Munich: Akademie, 1766. Reprinted, Munich: T. Marezell, 1964, pp. 339-40.

Exordium magnum cisterciense. See Conrad of Eberbach.

Gabler, J., ed. "Ein Brief des Wiener Dominikaners und Universitätsprofessors Leonhard Huntpichler an den Kartäuser Nikolaus Kempf von Straßburg." *AEKG*, 9 (1934), 135-36.

Gerson, Jean. *Ioannis Carlerii de Gerson, De mystica theologia.* Edited by André Combes. Lugano: Thesaurus Mundi, 1958.

___. *Oeuvres Complètes.* 10 vols. in 11. Edited by Palémon Glorieux. Paris: Desclée, 1960-73.

___. Vol. 2: *L'oeuvre épistolaire.* 1960.

___. Vol. 3: *L'ouevre magistrale.* 1962.

___. Vol. 5: *L'oeuvre oratoire.* 1963.

___. Vol. 9: *L'oeuvre doctrinale.* 1972.

___. Vol. 10: *L'oeuvre polémique.* 1973.

Giovanni da Mantua. *Iohannis Mantuani in Cantica Canticorum et de Sancta Maria Tractatus ad Comitissam Matildam.* Spicilegium Friburgense, 19. Edited by Bernhard Bischoff and Burkhard Taeger. Fribourg, Switz.: Universitätsverlag, 1973.

Glossa Ordinaria. PL 113-14. Cf. Nicholas of Lyra, below.

Gregory the Great. *Expositiones in Canticum Canticorum.* Edited by Patrick Verbraken. CCSL, 144. Turnhout: Brepols, 1963.

___. *Gregorii I Papae registrum epistolarum libri XIV.* PL 77: 441-1328. Edited by Paul Ewald and Ludo M. Hartmann. Monumenta Germaniae Historica: Epistolae. Vol. 1: *Libri I-VII*; Vol. 2: *Libri VIII-XIV.* Berlin: Weidmann, 1891, 1899. Reprinted 1978. Partially translated by James Barmby. NPNF. Series 2. Vol. 11 (1894, 1955).

___. *Regula pastoralis.* PL 77: 13-128. Translated by James Barmby. NPNF. Series 2. Vol. 11 (1894, 1955). Translated by Henry Davis in Ancient Christian Writers series, vol. 11. Washington, D.C.: Catholic University of America Press, 1950.

Gregory of Nazianzus. "In Defense of His Flight to Pontus and His Return." (= *Oration* II). Edited by J. Bernardi. SC, 247. Paris: Du Cerf, 1978, pp. 84-240. Translated by Charles G. Browne and James E. Swallow. NPNF. Series 2. Vol. 7 (1893, 1955), pp. 204-27.

Gregory of Nyssa. *Ascetical Works.* Translated by Virginia Woods Callahan. The Fathers of the Church, 58. Washington, D.C.: Catholic Univ. of America Press, 1967.

___. *Commentary on the Song of Songs.* Translated by Casimir McCambley. The Archbishop Iakovos Library of Ecclesiastical and Historical Sources, 12. Brookline, Mass.: Hellenic College Press, 1987.

___. *From Glory to Glory: Texts from Gregory of Nyssa's Mystical Writings.* Edited Jean Daniélou. Translated by Herbert Musurillo. New York: Charles Scribner's Sons, 1961.

Guibert de Nogent. *Autobiographie.* Edited by Edmond-René Labande. Les classiques de l'histoire de France au moyen âge. Paris: Société d'édition "les Belles Lettres," 1981.

Guigo I. *Coutumes de Chartreuse [Consuetudines Cartusienses].* Edited and translated by a Carthusian. SC, 313. Paris: Du Cerf, 1984.

——. *Les Meditations.* Translated and edited by a Carthusian. SC, 308. Paris: Du Cerf, 1983. Translated by John J. Jolin. Mediaeval Philosophical Texts in Translation, 6. Milwaukee: Marquette Univ. Press, 1951.

——. See also *Lettres des premiers chartreux,* below.

Guigo II. *Lettre sur la vie contemplative (L'échelle des moines); Douze Meditationes.* Edited by Edmund Colledge and James Walsh. Translated by a Carthusian. SC, 163. Série des Textes Monastiques d'Occident, 29. Paris: Du Cerf, 1970. Cf. Guigo II. *Ladder of Monks: A Letter on the Contemplative Life; Twelve Meditations.* Translated and edited by Edmund Colledge and James Walsh. Garden City, N.Y.: Doubleday-Image, 1978.

Guigo de Ponte. *De contemplatione.* 1 vol. in 2 pts. Edited by Philippe DuPont. AC, 72. 1985.

Heinrich Egher of Kalkar. *Het tractaat "Ortus et decursus ordinis cartusiensis" van Hendrik Egher van Kalkar.* Edited by Hendrina G. C. Vermeer. Diss., Leiden, 1929. Published at Wageningen: H. Veenman en Zonen, 1929.

Heinrich Heinbuche von Langenstein.

——. Hohmann, Thomas. *Heinrichs von Langenstein "Untersuchung der Geister" lateinisch und deutsch: Texte und Untersuchungen zur Übersetzungsliteratur aus der Wiener Schule.* MTU, 63. Munich: Artemis, 1977.

——. Lang, Albert, ed. "Die Katharinenpredigt Heinrichs von Langenstein." *Divus Thomas: Jahrbuch für Philosophie und spekulative Theologie,* 26 (1948), 123-59, 233-50.

——. Rudolf, Rainer, ed. *Heinrich von Langenstein, Erchantnuzz der Sund- nach österreichischen Handschriften herausgegeben.* Texte des späten Mittelalters und der frühe Neuzeit, 22. Berlin: E. Schmidt, 1969.

——. Sommerfeldt, Gustav, ed. "Des Magisters Heinrich von Langenstein Traktate 'De contemptu mundi'." *ZKTh,* 29 (1905), 404-12.

——. ——, ed. "Langensteins Brief *de vita solitarii,*" *ZKTh,* 30 (1906), 191-93.

Heinrich Totting von Oyta.

——. Lang, Albert, ed. *Heinrich Totting von Oyta: Quaestio de Sacra Scriptura et de veritatibus catholicis.* Opuscula et textus historiam ecclesiae eiusque vitam atque doctrinam illustrantia, series scholastica, fasc. XII. Münster i. W.: Aschendorff, 1932. Second edition 1953.

——. See also Nicholas Prünzlein von Dinkelsbühl, Sommerfeldt, ed.

Herp (Harphius), Hendrik. *Theologia mystica.* Cologne: M. Novesianus, 1538. Reprinted Farnborough: Gregg Press, 1966.

——. *Henri Herp: De processu humani profectus: Sermones de diversis materiis vitae contemplativae.* Edited by Georgette Epiney-Burgard. Veröffentlichungen des Instituts für Europäische Geschichte, Mainz, Abteilung für abendländische Religionsgeschichte, 106. Wiesbaden: Franz Steiner, 1982.

——. *Hendrik Herp O.F.M., Spieghel der volcomenheit.* 2 vols. Edited by Lucidus Verschueren. Antwerp: Uitgever Neerlandia, 1931.

Historia monachorum in Aegypto. Edited by A.-J. Festugière. Subsidia Hagiographica, 6. Brussels, 1961. Translated by Norman Russell as *The Lives of the Desert Fathers*. CS, 34. London: Mowbray, 1980; Kalamazoo: Cistercian Publications, 1980. Cf. Rufinus, below.

Holcot [Holkot], Robert. *Exploring the Boundaries of Reason: Three Questions on the Nature of God by Robert Holcot, O.P.* Edited by Hester G. Gelber. Studies and Texts, 62. Toronto: Pontifical Institute of Medieval Studies, 1983.

___. *Super sapientiam Salomonis*. Hagenau, 1494; reprinted Frankfurt: Minerva, 1974.

Hugh of Balma. *Viae Sion lugent [De mystica theologia; De triplici via]*. In *Cardinalis S. Bonaventurae Opera Omnia*. Vol. 8. Edited by A. C. Peltier. Paris: L. Vivès, 1864-71, pp. 2-53.

Huntpichler, Leonhard. See Gabler, J.

Jacob de Paradiso. *Opuscula inedita*. Edited by Stanislaw A. Porebski. Textus et studia historiam theologiae in Polonia excultae spectantia, 5. Warsaw: Akademia theologii Katolickiej, 1978.

___. *De dignitate pastorum et cura pastorali*. Innsbruck, UB, cod. 633, 174r-192v (Charterhouse of Schnals in South Tirol).

Jedin, Hubert, ed. "Contarini und Camaldoli." *Archivio italiano per la storia della pietà*, 2 (1959), 53-117.

Joachimsohn (Joachimsen), Paul, ed. *Hermann Schedels Briefwechsel, 1452-1478*. Bibliothek des litterarischen Vereins in Stuttgart, 196. Tübingen: Literarischer Verlag, 1893.

Johann of Eych. *Inpugnatorium speculi pastorum et animarum rectorum*. Clm 4403, fol. 24r (32r) - 32r (40r). Cf. Bernard of Waging.

John Cassian. *Collationes*. Edited and translated by E. Pichèry. SC, 42, 54, 64. Paris: Du Cerf, 1955, 1966, 1971. Translated by Edgar C. S. Gibson in NPNF. Series 2. Vol. 11, pp. 281-545. Partially translated by Colm Luibheid in *John Cassian: Conferences*. CWS. New York: Paulist, 1985.

___. *Institutiones coenobiorum*. Edited by J.-C. Guy. SC, 109. Paris: Du Cerf, 1965. Translated by Edgar C. S. Gibson in NPNF. Series 2. Vol. 11, pp. 163-290.

John Chrysostom. *De sacerdotio*. Edited by A. M. Malingrey. SC, 272. Paris: Du Cerf, 1980. Translated by W. R. W. Stephans. NPNF. Series 1. Vol. 9 (1889, 1956), pp. 33-83.

John Climacus. *The Ladder of Divine Ascent*. PG 88: 631-1164. Translated by Colm Luibheid and Norman Russell. CWS. New York: Paulist, 1982.

Kempf, Nicholas. See appendix A.

Lang, Albert. See Heinrich Heinbuche von Langenstein.

Laudemus (Carthusian chronicle). Edited in André Wilmart, "La chronique des premiers chartreux." *Revue Mabillon*, 16 (1926), 77-142.

Le Couteulx, Charles. *Annales ordinis cartusiensis ab anno 1084 ad annum 1429*. Second edition. 8 volumes. Montreuil-sur-Mer, 1887-91.

Le livre des XXIV philosophes. Edited and translated by Françoise Hudry. Collection Krisis. Brignoud: Editions Jerome Millon, 1989.

Lettres de premiers Chartreux. Vol. 1: *S. Bruno, Guigues, S. Anthelme*. Edited by a Carthusian. SC, 88. Paris: Du Cerf, 1962. Vol. 2: *Les moines de Portes*. Edited by a Carthusian. SC, 274. Paris: Du Cerf, 1980.

Lhotsky, Alphons, ed. *Acta facultatis artium universitatis Vindobonensis*. Vol. 1: *1385-1416*. Publikationen des Instituts für österreichische Geschichtsforschung, Reihe 6: Quellen zur Geschichte der Universität Wien, Abteilung 2. Vienna: Böhlau, 1968.

Liber XXIV philosophorum. See Baeumker under Secondary Sources, below. Cf. *Le Livre des XXIV philosophes*, above.

Luther, Martin. *De servo arbitrio*. WA 18: 600-787. ET in *Luther and Erasmus: Free Will and Salvation*. Translated by Philip S. Watson and B. Drewery. Library of Christian Classics, 17. Philadelphia: Westminster, 1969, pp. 101-334.

___. *De votis monasticis* (1521). In *WA*. Vol. 8. Weimar: Böhlaus Nachfolger, 1889, pp. 573-669. Translated by James Atkinson in *Luther's Works*. Vol. 44. Edited by Jaroslav Pelikan and Helmut T. Lehmann. Philadelphia: Fortress Press, 1966, pp. 243-400.

___. *Wider die himmlischen Propheten, von den Bildern und Sakrament* (1524-25). *WA* 18 (1908), 37-214. Translated by Conrad Bergendoff. *Luther's Works*. Vol. 40. Edited Helmut T. Lehmann and Jaroslav J. Pelikan. Philadelphia: Muhlenberg Press, 1958, pp. 79-223.

Martin of Senging. "Tuitiones pro observantia regulae Sancti Patris Benedicti in concilio Basileensi." In *Bibl. ascetica*. 8: 504-50.

Menhardt. See Nicholas Prünzlein von Dinkelsbühl.

Nicholas of Cusa. See Cusanus.

Nicholas of Lyra. *Postilla super totam Bibliam*. 4 vols. Straßburg, 1492. Reprinted Frankfurt a. Main: Minerva, 1971.

Nicholas Prünzlein von Dinkelsbühl.

___. Damerau, Rudolf, ed. *Texte zum Problem des Laienkelches: Nikolaus von Dinkelsbühl (1360-1433)*. I: *Tractatus contra errores Hussitarum*. II: *De sub utraque*. SGR, 6. Gießen: Wilhelm Schmitz, 1969.

___. ___, ed. *Der Galaterbriefkommentar des Nikolaus von Dinkelsbühl—Deutsch*. SGR, 8. Gießen: Schmitz, 1970.

___. ___, ed. *Der Herrngebetskommentar des Nikolaus von Dinkelsbühl*. Gießen: Schmitz, 1971.

___. Madre, Alois, ed. "Sermo magistri Nicolai ad clerum et ad religiosos De profectu et perfectione." In *Ecclesia militans: Studien zur Konzilien- und Reformationsgeschichte*. Vol. 1. Remigius Bäumer zum 70. Geburtstag gewidmet. Edited by Walter Brandmüller, Herbert Immenkötter, Erwin Iserloh. Paderborn: Schöningh, 1988, pp. 185-211.

___. Menhardt, Hermann. "Nikolaus von Dinkelsbühls deutsche Predigt vom Eigentum im Kloster." *ZDP*, 73 (1954), 1-39, 268-90.

___. Sommerfeldt, Gustav, ed. "Zwei politische *Sermones* des Heinrich von Oyta und des Nikolaus von Dinkelsbühl." *HJ*, 26 (1905), 318-27.

___. See also Binder, under Secondary Sources.

Nider, Johannes. *Formicarius*. Cologne, n.d. Reprinted with an introduction by Hans Biedermann. Graz: Akademische Druck und Verlagsanstalt, 1971.

___. *De reformatione religiosorum* [*Tractatus de reformatione status coenobitici*]. Edited Joannes Boucquetius [Boucquet]. Paris: Jean Petit, 1512; Antwerp: Plantin, 1612 [not seen]. [Manuscript copy in Salzburg, St. Peter, Stiftsbibliothek cod. b IX 7].

Origen. *Homiliae in Cantica Canticorum.* Edited by O. Rousseau. SC, 37. Paris: Du Cerf, 1953, 1966.

Palladius. *Historia lausiaca.* PG 34: 991-1262. Edited C. Butler. Texts and Studies, 6., parts 1-2. 2 vols. Cambridge: Cambridge Univ. Press, 1898, 1904. Latin translation in PL 73:1066-134 (= bk. 8 of *Vitae Patrum* as edited by Heribert Rosweyde).

Pelagius the Deacon. *Verba Seniorum.* PL 73:851-991 [= bk. 5 of *Vitae Patrum* as edited by Heribert Rosweyde]. Excerpts translated in Owen Chadwick, *Western Asceticism.*

Perkins, William. *The Works of William Perkins.* Edited Ian Breward. Appleford, Abingdon, Berkshire: Sutton Courtenay Press, 1970.

Peter Abailard. *Sic et Non: A Critical Edition.* Edited by Blanche B. Boyer and Richard McKeon. Chicago: Univ. of Chicago Press, 1976-77.

Peter the Venerable. *Letters of Peter the Venerable.* Edited by Giles Constable. Cambridge, Mass: Harvard Univ. Press, 1967.

Petrarca, Francesco. *De otio religioso.* Edited by G. Rotondi. Vatican City: Biblioteca Apostolica Vaticana, 1958. Reprinted in *Opere latine di Francesco Petrarca.* Vol. 1. Edited by Antonietta Bufano and others. Turin: Unione Tipografico-Editrice, 1975, pp. 568-809.

___. *De secreto conflictu curarum mearum* in *Francesco Petrarca Opere.* Edited by Giovanni Ponte. Milan: U. Mursia, 1968, pp. 432-597.

___. *Petrarch's Secretum.* With introduction, notes, and critical anthology by Davy A. Carozza and H. James Shey. American Univ. Studies, Series XVII, Classical Languages and Literatures, 7. New York: Peter Lang, 1989.

___. *De vita solitaria.* Edited Antonio Altamura. Studi e testi umanistici, Series 2: Testi e documenti, 1. Naples: Arti Graffiche Dottore Dino Amodio, 1943. Translated by Jacob Zeitlin as *The Life of Solitude by Francis Petrarch.* Champaign: Univ. of Illinois Press, 1924.

Petrus of Rosenheim. "Sermo de statu vitae monasticae sui temporis." In *Bibl. ascetica*, 2:81-94. See also Thoma, below.

Peuntner, Thomas. See Schnell.

Pez, Bernard, ed. *Thesaurus anecdotorum novissimus: Seu veterum monumentorum praecipue ecclesiasticorum ex germanicis bibliothecis adornata collectio recentissima.* Vol. 1. Augsburg: Philip, Martin, Johannes Veith, 1721.

Pez, Bernhard, and Wydemann, Leopold. Correspondence: "Peziana" collection. Melk, Stiftsarchiv (no shelf number).

Philo of Alexandria. *De specialibus legibus.* In *Philon d'Alexandrie. Oeuvres.* Vol. 24-25. Edited by André Mosès. Paris: Du Cerf, 1970.

Pirckheimer, Willibald. *Willibald Pirckheimers Briefwechsel.* 2 vols. Edited by Emil Reicke. Veröffentlichungen der Kommission zur Erforschung der Geschichte der Reformation und Gegenreformation, Reihe 1. Nürnberg, 1940, 1956.

Pseudo-Dionysius. *De divinis nominibus*; *De mystica theologia*; *Epistolas*; *De coelestia hierarchia*; *De ecclesiastica hierarchia.* In *Dionysiaca. Recueil donnant l'ensemble des traductions latines des ouvrages attribués au Denys l'Aréopagite.* 2 vols. Edited by Ph. Chevallier and others. Paris: Desclée de Brouwer, 1937, 1950. Translated by Colm Luibheid. *Pesudo-Dionysius: Complete Works.* CWS. New York: Paulist Press, 1987.

RB 1980: The Rule of St. Benedict in Latin and English with Notes. Edited by Timothy Fry and others. Collegeville, Minn.: Liturgical Press, 1981.

Reicke, Emil. See Pirckheimer, Willibald.

Robert of Tombelaine [Pseudo-Gregory the Great]. *Expositio in Cantica Canticorum.* PL 79:493-548.

Rode, Johannes. *Liber de bono regimine abbatis.* In *Bibl. ascetica,* 1: 158-204.

Rösler, Augustin, ed. and trans. *Der Kartäuser Nikolaus Kempf und seine Schrift über das rechte Ziel und die rechte Ordnung des Unterrichts.* Bibliothek der katholischen Pädagogik, 7. Freiburg: Herder, 1894.

Rudolf of Biberach. *Septem itineribus aeternitatis.* In *Bonaventurae opera omnia.* Vol. 8. Edited by A. C. Peltier. Paris: Louis Vivès, 1866, pp. 393-482. Cf. Margot Schmidt, editor. *De septem itineribus aeternitatis: Nachdruck der Ausgabe von Peltier 1866 mit einer Einleitung in die lateinischen Überlieferung und Corrigenda zum Text.* Mystik in Geschichte und Gegenwart, Abt. 1: Christliche Mystik, 1. Stuttgart-Bad Cannstatt: Frommann-Holzboog, 1985.

———. *Die siben strassen zu got: Revidierte hochalemannische Übertragung nach der Handschrift Einsiedeln 278 mit hochdeutscher Übersetzung.* Edited by Margot Schmidt. Spicilegium Bonaventurianum, 6. Florence: Quaracchi, 1969.

Rudolf, Rainer. See Heinrich Heinbuche von Langenstein.

Rufinus. *Historia Monachorum in Aegypto.* Edited by Dominicus Vallarsius. PL 21: 387-462.

Sancti Brunonis Vita antiquior auctore primorum quinque Cartusiae Priorum chronologo anonymo. PL 152: 481-92. Cf. *Acta Sanctorum,* Oct. III (6. Oct). Edited by J. Bollandus, G. Henschenius, D. Papebroch, and others. Antwerp: J.N. van der Beken, 1770. Reprinted Paris, 1868, pp. 703-7.

Schedel, Hermann. See Joachimsohn.

Schmidt, Margot. See Rudolf of Biberach, above.

Schnell, Bernhard. *Thomas Peuntner, "Büchlein von der Liebhabung Gottes": Edition und Untersuchungen,* MTU, 81. Munich: Artemis, 1984.

Sommerfeldt. See Heinrich Heinbuche von Langenstein; Nicholas Prünzlein von Dinkelsbühl.

Statuta ordinis cartusiensis a domino Guigone priore Cartusiae edita; Statuta antiqua ordinis cartusiensis in tribus partibus comprehensa; Statuta nova ordinis cartusiensis in tribus partibus antiquiorum partibus correspondentibus comprehensa; Tertia compilatio. Basel: Amerbach, 1510. Reprinted with consecutive pagination as *The Evolution of the Carthusian Statutes from the Consuetudines Guigonis to the Tertia Compilatio.* Volume 1: *Consuetudines Guigonis; Prima Pars Statutorum Antiquorum.* Volume 2: *Secunda Pars Statutorum Antiquorum; Tertia Pars Statutorum Antiquorum; Statuta Nova.* Volume 3: *Tertia Compilatio Statutorum Ordinis Cartusiensis; Repertorium Statutorum Ordinis Cartusiensis per ordinem alphabeti.* Volume 4: *Priuilegia Ordinis Cartusiensis et mutliplex confirmatio eiusdem; Nomina provinciarum et domorum Ordinis Cartusiensis.* AC 99.1-4. 1989.

Steyerer, Anton. "Collectanea historica Austriaca," part 6, Böhm index 86/6, in the Österreichisches Haus-, Hof-, und Staatsarchiv, Vienna, 377r-379v (new foliation).

Tauler, Johannes. *Die Predigten Taulers aus der Engelberger und der Freiburger Handschrift sowie aus Schmidts Abschriften der ehemaligen Straßburger Handschriften.* Edited by Ferdinand Vetter. Deutsche Texte des Mittelalters, 11. Berlin: Weidmannsche Buchhandlung, 1910.

Uiblein, Paul, ed. *Die Akten der Theologischen Facultät der Universität Wien (1396-1508),* vol. 1. Vienna: Verband der wissenschaftlichen Gesellschaften Österreichs, 1978.

Valla, Lorenzo. *De libero arbitrio.* Edited by Maria Anfossi. Opuscoli filosofici: testi e documenti inediti o rari pubblicati da Giovanni Gentile, 6. Florence: Leo S. Olschki, 1934.

___. *De professione religiosorum.* Thesaurus Mundi, 25. Edited by Mariarosa Cortesi. Padua, 1986. Translated by Olga Zorzi Pugliese as *"The Profession of the Religious" and the principal arguments from "The Falsely-Believed and Forged Donation of Constantine".* Renaissance and Reformation Texts in Translation, 1. Toronto: Centre for Reformation and Renaissance Studies, 1985.

Verba seniorum. See *Historia monachorum,* Palladius, Pelagius the Deacon, Rufinus, above.

Vitae patrum [Vitas patrum]. See *Historia monachorum,* Palladius, Pelagius the Deacon, Rufinus, above.

Waddell, Helen, trans. *The Desert Fathers.* Ann Arbor: Univ. of Michigan Press, 1957.

Wicks, Jared, ed. and trans. *Cajetan Responds: A Reader in Reformation Controversy.* Washington, D.C.: Catholic Univ. of America Press, 1978.

William of Saint-Thierry. *Aenigma Fidei.* PL 180: 397-440. Translated by John D. Anderson. CF 9. Washington, D.C.: Cistercian Publications, 1974.

___. *Epistola ad fratres de Monte Dei.* Edited by R. Thomas. *Lettre aux Frères du Mont-Dieu.* 2 vols. Pain de Cîteux, 33-34. Chambarand: Pain de Cîteaux, 1968. Translated by Theodore Berkeley. *The Golden Epistle: A Letter to the Brethren at Mont-Dieu.* CF, 12. Spencer, Mass.: Cistercian Publications, 1971.

___. *De natura et dignitate amoris.* PL 180:379-408. Edited by Robert Thomas. Pain de Cîteaux series, 23-24. Chambarand: Pain de Cîteaux, 1965. Translated by Thomas X. Davis, *The Nature and Dignity of Love.* CF, 30. Kalamazoo: Cistercian Publications, 1981.

Wittmer, Charles, and Meyer, J. Charles, eds. *Le livre de bourgeoisie de la ville de Strasbourg, 1440-1530,* 3 vols. Strasbourg and Zürich: P. H. Heitz, 1948.

Zerbolt, Gerard, of Zutphen. *De spiritualibus ascensionibus.* In *Maxima bibliotheca veterum patrum et antiquorum scriptorum ecclesiasticorum.* Vol. 26. Edited by M. de la Bigne (Martène and Durand). Lyon: Anissonios, 1677, pp. 234-289. Partially translated in John Van Engen, *Devotio Moderna: Selected Writings.* CWS. New York and Mahwah: Paulist Press, 1988.

Manuscript Catalogues and Aids

Böhm, Constantin Edlen von. *Die Handschriften des kaiserlichen Haus-, Hof-, und Staatsarchivs*. Vienna: Wilhelm Braumüller, 1873. *Supplement*. 1874.

Bursill-Hall, G. L. *A Census of Medieval Latin Grammatical Manuscripts*. Grammatica Speculativa, 4. Stuttgart-Bad Cannstatt: Frommann-Holzboog, 1981.

Catalogue général des manuscrits latins, Tome VI (no. 3536 à 3775b). Paris: Bibliothèque Nationale, 1975.

Catalogus codicum bibliothecae universitatis regiae scientiarum Budapestinensis. 2 vols. in 5 pts. Budapest: University, 1881-1910.

Catalogus codicum manu scriptorum bibliothecae regiae monacensis. Vol. 3-4: *Catalogus codicum latinorum bibliothecae regiae monacensis*, 2 vols. in 7 pts. Edited by C. Halm, G. Laubmann and others. Munich, 1868-1881.

Catalogus codicum manuscriptorum medii aevi latinorum qui in bibliotheca Jagellonica Cracoviae asservantur. 4 vols (to cod. 667). Cracov, 1980-88.

"Codicum manuscriptorum Bibliothecae Seitenstettensis." Bound photocopy of handwritten catalogue available at Hill Monastic Manuscript Library [= HMML], Collegeville, Minnesota.

Denis, Michael. *Codices manuscripti theologici bibliothecae palatinae Vindobonensis latini aliarumque occidentis linguarum*. 6 parts in 2 volumes. Vienna: Joan. Thomae Nob. de Trattnern, 1793-1802.

Descriptive Inventories of Manuscripts Microfilmed for the Hill Monastic Manuscript Library, Austrian Libraries. Vol. 1: *Geras, Güssing, Haus, Wilten, Innsbruck Wilten, Salzburg erzbischöfliches Konsistorialarchiv, Salzburg erzbischöfliches Priesterseminar, Salzburg Museum Carolino-Augusteum, Schlierbach, Schwaz*. Compiled by Donald Yates. Collegeville, Minn.: HMML, 1981.

Descriptive Inventories of Manuscripts Microfilmed for the Hill Monastic Manuscript Library, Austrian Libraries. Vol. 2: *St. Georgenberg-Fiecht*. Compiled by Peter Jeffrey and Donald Yates. Collegeville, Minn.: HMML, 1985.

Descriptive Inventories of Manuscripts Microfilmed for the Hill Monastic Manuscript Library, Austrian Libraries. Vol. 3: *Herzogenburg*. Compiled by Hope Mayo. Collegeville, Minn.: HMML, 1985.

Frioli, Donatella. *Biblioteca civica gambalunghiana*. In *Catalogo di manoscritti filosofici nelle biblioteche italiane, I: Firenze, Pisa, Poppi, Rimini, Trieste*. Edited by T. DeRobertis and others. Florence: Olschki, 1980.

_____. *I Codici del Cardinale Garampi nella Biblioteca Gambalunghiana di Rimini*. Collana di "Storie e storia", 5. Rimini: Maggioli Editore, 1986.

Glauche, Günter. See *Mittelalterliche Bibliothekskataloge Deutschlands und der Schweiz*.

Gottlieb, Theodor. See *Mittelalterliche Bibliothekskataloge Österreichs*.

Gruys, Albert, comp. *Cartusiana*. See the Key to Abbreviations.

Hain, Ludwig F. T. *Repertorium bibliographicum, in quo libri omnes ab arte typographica inventa usque ad annum MD. typis expressi, ordine alphabetico vel simpliciter enumerantur vel adcuratius recensentur.* Stuttgart and Paris, 1826-69. Reprinted Berlin: J. Altmann, 1925, and Milan: Görlich, 1948.

Die Handschriften der badischen Landesbibliothek Karlsruhe, VII: *Die Reichenauer Handschriften*, vol. 2: *Die Papierhandschriften.* Leipzig and Berlin: Teubner, 1914; reprinted 1971.

Helssig, Rudolf, ed. *Katalog der Lateinischen und deutschen Handschriften der Universitätsbibliothek zu Leipzig*, vol. 1: *Theologische Handschriften* [to cod. 486]. Leipzig: Salomon Hirzel, 1926-35.

Hohmann, Thomas. "Initienregister der Werke Heinrichs von Langenstein." *Traditio*, 32 (1976), 399-426.

Hübl, A. *Catalogus codicum manuscriptorum qui in bibliotheca monasterii B.M.V. ad scotos Vindobonae servantur.* Vienna, 1899.

Jungwirth, Augustin. "Katalog der Handschriften des Stiftes St. Peter in Salzburg." Bound photocopy of the partially handwritten catalogue available at Hill Monastic Manuscript Library, Collegeville, Minnesota.

Kern, Anton, ed. *Die Handschriften der Universitäts-bibliothek Graz.* Series: Handschriftenverzeichnisse österreichischer Bibliotheken, Steiermark, 2. Vienna: Druck und Verlag der österreichischen Staatsdruckerei, 1956.

Lehmann, Paul. See *Mittelalterliche Bibliothekskataloge Deutschlands und der Schweiz.*

Mairold, Maria. "Zur Bibliotheksgeschichte der Kartause Seitz." In *Die Kartäuser in Österreich.* Zweiter internationaler Kongress über die Kartäusergeschichte und -Spiritualität. Vol. 1. Edited by James Hogg. AC, 83.1. 1980, 23-47.

Mazal, O., and Unterkircher, F., eds. *Katalog der abendländischen Handschriften der Österreichischen Nationalbibliothek, Series Nova.* Vienna, 1963.

Mezy, Ladislaus, and Bolgár, Agnes. *Codices latini medii aevi bibliothecae universitatis Budapestinensis.* Budapest: Akadémiai Kiadó, 1961.

Mittelalterliche Bibliothekskataloge Deutschlands und der Schweiz. Vol. 2: *Bistum Mainz, Erfurt.* Edited by Paul Joachim Georg Lehmann. Munich: C. H. Beck, 1928.

Mittelalterliche Bibliothekskataloge Deutschland und der Schweiz. Vol. 4. Part 2: *Bistum Freising.* Edited by Günter Glauche. *Bistum Würzburg.* Edited by Hermannn Knaus. Munich: Beck, 1979.

Mittelalterliche Bibliothekskataloge Österreichs, 1: *Niederösterreich.* Edited by Theodor Gottlieb. Vienna: A. Holzhausen, 1915. [Cf. index volume compiled by Arthur Goldmann (Vienna: A. Holzhausen, 1929).] Partially reprinted by James Hogg as "Theodor Gottlieb's Edition of the Medieval Library Catalogue of the Charterhouse of Aggsbach, together with two brief notes concerning books from the Charterhouses of Gaming and Mauerbach." In *Spiritualität Heute und Gestern.* Vol. 7. AC, 35.7. 1990, pp. 1-99.

Petrarch.

___. Ullman, Berthold L., compiler. *Petrarch Manuscripts in the United States.* Censimento dei codici petrarcheschi, 1. Padua: Attenore, 1964.

___. Pellegrin, Elisabeth. *Manuscrits de Pétrarque dans les bibliothèques de France.* Censimento dei Codici Petrarcheschi, 2. Padua: Atenore, 1966. Originally appeared in *Italia medioevale e umanistica*, 4 (1961), 6 (1963), 7 (1964).

___. Besomi, Ottavio. *Codici Petrarcheschi nelle biblioteche svizzere.* Censimento dei codici petrarcheschi, 3. Padua: Attenore, 1967.

___. Sottili, Agostino. *I codici del Petrarca nella Germania occidentale*, 2 volumes. Censimento dei codici petrarcheschi, 4, 7. Padua: Antenore, 1971, 1978.

___. Mann, Nicholas. *Petrarch Manuscripts in the British Isles.* Censimento dei Codici Petrarcheschi, 6. Padua: Attenore, 1975.

___. Jansenas, Michael. *Petrarch in America: A Survey of Petrarchan Manuscripts.* Washington, D.C.: Folger Shakespeare Library, 1974; New York: Pierpont Morgan Library, 1974.

Pfeiffer, Hermann, and Cernik, Berthold. *Catalogus codicum manu scriptorum, qui in bibliothecae canonicorum regularium S. Augustini Claustroneoburgi asservantur.* Vol. 1: *Codices 1-260.* Vienna: Klosterneuburg, 1922. Vol. 2: *Codices 261-452.* Vienna: Klosterneuburg, 1931. [Six additional volumes of handwritten catalogues.]

Piccard, Gerhard. *Findbuch der Wasserzeichenkartei im Hauptstaatsarchiv Stuttgart.* Vol. 2: *Die Ochsenkopf Wasserzeichen.* Veröffentlichungen der staatlichen Archivverwaltung Baden-Württemberg, Sonderreihe: Die Wasserzeichenkartei Piccard im Hauptstaatsarchiv Stuttgart, Findbuch 2; Teil 3. Stuttgart: W. Kohlhammer, 1966.

Rose, V., and Schillmann, F. *Verzeichnis der lateinischen Handschriften der königlichen Bibliothek zu Berlin.* 3 vols. Berlin, 1893-1919.

Saenger, Paul H. *A Catalogue of the Pre-1500 Western Manuscript Books at the Newberry Library.* Chicago: Univ. of Chicago Press, 1989.

Schreiber, Heinrich. *Die Bibliothek der ehemaligen Mainzer Kartause, die Handschriften und ihre Geschichte.* Beiheft to Zentralblatt für Bibliothekswesen, 60. Leipzig: Harrassowitz, 1927.

Tabulae codicum manuscriptorum praeter graecos et orientales in bibliotheca palatina Vindobonensi asservatorum. 11 vols. Vienna, 1864-1912.

Secondary Sources

Alberigo, Giuseppe. "Vita attiva e vita contemplativa in un'esperienza del XVI secolo." *Studi Veneziani*, 16 (1974), 177-225.

Anderson, Luke. "Enthymeme and Dialectic: Cloister and Classroom." In *From Cloister to Classroom: Monastic and Scholastic Approaches to Truth.* The Spirituality of Western Christendom, 3. Edited by E. Rozanne Elder. CS, 90. Kalamazoo: Cistercian Publications, 1986, pp. 239-74.

___. "The Rhetorical Epistemology in Saint Bernard's Super Cantica." Unpublished paper read at the International Medieval Congress, Kalamazoo, 1990.

Anderson, Robert D. "Laying Bare Speculative Grammar: Some Remarks." *New Scholasticism*, 61 (1987), 13-24.

___. "Medieval Speculative Grammar: A Study of the Modistae." PhD diss., Medieval Institute, Univ. of Notre Dame, 1989.

Angerer, Joachim. See Primary Sources.

Aschbach, Joseph. *Geschichte der Wiener Universität im ersten Jahrhundert ihres Bestehen: Festschrift zu ihren fünfhundertjährigen Gründungsfeier*, 3 vols. Vienna: Verlag der königlichen und kaiserlichen Universität, 1865-88; reprinted Farnborough, Hampshire: Gregg Press, 1967.

Astell, Ann W. *The Song of Songs in the Middle Ages*. Ithaca: Cornell Univ. Press, 1990.

Aston, Margaret. "Wyclif and the Vernacular." In *From Ockham to Wyclif*. Edited by Anne Hudson and Michael Wilks. Oxford: Basil Blackwell for the Ecclesiastical History Society, 1987, pp. 281-330.

Auer, Johann. "Die aristotelische Logik in der Trinitätslehre der Spätscholastik: Bemerkungen zu einer Quaestio des Johannes Wuel de Pruck, Wien, 1422." In *Theologie in Geschichte und Gegenwart: Michael Schmaus zum sechzigsten Geburtstag dargebracht von seinen Freunden und Schülern*. Edited by Johann Auer and Hermann Volk. Munich: Karl Zink, 1957, pp. 457-96.

___. "Die *Theologia mystica* des Kartäusers Jakob von Jüterbog (+ 1465)." In *Die Kartäuser in Österreich*. Zweiter internationaler Kongress über die Kartäusergeschichte und -Spiritualität. Vol. 2. AC, 83.2. 1981, pp. 19-52.

Axters, Stephanus. *Geschiedenis van de Vroomheid in de Nederlanden*, vol. 3: *De Moderne Devotie, 1380-1550*. Antwerp: de Sikkel, 1956.

Bacht, H. "Luthers 'Urteil über die Mönchsgelübde' in ökumenischer Sicht." *Catholica* 21 (1967), 222-51.

Baeumker, Clemens. "Das pseudo-hermetische 'Buch der vierundzwanzig Meister' (Liber XXIV philosophorum): Ein Beitrag zur Geschichte des Neupythagoreismus und Neuplatonismus im Mittelalter." In *Abhandlungen aus dem Gebiete der Philosophie und ihrer Geschichte. Eine Festgabe zum 70. Geburtstag des Freiherrn Georg von Hertling von seinen Schülern und Verehrern*. Freiburg, 1913, pp. 17-40. Republished with corrections and expansion in *Studien und Charakteristiken zur Geschichte der Philosophie insbesondere des Mittelalters: Gesammelte Vorträge und Aufsätze von Clemens Baeumker*. Edited by Martin Grabmann. Beiträge zur Geschichte der Philosophie des Mittelalters, 24.1-2. Münster: Aschendorff, 1927, pp. 194-214.

Baier, Hermann. "Von der Reform des Abtes Friedrich von Wartenburg bis zur Säkularisation (1427-1803)." In *Die Kultur des Abtei Reichenau, Erinnerungschrift zur zwölfhundertsten Wiederkehr des Gründungsjahres des Inselklosters, 724-1924*, vol. 1. Edited by Konrad Beyerle. Munich: Verlag der Münchner Drucke, 1925. Reprinted Aalen: Scientia, 1974, pp. 213-62.

Baier, Walter. "Des Johannes Nicolai OCart (+ 1475) Passionstraktat, der fälschlich Nikolaus Kempf zugeschrieben wurde." In *Die Kartäuser in Österreich*. Zweiter internationaler Kongress über die Kartäusergeschichte und -Spiritualität. Vol. 1. AC, 83.1. 1980, pp. 155-79.

___. *Untersuchungen zu den Passionsbetrachtungen in der "Vita Christi" des Ludolf von Sachsen: Ein Quellenkritischer Beitrag zu Leben und Werk Ludolfs und zur Geschichte der Passionstheologie*. 3 vols. AC, 44.1-3. 1977.

Baldwin, John W. *Masters, Princes, and Merchants: The Social Views of Peter the Chanter and His Circle*. 2 vols. Princeton: Princeton Univ. Press, 1970.

___. *The Scholastic Culture of the Middle Ages, 1000-1300*. Lexington, Mass.: D. C. Heath and Company, 1971.

Ball, R. M. "Thomas Cyrcetur, a Fifteenth-Century Theologian and Preacher." *JEH*, 37 (1986), 205-39.

Baptist-Hlawatsch, Gabriele. *Das katechetische Werk Ulrichs von Pottenstein: sprachliche und rezeptionsgeschichtliche Untersuchungen*. Tübinger Texte zur Germanistik, 4. Tübingen: Niemeyer, 1980.

Baron, Hans. "Petrarch: His Inner Struggles and the Humanistic Discovery of Man's Nature." In *Florilegium Historiale: Essays Presented to Wallace K. Ferguson*. Edited by J. G. Rowe and W. H. Stockdale. Toronto: Univ. of Toronto Press, 1971, pp. 19-51.

___. *Petrarch's Secretum: Its Making and Its Meaning*. Medieval Academy Books, 94. Cambridge, Mass.: Medieval Academy of America, 1985.

Batlle, Columba M. *Die "Adhortationes sanctorum patrum" ("Verba seniorum") im lateinischen Mittelalter: Überlieferung, Fortleben, und Wirkung*. BGAM, 31. Münster i. W.: Aschendorff, 1971.

Bauch, Gustav. *Die Rezeption des Humanismus in Wien*. Breslau, 1903. Reprinted Aalen: Scientia, 1986.

Bauer, Erika. "Nikolaus von Dinkelsbühl: Handschriftenfund und Neuzuweisung." *ZDA*, 100 (1971), 159-61.

Baum, Wilhelm. *Nikolaus Cusanus in Tirol: Das Wirken des Philosophen und Reformators als Fürstbischof von Brixen*. Schriften des südtiroler Kulturinstitutes, 10. Bolzano: Athesia, 1983.

Becker, Petrus. *Das monastische Reformprogramm des Johannes Rode, Abtes von St. Matthias in Trier*. BGAM, 30. Münster i. W.: Aschendorff, 1970.

Bell, David N. *The Image and Likeness: The Augustinian Spirituality of William of Saint Thierry*. CS, 78. Kalamazoo: Cistercian Publications, 1984.

Bellot, Josef. "Das Benediktinerstift St. Ulrich und Afra in Augsburg und der Humanismus." *SMGB*, 84 (1973), 394-406.

Berg, Klaus. "Zur Geschichte der Bedeutungsentwicklung des Wortes Bescheidenheit." In *Würzburger Prosastudien I: Wort-, begriffs-, und textkundliche Untersuchungen*. Edited by the Forschungsstelle für deutsche Philologie der Universität Würzburg. Medium Aevum, Philologische Studien, 13. Munich: Fink, 1968, pp. 16-80.

Berger, David. "Mission to the Jews and Jewish-Christian Contacts in the Polemical Literature of the High Middle Ages." *AHR*, 91 (1986), 576-91.

Berlière, Ursmer. "La réforme de Melk au XVe siècle." *Revue Bénédictine*, 12 (1895), 204-13, 288-309.

Bernard-Maitre, H. "Un théoricien de la contemplation à la chartreuse parisienne de Vauvert: Pierre Cousturier dit Sutor (c. 1480-18 juin 1537)." *RAM*, 32 (1956), 174-95.

Bernards, Matthäus. "Zur Kartäusertheologie des 16. Jahrhunderts: Der Kölner Prior Petrus Blomevenna (+ 1536) und seine Schrift *De bonitate divina*." In *Von Konstanz nach Trient: Beiträge zur Geschichte der Kirche von den Reformkonzilien bis zum Tridentinum*. Festgabe für August Franzen. Edited by Remigius Bäumer. Paderborn: F. Schöningh, 1972, pp. 447-79.

Bernoulli, Carl Christoph. "Über unsere alten Klosterbibliotheken." *Basler Jahrbuch*. Basel: R. Reich, vormals C. Dettlofs Buchhandlung, 1895, pp. 79-91.

Best, Thomas W. *Jacob Bidermann*. Twayne's World Authors Series, 314. Boston: Twayne Publishers, 1975.

De Bhaldraithe, Eoin. "Michael Sattler, Benedictine and Anabaptist." *Downside Review*. 105 (April 1987), pp. 111-31.

Billanovich, Giuseppe. "Un ignoto fratello del Petrarca." *Italia medioevale e umanistica*, 25 (1982), 375-80.

Binder, Karl. "Eine Anthologie aus Schriften mittelalterlichen Wiener Theologen." In *Dienst an der Lehre: Studien zur heutigen Philosophie und Theologie*. Festschrift für Franz Kardinal König. Edited by the Katholisch-Theologische Fakultät der Universität Wien. Wiener Beiträge zur Theologie, 10. Vienna: Herder, 1965, pp. 201-61.

___. *Die Lehre des Nikolaus von Dinkelsbühl über die unbefleckte Empfängnis im Licht der Kontroverse*. Wiener Beiträge zur Theologie, 31. Vienna: Herder, 1970.

Black, Antony. "The Universities and the Council of Basle: Collegium and Concilium." In *Les Universités à la fin du moyen âge / The Universities in the Late Middle Ages*. Edited by Jozef IJsewijn and Jacques Paquet. Mediaevalia Lovaniensia, Series I, Studia 6. Publications de l'Institut d'Études Médiévales de l'Université Catholique de Louvain, 2e. série, vol. 2. Leuven: Louvain Univ. Press, 1978, pp. 511-23.

___. "The University and the Council of Basle: Ecclesiology and Tactics." *Annuarium Historiae Conciliorum*, 6 (1974), 341-51.

Bligny, Bernard. "La Grande Chartreuse et son ordre au temps du Grand Schisme et de la crise conciliaire (1378-1449)." In *Historia et spiritualitas Cartusiensis*. Colloquii Quarti Internationalis Acta, Gandavi-Antverpiae-Bruges, 16-19 Sept. 1982. Edited by Jan de Grauwe. Destelbergen: Grauwe, 1983, pp. 35-57.

___. *Saint Bruno, le premier chartreux*. Rennes: Ouest-France, 1984.

Bligny, Bernard, and Chaix, Gerald, editors. *La naissance des Chartreuses*. Actes du VIe Colloque International d'Histoire et de Spiritualité Cartusiennes, Grenoble, 12-15 septembre 1984. Grenoble: Editions des Cahiers de l'Alpe de la Société des Ecrivains dauphinois, 1986. See also Primary Sources.

Blumenberg, Hans. "*Curiositas* und *veritas*: Zur Ideengeschichte von Augustin, *Confessiones* X,35." *Studia patristica*. Vol. 6. Part 4. Edited by F. C. Cross. Berlin: Akademie Verlag, 1962, pp. 294-302.

___. *The Legitimacy of the Modern Age*. Translated by Robert M. Wallace. Cambridge, Mass.: MIT Press, 1983.

Böckmann, Aquinata. "Discretio im Sinne der Regel Benedikts und ihrer Tradition." *Erbe und Auftrag*, 52 (1976), 362-73.

Bonner, Gerald. "Augustine's Doctrine of Man: Image of God and Sinner." *Augustinianum*, 24 (1984), 495-514.

Bonorand, Conradin. "Abt Chilian Püttricher von St. Peter als Humanist." *SMGB*, 93 (1982), 270-87.

___. "Die Bedeutung der Universität Wien für Humanismus und Reformation, insbesondere in der Ostschweiz." *Zwingliana*, 12 (1965), 162-80.

Borst, Arno. *Mönche am Bodensee: 610-1525*. Sigmaringen: Jan Thorbecke, 1978.

Bouchard, Constance Brittain. *Sword, Miter, and Cloister: Nobility and the Church in Burgundy*. Ithaca: Cornell Univ. Press, 1987.

Bouchayer, Auguste. *Les chartreux: Maîtres de forges*. Grenoble: Didier and Richard, 1927.

Bouvet, Jean. "Le 'Soliloquium' d'Adam de Perseigne." *Collectanea Cisterciensia*, 50 (1988), 113-71.

Bouwsma, William J. *John Calvin: A Sixteenth-Century Portrait*. New York: Oxford University Press, 1988.

___. "Lawyers and Early Modern Culture," *AHR* 78 (1973), 303-27.

Bouyer, Louis. *History of Christian Spirituality*. Vol. 1: *Spirituality of the Fathers*. Translated by Mary P. Ryan. New York: Seabury, 1963.

Bouyer, Louis; Leclercq, Jean; and Vandenbroucke, François. *History of Christian Spirituality*. Vol. 2: *The Spirituality of the Middle Ages*. Translated by the Benedictines of Holme Eden Abbey. New York: Seabury Crossroad, 1968.

Boyle, Leonard E. *Pastoral Care, Clerical Education, and Canon Law, 1200-1400*. London: Variorum, 1981.

___. "Robert Grosseteste and the Pastoral Care." In *Medieval and Renaissance Studies*, 8. Proceedings of the Southeastern Institute of Medieval and Renaissance Studies, Summer, 1976. Edited by Dale B. J. Randall. Durham, N.C.: Duke Univ. Press, 1979. Reprinted in Boyle, *Pastoral Care, Clerical Education, and Canon Law, 1200-1400*. London: Variorum, 1981, ch. I.

Boyle, Marjorie O'Rourke. "Erasmus and the 'Modern' Question: Was He Semi-Pelagian." *ARG*, 75 (1984), 59-77.

Brann, Noel. *The Abbot Trithemius (1462-1516): The Renaissance of Monastic Humanism*. SHCT, 24. Leiden, Brill, 1981.

Braudel, Fernand. *Civilization and Capitalism, Fifteenth-Eighteenth Century*. Volume 1: *The Structures of Everyday Life: The Limits of the Possible*. Translated by Siân Reynolds. New York: Harper and Row, 1981.

Brown, Colin. *History and Faith: A Personal Exploration*. Grand Rapids: Academe [Zondervan], 1987.

Brown, D. Katherine. *Pastor and Laity in the Theology of Jean Gerson*. Cambridge: Cambridge Univ. Press, 1987.

Brown, Elizabeth A. R. "Georges Duby and the Three Orders." *Viator*, 17 (1986), 51-64.

Brown, Peter R. L. "Aspects of the Christianization of the Roman Aristocracy." *Journal of Roman Studies*, 51 (1961), 1-11. Reprinted in Brown, *Religion and Society in the Age of Saint Augustine* (New York: Harper and Row, 1972), 161-82.

___. *The Body and Society: Men, Women, and Sexual Renunciation in Early Christianity*. Lectures in the History of Religions, n.s., 13. New York: Columbia Univ. Press, 1988.

___. *The Making of Late Antiquity*. Chicago: Univ. of Chicago Press, 1978.

___. "The Notion of Virginity in the Early Church." In *Christian Spirituality: Origins to the Twelfth Century*. Edited by Bernard McGinn and John Meyendorff. New York: Crossroad, 1985, 427-43.

___. "Patrons of Pelagius: The Roman Aristocracy between East and West." *JTS*, n.s. 21 (1970), 56-72.

___. "The Rise and Function of the Holy Man in Late Antiquity." *Journal of Roman Studies*, 61 (1971), 80-101.

___. *The World of Late Antiquity*. London: Thames and Hudson, 1971; New York: Harcourt Brace Jovanovich, 1974.

Brunner, Otto. "Beiträge zur Geschichte des Fehdewesens im spätmittelalterlichen Österreichs." *JLNö*, 22 (1929), 431-507.

Bulaeus (Du Boulay), Caesarius. *Historia Universitatis Parisiensis* [1668]. Reprinted Frankfurt: Minerva, 1966.

Bullough, Vern L. "Achievement, Professionalization, and the University." In *Les Universités à la fin du moyen âge / The Universities in the Late Middle Ages*. Edited by Jozef IJsewijn and Jacques Paquet. Mediaevalia Lovaniensia, Series I, Studia 6. Publications de l'Institut d'Études Médiévales de l'Université Catholique de Louvain, 2e. série, vol. 2. Leuven: Louvain Univ. Press, 1978, pp. 497-510.

Burckhardt, Max. "Bibliotheksaufbau, Bücherbesitz und Leserschaft im spätmittelalterlichen Basel." In *Studien zum städtischen Bildungswesen des späten Mittelalters und der frühen Neuzeit*. Bericht über Kolloquien der Kommission zur Erforschung der Kultur des Spätmittelalters, 1978 bis 1981. Edited by Bernd Moeller, Hans Patze, and Karl Stackmann, compiled by Ludger Grenzmann. Abhandlungen der Akademie der Wissenschaften in Göttingen, Philologisch-Historische Klasse, 137. Göttingen: Vandenhoeck und Ruprecht, 1983, pp. 33-52.

Burger, Christoph. *Aedificatio, Fructus, Utilitas: Johannes Gerson als Professor der Theologie und Kanzler der Universität Paris*. Beiträge zur historischen Theologie, 70. Tübingen: J. C. B. Mohr, 1986.

Burrows, Mark S. "Jean Gerson after Constance: 'Via Media et Regia' as a Revision of the Ockhamist Covenant," *CH*, 59 (1990), 467-81.

___. *Jean Gerson and "De Consolatione Theologiae (1418): The Consolation of a Biblical and Reforming Theology for a Disordered Age*. Beiträge zur historischen Theologie, 78. Tübingen: J. C. B. Mohr, 1991.

Butler, E. Cuthbert. *Benedictine Monachism: Studies in Benedictine Life and Rule*. New York: Barnes and Noble, 1962; Cambridge: Speculum Historiale, 1961. Originally published New York and London: Longmans Green and Co., 1924.

___. *Western Mysticism: The Teaching of SS Augustine, Gregory, and Bernard on Contemplation and the Contemplative Life; Neglected Chapters in the History of Religion*. New York: E. P. Dutton, 1924. Reprinted with introduction by David Knowles, London: Constable, 1967.

Bynum, Caroline Walker. *"Docere Verbo et Exemplo": An Aspect of Twelfth-Century Spirituality*. Harvard Theological Studies, 31. Missoula: Scholars Press, 1979.

___. *Holy Feast and Holy Fast: The Religious Significance of Food to Medieval Women*. Berkeley: Univ. of California Press, 1987.

Cabassut, André. "Discretion." In *DSAM*, 3: 1311-30.

Cantelli, Silvia. "Il commento al Cantico dei Cantici di Giovanni da Mantova." *Studi medievali*, ser. 3, vol. 26 (1985), 101-84.

Carozza. See Petrarch, above.

Casagrande, Carla, and Vecchio, Silvana. *I peccati della lingua: Disciplina ed etica della parola nella cultura medievale*. Biblioteca Biographica. Rome: Istituto della Enciclopedia Italiana, 1987.

Casey, Michael. *Athirst for God: Spiritual Desire in Bernard of Clairvaux's Sermons on the Song of Songs*. CS, 77. Kalamazoo: Cistercian Publications, 1988.

Cervelli, Innocenzo. "Storiografia e problemi intorno alla vita religiosa e spirituale a Venezia nella prima metà del '500." *Studi veneziani*, 8 (1966), 447-76.

Chadwick, Owen. *John Cassian: A Study in Primitive Monasticism*. Cambridge: Cambridge Univ. Press, 1950. Second edition, 1968.

Chaix, Gérard. "Contributions cartusiennes aux débuts de la réforme Catholique dans les pays de langue Française (1560-1620)." *Revue d'histoire de l'Eglise de France*, 75 [= no. 194] (1989), 115-23.

___. *Réforme et Contre-Réforme Catholique: Recherches sur la Chartreuse de Cologne au XVIe siecle*. 3 vols. AC, 80. 1981.

___. "Sainte-Barbe, Cologne et l'empire au XVIe siecle." In *Die Kartäuser in Österreich*. Zweiter internationaler Kongress über die Kartäusergeschichte und -Spiritualität. Vol. 3. AC, 83. 1981, pp. 96-111.

___. "Les traductions de la Chartreuse de Cologne au XVIe siecle." In *Kartäusermystik und -mystiker: Dritter Internationaler Kongress über die Kartäusergeschichte und -spiritualität*. Vol. 5. AC, 55.5. 1982, pp. 67-78.

Châtillon, Jean. "La Bible dans les écoles du XIIe siècle." In *Le Moyen Age et la Bible*. Edited by Pierre Riché and Guy Lobrichon. Bible de tous les temps, 4. Paris: Beauchesne, 1984, pp. 163-97. Reprinted in Châtillon, *D'Isidore de Séville à Saint Thomas d'Aquin: Etudes d'histoire et de théologie*. Collected Studies Series, 225. London: Variorum, 1985, ch. 2.

Chenu, Marie-Dominique. *Nature, Man, and Society in the Twelfth Century*. Translated by Jerome Taylor and Lester K. Little. Chicago: Univ. of Chicago Press, 1968.

Christian Spirituality: Origins to the Twelfth Century. Edited by Bernard McGinn and John Meyendorff. World Spirituality: An Encyclopedic Quest, 16. New York: Crossroad, 1985.

Christian Spirituality: High Middle Ages and Reformation. Edited by Jill Raitt with Bernard McGinn and John Meyendorff. World Spirituality: An Encyclopedic Quest, 17. New York: Crossroad, 1987.

Clark, Elizabeth A. *Jerome, Chrysostom and Friends: Essays and Translation*. Studies in Women and Religion, 2. New York: Edwin Mellen, 1979.

Clark, Francis. *The Pseudo-Gregorian Dialogues*, 2 vols. SHCT, 37. Leiden: Brill, 1987.

___. "St. Gregory and the Enigma of the Dialogues: A Response to Paul Meyvaert" [with comment by Meyvaert]. *JEH*, 40 (1989), 323-46.

Cohen, Jeremy. *The Friars and the Jews: The Evolution of Medieval Anti-Judaism*. Ithaca: Cornell Univ. Press, 1982.

____. "Scholarship and Intolerance in the Medieval Academy: The Study and Evaluation of Judaism in European Christendom." *AHR*, 91 (1986), 592-613. Cf. Berger, David.

Colish, Marcia. "Systematic Theology and Theological Renewal in the Twelfth Century." *JMRS*, 18 (1988), 135-56.

Colledge, Edmund. "Meister Eckhart, His Times and His Writings." *The Thomist*, 42 (1978), 240-58.

Colledge, Edmund, and Marler, J. C. "*Tractatus magistri Johannis gerson de mistica theologia*: St. Pölten, Diözesanarchiv MS. 25." *Mediaeval Studies*, 41 (1979), 354-86.

Combes, André. *Essai sur la critique de Ruysbroeck par Gerson*. Vol. 1: *Introduction critique et dossier documentaire*. Vol. 2: *La première critique gersonienne du "De ornatu spiritualium nuptiarum"*. Vol. 3: *L'évolution spontanée de la critique gersonienne* (première partie). Vol. 4: *L'évolution spontanée de la critique gersonienne* (deuxième partie). Études de théologie et d'histoire de la spiritualité, 4, 5.1, 5.2, 6. Paris: J. Vrin, 1945, 1948, 1959, 1972.

____. *La théologie mystique de Gerson: Profil de son évolution*. 2 vols. Spiritualitas, 1-2. Rome: Desclée, 1963.

Congar, Yves. "Die Ekklesiologie des Hl. Bernhards." In *Bernhard von Clairvaux: Mönch und Mystiker*, Internationaler Bernhard-Kongress, Mainz, 1953. Edited by Joseph Lortz. Veröffentlichungen des Instituts für europäische Geschichte, 6. Wiesbaden: Steiner, 1955, pp. 79-97. French version: "L'ecclésiologie de S. Bernard." In *S. Bernard Théologien*. Actes du congrès de Dijon, 15-19 Septembre 1953. Second edition. Rome: Editiones cistercienses, 1955 (= *Analecta sacri ordinis cisterciensis*, 9, no. 3-4 [1953]), pp. 136-90.

____. "Les laics et l'ecclésiologie des 'ordines' chez les théologiens des XIe et XIIe siècles." In *I laici nella societas cristiana dei secoli XI e XII*. Atti della terza Settimana internazionale di studio Mendola, 21-27 Agosto 1965. Pubblicazioni dell' Università Cattolica del Sacro Cuore, Contributi 35: Varia 5. Miscellanea del Centro di Studi Medioevali, 5. Milan: Editrice Vita e Pensiero, 1968, pp. 83-117.

Connolly, James L. *John Gerson: Reformer and Mystic*. Recueil de travaux publiés par les membres des conférences d'histoire et de philologie, 2, série, fasc. 12. Leuven: Librairie Universitaire, 1928.

Constable, Giles. "Petrarch and Monasticism." In *Francesco Petrarca: Citizen of the World*. Proceedings of the World Petrarch Congress, Washington, D.C., April 6-13, 1974. Edited by Aldo S. Bernardo. Padua: Editrice Antenore, 1980, and Albany: State Univ. of New York Press, 1980, pp. 53-99. Reprinted as the last chapter in Constable, *Monks, Hermits, and Crusaders in Medieval Europe*. London: Variorium, 1988.

____. "Twelfth-Century Spirituality and the Late Middle Ages." In *Medieval and Renaissance Studies*. Vol. 5. Edited by Osbourne B. Hardison, Jr. Chapel Hill: Univ. of North Carolina Press, 1971, pp. 27-60. Reprinted in Constable, *Religious Life and Thought (11th-12th Centuries)*. London: Variorum Reprints, 1979, ch. XV.

Cormeau, Christoph. "Wiens Universität und die deutschen Prosatexte im Umkreis Heinrichs von Langenstein." In *Milieux universitaires et mentalité urbaine au moyen âge*. Colloque du Département d'Études Médiévales de Paris-Sorbonne et de l'université de Bonn. Edited by Daniel Poirion. Cultures et civilisations médiévales, 6. Paris: Presses de l'université de Paris-Sorbonne, 1987, pp. 35-45.

Courtenay, William J. "*Antiqui* and *Moderni* in Late Medieval Thought." *JHI*, 48 (1987), 3-10.

___. "The Bible in the Fourteenth Century: Some Observations." *CH*, 54 (1985), 176-87.

___. "Inquiry and Inquisition: Academic Freedom in Medieval Universities." *CH*, 58 (1989), 168-81.

___. "The Reception of Ockham's Thought at the University of Paris." In *Preuve et raisons à l'université de Paris: Logique, ontologie et théologie au XIVe siècle.* Edited by Zénon Kaluza and Paul Vignaux. Paris: J. Vrin, 1984, pp. 43-64.

___. *Schools and Scholars in Fourteenth-Century England*. Princeton: Princeton Univ. Press, 1987.

Cousins, Ewert. "Francis of Assisi: Christian Mysticism at the Crossroads." In *Mysticism and Religious Traditions*. Edited by Steven T. Katz. New York: Oxford, 1983, 163-90.

Cranz, F. Edward. "Cusanus, Luther, and the Mystical Tradition." In *The Pursuit of Holiness in Late Medieval and Renaissance Religion*. Edited by Charles Trinkaus and Heiko A. Oberman. SMRT, 10. Leiden: Brill, 1974, pp. 93-102.

___. "The Transmutation of Platonism in the Development of Nicolaus Cusanus and of Martin Luther." In *Nicolo Cusano agli inizi del mondo moderno*. Atti del congresso internazionale in occasione del V centenario della morte di Nicolo Cusano, Bressanone, 6-10 settembre 1964. Facolta di magistero dell'Universita di Padova, XII. Florence: Sansoni, 1970, pp. 73-102.

Cremascoli, G. "Se i *Dialogi* siano opera di Gregorio Magno: due volumini per una *vexata quaestio.*" *Benedictina*, 36 (1989), 179-92.

Csendes, Peter, and Größing, Helmut. "Schrifttum zur Geschichte Wiens (1954-1974)." *MIÖG*, 83 (1975), 415-72.

___. *Wien in den Fehden der Jahre 1561-63*. Militärhistorische Schriftenreihe, Heft 28. Vienna: Österreichischer Bundesverlag, 1974.

Deblaere, Albert. "Humanisme chrétien et vocation monastique." *Studia missionalia*, 28 (1979), 97-132.

Dekkers, Eloi. "'Discretio' chez Saint Benoît et Saint Grégoire." *Collectanea Cisterciensia*, 46 (1984), 79-88.

Delumeau, Jean. *Rassurer et protéger: Le sentiment de sécurité dans l'Occident d'autrefois*. Paris: Fayard, 1989.

Deseille, Placide. "Théologie de la vie monastique selon saint Bernard." In *Vie Monastique* (1961), 503-25.

Despland, Michel. *La religion en occident: Evolution des idées et du vécu*. Héritage et projet, 23. Montreal: Fides, 1979.

DiLorenzo, Raymond D. "Rational Research in the Rhetoric of Augustine's *Confessio.*" In *From Cloister to Classroom: Monastic and Scholastic Approaches to Truth.* [= The Spirituality of Western Christendom, 3.] Edited by E. Rozanne Elder. CS, 90. Kalamazoo: Cistercian Publications, 1986, pp. 1-26.

Dörries, H. "The Place of Confession in Early Monasticism." In *Studia Patristica.* Vol. 5 (Oxford Conference, 1959). Part 3: *Liturgica, Monastica et Ascetica, Philosophica.* Edited by F. L. Cross. Berlin: Akademie-Verlag, 1962, pp. 284-311.

Dohna, Lothar Graf zu, and Wetzel, Richard. "Die Reue Christi: Zum theologischen Ort der Buße bei Johann von Staupitz." *SMGB*, 94 (1983), 457-82.

Dolfen, Christian. *Die Stellung des Erasmus von Rotterdam zur scholastischen Methode.* DTheol. diss., Univ. of Münster, 1936. Published at Osnabrück: Meinders und Elstermann, 1936.

Dondaine, H.-F. "L'objet et le 'medium' de la vision béatifique chez les théologiens du XIIIe siècle." *RTAM*, 19 (1952), 60-130.

Douglass, E. Jane Dempsey. *Justification in Late Medieval Preaching: A Study of John Geiler of Keisersberg.* SMRT, 1. Leiden, 1966. Second edition, 1989.

Dubois, Jacques. "L'institution des convers au XIIe siècle, forme de la vie monastique propre aux laïcs." In *I laici nella "societas cristiana" dei secoli XI e XII.* Atti della terza settimana internazionale di studio, Mendola, 21-27 agosto 1965. Milan, 1968, 183-261. Abridged and translated as "The Laybrothers' Life in the Twelfth Century: A Form of Lay Monasticism." *CS*, 7 (1972), 161-213.

___. "Quelques problèmes de l'histoire de l'ordre des Chartreux à propos de livres recents." *Revue d'histoire ecclésiastique*, 63 (1968), 27-54.

Duby, Georges. *The Chivalrous Society.* Translated by Cynthia Postan. Berkeley: Univ. of California Press, 1977.

___. *The Three Orders: Feudal Society Imagined.* Translated by Arthur Goldhammer. Chicago: Univ. of Chicago Press, 1980.

Duggan, Lawrence G. "Fear and Confession on the Eve of the Reformation." *ARG*, 75 (1984), 153-75.

Dumont, Charles. "Saint Aelred: The Balanced Life of the Monk." *Monastic Studies*, 1 (1963), 25-38. Originally: "L'équilibre humain de la vie cistercienne d'après le Bienhereux Aelred de Rievaulx." *Collectanea O.C.S.O.*, 18 (1956), 177-89.

DuPont, Philippe. "L'ascension mystique chez Guiges du Pont." In *Kartäusermystik und -mystiker*, Dritter Internationaler Kongress über die Kartäusergeschichte und -spiritualität. Vol. 1. Edited by James Hogg. AC, 55.1. 1981, pp. 47-80.

Dupraz, Joelle. "Bovinant, une mine de fer dans les limites du désert de la Grande Chartreuse (XIIème-XVIIIème siècles)." In *La naissance des Chartreuses.* Actes du VIe Colloque International d'Histoire et de Spiritualité Cartusiennes, Grenoble, 12-15 septembre 1984. Edited by Bernard Bligny and Gerald Chaix. Grenoble: Editions des Cahiers de l'Alpe de la Société des Ecrivains dauphinois, 1986, pp. 489-500.

Eichler, F. "Groß, Erhart," in *Verfasserlexikon.* Rev. ed. Vol. 2: cols. 102-6.

Elie, Hubert. *Les éditions des statuts de l'ordre des Chartreux.* Lausanne: F. Rouge, 1943.

Ellul, Jacques. *La Technique, ou l'enjeu du siècle.* Paris: Armand Colin, 1954. Translated by John Wilkinson as *The Technological Society.* New York: Knopf, 1964.

Elm, Kaspar. "Die Bruderschaft vom gemeinsamen Leben: Eine geistliche Lebens-form zwischen Kloster und Welt, Mittelalter und Neuzeit." *Ons geestelijk Erf*, 59 (1985), 470-96.

____. "Mendikanten und Humanisten im Florenz des Tre- und Quattrocento." In *Die Humanisten in ihrer politischen und sozialen Umwelt*. Edited by Otto Herding and Robert Stupperich. Kommission für Humanismusforschung, Mitteilung 2. Boppard: Kommission für Humanismusforschung, 1976, pp. 51-85.

____. "Reform- und Observanzbestrebungen im spätmittelalterlichen Ordenswesen." In *Reformbemühungen und Observanzbestrebungen im spätmittelalterlichen Ordenswesen*. Edited by Kaspar Elm. Berliner Historische Studien, 14. Or-densstudien, 6. Berlin: Duncker und Humblot, 1989, pp. 3-19.

____. "Verfall und Erneuerung des Ordenswesen im Spätmittelalter." In *Untersuch-ungen zu Kloster und Stift*. Edited by the Max-Planck-Institut für Geschichte in the series Veröffentlichungen des Max-Planck-Instituts für Geschichte, 68. Studien zur Germania Sacra, 14. Göttingen: Vandenhoeck und Ruprecht, 1980, pp. 188-238.

Emery, Kent, Jr. "Lovers of the World and Lovers of God and Neighbor: Spiritual Commonplaces and the Problem of Authorship in the Fifteenth Century." In *Historia et spiritualitas Cartusiensis*. Colloquii Quarti Internationalis Acta, Gh-ent-Antwerp-Bruges, 16-19 Sept. 1982. Edited by Jan de Grauwe. Destelbergen: de Grauwe, 1983, pp. 177-219.

____. "Twofold Wisdom and Contemplation in Denys of Ryckel (Dionysius Car-tusiensis, 1402-71)." *JMRS*, 18 (1988), 99-134.

Émery, P. Y. "Luther et le monachisme." *Verbum Caro*, 78 (1966), 82-90.

Emmen, Aquilin. "Heinrich von Langenstein und die Diskussion über die Empfäng-nis Mariens." In *Theologie in Geschichte und Gegenwart: Michael Schmaus zum sechzigsten Geburtstag dargebracht von seinen Freunden und Schülern*. Edited by Johann Auer and Hermann Volk. Munich: Karl Zink, 1957, pp. 625-50.

Engelbert, Pius. "Neue Forschungen zu den 'Dialogen' Gregors des Großen: Ant-wort auf Clark's These." *Erbe und Auftrag*, 65 (1989), 376-93.

Erdinger, Anton. "Beiträge zur Geschichte der Karthause und der Pfarre Gaming." *Geschichtliche Beilagen zu den Consistorial-Currenden der Diözese St. Pölten*, 5 (1895), 1-109.

Esnault, René H. "Kontinuität von Kirche und Mönchtum bei Luther." In *Kirche, Mystik, Heiligung, und das Natürliche bei Luther*. Vorträge des Dritten Interna-tionalen Kongresses für Lutherforschung, Järvenpää, Finland, 11-16 August 1966. Edited by Ivar Asheim. Göttingen: Vandenhoeck und Ruprecht, 1967, pp. 122-42.

____. *Luther et le monachisme aujourd'hui*. Nouvelle série théologique, 17. Geneva: Labor et Fides, 1964.

Etaix, Raymond. "L'homiliaire Cartusien." *Sacris Erudiri*, 13 (1962), 67-112.

____. "Le lectionnaire cartusien pour le réfectoire." *Revue d'études Augustiniennes*, 23 (1977), 272-303.

Evans, G. R. *Old Arts and New Theology: The Beginnings of Theology as an Aca-demic Discipline*. Oxford: Clarendon, 1980.

Ewig, Eugen. *Die Anschaungen des Kartäusers Dionysius von Roermond über den christlichen Ordo in Staat und Kirche.* Bonn: Ludwig Leopold, 1936 [Dissertation at Bonn].

Falk. F. "Der mittelrheinische Freundeskreis des Heinrichs von Langenstein." *HJ*, 15 (1894), 517-28.

Febvre, Lucien. "Pour l'histoire d'un sentiment: Le besoin de sécurité." *Annales: Economies, Sociétés, Civilisations,* 11 (1956), 244-47.

___. *The Problem of Unbelief in the Sixteenth Century: The Religion of Rabelais.* Translated by Beatrice Gottlieb. Cambridge, Mass.: Harvard Univ. Press, 1982.

Feiss, Hugh. "St. Bernard's Theology of Baptism and the Monastic Life." *CS*, 25 (1990), 79-91.

Ferguson, Wallace K. *The Renaissance in Historical Thought.* Cambridge, Mass.: Harvard Univ. Press, 1948.

Fine, Jr., John V. A. *The Late Medieval Balkans: A Critical Survey from the Late Twelfth Century to the Ottoman Conquest.* Ann Arbor: Univ. of Michigan Press, 1987.

Fletcher, J. M. "Wealth and Poverty in the Medieval German Universities with Particular Reference to the University of Freiburg." In *Europe in the Late Middle Ages.* Edited by J. R. Hale, J. R. L. Highfield, and B. Smalley. Evanston, Ill.: Northwestern Univ. Press, 1965, pp. 410-36.

Fodor, Adrienne. "Die Bibliothek der Kartause Lechnitz in der Zips vor 1500." *Armarium: Studia ex historia scripturae librorum et ephemeridum* (1977), 1-22.

Fontaine, Jacques. "Valeurs antiques et valeurs chrétiennes dans la spiritualité des grands proprietaires terriens à la fin du IVe siècle occidental." In *Epektasis: Mélanges Patristiques offerts au Cardinal Jean Daniélou.* Paris: Beauchesne, 1972, pp. 571-95.

Fragnito, Gigliola. "Cultura umanistica e riforma religiosa: il 'De officio viri boni ac probi episcopi' di Gasparo Contarini." *Studi veneziani,* 11 (1969), 75-189.

Frank, Barbara. "Subiaco, ein Reformkonvent des späten Mittelalters: Zur Verfassung und Zusammensetzung der Sublacenser Mönchsgemeinschaft in der Zeit von 1362 bis 1514." *QFIAB*, 52 (1972), 526-656.

___. *Das Erfurter Peterskloster im 15. Jahrhundert: Studien zur Geschichte der Klosterreform und der Bursfelder Union.* Veröffentlichungen des Max-Planck-Instituts für Geschichte, 34. Studien zur Germania Sacra, 11. Göttingen: Vandenhoeck und Ruprecht, 1973.

Frank, Isnard W. *Der antikonziliaristische Dominikaner Leonhard Huntpichler: Ein Beitrag zum Konziliarismus der Wiener Universität im 15. Jahrhundert.* AöG, 131. Vienna: Verlag der österreichischen Akademie der Wissenschaften, 1976.

___. *Hausstudium und Universitätsstudium der Wiener Dominikaner bis 1500.* AöG, 127. Vienna: Böhlau, 1968.

Frank, Karl Suso. *[Aggelikos Bios]: Begriffsanalytische und begriffsgeschichtliche Untersuchung zum "engelgleichen Leben" im frühen Mönchtum.* BGAM, 26. Münster im Westfalen: Aschendorff, 1964.

___. "Vom Kloster als scola dominici servitii zum Kloster ad servitium imperii." *SMGB*, 91 (1980), 80-97.

Frieß, Edmund. "Zur sozialem und wirtschaftlichen Lage der gutsherrlichen Leute am Fuße des Ötschers nach dem Bauernsturme: Das Gesinde in der Gutsherr-schaft der Kartause Gaming zu Ausgang des 16. Jahrhunderts." *JLNö*, n.F. 21 (1928), 172-88.

Frioli, Donatella. "Il 'Tractatus de affectibus formandis' di Nicola Kempf, un'opera che si riteneva perduta." *Studi Medievali*, ser. 3, vol. 30 (1989), 367-404.

Froehlich, Karlfried. "Justification Language and Grace: The Charge of Pelagianism in the Middle Ages." In *Probing the Reformed Tradition: Historical Studies in Honor of Edward A. Dowey, Jr.*. Edited by Elsie Anne McKee and Brian G. Armstrong. Louisville: Westminster/John Knox, 1989, pp. 21-47.

Gabriel, Astrik L. "Preparatory Teaching in the Parisian Colleges during the Four-teenth Century." *Revue de l'Université de Ottawa*, 21 (1951), 449-83. Reprinted in Gabriel, *Garlandia: Studies in the History of the Mediaeval University*. Notre Dame: Mediaeval Institute, 1969; Frankfurt: Josef Knecht, 1969, pp. 97-124.

Gall, Franz. *Alma Mater Rudophina, 1365-1965: Die Wiener Universität und ihre Studenten*. Vienna: Austria Press, 1965.

___. *Die alte Universität*. Wiener Geschichtsbücher, 1. Vienna, Hamburg: Zsolnay, 1970.

___. "Gründung und Anfänge der Wiener Universität." In *Les universités européen-nes du XIVe au XVIIIe siècle*. Études et documents publiées par l'Institut d'His-toire de la Faculté de Genève, 4. Geneva: Droz, 1967, pp. 48-55.

Ganzer, Klaus. "Zur monastischen Theologie des Johannes Trithemius." *HJ*, 101 (1981), 384-21.

___. "Monastischer Reform und Bildung: Ein Traktat des Hieronymus Aliotti (1412-1480) über die Studien der Mönche." In *Reformatio Ecclesiae: Beiträge zu kirchlichen Reformbestrebungen von der Alten Kirche bis zur Neuzeit: Festgabe für Erwin Iserloh*. Edited by Remigius Bäumer. Paderborn: Schöningh, 1980, pp. 181-99.

Gavigan, Johannes. "De doctoribus theologiae O.S.A. in universitate Vindobonensi." *Augustinianum*, 5 (1965), 271-364.

Geary, Patrick J. *Before France and Germany: The Creation and Transformation of the Merovingian World*. New York: Oxford Univ. Press, 1988.

Gehl, Paul F. "Competens Silentium: Varieties of Monastic Silence in the Medieval West." *Viator*, 18 (1987), 125-60.

___. "Mystical Language Models in Monastic Educational Psychology." *JMRS*, 14 (1984), 219-43.

Geith, Karl-Ernst. "Elisabeth Kempf (1415-1485), Priorin und Übersetzerin in Unter-linden zu Colmar." *Annuaire de Colmar*, 29 (1980-81), pp. 47-73.

Gelber, Hester G. "Logic and the Trinity: A Clash of Values in Scholastic Thought, 1300-1335." PhD diss., Univ. of Wisconsin, 1974.

Gerz-von Büren, Veronika. *La Tradition de l'oeuvre de Jean Gerson chez les Char-treux: La Chartreuse de Bâle*. Institut de recherches et d'histoire des textes, Bibliographies, Colloques, Travaux préparatoires. Paris: Centre National de la Recherche Scientifique, 1973.

Ghellinck, Joseph de. "Les catalogues de bibliothèques médiévales chez les char-treux et un guide de lectures spirituelles." *RAM*, 25 (1949), 284-98.

___. *Le mouvement théologique du XIIe siècle, sa préparation lointaine avant et autour de Pierre Lombard, ses rapports avec les initiatives des canonistes.* 2nd Edition. Museum Lessianum—Section Historique, 10. Bruges, 1948. Reprinted Brussels: Culture et civilisation, 1969.

Gieraths, Gundolf. "Johannes Nider, O.P., und die 'Deutsche Mystik' des 14. Jahrhunderts." *Divus Thomas: Jahrbuch für Philosophie und spekulative Theologie,* 30 (1952), 321-46.

Gilbert, Felix. "Religion and Politics in the Thought of Gasparo Contarini." In *Action and Conviction in Early Modern Europe: Essays in Memory of E. H. Harbison.* Edited by T. K. Rabb and J. E. Seigel. Princeton: Princeton Univ. Press, 1969, pp. 90-116.

Gilbert, Neal W. "Comment." *JHI,* 48 (1987), 41-50.

___. "Ockham, Wyclif, and the 'Via Moderna'," in *Antiqui et Moderni: Traditionsbewußtsein und Fortschrittsbewußtsein im späten Mittelalter.* Edited by Albert Zimmermann. Miscellanea Mediaevalia, 9. Berlin: De Gruyter, 1974, pp 85-125.

Gillespie, Vincent. "Cura Pastoralis in Deserto." In *De Cella in Seculum: Religious and Secular Life and Devotion in Late Medieval England.* Edited by Michael G. Sargent. Cambridge: D. S. Brewer, 1989, pp. 161-81.

Gillet, Robert. "Spiritualité et place du moine dans l'église selon saint Grégoire le Grand." In *Vie monastique,* pp. 323-52.

Gilson, Etienne. *La théologie mystique de Saint Bernard.* Paris, 1934. Second edition 1947. Translated by A. Downes as *The Mystical Theology of Saint Bernard.* New York: Sheed and Ward, 1940.

Girgensohn, Dieter. *Peter von Pulkau und die Wiedereinführung des Laienkelches: Leben und Wirken eines Wiener Theologen in der Zeit des großen Schismas.* Veröffentlichungen des Max-Planck-Instituts für Geschichte, 12. Göttingen: Vandenhoeck und Ruprecht, 1964.

Gleason, Elisabeth G. See Minnich, Nelson H.

Glorieux, Palémon. "Gerson et les Chartreux." *RTAM,* 28 (1961), 115-53.

Glückert, Ludwig. "Hieronymus von Mondsee (Magister Johannes de Werdea): Ein Beitrag zur Geschichte des Einflusses der Wiener Universität im 15. Jahrhundert." *SMGB,* 48 [n.F. 17] (1930), 98-201.

Gómez, Ildefonso M. "Los Cartujos y los estudios." *Los monjes y los estudios* (IV Semana de Estudios monasticos). Poblet, 1963, pp. 163-207.

Grabmann, Martin. "Bernhard von Waging (+ 1472), Prior von Tegernsee, ein bayerischer Benediktinermystiker des 15. Jahrhunderts." *SMGB,* n.F. 60 (1946), 82-98.

___. "Die Erklärung des Bernhard von Waging O.S.B. zum Schlußkapitel von Bonaventuras *Itinerarium mentis in Deum." Franziskanische Studien,* 8 (1921), 125-35.

Grafton, Anthony, and Jardine, Lisa. *From Humanism to the Humanities: Education and the Liberal Arts in Fifteenth- and Sixteenth-Century Europe.* Cambridge, Mass.: Harvard Univ. Press, 1986.

Grant, Georg Parkin. *Lament for a Nation.* 1965. Republished Ottawa: Carlton Univ. Press, 1978.

___. *Technology and Empire.* Toronto: House of Anansi, 1969.

Grausam, George. "Weiteres Schrifttum zur Geschichte der Kartausen Niederöster-reichs Aggsbach, Gaming, und Mauerbach." *Unsere Heimat*, n.F. 39 (1968), 234-37.

Grausem, J. P. "Le *De contemplatione* du chartreux Guiges du Pont (+ 1297)." *RAM*, 10 (1929), 259-89.

Greenfield, Concetta Carestia. *Humanist and Scholastic Poetics, 1250-1500*. Toronto: Univ. of Toronto Press, 1981.

Greven, Joseph. *Die kölner Kartause und die Anfänge der katholischen Reform in Deutschland*. Edited by Wilhelm Neuss. Katholisches Leben und Kämpfen im Zeitalter der Glaubensspaltung, 6. Münster: Aschendorff, 1935.

Grössing, Helmuth. "*Astronomus poeta*: Georg von Peuerbach als Dichter." *JVGSW*, 34 (1978), 54-66.

Großmann, Karl. "Begründung der modernen Himmelskunde durch die Wiener Mathematikerschule des 15. Jahrhunderts: Ein Kulturbild aus dem spätmittelal-terlichen Wien." *JVGSW*, 21/22 (1965/66), 209-10.

____. "Die Frühzeit des Humanismus in Wien bis zu Celtis Berufung 1497." *JLNö*, 22 (1929), 150-325.

Gründler, Otto. "*Devotio moderna atque antiqua*: The Modern Devotion and Carthu-sian Spirituality." In *The Roots of the Modern Christian Tradition*. Edited by E. Rozanne Elder. The Spirituality of Western Christendom, 2. Kalamazoo: Cister-cian Publications, 1984, pp. 27-45.

Grundmann, Herbert. "Neue Beiträge zur Geschichte der religiösen Bewegungen im Mittelalter." *Archiv für Kulturgeschichte*, 37 (1955), 129-82.

____. "Die geschichtliche Grundlagen der deutschen Mystik." *DVfLG*, 12 (1934), 400-29. Reprinted in *Altdeutsche und altniederländische Mystik*. Edited by Kurt Ruh. Darmstadt: Wissenschaftliche Buchgesellschaft, 1964, pp. 72-99.

____. *Religiöse Bewegungen im Mittelalter: Untersuchungen über die geschichtliche Zusammenhänge zwischen der Ketzerei, den Bettelorden und der religiösen Grundlagen der deutschen Mystik*. Historische Studien, 267. Berlin: Ebering, 1935. Second edition, Hildesheim, 1961.

Grünewald, Stanislaus. *Franziskanische Mystik: Versuch zu einer Darstellung mit besonderer Berücksichtigung des Heiligen Bonaventura*. Munich: Naturrechts-Verlag, 1936.

Guimet, F. "*Caritas ordinata* et *amor discretus* dans la théologie trinitaire de Richard de Saint-Victor." *Revue du Moyen Age Latin*, 4 (1948), 225-36.

Guinan, Patricia A. "Carthusian Prayer and Hugh of Balma's *Viae Sion Lugent*." PhD diss., Medieval Institute, Univ. of Notre Dame, 1985.

Gumbel, Hermann. "Moser, Ludwig," in *Verfasserlexikon*. Rev. ed. Vol. 3, cols. 434-37.

Gumbert, P. J. *Die Utrechter Kartäuser und ihre Bücher im frühen fünfzehnten Jahr-hundert*. Leiden: Brill, 1974.

Haas, Alois Maria. "Die deutsche Mystik im Spannungsbereich von Theologie und Spiritualität." In *Literatur und Laienbildung im Spätmittelalter und in der Re-formationszeit, Symposion Wolfenbüttel 1981*. Edited by Ludger Grenzmann and Karl Stackmann. Germanistische-Symposien-Berichtsbände, 5. Stuttgart: J. B. Metzlersche Verlagsbuchhandlung, 1984, pp. 604-42.

___. "Schools of Late Medieval Mysticism." In *Christian Spirituality: High Middle Ages and Reformation.* Edited by Jill Raitt, Bernard McGinn, and John Meyendorff. World Spirituality: An Encyclopedic Quest, 17. New York: Crossroad, 1987, pp. 140-75.

Hacker, Paul. "Martin Luther's Notion of Faith." In *Catholic Scholars Dialogue with Luther.* Edited by Jared Wicks. Chicago: Loyola Univ. Press, 1970, pp. 85-106, 194-98. Originally appeared in Hacker, *Das Ich im Glauben bei Martin Luther.* Graz: Styria Verlag, 1966. Translated as *The Ego in Faith: Martin Luther and the Origins of Anthropocentric Religion.* Chicago: Loyola Univ. Press, 1970.

Häfele, Gallus M. *Franz von Retz: Ein Beitrag zur Gelehrtengeschichte des Dominikanerordens und der Wiener Universität am Ausgange des Mittelalters.* Innsbruck: Tyrolia, 1918.

Hägglund, Bengt. "The Background of Luther's Doctrine of Justification in Late Medieval Theology." *Lutheran World,* 8 (1961), 24-46. Reprinted in Facet Books Series. Philadelphia: Fortress, 1971.

Haller, Walter H. *Studien zur Ludwig Moser, Kartäusermönch in Basel.* Fribourg, Switzerland: Paulus Druckerei, 1967.

Hallier, Amédée. *The Monastic Theology of Aelred of Rievaulx: An Experiential Theology.* Translated by Columban Heaney. CS, 2. Shannon, Ireland: Irish Univ. Press, 1969.

Halpérin, Jean. "La notion de sécurité dans l'histoire économique et sociale." *Revue d'histoire économique et sociale,* 30 (1952), 7-25.

Hamm, Berndt. *Frömmigkeitstheologie am Anfang des 16. Jahrhunderts: Studien zu Johannes von Paltz und seinem Umkreis.* Beiträge zur historischen Theologie, 65. Tübingen: J. C. B. Mohr, 1982.

___. "Lazarus Spengler und Martin Luthers Theologie." In *Martin Luther: Probleme seiner Zeit.* Edited by Volker Press and Dieter Stievermann. Spätmittelalter und frühe Neuzeit, 16. Stuttgart: Klett-Cotta, 1986, pp. 124-36.

___. *Promissio, Pactum, Ordinatio: Freiheit und Selbstbindung Gottes in der scholastischen Gnadenlehre.* Beiträge zur historischen Theologie, 54. Tübingen: J. C. B. Mohr, 1977.

___. "Was ist reformatorische Rechtfertigungslehre?" *ZThK,* 83 (1986), 1-38.

Hammermayer, Ludwig. "Die Forschungszentren der deutschen Benediktiner und ihre Vorhaben." In *Historische Forschung im 18. Jahrhundert: Organisation, Zielsetzung, Ergebnisse,* 12. Deutsch-Französisches Historikerkolloquium des deutschen Instituts Paris. Edited by Karl Hammer and Jürgen Voss. Pariser historische Studien, 13. Bonn: Ludwig Röhrscheid, 1976, pp. 122-91.

Hantsch, Hugo. *Geschichte Österreichs,* vol. 1: *Bis 1648.* Graz, Vienna, Cologne: Styria, 1969.

___. "Bernhard Pez und Abt Berthold Dietmayr." *MIÖG,* 71 (1963), 128-39.

Haselbach, Karl. "Die Kartause von Gaming," *Blätter des Vereins für Landeskunde von Niederösterreich,* n.F. 12 (1878), 244-60.

Haskins, Charles H. *The Renaissance of the Twelfth Century.* Cambridge, Mass.: Harvard Univ. Press, 1927.

Hausherr, Irénée. *Penthos: The Doctrine of Compunction in the Christian East.* Translated by Anselm Hufstader. CS, 53. Kalamazoo: Cistercian Publications, 1982.

_____. *Spiritual Direction in the Early Christian East.* Translated by Anthony P. Gythiel. Cistercian Studies Series, 116. Kalamazoo: Cistercian Publications, 1990.

Heath, Terence. "Logical Grammar, Grammatical Logic, and Humanism in Three German Universities." *SR*, 18 (1971), 9-64.

Heerwagen, Heinrich. "Die Kartause in Nürnberg, 1380—1525." *Mitteilungen des Vereins für Geschichte der Stadt Nürnberg*, 15 (1902), 88-132.

Heilig, Konrad Josef. "Kritische Studien zum Schrifttum der beiden Heinriche von Hessen." *Römische Quartalschrift für christliche Altertumskunde und für Kirchengeschichte*, 40 (1932), 105-76.

Heimbucher, Max. *Die Orden und Kongregationen der katholischen Kirche.* 3 vols. Paderborn: Schöningh, 1907.

Heinzelmann, Martin. *Bischofsherrschaft in Gallien: Zur Kontinuität römischer Führungsschichten vom 4. bis zum 7. Jahrhundert. Soziale, prosopographische und bildungsgeschichtliche Aspekte.* Beihefte der Francia, 5. Munich: Artemis, 1976.

Heitmann, Klaus. *Fortuna und Virtus: Eine Studie zu Petrarcas Lebensweisheit.* Cologne: Böhlau, 1958.

Heldwein, Johannes. *Die Klöster Bayerns am Ausgange des Mittelalters.* Munich: J. Lindauersche Buchhandlung, 1913.

Helmrath, Johannes. *Das Basler Konzil 1431-1449: Forschungsstand und Probleme.* Kölner historische Abhandlungen, 32. Cologne: Böhlau, 1987.

Henkel, Nikolaus. "Leipzig als Übersetzungszentrum am Ende des 15. und Anfang des 16. Jahrhundert." In *Literatur und Laienbildung im Spätmittelalter und in der Reformationszeit, Symposion Wolfenbüttel 1981.* Edited by Ludger Grenzmann and Karl Stackmann. Germanistische-Symposien-Berichtsbände, 5. Stuttgart: J. B. Metzlersche Verlagsbuchhandlung, 1984, pp. 559-78.

Henry, E. "Gerson dans l'exil du 15. mai 1418 au 15. novembre 1419." *Travaux de l'academie impériale de Reim*, 25 (1857), 335-52.

Hess, Günter, with manuscript analysis by Urusula Hess. "Spektator-Lector-Actor: Zum Publikum von Jacob Bidermann's *Cenodoxus*." *Internationales Archiv für Sozialgeschichte der deutschen Literatur*, 1 (1976), 30-106.

Hillenbrand, Eugen. "Arnoldi, von Alfeld, Heinrich." In *Verfasserlexikon*. Rev. ed. Vol. 1, cols. 487-89.

Hilpisch, Stephan. *Geschichte des Benediktinischen Mönchtums.* Freiburg i. Br.: Herder, 1929. Translated by J. Doyle, *Benedictines through Changing Centuries.* Collegeville, Minn.: St. John's Abbey, 1958.

Hiss, Wilhelm. *Die Anthropologie Bernhards von Clairvaux.* Berlin: De Gruyter, 1964.

Hocquard, Gaston. "Les idées maîtresses des *Meditations* du Prieur Guiges Ier." In *Historia et Spiritualitas Cartusiensis.* Acta Colloquii Quarti Internationalis, Ghent-Antwerp-Bruges, 16-19 Septembre 1982. Edited by Jan de Grauwe. Destelbergen: de Grauwe, 1983, pp. 247-56.

Hödl, Ludwig. "Die dialektische Theologie des 12. Jahrhunderts." In *Arts libéraux et philosophie.* Actes IVe congrès international de philosophie médiévale, université de montréal, 27 Aug. - 2 Sept. 1967. Montreal: Institute d'études médiévales, 1969; Paris: J. Vrin, 1969, pp. 137-47, discussion, pp. 148-56.

Hörmer, Alois. "Der Kartäuser Nikolaus Kempf als Seelenführer: Ein Beitrag zur Aszese des Spätmittelalters." DTheol dissertation, Univ. of Vienna, Katholische theologische Fakultät, 1959.

Höver, Werner. *Theologia Mystica in altbairischer Übertragung. . . Studien zum Übersetzungswerk eines Tegernseer Anonymus aus der Mitte des 15. Jahrhunderts.* MTU, 36. Munich: Beck, 1971.

Hoffmann, Brunhilde. "Die Aufhebung der Kartause Gaming. DPhil dissertation in history, Univ. of Vienna, 1948. Published as AC, 58. 1981.

Hoffmann, Fritz. "Robert Holcot—Die Logik in der Theologie." In *Die Metaphysik im Mittelalter: Ihr Ursprung und ihre Bedeutung.* Vorträge des II. Internationalen Kongresses für mittelalterliche Philosophie, Köln, 31. August - 6. September 1961. Edited by Paul Wilpert. Miscellanea Mediaevalia, 2. Berlin: De Gruyter, 1963, pp. 624-39.

Hogg, James. *Die ältesten consuetudines der Kartäuser.* AC, 1. Berlin, Salzburg: Hogg, 1973.

____. "The Carthusians and the 'Rule of St. Benedict'." In *Itinera Domini: Gesammelte Aufsätze aus Liturgie und Mönchtum.* Festschrift Emmanuel von Severus O.S.B. Münster: Aschendorff, 1988, pp. 281-318.

____. *Dom Edmund Gurdon: A Memoir.* AC, 129. 1988, pp. 91-144.

____. "The Dormitorium Dilecti Dilecti of Richard Methley of Mount Grace Charterhouse, transcribed from the Trinity College Cambridge MS. O. 2. 56." In *Kartäusermystik und -Mystiker.* Dritter internationaler Kongress über die Kartäusergeschichte und -Spiritualität. Vol. 5. AC, 55.5. 1982, pp. 79-103.

____. "Everyday Life in the Charterhouse in the Fourteenth and Fifteenth Centuries." In *Klösterliche Sachkultur des Spätmittelalters.* Internationaler Kongress Krems an der Donau, 18. bis 21. September 1978. Vienna: Österreichische Akademie der Wissenschaften, 1980, 113-46.

____. "Gaming," *DHGE,* vol. 19 (1981), cols. 988-97.

____. "Geirach," *DHGE,* vol. 20 (1984), cols. 258-62.

____. "Hugh of Balma and Guigo du Pont." In *Kartäuserregel und Kartäuserleben.* Internationaler Kongress vom 30. Mai bis 3. Juni, 1984, Stift Heiligenkreuz. AC, 113.1. 1984, pp. 61-88.

____. "Mount Grace Charterhouse and Late Medieval English Spirituality." In *Collectanea Cartusiana.* Vol. 3. AC, 82.3. 1980, pp. 1-43.

____. "A Mystical Diary: The *Refectorium salutis* of Richard Methley of Mount Grace Charterhouse." In *Kartäusermystik und -Mystiker.* Dritter internationaler Kongress über die Kartäusergeschichte und -Spiritualität. Vol. 1. AC, 55.1. 1981, pp. 208-38.

____. "The *Schola amoris languidi* of Richard Methley of Mount Grace Charterhouse transcribed from the Trinity College Cambridge MS. O. 2. 56." In *Kartäusermystik und -Mystiker.* Dritter internationaler Kongress über die Kartäusergeschichte und -Spiritualität. Vol. 2. AC, 55.2. 1981, pp. 138-65.

____. "The Ways of God to Man: The Carthusian Chronicle of Universal History in Oxford Bodleian Library MS. E. Museo 160." In *Kartäuserliturgie und Kartäuserschrifttum.* Vol. 4. AC 116.4. 1989, pp. 152-63.

Hohmann, Thomas. *Heinrichs von Langenstein "Untersuchung der Geister" lateinisch und deutsch: Texte und Untersuchungen zur Übersetzungsliteratur aus der Wiener Schule.* MTU, 63. Munich: Artemis, 1977.

———. "'Die recht gelerten maister': Bemerkungen zur Übersetzungsliteratur des Wiener Schule des Spätmittelalters." In *Die österreichische Literatur: Ihr Profil von den Anfängen im Mittelalter bis ins 18. Jahrhundert (1050-1750).* Vol. 1. Edited by Herbert Zeman. Graz: Akademische Druck- und Verlagsanstalt, 1986, pp. 349-65.

———. "Texte unter dem Namen 'Heinrich von Langenstein'." In *Würzburger Prosa-Studien* [Kurt Ruh zum 60. Geburtstag], vol. 2. Edited Peter Kesting. Medium Aevum, 31. Munich: Wilhelm Fink, 1975, pp. 219-36.

Honemann, Volker. "Aspekte des 'Tugendadels' im europäischen Spätmittelalter." In *Literatur und Laienbildung im Spätmittelalter und in der Reformationszeit, Symposion Wolfenbüttel 1981.* Edited by Ludger Grenzmann and Karl Stackmann. Germanistische-Symposien-Berichtsbände, 5. Stuttgart: J. B. Metzlersche Verlagsbuchhandlung, 1984, pp. 274-86, discussion, pp. 287-88.

———. "The Reception of William of St. Thierry's *Epistola ad fratres de Monte Dei* during the Middle Ages." In *Cistercians in the Late Middle Ages.* Edited by E. Rozanne Elder. Cistercian Studies Series, 64. Studies in Medieval Cistercian History, 6. Kalamazoo: Cistercian Publications, 1981, pp. 5-18.

Horsfield, Robert. "*The Pomander of Prayer*: Aspects of Late Medieval English Carthusian Spirituality and Its Lay Audience." In *De Cella in Seculum: Religious and Secular Life and Devotion in Late Medieval England.* Edited by Michael G. Sargent. Cambridge: D. S. Brewer, 1989, 205-13.

Hossfeld, Max. "Johannes Heynlin aus Stein: Ein Kapitel aus der Frühzeit des deutschen Humanismus." *Basler Zeitschrift für Geschichte und Altertumskunde,* 6 (1907), 309-56, and 7 (1908), 79-219, 235-398.

Hubalek, Franz. "Aus dem Briefwechsel des Johannes Schlitpacher von Weilheim (der Kodex 1767 der Stiftsbibliothek Melk)." DPhil diss., Univ. of Vienna, 1963.

Irvine, Martin. "Bede the Grammarian and the Scope of Grammatical Studies in Eighth-Century Northumbria." *Anglo-Saxon England,* 15 (1986), 15-44.

Isaacson, Michael. "Passion Play." *Universitas* (St. Louis University), 16, no. 3 (Spring 1991), 10-12.

Ivánka, Endre von. "Der 'Apex Mentis'." *ZkTh,* 72 (1950), 147-66. Reprinted in *Plato Christianus.* Einsiedeln: Johannes Verlag, 1964, pp. 315-38. Reprinted in *Platonismus in der Philosophie des Mittelalters.* Edited by Werner Beierwaltes. Wege der Forschung, 197. Darmstadt: Wissenschaftliche Buchgesellschaft, 1969, pp. 121-46.

———. "La Structure de l'âme selon S. Bernard." In *Saint Bernard Théologien.* Actes du congrès de Dijon, 15-19 Septembre 1953. Rome: Editiones Cistercienses, 1955, pp. 202-8.

———. "Zur Überwindung des Neuplatonischen Intellektualismus in der Deutung der Mystik: Intelligentia oder Principalis Affectio." *Scholastik,* 30 (1955), 185-94. Reprinted in *Plato Christianus,* pp. 352-63. Reprinted in *Platonismus in der Philosophie des Mittelalters,* pp. 147-60.

Jaeger, C. Stephen. *The Origins of Courtliness: Civilizing Trends and the Formation of Courtly Ideals, 939-1210*. Philadelphia: Univ. of Pennsylvania Press, 1985.

Janz, Denis R. *Luther and Late Medieval Thomism: A Study in Theological Anthropology*. Waterloo, Ontario: Wilfrid Laurier Univ. Press, 1983.

Jardine, Lisa. See Grafton, Anthony.

Jaroschka, Walter. "Thomas Ebendorfer als Theoretiker des Konziliarismus." *MIÖG*, 71 (1963), 87-98.

Jedin, Hubert. *Geschichte des Konzils von Trient*. Vol. 1: *Der Kampf um das Konzil*. Freiburg i. Br.: Herder, 1949. Translated by Ernest Graf as *History of the Council of Trent*. Vol. 1. St. Louis: Herder, 1957.

___. "Ein 'Turmerlebnis' des jungen Contarinis." *HJ*, 70 (1951), 115-30. Reprinted in Jedin, *Kirche des Glaubens, Kirche der Geschichte: Ausgewählte Aufsätze und Vorträge*. Vol. 1. Freiburg: Herder, 1966, pp. 167-80.

Joachimsohn (Joachimsen), Paul. "Aus der Bibliothek Sigismund Gossembrots." *Centralblatt für Bibliothekswesen*, 11 (1894), 249-68, 297-307.

___. *Die humanistische Geschichtsschreibung in Deutschland*. Vol. 1: *Die Anfänge: Sigismund Meisterlin*. Bonn: P. Hanstein, 1895.

___. See also Primary Sources.

Jones, Cheslyn; Wainwright, Geoffrey; Yarnold, Edward, editors. *The Study of Spirituality*. New York: Oxford Univ. Press, 1986.

Kaluza, Zenon. "Le Chancelier Gerson et Jérôme de Prague." *AHDL*, 59 (1984), 81-126.

___. *Les querelles doctrinales a Paris: Nominalistes et realistes aux confins du XIVe et du XVe siècles*. Bergamo: Pierluigi Lubrina Editore, 1988.

Karpp, Heinrich. "Ein Bibellob aus der Basler Konzilsuniversität." In *Studien zur Geschichte und Theologie der Reformation: Festschrift für Ernst Bizer*. Edited by Luise Abramowski. Neukirchen: Neukirchner Verlag, 1969, pp. 79-96.

Katschthaler, Eduard. "Melk" in *Topographie von Niederösterreich*. Vol. 6. Vienna: Seidel, 1909, pp. 370-508.

___. *Über Bernhard Pez und dessen Briefnachlaß*. In *39. Jahresbericht des k[öniglichen]. [und] k[aiserlichen]. Obergymnasiums der Benedictiner zu Melk*. Melk: R. Brzezowsky [Selbstverlag des Gymnasiums], 1889, pp. 5-106.

Keiblinger, Ignaz. *Geschichte des Benedictiner-Stiftes Melk in Niederösterreich, seiner Besitzungen und Umbgebung*. Second edition. 2 vols. Vienna: F. Beck, 1867-68. Originally published, 1851.

Kellner, Altman. *Das Profeßbuch des Stiftes Kremsmünster*. Kremsmünster: Stift, 1968.

Kellner, H. "Jakobus von Jüterbogk, ein deutscher Theologe des 15. Jahrhunderts." *Theologischer Quartalschrift*, 48 (1866), 315-48.

Kellner, Hans. *Language and Historical Representation: Getting the Story Crooked*. Madison: Univ. of Wisconsin Press, 1989.

Kennan, Elizabeth T. "The *De consideratione* of St. Bernard of Clairvaux and the Papacy in the Mid-twelfth Century: A Review of Scholarship." *Traditio*, 23 (1967), 73-115.

___. "Introduction." In Bernard of Clairvaux, *Five Books on Consideration: Advice to a Pope*. Translated by John D. Anderson and Elizabeth T. Kennan. CF, 37. Kalamazoo: Cistercian Publications, 1976, pp. 1-18.

Kieckhefer, Richard. "Meister Eckhart's Conception of Union with God." *Harvard Theological Review*, 71 (1978), 203-25.

Kink, Rudolf. *Geschichte der kaiserlichen Universität zu Wien*. 2 vols. Vienna: Carl Gerold und Sohn, 1854. Reprinted Frankfurt a. M.: Minerva, 1969.

Kinneavy, James L. *Greek Rhetorical Origins of the Christian Faith*. Oxford: Oxford Univ. Press, 1987.

Klapper, Joseph. *Der Erfurter Kartäuser Johannes Hagen*: I. Teil: *Leben und Werk*. II. Teil: *Verzeichnis seiner Schriften mit Auszügen*. Erfurter Theologische Studien, 9-10. Leipzig: St. Benno Verlag, 1961.

Klein, Alessandro. *Meister Eckhart: La dottrina mistica della giustificazione*. Biblioteca di filosofia: Ricerche, 4. Milan: U. Mursia Editore, 1978.

Klein, Klaus. "Frühchristliche Eremiten im Spätmittelalter und in der Reformationszeit: Zu Überlieferung und Rezeption der deutschen 'Vitaspatrum'-Prosa." In *Literatur und Laienbildung im Spätmittelalter und in der Reformationszeit, Symposion Wolfenbüttel 1981*. Edited by Ludger Grenzmann and Karl Stackmann. Germanistische-Symposien-Berichtsbände, 5. Stuttgart: J. B. Metzlersche Verlagsbuchhandlung, 1984), pp. 686-95, discussion, p. 696.

Kleineidam, Erich. "Die theologische Richtung der Erfurter Kartäuser am Ende des 15. Jahrhundert: Versuch einer Einheit der Theologie." In *Miscellanea Erfordiana*. Erfurter theologische Studien, 12. Leipzig: St. Benno Verlag, 1962, pp. 247-71. Reprinted in Zadnikar and Wienand, eds., *Die Kartäuser*, pp. 185-202.

Kloczowski, Jerzy. "Le conciliarisme á l'université de Cracovie au XVe siècle et ses prolongements au XVIe siècle." In *The Church in a Changing Society: Conflict, Reconciliation, or Adjustment?*. Proceedings of the CIHEC [Commission internationale d'histoire ecclésiastique comparée] Conference in Uppsala, August 17-21, 1977. Publications of the Swedish Society of Church History, n.s. 30. Uppsala: Almqvist and Wiksell, 1978, pp. 223-26.

Kneller, C. A. "Eine mittelalterliche Abhandlung über die Gewissensrechenschaft." *ZAM*, 1 (1926), 92-95.

Knoll, Paul W. "The University of Cracow in the Conciliar Movement." In *Rebirth, Reform, and Resiliance: Universities in Transition, 1300-1700*. Edited by James M. Kittelson and Pamela J. Transue. Columbus: Ohio State Univ. Press, 1984, pp. 190-212.

Knowles, David. *The English Mystical Tradition*. London: Burns and Oates, 1964; New York: Harper and Brothers, 1964.

___. "The Influence of Pseudo-Dionysius on Western Mysticism." In *Christian Spirituality: Essays in Honour of Gordon Rupp*. Edited by Peter Brooks. London: S.C.M. Press, 1975, pp. 79-94.

Knowles, David, and W. F. Grimes. *Charterhouse: The Medieval Foundation in the Light of Recent Discoveries*. London: Longmans, Green and Co., 1954.

Koch, Josef. *Nikolaus von Kues und seine Umwelt*. Sitzungsberichte der Heidelberger Akademie der Wissenschaften. Jahrgang 1944/48, 2. Abhandlung. Heidelberg: Carl Winter, 1948.

Kogler, A.-Ch. "Mémoire sur la composition et l'origine des divers recueils de privilèges généraux de l'ordre des chartreux." *Revue Mabillon*, 19 (1929), 131-60.

Kohl, Benjamin A. "Humanism and Education." In *Renaissance Humanism: Foundations, Forms, and Legacy*. Edited by Albert Rabil, Jr.. Vol. 3: *Humanism and the Disciplines*. Philadelphia: Univ. of Pennsylvania Press, 1988, pp. 5-22.

Koller, Gerda. *Princeps in Ecclesia: Untersuchungen zur Kirchenpolitik Herzog Albrechts V von Österreich*. AöG, 124. Vienna: Böhlau, 1964.

Kraume, Herbert. *Die Gerson-Übersetzungen Geilers von Kaysersberg: Studien zur deutschsprachigen Gerson-Rezeption*. Munich: Artemis, 1980.

Kraybill, Donald B. *The Riddle of Amish Culture*. Baltimore: Johns Hopkins Univ. Press, 1989.

Krebs, Engelbert. "Kempf, Nikolaus von." *Verfasserlexikon*. First edition. Vol. 2, cols. 784-86. Bibliographic supplement in vol. 5 (1955), col. 511.

Kren, Claudia. "Patterns in Arts Teaching at the Medieval University of Vienna." *Viator*, 18 (1987), 321-36.

Kreuzer, Georg. *Heinrich von Langenstein: Studien zur Biographie und zu den Schismatraktaten unter besonderer Berücksichtigung der Epistola pacis und der Epistola concilii pacis*. Quellen und Forschungen aus dem Gebiet der Geschichte, n.F., 6. Paderborn: Schöningh, 1987.

Kristeller, Paul Oskar. "The Contribution of Religious Orders to Renaissance Thought and Learning. *American Benedictine Review*, 21 (1970), 1-54. Reprinted in Kristeller, *Medieval Aspects of Renaissance Learning: Three Essays*. Edited by Edward P. Mahoney. Durham, N.C.: Duke Univ. Press, 1974, pp. 95-158.

———. *Renaissance Thought and Its Sources*. Edited by Michael Mooney. New York: Columbia Univ. Press, 1979.

Kropff, Martin. *Bibliotheca Mellicensis seu vitae et scripta inde a sexcentis . . . annis Benedictina Mellicensium*. Vienna: Johannes Pauli Kraus, 1747.

Krynen, Jean. "La pratique de la theorie de l'amour sans connaissance dans le *Viae Sion lugent* d'Hughes de Balma." *RAM*, 40 (1964), 161-83.

Kurt, Joachim. "Die Reformation und ihre Auswirkung auf die Erfurter Kartause zur Zeit von 1517-1555." In *Die Kartäuser und die Reformation*. Internationaler Kongress vom 24. bis 27. August 1983. Vol. 1. AC, 108.1. 1984, pp. 92-118.

Ladner, Gerhart B. "Homo Viator: Medieval Ideas on Alienation and Order." *Speculum*, 42 (1967), 233-59.

———. *The Idea of Reform: Its Impact on Christian Thought and Action in the Age of the Fathers*. Cambridge, Mass.: Harvard Univ. Press, 1959.

———. "Die mittelalterliche Reform-Idee und ihr Verhältnis zur Idee der Renaissance." *MIÖG*, 60 (19520, 31-59.

Lang, Albert. *Heinrich Totting von Oyta: Ein Beitrag zur Entwicklungsgeschichte der ersten deutschen Universitäten und zur Problemgeschichte des Spätmittelalters*. BGPhMA, 33.4-5. Münster i. W.: Aschendorff, 1937.

———. "Die Universität als geistiger Organismus nach Heinrich von Langenstein." *Divus Thomas: Jahrbuch für Philosophie und spekulative Theologie*, 27 (1949), 41-86.

___, ed. See Primary Sources, Heinrich von Langenstein.

Lang, Justin. *Die Christologie bei Heinrich von Langenstein*. Freiburger theologische Studien, 85. Freiburg i. Br.: Herder, 1966.

Lang, Peter Thaddäus. "Wurfel, Wein und Wettersegen: Klerus und Gläubige im Bistum Eichstätt am Vorabend der Reformation." In *Martin Luther: Probleme seiner Zeit*. Edited by Volker Press and Dieter Stievermann. Spätmittelalter und frühe Neuzeit, Tübinger Beiträge zur Geschichtsforschung, 16. Stuttgart: Klett-Cotta, 1986, pp. 219-43.

Lawless, George. *Augustine and His Monastic Rule*. Oxford: Clarendon, 1987.

___. "Psalm 132 and Augustine's Monastic Ideal." *Angelicum*, 59 (1982), 526-39.

Leclercq, Jean. "Introduction." In Bernard of Clairvaux, *On the Song of Songs*. Vol. 2. Translated by Kilian Walsh. CF, 7. Kalamazoo: Cistercian Publications, 1976, pp. vii- xxx.

___. "Introduction." in *Bernard of Clairvaux: Selected Works*. Translated by G. R. Evans. CWS. New York: Paulist, 1987, pp. 13-57.

___. "The Bible and the Gregorian Reform." *Concilium*, 17 (1966), 63-67.

___. "*Curiositas* and the Return to God in St. Bernard of Clairvaux." *CS*, 25 (1990), 92-100. Translated by Sister Susan van Winkle. Originally published in *Bivium* (1983).

___. *The Love of Learning and the Desire for God: A Study of Monastic Culture*. Translated by Catharine Misrahi. New York: Fordham Univ. Press, 1961. Originally published as *L'Amour des lettres et le désir de Dieu*. Paris: Du Cerf, 1957.

___. "Monastic and Scholastic Theology in the Reformers of the Fourteenth to the Sixteenth Century." In *From Cloister to Classroom: Monastic and Scholastic Approaches to Truth*. The Spirituality of Western Christendom III, CS, 90. Kalamazoo: Cistercian Publications, 1986), 178-201.

___. *Monks and Love in Twelfth-Century France: Psycho-Historical Essays*. Oxford: Clarendon, 1979.

___. "Naming the Theologies of the Early Twelfth Century." *Mediaeval Studies,* 53 (1991), 327-36.

___. *Monks on Marriage: A Twelfth-Century View*. New York: Seabury, 1982.

___. *Otia monastica: Etudes sur le vocabulaire de la contemplation au moyen âge*. Studia Anselmiana, 51. Rome: Pontificum Institutum S. Anselmi and Herder, 1963.

___. *Saint Bernard mystique*. Paris: Desclée de Brouwer, 1948.

___. "Temi monastici nell'opera del Petrarca." *Lettere italiane*, 43 (1991), 42-54.

Lees, Rosemary Ann. *The Negative Language of the Dionysian School of Mystical Theology: An Approach to the "Cloud of Unknowing."* 2 vols. AC, 107. 1983.

Lefebvre, Joël. "Le poète, la poèsie, et la poètique: Elements pour une définition et pour une datation de l'humanisme allemand." In *L'humanisme allemand (1480-1540)*. XVIIIe Colloque Internationale de Tours. Edited by Joël Lefebvre and Jean-Claude Margolin. Humanistische Bibliothek, Reihe 1: Abhandlungen, 38. De Pétrarque à Descartes, 37. Munich: Fink, 1979; Paris: J. Vrin, 1979, pp. 285-301.

Leff, Gordon. *Paris and Oxford Universities in the Thirteenth and Fourteenth Centuries: An Institutional and Intellectual History*. New York: John Wiley and Sons, 1968.

LeGoff, Jacques. "Apostolat mendiant et fait urbain dans la France médiévale: L'implantation des Ordres Mendiants, Programme questionnaire pour une enquête." *Annales: Economies, Sociétés, Civilisations*, 23 (1968), pp. 335-52.

____. "How Did the Medieval University Conceive of Itself," and "The Universities and the Public Authorities in the Middle Ages and the Renaissance." In *Time, Work, and Culture in the Middle Ages*. Translated by Arthur Goldhammer. Chicago: Univ. of Chicago Press, 1980, pp. 122-34, 135-49, 318-24.

Lehmann, Paul Joachim Georg. "Bücherliebe und Bücherpflege bei den Kartäusern." In *Miscellanea Francesco Ehrle*. Vol. 4: *Paleografia e diplomatica*. Studi e testi, 41. Rome: Bibliotheca apostolica Vaticana, 1924, pp. 364-89. Reprinted in Lehmann, *Erforschung des Mittelalters: Ausgewählte Abhandlungen und Aufsätze*. Vol. 3. Stuttgart: Hiersemann, 1960, pp. 121-42.

Lekai, Louis J. *The Cistercians: Ideals and Reality*. Kent, Ohio: Kent State Univ. Press, 1977.

Leloir, Louis. "La sagesse des ancien moines." *Studia missionalia*, 28 (1979), 61-95.

Lemmer, Manfred. "Brant, Sebastian." *Verfasserlexikon*. Rev. ed. Vol. 1, cols. 992-1005.

Lentner, Leopold. "'Stella clericorum': Ein Pastoralbuch des späten Mittelalters aus den Handschriften und Inkunabeln in der österreichischen Nationalbibliothek." In *Dienst an der Lehre: Studien zur heutigen Philosophie und Theologie*. Festschrift Franz Kardinal König. Edited by the Katholisch-Theologische Fakultät der Universität Wien. Wiener Beiträge zur Theologie, 10. Vienna: Herder, 1965, pp. 263-74.

Leroux, Jean-Marie. "Monachisme et communauté chrétienne d'après Saint Jean Chrysostome." In *Vie Monastique*, 143-90.

Lewis, C. S. *English Literature in the Sixteenth Century*. Oxford History of English Literature, 3. New York: Oxford Univ. Press, 1954.

Lhotsky, Alphons. *Quellenkunde zur mittelalterliche Geschichte Österreichs. MIÖG, Ergänzungsband*, 19. Vienna: Böhlau, 1963.

____. *Thomas Ebendorfer: Ein österreichischer Geschichtsschreiber, Theologe, und Diplomat des 15. Jahrhunderts*. Schriftenreihe der Monumenta Germaniae Historica, 15. Stuttgart: Hiersemann, 1957.

____. *Umriß einer Geschichte der Wissenschaftspflege im alten Niederösterreich im Mittelalter*. Forschungen zur Landeskunde von Niederösterreich, 17. Vienna: Verein für Landeskunde von Niederösterreich und Wien, 1964.

____. *Die Wiener Artistenfakultät, 1365-1497*. Sitzungsberichte der Wiener Akademie der Wissenschaften, philosophisch-historische Klasse, 247.2. Vienna: Böhlau, 1965.

____. "Zur Frühgeschichte der Wiener Hofbibliothek," *MIÖG*, 59 (1951), 329-63. Reprinted in Lhotsky, *Aufsätze und Vortrage*. Vol. 1. Munich: Oldenbourg, 1970, pp. 170-84.

____, ed. See Primary Sources.

Lickteig, Franz-Bernard. "The German Carmelites at the Medieval Universities." PhD diss., Catholic Univ. of America, 1977. Published in the series Textus et Studia Historica Carmelitana, 13. Rome, 1981.

Lienhard, Joseph T. "The 'Discernment of Spirits' in the Early Church." *Theological Studies*, 41 (1980), 505-29.

___. *Paulinus of Nola and Early Western Monasticism.* Theophania: Beiträge zur Religions- und Kirchengeschichte des Altertums, 28. Cologne and Bonn: Peter Hanstein Verlag, 1977.

Lindner, Pirmin. "Familia S. Quirini in Tegernsee." *Oberbayerisches Archiv für vaterländische Geschichte,* 50 (1897), 18-130. Continued in *Ergänzungsband zum 50. Band* (1898), 1-318.

___. "Das Profeßbuch der Benediktinerabtei Mondsee." *Archiv für die Geschichte der Diözese Linz,* 2 (1905), 133-99.

___. "Profeßbuch der Benediktinerabtei St. Peter in Salzburg (1149-1856)." *Mitteilungen der Gesellschaft für Salzburger Landeskunde,* 46 (1906), 1-128.

Linsenmayer, A. "Johannes Geuß, ein Prediger des 15. Jahrhunderts." *Theologisch-praktische Monats-Schrift,* 3 (1893), 825-32.

Little, Lester K. *Religious Poverty and the Profit Economy in Twelfth-Century Europe.* Ithaca, N.Y.: Cornell Univ. Press, 1978.

___. "Pride Goeth before Avarice: Social Change and the Vices in Latin Christianity." *AHR,* 76 (1971), 16-49.

___. See also Rosenwein, Barbara H.

Lockhart, Robin Bruce. *Halfway to Heaven: The Hidden Life of the Sublime Carthusians.* New York: Vanguard Press, 1985.

Lohse, Bernhard. *Mönchtum und Reformation: Luthers Auseinandersetzung mit dem Mönchsideal des Mittelalters.* Forschungen zur Kirchen- und Dogmengeschichte, 12. Göttingen: Vandenhoeck und Ruprecht, 1963.

Loos, Erich. "Die Hauptsünde der *acedia* in Dantes *Commedia* und in Petrarcas *Secretum*: Zum Problem der italienischen Renaissance." In *Petrarca, 1304-1374: Beiträge zu Werk und Wirkung.* Edited by Fritz Schalk. Frankfurt a. M.: Vittorio Klostermann, 1975, pp. 156-83.

Lorch, Maristella. "Petrarch, Cicero, and the Classical Pagan Tradition." In *Renaissance Humanism: Foundations, Forms, and Legacy.* Edited by Albert Rabil, Jr. Vol. 3: *Humanism in Italy.* Philadelphia: Univ. of Pennsylvania Press, 1988, pp. 71-94.

Lorenz, Rudolf. "Die Anfänge des abendländischen Mönchtums im 4. Jahrhundert." *ZKG,* 77 (1966), 1-61.

Lourdaux, Willem. "Kartuizers — Moderne Devoten: Een Probleem van Afhankelijkheid." *Ons geestelik Erf* 37 (1963), 402-18.

Lytle, Guy Fitch. "Universities as Religious Authorities in the Later Middle Ages and Reformation." In *Reform and Authority in the Medieval and Reformation Church.* Edited by Guy Fitch Lytle. Washington, D.C.: Catholic Univ. of America Press, 1981, pp. 69-97.

McClain, Joseph P. *The Doctrine of Heaven in the Writings of St. Gregory the Great.* Catholic University of America, Studies in Sacred Theology, 2nd series, no. 95. Washington, D.C.: Catholic Univ. of America, 1956.

McClure, George W. "Healing Eloquence: Petrarch, Salutati, and the Physicians." *JMRS,* 15 (1985), 317-46.

McGinn, Bernard. *The Golden Chain: A Study in the Theological Anthropology of Isaac of Stella.* CS, 15. Washington, D.C.: Cistercian Publications, 1972.

McGrath, Alister E. *Iustitia Dei: A History of the Christian Doctrine of Justification.* 2 vols. Cambridge: Cambridge Univ. Press, 1986.

____. *Luther's Theology of the Cross.* Oxford: Blackwell, 1985.

McGuire, Brian Patrick. *Friendship and Community: The Monastic Experience, 350-1250,* Cistercian Studies, 95. Kalamazoo: Cistercian Publications, 1988.

McSorley, Harry J. *Luther Right or Wrong? An Ecumenical-Theological Study of Luther's Major Work, The Bondage of the Will.* New York: Newman Press, and Minneapolis: Augsburg Publishing House, 1969.

Machilek, Franz. "Ein Eichstätter Inquisitionsverfahren aus dem Jahre 1460." In *Jahrbuch für fränkische Landesforschung,* 34/35 [Festschrift für Gerhard Pfeiffer] (1974/75), pp. 417-46.

____. "Klosterhumanismus in Nürnberg um 1500." *Mitteilungen des Vereins für Geschichte der Stadt Nürnberg,* 64 (1977), 10-45.

Mackensen, Heinz. "Contarini's Theological Role at Ratisbon in 1541." *ARG,* 51 (1960), 36-57.

Madre, Alois. *Nikolaus von Dinkelsbühl: Leben und Schriften: Ein Beitrag zur theologischen Literaturgeschichte.* BGPhMA, 40.4. Münster i. W.: Aschendorff, 1965 [dissertation, Würzburg, 1943].

Madre, Alois, ed. See Primary Sources, Nicholas Prünzlein von Dinkelsbühl.

Maierù, Alfonso. "Logic and Trinitarian Theology: *De Modo Predicandi ac Sylogizandi in Divinis.*" In *Meaning and Inference in Medieval Philosophy,* Studies in Memory of Jan Pinborg. Edited by Norman Kretzmann. Synthese Historical Library/Texts and Studies in the History of Logic and Philosophy, 32. Dordrecht and Boston: Kluwer Academic Publishers, 1989, pp. 247-95.

____. "Logique et théologie trinitaire dans le moyen-âge tardif: deux solutions en présence." In *The Editing of Theological and Philosophical Texts from the Middle Ages.* Acts of the Conference arranged by the Department of Classical Languages, University of Stockholm, 29-31 August 1984. Edited by Monika Asztalos. Acta Universitatis Stockholmiensis, Studia Latina Stockholmiensia, 30. Stockholm: Almqvist and Wiksell, 1986, pp. 185-212.

____. "Logique et théologie trinitaire: Pierre d'Ailly." In *Preuve et raisons à l'université de Paris: Logique, ontologie et théologie au XIVe siècle.* Edited by Zénon Kaluza and Paul Vignaux. Paris: J. Vrin, 1984, pp. 253-68.

Malone, Edward E. "Martyrdom and Monastic Profession as a Second Baptism." In *Vom christlichen Mysterium: Gesammelte Aufsätze zum Gedächtnis von Odo Casel, O.S.B.* Edited by A. Mayer, Jr., J. Quasten, and B. Neunheuser. Düsseldorf: Patmos, 1951, pp. 115-34.

____. *The Monk and the Martyr: The Monk as the Successor of the Martyr.* Washington, D.C.: Catholic University of America Press, 1950.

Mann, Nicholas. "Recherches sur l'influence et la diffusion du 'De remediis' de Pétraque aux Pays-Bas." In *The Late Middle Ages and the Dawn of Humanism Outside Italy.* Edited by G. Verbeke, and J. IJsewijn. Leuven: Louvain Univ. Press, 1972, pp. 78-88.

Manns, Peter. "Absolute and Incarnate Faith—Luther on Justification in the Galatians' Commentary of 1531-1535." In *Catholic Scholars Dialogue with Luther.* Edited by Jared Wicks. Chicago: Loyola Univ. Press, 1970, pp. 121-56, 205-23.

Originally appeared in German in *Reformata Reformanda* (Jedin Festschrift). Münster: Aschendorff, 1965.

———. "Zum Gespräch zwischen M. Luther und der katholischen Theologie: Begegnung zwischen patristisch-monastischer und reformatorische Theologie an der Scholastik vorbei." In *Thesaurus Lutheri: Auf der Suche nach neuen Paradigmen der Luther-Forschung.* Referate des Luther-Symposions in Finnland, 11.-12. November 1986. Edited by Tuoma Mannermaa, Anja Ghiselli, and Simo Peura. Helsinki, 1987, pp. 63-154. Reprinted in Manns, *Vater im Glauben: Studien zur Theologie Martin Luthers,* Festgabe zum 65. Geburtstag am 10 März 1988. Edited by Rolf Decot. Veröffentlichungen des Instituts für europäische Geschichte Mainz, 131. Stuttgart: Franz Steiner Verlag Wiesbaden, 1988, pp. 441-532.

Markowski, Mieczyslaw. "Abhandlungen zur Logik an der Universität Wien in den Jahren 1365-1500." *Studia Mediewistyczne,* 22, no. 1 (1983), 53-77.

———. *Buridanica quae in codicibus manu scriptis bibliothecarum Monacensium asservantur.* Wroclaw etc.: Polish Academy of Sciences, 1981.

———. "L'influence de Jean Buridan sur les universités d'Europe Central." In *Preuve et raisons à l'université de Paris: Logique, ontologie et théologie au XIVe siècle.* Edited by Zénon Kaluza and Paul Vignaux. Paris: J. Vrin, 1984, pp. 149-63.

———. "Jean Buridan est-il l'auteur des questions sur les 'Seconds analytiques'?" *Mediaevalia philosophica polonorum,* 12 (1966), pp. 16-30.

———. "Johannes Buridans Kommentare zu Aristoteles' Organon in Mitteleuropas Bibliotheken." In *The Logic of Jean Buridan.* Acts of the Third European Symposium on Medieval Logic and Semantics, Copenhagen 16.-21. November 1975. Edited by Jan Pinborg. Opuscula Graecolatina (Supplementa Musei Tusculani), 9. Copenhagen: Museum Tusculanum, 1976, pp. 9-20.

Marks, Richard B. *The Medieval Manuscript Library of the Charterhouse of St. Barbara in Cologne.* 2 vols. AC, 21-22. 1974.

Martin, Dennis D. "A Foretaste of the Kingdom: Mystical Theology in Nikolaus Kempf's *De ostensione regni Dei.*" In *Kartäusermystik und -mystiker,* Dritter Internationaler Kongress über die Kartäusergeschichte und -spiritualität, vol. 5. Edited by James Hogg. AC, 55.5. 1982.

———. "Catholic Spirituality and Anabaptist and Mennonite Spirituality." *Mennonite Quarterly Review,* 62 (1988), 5-25.

———. "Kempf, Nicholas, von Straßburg." in *Verfasserlexikon.* Rev. ed. Vol. 4, cols. 1117-23.

———. "Kydrer, Wolfgang, von Salzburg." *Verfasserlexikon.* Rev. ed. Vol. 5, cols. 474-77.

———. "Popular and Monastic Pastoral Issues in the Later Middle Ages." *CH,* 56 (1987), 320-32.

———. "Der 'Tractat von der lieb gots und des Nächsten' in cgm 780 und 394." *ZDA,* 108 (1979), 258-66.

———. "*Trahere in Affectum*: Praxis-Centered Theological Education in the Fifteenth Century." *Religious Education,* 85 (1990), 604-16.

———. "*Via Moderna,* Humanism, and the Hermeneutics of Late Medieval Monastic Life." *Journal of the History of Ideas,* 51 (1990), 179-97.

___. "The Writings of Nikolaus Kempf of Straßburg, ca. 1437-1468." In *Die Kartäuser in Österreich*. Zweiter internationaler Kongress über die Kartäusergeschichte und -Spiritualität. Vol. 1. AC, 83.1 1980, 127-54.

Martin, Lawrence T. "Bede's Structural Use of Wordplay as a Way to Truth." In *From Cloister to Classroom: Monastic and Scholastic Approaches to Truth* (= The Spirituality of Western Christendom, 3). Edited by E. Rozanne Elder. CS, 90. Kalamazoo: Cistercian Publications, 1986, pp. 27-46.

Martín, T. H. "Los misticos alemanes en la España del XVI y XVII." *Revista de Espiritualidad*, 48 (1989), 111-28.

Maschek, Hermann. "Der Verfasser des Büchleins von der Liebhabung Gottes." *Zentralblatt für Bibliothekswesen*, 53 (1936), 361-68.

Mathisen, Ralph W. *Ecclesiastical Factionalism and Religious Controversy in Fifth-Century Gaul*. Washington, D.C.: Catholic Univ. of America Press, 1989.

___. "Petronius, Hilarius, and Valerianus: Prosopographical Notes on the Conversion of the Roman Aristocracy." *Historia: Zeitschrift für alte Geschichte* (Wiesbaden), 30 (1980), 106-12.

Matter, E. Ann. *The Voice of My Beloved: The Song of Songs in Western Medieval Christianity*. Philadelphia: Univ. of Pennsylvania Press, 1990.

Matthias von Scarpatetti, Beat. "Heynlin, Johannes, de Lapide." *Verfasserlexikon*. Rev. ed. Vol. 3, cols. 1213-19.

Mayer, Anton. "Aus dem geistigen Leben Niederösterreichs im 15. Jahrhundert." In *Festgabe zum 100-jährigen Jubiläum des Schottengymnasiums*. Vienna: Wilhelm Braumüller, 1907, 187-201.

Mehl, James V. "Hermann von dem Busche's *Vallum humanitatis* (1518): A German Defense of the Renaissance *Studia Humanitatis*." *Renaissance Quarterly*, 42 (1989), 480-506.

Meier, Ludger. *Die Werke des Erfurter Kartäusers Jakob von Jüterbog in ihrer handschriftlichen Überlieferung*. BGPhMA, 37.5. Münster i. W.: Aschendorff, 1955.

Melczer, William. "Albrecht von Eyb (1420-1475) et les racines italiennes du premier humanisme allemand." In *L'Humanisme allemand (1480-1540)*. XVIIIe Colloque Internationale de Tours. Edited by Joël Lefebvre and Jean-Claude Margolin. Humanistische Bibliothek, Reihe 1: Abhandlungen, 38. De Pétrarque à Descartes, 37. Munich: Fink, 1979; Paris: J. Vrin, 1979, pp. 31-44.

Mertens, Dieter. "Früher Buchdruck und Historiographie: Zur Rezeption historiographischer Literatur im Bürgertum des deutschen Spätmittelalters beim Übergang vom Schreiben zum Drucken." In *Studien zum städtischen Bildungswesen des späten Mittelalters und der frühen Neuzeit*. Bericht über Kolloquien der Kommission zur Erforschung der Kultur des Spätmittelalters 1978 bis 1981. Edited by Bernd Moeller, Hans Patze, Karl Stackmann. Abhandlungen der Akademie der Wissenschaften in Göttingen, philologisch-historische Klasse, dritte Folge, no. 137. Göttingen: Vandenhoeck und Ruprecht, 1983, pp. 83-111.

___. *Iacobus Carthusiensis: Untersuchungen zur Rezeption der Werke des Kartäusers Jakob von Paradies*. Veröffentlichungen des Max-Planck-Instituts für Geschichte, 50. Studien zur Germania Sacra, 13. Göttingen: Vandenhoeck und Ruprecht, 1976.

___. "Jakob von Paradies (1381-1465) über die mystische Theologie." In *Kartäus-ermystik und -Mystiker*, Dritter Internationaler Kongress über die Kartäus-ergeschichte und -spiritualität. Vol. 5. AC, 55.5. 1982, pp. 31-46.

___. "Kartäuser-Professoren." In *Die Kartäuser in Österreich*. Zweiter internation-aler Kongress über die Kartäusergeschichte und -Spiritualität. Vol. 3. AC, 83.3. 1981, pp. 75-87.

___. "Riforma monastica e potere temporale nella Germania sud-occidentale prima della Riforma." In *Strutture ecclesiastiche in Italia e in Germania prima della Riforma*. Edited by Paolo Prodi and Peter Johanek. Annali dell'Istituto storico italo-germanico, Quaderno 16. Bologna: Società editrice il Mulino, 1984, pp. 171-205.

Meyer, Andreas. "Das Wiener Konkordat von 1448—Eine erfolgreiche Reform des Spätmittelalters." *QFIAB*, 66 (1986), 108-51.

Meyvaert, Paul. "The Enigma of Gregory the Great's *Dialogues*: A Response to Francis Clark." *JEH*, 39 (1988), 335-81.

Michiels, Guibert. "Robert de Tombelaine." In *DSAM*. Vol. 13, cols. 828-31.

Mieth, Dietmar. *Die Einheit von vita activa und vita contemplativa in den deutschen Predigten und Traktaten Meister Eckharts und bei Johannes Tauler: Unter-suchungen zur Struktur des christlichen Lebens*. Studien zur Geschichte der katholischen Moraltheologie, 15. Regensburg: Pustet, 1969.

Minnich, Nelson H., and Gleason, Elisabeth G. "Vocational Choices: An Unknown Letter of Pietro Querini to Gasparo Contarini and Niccolò Tiepolo (April, 1512)." *Catholic Historical Review*, 75 (1989), 1-20.

Mohrmann, Christine. "Observations sur la langue et le style de Saint Bernard." In *S. Bernardi Opera*. Vol. 2 (1958), pp. IX-XXXIII.

___. "Le Style de Saint Bernard." In Christine Mohrmann. *Etudes sur le latin des chrétiens*. Vol. 2. Storia e letteratura, 87. Rome: Edizioni di Storia e Letteratura, 1961, pp. 347-67. Originally appeared as "Le style de S. Bernard." In *San Ber-nardo: Pubblicazione commemorativa nell'VIII centenario della sua morte*. Pubblicazioni dell'Università Cattolica de S. Cuore, n.s., 46. Milan: Vita e pen-siero, 1954, pp. 166-184.

Molloy, Noel. "Hierarchy and Holiness: Aquinas on the Holiness of the Episcopal State." *The Thomist*, 39 (1975), 1-55.

Mornet, Elisabeth. "'Pauperes scolares': Essai sur la condition matérielle des étudi-ants scandinaves dans les universités aux XIVe et XVe siècles." *Le Moyen Age*, 84 (1978), 53-102.

Morrison, Karl F., "Hermeneutics and Enigma: Bernard of Clairvaux's *De Consid-eratione*." *Viator*, 19 (1988), 129-51.

___. *"I Am You": The Hermeneutics of Empathy in Western Literature, Theology, and Art*. Princeton: Princeton Univ. Press, 1988.

___. *The Mimetic Tradition in the West*. Princeton: Princeton Univ. Press, 1982.

Moulin, Léo. "Note sur les particularités de l'ordre cartusien." In *Historia et Spiritu-alitas Cartusiensis*. Acta Colloquii Quarti Internationalis, Ghent-Antwerp-Bruges, 16-19 Septembre 1982. Edited by Jan de Grauwe. Destelbergen: de Grauwe, 1983, pp. 283-88.

Müller, Alois. "Personalien zur Geschichte der nieder-österreichischen Karthausen Mauerbach, Gaming, und Aggsbach." *Blätter des Vereins für Landeskunde von Niederösterreich*, n.F. 11 (1877), 166-71.

Müller, Günter. *Deutsche Dichtung von der Renaissance bis zum Ausgang des Barock*. Darmstadt: Hermann Gentner, 1957. Originally published 1927.

___. "Zur Bestimmung des Begriffs 'altdeutsche Mystik'." *DVfLG*, 4 (1926), 97-127. Reprinted in *Altdeutsche und altniederländische Mystik*. Edited by Kurt Ruh. Darmstadt: Wissenschaftliche Buchgesellschaft, 1964, pp. 1-34.

Müller, Winfried. "Die Anfänge der Humanismusrezeption in Kloster Tegernsee." *SMGB*, 92 (1981), 28-90.

Mulligan, R. W. "*Ratio superior* and *ratio inferior*: The Historical Background." *New Scholasticism*, 29 (1955), 1-32.

Mursell, Gordon. "Love of the World in the *Meditations* of Guigo I." In *De Cella in Saeculum: Religious and Secular Life and Devotion in Medieval England*. Edited by Michael G. Sargent. Cambridge, England: D. S. Brewer, 1989, pp. 59-65.

___. *The Theology of the Carthusian Life in the Writings of St. Bruno and Guigo I*. AC, 127. 1988.

Muscatine, Charles. *The Old French Fabliaux*. New Haven: Yale Univ. Press, 1986.

Muschg, Walter. *Die Mystik in der Schweiz, 1200-1500*. Frauenfeld, and Leipzig: Huber, 1935.

Mussafia, Adolf. "Über die Quelle des altfranzösischen 'Dolopathos'." *Sitzungsberichte der kaiserlichen Akademie der Wissenschaften* [Vienna]. Phil.-historische Classe, 48 (1864), pp. 246-67.

Nauwelaerts, M. A. "Rodolphe Agricola et le Pétrarquisme aux Pays-Bas." In *The Late Middle Ages and the Dawn of Humanism Outside Italy*. Edited by G. Verbeke and J. IJsewijn. Leuven: Louvain Univ. Press, 1972, pp. 171-81.

Neiman, A. M. "The Arguments of Augustine's 'Contra Academicos'." *Modern Schoolman*, 59 (1982), 255-78.

___. "Augustine's Philosophizing Person: The View at Cassiciacum." *New Scholasticism*, 58 (1984), 236-55.

Neuhauser, Walter. "Beiträge zur Bibliotheksgeschichte der Kartause Schnals." In *Die Kartäuser in Österreich*. Zweiter internationaler Kongress über die Kartäusergeschichte und -Spiritualität. Vol. 1. Edited by James Hogg. AC, 83.1 1980, pp. 48-126.

Neuschel, Kristen B. *Word of Honor: Interpreting Noble Culture in Sixteenth-Century France*. Ithaca, N.Y.: Cornell Univ. Press, 1989.

Newald, Richard. "Beiträge zur Geschichte des Humanismus in Oberösterreich." *Jahrbuch des Oberösterreichischen Musealvereins*, 81 (1926), 154-223. Reprinted in Newald, *Probleme und Gestalten des deutschen Humanismus*. Edited by Hans-Gert Roloff. Berlin, 1963, pp. 67-112.

Newen von Newenstein, Joseph Karl. *Pandectae saeculares dum sacratissima familia Cartusiana quae Gemnici floret*. Vienna: van Ghelen, 1732.

Niederberger, Othmar, and Jelenik, Heinrich. *Die Kartause Gaming*. Heimaturkunde des Bezirkes Scheibbs, Bildband II, AC, 58.2. 1981.

Nissen, Peter J. A. "De Moderne Devotie en het Nederlands-Westfaaalse Doper-dom." In *De Doorwerking van de Moderne Devotie: Windesheim 1387-1987.* Ed. P. Bange, C. Graafland, A. J. Jelsma, A. G. Weiler. Hilversum: Uitgeverij Verloren, 1988, pp. 95-118.

Nürnberg, Rosemarie. *Askese als sozialer Impuls: Monastisch-asketische Spiritu-alität als Wurzel und Triebfeder sozialer Ideen und Aktivitäten der Kirche in Südgallien im 5. Jahrhundert.* Hereditas: Studien zur Alten Kirchengeschichte, 2. Bonn: Borengässer, 1988.

Oberman, Heiko A. *Contra vanam curiositatem: Ein Kapitel der Theologie zwischen Seelenwinkel und Weltall.* Zürich: Theologischer Verlag, 1973.

____. "Gabriel Biel and Late Medieval Mysticism." *CH*, 30 (1961), 259-87.

____. "Die Gelehrten die Verkehrten: Popular Response to Learned Culture in the Renaissance and Reformation." In *Religion and Culture in Renaissance and Reformation.* Edited by Steven Ozment. Sixteenth Century Essays and Studies, 11. St. Louis: Sixteenth Century Studies, 1989.

____. *The Harvest of Medieval Theology.* Cambridge, Mass.: Harvard Univ. Press, 1963. Rev. edition, Grand Rapids: Eerdmans, 1967. Reprinted Durham, N.C.: Labyrinth Press, 1983.

____. *Luther: Mensch zwischen Gott und Teufel.* Berlin: Severin und Siedler, 1983. Translated by Eileen Walliser-Schwarzbart as *Luther: Man Between God and the Devil.* New Haven: Yale, 1989.

____. "Reformation and Revolution: Copernicus' Discovery in an Era of Change." In *The Cultural Context of Medieval Learning.* Proceedings of the First Interna-tional Conference on Philosophy, Science, and Theology in the Middle Ages—September 1973. Edited by John E. Murdoch and Edith Dudley Sylla. Boston Studies in the Philosophy of Science, 26. Synthese Library, 76. Dordrecht: D. Reidel, 1975, pp. 397-429, discussion 429-35.

____. "Simul Gemitus et Raptus: Luther und die Mystik." In *Kirche, Mystik, Heiligung, und das Natürliche bei Luther.* Vorträge des Dritten Internationalen Kongresses für Lutherforschung, Järvenpää, Finland, 11-16 August 1966. Ed-ited by Ivar Asheim. Göttingen: Vandenhoeck und Ruprecht, 1967, pp. 24-59. Original English version published in *The Reformation in Medieval Perspective.* Edited by Steven Ozment. Chicago: Quadrangle, 1971, pp. 219-51.

____. "The Stubborn Jews: Timing the Escalation of Antisemitism in Late Medieval Europe." *Yearbook* of the Leo Baeck Institute, 34. London, 1989, pp. xi-xxv.

____. "University and Society on the Threshold of Modern Times: The German Con-nection." In *Rebirth, Reform, and Resiliance: Universities in Transition, 1300-1700.* Edited by James M. Kittelson and Pamela J. Transue. Columbus: Ohio State Univ. Press, 1984, pp. 19-41.

____. "*Via antiqua* and *via moderna*: Late Medieval Prolegomena to Early Reforma-tion Thought." In *From Ockham to Wyclif.* Edited by Anne Hudson and Mi-chael Wilks. Oxford: Basil Blackwell for the Ecclesiastical History Society, 1987, pp. 445-64. Reprinted in *JHI*, 48 (1987), 23-40.

____. *Werden und Wertung der Reformation: Vom Wegestreit zum Glaubenskampf.* Tübingen: J. C. B. Mohr, 1977. Second edition, 1979. Translated by Dennis

Martin as *Masters of the Reformation: The Emergence of a New Intellectual Climate in Europe.* Cambridge: Cambridge Univ. Press, 1981.

___. "Wir sein pettler. Hoc est verum: Bund und Gnade in der Theologie des Mittelalters und der Reformation." *ZKG*, 78 (1967), 232-52. Reprinted in Oberman, *Die Reformation: Von Wittenberg nach Genf.* Göttingen: Vandenhoeck and Ruprecht, 1986, 90-112.

O'Connell, Robert J. *Art and the Christian Intelligence in St. Augustine.* Cambridge, Mass.: Harvard Univ. Press, 1978.

Oediger, Friedrich Wilhelm. *Über die Bildung der Geistlichen im späten Mittelalter.* Studien und Texte zur Geistesgeschichte des Mittelalters, 2. Leiden: Brill, 1953.

___. "Über die Klerusbildung im Spätmittelalter." *HJ*, 50 (1930), 145-88.

Ohly, Friedrich. *Hohelied-Studien: Grundzüge einer Geschichte der Hoheliedauslegung des Abendlandes bis um 1200.* Schriften der Wissenschaftlichen Gesellschaft an der Johann Wolfgang Goethe-Universität Frankfurt am Main, Geisteswissenschaftliche Reihe, Nr. 1. Wiesbaden: Franz Steiner, 1958.

Olphe-Galliard, M. "Vie contemplative et vie active d'après Cassien." *RAM*, 16 (1935), 252-88.

O'Malley, John W. *Giles of Viterbo on Church and Reform: A Study in Renaissance Thought.* SMRT, 5. Leiden: Brill, 1968.

___. "Historical Thought and the Reform Crisis of the Early Sixteenth Century." *Augustinian Heritage*, 35 (1989), 143-62.

O'Meara, John J. *The Young Augustine: The Growth of St. Augustine's Mind up to His Conversion.* New York: Alba House, 1965.

Ong, Walter J. *Orality and Literacy: The Technologizing of the Word.* London and New York: Methuen, 1982.

___. *Ramus, Method, and the Decay of Dialogue.* Cambridge, Mass.: Harvard Univ. Press, 1958.

Overfield, James. *Humanism and Scholasticism in Late Medieval Germany.* Princeton: Princeton Univ. Press, 1984.

___. "Nobles and Paupers at German Universities to 1600." *Societas: A Review of Social History*, 7 (1974), 175-210.

Ozment, Steven E. *The Age of Reform, 1250-1550: An Intellectual and Religious History of Late Medieval and Reformation Europe.* New Haven: Yale Univ. Press, 1980.

___. *Homo Spiritualis: A Comparative Study of the Anthropology of Johannes Tauler, Jean Gerson, and Martin Luther, 1509-1516, in the Context of their Theological Thought.* SMRT, 6. Leiden: Brill, 1969.

___. *Mysticism and Dissent: Religious Ideology and Social Protest in the Sixteenth Century.* New Haven: Yale Univ. Press, 1973.

___. "Mysticism, Nominalism, and Dissent." In *The Pursuit of Holiness in Late Medieval and Renaissance Religion.* Edited by Charles Trinkaus and Heiko A. Oberman. SMRT, 10. Leiden: Brill, 1974, pp. 67-92.

___. *The Reformation in the Cities: The Appeal of Protestantism to Sixteenth-Century Germany and Switzerland.* New Haven: Yale Univ. Press, 1975.

___. "The University and the Church: Patterns of Reform in Jean Gerson." *Medievalia et Humanistica*, n.s. 1 (1970), 111-26.

Pablo Maroto, Faustino de. "Amor y conocimiento en la vida mística, según Hugo de Balma." *Revista de espiritualidad*, 24 (1965), 399-447.

Padover, S. K. "German Libraries in the Fourteenth and Fifteenth Centuries." In *The Medieval Library*. Edited by James Westfall Thompson. Chicago: Univ. of Chicago Press, 1939. Reprinted with supplement by Blanche B. Boyer. New York: Hafner Publishing Co., 1965, pp. 453-76.

Palmer, Nigel. "Ein Handschriftenfund zum Übersetzungswerk Heinrich Hallers und die Bibliothek des Grafen Karl Mohr." *ZdA*, 102 (1974), 49-66.

Paquet, Jacques. "Recherches sur l'universitaire 'pauvre' au moyen âge." *Revue Belge de Philologie et d'histoire*, 56 (1978), 301-53.

——. "L'universitaire 'pauvre' au moyen âge: problèmes, documentation, questions de méthode." In *Les Universités à la fin du moyen âge / The Universities in the Late Middle Ages*. Edited by Jozef IJsewijn and Jacques Paquet. Mediaevalia Lovaniensia, Series I, Studia 6. Publications de l'Institut d'Études Médiévales de l'Université Catholique de Louvain, 2e. série, vol. 2. Leuven: Louvain Univ. Press, 1978, pp. 399-425.

Parente, James A., Jr. *Religious Drama and the Humanist Tradition: Christian Theater in Germany and in the Netherlands, 1500-1680*. SHCT, 39. Leiden: Brill, 1987.

Pascoe, Louis B. "Jean Gerson: Mysticism, Conciliarism, and Reform." *Annuarium Historiae Conciliorum*, 6 (1974), 135-53.

Passmann, Antonin. "Die Kartause zu Straßburg, IV: Geistiges Leben in der Kartause." *Archives de l'église d'Alsace*, 26 (1959), 141-51.

Pasztor, Edith. "Ideale del monachesimo ed età dello Spirito come realtà spirituale e forma d'Utopia." In *L'età dello Spirito e la fine dei tempi in Gioacchino da Fiore e nell Gioachimismo medievale*. Atti del II Congresso Internazionale di Studi Gioachimiti, 6-9 settembre 1984. Edited by Antonio Crocco. S. Giovanni in Fiore, Italy: Centro Internazionale di Studi Gioachimiti, 1986, pp. 55-124.

Pater, Calvin Augustine. "Melchior Hoffman's Explication of the Songs [!] of Songs." *ARG*, 67 (1977), 173-91.

Paulhart, Herbert. *Die Kartause Gaming zur Zeit des Schismas und der Reformkonzilien*. AC, 5. 1972.

——. "Schrifttum zur Geschichte der niederösterreichischen Kartausen Aggsbach, Gaming, und Mauerbach." *Unsere Heimat, Monatsblatt des Vereins für Landeskunde von Niederösterreich und Wien*, n.F. 39 (1968), 129-32.

Paulus, Nikolaus. "Ein mittelalterliches Büchlein von der Liebe Gottes." *ZAM*, 3 (1928), 69-72.

——. "Der Kartäuser Nikolaus Kempf von Straßburg und seine Schrift über die rechte Art und Weise zu studieren." *AEKG*, 3 (1928), 22-46.

——. "Wer ist der Verfasser des Alphabetum divini amoris?" *ZAM*, 3 (1928), 157-60.

Payer, Pierre J. "Prudence and the Principles of Natural Law: A Medieval Development." *Speculum*, 54 (1979), 55-70.

Pennington, M. Basil, ed. *Monastery: Prayer, Work, Community*. San Francisco: Harper and Row, 1983.

Percival, W. Keith. "Renaissance Grammar." In *Renaissance Humanism: Foundations, Forms, and Legacy*. Edited by Albert Rabil, Jr. Vol. 3: *Humanism and the Disciplines*. Philadelphia: Univ. of Pennsylvania Press, 1988, pp. 67-83.

Perger, Richard. "Wolfgang Holzer: Aufstieg und Fall eines Wiener Politikers im 15. Jahrhundert." *JVGSW*, 41 (1985), 7-61.

Persoons, Ernest. "Handschriften uit Kloosters in de Nederlanden in Wenen." *Archives et bibliothèques de Belgique*, 38 (1967), 59-107.

Pesch, Otto H., and Peters, Albrecht. *Einführung in die Lehre von Gnade und Rechtfertigung.* Darmstadt: Wissenschaftliche Buchgesellschaft, 1981.

Petreius, Theodorus. *Bibliotheca Cartusiana sive illustrium sacri cartusiensis ordinis scriptorum catalogus.* Cologne: M. Hieratum, 1609. Reprinted Farnborough, Hampshire: Gregg Press, 1968.

Pfeiffer, Gerhard, ed. *Nürnberg—Geschichte einer europäischen Stadt.* Munich: C. H. Beck, 1971.

Pinborg, Jan. *Logik und Semantik im Mittelalter: Ein Überblick.* Stuttgart-Bad Cannstatt: Frommann-Holzboog, 1972.

Posada, Gerardo. *Der Heilige Bruno: Vater der Kartäuser; Ein Sohn der Stadt Köln.* Translated by Hubertus Maria Blüm, with contributions by Adam Wienand and Otto Beck. Cologne: Wienand, 1987.

Post, Richardus Regnerus. *The Modern Devotion: Confrontation with Reformation and Humanism.* SMRT, 3. Leiden: Brill, 1968.

Prinz, Friedrich. *Frühes Mönchtum im Frankenreich: Kultur und Gesellschaft in Gallien, den Rheinlanden und Bayern am Beispiel der monastischen Entwicklung (4. bis 8. Jahrhundert).* Munich: Oldenbourg, 1965.

Procter, Robert E. *Education's Great Amnesia: Reconsidering the Humanities from Petrarch to Freud.* Bloomington: Indiana Univ. Press, 1988.

____. "The *Studia Humanitatis*: Contemporary Scholarship and Renaissance Ideals." *Renaissance Quarterly*, 43 (1990), 813-18.

Puschnig, Reiner. "Zur Geschichte des untersteiriscchen Klosters Geirach: Fünf bisher unbekannte Urkunden." *Zeitschrift des historischen Vereins für Steiermark*, 34 (1941), 13-32.

Quivy, Paul, and Thiron, Joseph. "Robert de Tombelaine et son commentaire sur le Cantique des Cantiques." In *Le millénaire monastique du Mont-Saint-Michel.* Vol. 2: *Vie montoise et rayonnement intellectuel.* Paris: P. Lethielleux, 1967, pp. 347-56.

Rabensteiner, Augustin. "Beiträge zur Reformgeschichte der Benediktinerklöster im 15. Jahrhundert." *SMBO*, 10 (1889), 414-22.

Rabil, Albert, Jr. "The Significance of 'Civic Humanism' in the Interpretation of the Italian Renaissance." In *Renaissance Humanism: Foundations and Forms.* Edited by Albert Rabil, Jr. Vol. 1: *Humanism in Italy.* Philadelphia: Univ. of Pennsylvania Press, 1988, pp. 141-74.

Rabil, Albert, Jr., editor. *Renaissance Humanism: Foundations, Forms, and Legacy.* 3 vols. Philadelphia: Univ. of Pennsylvania Press, 1988.

Rapp, Francis. "Chartreux et ville dans l'Empire: le cas de Strasbourg." In *La naissance des chartreuses.* VIe Colloque International d'Histoire et de Spiritualité Cartusiennes. Edited by Bernard Bligny and Gérald Chaix. Grenoble: Editions des Cahiers de l'Alpe, 1986, pp. 237-58.

Rashdall, Hastings. *The Universities of Europe in the Middle Ages.* 3 vols. Revised by F. M. Powicke and A. B. Emden. Oxford: Oxford Univ. Press, 1936.

Redlich, Virgil. *Tegernsee und die deutsche Geistesgeschichte des 15. Jahrhundert.* Schriftenreihe zur bayerischen Landesgeschichte, 9. Munich: Kommission für Bayerischen Landesgeschichte, 1931. Reprinted Aalen: Scientia, 1974.

____. "Eine Universität auf dem Konzil in Basel." *HJ,* 49 (1929), 42-101.

Reeves, Marjorie. "The Originality and Influence of Joachim of Fiore." *Traditio,* 36 (1980), 269-316.

Reeves, Marjorie, and Hirsch-Reich, Beatrice. *The "Figurae" of Joachim of Fiore.* Oxford: Clarendon, 1972.

Reimann, Arnold. *Die älteren Pirckheimer: Geschichte eines Nürnberger Patriziergeschlechtes im Zeitalter des Frühumanismus bis 1501.* Edited by H. Rupprich. Introduction by Gerhard Ritter. Leipzig: Koehler und Amelang, 1944.

Reiter, Ernst. "Rezeption und Beachtung von Basler Dekreten in der Diözese Eichstätt unter Bischof Johann von Eych (1445-1464)." In *Von Konstanz nach Trient: Beiträge zur Geschichte der Kirche von der Reformkonzilien bis zum Tridentinum.* Festschrift für August Franzen. Edited by Remigius Bäumer. Paderborn: Schöningh, 1972, pp. 215-32.

Renaudet, Augustin. *Préréforme et humanisme à Paris pendant les premières guerres d'Italie (1494-1517).* Second edition. Bibliothèque Elzévirienne, n.s.: Etudes et documents. Paris: Librairie d'Argences, 1953.

Renna, Thomas J. "Bernard versus Abelard: An Ecclesiological Conflict." In *Simplicity and Ordinariness.* Edited by John R. Sommerfeldt. CS, 61. Studies in Medieval Cistercian History, 4. Kalamazoo: Cistercian Publications, 1980, pp. 94-138.

____. "Wyclif's Attacks on the Monks." In *From Ockham to Wyclif.* Edited by Anne Hudson and Michael Wilks. Studies in Church History, Subsidia 5. Oxford: Basil Blackwell for the Ecclesiastical History Society, 1987, pp. 267-80.

Rennhofer, Friedrich. *Die Augustiner-Eremiten in Wien: Ein Beitrag zur Kulturgeschichte Wiens.* Cassiciacum, 13. Würzburg: Augustinus Verlag, 1956.

Repgen, Konrad. "'Reform' als Leitgedanke kirchlicher Vergangenheit und Gegenwart." *RQ,* 84 (1989), 5-30.

Rice, Eugene F., Jr. "Jacques Lefèvre d'Etaples and the Medieval Christian Mystics." In *Florilegium Historiale: Essays presented to Wallace K. Ferguson.* Edited by J. G. Rowe and W. H. Stockdale. Toronto: Univ. of Toronto Press, 1971, pp. 90-124.

Riedlinger, Helmut. *Die Makellosigkeit der Kirche in den lateinischen Hoheliedkommentaren des Mittelalters.* BGPhMA, 38.3. Münster i. W.: Aschendorff, 1958.

Rösler. See Primary Sources, above.

Rosenwein, Barbara H. *Rhinoceros Bound: Cluny in the Tenth Century.* Philadelphia: Univ. of Pennsylvania Press, 1982.

Rosenwein, Barbara H., and Little, Lester K. "Social Meaning in the Monastic and Mendicant Spiritualities." *Past and Present,* 63 (1974), 4-32.

Ross, James Bruce. "Gasparo Contarini and His Friends." *SR,* 17 (1970), 192-232.

Roßmann, Heribert. *Die Geschichte der Kartause Aggsbach bei Melk in Niederösterreich.* AC, 30. 1976.

___. "Leben und Schriften des Kartäusers Vinzenz von Aggsbach." In *Die Kartäuser in Österreich*. Zweiter internationaler Kongress über die Kartäusergeschichte und -Spiritualität. Vol. 3. AC, 83.3. 1981, pp. 1-20.

___. "Der Magister Marquard Sprenger in München und seine Kontroversschriften zum Konzil von Basel und zur mystischen Theologie." In *Mysterium der Gnade*, Festschrift J. Auer. Edited by H. Roßmann and J. Ratzinger. Regensburg: Pustet, 1975, pp. 350-411.

___. "Die Stellungnahme des Kartäusers Vinzenz von Aggsbach zur mystischen Theologie des Johannes Gerson." In *Kartäusermystik und -mystiker*. Dritter internationaler Kongress über die Kartäusergeschichte und -Spiritualität. Vol. 5. AC, 55.5. 1982, pp. 5-30.

___. "Der Tegernseer Benediktiner Johannes Keck über die mystische Theologie." In *Das Menschenbild des Nikolaus von Kues und der christlichen Humanismus*, Festgabe R. Haubst. Edited by Martin Bodewig, Josef Schmitz, and Reinhold Weier. [= *Mitteilungen und Forschungsbeiträge der Cusanusgesellschaft*, 13]. Mainz: Grünewald, 1978, pp. 330-52.

Rott, Jean. "L'humanisme et la réforme pédagogique en Alsace." In *L'humanisme en Alsace*. Association Guillaume Budé, Congrès de Strasbourg, 20-22. avril 1938. Paris: Société d'édition "Les Belles Lettres," 1939, pp. 64-82.

Rousseau, Philip. *Acetics, Authority, and the Church in the Age of Jerome and Cassian*. Oxford: Oxford Univ. Press, 1978.

___. *Pachomius: The Making of a Community in Fourth-Century Egypt*. The Transformation of the Classical Heritage, 6. Berkeley: Univ. of California Press, 1985.

___. "The Spiritual Authority of the 'Monk-Bishop': Eastern Elements in Some Western Hagiography of the Fourth and Fifth Centuries." *JTS*, n.s. 22 (1971), 380-419.

Rowan, Steven. "Chronicle as Cosmos: Hartmann Schedel's Nuremberg Chronicle, 1493." In *Literatur und Kosmos: Innen- und Außenwelten in der deutschen Literatur des 15. bis 17. Jahrhunderts*. Edited by Gerhild Scholz Williams and Lynne Tatlock. (= *Daphnis*, 15, no. 2-3 [1986]). Amsterdam: Rodopi, 1986, pp. 127-59.

Rublack, Hans-Christoph. "Die Rezeption von Luthers *De votis monasticis iudicium*." In *Reformation und Revolution: Beiträge zum politischen Wandel und den sozialen Kräften am Beginn der Neuzeit*. Festschrift für Rainer Wohlfeil zum 60. Geburtstag. Stuttgart: Franz Steiner, 1989, pp. 224-37.

Ruello, Francis. "Statut et rôle de l'*intellectus* et de l'*affectus* dans la *Theologie mystique* de Hughes de Balma." In *Kartäusermystik und -mystiker*. Dritter Internationaler Kongress über die Kartäusergeschichte und -spiritualität. Vol. 1. AC, 55.1. 1981, pp. 1-46.

Ruether, Rosemary Radford. *Gregory of Nazianzus: Rhetor and Philosopher*. Oxford: Clarendon, 1969.

Rüthing, Heinrich. *Der Kartäuser Heinrich Egher von Kalkar, 1328-1408*. Veröffentlichungen des Max-Planck-Instituts für Geschichte, 18. Studien zur Germania Sacra, 8. Göttingen: Vandenhoeck und Ruprecht, 1967.

___. "Die Kartäuser und die spätmittelalterlichen Ordensreformen." In *Reformbemühungen und Observanzbestrebungen im spätmittelalterlichen Ordenswe-*

sen. Edited by Kaspar Elm. Berliner Historische Studien, 14. Ordensstudien, 6. Berlin: Duncker und Humblot, 1989, pp. 35-58.

___. "Kempf, Nicolas." *DSAM.* Vol. 8. Paris: Beauchesne, 1974, cols. 1699-1703.

___. "'Die Wächter Israels': Ein Beitrag zur Geschichte der Visitationen im Kartäuserorden." In Zadnikar and Wienand, *Die Kartäuser* (1983), pp. 169-83.

___. "Zur Geschichte der Kartausen in der Ordensprovinz Alemannia inferior von 1320 bis 1400." In Zadnikar and Wienand, *Die Kartäuser* (1983), pp. 139-67 [= chapter one of Rüthing, *Der Kartäuser Heinrich Egher von Kalkar, 1328-1408*].

Ruh, Kurt. *Bonaventura Deutsch: Ein Beitrag zur deutschen Franziskaner-mystik und -Scholastik.* Bibliotheca Germanica, 7. Bern: Francke Verlag, 1956.

___. "Zur Grundlegung einer Geschichte der Franziskanischen Mystik." In *Altdeutsche und altniederländische Mystik.* Edited Kurt Ruh. Wege der Forschung, 23. Darmstadt: Wissenschaftliche Buchgesellschaft, 1964, pp. 240-74.

Rupprich, Hans. *Das Wiener Schrifttum des ausgehenden Mittelalters.* Sitzungsberichte der österreichischen Akademie der Wissenschaften, philosophisch-historische Klasse, 228.5. Vienna: R. M. Rohrer for the Akademie, 1954.

Russell, Kenneth C. "Acedia—The Dark Side of Commitment." *Review for Religious,* 47 (1988), 730-37.

___. "Roots of the Noonday Demon." *Sisters Today,* 56 (1984-85), 417-22.

Saenger, Paul. "Books of Hours and the Reading Habits of the Later Middle Ages." *Scrittura e civiltà,* 9 (1985), 239-69.

___. "Physiologie de la lecture et séparation des mots." *Annales, Sociétés, Économies, Civilisations,* 44 (1989), 939-52.

___. "Silent Reading: Its Impact on Late Medieval Script and Society." *Viator,* 13 (1982), 367-414.

Sargent, Michael G., ed. *De Cella in Saeculum: Religious and Secular Life and Devotion in Late Medieval England.* Wolfeboro, N.H., and Woodbridge, Suffolk: Boydell and Brewer, 1989.

___. "The Self-Verification of Visionary Phenomena: Richard Methley's *Experimentum veritatis.*" In *Kartäusermystik und -Mystiker.* Dritter internationaler Kongress über die Kartäusergeschichte und -Spiritualität. Vol. 2. AC, 55.2. 1981, pp. 121-37.

Schäffauer, F. "Nikolaus von Dinkelsbühl als Prediger: Ein Beitrag zur religiösen Kulturgeschichte des ausgehenden Mittelalters." *Theologische Quartalschrift,* 115 (1934), 405-39, 516-47.

Schalk, Karl. *Aus der Zeit des Österreichischen Faustrechts, 1440-1463.* Abhandlungen zur Geschichte und Quellenkunde der Stadt Wien, 3. Vienna: A. Holzhausen, 1919.

Schellhorn, Maurus. "Die Petersfrauen: Geschichte des ehemaligen Frauenkonventes bei St. Peter in Salzburg, ca. 1130-1583." *Mitteilungen der Gesellschaft für Salzburger Landeskunde,* 65 (1925), 164-85.

Schenck, Mary Jane Stearns. *The Fabliaux: Tales of Wit and Deception.* Purdue University Monographs in Romance Languages, 24. Amsterdam and Philadelphia: Benjamins, 1987.

Schieler, Karl. *Magister Johannes Nider aus dem Orden der Prediger-Brüder: Ein Beitrag zur Kirchengeschichte des 15. Jahrhunderts.* Mainz: Franz Kirchheim, 1885.

Schillmann, Fritz. "Neue Beiträge zu Jakob von Jüterbock." *ZKG*, 35 (1914), 64-76, 363-71.

Schindler, David, editor. *Hans Urs von Balthasar: His Life and Work.* San Francisco: Communio Books and Ignatius Press, 1991.

Schmidt, Margot. "'Discretio' bei Hildegard von Bingen als Bildungselement." In *Spiritualität Heute und Gestern.* Vol. 2. AC, 35.2. 1983, 73-94.

———. "Nikolaus von Kues im Gespräch mit den Tegernseer Mönchen über Wesen und Sinn der Mystik." In *Das Sehen Gottes nach Nikolaus von Kues.* Akten des Symposions in Trier vom 25. bis 27. September 1986. Edited by Rudolf Haubst. (= *Mitteilungen und Forschungsbeiträge der Cusanus-Gesellschaft,* 18). Trier: Paulinus-Verlag, 1989, pp. 25-49.

Schmitt, Jean-Claude. "Où en est l'enquête 'Ordres mendiants et urbanisation dans la France médiévale'?" In *Stellung und Wirksamkeit der Bettelorden in der städtischen Gesellschaft.* Edited by Kaspar Elm. Berliner Historische Studien, 3. Ordensstudien, 2. Berlin: Duncker und Humblot, 1981, pp. 13-18.

Schmitz, Philibert. *Geschichte des Benediktinerordens.* Vol. 3: *Die äußere Entwicklung des Ordens vom Wormser Konkordat (1122) bis zum Konzil von Trient.* Translated by Raimund Tschudy. Einsiedeln and Zürich, 1955. Originally published in French, 1948.

Schnell, Bernhard. See Primary Sources.

Schramb, Anselm. *Chronicon Mellicense seu annales monasterii Mellicensis utrumque statum, imprimis Austriae cum successione principium etc.* Vienna: Johann Georg Schlegel, 1702.

Schrauf, Karl. *Die Geschichte der Wiener Universität in ihren Grundzügen.* Vienna: A. Holzhausen, 1901.

Schreiber, Heinrich. *Die Bibliothek der ehemaligen Mainzer Kartause.* Zentralblatt für Bibliothekswesen, Beiheft, 60. Leipzig: Harrassowitz, 1927.

Schreiner, Klaus. "Benediktinische Klosterreform als zeitgebundene Auslegung der Regel." *Blätter für württembergische Kichengeschichte,* 86 (1986), pp. 107-95.

———. "Mönchsein in der Adelsgesellschaft des hohen und späten Mittelalters: Klösterliche Gemeinschaftsbildung zwischen spiritueller Selbstbehauptung und sozialer Anpassung." *Historische Zeitschrift,* 248, no. 3 (1989), 557-621.

Schröder, A. "Der Humanist Veit Bild, Mönch bei St. Ulrich." *Zeitschrift des historischen Vereins für Schwaben und Neuburg,* 20 (1893), 173-227.

Schwab, Johann B. *Johannes Gerson, Professor der Theologie und Kanzler der Universität Paris: Eine Monographie.* Würzburg: Stahel, 1858.

Schwarz, Reinhard. "Luther's Inalienable Inheritance of Monastic Theology." *American Benedictine Review,* 39 (1988), 430-50.

Schwinges, Rainer Christoph. "Pauperes an deutschen Universitäten des 15. Jahrhunderts." *Zeitschrift für historische Forschung,* 8 (1981), 285-309.

———. *Deutsche Universitätsbesucher im 14. und 15. Jahrhundert: Studien zur Sozialgeschichte des alten Reiches.* Veröffentlichungen des Instituts für Europäische Geschichte Mainz, 123. Beiträge zur Sozial und Verfassungsgeschichte des Alten Reiches, 6. Stuttgart and Wiesbaden: Franz Steiner, 1986.

Scribner, Robert W. "Civic Unity and the Reformation in Erfurt." *Past and Present*, 66 (1975), pp. 29-60.

Séjourné, P. "Pez (Bernard)," and "Pez (Jérôme)." In *DThC*, 12 (1933), cols. 1356-64, 1564-65.

Sexauer, Wolfram D. *Frühneuhochdeutsche Schriften in Kartäuserbibliotheken: Untersuchungen zur Pflege der volkssprachlichen Literatur in Kartäuserklöstern des oberdeutschen Raums bis zum Einsetzen der Reformation.* Europäische Hochschulschriften, Reihe I, 247. Frankfurt a. M.: Bern, 1978.

Shank, Michael H. *"Unless You Believe, You Will Not Understand": Logic, University, and Society in Late Medieval Vienna.* Princeton: Princeton Univ. Press, 1988.

Smahel, Frantisek. "Krise und Revolution: Die Sozialfrage im vorhussitischen Böhmen." In *Europa 1400: Die Krise des Spätmittelalters.* Edited by Ferdinand Seibt and Winfried Eberhard. Stuttgart: Klett-Cotta, 1984, pp. 65-81.

Smalley, Beryl. "Essay I." In *Medieval Exegesis of Wisdom Literature: Essays by Beryl Smalley.* Edited by Roland E. Murphy. Scholars Press Reprints and Translations Series. Atlanta: Scholars Press, 1986, pp. 1-38. Originally appeared in *Dominican Studies* 2 (1949), 318-355.

Snyder, C. Arnold. *The Life and Thought of Michael Sattler.* Scottdale: Herald Press, 1984.

———. "Michael Sattler, Benedictine: Dennis Martin's Objections Reconsidered." *Mennonite Quarterly Review*, 61 (1987), 251-79.

Sommerfeldt, Gustav. "Aus der Zeit der Begründung der Universität Wien." *MÖIG*, 29 (1908), 302-89.

Sommerfeldt, John R. "Bernard of Clairvaux: The Monk and Society." In *The Spirituality of Western Christendom.* Edited by E. Rozanne Elder. CS, 30. Kalamazoo: Cistercian Publications, 1976, pp. 72-84.

———. "Charismatic and Gregorian Leadership in the Thought of Bernard of Clairvaux." In *Bernard of Clairvaux: Studies presented to Dom Jean Leclercq.* Edited by M. Basil Pennington. CS, 23. Washington, D.C.: Cistercian Publications, 1973, pp. 73-90.

———. "Consistency of Thought in the Works of Bernard of Clairvaux." PhD diss., Univ. of Michigan, 1960.

———. "Social Theory of Bernard of Clairvaux." In *Studies in Medieval Cistercian History.* Edited by M. Basil Pennington. CS, 13. Shannon, Ireland: Irish Univ. Press, 1971, pp. 35-48.

Southern, Richard W. *The Making of the Middle Ages.* London: Hutchinson, 1953; New Haven: Yale, 1953.

———. *Robert Grosseteste.* Oxford: Clarendon, 1986.

Spaapen, B. "Kartuizer-Vroomheid en Ignatiaanse Spiritualiteit." *Ons geestelijk Erf*, 30 (1956), 339-66; 31 (1957), 129-49.

Spidlik, Tomas. *The Spirituality of the Christian East: A Systematic Handbook.* CS, 79. Kalamazoo: Cistercian Publications, 1986.

Spitz, Lewis. *The Religious Renaissance of the German Humanists.* Cambridge, Mass.: Harvard Univ. Press, 1963.

Spreitz, Edmund Ferdinand. "Zur ältesten Geschichte der Kartause Gaming." DPhil dissertation in history, Univ. of Vienna, 1929. Published as AC, 58.4. 1986.

Srbik, Robert Ritter von. *Maximilian I und Gregor Reisch.* Edited Alphons Lhotsky. Schriften des D. Dr. Josef Mayer-Gunthof-Fonds, 1 [= AöG, 122.2]. Vienna: Böhlau, in Kommission für die österreichischen Akademie der Wissenschaften, 1961.

Stamm, Heinz-Meinolf. *Luthers Stellung zum Ordensleben.* Veröffentlichungen des Instituts für Europäische Geschichte, Mainz, 101. Wiesbaden: Steiner, 1980.

Steer, Georg. "Die Stellung des 'Laien' im Schrifttum des Straßburger Gottesfreundes Rulman Merswin und der deutschen Dominkanermystiker des 14. Jahrhunderts." In *Literatur und Laienbildung im Spätmittelalter und in der Reformationszeit, Symposion Wolfenbüttel 1981.* Edited by Ludger Grenzmann and Karl Stackmann. Germanistische-Symposien-Berichtsbände, 5. Stuttgart: J. B. Metzlersche Verlagsbuchhandlung, 1984, pp. 643-60.

Steinmetz, David C. *Luther and Staupitz.* Durham, N.C.: Duke Univ. Press, 1980.

___. *Luther in Context.* Bloomington: Indiana Univ. Press, 1986.

___. *Misericordia Dei: The Theology of Johannes von Staupitz in its Late Medieval Setting.* SMRT, 4. Leiden: Brill, 1968.

___. "Religious Ecstasy in Staupitz and the Young Luther." *Sixteenth Century Journal,* 11 (1980), 23-37.

Steneck, Nicholas H. *Science and Creation in the Middle Ages: Henry of Langenstein (d. 1397) on Genesis.* Notre Dame, Ind.: Univ. of Notre Dame Press, 1976.

Stieber, Joachim W. *Pope Eugenius IV, the Council of Basel, and the Secular and Ecclesiastical Authorities in the Empire.* SHCT, 13. Leiden: Brill, 1978.

Stievermann, Dieter. *Landesherrschaft und Klosterwesen im spätmittelalterlichen Württemberg.* Sigmaringen: Jan Thorbecke, 1989.

Stinger, Charles L. *Humanism and the Church Fathers: Ambrogio Traversari (1386-1439) and Christian Antiquity in the Italian Renaissance.* Albany, N.Y.: State Univ. of New York Press, 1977.

___. "St. Bernard and Pope Eugenius IV (1431-1447)." In *Cistercian Ideals and Reality.* Edited by John R. Sommerfeldt. CS, 60. Studies in Medieval Cistercian History, 3. Kalamazoo: Cistercian Publications, 1978, pp. 329-343.

Stock, Brian. "Experience, Praxis, Work, and Planning in Bernard of Clairvaux: Observations on the *Sermones in Cantica.*" In *The Cultural Context of Medieval Learning,* Proceedings of the First International Conference on Philosophy, Science, and Theology in the Middle Ages—September 1973. Edited by John E. Murdoch and Edith Dudley Sylla. Boston Studies in the Philosophy of Science, 26. Synthese Library, 76. Dordrecht: D. Reidel, 1975, pp. 219-62, discussion pp. 262-68.

___. *The Implications of Literacy: Written Language and Models of Interpretation in the Eleventh and Twelfth Centuries.* Princeton: Princeton Univ. Press, 1983.

Stoelen, Anselme. "Les commentaires scripturaires attribuées à Bruno le Chartreux." *RTAM,* 25 (1955), 177-247.

Stöller, Ferdinand. "Österreich im Kriege gegen die Hussiten (1420-1436)." *JLNö,* 22 (1929), 1-87.

Strauss, Gerald. *Manifestations of Discontent in Germany on the Eve of the Reformation.* Bloomington: Indiana Univ. Press, 1971.

Straw, Carole. *Gregory the Great: Perfection in Imperfection.* Berkeley: Univ. of California Press, 1988.

Sullivan, Donald. "Nicholas of Cusa as Reformer: The Papal Legation to the Germanies, 1451-52." *Mediaeval Studies*, 36 (1974), 382-428.

Sullivan, John Edward. *The Image of God: The Doctrine of St. Augustine and Its Influence.* Dubuque: Priory Press, 1963.

Swenden, Karel. "Dionysius van Rijkel—Biografische Nota." *Ons geestelijk Erf*, 24 (1950), 170-81.

Tarot, Rolf. "Jakob Bidermanns *Cenodoxus.* Diss., Cologne, 1960. Published Düsseldorf: Triltsch, 1960. See also Bidermann, under Primary Sources.

Taylor, Charles. *Sources of the Self: The Making of the Modern Identity.* Cambridge, Mass.: Harvard Univ. Press, 1989.

Telesca, William J. "The Cistercian Abbey in Fifteenth Century France: A Victim of Competing Jurisdictions of Sovereignty, Suzerainty, and Primacy." In *Cistercians in the Late Middle Ages.* Edited by E. Rozanne Elder. CS, 64. Studies in Medieval Cistercian History, 6. Kalamazoo: Cistercian Publications, 1981, pp. 38-58.

____. "The Cistercian Dilemma at the Close of the Middle Ages: Gallicanism or Rome." In *Studies in Medieval Cistercian History presented to Jeremiah F. O'Sullivan.* Edited by M. Basil Pennington. CS, 13. Kalamazoo: Cistercian Publications, 1971, pp. 163-85.

Tentler, Thomas N. *Sin and Confession on the Eve of the Reformation.* Princeton: Princeton Univ. Press, 1977.

Thoma, Franz X. "Die Briefe des Petrus von Rosenheim an Abt Kasper Ayndorffer von Tegernsee während der Klosterreform in Südbayern, 1426-1431." *Oberbayerisches Archiv für vaterländische Geschichte*, 67 (1930), 1-20.

____. "Petrus von Rosenheim, O.S.B.: Ein Beitrag zur Melker Reformbewegung." *SMGB*, 45 (1927), 94-222.

Thompson, E. Margaret. *The Carthusian Order in England.* London: S.P.C.K. 1930; New York: Macmillan, 1930.

Toews, John B. "Pope Eugenius IV and the Concordat of Vienna (1448)—An Interpretation." *CH*, 34 (1965), 178-94.

Topographie von Niederösterreich. Edited by the Verein für Landeskunde von Niederösterreich, vol. 3. Vienna: Seidel, 1893.

Trapp, Damasus. "Augustinian Theology of the Fourteenth Century: Notes on Editions, Marginalia, Opinions, and Book-lore." *Augustiniana*, 6 (1956), 146-274.

Trinkaus, Charles. "*Antiquitas* versus *Modernitas*: An Italian Humanist Polemic and Its Resonance." *JHI*, 48 (1987), 11-22.

____. "Erasmus, Augustine, and the Nominalists." *ARG*, 67 (1976), 5-32. Reprinted in Trinkaus, *The Scope of Renaissance Humanism.* Ann Arbor: Univ. of Michigan Press, 1983, pp. 274-301.

____. "Humanist Treatises on the Status of the Religious: Petrarch, Salutati, Valla." *SR*, 11 (1964), 7-45. Reprinted in Trinkaus, *The Scope of Renaissance Humanism.* Ann Arbor: Univ. of Michigan Press, 1983, pp. 195-236.

____. *In Our Image and Likeness: Humanity and Divinity in Italian Humanist Thought.* 2 vols. Chicago: Univ. of Chicago Press, 1970.

____. "Italian Humanism and the Problem of 'Structures of Consciousness'." *JMRS*, 2 (1972), 19-33.

___. "Luther's Hexameral Anthropology." In *Continuity and Discontinuity in Church History. Essays Presented to George Hunston Williams*. Edited by E. Forrester Church and Timothy George. Leiden: E. J. Brill, 1979, pp. 150-68. Reprinted in Trinkaus, *The Scope of Renaissance Humanism*. Ann Arbor: Univ. of Michigan Press, 1983, pp. 404-21.

___. *The Poet as Philosopher: Petrarch and the Formation of Renaissance Consciousness*. New Haven: Yale, 1979.

___. "The Problem of Free Will in the Renaissance and the Reformation." *JHI*, 10 (1949), 51-62. Reprinted in Trinkaus, *The Scope of Renaissance Humanism*. Ann Arbor: Univ. of Michigan Press, 1983, pp. 263-73.

Trout, Dennis E. "Augustine at Cassiciacum: *Otium honestum* and the Social Dimensions of Conversion." *Vigiliae Christianae*, 42 (1988), 132-46.

Tuck, J. Anthony. "Carthusian Monks and Lollard Knights: Religious Attitudes at the Court of Richard II." *Studies in the Age of Chaucer*, Proceedings, no. 1 (1984): *Reconstructing Chaucer*. Edited by Paul Strohm and Thomas J. Heffernan. Knoxville, Tenn.: New Chaucer Society, 1984, pp. 149-61.

Uiblein, Paul. "Beiträge zur Frühgeschichte der Universität Wien." *MIÖG*, 71 (1963), 284-310.

___. "Die österreichische Landesfürsten und die Wiener Universität im Mittelalter." *MIÖG*, 72 (1964), 382-408.

___. "Zu den Beziehungen der Wiener Universität zu anderen Universitäten im Mittelalter." In *Les Universités à la fin du moyen âge / The Universities in the Late Middle Ages*. Edited by Jozef IJsewijn and Jacques Paquet. Mediaevalia Loraniensia, Series I, Studia 6. Publications de l'Institut d'Études Médiévales de l'Université de Louvain, 2nd series, vol. 2. Leuven: Louvain Univ. Press, 1978, pp. 168-69.

___. "Zur Lebensgeschichte einiger Wiener Theologen des Mittelalters," *MIÖG*, 74 (1966), 95-107.

Uiblein, ed. See Primary Sources.

Valentin, Jean-Marie. *Le théatre des Jesuites dans les pays de langue allemande (1554-1680): Salut des âmes et ordre des cités*. 3 vols. Publications universitaires européennes, série 1: Langues et littérature allemandes, vol. 255.1-3. Bern: Peter Lang, 1978.

Valentini, Eugenio. "La dottrina della vocazione nel Ven. Nicolao de Argentina." *Salesianum*, 15 (1953), 244-59.

Vallée, Gérard. "Luther and Monastic Theology: Notes on *Anfechtung* und *compunctio*." *ARG*, 75 (1984), 290-97.

Van Dam, Raymond. *Leadership and Community in Late Antique Gaul*. The Transformation of the Classical Heritage, 8. Berkeley: Univ. of California Press, 1985.

Van den Eynde, Damian. "Literary Note on the Earliest Scholastic Commentarii in Psalmos." *Franciscan Studies*, 14 (1954), 121-54.

___. "Complementary Note on the Earliest Scholastic Commentarii in Psalmos." *Franciscan Studies*, 17 (1957), 149-72.

Van der Meer, Frederik. *Augustine the Bishop: The Life and Work of a Father of the Church*. Translated by Brian Battershaw and G. R. Lamb. New York: Sheed and Ward, 1961.

Van Dülmen, Richard. "Die Gesellschaft Jesu und der bayerische Späthumanismus: Ein Überblick mit dem Briefwechsel von J. Bidermann." *Zeitschrift für bayerische Landesgeschichte*, 37 (1974), 358-415.

Van Engen, John H. "Images and Ideas: The Achievements of Gerhart Burian Ladner, with a Bibliography of his Published Works." *Viator*, 20 (1989), 85-115.

___. *Rupert of Deutz*. Publications of the UCLA Center for Medieval and Renaissance Studies, 18. Berkeley: Univ. of California Press, 1983.

Van Fleteren, Frederick. "Augustine and the Possibility of the Vision of God in this Life." *Studies in Medieval Culture*, vol. 11. Kalamazoo: Medieval Institute, 1977, 9-16.

Vancsa, Max. "Das Fünfzehnte Jahrhundert." In *Geschichte der Stadt Wien*, vol. 2. Edited by the Historischer Verein der Stadt Wien. Vienna: A. Holzhausen, 1904, pp. 518-48.

Vandenbroucke, François. "Henri de Langenstein." In *DSAM*, 7 (1969), cols. 215-19.

Vanis, Jaroslav. "Die Kartäuser in den böhmischen Ländern," *Analecta Cartusiana*, n.s. 1, no. 2 (1989), 105-12.

Vansteenberghe, Edmond. *Autour de la docte ignorance*. BGPhMA, 14. Münster i. W.: Aschendorff, 1915.

Vasoli, Cesare. "Les débuts de l'humanisme a l'université de Paris." In *Preuve et raisons à l'université de Paris: Logique, ontologie et théologie au XIVe siècle*. Edited by Zénon Kaluza and Paul Vignaux. Paris: J. Vrin, 1984, pp. 269-86.

Vauchez, André. *La spiritualité du moyen age occidental VIIIe-XIIe siècle*. Paris: Presses Universitaires de France, 1975.

Verheijen, Luc. *Nouvelle approche de la Règle de Saint Augustin*. Bégrolles en Mauges: Editions Monastiques (Abbaye de Bellefontaine), 1980. Leuven: Institut Historique Augustinien, 1988. Trans. as *La Regola di S. Agostino: Studi e Ricerche*. Translated by Bernadette Caravagii. Edited by Giovanni Scanavino. Palermo: Edizioni Augustinus, 1986. Chapter six was published separately as *Saint Augustine's Monasticism in the Light of Acts 4.32-35*. The Saint Augustine Lecture, 1975. Villanova, Pa.: Villanova University Press, 1979.

Verbraken, P. "Les Dialogues de Saint Grégoire le Grand sont-ils apocryphes?" *Revue Bénédictine*, 98 (1988), pp. 272-77.

Vermeer. See Heinrich Egher van Kalkar under Primary Sources.

Verschueren, Lucidus. *De Bibliotheek der Kartuizers van Roermond*. Historische Tijdschrift, Series Studien, 6. Tilburg: Drukkerij Henri Bergmans, 1941. See also Primary Sources, Hendrik Herp.

Viller, Marcel. "Lectures spirituelles de Jérome de Mondsee." *RAM*, 13 (1932), 374-88.

___. "Nider est-il l'auteur de l'alphabetum divini amoris?" *RAM*, 4 (1923), 367-78.

Voci, Anna Maria. *Petrarca e la vita religiosa: il mito umanista della vita eremitica*. Studi di storia moderna e contemporanea, 13. Rome: Istituto storico italiano per l'età moderna e contemporanea, 1983.

Vos de Wael. See Denys of Rijkel under Primary Sources.

Wainwright, Geoffrey. See Jones, Cheslyn.

Walsh, James J. "Introduction." In *The Cloud of Unknowing.* Edited by James Walsh. CWS. New York: Paulist Press, 1981, pp. 1-97.

___. "'Sapientia Christianorum': The Doctrine of Thomas Gallus Abbot of Vercelli on Contemplation." Dissertatio ad Lauream in Facultate Theologica, Pontifical Gregorian University, Rome, 1957.

___. "Thomas Gallus et l'effort contemplatif." *RHSp,* 51 (1975), 17-42.

Walsh, Katherine. "From 'Victims' of the Melk Reform to Apostles of the Counter-Reformation: The Irish Regular Clergy in the Habsburg Dominians." In *The Churches, Ireland and the Irish.* Edited by W. J. Sheils and Diana Wood. Papers read at the 1987 Summer Meeting and the 1988 Winter Meeting of the Ecclesiastical History Society, Studies in Church History, vol. 25. Oxford: Basil Blackwell for the Ecclesiastical History Society, 1989, pp. 69-88.

___. "The Observance: Sources for a History of the Observant Reform Movement in the Order of Augustinian Friars in the Fourteenth and Fifteenth Centuries." *Rivista di Storia della chiesa in Italia,* 31 (1977), 40-67.

___. "Vom Wegestreit zur Häresie: Zur Auseinandersetzung um die Lehre John Wyclifs in Wien und Prag an der Wende zum 15. Jahrhundert." *MIÖG,* 94 (1986), 25-47.

Wappeler, Anton. *Geschichte der theologischen Fakultät der königlichen und kaiserlichen Universität zu Wien.* Vienna: Wilhelm Braumüller, 1884.

Wattenbach, W. "Sigismund Gossembrot als Vorkämpfer der Humanisten und seine Gegner." *Zeitschrift für die Geschichte des Oberrheins,* 25 (1873), 36-69.

Weber, Alison. *Teresa of Avila and the Rhetoric of Femininity.* Princeton: Princeton University Press, 1990.

Weber, Richard K. "The Search for Identity and Community in the Fourteenth Century." *The Thomist,* 42 (1978), 182-96.

Weidenhiller, Egino. *Untersuchungen zur deutschsprachigen katechetischen Literatur des späten Mittelalters.* MTU, 10. Munich: C. H. Beck, 1965.

Wenzel, Siegfried. "Petrarch's Accidia." *SR,* 8 (1961), 36-48.

___. *The Sin of Sloth: 'Acedia' in Medieval Thought and Literature.* Chapel Hill, N.C.: Univ. of North Carolina Press, 1967.

Wetzel, Richard. See Dohna, Lothar Graf zu, above.

White, Graham. "Pelagianisms." *Viator,* 20 (1989), 233-54.

White, Hayden F. "The Gregorian Ideal and Bernard of Clairvaux." *JHI,* 21 (1960), 321-48.

Wichner, Jakob. *Geschichte des Benediktinerstiftes Admont,* Vol. 3: *1297-1466.* Graz: the author, 1878.

Wicks, Jared. "Luther (Martin)." *DSAM,* vol. 9 (1976), cols. 1206-43.

___. *Luther and His Spiritual Legacy.* Theology and Life series, 7. Wilmington, Del.: Michael Glazier, 1983.

___. *Man Yearning for Grace: Luther's Early Spiritual Teaching.* Washington: Corpus Books, 1968.

Wienand, Adam. "Ein Loblied auf die Kartäuser von Sebastian Brant, Basel." In *Die Kartäuser: Der Orden der schweigenden Mönche.* Edited by Marijan Zadnikar and Adam Wienand. Cologne: Wienand, 1983.

Wiener, Philip P., et al., eds. *Dictionary of the History of Ideas.* New York: Scribners, 1973.

398   BIBLIOGRAPHY

Wiesinger, Peter. "Zur Autorschaft und Entstehung des Heinrich von Langenstein
    zugeschriebenen Traktats 'Erkanntnis der Sünde'." *ZDP*, 97 (1978), 42-60.
Williams, George H. *Wilderness and Paradise in Christian Thought: The Biblical
    Theme of the Desert in the History of Christianity and the Paradise Theme in
    the Theological Idea of the University.* New York: Harper and Brothers, 1962.
Williams-Krapp, Werner. "Laienbildung und volkssprachliche Hagiographie im
    späten Mittelalter." In *Literatur und Laienbildung im Spätmittelalter und in der
    Reformationszeit, Symposion Wolfenbüttel 1981.* Edited by Ludger Grenzmann
    and Karl Stackmann. Germanistische-Symposien-Berichtsbände, 5. Stuttgart: J.
    B. Metzlersche Verlagsbuchhandlung, 1984), pp. 697-707.
Wilmart, André. "L'appel a la vie cartusienne suivant Guiges l'ancien." *RAM*, 14
    (1933), 337-48.
___. "La chronique des premiers chartreux." *Revue Mabillon*, 16 (1926), 77-142.
___. "Les écrits spirituelles des deux Guiges." *RAM*, 5 (1924), 59-79, 127-58. Re-
    printed in Wilmart, *Auteurs spirituels et textes dévots du moyen âge latin,
    Études d'histoire littéraire.* Paris: Librairie Bloud et Gay, 1932, pp. 217-60.
Wilpert, Paul. "Bernhard von Waging, Reformer vor der Reformation." In *Festgabe
    für seine königliche Hoheit Kronprinz Rupert von Bayern.* Munich-Pasing: Ver-
    lag Bayerische Heimatforschung, 1954, pp. 260-75.
___. "Vita Contemplativa und Vita Activa: Eine Kontroverse des 15. Jahrhunderts."
    *Passauer-Studien: Festschrift für Bischof Dr. Dr. Konrad Landersdorfer O.S.B.
    zum 50. Jahrestag seiner Priesterweihe*, dargeboten von der Philosophisch-
    Theologische Hochschule Passau, 1953. Passau: Verlag Passavia, 1953, pp.
    209-27.
Winklhofer, Alois. "Johannes vom Kreuz und die Surius-Übersetzung der Werke
    Taulers." *Theologie in Geschichte und Gegenwart: Michael Schmaus zum
    sechzigsten Geburtstag dargebracht von seinen Freunden und Schülern.* Edited
    by Johann Auer and Hermann Volk. Munich: Karl Zink, 1957, pp. 317-48.
Winner, Gerhard. *Die Klosteraufhebungen in Niederösterreich und Wien.* Forsch-
    ungen zur Kirchengeschichte Österreichs, 3. Vienna, Munich: Oldenbourg,
    1967.
___. "Zur Bibliotheksgeschichte des ehemaligen Augustiner-Chorherrenstiftes St.
    Pölten." In *Translatio Studii: Manuscript and Library Studies Honoring Oliver
    L. Kapsner, O.S.B.* Edited by Julian G. Plante. Collegeville: St. John's Univ.
    Press, 1973, pp. 48-74.
Winter, Sean F. "Michael Sattler and the Schleitheim Articles: A Study in the Back-
    ground to the First Anabaptist Confession of Faith." *The Baptist Quarterly*, 34
    (1991), 52-66.
Witt, Ronald G. "Medieval Italian Culture and the Origins of Humanism as a Stylis-
    tic Ideal." In *Renaissance Humanism: Foundations, Forms and Legacy.* Vol. 1:
    Humanism in Italy. Edited by Albert Rabil, Jr. Philadelphia: Univ. of Pennsyl-
    vania Press, 1988, pp. 29-70.
Workman, Herbert B. *The Evolution of the Monastic Ideal from the Earliest Times
    down to the Coming of the Friars: A Second Chapter in the History of Christian
    Renunciation.* London: Epworth Press, 1927. Reprinted with introduction by
    David Knowles. Boston: Beacon Press, 1962.

Worstbrock, Franz Josef. "Geuß (Gaws, Gews, Geiz, Geyss), Johannes." In *Verfasserlexikon*. Rev. ed. Vol. 3, cols. 37-41.

Yarborough, Anne. "Christianization in the Fourth Century: The Example of Roman Women." *CH*, 45 (1976), 149-65.

Yarnold, Edward. "*Duplex Iustitia*: The Sixteenth Century and the Twentieth." In *Christian Authority: Essays in Honor of Henry Chadwick*. Edited by G. R. Evans. Oxford: Clarendon, 1988, pp. 204-23.

Yarnold. See also Jones, Cheslyn.

Zadnikar, Marijan, and Wienand, Adam, eds. *Die Kartäuser: Der Orden der schweigenden Mönche*. Cologne: Wienand, 1983.

Zeibig, Hartmann J. *Beiträge zur Geschichte der Wirkung des Basler Concils in Österreich*. Sitzungsberichte der Wiener Akademie der Wissenschaften, Phil.-Hist. Klasse, 8. Vienna, 1852, pp. 515-618.

Zeißberg, H. R. von. "Zur Geschichte der Karthause Gaming in Österreich u. d. Enns." *Achiv für österreichische Geschichte*, 60 (1880), 565-96.

Zibermayr, Ignaz. *Die Legation des Kardinals Cusanus in Österreich und die Ordensreform in der Kirchenprovinz Salzburg*. Reformationsgeschichtliche Studien und Texte, 29. Münster i. W.: Aschendorff, 1914.

___. "Die Reform von Melk: Aus Anlaß 500-jährigen Gedenkens ihrer Begründung." *SMGB*, 39 (1918), 171-74.

___. "Johann Schlitpacher's Aufzeichnungen als Visitator der Benediktinerklöster in der Salzburger Kirchenprovinz: Ein Beitrag zur Geschichte der Cusanischen Klosterreform (1451-1452)." *MÖIG*, 30 (1909), 258-79.

Zimdars-Swartz, Sandra. "Joachim of Fiore and the Cistercian Order: A Study of *De vita sancti Benedicti*." In *Simplicity and Ordinariness*. Edited by John R. Sommerfeldt. CS, 61. Studies in Medieval Cistercian History, 4. Kalamazoo: Cistercian Publications, 1980, pp. 293-309.

Zimmermann, Harald. "Romkritik und Reform in Ebendorfers Papstchronik." In *Reformatio Ecclesiae: Beiträge zu kirchlichen Reformbemühungen von der Alten Kirche bis zur Neuzeit: Festgabe für Erwin Iserloh*. Edited by Remigius Bäumer. Paderborn: Schöningh, 1980, pp. 169-80.

Zippel, Gianni. "Gli inizi dell'Umanesimo tedesco e l'Umanesimo italiano, nel XV secolo." *Bollettino dell'Istituto storico italiano per il medio evo e archivio muratoriano*, 75 (1963), 345-89.

Zoepfl, Friedrich. "Der Humanismus am Hof der Fürstbischöfe von Augsburg." *HJ*, 62 (1949), 671-708.

Zschoch, Hellmut. *Klosterreform und monastische Spiritualität im 15. Jahrhundert: Conrad von Zenn OESA (+ 1460) und sein Liber de vita monastica*. Beiträge zur historischen Theologie, 75. Tübingen: J. C. B. Mohr, 1988.

Zumkeller, Adolar. *Augustine's Ideal of the Religious Life*. New York: Fordham Univ. Press, 1986.

INDEX OF MANUSCRIPTS

Sigla

B*: Budapest:
> B1: Egyetemi Könyvtár (University Library), cod. 72 (Lövöld)
> B2: Egyetemi Könyvtár (University Library), cod. 77 (Lethenkow)
> B3: Országos Széchényi Könyvtár (Nat. Lib.), cod. 387 (Seitz)

F: Fulda, Hessische Landesbibliothek, Aa 114

G*: Graz, Universitätsbibliothek
> G1: cod. 262 (Seitz)
> G2: cod. 559 (Seitz)

La: Lambach, Stiftsbibliothek, MS chartac. 259

MkA: Melk, Stiftsarchiv "De proponentibus" (no shelf number)

Mk*: Melk, Stiftsbibliothek
> MkP2: cod. 683 (766)
> Mk1: cod. 1093 (423)
> Mk2: cod. 878 (722)
> Mk3: cod. 1562 (614)

M*, T*: Munich, Bayerische Staatsbibliothek
> M1: clm 3034 (Andechs)
> M2a: clm 4728 (Benediktbeuren)
> M2b: clm 5827 (Ebersberg)
> M4: clm 7531 (Indersdorf)
> M6: clm 16196 (St. Nikolaus in Passau)
> M7: clm 21625 (Weihenstephan)
> T1: clm 18555b (Tegernsee)
> T2: clm 18563 (Tegernsee)
> T3: clm 18211 (Tegernsee)

P: Paris, Bibliothèque National, Latin 3619

Pk: Parkminster, St. Hugh's Charterhouse, cod. D 150 (b 16 b)

R: Rein, Stiftsbibliothek, cod. 77

Ri: Rimini, Biblioteca Civica Gambalunga, cod. 71

S: St. Pölten, Bischöfl. Alumnats-Bibl. (Priestersem.), cod. 77

V*: Vienna, Nationalbibliothek
> V1: cvp 4259 (University; Gaming?)
> V2: cvp 4742 (Aggsbach)
> V3: cvp 4736
> V5: cvp 13904 (Gaming?)

VS1: Vienna, Schottenstift, Stiftsbibliothek, cod. 336 (296)

Index of Manuscripts

Note: Manuscripts mentioned solely as a result of citations from secondary literature or from catalogues are not indexed above (many of these are found together on pp. 304-7).

INDEX OF PERSONS AND PLACES

INDEX OF SUBJECTS

11:28-30, pp. 21, 94, 94 n.70, 150 n.121;
Mt 19, pp. 17, 98, 203
Scriptures, 119; exegesis, 81; exposition of,
197; four senses, 81, 81 n.25; as honey,
Kempf, 52, 83, 30 n.43; role in theology,
91 n.58
Secular clergy, 96; Gerson on, 92, 94; turned
monks, 100, 104 n.94
Securitas, 11, 71, 87 n.44, 93, 93 n.66, 96,
127, 203, 210, 212, 217, 225, 237; Bernard
of Waging and Johann of Eych, 218 n.116;
of monastic life, 255; true and false, 266;
See also Monastic life, fallibility of; Risk
Seeking. *See* Yearning
Self, 2, 11, 15, 16, 21; love of, 161. *See also*
Extrinsic self; Intrinsic self
Self-abandonment, 245
Self-deception, 127, 141
Self-denial, 162
Self-examination, 83, 127, 164
Self-judgment, 134, 140, 164
Self-knowledge, 87, 118, 120, 161
Semantic logic, 41
Semimonastic life, Petrarch, 245
Seniores, 132; and *iuniores*, monastic, 124
Signs, creation as, 166-67
Silence, 17-18, 270, 282
Similitudo Dei, 169, 170
Simplicity, 46, 65, 69, 168, 172, 193. *See
also* Curiosity; Learning
Sin, 78, 170; awareness of, 134, 150; cardi-
nal, 15, 78, 264; consciousness of, 255,
260, 267; the Fall, 161, 165, 176 n.69; fall-
ing into, 75 n.14; mortal, 129; venial, 143,
162. *See also* Anger; Envy; Original Sin;
Pride
Social change, late medieval, 86, 98 n.82
Sola fide, 135, 136, 149
Sola gratia, 165, 176, 184, 185, 261. *See
also* Grace
Solitude, 1, 85-87; Petrarch, 245-247
Song of Songs. *See* Scriptural exegesis
Soteriology, 17, 20, 97, 135, 136, 145, 157,
158, 165, 182; monastic, 146, 242, 270;
mystical, 170; Petrarch, 253, 254, 255. *See
also Ex puris naturalibus*; Grace; Justification; Salvation; *Sola gratia*
Soul, powers of. *See* Psychology, theological
Speculative theology, 13, 80. *See also* Affective theology; Scholastic theology
Spiritual digestion. *See* Reading
Spiritual direction, 15, 16, 29, 54, 59, 60, 94,
115, 125, 127, 129, 130, 148, 207, 241,
246, 247, 260, 282, 284. *See also* Extrinsic
counsel

Subditi (subjects). *See* Leadership, in monas-
tery
Supererogation, 95, 95 n.72, 126
Superiors. *See* Leadership, in monastery
Synderesis, 171

Temperance. *See* Moderation
Terminism. *See Via moderna*
Territorial states and monastic reform, 61
Tasting,30 n.43, 82, 92, 219
Textual criticism, and Carthusians, 70, 114
n.4
Textuality and Monasticism, 261 n.5, 262,
262 n.9. *See also* Literacy
Theologian, ideal, 38, 76, 82, 83
Theology, 71-85 passim; academic dangers
of, 46, 89,. ch. 3; incarnational, 93; logic
in, 42, 66; love as goal of, 73, 75; in mon-
astery, 92; reform of, 91; Scripture, 77.
See also Affective theology; Monastic the-
ology; Rhetorical theology; Scholastic the-
ology
Theology, prescholastic/patristic, 48, 54, 57,
60, 97
Threefold path (purgative, illuminative, uni-
tive), 145, 161, 162, 163, 165, 166, 170; il-
lumination, 163, 165, 166, 167, and union,
second degree of, 162; purgation, third de-
gree, 163; purgative, three degrees of, 170.
See also Mystical theology
Tongue, sins of, 294, 294 n.50
Tourism, Grande Chartreuse, 3
Tradition, 8, 9; as means of change, 223
Translations. *See* Kempf, Nicholas; Vernacu-
lar literature
Trier. See Johannes Rode
Trinity, 141; logical argumentation for, 43,
47, 48, 59
Tristitia. See *Acedia*
Trust. *See* Confidence; *Discretio*
Turks, 36, 106
Tutelage. *See* Childlikeness; Freedom

Union, Unitive way. *See* Mystical union
Universals, 42
Universities, English theological faculties,
47, 47 n.37; German, 40
University education, Kempf on dangers of,
29, 72-91
University, relations between disciplines, 73
Unknowing union. *See* Mystical union, cog-
nition and affectivity
Urban charterhouses, 112, 230, 230 n.164,
233, 235, 236, 238
Urban culture, 2, 12, 214, 220, 221, 223,
247, 257

NOTE: In lieu of a Scripture Index, the main discussions of scripture passages are indexed under "Scriptural exegesis," above.

Studies in the History
of Christian Thought

EDITED BY HEIKO A. OBERMAN

1. McNEILL, J. J. *The Blondelian Synthesis*. 1966. Out of print
2. GOERTZ, H.-J. *Innere und äussere Ordnung in der Theologie Thomas Müntzers*. 1967
3. BAUMAN, Cl. *Gewaltlosigkeit im Täufertum*. 1968
4. ROLDANUS, J. *Le Christ et l'Homme dans la Théologie d'Athanase d'Alexandrie*. 2nd ed. 1977
5. MILNER, Jr., B. Ch. *Calvin's Doctrine of the Church*. 1970. Out of print
6. TIERNEY, B. *Origins of Papal Infallibility, 1150-1350*. 2nd ed. 1988
7. OLDFIELD, J. J. *Tolerance in the Writings of Félicité Lamennais 1809-1831*. 1973
8. OBERMAN, H. A. (ed.) *Luther and the Dawn of the Modern Era*. 1974. Out of print
9. HOLECZEK, H. *Humanistische Bibelphilologie bei Erasmus, Thomas More und William Tyndale*. 1975
10. FARR, W. *John Wyclif as Legal Reformer*. 1974
11. PURCELL, M. *Papal Crusading Policy 1244-1291*. 1975
12. BALL, B. W. *A Great Expectation*. Eschatological Thought in English Protestantism. 1975
13. STIEBER, J. W. *Pope Eugenius IV, the Council of Basel, and the Empire*. 1978. Out of print
14. PARTEE, Ch. *Calvin and Classical Philosophy*. 1977
15. MISNER, P. *Papacy and Development*. Newman and the Primacy of the Pope. 1976
16. TAVARD, G. H. *The Seventeenth-Century Tradition*. A Study in Recusant Thought. 1978
17. QUINN, A. *The Confidence of British Philosophers*. An Essay in Historical Narrative. 1977
18. BECK, J. *Le Concil de Basle (1434)*. 1979
19. CHURCH, F. F. and GEORGE, T. (ed.) *Continuity and Discontinuity in Church History*. 1979
20. GRAY, P. T. R. *The Defense of Chalcedon in the East (451-553)*. 1979
21. NIJENHUIS, W. *Adrianus Saravia (c. 1532-1613)*. Dutch Calvinist. 1980
22. PARKER, T. H. L. (ed.) *Iohannis Calvini Commentarius in Epistolam Pauli ad Romanos*. 1981
23. ELLIS, I. *Seven Against Christ*. A Study of 'Essays and Reviews'. 1980
24. BRANN, N. L. *The Abbot Trithemius (1462-1516)*. 1981
25. LOCHER, G. W. *Zwingli's Thought*. New Perspectives. 1981
26. GOGAN, B. *The Common Corps of Christendom*. Ecclesiological Themes in Thomas More. 1982
27. STOCK, U. *Die Bedeutung der Sakramente in Luthers Sermonen von 1519*. 1982
28. YARDENI, M. (ed.) *Modernité et nonconformisme en France à travers les âges*. 1983
29. PLATT, J. *Reformed Thought and Scholasticism*. 1982
30. WATTS, P. M. *Nicolaus Cusanus*. A Fifteenth-Century Vision of Man. 1982
31. SPRUNGER, K. L. *Dutch Puritanism*. 1982
32. MEIJERING, E. P. *Melanchthon and Patristic Thought*. 1983
33. STROUP, J. *The Struggle for Identity in the Clerical Estate*. 1984
34. 35. COLISH, M. L. *The Stoic Tradition from Antiquity to the Early Middle Ages*. 1.2. 2nd ed. 1990
36. GUY, B. *Domestic Correspondence of Dominique-Marie Varlet, Bishop of Babylon, 1678-1742*. 1986
37. 38. CLARK, F. *The Pseudo-Gregorian Dialogues*. I. II. 1987
39. PARENTE, Jr., J. A. *Religious Drama and the Humanist Tradition*. 1987
40. POSTHUMUS MEIJES, G. H. M. *Hugo Grotius, Meletius*. 1988
41. FELD, H. *Der Ikonoklasmus des Westens*. 1990
42. REEVE, A. and SCREECH, M.A. (eds.) *Erasmus' Annotations on the New Testament*. 1990
43. KIRBY, W.J.T. *Richard Hooker's Doctrine of the Royal Supremacy*. 1990
44. GERSTNER, J.N. *The Thousand Generation Covenant*. Reformed Covenant Theology. 1990
45. CHRISTIANSON, G. and IZBICKI, T.M. (eds.) *Nicholas of Cusa*. 1991
46. GARSTEIN, O. *Rome and the Counter-Reformation in Scandinavia*. 1553-1622. 1992
47. GARSTEIN, O. *Rome and the Counter-Reformation in Scandinavia*. 1622-1656. 1992
48. PERRONE COMPAGNI, V. (ed.) *Cornelius Agrippa, De occulta philosophia Libri tres*. 1992
49. MARTIN, D.D. *Fifteenth-Century Carthusian Reform*. The World of Nicholas Kempf. 1992

Prospectus available on request

E. J. BRILL — P.O.B. 9000 — 2300 PA LEIDEN — THE NETHERLANDS